IFIP Advances in Information and Communication Technology

664

Editor-in-Chief

Kai Rannenberg, Goethe University Frankfurt, Germany

Editorial Board Members

TC 1 – Foundations of Computer Science
Luís Soares Barbosa, University of Minho, Braga, Portugal

TC 2 – Software: Theory and Practice
Michael Goedicke, University of Duisburg-Essen, Germany

TC 3 – Education
Arthur Tatnall, Victoria University, Melbourne, Australia

TC 5 – Information Technology Applications
Erich J. Neuhold, University of Vienna, Austria

TC 6 – Communication Systems
Burkhard Stiller, University of Zurich, Zürich, Switzerland

TC 7 – System Modeling and Optimization
Fredi Tröltzsch, TU Berlin, Germany

TC 8 – Information Systems
Jan Pries-Heje, Roskilde University, Denmark

TC 9 – ICT and Society
David Kreps, National University of Ireland, Galway, Ireland

TC 10 – Computer Systems Technology
Ricardo Reis, Federal University of Rio Grande do Sul, Porto Alegre, Brazil

TC 11 – Security and Privacy Protection in Information Processing Systems
Steven Furnell, Plymouth University, UK

TC 12 – Artificial Intelligence
Eunika Mercier-Laurent, University of Reims Champagne-Ardenne, Reims, France

TC 13 – Human-Computer Interaction
Marco Winckler, University of Nice Sophia Antipolis, France

TC 14 – Entertainment Computing
Rainer Malaka, University of Bremen, Germany

IFIP – The International Federation for Information Processing

IFIP was founded in 1960 under the auspices of UNESCO, following the first World Computer Congress held in Paris the previous year. A federation for societies working in information processing, IFIP's aim is two-fold: to support information processing in the countries of its members and to encourage technology transfer to developing nations. As its mission statement clearly states:

IFIP is the global non-profit federation of societies of ICT professionals that aims at achieving a worldwide professional and socially responsible development and application of information and communication technologies.

IFIP is a non-profit-making organization, run almost solely by 2500 volunteers. It operates through a number of technical committees and working groups, which organize events and publications. IFIP's events range from large international open conferences to working conferences and local seminars.

The flagship event is the IFIP World Computer Congress, at which both invited and contributed papers are presented. Contributed papers are rigorously refereed and the rejection rate is high.

As with the Congress, participation in the open conferences is open to all and papers may be invited or submitted. Again, submitted papers are stringently refereed.

The working conferences are structured differently. They are usually run by a working group and attendance is generally smaller and occasionally by invitation only. Their purpose is to create an atmosphere conducive to innovation and development. Refereeing is also rigorous and papers are subjected to extensive group discussion.

Publications arising from IFIP events vary. The papers presented at the IFIP World Computer Congress and at open conferences are published as conference proceedings, while the results of the working conferences are often published as collections of selected and edited papers.

IFIP distinguishes three types of institutional membership: Country Representative Members, Members at Large, and Associate Members. The type of organization that can apply for membership is a wide variety and includes national or international societies of individual computer scientists/ICT professionals, associations or federations of such societies, government institutions/government related organizations, national or international research institutes or consortia, universities, academies of sciences, companies, national or international associations or federations of companies.

More information about this series at https://link.springer.com/bookseries/6102

Duck Young Kim · Gregor von Cieminski ·
David Romero (Eds.)

Advances in Production Management Systems

Smart Manufacturing and Logistics Systems: Turning Ideas into Action

IFIP WG 5.7 International Conference, APMS 2022
Gyeongju, South Korea, September 25–29, 2022
Proceedings, Part II

Editors
Duck Young Kim (iD)
Pohang University of Science and
Technology
Pohang, Korea (Republic of)

Gregor von Cieminski (iD)
ZF Friedrichshafen AG
Friedrichshafen, Germany

David Romero (iD)
Tecnológico de Monterrey
Mexico City, Mexico

ISSN 1868-4238   ISSN 1868-422X (electronic)
IFIP Advances in Information and Communication Technology
ISBN 978-3-031-16413-2   ISBN 978-3-031-16411-8   (eBook)
https://doi.org/10.1007/978-3-031-16411-8

This Springer imprint is published by the registered company Springer Nature Switzerland AG
The registered company address is: Gewerbestrasse 11, 6330 Cham, Switzerland

Preface

Over the past few years, we have been going through tough times with the COVID-19 pandemic. This coincides with other fundamental risks to the global economy. If we look at the manufacturing and logistics industries, we have experienced an ever more challenging environment in the global supply chains and networks. Sustainable energy management and global environmental issues are no longer just regulations but top priorities for competitiveness and even survival. Most manufacturers and logistics providers have nowadays to operate in very volatile, uncertain, complex, and ambiguous market conditions. For example, product lifecycles are becoming shorter and shorter; customers' demands are turning out to be highly unpredictable and unbounded; raw material and energy prices are being subject to sharp increases; and transport, logistics, and distribution systems are being demanded with almost impossible delivery times, all threatening the break-even point of manufacturing and logistics enterprises.

To meet these urgent business and operational challenges, many studies on manufacturing and logistics management systems have been conducted in academia. Some research topics such as Industry 4.0, digital transformation, and cyber-physical production systems are buzzwords in many consulting firms without concrete action plans. Therefore, the International Conference on Advances in Production Management Systems (APMS 2022) in Gyeongju, South Korea, aimed to bridge the gap between academia and industry in the development of next-generation smart and sustainable manufacturing and logistics systems. The conference spotlighted internationally renowned keynote speakers from academia and industry, and the active participation of manufacturers, their suppliers, and logistics service providers.

A large international panel of experts reviewed 153 submissions (with a minimum of two single-blind reviews per paper) and selected the best 139 papers to be included in the proceedings of APMS 2022, which are organized into two parts. The topics of special interest in the first part include AI and Data-driven Production Management; Smart Manufacturing and Industry 4.0; Simulation and Model-driven Production Management; Service Systems Design, Engineering and Management; Industrial Digital Transformation; Sustainable Production Management; Digital Supply Networks; and Urban Mobility and City Logistics.

The conference featured special sessions to empathize with the real challenges of today's industry, and accordingly, to exchange valuable knowledge and promote discussions about new answers while emphasizing how to turn technological advances into business solutions. The following important topics were actively discussed in the special sessions and these topics are included in the second part of the APMS 2022 proceedings: Development of Circular Business Solutions and Product-Service Systems through Digital Twins; "Farm-to-Fork" Production Management in Food Supply Chains; Digital Transformation Approaches in Production Management; Smart Supply Chain and Production in Society 5.0 Era; Service and Operations Management in the

Context of Digitally-enabled Product-Service Systems; Sustainable and Digital Servitization; Manufacturing Models and Practices for Eco-efficient, Circular and Regenerative Industrial Systems; Cognitive and Autonomous AI in Manufacturing and Supply Chains; Operators 4.0 and Human-Technology Integration in Smart Manufacturing and Logistics Environments; Cyber-Physical Systems for Smart Assembly and Logistics in Automotive Industry; and Trends, Challenges and Applications of Digital Lean Paradigm.

APMS 2022 was supported by the International Federation of Information Processing (IFIP), and it was organized by the IFIP Working Group 5.7 on Advances in Production Management Systems (APMS) established in 1978, the Department of Industrial and Management Engineering of Pohang University of Science and Technology (POSTECH), the Korean Institute of Industrial Engineers (KIIE), and the Institute for Industrial Systems Innovation of Seoul National University. The conference was also supported by four leading journals: Production Planning & Control (PPC), the International Journal of Production Research (IJPR), the International Journal of Logistics Research and Applications (IJLRA), and the International Journal of Industrial Engineering and Management (IJIEM).

We would like to give very special thanks to the members of the IFIP Working Group 5.7, the Program Committee, the Organizing Committee, and the Advisory Board, along with the reviewers of each submission. Finally, we deeply appreciate the generous financial support from our sponsors, namely, Pohang Iron and Steel Company (POSCO), POSTECH, and the Institute for Industrial Systems Innovation of Seoul National University.

September 2022

Duck Young Kim
Gregor von Cieminski
David Romero

Organization

Honorary Co-chairs

Dimitris Kiritsis	École Polytechnique Fédérale de Lausanne, Switzerland
Chi-Hyuck Jun	Pohang University of Science and Technology, South Korea

Conference Chair

Duck Young Kim	Pohang University of Science and Technology, South Korea

Conference Co-chair

Gregor Von Cieminski	ZF Friedrichshafen, Germany

Program Chair

David Romero	Tecnológico de Monterrey, Mexico

Organizing Committee Chair

Minseok Song	Pohang University of Science and Technology, South Korea

Program Committee

Dong Ho Lee	Hanyang University, South Korea
Sang Do Noh	Sungkyunkwan University, South Korea
Kyungsik Lee	Seoul National University, South Korea
Hong-Bae Jun	Hongik University, South Korea
Xuehao Feng	Zhejiang University, China
Thorsten Wuest	West Virginia University, USA
Paolo Gaiardelli	University of Bergamo, Italy
Mélanie Despeisse	Chalmers University of Technology, Sweden

Advisory Board

Alexandre Dolgui	IMT Atlantique, France
Bojan Lalić	University of Novi Sad, Serbia
Farhad Ameri	Texas State University, USA

Ilkyeong Moon	Seoul National University, South Korea
Hermann Lödding	Technische Universität Hamburg, Germany
Marco Taisch	Politecnico di Milano, Italy
Andrew Kusiak	University of Iowa, USA
Volker Stich	RWTH Aachen, Germany
Vittal Prabhu	Pennsylvania State University, USA
Jai-Hyun Byun	Gyeongsang National University, South Korea

Organizing Committee

Dong Gu Choi	Pohang University of Science and Technology, South Korea
Kwangmin Jung	Pohang University of Science and Technology, South Korea
Kwangyeol Ryu	Pusan National University, South Korea
Jongho Shin	Chosun University, South Korea
Sujeong Baek	Hanbat National University, South Korea

Marco Garetti Doctoral Workshop Co-chairs

| David Romero | Tecnológico de Monterrey, Mexico |
| Jannicke Baalsrud Hauge | KTH Royal Institute of Technology, Sweden, and BIBA, Germany |

Contents – Part II

Digital Transformation Approaches in Production Management

Smart Supply Chain and Production in Society 5.0 Era

Service and Operations Management in the Context of Digitally-Enabled Product-Service Systems

Sustainable and Digital Servitization

Manufacturing Models and Practices for Eco-Efficient, Circular and Regenerative Industrial Systems

Cognitive and Autonomous AI in Manufacturing and Supply Chains

Operators 4.0 and Human-Technology Integration in Smart Manufacturing and Logistics Environments

Cyber-Physical Systems for Smart Assembly and Logistics in Automotive Industry

Trends, Challenges and Applications of Digital Lean Paradigm

Contents – Part I

Smart Manufacturing and Industry 4.0

Simulation and Model-Driven Production Management

Service Systems Design, Engineering and Management

Industrial Digital Transformation

Sustainable Production Management

Digital Supply Networks

Urban Mobility and City Logistics

Development of Circular Business Solutions and Product-Service Systems Through Digital Twins

Servitized Cloud-Based Simulation of Evaporation Plants: Model-Based Design Tools Supporting Circular Bioeconomy

Claudio Sassanelli[1]([✉]) [iD], Paolo Greppi[2] [iD], Giorgio Mossa[1] [iD], and Sergio Terzi[3] [iD]

[1] Department of Mechanics, Mathematics and Management, Politecnico di Bari, Via Orabona 4, 70125 Bari, Italy
{claudio.sassanelli,giorgio.mossa}@poliba.it
[2] Simevo Srl, Via Vincenzo Cesati 12, 13100 Vercelli, Italy
paolo.greppi@simevo.com
[3] Department of Management, Economics and Industrial Engineering, Politecnico di Milano, Piazza Leonardo da Vinci, 32, 20133 Milan, Italy
sergio.terzi@polimi.it

Abstract. Continuous industrial processes will play a key role for the sustainable transition worldwide. Different flows of matter and energy must be recovered through these systems and integrated in a Circular Economy fashion. To foster in such a virtuous trend the involvement of companies, mostly SMEs (often lacking critical assets, funds, technologies or knowledge), the continuous processes should be packaged, servitized and marketed as plants-as-a-service. Model-based design (MBD) tools can provide test before invest and decision support in the feasibility and procurement phases, as well as optimization and self-diagnosing during operation, in a cyber-physical system (CPS) setting. To ease their provision, a cloud-based collaboration platform, enabling providers to deploy tools in a sandbox, has been developed by the HUBCAP project. The purpose of this paper is to introduce the web application tool built for the evaporation process simulation, validated against real-world performance data for the reference evaporation plant, and deployed to the HUBCAP platform. To structure it, data collection, filtration, processing, and reporting have been performed on the full-scale pilot plant (the EVAPOSIM experiment), a triple-effect evaporator operating in counterflow and vacuum condition. To explore the sustainability of their plant, companies can use this MBD tool through the sandbox of the HUBCAP platform under a servitized (use- or result-oriented) business model (software as a service).

Keywords: Bioeconomy · Circular economy · Model-based design · Evaporation plant · Digital platform · Sandbox · Product-service systems · Software as a service

1 Introduction

Continuous industrial processes (e.g., biogas upgrading [1], hydrogen as energy carrier [2], industrial wastewater recovery [3] can play a key role for the sustainable transition

© IFIP International Federation for Information Processing 2022
Published by Springer Nature Switzerland AG 2022
D. Y. Kim et al. (Eds.): APMS 2022, IFIP AICT 664, pp. 3–10, 2022.
https://doi.org/10.1007/978-3-031-16411-8_1

worldwide. Different flows of matters and energy are indeed intended to be recovered through these systems under a Circular Economy (CE) and Bioeconomy fashion [4]. To foster in such a virtuous trend the involvement of companies, mostly SMEs (often lacking critical assets, funds, technologies or knowledge) and push the transitioning of manufacturing plants into a cyber-physical system (CPS) setting, it becomes essential to provide test before investing tools [5]. Enriched with digital model-based design (MBD) tools [6], such tools can provide decision support and can help to find the most suitable set-points to optimally use the infrastructure under analysis in multiple domains (e.g., energy management, manufacturing process, real-time optimization [5, 7]). To ease their provision, a cloud-based collaboration plat-form, enabling tool providers (companies, research organizations, and Digital Innova-tion Hubs (DIHs)) to deploy tools in a sand-box [6], has been developed by the HUBCAP project [8]. For example, concerning evaporation process, once the plant has been designed and implemented, the main issue is to understand how to make it run efficiently, through a decision-making system to look at daily operation in real time able [9].

However, even simpler solutions are still needed and also a visualization interface able to easily show results to the human operators needs to be developed to involve them into the decision-making process. In addition, such a tool has not been tested online. Therefore, the purpose of this paper is to introduce EVAPOSIM, a web application tool built for the evaporation process simulation, validated against real-world performance data for a reference evaporation plant, and deployed to the HUBCAP platform. To explore the sustainability of their plant, companies can use this MBD tool through the sandbox of the HUBCAP platform under a servitized (use- or result-oriented) business model (software-as-a-service (SaaS)).

The paper is structured as follows. Section 2 introduces the concept of (bio-) economy in the evaporation plants context and the servitized digital platform deploying MBD to develop CPS. Section 3 presents the research methodology, detailing how the tool has been built based on data collection from a real case. Section 4 presents the tool and Sect. 5 discusses its functionalities. Finally, Sect. 5 concludes the paper.

2   Research Context

2.1   Evaporation Plants and Circular Economy

Industrial wastewaters and landfill leachates are among the most polluted water steams produced by human activity. They can be treated with a combination of several processes (membrane separation, electrochemical and physicochemical processes), to recover a concentrated solution to be disposed of and a purified water stream. Evaporation is one of those treatment processes, whereby a more concentrated solution is obtained from a more dilute solution by evaporation of the solvent (i.e., in the case of wastewater treatment). In this sense, the terms evaporation and concentration are often used synonymously. The input is the diluted solution, the output is the evaporated solvent and, as a residue, the concentrated solution. The concentration of the final solution depends on the amount of evaporated solvent. Evaporation requires large amounts of low-thermal-level heat, required to boil off the solvent and then remove it as vapor from the solution that is gradually becoming concentrated. The relevance for the CE of evaporation applied to the treatment of landfill leachates is twofold. From one hand the purified water can be reused following the CE principles, in relation to its specification preferably as a feedstock or auxiliary in industrial processes or on the landfill site itself. On the other hand, the low-thermal-level heat can be obtained by recovering thermal wastes elsewhere on the site, for example the thermal exhaust from a cogeneration plant fed with the locally produced landfill gas.

2.2 Servitized Digital Platforms: Model-Based Design Models and Tools

The HUBCAP project developed a collaboration platform, based on the DIHIWARE collaboration platform (a web portal offering several social collaboration features already used in previous European funded projects), under the shape of a web-portal offering portfolios of services [10] and MBD assets (models and tools) to be adopted in the CPSs' development. These services and assets are offered for experimentation in a test before invest approach through a sandbox enabling users to access them in a ready to use way. The platform aims at attracting end-users interested in adopting MBD assets, aggregating them in a community composed of DIHs, providers of MBD assets and developers of CPS solutions. Through its platform, HUBCAP is providing several streams of funding to lower entry barriers for European SMEs interested in adopting MBD in the development process of their CPSs. However, in the future, the use of the HUBCAP platform will be open to a wider worldwide user base community of MBD asset providers and consumers, offering assets according to a SaaS business model.

3   Research Methodology

To develop the tool, data collection, filtration, processing, and reporting have been performed on the full-scale pilot plant (the EVAPOSIM experiment), a triple-effect evaporator operating in counterflow and vacuum condition. Over 40 sensors, distributed throughout the whole process, collect data and load them into the plant supervisor system and can be easily retrieved by plant operator and manager.

The evaporation plant is installed close to a landfill that collects municipal solid waste and nonhazardous special waste. The flow scheme of the plant and its top view are shown in Fig. 1 and 2. The landfill produces approximately 280 t/day of leachate characterized by high concentrations of chemical oxygen demand, ammonia, heavy metals, perfluoroalkyl substances and chlorides. The leachate is first treated with a reverse osmosis plant, producing about 208 t/day of permeate with characteristics suitable for discharge into surface waters and 72 t/day of retentate which is sent to the evaporation plant with a dry matter (DM) concentration of about 3.5%. The quantity of distillate produced is approximately 60 t/day, while the final quantity of concentrate with a DM concentration of approximately 20% is 12 t/day. The distillate in this case is recirculated to the head of the osmosis plant, but could be reused after conditioning in the industrial processes.

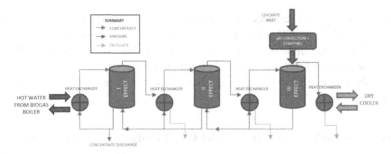

Fig. 1. Flow scheme of the evaporation plant in object [credits: NBT Bulgaria EOOD]

Fig. 2. Evaporation plant: top view [credits: NBT Bulgaria EOOD]

3.1 Data Selection and Criteria

The evaporator plant has installed a set of sensors and instruments that are fundamental to control the evaporation process and help to analyse its status. All the plant works on functional logics that control its automatism: these logics are written into the Programmable Logic Controller (PLC) control system. The plant operator works on the Supervisory Control And Data Acquisition (SCADA) system, the interface between the operator and the control systems PLC able to change some set points and take the data necessary for work. The data recorded by the system (stored in the SCADA and graphed for immediate viewing at the operator panel or with remote access to the plant) are temperatures, flow rates, density, electrical conductivity, pressures, and other parameters. The data used for the EVAPOSIM experiment refer to the year 2020, during which the plant was in the start-up and commissioning phase and different plant operating modes were possible (making data collection accurate and verified on site).

3.2 Data Extraction Preparation, Filtering and Range Definition

The data collected by SCADA are saved into external storage unit that can be taken directly from operator panel, or, for a more specific analysis, extracted from storage unit and copied to a PC into a.csv file (containing max. 500k records). When the file unit is full, a new one is created by SCADA and new data are saved. Given the large amount of data to be processed, it was decided to process these files in spreadsheets. It is also essential to choose which measuring instruments are of interest for the model validation. The purpose of data selection was to find data that can be assumed acceptable for the EVAPOSIM project. Data preparation and filtering is an important step prior to processing and involves reformatting data, making corrections to data and the combining of data sets. The selected data are:

- Temperature, to understand the heating status of the plant, the heat exchange efficiency in the heat exchangers, the operating temperature of effects.
- Pressure, regulating the evaporation process, connected with temperature of all the system (with lower pressure value the effect needs less temperature to evaporate).
- Volume of inlet and outlet, to define the evaporator concentration performance.
- Density of concentrate, controlling the discharge set point (connected to the %DM).
- Electric conductivity of distillate, showing the "quality" of distillate, the amount of salts inside the distillate and so the purity of the evaporate.

It is possible to look at the different modes of operations where specific days and precise times were chosen to analyse the functionality of the plant. During these periods there was a precise control of the plant by specialised technicians, who were able to validate the accuracy of the instrumental measurements and plant operativity. In addition, the evaporator was performing adequately without any anomalies and the data was in line with the design performance. All these indications allowed to validate the parameters recorded in different operating conditions. To make useful the chosen modes of operations for software development, operating windows during the designated running day were identified, choosing working windows as steady state of the plant.

4 Results

The EVAPOSIM experiment was run to enable the cloud-based simulation of evaporation plants and deliver the related web-app. The simulation approach used is:

- first-principle-based (the behaviour of the physical system is described a-priori using fundamental laws (e.g., mass and energy conservation) and empirical engineering correlations from textbooks and literature (e.g., reaction kinetics)),
- steady-state (the process is assumed in steady operation, i.e. all intensive variables and the fluxes of extensive properties are constant in time (so unsuitable for transients processes, control system design, or processes inherently unsteadily operating)),
- concentrated-parameters (it is assumed that each unit can be represented as a homogeneous portion of matter (this drastic simplification is widely employed in process engineering, most in the Continuously Stirred Tank Reactor (CSTR))),
- process simulation (the scope of the simulation is an entire process or plant unit (not a single device), accepting coarse-grained, less detailed results in exchange).

The application of this simulation approach to continuous evaporation plants is well-established and gives accurate results. In a previous project, the LIBPF™ process simulation technology was successfully used to model a triple-effect evaporator operating in counterflow and vacuum conditions during the design phase. This process model was the starting point and was validated against real-world performance data (collected, filtered, and pre-processed from a reference evaporation plant in operation).

4.1 Web Applications

The EVAPOSIM web-app is simple-to-use, customized web applications for the cloud-based simulation of the evaporation plant and the demo process respectively. They make the process models more accessible so that non-experts can prioritize and optimize decisions in the proposal and design phases of new plants. Both are based on pretty much the same code base and work in a similar way. The users can configure simulation cases (full load, partial load, high concentration, etc.), run simulations, and graphically examine results. Figure 3 reports screenshots of the web-app.

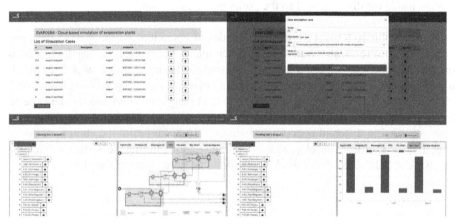

Fig. 3. Top-left: start page of the EVAPOSIM web-app; Top-right: new case creation form of the EVAPOSIM web-app; Bottom-left: case detail page of the EVAPOSIM web-app with PFD view; Bottom-right: case detail page of the EVAPOSIM web-app with bar chart view.

4.2 Demo Process Model

The demo process model has been deployed to the HUBCAP platform a demo instance of the web application so that new adopters can test it and evaluate its suitability for their customized applications.

Three requirements have been defined (it should be: 1) relevant to perspective adopters; 2. Non-confidential and validated against publicly available data; 3. Easy to grasp). Based on a screening of the continuous industrial processes in relation to the CE, renewable hydrogen electrolysers have been identified as most relevant.

Electrolysis is an electrochemical process that uses direct electric current to drive an otherwise non-spontaneous chemical reaction, such as the decomposition of water in hydrogen and oxygen. Alkaline water electrolysis employs Nickel-based electrodes separated by a diaphragm (to make sure the product gases are separated), and immersed in a concentrated alkaline solution of potassium hydroxide as electrolyte, and does not require the costly and rare precious metals as catalyzers. Alkaline water electrolysis plants are operated under pressure (typically 30 bar) and at mild temperature (around 60–90 °C). Currently, this is the most mature electrolysis technology and it is commercially available up to the range of 10-MW plants. Therefore, the alkaline water electrolysis was implemented as demo process and validated [11].

5 Discussion and Conclusions

This paper reports the work conducted to develop EVAPOSIM, a cloud-based simulation tool of evaporation plants into a cloud-based platform. EVAPOSIM makes the evaporation process model more accessible so that non-experts can prioritize and optimize decisions in the proposal and design phases of new plants.

With the same methodology, models for other processes and plants relevant for the CE (such as water electrolysis, membrane separations, fuel cells, steam reforming, cogeneration etc.) can be created and provided for servitized, cloud-based simulation.

The process model can be used in all phases of a project: in the feasibility phase to estimate plant size and capital costs; in the proposal phase to estimate operating costs (mainly electrical and thermal energy consumptions) and key performance parameters (conversion efficiency and hydrogen production); in the design phase to guide the equipment sizing and selection; in the operator training phase, to help bring up to speed the operators on the new technology; during operation for on-line monitoring to troubleshoot and optimize the plant.

The development of the tool started taking as reference an evaporation plant installed into a landfill that collects municipal solid waste and nonhazardous special waste. The tool will be provided in a cloud asset (the HUBCAP platform), to impel its function of testing before investing for a wide range of evaporation plants.

Its use should facilitate users to realize the actual effects of CE and Bioeconomy, giving evidence of which could be the flows of materials and energy related to a specific setting of the plant and of the wastes adopted. Indeed, the main outcome for the users will be the very fast evaluation of the economic and environmental sustainability of the plant analyzed before investing in a specific technology. On the other side, the usage of this tool in a cloud-based environment concurs at facilitating and impelling the provision of such MBD simulation tools through a PSS business model. The tool provider can offer the SaaS, obtaining revenues based on its use or result. In addition, the paper aims at facilitating the adoption of other tools and at attracting other models and tools interested in finding new partners and applications in the energy domain.

The main future work could be the implementation of the functionality of collecting real-time data from the sensors, obtaining a digital twin of the plant. This could first support the internal measurement of the circular flows going through the plant and second trigger a more effective alignment of the plant resources with its external stakeholders, paving the way towards a Circular Bioeconomy community [12]. Finally, the main issue to be faced to exploit this tool is the need of dedicated process managers fostering the transfer of tacit knowledge and experience belonging to the experts operating on the plants to feed the plant automated system. Therefore, a new business model is needed where software providers become the integrator of those advanced systems. In this context, a big contrast is raised between SMEs (typically flexible) and big companies (instead rigid and more reluctant to upset their processes).

Acknowledgments. This work was supported by the HUBCAP Innovation Action funded by the European Commission's Horizon 2020 Programme under GA 872698.

References

1. Vo, T.T.Q., Wall, D.M., Ring, D., Rajendran, K., Murphy, J.D.: Techno-economic analysis of biogas upgrading via amine scrubber, carbon capture and ex-situ methanation. Appl. Energy **212**, 1191–1202 (2018). https://doi.org/10.1016/j.apenergy.2017.12.099
2. Turner, J.A.: Sustainable hydrogen production. Science (80-.) **305**(5686), 972–974 (2004). https://doi.org/10.1126/SCIENCE.1103197
3. Gherghel, A., Teodosiu, C., De Gisi, S.: A review on wastewater sludge valorisation and its challenges in the context of circular economy. J. Clean. Prod. **228**, 244–263 (2019). https://doi.org/10.1016/J.JCLEPRO.2019.04.240
4. D'Adamo, I., et al.: Bioeconomy of sustainability: drivers, opportunities and policy implications. Sustainability **14**(1), 1–7 (2022). https://doi.org/10.3390/su14010200
5. Macedo, H.D., Sassanelli, C., Larsen, P.G., Terzi, S.: Facilitating model-based design of cyber-manufacturing systems (2021). https://doi.org/10.1016/j.procir.2021.11.327
6. Larsen, P.G., et al.: A cloud-based collaboration platform for model-based design of cyber-physical systems (2020). https://orcid.org/0000-0001-7041-1807
7. Greppi, P., Bosio, B., Arato, E.: A steady-state simulation tool for MCFC systems suitable for on-line applications. Int. J. Hydrog. Energy **33**(21), 6327–6338 (2008). https://doi.org/10.1016/J.IJHYDENE.2008.07.018
8. HUBCAP project (2020). https://www.hubcap.eu/. Accessed 14 Jan 2022
9. Krämer, S., Engell, S.: Resource efficiency of processing plants: monitoring and improvement (2018)
10. Sassanelli, C., Terzi, S.: The D-BEST reference model: a flexible and sustainable support for the digital transformation of small and medium enterprises. Glob. J. Flex. Syst. Manag. **40171**(307) (2022). https://doi.org/10.1007/s40171-022-00307-y
11. Sánchez, M., Amores, E., Abad, D., Rodríguez, L., Clemente-Jul, C.: Aspen plus model of an alkaline electrolysis system for hydrogen production. Int. J. Hydrog. Energy **45**(7), 3916–3929 (2020). https://doi.org/10.1016/J.IJHYDENE.2019.12.027
12. D'adamo, I., Sassanelli, C.: Biomethane community: a research agenda towards sustainability. Sustainability **14**(4735), 1–22 (2022). https://doi.org/10.3390/SU14084735

The Digital Twin Application
for Micro-Tool Wear Monitoring
with Open-Source CAD System

Christiand[1,2], Gandjar Kiswanto[1(✉)], and Ario Sunar Baskoro[1]

[1] Universitas Indonesia, Depok, Indonesia
gandjar_kiswanto@eng.ui.ac.id
[2] Universitas Katolik Indonesia Atma Jaya, Tangerang Selatan, Indonesia
https://robot.atmajaya.ac.id, https://www.ui.ac.id

Abstract. The digital twin technology offers a tight coupling between the simulated process and the actual world events. In the field of tool wear monitoring (TWM), such system characteristic is essential to maintain the accuracy of the wear prediction by taking into account the actual condition data during the machining process. This paper presents the implementation of the digital twin technology where the micro-milling machining process is simulated by using the spindle controller, spindle motor, and cutting torque model. The wear monitoring was performed by comparing the spindle motor's simulated and real-time electric current. A virtual environment was developed using FreeCAD - an open-source CAD system, to represent the processes and objects involved in the machining. The digital twin framework ensures that the simulation and real-time data were synchronized in the virtual environment. This paper focuses on the building blocks and technical implementation in realizing a digital twin application in the domain of micro-tool wear monitoring.

Keywords: Digital twin · Tool wear monitoring · Micro-milling · FreeCAD

1 Introduction

Tool wear monitoring (TWM) has been actively researched for two decades. The research aimed to develop a system or method that accurately predicts the actual wear of the tool during the machining process. TWM system has an important role in achieving the properties of high-quality machining, i.e., excellent surface integrity, accuracy, and cost-efficiency. TWM systems were mostly developed for the macro-machining application, such as macro-milling or micro-turning. However, the increasing demand for miniaturization of many advanced

© IFIP International Federation for Information Processing 2022
Published by Springer Nature Switzerland AG 2022
D. Y. Kim et al. (Eds.): APMS 2022, IFIP AICT 664, pp. 11–18, 2022.
https://doi.org/10.1007/978-3-031-16411-8_2

devices with micro-feature, such as bio-sensor with their micro-fluidic channel, has stimulated the expansion of TWM research to the micro-machining domain. In particular, many recent works of TWM development were focused on improving the micro-machining quality for micro-milling applications due to the advantages of micro-milling compared to other micro-fabrication methods. Some of the micro-milling advantages are macro-milling technique derivation and the ability to process 3D-complex geometry with various materials. However, micro-milling is very susceptible to tool breakage due to the rapid wear during the machining and the downsized dimension of the tool. Therefore, the TWM system is needed and has become an important part of the high-quality micro-milling process.

Industry 4.0 has brought one key-enabler technology named **digital twin** (DT) to seamlessly combine the simulation and the real world for providing various services. This new technology allows the development of a new class of TWM methods that combines simulation and real-time data simultaneously. Within the future smart factory of Industry 4.0, the digital twin approach is very plausible since the computing power for the simulation process equipped with a high-speed sensors network will be common in the machining environment of the future smart factory. Thus, both simulation and real-time data acquisition can be executed and integrated seamlessly. Even more, the DT-based TWM may anticipate and benefit the advancement in the field of industrial sensors in the future since the newly developed sensors can be easily integrated into the existing sensor networks.

This paper presents the development of a DT-based TWM system for the micro-milling application. The micro-milling process was simulated by using the spindle motor model, the spindle controller model, and the cutting torque model. The wear monitoring was performed by comparing the simulated and the real-time electric current from the built-in sensor of the spindle motor. The virtual environment was built by using FreeCAD - an open-source CAD system. The development was targeted for the broad range of machining sites to represent the micro-milling process and all the machining objects. The DT synchronizes the data from the simulation and real-time data acquisition inside the virtual environment. The presentation of this paper focuses on the building blocks and technical implementation in realizing a digital twin application in the domain of micro-tool wear monitoring.

2   Literature Review

2.1   Digital Twin in Manufacturing Applications

The digital twin (DT) technology has been adopted for several manufacturing applications with some specific goals. Aivaliotis et al. developed a DT system for the predictive maintenance of industrial robot [1]. The robot gearbox parameters' iterative fine-tuning was performed using the DT system. Kannan et al. predicted the wear of the grinding wheel by using a DT system [2]. The predictive model of the grinding redress was constructed from the auto-regression moving average (ARMA). The model was selected due to the static properties of the motor spindle signal in the time series. Botkina et al. have developed a DT system for cutting tool [3]. In their system, the information of the physical tool was continuously and digitally updated during the machining process. The data representation and exchange of the cutting tool followed ISO 13399 standard. The updated information of the cutting tool was targeted for precise process simulation, control, and analysis. Eventually, the result of the DT system gave benefits for the continuous improvement of the production process. The aforementioned DT systems show that the application needs at minimally three major building blocks, i.e., a) **the object to be imitated**, b) **the digital twin**, c) **the communication means between the imitated object and the digital twin**.

2.2 Digital Twin Building Block

The digital twin building block contains information to model the real object digitally. The digital model can represent the process (dynamics, state propagation) related to the objects [1], the physic (shape, form, geometry) of the objects [3], or the properties (surface roughness) of the objects [4]. The model can be generated from the industrial standard, physics law derivation, or empirical equation from the experiments. In order to monitor the variable of interest, the digital twin often contains a virtual environment to report the latest status of the simulation and the incoming real-time data. The virtual environment is obviously needed for the applications where the motion or object changes should be visually presented to the DT users. At a minimum, the digital twin has a user interface, e.g., a software dashboard, to monitor the variable of interest. Cai et al. presented the technique to build a DT system and fused the sensor information in the cyber-physical manufacturing [4]. Their DT system has a virtual machine to visualize the running process and a data acquisition module to get the 3-axes accelerometer data for monitoring the surface roughness of the workpiece.

2.3 Virtual Environment for the Digital Twin

There are many methods to build a virtual environment for the DT application. As suggested by Cai et al., the developments of virtual environments may take reference from the previous works of virtual system developments, such as Virtual Assembly [5], Virtual Tooling [6] and Virtual Prototyping [7]. Most of the virtual environments were developed with 3D graphic libraries on some programming language and separated from the CAD system. However, as a matter of fact, the CAD system was the initial place where the virtual object was designed. For the reason of seamless interoperability and further expandability, the virtual environment for DT would be more appropriate to work inside the CAD system. FreeCAD - an open-source CAD system that offers functionality to develop specific modules inside its 3D graphic environment [8]. The virtual environment development for various engineering applications has been reported using FreeCAD as the virtual environment [9,10]. Compared to OpenSCAD -

another open-source cad system, FreeCAD has advantages in exporting the standard parametric models, Python programming, and combining external models to its 3D graphic interface [11].

2.4 Micro-milling Model for the Digital Twin

The micro-milling process can be modeled by using the mechanistic model with the tool wear as the contributing factor [12,13]. Later, the micro-tool wear information is inferred by comparing the cutting force data from the actual machining and the simulation. However, acquiring the cutting force data is costly in micro-milling due to the high price of the force sensor with the micro-meter specification. Alternatively, the micro-milling process can be modeled by using the information from the built-in sensors of the machining devices, e.g., torque and electrical current sensors of the motor spindle [14]. This strategy cuts down the cost of the sensor installation. As far as the tool wear is concerned, the data-driven method can actually generate the model relating the tool wear and the input data from various sensors, such as cutting force, vibration, acoustic emission, and power sensors [15,16]. However, such a data-driven approach will lose the concept of DT where the imitated object should ideally represent and be derived from the actual phenomena of the process, i.e., using physic (mechanic) law.

3 Methodology

3.1 System Architecture

The system architecture of DT-based tool wear monitoring (Fig. 1) follows the building blocks explained in the Subsect. 2.1 and 2.2. The system consists of the

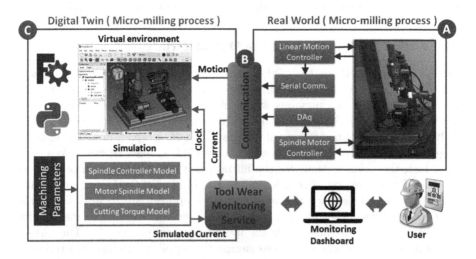

Fig. 1. The system architecture for micro-tool wear monitoring with digital twin

three big blocks, i.e., a) the object to be imitated, b) the digital twin, and c) the communication. The micro-milling machine is a miniaturized 5-DOF (degree of freedom) CNC machine with a linear resolution of 1 μm. The motor controller provides position (x, y, z, γ, β) information through the RS-232 serial communication. The spindle uses a high-speed brushless DC motor with 80000 rpm maximum speed and air coolant. The data acquisition (DAq) module gathers real-time information on the spindle's working condition through the GPIO port. The spindle information consists of the torque (T), current (i), and speed (ω) in real-time.

3.2   Micro-milling Simulation

The simulation uses the spindle motor model in Eq. (1), the spindle controller model in Eq. (2)–(3), and the cutting torque model in Eq. (4)–(5) to represent the imitated micro-milling process. The formulation of the models has been taken from our previous work in [17]. Machining parameters are known prior to the simulation run. The micro-tool wear monitoring is performed by comparing the real electric current from the built-in current sensor of the spindle to the simulated current from the simulation. The difference between the two electric current values can infer the abnormality and wear progression profile. The numerical engine for the simulation uses XCOS dynamic system library from SciLab.

$$J_m \frac{d^2\theta(t)}{dt^2} + B_m \frac{d\theta(t)}{dt} = K_T \cdot i(t) - T_c(t) \tag{1}$$

$$i(t) = K_p e(t) + K_i \int_0^\tau e(\tau)\, d\tau + K_d \frac{de(t)}{dt} \tag{2}$$

$$e(t) = \omega_{ref}(t) - \omega(t) \tag{3}$$

$$T_c(t) = g(t) \cdot \begin{cases} a_1 e^{a_2 t} + a_3; & \text{for rise} \\ b_1 \log(t) + b_2; & \text{for steady} \\ c_1 t^2 + c_2 t + c_3; & \text{for fall} \end{cases} \tag{4}$$

$$g(t) = \begin{cases} 1, & t_c^{start} \le t \le t_c^{end} \\ 0, & else \end{cases} \tag{5}$$

3.3   Virtual Environment

The environment of the micro-milling was built inside the FreeCAD. All the 3D object files were imported to the FreeCAD in assembly mode. The 3D environment of micro-milling consists of the CNC machine and workpiece 3D models. For the CNC motion simulation, the CNC machine's kinematic chain should be defined by arranging the hierarchy of the kinematic joints and links (bodies). Figure 2 shows the example of the 1-DOF kinematic chain definition with two links ($Link1$, $Link2$) and one joint ($J12$). This work only used the primitive types of joint, i.e., revolute and prismatic. To realize such an idea in the FreeCAD system, the body coordinate with respect to the world coordinate (H^{world}) was assigned by using an entity named **part**. Then, each imported body was attached to the **part** entity coincidently. FreeCAD stores the local coordinate of each entity (H) relative to the coordinate of the parent entity. Therefore, actuating the intermediate part (e.g., $J12$) between the two connected parts (e.g., $J1$, $J2$) has the similar effect of having one primitive joint with variable θ. The refresh event of the virtual environment depends on the clock signal issued by the simulation block (see Fig. 1).

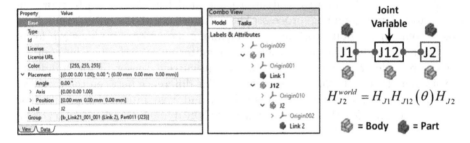

Fig. 2. Kinematics definition for the virtual environment

4   Experiment and Result

The machining experiment was conducted with the three sets of machining parameters as reported in the Table.1 of our previous work [17]. For the analysis purpose, the time-stamped data of the motor position and spindle information were recorded into the files. Then, each data entry from the files was replayed sequentially in the simulation according to the time stamp. The current presentation emphasizes the quality of the simulation and real-time data synchronization in a virtual environment. In particular, the activation function of cutting torque from the Eq. (5) was executed based on the collision event between the virtual micro-tool with the virtual workpiece in the FreeCad as the virtual environment. The collision volume became the substitution for the uncut chip thickness (UCT) to calculate the simulated cutting torque.

Figure 3 shows the synchronization between the real-time data and the simulation. Point A in Fig. 3 is the starting event when the collision is about to occur with partial tool immersion. Point B is the event boundary when the tool was in full contact with the workpiece. The event triggering mechanism came from the micro-milling machine's motor controller's real-time position data. This mechanism realized the concept of a digital twin where the simulation and real-time events are integrated and coupled in one process. The tool wear monitoring was performed by observing the spindle electric current during the machining process. Abnormality of the wear progression can be detected by comparing the simulated and actual electric current of the motor spindle. Compared to the torque sensor, the electric current sensor is more economical. The experiment has shown the tight interaction between the simulation, the real world, and the targeted service.

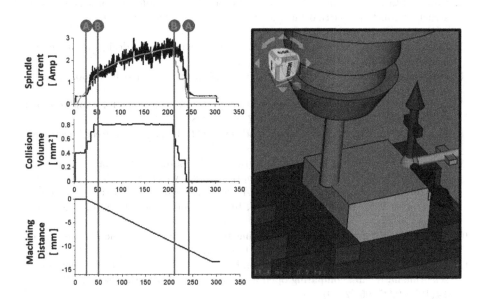

Fig. 3. Experiment result

5 Conclusion

The development of a tool wear monitoring system using digital twin technology with an open-source CAD system has been presented. The micro-tool wear monitoring was realized by observing the simulated electric current of the spindle motor. The digital twin of the micro-milling process was developed based on the three digital models, i.e., the spindle motor model, spindle controller model, and cutting torque model. The integration of real-time position data into the simulation was useful for calculating the virtual collision volume to simulate the cutting torque. The proposed system becomes an example for further works on the realization of various services in machining by using digital twin technology.

Acknowledgement. This work has been supported by Beasiswa Pendidikan Indonesia (BPI) from Indonesia Endowment Fund for Education (LPDP).

References

1. Aivaliotis, P., Georgoulias, K., Arkouli, Z., Makris, S.: Methodology for enabling digital twin using advanced physics-based modelling in predictive maintenance. Procedia CIRP **81**, 417–422 (2019)
2. Kannan, K., Arunachalam, N.: A digital twin for grinding wheel: an information sharing platform for sustainable grinding process. J. Manuf. Sci. Eng. **141**(2) (2019)
3. Botkina, D., Hedlind, M., Olsson, B., Henser, J., Lundholm, T.: Digital twin of a cutting tool. Procedia CIRP **72**, 215–218 (2018)
4. Cai, Y., Starly, B., Cohen, P., Lee, Y.S.: Sensor data and information fusion to construct digital-twins virtual machine tools for cyber-physical manufacturing. Procedia Manuf. **10**, 1031–1042 (2017)
5. Ong, S., Pang, Y., Nee, A.: Augmented reality aided assembly design and planning. CIRP Ann. **56**(1), 49–52 (2007)
6. Altintas, Y., Cao, Y.: Virtual design and optimization of machine tool spindles. CIRP Ann. **54**(1), 379–382 (2005)
7. Choi, S., Cheung, H.: A versatile virtual prototyping system for rapid product development. Comput. Ind. **59**(5), 477–488 (2008)
8. FreeCAD: Your own 3d parametric modeler (2022). https://www.freecadweb.org/. Accessed 12 Apr 2022
9. Gayer, D., O'Sullivan, C., Scully, S., Burke, D., Brossard, J., Chapron, C.: FreeCAD visualization of realistic 3d physical optics beams within a CAD system-model. In: Millimeter, Submillimeter, and Far-Infrared Detectors and Instrumentation for Astronomy VIII, vol. 9914, p. 99142Y. International Society for Optics and Photonics (2016)
10. Li, J.Y., et al.: FreeCAD based modeling study on MCNPX for accelerator driven system. Prog. Nucl. Energy **107**, 100–109 (2018)
11. Machado, F., Malpica, N., Borromeo, S.: Parametric CAD modeling for open source scientific hardware: comparing openSCAD and freeCAD Python scripts. Plos One **14**(12), e0225795 (2019)
12. Liu, T., Zhu, K., Wang, G.: Micro-milling tool wear monitoring under variable cutting parameters and runout using fast cutting force coefficient identification method. Int. J. Adv. Manuf. Technol. **111**(11), 3175–3188 (2020)
13. Li, G., Li, S., Zhu, K.: Micro-milling force modeling with tool wear and runout effect by spatial analytic geometry. Int. J. Adv. Manuf. Technol. **107**(1), 631–643 (2020)
14. Kaneko, K., Nishida, I., Sato, R., Shirase, K.: A practical method to monitor tool wear in end milling using a changing cutting force model that requires no additional sensors. J. Adv. Mech. Des. Syst. Manuf. **15**(6), JAMDSM0077 (2021)
15. Bagri, S., Manwar, A., Varghese, A., Mujumdar, S., Joshi, S.S.: Tool wear and remaining useful life prediction in micro-milling along complex tool paths using neural networks. J. Manuf. Process. **71**, 679–698 (2021)
16. Tansel, I., et al.: Tool wear estimation in micro-machining: Part I: tool usage-cutting force relationship. Int. J. Mach. Tools Manuf. **40**(4), 599–608 (2000)
17. Kiswanto, G., et al.: Digital twin approach for tool wear monitoring of micro-milling. Procedia CIRP **93**, 1532–1537 (2020)

A Framework to Address Complexity and Changeability in the Design of Circular Product-Service Systems

Alessandro Bertoni(✉) [ID] and Raj Jiten Machchhar [ID]

Department of Mechanical Engineering, Blekinge Institute of Technology, 37179 Karlskrona, Sweden
alessandro.bertoni@bth.se

Abstract. The design of a circular PSS solution goes beyond the traditional perspective of circular product design encompassing multiple complexity dimensions that need to be considered and addressed in the early stages of design. The paper provides a literature-based outlook on the levels of complexity to be faced when making decisions in early PSS design by positioning the concept of changeability inherited from the systems engineering literature into the context of the design of circular PSS. The paper ultimately stresses the need to consider the changeability of PSS as a relevant dimension in the assessment of its circularity potential. It does so by proposing a framework for the design of circular PSS solutions, summarizing the main design strategies and approaches currently described in the literature to mitigate the uncertainties generated by PSS complexity.

Keywords: Changeability · Product-service systems · Complexity · Circularity

1 Introduction

Governmental institutions and researchers agree that a move toward circular economy systems would contribute to the achieving of the sustainable development goals defined by the United Nations [1]. Manufacturing companies play a key role in realizing sustainability ambitions and a consistent research effort has been spent on identifying what are the fundamental criteria upon which circular economy is defined and measured in the industry (e.g., [2]). From a product development perspective, circularity consideration makes early decisions more and more difficult, increasing the level of complexity of the design problem, now addressing the development of a complex system featuring the combination of product and service components (i.e., developing Product-Service Systems solutions or PSS) to be delivered in a lifespan that could, in some cases, extend over several decades. In such contexts, the translation of high-level circularity considerations into specific product requirements that guide design decisions is a challenging task. Methods to promote the development of circular systems have been proposed in literature both from a business development and a product development perspective (e.g. [3, 4]). However, the literature still does not provide a comprehensive outlook on how

© IFIP International Federation for Information Processing 2022
Published by Springer Nature Switzerland AG 2022
D. Y. Kim et al. (Eds.): APMS 2022, IFIP AICT 664, pp. 19–25, 2022.
https://doi.org/10.1007/978-3-031-16411-8_3

to deal with the new uncertainties introduced by circularity considerations during the early engineering design of PSS. In this regard, one of the challenges is the lack of literature elucidating the complexities that exist in and around the inferred PSS. To bridge this knowledge gap, the paper aims to provide a comprehensive outlook on the level of complexity introduced by PSS, stressing the need to consider the changeability of PSS as a relevant dimension in the assessment of its circularity potential. As a result, the paper positions the concept of changeability in relation to the available literature about the design of circular solutions and in relation to the literature concerning systems complexity and changeability in systems engineering. Ultimately the paper summarizes the main available design strategies and approaches currently described in the literature to mitigate the uncertainties generated by PSS complexity.

The definition of the research problem and objective is the results of a participatory action research approach in collaboration with two major Swedish companies operating in the aerospace and construction machinery industry. Qualitative data were gathered through semi-structured interviews, workshops, and focus groups, initially to compile a comprehensive descriptive analysis, although the contribution of this paper shall be seen as largely based on literature review and synthesis. A narrative-styled literature review, complemented by a snowballing technique, was performed in the field of PSS and systems engineering. The choice of not performing a more structured and formalized systematic review was driven by the acknowledgment of the high variety of synonyms of changeability, flexibility and adaptability available in literature, that led, in a first step, to an unmanageable number of publications from multiple research fields.

2 Literature Review

2.1 Design of Circular PSS Solutions

The academic discussion about how to design circular products can be framed into the broader research effort of developing and implementing methods for sustainability quantification. In product design, this translates into the capability of integrating new methods and approaches into the current well-established engineering practices. In such a context a broad range of engineering methods have flourished under the umbrella of Eco-design (e.g. [5]), Design for Sustainability (e.g. [6]), Design for environment (e.g. [7]), Sustainable Product development (e.g. [8]) and Design for Circularity (e.g. [4]). The latter has focused on understanding what the features of a circular economy system are, and therefore, what kind of circular economy indicators can be introduced to measure the circularity of a product or a system. To enable this, the Ellen McArthur Foundation published a list of material circularity indicators at the product level and at the company level [3]. Pauliuk [9] stressed the importance of circular strategies to be monitored from a higher system perspective, to avoid defining indicators that would bring companies' decisions in the wrong direction. This highlights the need to have the right indicators used in the correct context and with a suitable level of granularity based on the specific focus of the design activity. Den Hollander et al. [4] argued that circular product design is guided by the Inertia Principle, prescribing product integrity to be the main design objective to be pursued and to be preferred to product recyclability. Based on this they defined circular product design as the combination of both design for integrity (i.e. aiming at resisting, postponing, and reversing obsolescence at the product and component level), and design for recycling, aiming at preventing and reversing obsolescence at a material level.

2.2 Complexity and Changeability in Systems Design

In the realm of systems engineering, Magee and de Weck [10 p. 2] defined a complex system as "a system with numerous components and interconnections, interactions or interdependencies that are difficult to describe, understand, predict, manage, design, and/or change". Further, Gaspar et al. [11] defined the complexity of a system as the quantity of information necessary to define a system, understand the interdependencies, and predict future scenarios. In such a context, five essential aspects for engineering a complex system were proposed by Rhodes and Ross [12], namely, structural, behavioral, contextual, temporal, and perceptual complexity. Addressing such complexities reflects the primary need to deliver desired value to all the associated stakeholders throughout the lifecycle [12]. In such a context changeability is a property of the system to reach various conceivable states to allow a robust value delivery during the operational stage while embracing changes in the operational context [13]. Changeability is a collection of many change-related "ilities" such as adaptability, flexibility, scalability, etc. and it is acknowledged as an over-arching property of the system of being able to either change the "form" or "function" of the system to bring about a change in the operation as a response to changes in the context [13]. Changeability is highly related to the complexity of the system; however, changeability excludes change-related ilities outside the operational life of the system thus excluding factors such as "remanufacturing" or "recycling", that fall inside the "traditional" boundaries of design for remanufacturing and recyclability.

3 Defining Changeability in the Design of Circular PSS Solutions

The existing literature shows some limitations in supporting the design of circular PSS solutions. Firstly, limited methods and tools are capable of identifying and assessing circularity in early design phases, which requires linking PSS circularity with stakeholder needs, as well as potential business implications, that may change over time. Secondly, when working on the conceptual design of PSS components (or sub-systems), engineers work with requirements that seldom reflect the overall design rationale of circular solutions. Thirdly, even if circularity-related product requirements are in place there is a lack of understanding about the value robustness of a circularity solution along its lifecycle, that is, about how the PSS solution will deal with the behavioral, structural, contextual, perceptual, and temporal complexity, or, in other words, about how "changeable" a PSS solution will be.

Based on such considerations Fig. 1 proposes a framework for design of circular PSS solutions, positioning design for PSS changeability as a complementary dimension to design for integrity and recycling. The framework adds the "Design for PSS changeability" dimension (bottom part of Fig. 1) listing potential design strategies and potential methods to mitigate the negative impact of five levels of system complexity. The complexity levels are derived from the work by Rhodes and Ross [12] further investigated by authors in the field of aerospace and maritime engineering (e.g. [11, 13, 14, 15]), while the potential design strategies and methods to mitigate the negative effect of complexity in design decision making are derived from the available scientific literature in the field. In detail the five levels of complexity are:

Structural Complexity. Defined by the system components and their relationship. The structural complexity is determined by the decision made by engineers and designers in PSS design; thus, it is normally in the control of decision-makers. Structural complexity is often addressed and reduced by applying strategies for modular product and service design, that are claimed to be able to mitigate changes and conflicting requirements. In this regard, an example of concept selection for elevators provided as PSS is presented in literature by [16]. Here the selection of proper PSS module instances which are a function of product and service modules combined into a solution under relevant constraints is the design strategy to address the structural complexity of the product while developing as PSS solution [16].

Behavioral Complexity. Defined as the complexity given by the multiple parts of the designed system that concurrently operate to deliver the intended value. Such definition does not encompass external factors that can influence the system under design, thus also the behavioral complexity can be considered as a parameter in the control of the decision-makers. Model-based systems engineering (MBSE) is one of the known approaches to simulate such behavior while systems are still in the design stage. Based on the use of "executable" models (often based on SysML or UML language), MBSE is increasingly adopted in industry to address the behavioral complexity of complex systems.

Contextual Complexity includes all external factors that can influence the behavior of the system. Contextual complexity is focused on understanding the influence of external stimuli and it has been the focus of research for many decades. The challenge is that the decision-makers can manage the uncertainties internal to the system to a certain level, but the external uncertainties are beyond the control of the decision-makers, thus making it cumbersome to build a system capable of handling these uncertainties. This viewpoint is preserved in PSS design, where many researchers have actively acknowledged the changing context and its influence on the lifecycle of the [17]. Emerging design strategies dealing with PSS contextual complexity encompass the use of scenario simulations based on agent-based and discrete event modeling (e.g. [18]) or the creation of environmental interaction models [19].

Temporal Complexity. Temporal complexity escalates the concept of contextual complexity by introducing a time dimension in the system-context interaction. Researchers agree on the unexploited potential of the PSS value delivery given by the lack of integration of long-term thinking during the design, stating that PSS must include a lifecycle or through-life perspective, (e.g. [20]). In such a context, scenario-based simulations linked to the development of digital twins are seen as the potential strategies to deal with temporal complexity in PSS design. In particular, the literature identifies as a potential future scenario the use of virtual "beta prototypes" of PSS (also defined as "fake twins" [21]) capable of simulating radical changes in the PSS hardware while running in parallel with the entity that exists in reality. This is based on the idea that, through the accumulation of data, the virtual models will reach a tipping point showing when a fake twin (i.e., a radical redesign of the original PSS concept) will become more value-adding for both the provider and its customers, considering investments, switching costs, risks and more in the equation.

Perceptual Complexity. Such complexity is generated by the differences in the opinion of the stakeholders about the value of a system. The essence of perceptual complexity is the dynamics of expectations from the system through time [11]. Work in the field of PSS prototyping has focused on PSS perception by crating shared stakeholders' experiences and providing a sense of full scalability of PSS solutions [22]. Additionally, virtual reality applications have been proposed to replicate intangible and subjective customers' experiences during PSS testing [23], although the use of such technology to address the perceptual complexity in PSS design is still in its infancy.

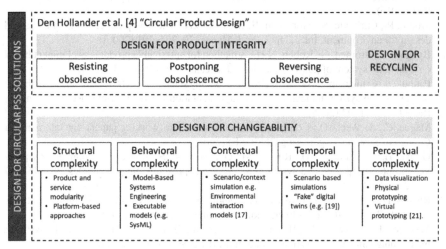

Fig. 1. Framework for Design for PSS circular solution positioning "Design for PSS changeability" in relation to circular product design.

4 Conclusions

The design of a circular PSS solution goes beyond the traditional perspective of circular product design encompassing multiple complexity dimensions that need to be considered and addressed in the early stages of design. The paper has presented an outlook on various levels of complexities that affect PSS design stressing the need to consider the changeability of PSS as an integral part of the effort toward designing new circular solutions, complementing the established approach for circular product design available in literature. The paper positions its contribution in between the field of PSS design and systems engineering and shall be seen as a tentative to provide a framework of reference around which to further develop future research efforts in the field.

References

1. United Nations General Assembly: Transforming our world: The 2030 agenda for sustainable development (2015). https://www.unfpa.org/resources/transforming-our-world-2030-agenda-sustainable-development. Accessed 29 Apr 2022
2. EASAC European Academies' Science Advisory Council: Indicators for Circular Economy. The Clyvedon Press Ltd., Cardiff (2016)
3. MacArthur, E., Zumwinkel, K., Stuchtey M.R.: Growth within: a circular economy vision for a competitive Europe. Ellen MacArthur Foundation (2015)
4. Den Hollander, M.C., Bakker, C.A., Hultink, E.J.: Product design in a circular economy: development of a typology of key concepts and terms. J. Ind. Ecol. **21**(3), 517–525 (2017)
5. Pigosso, D.C., Rozenfeld, H., McAloone, T.C.: Ecodesign maturity model: a management framework to support ecodesign implementation into manufacturing companies. J. Clean. Prod. **59**, 160–173 (2013)
6. Bhamra, T., Lofthouse, V.: Design for Sustainability: A Practical Approach. Routledge, Milton Park (2016)
7. Sroufe, R., Curkovic, S., Montabon, F., Melnyk, S.A.: The new product design process and design for environment. Int. J. Oper. Prod. Manag. **20**, 267–291 (2000)
8. Byggeth, S., Broman, G., Robèrt, K.H.: A method for sustainable product development based on a modular system of guiding questions. J. Clean. Prod. **15**(1), 1–11 (2007)
9. Pauliuk, S.: Critical appraisal of the circular economy standard BS 8001: 2017 and a dashboard of quantitative system indicators for its implementation in organizations. Resour. Conserv. Recycl. **129**, 81–92 (2018)
10. Magee, C., de Weck, O.: Complex system classification (working paper). In: International Council of Systems Engineering (INCOSE) (2004)
11. Gaspar, H.M., Rhodes, D.H., Ross, A.M., Ove Erikstad, S.: Addressing complexity aspects in conceptual ship design: a systems engineering approach. J. Ship Prod. Des. **28**, 145–159 (2012)
12. Rhodes, D.H., Ross, A.M.: Five aspects of engineering complex systems emerging constructs and methods. In: 2010 IEEE International Systems Conference. pp. 190–195 (2010)
13. Mekdeci, B., Ross, A.M., Rhodes, D.H., Hastings, D.E.: Pliability and viable systems: maintaining value under changing conditions. IEEE Syst. J. **9**, 1173–1184 (2015)
14. Gaspar, H.M., Hagen, A., Erikstad, S.O.: On designing a ship for complex value robustness. Ship Technol. Res. **63**, 14–25 (2016)
15. Ross, A.M., Rhodes, D.H., Hastings, D.E.: Defining changeability: reconciling flexibility, adaptability, scalability, modifiability, and robustness for maintaining system lifecycle value. Syst. Eng. **11**, 246–262 (2008)
16. Song, W., Sakao, T.: A customization-oriented framework for design of sustainable product/service system. J. Clean. Prod. **140**, 1672–1685 (2017)
17. Richter, A., Sadek, T., Steven, M.: Flexibility in industrial product-service systems and use-oriented business models. CIRP J. Manuf. Sci. Technol. Ind. Prod. Serv. Syst. **3**, 128–134 (2010)
18. Rondini, A., Tornese, F., Gnoni, M.G., Pezzotta, G., Pinto, R.: Hybrid simulation modelling as a supporting tool for sustainable product service systems: a critical analysis. Int. J. Prod. Res. **55**, 6932–6945 (2017)
19. Zhang, H., Qin, S., Li, R., Zou, Y., Ding, G.: Environment interaction model-driven smart products through-life design framework. Int. J. Comput. Integr. Manuf. **33**, 360–376 (2020)
20. Gaiardelli, P., et al.: Product-service systems evolution in the era of Industry 4.0. Serv. Bus. **15**(1), 177–207 (2021). https://doi.org/10.1007/s11628-021-00438-9

21. Bertoni, M., Bertoni, A.: Designing solutions with the product-service systems digital twin: what is now and what is next? Comput. Ind. **138**, 103629 (2022)

22. Bertoni, A., Ruvald, R.: Physical prototypes to foster value co-creation in product-service systems conceptual design: a case study in construction equipment. In: Camarinha-Matos, L.M., Boucher, X., Afsarmanesh, H. (eds.) PRO-VE 2021. IAICT, vol. 629, pp. 382–389. Springer, Cham (2021). https://doi.org/10.1007/978-3-030-85969-5_35

23. Peruzzini, M., Mengoni, M., Raponi, D.: How to use virtual prototyping to design product-service systems. In: 2016 12th IEEE/ASME International Conference on Mechatronic and Embedded Systems and Applications (MESA), pp. 1–6. IEEE (2016)

Information Systems and Circular Manufacturing Strategies: The Role of Master Data

Terje Andersen[1]([⊠]) [iD], Gianmarco Bressanelli[2] [iD], Nicola Saccani[2] [iD], and Benedetta Franceschi[2] [iD]

[1] Molde University College - Specialized University in Logistics, P.O. Box 2110, NO-6402 Molde, Norway
Terje.Andersen@himolde.no
[2] RISE Laboratory, Department of Mechanical and Industrial Engineering, Università degli Studi di Brescia, Via Branze 38, 25123 Brescia, Italy

Abstract. In the transition towards a more sustainable future, circular economy is a key concept. Manufacturers play a key role in this transition, and different circular manufacturing strategies rely on digital technologies and information systems to be fulfilled. These systems and technologies need master data, basic data a firm's business activities are based on, to work. However, manufacturing companies still have little knowledge on which master data are needed, and how these data can support decisions in circular manufacturing strategies. In this paper, we bridge different circular manufacturing strategies with important master data elements in a framework for master data management. The basis for the framework is scientific literature within the domains of circular manufacturing strategies and information systems. The framework can be used by researchers to explore master data requirements for different strategies, and by practitioners to get an overview of data requirements for different circular manufacturing strategies.

Keywords: Circular manufacturing · Master data · Master data management

1 Introduction

In the transition to a more sustainable future, circular economy (CE) is an important approach. The idea of CE is to move from a traditional linear economic model characterized by a take-make-use-and-dispose approach to a CE model, in which materials and the embodied energy of products remain in a restorative system for as long as possible [1]. Literature are connecting the CE transition to extensive use of digital technologies [2]. New emerging technologies as internet of things (IoT), cloud computing, additive manufacturing, blockchain, and augmented and virtual reality are, among others, mentioned as enabling technologies for CE [3]. These technologies, together with cyber-physical systems, digital twins, big data and analytics, and autonomous robots are also important for the future of manufacturing, labeled Industry 4.0 [4]. System integration is often

© IFIP International Federation for Information Processing 2022
Published by Springer Nature Switzerland AG 2022
D. Y. Kim et al. (Eds.): APMS 2022, IFIP AICT 664, pp. 26–33, 2022.
https://doi.org/10.1007/978-3-031-16411-8_4

mentioned as another important building block for Industry 4.0 [5]. Manufacturing companies play an important role in this transition since they usually are the focal actor who manages upstream and downstream activities in the supply chain [6]. Different strategies have been conceptualized for the CE, ranging from recover to refuse [7] and, within the supply chain, a set of strategies specifically for circular manufacturing (CM) has been identified [8]. Manufacturing companies rely on a portfolio of information systems to support their operation and business processes [9], and all these systems and technologies need master data to work.

However, manufacturing companies have little knowledge on which master data are needed, and on how these data can support decisions in CM strategies. In addition, they have little visibility and access to these data – especially for long, complex supply chains – and the management of master data is still a practical issue in companies. Unfortunately, scientific literature still overlooks this domain, and the role of master data and master data management in the context of CM strategies has received very little attention to date. A resent research from Acerbi et al. [10] propose a data model for CM. Our work focusses on the need for master data, and is guided by the following research question: *which master data is needed for the different CM strategies?* For this purpose, a framework for master data management (MDM) for CM strategies is proposed, based on a literature review. The organization of the rest of the paper is as follows. In Sect. 2, we present background information on CM strategies and MDM. In Sect. 3, we introduce and discuss our framework for MDM for CM strategies. Lastly, Sect. 4 holds the conclusion, including limitations and suggestions for further research.

2   Background

The main idea of CE is to move from a traditional linear business model characterized by a take-make-use-dispose approach to a circular model in which materials and energy remain in a restorative system [1, 11]. Manufacturers play a key role in this transition, managing activities both upstream the supply chain to suppliers and downstream to customers, and in addition interact with other actors. Today's supply chains are recognized as complex, often global, and with a high degree of specialization [12, 13].

CE can be achieved by implementing different circular strategies. Blomsma et al. [14] divide these strategies into preventive strategies, loop-closing strategies, loop-extending strategies, and longevity strategies. Potting et al. [7] use the "R's and Re's" categories when they describe 10 different Re strategies from Refuse (R0) to Recover (R9) arguing for implementing an as high circular strategy as possible (low R). Given the relevance of manufacturing companies for the CE, the concept of CM has been recently established. Acerbi and Taisch [15] define the goal for CM to "reduce resources consumption, to extend resources lifecycles and to close the resources loops, by relying on manufacturers' internal and external activities that are shaped in order to meet stakeholders' needs". In addition, they propose the following CM strategies for manufacturers: circular design, remanufacturing, disassembly, reuse, recycle, resource efficiency, cleaner production, servitization-based business models, industrial symbiosis, and closed-loop supply chain.

Information Systems (IS) has been an important success factor for supply chain management. Magal and Word [16] define IS as "computer-based systems that capture, store, and retrieve data associated with process activities […] IS also organize these data into meaningful information that organizations use to support and assess these activities". Manufacturing companies have a portfolio of IS to support their operation and business processes [9]. Examples are computer aided design (CAD) for product development, customer relationship management (CRM) for interaction downstream the supply chain, product lifecycle management (PLM) for total management of products in all their lifecycle [17], advanced planning and scheduling (APS), manufacturing execution system (MES) and supervision, control, and data acquisition (SCADA) for the manufacturing process. Enterprise resource planning (ERP) has an important role in a company, both for internal planning and control and for collaboration along the supply chain [18]. The different systems have different purposes and target different processes within a company. For instance, SCM work upstream the supply chain, CRM downstream, PLM adopt a product development perspective, while MES target the manufacturing process on the shop floor. One way to define this IS ecosystem is using the product, process (production) and profit (business or enterprise) dimensions, where different IS support different activities within each dimension [19] and the automation pyramid (ISA 95) represent the connection between the dimensions. In addition, information systems can be vertically integrated (inside a company), and horizontally integrated among companies in the supply network.

Master data is basic data a firm's business activities are based on. Magal and Word [16] define master data as "key entities with whom an organization interacts" like customer data, supplier data and product data. As contrast to transaction data, master data typically describes basic characteristics of objects and is relatively static, meaning that they do not change much over time. As a result, master data usually remain largely unaltered, are quite constant regarding volume, and are the basis for transaction data [20]. Since the complexity in companies and supply chains is constantly increasing, also the number of IS in use in manufacturing companies is augmenting. In addition, these IS are often integrated with Industry 4.0 technologies as robots, IoT, big data and analytics, where the IS may serve as master data managers while the industry 4.0 technologies will generate a huge amount of transaction data [19]. All these IS need master data to work. This has led to an increased relevance for MDM, defined as best practices to manage master data where the main purpose is to secure master data's quality and that these data are updated to support transactions and business operations [21].

3 A Framework for Master Data Management for Circular Manufacturing Strategies

Based on a preliminary literature review, we propose a framework for MDM for CM strategies in Fig. 1. The first column refer to the CM strategies (adapted from Polenghi et al. [8]) and to the life cycle phases Begin of Life (BoL), Middle of Life (MoL) and End of Life (EoL). The second column refer to the business process related to the CM strategy and MDM. This can be firm internal processes or inter-company processes. The third column refer to the product, process, or business domain. The Information System and Master Data element columns are discussed hereafter. For the EoL activities, we have only included the supply chain activities between actors, not specific activities for the different strategies (reuse, remanufacturing, disassembly, recycle or waste management). The last column holds examples of master data for the specific CM strategi.

CM strategy/LC phase	Activity	Domain	Information System	Master Data element	Examples
Circular design, BoL	Product development	Product	CAD/CAE/ PLM	MD for products	Products, BoMs
Cleaner production, BoL	Manufacturing	Process Product	ERP/MES	MD for products MD for manufacturing	Products, BoMs Routing, CO2 emission pr product
Resource efficiency, BoL	Manufacturing	Process	ERP/MES/ EDI/BC	MD for products MD for manufacturing	Products, BoMs Routing, CO2 emission pr product
Servitization, MoL	Product usage	Business	Platforms/ ERP/PLM	MD for product usage	Customer data, MD for max utilization of products
Resource efficiency, MoL	Product usage	Product	Platforms/ ERP/PLM	MD for product usage	MD for energy usage CO2 emission pr product
Reuse, EoL	Return to service provider, reuse	Process Product	PLM (CLSC) BC (OLSC)	MD for products MD for product usage	MD for max utilization of products
Remanufacturing, EoL	Return to manufacturer	Process Product	PLM (CLSC) BC (OLSC)	MD for products MD for product usage	Material composition MD for utilisation of parts
Disassembly, EoL	Return to manufacturer	Process Product	PLM (CLSC) BC (OLSC)	MD for products MD for product usage	Material composition MD for utilisation of parts
Recycling, EoL	Return to parts manufacturer	Process Product	PLM (CLSC) BC (OLSC)	MD for products MD for product usage	Material composition MD for utilisation of material
Waste management, EoL	Return to waste handler	Process Product	PLM (CLSC) BC (OLSC)	MD for products MD for product usage	Material composition

Fig. 1. A framework for master data management for circular manufacturing strategies

Circular design has its origin in the product development process. Traditionally computer aided design (CAD) and computer aided engineering (CAE) were the Information systems supporting this business process. Later on product data management (PDM) and product lifecycle management (PLM) systems has evolved [22]. Varl et al. [23] argue for CAD and PLM as tools supporting customized product development, a product development approach with similarities to circular design. Myung [24] identified the following master data for PLM: Parts Data, Design Data, BOM, Docs/Specification, Configuration Data, Work Instructions, Product Quality Data, Product Compliance Data, Product Service Data. In the construction industry, Building Information Models (BIMs) is established, holding information about size, volume, weight, time, costing, facility management, maintenance, and operation [25, 26] of buildings, or its components.

While circular design focus on closing the loop with a Cradle to Cradle approach in the design phase of a product, **cleaner production** has the goal to minimize the environmental impact in production [27]. Information systems in this process are the typical systems from the automation pyramid, ERP and MES. Basic business processes supported by an ERP system are procurement, fulfillment and production process [16]. Basic master data for these processes are product data, supplier data, customer data, BOM's, routing and work centers [28].

Resource efficiency in the BoL phase can be internal production [28], or activities along the supply chain. As for cleaner production, the automation pyramid is important to measure resource efficiency on a product level. In addition, information from upstream and downstream supply chain actors are valid for measuring resource efficiency. For supply chain activities, information sharing techniques and standards are dominating. Electronic data interchange (EDI) is still an important standard [29], however interest in implementation of blockchain technology for supply chain collaboration is increasing [30].

Servitization or Product Service Systems is not only a CM strategy, but a business model, where a products functionality is delivered rather than the product itself [31]. Here the need for master data is moved to the use phase of a product. Data for measurement of the usage of the product or service is important. This can be done by a digital platform for measurement and value added services [32]. Data needed is related to customer, usage, and condition of the product, eventually suppliers involved in the delivery of the service. The **resource efficiency** in the use phase of a product differs from the resource efficiency in the production phase. In a servitization business model with a platform approach, it is natural that the platform hold this information [32]. For traditional sales, where the ownership of the goods is transferred from the supplier to the customer, either the customer/owner or the supplier can measure the resource efficiency. This will need computation capabilities not usually available among consumers. If these measurements is done by the supplier, they will have a PLM approach focusing on the customer and the goods sold [33], If it is done by the owner of the goods, an ERP approach seems to be reasonable, where the goods is an asset in the company owning the goods [8].

The last CM strategies are connected to the EoL phase of a product. According to the CE butterfly model [34], material shall flow back to service provider (**reuse**), product manufacturer (**remanufacturing, disassembly**) and parts manufacturer (**recycle**). All of these strategies will need some kind of supply chain coordination to be able to follow the "Rs" hierarchy among the strategies[35]. The communication need will depend on if the loop is closed, meaning that the same actor handles the EoL treatment as placed the goods to the marked, or open if not [36]. In both cases, flow of information from the BoL and MoL phase may have relevance [37], but technologies used for this flow may differ. In a closed-loop supply chain, it should be expected that the manufacturer or service provider have followed the product via their PLM systems. In an open-loop supply chain this is not expected since the original manufacturer or service provider are not connected to the EoL treatment. Here, blockchain technology may be a solution [37].

The last CM strategy, **waste management** is a non-preferred strategy. The overall goal for CE is to prevent waste [34]. However, waste must be handled in an optimal way. Waste management face some of the same challenges as other open-loop supply chain challenges. Digital Product Passport (DPP) may solve some of the issues related to product lifecycle information flow in the supply chain [38].

4   Conclusion

This paper presented a framework for master data management for different CM strategies. In our point of view information flow is, together with flow of products and value the three main flows for supply chain performance [39]. Enterprises are using IS to enable this information flow [17, 18]. For CM, new and extended information flow is needed, valid for all product lifecycle phases [8, 40]. However, the needs are different both related to lifecycle phases, activities and technology used. Manufacturers are in a unique position for improved circularity. Depending on the level of Supply Chain integration, they have information about the product they manufacture, and the actors upstream and downstream the supply chain [12, 13, 17]. Future manufacturing will increase IS integration, both horizontal and vertical [11]. Thus, frameworks are needed to understand the different needs for future manufacturing: our framework documents different master data needs for different CM strategies, and it can thus guide future research in different perspectives for different CM strategies. The framework shows that there are different IS and technologies, activities to be supported by digital technology and IS, leading to different master data to focus on, based on the different CM strategies.

Nevertheless, our research has limitations. The findings follow a preliminary literature search. A more structured approach for the collection of current literature would make this study more robust. In addition, the framework is purely based on scientific research. The topic covered in this research is also on the agenda both for the manufacturing industry, and for software and digital technology providers. Including grey literature may give new insight. Moreover, the framework has not been validated in real use. Using a case study including the use of the framework to validate its usability would make the framework more robust. All these issues are under consideration for further research to strength the study.

References

1. Geissdoerfer, M., Savaget, P., Bocken, N.M.P., Hultink, E.J.: The circular economy – a new sustainability paradigm? J. Clean. Prod. **143**, 757–768 (2017)
2. Tukker, A.: Product services for a resource-efficient and circular economy – a review. J. Clean. Prod. **97**, 76–91 (2015)
3. Bressanelli, G., Pigosso, D.C.A., Saccani, N., Perona, M.: Enablers, levers and benefits of circular economy in the electrical and electronic equipment supply chain: a literature review. J. Clean. Prod. **298**, 126819 (2021)
4. Lasi, H., Fettke, P., Kemper, H.-G., Feld, T., Hoffmann, M.: Industry 4.0. Bus. Inf. Syst. Eng. **6**(4), 239–242 (2014)
5. Gerbert, P., Lorenz, M., Rüßmann, M., Waldner, M., Justus, J.: Industry 4.0-The Future of Productivity and Growth in Manufacturing Industries. The Boston Consulting Group (2015)
6. Brintrup, A., Ledwoch, A.: Supply network science: emergence of a new perspective on a classical field. Chaos Interdiscip. J. Nonlinear Sci. **28**(3), 033120 (2018)
7. Potting, J., Hekkert, M., Worrell, E., Hanemaaijer, A.: Circular Economy: Measuring Innovation in the Product Chaing–Policy Report. PBL Netherlands Environmental Assessment Agency (2017)
8. Polenghi, A., Acerbi, F., Roda, I., Macchi, M., Taisch, M.: Enterprise information systems interoperability for asset lifecycle management to enhance circular manufacturing. IFAC-PapersOnLine **54**(1), 361–366 (2021)
9. Bowersox, D., Closs, D., Drayer, R.: The digital transformation: technology and beyond. Supply Chain Manag. Rev. (2005). service.boulder.ibm.com
10. Acerbi, F., Sassanelli, C., Taisch, M.: A conceptual data model promoting data-driven circular manufacturing. Oper. Manag. Res. (2022)
11. Masi, D., Day, S., Godsell, J.: Supply chain configurations in the circular economy: a systematic literature review. Sustainability **9**, 1602 (2017)
12. Boccaletti, S., et al.: The structure and dynamics of multilayer networks. Phys. Rep. **544**(1), 1–122 (2014)
13. Bortolini, M., Galizia, F.G., Mora, C.: Reconfigurable manufacturing systems: literature review and research trend. J. Manuf. Syst. **49**, 93–106 (2018)
14. Blomsma, F., Kjaer, L., Pigosso, D., McAloone, T., Lloyd, S.: Exploring circular strategy combinations - towards understanding the role of PSS. Procedia CIRP **69**, 752–757 (2018)

15. Acerbi, F., Taisch, M.: A literature review on circular economy adoption in the manufacturing sector. J. Clean. Prod. **273**, 123086 (2020)
16. Magal, S., Word, J.: Essentials of Business Processes and Information Systems. Wiley, Hoboken (2009)
17. Madenas, N., Tiwari, A., Turner, C., Woodward, J.: Information flow in supply chain management: a review across the product lifecycle. CIRP J. Manuf. Sci. Technol. **7**, 335–346 (2014)
18. Nair, P., Raju, V., Anbuudayashankar, S.: Overview of information technology tools for supply chain management. CSI Commun. (2009). Citeseer
19. Li, Q., et al.: Smart manufacturing standardization: architectures, reference models and standards framework. Comput. Ind. **101**, 91–106 (2018)
20. Otto, B., Hüner, K.: Functional Reference Architecture for Corporate Master Data Management, St. Gallen (2009)
21. Alharbi, A.: Master data management. J. Inf. Syst. Technol. Plan. **8**(19), 95–101 (2016)
22. Romero, D., Vernadat, F.: Enterprise information systems state of the art: past, present and future trends. Comput. Ind. **79**, 3–13 (2016)
23. Varl, M., Duhovnik, J., Tavčar, J.: Customized product development supported by integrated information. J. Ind. Inf. Integr. **25**, 100248 (2022)
24. Myung, S.: Master data management in PLM for the enterprise scope. In: Bouras, A., Eynard, B., Foufou, S., Thoben, K.-D. (eds.) PLM 2015. IAICT, vol. 467, pp. 771–779. Springer, Cham (2016). https://doi.org/10.1007/978-3-319-33111-9_70
25. Redmond, A., Hore, A., Alshawi, M., West, R.: Exploring how information exchanges can be enhanced through cloud BIM. Autom. Constr. **24**, 175–183 (2012)
26. Gourlis, G., Kovacic, I.: Building information modelling for analysis of energy efficient industrial buildings – a case study. Renew. Sustain. Energy Rev. **68**, 953–963 (2017)
27. Fresner, J.: Cleaner production as a means for effective environmental management. J. Clean. Prod. **6**(3), 171–179 (1998)
28. Magal, S., Word, J.: Integrated Business Processes with ERP Systems. Wiley, Hoboken (2011)
29. Cecere, L.: EDI: Workhorse of the Value Chain–A Closer Look at B2B Connectivity Benchmarks in the Extended Supply Chain. Supply Chain Insights LLC (2013)
30. Wang, Y., Singgih, M., Wang, J., Rit, M.: Making sense of blockchain technology: how will it transform supply chains? Int. J. Prod. Econ. **211**, 221–236 (2019)
31. Bocken, N.M.P., Short, S.W., Rana, P., Evans, S.: A literature and practice review to develop sustainable business model archetypes. J. Clean. Prod. **65**, 42–56 (2014)
32. Cenamor, J., Rönnberg Sjödin, D., Parida, V.: Adopting a platform approach in servitization: leveraging the value of digitalization. Int. J. Prod. Econ. **192**, 54–65 (2017)
33. Sakao, T., Nordholm, A.K.: Requirements for a product lifecycle management system using Internet of Things and big data analytics for product-as-a-service. Front. Sustain., 70 (2021)
34. Ellen-MacArthur-Foundation, E.: Towards the circular economy. Economic and business rationale for an accelerated transition (2013)
35. Andersen, T.: A comparative study of national variations of the European WEEE directive: manufacturer's view. Environ. Sci. Pollut. Res. (2021)
36. Gou, Q., Liang, L., Huang, Z., Xu, C.: A joint inventory model for an open-loop reverse supply chain. Int. J. Prod. Econ. **116**(1), 28–42 (2008)
37. Andersen, T., Jæger, B.: Circularity for electric and electronic equipment (EEE), the edge and distributed ledger (Edge&DL) model. Sustainability **13**(17), 9924 (2021)
38. Adisorn, T., Tholen, L., Götz, T.: Towards a digital product passport fit for contributing to a circular economy. Energies **14**(8), 2289 (2021)

39. Lambert, D.M., Cooper, M.C., Pagh, J.D.: Supply chain management: implementation issues and research opportunities. Int. J. Logist. Manag. **9**(2), 1–20 (1998)
40. de Oliveira, S.F., Soares, A.L.: A PLM vision for circular economy. In: Camarinha-Matos, L., Afsarmanesh, H., Fornasiero, R. (eds.) PRO-VE 2017. IFIP AICT, vol. 506, pp. 591–602. Springer, Cham (2017). https://doi.org/10.1007/978-3-319-65151-4_52

Application of Total Cost of Ownership Driven Methodology for Predictive Maintenance Implementation in the Food Industry

Irene Roda[1(✉)], Simone Arena[2], Macchi Macchi[1], and Pier Francesco Orrù[2]

[1] Dipartimento di Ingegneria Gestionale, Politecnico di Milano, Piazza Leonardo da Vinci 32, Milan, Italy
irene.roda@polimi.it

[2] Dipartimento di Ingegneria Meccanica, Chimica e dei Materiali, University of Cagliari, Via Marengo 2, Cagliari, Italy

Abstract. The Industry 4.0 has boosted technological advancements leading to the development of predictive maintenance solutions in the manufacturing sector. In this scenario, companies are dealing with complex decision-making problems involving investments in technological solutions and data analytics modelling implementation. Therefore, there is a need for strategic guidance for defining the best investments options through a technical-economic approach based on system modelling and lifecycle perspective. This paper presents the implementation within a relevant Italian food company of a methodology developed to evaluate predictive maintenance implementation scenarios based on alternative condition monitoring solutions, under the lenses of Total Cost of Ownership. Technical systemic performances are evaluated through Monte Carlo simulation based on the Reliability Block Diagram (RBD) model of the system. The results provide concrete evidence of effective applicability of the methodology guiding decision-makers toward a solution for improving technical system performances and reducing lifecycle costs.

Keywords: Predictive maintenance · Total cost of ownership · Condition monitoring · Decision-making

1 Introduction

Predictive maintenance solutions have become widely adopted in the manufacturing sector thanks to the possibilities provided by the new technological advancements and data analytics developments [1, 2]. Indeed, it can not only reduce the failure rate of machinery, but also it allows to extend the service lifetime and globally, plays a fundamental role in cost reduction and business performance improvement [3]. For its practical deployment, it is necessary for decision-makers to comprehensively evaluate the technology, considering holistically all issues of safety, availability, and cost-effectiveness [4–6]. In this context, safety life cycle and dependability concepts are key aspects that have a significant

D. Y. Kim et al. (Eds.): APMS 2022, IFIP AICT 664, pp. 34–40, 2022.
https://doi.org/10.1007/978-3-031-16411-8_5

impact on decision-making process thus, their evaluation has been widely investigate in literature through reliability model. Reliability Block Diagram (RBD) model is one of the most used techniques [7–9]. Moreover, in the manufacturing industry, companies nowadays are facing a vast offer of solutions for predictive maintenance by technology providers and are expressing the need for having formal guidelines to understand where to address their investments [10–12]. Particularly, the adoption of the total cost of ownership (TCO) to support decision-making within the asset management framework is one of the most suitable accounting techniques in different industrial application [13–17]. In [1], we proposed a methodology to combine technical performance analysis with economic evaluation, representing a structured approach that supports the implementation of predictive maintenance activities in industrial applications. This paper aims to provide a more detailed overview of the application case that was developed within the production plant of a leading food company to demonstrate the applicability of the methodology and its main benefits. In the following Sect. 2, the main steps of the proposed methodology are described, in Sect. 3 the application case within the food sector is described, and finally, the main findings are commented in Sect. 4.

2 Methodology Overview

This paper refers to the methodology presented in [1], which is aimed to support industrial engineers in defining which is the best solution for installing in the industrial system technologies for collecting monitoring data and which type of solution to select, for predictive maintenance implementation. In particular, the methodology is made up of 10 main steps as depicted in Fig. 1.

The first step consists of the identification of the context in which predictive maintenance activities should be introduced, defining the asset system to be analysed and modelled. The second step is aimed to build the Cost Breakdown Structure for the Total Cost of Ownership (TCO) model of the reference asset system. Step 3 consists of system modelling implementing a Failure Mode and Effect and Criticalities Analysis (FMECA) for getting information on asset components degradation and its detectability, and the Reliability Block Diagram (RBD) to model the entire system including the impact of each component failure at system level. Step 4 is dedicated to data collection including technical and economic data. After that, in step 5, Monte Carlo simulation is used to evaluate and compare several scenarios derived from different condition monitoring (CM) systems. This step is run for the case base scenario, enabling identified critical components within the system, and for any alternative scenarios defined in the following step, through an iterative procedure, enabling evaluating alternative CM solutions. Based on criticality analysis of system components carried out in step 5, step 6 allows defining several scenarios (derived from different CM techniques on critical equipment). In this step alternative types and installation locations of tools to monitor asset health and different expected level of quality of capability of the diagnosis and prognosis process can be evaluated. Moreover, the economic impact of the solution is considered. These elements are input for running again step 5 (simulation) for each alternative scenario and evaluating the impact of condition monitoring measurement systems on the system performance during its lifecycle. Step 7 allows evaluating each single scenario through

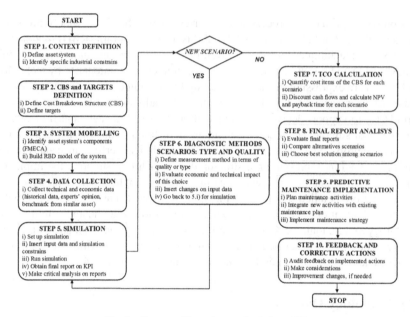

Fig. 1. Proposed iterative methodology [1].

TCO. After the analysis of the results obtained in each scenario (step 8), the predictive maintenance activities based on the CM systems as chosen can be planned and implemented in step 9. Last step identifies feedback and review on performed maintenance activities and corrective actions and it is not reported in this work.

3   Application Case

The proposed methodology was applied at the Beginning of Life (BOL) stage of a production line of an industrial plant recently installed by a large food company, producing cocoa panels. The line enables the whole production process, starting from raw material collection to finished good packaging as reported in Fig. 2.

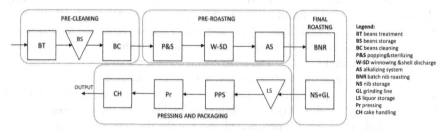

Fig. 2. Schematic representation of cocoa production process

The analysis is performed through a differential evaluation between the AS-IS base case, considered as the reference scenario, and the proposed scenarios based on alternative solutions for improving technical and economic performances. Thus, these solutions are achieved by the implementation of CM measurement techniques on critical machines. Through the methodology, the implementation of the first five steps, was done by the use of a Reliability Engineering software (R-MES ©) which supports Reliability Block Diagram modelling and Monte Carlo Simulation. The application of the methodology is briefly described step by step hereafter.

STEP 1 - The company has provided technical accurate chart (P&I diagrams) of the line. During first two phases cleaning and de-bacterizing machines are used to eliminate impurities and wastes from cocoa beans, avoiding reduction of output quality; while, during last two phases, machines are dedicated to roasting of cocoa nib and to mechanical treatments of liquid cocoa mass, through milling and pressing stages, to obtain cocoa panels and cocoa butter. In this step, the context and assumptions were clarified: (i) industrial plant works continuously 24/7; (ii) based on company experts' opinion, production process does not present quality problems in terms of product scraps or reduction of speed.

STEP 2 - In this step, the cost items are identified for the CBS of the TCO model, and they are: investment cost, involving acquisition and wiring cost of CM systems and related planned plant downtime (design, construction, and installation phase), Utilization and Maintenance costs, including costs related to production losses due to failures and production stoppage and to energy consumption due to installation of new diagnostic techniques (utilisation and maintenance phase) and, finally, dismissing costs or the possibility of recovering CM systems inside production plant (disposal). The technical parameters required for the estimation of the cost items are the Time to Repair (TTR) and the Time between Failure (TBF) of the different machines in the line and their Availability.

STEP 3 - The system modelling phase is performed through: (i) the identification of the department areas, that compose the production line of cocoa, to make the list of significant components and elements, and (ii) the identification of impacts of failure effects for each component's failure modes, for building the RBD model of the line. Six department areas have been identified including 95 equipment's overall.

STEP 4 - Being at the BOL stage of the line, no failure historical data are available. For this reason for the technical data acquisition we relied on maintenance experts' opinions on asset behaviour considering other similar lines in other plants of the company and on benchmark data from similar assets derived from literature research. For this, a wide research was carried out to identify similar processes in the food sector, using similar machines. Summarizing the technical data collection, 95 components are considered, and for each of it the best fitting for probability distributions of two required variables (TBF and TTR) was modelled based on the data collected.

STEP 5 - This step represents the innovative aspect of the proposed methodology since it allows overcoming the criticalities associated with the lack of historical data by estimating several scenarios a priori through Monte-Carlo simulation technique. The simulation process is performed to assess the impact of equipment failure on the entire production system aiming at identifying critical assets and the system expected Availability. According to RBD modelling, R-MES software is adopted firstly to estimate the availability for the whole production system in the AS-IS scenario which is used as reference value. In this case, a mean value of 81.57% was achieved. Subsequently, based on overall technical performances, a critical analysis of each component involved in production process is carried out to identify equipment with the highest impact on overall system availability. In detail, most critical components are: 4 hydraulic units, 4 cake conveyors and 2 mills, having the lowest impact on system availability among the analysed assets (=0.990).

STEPS 6 and 7 - These steps involve two different tasks: (i) generation of scenarios for the implementation of CM systems on the critical assets identified in step 5, and (ii) ΔTCO calculation obtained as the difference between the TCO for each generated scenario and the reference AS-IS situation. For this case, two different scenarios are depicted and each of it is analysed in terms of type of CM systems to install and quality of its diagnostic capabilities, considering the following cases: (I) best operating condition (hypothesizing ideal operative condition of the adopted CM system); (ii) worst operating condition (hypothesizing that CM systems are not perfect in detecting failures and also, delays could affect restoration activities). In particular, the following scenarios are selected:

- Scenario 1a/1b: implementation of pressure sensors on 4 hydraulic units (Best operating condition/Worst operating condition);
- Scenario 2a/2b: implementation of inductive sensors on 4 cake conveyors and vibration analysis sensors on 2 mills (Best operating condition/ Worst operating condition).

Each scenario is evaluated by considering three different parameters, i.e., availability, pay-back time, and total annual equivalent cost (AEC) (Fig. 3).

The parameters of the probability density functions of TBF and TTR were modified for representing the best and worst operating condition scenario (Roda et al. 2019) as depicted in the following Fig. 2.

STEP 8 - In this step, the achieved results for the generated scenarios are summarized ad reported in Table 1. The achieved results showed that the generated scenarios provide an increment of the overall system availability thus, all the proposed solutions are cost-effective compared to the AS-IS condition, even under the worst operating conditions scenarios. It can be noticed that several differences exist by comparing separately the cases in best and worst operating conditions. Indeed, in both cases, best solution is scenario 2 because, despite a higher investment due to the higher cost of vibration analysis systems, it provides a higher increment of technical system performances. Concerning the economic aspect, scenario 2 turns out to be the best solution since TCO value, and consequently, AEC_{tot} is the lowest. Thus, it represents the best investment considering the entire plant life-cycle and it can provide a high reduction of production losses costs. Moreover, the pay-back time showed the same values by considering the best and worst operating conditions separately.

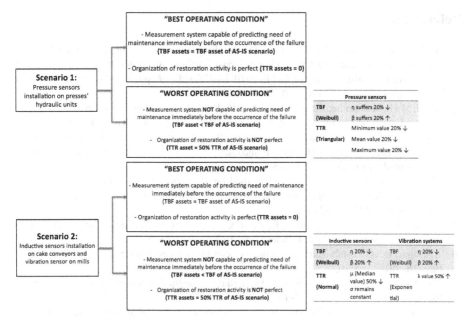

Fig. 3. Summary of proposed scenarios and assumptions

Table 1. Summary of achieved results for the proposed scenarios

	Δ Availability	AEC$_{tot}$	Pay-back time
Scenario 1a (*Best Op. Cond.*)	+1.88%	−58851 €	<1 year
Scenario 1b (*Worst Op. Cond.*)	+0.64%	−16488 €	<2 year
Scenario 2a (*Best Op. Cond.*)	+2.32%	−73246 €	<1 year
Scenario 2b (*Worst Op. Cond.*)	+0.76%	−19951 €	<2 year

4 Discussion and Conclusions

This work reports the application of the methodology proposed by [1], to a real industrial case in a leading food company. The methodology provides support for the decision-making process for the implementation of predictive maintenance through the integration of technical performance analysis (RAM analysis) with economic evaluation (TCO approach) based on simulation. The case study provides concrete evidence of the applicability of the established methodology, highlighting its potentials to be applied in cases where no historical data are available as well. In accordance with company experts' opinion, the defined methodology represents a good decision-making support to identify critical components where predictive maintenance should be implemented. In fact, it allows to manage a better utilisation of resources avoiding the installation of CM systems on machines and components, that are not critical from a system level perspective.

References

1. Roda, I., Arena, S., Macchi, M., Orrù, P.F.: Total cost of ownership driven methodology for predictive maintenance implementation in industrial plants. In: Ameri, F., Stecke, K.E., von Cieminski, G., Kiritsis, D. (eds.) APMS 2019. IAICT, vol. 566, pp. 315–322. Springer, Cham (2019). https://doi.org/10.1007/978-3-030-30000-5_40
2. Abidi, M.H., Mohammed, M.K., Alkhalefah, H.: Predictive maintenance planning for industry 4.0 using machine learning for sustainable manufacturing. Sustainability 14, 3387 (2022)
3. Nikolic, B., Ignjatic, J., Suzic, N., Stevanov, B., Rikalovic, A.: Predictive manufacturing systems in industry 4.0: trends, benefits and challenges. In: Proceedings of the 28th DAAAM International Symposium, pp. 796–802 (2017)
4. Meng, H., Liu, X., Xing, J., Zio, E.: A method for economic evaluation of predictive maintenance technologies by integrating system dynamics and evolutionary game modelling. Reliab. Eng. Syst. Saf. 222, 108424 (2022)
5. Faccio, M., Persona, A., Sgarbossa, F., Zanin, G.: Industrial maintenance policy development: a quantitative framework. Int. J. Prod. Econ. 147, 85–93 (2014)
6. Al-Najjar, B.: On establishing cost-effective condition-based maintenance. J. Qual. Maint. Eng. 18, 401–416 (2012)
7. Guo, H., Yang, X.: A simple reliability block diagram method for safety integrity verification. Reliab. Eng. Syst. Saf. 92, 1267–1273 (2007)
8. Kaczor, G., Młynarski, S., Szkoda, M.: Verification of safety integrity level with the application of Monte Carlo simulation and reliability block diagrams. J. Loss Prev. Process Ind. 41, 31–39 (2016)
9. Carnevali, L., Ciani, L., Fantechi, A., Gori, G., Papini, M.: An efficient library for reliability block diagram evaluation. Appl. Sci. 11, 4026 (2021)
10. Beebe, R.S.: Predictive Maintenance of Pumps Using Condition Monitoring. Elsevier Science & Technology Books (2004). ISBN 1856174085
11. Bousdekis, A., Lepenioti, K., Apostolou, D., Mentzas, G.: Decision making in predictive maintenance: literature review and research agenda for industry 4.0. IFAC PapersOnLine 52, 607–612 (2019)
12. Arena, S., Florian, E., Zennaro, I., Orrù, P.F., Sgarbossa, F.: A novel decision support system for managing predictive maintenance strategies based on machine learning approaches. Saf. Sci. 146, 105529 (2022)
13. Ferrin, B.G., Plank, R.E.: Total cost of ownership models: an exploratory study. J. Supply Chain Manag. 38, 18–63 (2022)
14. Hurkens, C.A.M., Valk, W., Wynstra, F.: Total cost of ownership in the services industry: a case study. J. Supply Chain Manag. 42, 27–37 (2006)
15. Zachariassen, F., Arlbjørn, J.S.: Exploring a differentiated approach to total cost of ownership 111 (2011). ISBN 0263557111111
16. van Velzen, A., Annema, J.A., van de Kaa, G., van Wee, B.: Proposing a more comprehensive future total cost of ownership estimation framework for electric vehicles. Energy Policy 129, 1034–1046 (2019)
17. Franzò, S., Nasca, A., Chiesa, V.: Factors affecting cost competitiveness of electric vehicles against alternative powertrains: a total cost of ownership-based assessment in the Italian market. J. Clean. Prod. 363, 132559 (2022)

"Farm-to-Fork" Production Management in Food Supply Chains

Precision Agriculture Impact on Food Production in Brazil

André Henrique Ivale$^{(\boxtimes)}$ ⓘ and Irenilza de Alencar Nääs ⓘ

Paulista University, Rua Dr. Barcelar 1212, São Paulo, Brazil
andre.ivale@aluno.unip.br, irenilza.naas@unip.edu.br

Abstract. The present study aims to analyze the impact of Precision Agriculture (PA) on food production in Brazil. We applied the multicriteria group decision using the Analytical Hierarchy Process (AHP) to weigh several selected criteria. The group consensus was very high (91.9%). The most critical criteria in level 1 was the machinery input (48.9%), followed by software (44.4%) and human resources (6.7%). In level 2, within the machinery criterion, the sub-criteria soil was the most critical (31.9%), followed by pest control (28.5%). In level 2, within the software criterion, the sub-criteria input management was the most critical one (48.4%), followed by product management (42.3%). The four most significant global priorities are the sub-criteria soil (31.9%), Input management (21.5%), Product management (18.8%), and Pest control (13.9%). Results indicated that the use of PA in grain crops has a high impact on food production (71.1%).

Keywords: Multicriteria analysis · Agriculture 4.0 · Grain production

1 Introduction

The UN's 2030 agenda aims for sustainable development [1], and some actions are needed to increase world food production. However, current production rates meet consumer demands but do not necessarily feed the world population [2]. Information technology (IT) tools have impacted the industrial sector and the agriculture segment in the same way, and it is named Precision Agriculture (PA). PA's use focuses on boosting productivity rates, reducing labor costs, improving work quality and worker safety, and reducing environmental impacts [3, 4].

PA is a group of agricultural practices that uses information technology (IT) based on spatial and temporal variability. Such methods manage the agricultural production system carefully, not only in applying inputs or various mappings but also in all the processes involved in production [5, 6]. Thus, the potential of PA generates economic and environmental benefits [7, 8].

The Analytical Hierarchy Process (AHP) is a multicriteria decision-making approach that includes qualitative information (in the form of judgments) with accessible quantitative data. AHP is a decision-making tool that can help define the general decision operation by decomposing a complex question into a multi-level hierarchical structure

© IFIP International Federation for Information Processing 2022
Published by Springer Nature Switzerland AG 2022
D. Y. Kim et al. (Eds.): APMS 2022, IFIP AICT 664, pp. 43–49, 2022.
https://doi.org/10.1007/978-3-031-16411-8_6

of objectives, criteria, sub-criteria, and alternatives [9, 10]. Applications of AHP have been reported in various fields [11–13]. AHP hierarchic structure reproduces the actual trend of the human mind to sort out elements of a system [10]. AHP is a helpful tool for decision-making when professionals deal with complex and interactive systems [14, 15]. The present study aimed to evaluate PA use's impact on Brazil's food crop production. This case study is based on grain production (soybeans, corn, and rice).

2   Methods

We applied the Analytical Hierarchy Process (AHP) to analyze PA techniques' impact on Brazil's food production. First, we invited three experts to rate the criteria and weigh them towards the adequate answer of the perceived impact, as shown in Fig. 1. The inputs from the group of three experts were computed using the defined concepts (Table 1). The AHP-OS online software [16] was used to process the calculations.

Figure 1 was developed from a literature review carried out on published articles concerning PA and the technologies involved in food production, where the following criteria were selected (1) related topic addressed, (2) year of publication and (3) number of citations. From the literature reviewed, the most used technologies were extracted and divided into criteria and sub-criteria, as identified in Table 1, for later judgment and impact measurement according to the experts. The profile of the specialists were determined as (1) expertise with the PA use and application; (2) presented publication on PA use and application; and (3) proper knowledge on the judgment of the criteria.

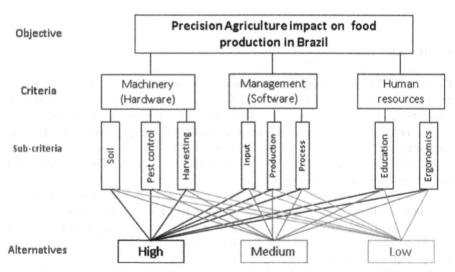

Fig. 1. Scheme of the AHP goal selected criteria, and alternatives for choosing the impact of PA on food production in Brazil

A set of pairwise comparison matrices (A; Eq. 1) was built. Each element on an upper level was used to compare the elements in the level below [9, 10]. The decision of relative weights (w_i) of all pairs of the n elements and these decisions are included as a number (a_{ij}) in a square matrix A (i.e., the comparison matrix):

$$A = (a_{ij}), \ (i, j = 1, 2 \ldots, \text{n}) \tag{1}$$

where aij = wi/wj and aij = 1/aji. The parameters for the pairwise comparison followed a 1-9 scale [9], where: 1 = not a priority; 2 = no to moderate; 3 = moderate; 4 = moderate to high; 5 = high; 6 = high to very high; 7 = very high; 8 = very high to greatest; 9 = highest priority. The weight was assigned to the $(i, j)^{th}$ position of the pairwise matrix chosen to compare with high sensitivity. The reciprocal of the assigned number was automatically given to the $(j, i)^{th}$ position. The highest eigenvalue (λ_{max}) was used to determine the consistency index (CI, Eq. 2).

$$CI = (\lambda_{max} - n) / (n - 1) \tag{2}$$

Table 1 shows the concepts used for each factor to help normalize the group participants' criteria weight.

Table 1. Selected criteria, sub-criteria, their description, and the references used to support the decision.

Factors	Factor's description	References
Machinery (Hardware)		
Soil	Agricultural machinery with onboard electronics (plowers and seeders) and an automated steering system. Remotely Piloted Aircraft (RPAs) or Unmanned Aerial Vehicles (UAVs) act in the mapping using a global positioning system (GPS). Sensors to measure organic matter, soil characteristics, and contaminations. Seal mapping using electrical conductivity (ECa) measurements	[17–21]
Pest control	Sensing and mapping to measure productivity, fertility, and compaction attributes, based on topography, terraces, and soil type, for later dosing and localized application. Monitoring of temporal variability Survey of diseases and diseases through RPAs or UAVs. Optical sensors and sprayers for localized application. Use of multispectral images, together with GIS tools	[22, 23]
Harvesting	Combines equipped with GNSS (Global Navigation Satellite System) and productivity sensors. Harvesters with autopilot and harvest monitor	[24, 25]
Software		
Input management	Images linked to the interpolation and transformation of data to generate maps of indexes, the health of the crops, soil conditions and management, and even crop productivity estimates. Use of data for decision-making, climate forecast, phytosanitary management, and financial market perspectives. Use the Graphical Information System (GIS), geostatistics, and data mining in databases	[18, 26–30]
Production management	Productivity sensors used on production. Use of the Variable Rate Technology (VRT) as inputs at a variable rate. Modeling via geographic information system (SIG)	[24, 25]

(continued)

Table 1. (*continued*)

Factors	Factor's description	References
Process management	Analytical methods and solutions to process data and build support systems for decision-making in crop management. Use of the Internet of Things. IoT, sensors, and implements reduce operating costs, increase productivity, and create new business opportunities and services. Use computational tools based on artificial intelligence	[31, 32]
Human resources		
Education	Agricultural production must integrate several areas of knowledge. The education of rural producers directly impacts the adoption of new technologies	[26, 33]
Ergonomics	Use machines and tools to aid in workers' activities and automate exhaustive work	[34]

3   Results and Discussion

Table 2 shows the hierarchy found by the consultant group. The most critical criteria in level 1was the machinery input (48.9%), followed by software (44.4%) and human resources (6.7%). In level 2, within the machinery criterion, the sub-criteria soil was the most critical (31.9%), followed by pest control (28.5%). In level 2, within the software criterion, the sub-criteria input management was the most critical one (48.4%), followed by product management (42.3%). The four most significant global priorities are the sub-criteria soil (31.9%), Input management (21.5%), product management (18.8%), and pest control (13.9%).

Table 2. Decision hierarchy of the criteria with corresponding weights.

Decision Hierarchy						
Level 0	Level 1	Level 2	Glb Prio.	High	Average	Low
Precision Agriculture impact on food producti	Machinery (Hardware) 0.489	Soil 0.653	31.9%	0.740	0.195	0.065
		Pest control 0.285	13.9%	0.762	0.176	0.063
		Harvesting 0.062	3.0%	0.475	0.443	0.082
	Software 0.444	Input mgmt 0.484	21.5%	0.745	0.166	0.090
		Prod mgmt 0.423	18.8%	0.681	0.216	0.103
		Process mgmt 0.092	4.1%	0.513	0.309	0.179
	Human resources 0.067	Education 0.875	5.9%	0.658	0.202	0.139
		Ergonomics 0.125	0.8%	0.717	0.212	0.072
			1.0	71.1%	20.3%	8.7%

Table 3 presents the overall group results and the values registered by each consultant. There was a slight variation amongst the experts' results; however, the AHP group consensus was high (91.9%).

Table 3. Overall results from the group weigh.

Participants	High (%)	Average (%)	Low (%)	CImax (%)
Group	71.1	20.3	8.7	11.9
Consultant 1	69.8	16.2	14.0	30.8
Consultant 2	72.0	21.9	6.1	66.2
Consultant 3	67.7	24.7	7.6	8.4

PA is paving the way for big data in agricultural production [18, 32]. Clear documentation of such practices based on new technologies, possibly combined with other technologies such as blockchain, will strengthen the role of these certifications. Such measures can play a significant role in both conventional and organic farming [34]. Additionally, insurance products could become more effective when information unevenness can be decreased when providing information on yields, input use, and environmental conditions to insurance companies.

Worldwide, there are two major issues related to food production. First, enough food needs to be produced to feed the increasing population. Second, the environmental issue needs to be addressed due to the overuse of antimicrobials, fertilizers, and pesticides contributing to the greenhouse effetc, directly impacting the soil quality and contamination of the water sources. However, the AP application can contribute to measuring and quantifying the ideal amount for each application, avoiding excess and the environmental impact [22, 23].

A crucial aspect needed for the increasing uptake of PA is the improvement of decision support systems and software solutions that assist farmers in most efficiently administrating their purchases, planning requirements, and cost calculations [23, 31]. The overall vision is to come from precision to decision-making. The advent of machine-learning and deep-learning possibilities has improved the power and consistency of such decision support systems in crops mainly related to chemicals application [4, 5, 8, 28].

An increased interlinkage of agricultural production with upstream industries based on PA technologies might create incentives for more robust vertical adoption in the agrifood sector [7, 8]. For instance, highly integrated firms might realize the required integrated data systems more efficiently [18]. The increasing transparency of farming practices and the need to disclose some practices and adjust them to consumer needs might lead to more substantial incentives for backward integration.

The results obtained are based on the judgment of experts based on a literature review. It is recommended for future studies to compare the data obtained with real data on precision agriculture productivity, as well as the impact of each applied technology (criteria and sub-criteria). It is also suggested to explore and survey the impact of using artificial intelligence for decision-making supported by bigdata, as it is one of the most used emerging technologies today.

4 Final Remarks

Advanced technologies will possibly increase the capital intensity of PA, and this could mean that just a few farms can afford it. As a result, this may lead to concentration and rising inequality in the agricultural sector. To avoid such an outcome, diverse technologies must be available for different agricultural systems, ranging from small to large-scale farms and crops. Moreover, different forms of cooperation and PA technology distribution can enable many farms to benefit from the technologies. In developing countries, education is probably the most critical field to expand the potential use of PA. Results indicated that the use of PA might present a high impact on food production in Brazil.

References

1. UM-Brasil. Transformando nosso mundo: a agenda 2030 para o desenvolvimento sustentável (2016). Disponível em: https://brasil.un.org/pt-br/download/50190/91863. Acesso em 12 de novembro de 2021
2. de Oliveira, V.C., et al.: Tipificação da produção de grãos na Amazônia. Embrapa Territorial-Artigo em anais de congresso (ALICE). In: Congresso Interinstitucional De Iniciação Científica 12, 2018, Campinas. Anais... Campinas: Instituto Agronômico (IAC) (2018)
3. Massruhá, S.M.F.S., de Andrade Leite, M.A.: Agro 4.0-rumo à agricultura digital. Embrapa Informática Agropecuária-Artigo em anais de congresso (ALICE). In: Magnoni Júnior, L., et al. (Org.). JC na Escola Ciência, Tecnologia e Sociedade: mobilizar o conhecimento para alimentar o Brasil, 2nd edn. Centro Paula Souza, São Paulo (2017)
4. Chlingaryan, A., Sukkarieh, S., Whelan, B.: Machine learning approaches for crop yield prediction and nitrogen status estimation in precision agriculture: a review. Comput. Electron. Agric. **151**, 61–69 (2018)
5. Cassman, K.G.: Ecological intensification of cereal production systems: yield potential, soil quality, and precision agriculture. Proc. Natl. Acad. Sci. U.S.A. **96**, 5952–5959 (1999)
6. Miranda, E.: Modelagem e mapas de capacidade de suporte de carga de solos cultivados com cana-de-açúcar. 2006. 97 f. Tese (Doutorado em Agronomia) - Faculdade de Ciências Agronômicas-UNESP, Botucatu (2006)
7. Silva, C.B., et al.: Economic feasibility of precision agriculture in Mato Grosso do Sul State, Brazil: a case study. Precision Agric. **8**, 255–265 (2007)
8. Bramley, R.G.V.: Lessons from nearly 20 years of precision agriculture research, development, and adoption as a guide to its appropriate application. Crop Pasture Sci. **60**, 197–217 (2009)
9. Saaty, T.L.: Rank from comparisons and from ratings in the analytic hierarchy/network processes. Eur. J. Oper. Res. **168**, 557–570 (2006)
10. Saaty, T.L.: Decision making with the analytic hierarchy process. Int. J. Serv. Sci. **1**, 83 (2008)
11. Büyüközkan, G., Feyzioğlu, O., Nebol, E.: Selection of the strategic alliance partner in logistics value chain. Int. J. Prod. Econ. **113**, 148–158 (2008)
12. Chavez, M.D., et al.: Assessment of criteria and farming activities for tobacco diversification using the analytical hierarchical process (AHP) technique. Agric. Syst. **111**, 53–62 (2012)
13. Nguyen, A.T., et al.: Quantifying the complexity of transportation projects using the fuzzy analytic hierarchy process. Int. J. Proj. Manag. **33**, 1364–1376 (2015)

14. Rosado Júnior, A.G., et al.: Building consolidated performance indicators for an agribusiness company: a case study. Rev. Bras. Zootec. **40**, 454–461 (2011)
15. García, J.L., et al.: Multi-attribute evaluation and selection of sites for agricultural product warehouses based on an analytic hierarchy process. Comput. Electron. Agric. **100**, 60–69 (2014)
16. Goepel, K.D.: Implementation of an online software tool for the analytic hierarchy process (AHP-OS). Int. J. Anal. Hierarchy Process **10**(3), 469–487 (2018)
17. Giotto, E., et al.: Agricultura de Precisão: com o Sistema CR Campeiro 6, Santa Maria (2007)
18. Nicocelli Netto, M.: Plataformas, Consoles e Softwares. In: Queiroz, D.M., et al. (eds.) Agricultura Digital, 1st edn., pp. 286–307. Universidade Federal de Viçosa, Viçosa (2020)
19. Rabello, L.M., De Campos Bernardi, A.C., Inamasu, R.Y.: Condutividade elétrica aparente do solo. In: de Campos Bernardi, A.C., et al. (eds.) Agricultura de precisão: resultados de um novo olhar, pp. 48–57. Embrapa, Brasília, DF (2014)
20. Bassoi, L.H., Inamasu, R.Y. (ed.): Agricultura de precisão: resultados de um novo olhar, pp. 48–57. Embrapa, Brasília, DF (2014)
21. Hemming, J., Rath, T.: Computervision- based weed identification under field conditions using controlled lighting. J. Agric. Eng. Res. **78**, 233–243 (2001)
22. Rampim, L., et al.: Unidades de Manejo em Sistema de Agricultura de Precisão na Cultura da Soja. Scientia Agraria Paranaensis **11**(Supl.), 70–83 (2012)
23. Raun, W.R., et al.: Optical sensor-based algorithm for Crop nitrogen fertilization. Commun. Soil Sci. Plant Anal. **36**(19–20), 2759–2781 (2005)
24. Pires, J.l.F., et al.: Discutindo agricultura de precisão: aspectos gerais, 18 p. Embrapa trigo, Passo Fundo (2004). Documentos Online, 42. Disponível em: http://www.cnpt.embrapa.br/biblio/do/p_do42.htm. Acesso em: 17 jun. 2010
25. Coelho, J.P.C., Silva, J.R.M.: Agricultura de Precisão. AJAP, Lisboa (2009)
26. Massruhá, S.M.F.S., et al.: Tecnologias da informação e comunicação e suas relações com a agricultura, 1 edn., p. 411. Embrapa Informática Agropecuária, Brasília, DF (2014)
27. Resende, A.V., Bassoi, L.H., Inamasu, R.Y. (org.): Agricultura de precisão: resultados de um novo olhar, pp. 84–95. Embrapa, Brasília, DF (2014)
28. Budiharto, W., et al.: A review and progress of research on autonomous drone in agriculture, delivering items and geographical information systems (GIS). In: 2nd World Symposium on Communication Engineering (WSCE), pp. 205–209 (2019)
29. Grego, C.R., Oliveira, R.P., Vieira, S.R.: Geoestatística aplicada a Agricultura de Precisão. In: Bernardi, A.C.C., et al. (eds.) Agricultura de precisão: resultados de um novo olhar, pp. 74–83. Embrapa, Brasília, DF (2014)
30. Majumdar, J., Naraseeyappa, S., Ankalaki, S.: Analysis of agriculture data using data mining techniques: application of big data. J. Big Data **4**(1), Article no. 20 (2017). https://doi.org/10.1186/s40537-017-0077-4
31. Massruhá, S.M.F.S., Leite, M.A.A.: Agro 4.0 – Rumo à Agricultura Digital. Controle & Instrumentação, no. 235, pp. 56–59 (2018)
32. Bazzi, C.L., et al.: Management zones definition using soil chemical and physical attributes in a soybean area. Engenharia Agrícola **33**(5), 952–964 (2013)
33. Bassoi, L.H., et al.: Agricultura de precisão e agricultura digital. Revista Digital de Tecnologias Cognitivas **20**, 17–36 (2019)
34. Li, J., Jiao, X., Jiang, H., Song, J., Chen, L.: Optimization of irrigation scheduling for maize in an arid oasis based on simulation-optimization model. Agronomy **10**(7), 935 (2020)

Farm Management of Pig Production: Mobile Application Development Concept

Elton Gil R. Muachambi⬤, André Henrique Ivale(✉) ⬤, Raquel B. T. R. da Silva⬤,
and Irenilza de Alencar Nääs⬤

Paulista University, Rua Dr. Barcelar 1212, São Paulo, Brazil
{elton.muachambi,andre.ivale}@aluno.unip.br,
irenilza.naas@unip.edu.br

Abstract. To ensure the farmer follows up on the new consumer demand for pork traceability and welfare during production, we developed a concept of applying the good practices during on-farm pig production. The productive meat sector has undergone technological transformations in recent years by searching for products with better quality, social responsibility, and sustainability. The worldwide good-practice norms are already known, and further information is already published by breeders, technical manuals, and scientific papers. New advancements in information and communication tools (ITC) can allow farmers to access real-time farm data and check their compliance with the established good-practices norms. The present study aims to conceptualize a digital solution suitable for evaluating the compliance of the pig farming management conditions. A mobile application will be made based on the standards of good practices as a digital transformation. The producer will be able to continuously check in real-time through the mobile application, assuring that his herd complies with the worldwide standards during production.

Keywords: Mobile app · Pig farm · Good practices of production · Technology

1 Introduction

Brazilian swine farming is among the ten largest meat exporters. However, it faces numerous challenges; animal welfare stands out due to the high-value investment in technologies, management, and facilities to promote well-being as agreed with the European Union [1, 2]. Consumer behavior change has encouraged the automation of farms, causing the productive sector to suffer transformations in the search for better quality products and sustainability in recent years. Pig farming is an activity practiced in several regions of the world, and pork is the most consumed meat worldwide.

Animal production standards rely on worldwide norms based mainly on EU norms, legislation, and farm assurance schemes. The EU norms are based on scientific information and aim to safeguard the species' welfare [3]. Variations in environmental factors such as sunlight, temperature, metabolism characteristics, humidity, and thermal regulation can cause imbalances in the animal's body, and temperature causes stress. It is

© IFIP International Federation for Information Processing 2022
Published by Springer Nature Switzerland AG 2022
D. Y. Kim et al. (Eds.): APMS 2022, IFIP AICT 664, pp. 50–56, 2022.
https://doi.org/10.1007/978-3-031-16411-8_7

considered one factor that negatively affects animal production [4]. These factors compromise feed consumption, growth, the composition of animal products, fertility, and mortality, impacting productivity and profit [5].

All the losses caused by problems related to the lack of instruction in the Manuals of Good Practices can reach 0.15% of the animals unloaded in the slaughterhouses. Although this rate may seem small, the swine production chain has large proportions, where Brazil is the fourth-largest pork producer in the world, this percentage represents very significant annual losses, with approximately R$ 30 million [6, 7]. According to data from the Business Benchmark on Farm Animal Welfare [8, 9], consumer demand is increasingly growing worldwide regarding product quality and concern for animal welfare, making it a critical point that affects buying decisions.

New Technologies are helping livestock production for both efficiency and more focus on the welfare of the animals. These advances are necessary to ensure innovations from applications using cameras, microphones, and sensors to enhance the farmers' presence in everyday farming and technology for remote livestock monitoring. With the increasing use of mobile technology, the mobile application allows the ability to track individual livestock in real-time [10] automatically. Methods based on newly developed technology, such as sensor and machine vision technology, are non-contact and developed as an alternative to direct measurement methods [11–13]. Advanced technology increases productivity and improves production quality [14, 15]. The general application of digital contributes to the rapid development of indirect measurement methods [16, 17].

This study aims to conceptualize a digital solution suitable for pig farming. A mobile application will be made based on the standards of good practices as a digital transformation. From there, the producer will be able to know through the mobile application if his farm complies with the pork standards of production.

2 Methods

2.1 Mobile App Conceptualization

The digital mobile App conceptualization phase involves drafting the scope of that project and the documentation of all the desired features and requirements [18]. Creating the real digital is critical for successful product development, as it forms the fundamental basis of the project. The digital conceptualization of a couple of scattered ideas and visions requires an extensive amount of knowledge on how to target an audience and how the market of digital products functions [19]. This is an essential part of the problem when creating a tailored solution.

The application development software platform in swine farming is responsible for coding the application and executing management to develop and monitor results obtained on the farm. Android Studio will obtain better results in developing the software application providing agility and flexibility, enabling the system to analyze the conditions and variations of the development index to assist the farmer in monitoring management through physiological data and measurements [20–22]. The software will define evaluation criteria of management and control of the development of the animal, where the software monitors the interfaces of the storage and treatment of data based on the information comparing control methods and parameters of its development. Figure 1 shows the mobile conceptualization scope.

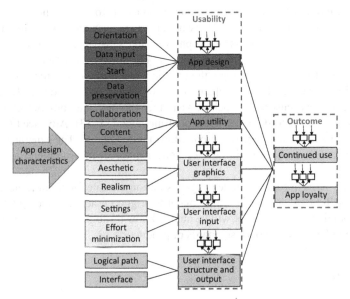

Fig. 1. Structural model of the mobile App. Adapted from [23]

2.2 App Development

The variables or classes included in the application are shown in Fig. 2. The associations between the application classes were based on the most critical factors in the pig farm production process.

We propose the input of the region characteristics (where the farm is located), the housing characteristics (height of the building, herd density - pigs/m^2, roof material, management data), data on housing temperature, and air velocity. The input will also come from data on drinkers, feeders, water quality, and specific details of management. We will give weights to each input based on the literature, and a final score is proposed based on the good practices used.

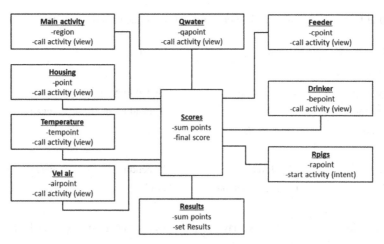

Fig. 2. Proposed flowchart of the App Pig's development

The calculation of the final score (scores) resulting from the diagnosis of a swine production good practices by the App is obtained by assigning weights to each class/variable or question. According to the production phase (week), the different categories of questions are based on factors of importance. Thus, scores are calculated according to the chosen region and the production phase (Eq. 1).

$$S_n = x1q_1 + x2q_2 + x3q_3 + \ldots xnq_n \tag{1}$$

where S_n = diagnostic score of good practices in n weeks of production and q = questions asked to a farmer. The weights attributed to each question are proportional to the importance of the question.

The interaction diagram between the user and the App functions like this: (1) the user selects the region the farm is located; (2) the user enters the answers to the questions corresponding to the phase of the production process in which the batch is located; (3) after answering all the questions, the user receives an output answer with scores of good production practices is presented. The questions will be related to parameters considered for the elaboration of the questions about good practices of production, were about rearing environment, the temperature and relative humidity of the environment, the airspeed, the amount and quality of water flow from drinking fountains, the regulation and flow of feeders, and the quality of the water. The weights (1 to 5) will be given following the instructions shown in Table 1. The idea is to give a higher weight to the highest impact the compliance with that specific variable affects the total output.

Table 1. Variables, limits, and observations related to the importance of the attribute.

Variable	Limits	Observation
Rearing environment		
– temperature	25–20 °C	Depending on the age range [2, 5, 24]
– relative humidity	60–85%	Depending on the age range [1, 24]
– air speed	0.8–1.5 m/s	[4, 24]
Water		
– quantity	~8.5 L/day	Depending on the age range [7, 12, 24]
– quality	Clean and potable	[24]
Feeder		
– feed quantity	~1.9–3.0 kg/day	Depending on the age range [24]
– feed quality	With proper components	[3]

2.3 Mobile App Concept Results

The schematic of the Pig's App concept and use is shown in Fig. 3. This mobile application will be used in an integrated analysis platform for producers and technicians in pig production based on the (24, 25).

Figure 3 shows the schematic of the mobile application concept that transforms data entered by the user into information on the farm level and allows users to collect and communicate best practice diagnostic recommendations digitally, providing real-time production analysis.

The methodology used in developing the swine application is customized and optimized in the procedures for monitoring swine development in swine farming by analyzing the monitoring processes through the usability and functionality of the application activities. According to [26], the App guarantees improvements and adaptations of the execution according to the user's needs, benefiting his purposes.

The application structure is related to the swine monitoring system provided in the graphical interface. More information is applied to the functions of the concepts of understanding the user interface, the use of monitoring and development of the swine is interconnected in the connection of the physical part and the logical part of the software. Software is the visible part of the system that interacts in the user interface communication system in a direct communication system—providing usability and ease of platform interaction and performing tasks in monitoring the pig growth.

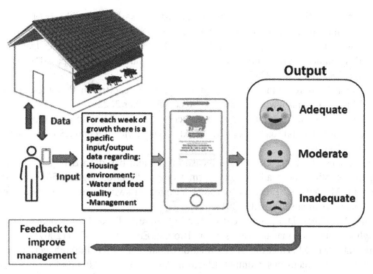

Fig. 3. Schematic of the App concept with the input data and the output results as input for decision-making.

3   Final Remarks

We conceptualize a mobile application based on standards of good practices for pork production, allowing farmers to comply with the norms and evaluate the herd in real time. Such an initiative might increase farmer control of the herd and reduce losses in pig farming since the farmer might follow up continuously on the data.

Using mobile data to record quantitative and qualitative data might enable analyzing environmental and swine management data. It might also prioritize and communicate technical visits and share the diagnosis with the entire management team.

It might manage and track essential communications from the farm with the technical team/company, visualize the best practices indicator with easy-to-view information, make decisions guided by insights and reduce losses in the production process.

References

1. Pandolfi, F., Stoddart, K., Wainwright, N., Kyriazakis, I., Edwards, S.: The 'Real Welfare' scheme: benchmarking welfare outcomes for commercially farmed pigs. Animal **11**(10), 1816–1824 (2017)
2. . Wilson, M.: Heat stress, trace minerals and gut health. Revista Pig Progress (2019)
3. Lara, L.J., Rostagno, M.H.: Impact of heat stress on poultry production. Animals **3**(2), 356–369 (2013)
4. Van Lankveld, A., Schaumberger, S.: How to overcome heat stress in Pigs. Revista Pig Progress, vol. 31, no. 5 (2016)
5. Mikovits, C., et al.: Impacts of global warming on confined livestock systems for growing-fattening pigs: simulation of heat stress for 1981 to 2017 in central Europe. Int. J. Biometeorol. **63**(2), 221–230 (2018). https://doi.org/10.1007/s00484-018-01655-0

6. Galvão, A.T., da Silva, A.D.S.L., Pires, A.P., de Morais, A.F.F., Neto, J.S.N.M., de Azevedo, H.H.F.: Bem-estar animal na suinocultura: Revisão. Pubvet **13**, 148 (2019)
7. Dalla Costa, O.A., Ludke, J.V., Costa, M.J.R.P., Faucitano, L., Peloso, J.V., Dalla Roza, D.: Efeito das condições pré-abate sobre a qualidade da carne de suínos pesados. Archivos de Zootecnia **59**(227), 391–402 (2010)
8. Farm Animal Welfare Council. Farm animal welfare in Great Britain: Past, present and future, pp. 1–59 (2009). http://www.fawc.org.uk. Accessed 5 Apr 2022
9. Verma, P., Sinha, N.: Integrating perceived economic well-being to technology acceptance model: the case of mobile based agricultural extension service. Technol. Forecast. Soc. Change **126**, 207–216 (2018)
10. Shi, C., Zhang, J., Teng, G.: Mobile measuring system based on LabVIEW for pig body components estimation in a large-scale farm. Comput. Electron. Agric. **156**, 399–405 (2019)
11. Benjamin, M., Yik, S.: Precision livestock farming in swine welfare: a review for swine practitioners. Animals **9**(4), 133 (2019)
12. Parsons, D.J., Green, D.M., Schofield, C.P., Whittemore, C.T.: Real-time control of pig growth through an integrated management system. Biosyst. Eng. **96**, 257–266 (2007)
13. Stajnko, D., Brus, M., Hočevar, M.: Estimation of bull live weight through thermographically measured body dimensions. Comput. Electron. Agric. **61**, 233–240 (2008)
14. Brown-Brandl, T.M., et al.: Shepherd. Heat and moisture production of modern swine. ASHRAE **120**, 469–489 (2014)
15. Banhazi, T.M., et al.: Precision livestock farming: an international review of scientific and commercial aspects. Int. J. Agric. Biol. Eng. **5**, 1–9 (2012)
16. Chen, X., Jia, J., Gao, W., Ren, Y., Tao, S.: Selection of an index system for evaluating the application level of agricultural engineering technology. Pattern Recognit. Lett. **109**, 12–17 (2017). https://doi.org/10.1016/j.patrec.2017.09.028
17. de Oliveira Júnior, A.J., de Souza, S.R.L., da Cruz, V.F., Vicentin, T.A., Glavina, A.S.G.: Development of an android App to calculate thermal comfort indexes on animals and people. Comput. Electron. Agric. **151**, 175–184 (2018)
18. Navas, T.O., et al.: Estresse por calor na produção de frangos de corte. Nutritime **13**(1) 2016
19. Carmona, M.A., Sautua, F.J., Pérez-Hernández, O., Mandolesi, J.I.: AgroDecisor EFC: first Android™ app decision support tool for timing fungicide applications for management of late-season soybean diseases. Comput. Electron. Agric. **144**, 310–313 (2018)
20. Google. Android Studio. https://developer.android.com/studio/index.html. Accessed Feb 2022, 2018
21. De Roo, N., Anderson, J., Krupnik, T.: On-farm trials for development impact? The organization of research and the scaling of agricultural technologies. Exp. Agric., 1–22 (2017)
22. Kamilaris, A., Kartakoullis, A., Prenafeta-Boldú, F.X.: A review on the practice of big data analysis in agriculture. Comput. Electron. Agric. **143**, 23–37 (2017)
23. Hoehle, H., Venkatesh, V.: Mobile application usability: conceptualization and instrument development. MIS Q. **39**, 435–472 (2015)
24. do Amaral, A.L., da Silveira, P.R.S., de Lima, G.J.M.M.: Boas práticas de produção de suínos. Embrapa Suínos e Aves-Circular Técnica (Infoteca-E 2006)
25. Baumüller, H.: Facilitating agricultural technology adoption among the poor: the role of service delivery through mobile phones. ZEF Working Paper Series No. 93 (2012)
26. Raymond, E.S.: A Brief History of Hackerdom. The Cathedral and the Bazaar: Musings on Linux and Open Source by an Accidental Revolutionary. O'Reilly & Associates, Sebastopol (1999)

Professional Guidance of the DPOs-BR in Corporate Governance in Logistics Chains

Liliam Sayuri Sakamoto[1]([✉]) [iD], Jair Minoro Abe[1] [iD], Jonatas Santos de Souza[1] [iD], Nilson Amado de Souza[1] [iD], Aparecido Carlos Duarte[1] [iD], Edvania Tarkiainem[2] [iD], and Luigi Pavarini de Lima[3] [iD]

[1] Paulista University, 1212, Dr. Bacelar Street, São Paulo, SP, Brazil
liliasakamoto@gmail.com
[2] IMF Smart Education, 25, Bernardino Obregón Street, Madrid, España
[3] Institute of Mathematics and Statistics (IME) - University of São Paulo - USP, 1010, Matão Street, São Paulo, SP, Brazil

Abstract. Currently, DPO (Data Protection Officer) professionals are working in sectors of the economy in the adaptation of the LGPD (Brazilian General Data Protection Law) in Brazil with the use of best management practices. Companies with consolidated corporate governance admit the incorporation of the LGPD (Brazil's General Data Protection Law) into their strategy, with highly trained professionals to consolidate leadership and monitor results. The commitment to enhance the structures that serve logistics companies is preferably used only by highly trained professionals, including internationally. In this sense, it was sought to list points that the sector should develop throughout the adaptation and especially in a continuous way to help achieve the objective within the institution. Data provided and collected in 2022 by the ANPPD (National Association of Data Privacy Professionals) from the almost 4 thousand (associates) trained professionals working in the Brazilian market show us that service sectors (50%) are using professionals trained in the LGPD, as well as in commerce (17%), in the industry (15%), in other segments (14%), and even showed in particular growth in agribusiness (4%) of professionals both in awareness and adaptation of the LGPD. And as strengths that must be followed in both awareness and adequacy, are the continuous improvement in acculturation processes, creation of orientation guides, training, until its implementation by outsourcing (DPO-as-a-Service), and professional responsibilities trained in LGPD and recognized by the CBO (Brazilian Classification of Occupations).

Keywords: Brazilian general data protection law · Protection · Logistics · Corporate governance · Professional guidance

1 Introduction

Identifying the core recognition aspect and its risks sectors in internal and external controls in corporate governance is one of the improvement challenges to DPO – Data

© IFIP International Federation for Information Processing 2022
Published by Springer Nature Switzerland AG 2022
D. Y. Kim et al. (Eds.): APMS 2022, IFIP AICT 664, pp. 57–65, 2022.
https://doi.org/10.1007/978-3-031-16411-8_8

Protection Officer in the enterprises in Brazil in compliance with LGPD (Brazil's General Data Protection Law) [3]. The external segments can be converted into better observance throughout Society, with a focus on Corporate Social Responsibility.

In Brazil, advances achieved by the capital market in Brazilian companies began with the Law n° 6.404/1976 and the creation in 1976 of the Brazilian Securities and Exchange Commission, like SEC - Securities and Exchange Commission in the USA. In 1995 with the Brazilian Institute of Corporate Governance (IBGC), and later in the 1988 Constitution [4] and with the national environmental policy. Brazilian business sectors are using the best market practices through Corporate Governance of Information and Technology with the support of specialists recognized by the Brazilian Classification of Occupations [5]. This study aims to elicit the main sectors of the Brazilian economy that are acting in the awareness, adequacy of LGPD and motivators of regulations as well as guidance by experts in LGPD in supply chain too.

1.1   Corporate Governance

Corporate Governance is due to the fact of mitigating misconduct that occurs within the Companies. The path pursued by the implementation and continuous improvement is based on its level of quality (transparency in business conduct, trained professional), and adequacy to regulation. And so, the guarantee of shareholders' rights is allowed [6].

Researchers point out that Corporate Governance allied to Corporate Social Responsibility and Information Technology (IT) brings significant gains for all those involved (Company Departments, Shareholders, Society). Therefore, when implemented by trained managers [9] internationally to work in the public and private sectors. Corporate Governance allied to Information Technology contributes to the improvement of Brazilian companies, as it allows providing all necessary support for strategic definitions under the responsibility of top management. In other countries, this contribution creates many governance innovations for assertive decisions.

COBIT 2019 is a Framework with a structure of Governance and Management internal control objectives [10], it is divided into two parts that address the corporate aspects that are Governance and Management. This guideline helps integrate standards, other guidelines, regulations, and best practices like Six Sigma, ITIL, PMBOOK, Sarbanes-Oxley regulations and community contribution.

Each part is organized into domains, in the Governance part there is only 1 domain and in the Management part, there are 4 domains. In EDM - Evaluate, Direct, and Monitor - Governance domain, there are 5 objectives: Ensured Governance Framework Setting and Maintenance, Ensured Benefits Delivery, Ensured Risk Optimization, Ensured Resource Optimization, and Ensured Stakeholder Engagement [10].

In Management 4 domains: APO - Align, Plan and Organize, BAI - Build, Acquire and Implement, DSS - Deliver, Service and Support, and MEA - Monitor, Evaluate and Assess, there are 35 control objectives. Inside its control objective, there is a description, and this purpose is described as a waterfall model, beginning with Enterprise Goals and this corporate alignment, with example metrics for each enterprise goal match to other example metrics for alignment goals [10].

It Control objective is organized by processes or tasks with organizational structures (Information Flows and Items) and presents the detail of people, skills, competencies, policies, procedures, culture, ethics and behavior, services, infrastructure, and applications. The innovation in this COBIT 2019 version is the addition of Design Factors and Focus Area to tailor the framework to priority objectives, adapt the guidance from the specific focus area, and target the capability and performance customized for each organization, see Fig. 1 [10].

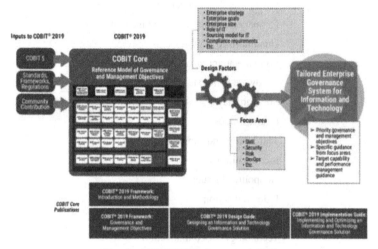

Fig. 1. COBIT 2019 framework [10]

IT Governance Models have been highlighted with the use of frameworks (Model of the Center for Information Systems Research (CISR) of MIT, COBIT 2019 - Control Objectives for Information and related Technology of ISACA- Information Systems Audit and Control Association, Corporate Governance of Information and Technology) as a means of support [10], with a focus aligned with the Company's business. In COBIT 2019, the corporate objectives in item 03 (EG-Enterprise Goals) stand out for dealing with the financial part and its compliance with external laws and regulations.

In COBIT® 2019, one of the models [10] used by Brazilian companies with an emphasis on the design factor, corporate objectives (EG-Enterprise Goals), and especially in the 19 risk categories shown in Table 1 [10]. These risks must be addressed by the DPO, which will be one of the main governance actors.

Table 1. Risk category COBIT® 2019.

Item	Risk category
1	Making IT investment decisions
2	Program and project lifecycle management
3	IT costs and oversight
4	IT expertise, skills, and behaviors
5	Enterprise IT Architecture
6	IT operational infrastructure incidents
7	Unauthorized actions
8	Software adoption and usage issues
9	Hardware incidents
10	Software flaws
11	Logical attacks
12	Third party and supplier incidents
13	Incompatibility
14	Geopolitical issues
15	Industrial action
16	Action of nature
17	Technology-based innovation
18	Environmental issues
19	Data and information management

1.2 Supply Chain Management and Logistics

A Supply Chain Management (SCM) is characterized by the standardization of operations integrated with several processes of purchase/sale, transport, storage, and distribution. This supply chain deals with flows and information [2] and is subject to compliance with the LGPD [3] because sensitive data travel between internal and external processes.

One of the bottlenecks in Brazil in terms of logistics costs is in agribusiness due to the production volume and distances between those who produce and their destinations. The sector in constant evolution seeks improvements in its processes with a Corporate Governance in the adaptation of commercial partners, suppliers, and farmers to adequate social-environmental practices.

Agribusiness evolves and updates itself, as does the awareness [16] of LGPD by trained DPO professionals [15] and its importance [17]. New processes are attributed to the use of the Artificial Intelligence technique [14] for prediction as support, and analysis [18]. Faced with these technological advances in the agribusiness sector, there has been a significant improvement in decision-making.

The adequacy of the LGPD [3], by producers still treated with costs, move towards the awareness of understanding as an investment, since agribusiness deals from confidential information of employees, suppliers, and customers to the culture of using paper to record personal data that are subject to LGPD [3].

Precision agriculture is also a point of attention as they are susceptible to data leaks and the possibility of having their entire operation interrupted. In this sense, as a response, the sector incorporates Corporate Governance allied to Information Technology.

In systemic terms, a strong ally in the supply chain is the ERP Enterprise Resource Planning tool for logistics [11] that allows numerous advantages, such as real-time information, identification of bottlenecks in processes, better inventory control, reduction in delivery time, compliance with the LGPD [3].

Professional DPOs guide the use of ERP systems approved by the association [1] with methodological quality [7] in their evaluation, as it has been a differential in standardization, and data integration as support in the adequacy by the small company.

And another differentiator for the DPO in the supply chain is knowing about KGM - knowledge governance mechanisms [13] using agri-food supply chain (AFSC) [8].

1.3 LGPD Regulation

Amends the Federal Constitution [11] to include the protection of personal data among fundamental rights and guarantees and to establish the exclusive competence of Brazil to legislate on the protection and processing of personal data.

The regulation of the Law in Brazil has been used as a complement to the understanding of the Law. It is worth remembering that no regulation takes away the right of the Law, as there are always unfounded attempts by parts of regulatory authorities.

We have recently managed to advance and regulate small businesses: Resolution CD/ANPD [12]. Approves the Regulation implementing Law No. 13.709, of August 14, 2018, General Law for the Protection of Personal Data (LGPD) [3], for small treatment agents (micro-companies, small companies, startups, legal entities governed by private law, including non-profits organizations).

In terms of regulations and ordinances, we are at the beginning because we have a long way to go on several points such as the definition of the Anonymization technique[16], portability standard, legacy base sharing, international agreements for data transfer, revocation in the punishment of DPO, among others in its Art.41, §2, III [3], violations in the Brazilian electoral context, and including the performance of inspection by the recently created National Data Protection Authority (ANPD).

Main Motivator for Regulation of the LGPD [3]. Much is researched on the real reasons that lead companies to adhere to adequacy after the awareness stage. The result of a discussion on the topic "Motivator for Regulation" is elicited (see Fig. 2) and shows that the main one is the fear of Fines (36%), followed by Pressure from Customers (26%), Pressure from Customers Regulators (24%), Employee Pressure (10%), International Pressure (2%), Others (2%).

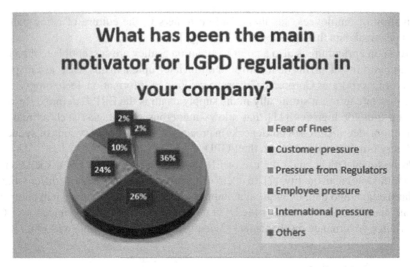

Fig. 2. Main motivator for regulation of LGPD in Companies. (Author).

2 Methodology

The methodology used was the literature review of Corporate Governance, LGPD Regulation e Supply Chain Management and Logistics. It was allied to an analysis of exploratory statistical research conducted by ANPPD on the training of professionals working with data protection and privacy, such as DPOs, mainly working in the supply chain area.

3 Professional Guidance for DPOs

3.1 Data Protection Officer Occupation

In 2016 in Europe, the European Regulation on Privacy of Personal Data [8] was created and served as a model in 2018 for Brazil. This model was the basis for the creation of the General Law on Personal Data Privacy-LGPD [3]. The purpose of the Law is to protect the fundamental rights of freedom and privacy and the free development of the personality of the natural person.

The LGPD – General Personal Data Privacy Law [3] was authorized in 2018, sanctioned by the then President of the Republic Michel Temer on August 14, 2018, taking full force in 2020.

The laws agree that for companies to adapt, it is necessary to involve areas such as IT/Information Security and regulation. And for that, they bring as a requirement a professional responsible for the privacy of personal data, the Data Privacy Officer in Brazil, known worldwide as DPO – Data Protection Officer.

And by LGPD Law in its Section II - Person in Charge of the Processing of Personal Data, its Art.41, §2, III [3] the professional is responsible for guiding and acting in the activities: accept complaints, receive communications, guide employees, and perform other duties. Important and recognized functions [5] by the Brazilian Classification of Occupations.

The Brazilian Classification of Occupations – CBO [5], established by ministerial decree no. 397, of October 9, 2002, aims to identify occupations in the labor market, for classification purposes with administrative and household records:

- CBO Code: 1421-35 – Personal Data Protection Officer.

3.2 Profissional Training

And as strengths that must be followed in awareness and adequacy, they range from continuous improvement in acculturation, and guidance guides, to their implementation by outsourcing and responsibilities of the professional training in the LGPD [3].

These points are the major contribution of DPOs in Brazil as recognized by the CBO [5] (Brazilian Classification of Occupations) body. Due to the recognition of the profession, there is also a growing demand in the service format (DPO as a Service) in hiring a data privacy specialist to fill the role, ensuring compliance with a fundamental point of the General Data Protection Law [16].

About Sector with DPO, Brazilian companies shown in Table 2 reflect the use of IT support (Information Technology). The professionalism of the DPO has been a benchmark among the sectors. The service sector has come out ahead with 50% of the market, just as agribusiness already appears in the survey as initially active with DPO.

Table 2. IT Governance Sectors - 2022 (Author).

Item	Sector	Representation
1st	Services	50%
2nd	Business	17%
3rd	Industry	15%
4th	Others	14%
5th	Agribusiness	4%

4 Conclusion

This research study presented training on data privacy controls to DPO professionals in controllers to help reduce the penalty of fines (36%).

Another point raised in this semester of 2022 was the emergence of agribusiness (4%) in the search for awareness and adequacy of the LGPD through trained professionals.

The data showed that lessons learned by the Corporate Governance of Information and Technology are standing out in the service sector (50%) in the pursuit of LGPD.

Acknowledgements. We thank the research group Paraconsistent logic and artificial intelligence maintained by the Paulista University and conducted by researcher Dr. Abe. This study was financed in part by the Coordination for the Improvement of Higher Education Personnel - Brazil (CAPES) -Financial Code 001.

References

1. ANPPD – Associação Nacional dos Profissionais de Privacidade de Dados. https://anppd.org/noticia/anppd-homologa-seu-1-software-para-conformidade-a-lgpd-09-09-2021. Accessed 11 Feb 2021
2. Ballou, R.H.: Gerenciamento da cadeia de Suprimento/Logística Empre-sarial, 5th edn. Porto Alegre (2006)
3. Brasil. Lei Geral de Proteção de Dados Pessoais (LGPD). Lei nº 13.709, de 14 de agosto de 2018. http://www.planalto.gov.br/ccivil_03/_ato2015-2018/2018/lei/L13709.htm. Accessed 09 Feb 2022
4. Brasil. Constituição Federal, de 1988. http://www.planalto.gov.br/ccivil_03/constituicao/constituicao.htm. Accessed 09 Feb 2022
5. CBO - Classificação Brasileira de Ocupações - 5.1.7 (mtecbo.gov.br). https://anppd.org/noticia/cargo-de-dpo-agora-tem-cbo-03-08-2021. Accessed 1 Feb 2022
6. Crisóstomo, V.L., Brandão, I.F.: The ultimate controlling owner and corporate governance in Brazil. Corp. Gov. Int. J. Bus. Soc. **19**(1), 120–140 (2019)
7. de Alencar Nääs, I., et al.: Lameness prediction in broiler chicken using a machine learning technique. Inf. Process. Agric. **8**(3), pp. 409–418 (2021). ISSN 2214-3173. https://doi.org/10.1016/j.inpa.2020.10.003. https://www.sciencedirect.com/science/article/pii/S2214317320302092
8. de Lima, L.A., Abe, J.M., Martinez, A.A.G., de Frederico, A.C., Nakamatsu, K., Santos, J.: Process and subprocess studies to implement the paraconsistent artificial neural networks for decision-making. In: Jain, V., Patnaik, S., Popenţiu Vlădicescu, F., Sethi, I.K. (eds.) Recent Trends in Intelligent Computing, Communication and Devices. AISC, vol. 1006, pp. 503–512. Springer, Singapore (2020). https://doi.org/10.1007/978-981-13-9406-5_61. 2019 Print ISBN 978-981-13-9405-8. ISBN 978-981-13-9406-5
9. de Souza, J.S., Abe, J.M., de Lima, L.A., de Souza, N.A.: The general law principles for protection the personal data and their importance. In: 7th International Conference on Computer Science, Engineering, and Information Technology (CSEIT 2020) (2020). Computer Science & Information Technology (CS & IT), Copenhagen, Denmark, Anais 2020. vol. 10, p. 109. https://doi.org/10.5121/CSIT.2020.101110. https://arxiv.org/abs/2009.14313
10. de Souza, J.S., et al.: The Brazilian law on personal data protection. Int. J. Net. Secur. Appl. (IJNSA) **12** (2020). SSRN https://ssrn.com/abstract=3949175
11. Dora, M., et al.: Critical success factors influencing artificial intelli-gence adoption in food supply chains. Int. J. Prod. Res., 1–20 (2021)
12. European Comission GDPR - General Data Protection Regulation (2016). https://gdpr-info.eu/. Accessed 11 Feb 2022
13. Gangi, F., Meles, A., Monferrà, S., Mustilli, M.: Does corporate social responsibility help the survivorship of SMEs and large firms? Glob. Finance J. **43**, 100402 (2020)

14. ISACA: Information Systems Audit and Control Association – COBIT 2019: Introduction and Methodology. ISACA, Rolling Meadows (2019b)
15. Lima, L.A., et al.: DPO no Brasil sob a ótica da LGPD – Lei Geral de Proteção de Dados. Instituto EXIN-Ministry of Economic Affairs in The Netherlands (2020). https://www.exin.com/br-pt/dpo-no-brasil-sob-a-otica-da-lgpd-lei-de-protecao-dedados/
16. PEC 17/2019- Proposta de Emenda à Constituição 1988. Available in: https://www.camara.leg.br/proposicoesWeb/fichadetramitacao?idProposicao=2210757. Accessed on: 10/02/2022
17. RESOLUTION CD/ANPD No. 2, 27 January 2022. https://www.in.gov.br/en/web/dou/-/resolucao-cd/anpd-n-2-de-27-de-janeiro-de-2022-376562019#:~:text=A%20ANPD%20poder%C3%A1%20determinar%20ao,os%20riscos%20para%20os%20titulares. Accessed 10 Feb 2022
18. Zhao, G., et al.: The impact of knowledge governance mecha-nisms on supply chain performance: empirical evidence from the agri-food industry. Prod. Plan. Control **32**(15), 1313–1336 (2021)

How Technologies Are Working
in the Coffee Sector

Paula Ferreira da Cruz Correia$^{(\boxtimes)}$ [ID] and João Gilberto Mendes dos Reis [ID]

RESUP - Research Group in Supply Chain Management - Postgraduate Program in
Production Engineering, Universidade Paulista - UNIP, São Paulo, Brazil
paulafecruz@gmail.com

Abstract. The world's population is estimated to exceed 9 billion people by 2050. A rapid and safe increase in food production associated with
the use of agro-industrial technologies is necessary. The aim of this article
is to investigate the use of technologies in the coffee sector. Recognizing
the need for a concise and accessible source of literature to disseminate
the findings about the coffee sector regarding new technologies. It collects
abstracts of articles from 2017 up to 2022 systematically raising important issues to be studied. The coffee sector brings proposals on the use of
different technologies and how to use them. A gap is evident for studies.
The quality of the grains is emphasized, but no studies which corroborate
to the competitiveness of the segment are presented. The results suggest
investments in the agro-industrial sector to promote competitiveness and
offer products with higher quality and competitive prices.

Keywords: Coffee · 4.0 Industry · Market competition

1   Introduction

The United Nations estimates that by 2050 the world population will exceed
9 billion people [1]. Therefore, it is necessary a quick and safe increase in food
production [2]. It leads to the use of technologies which are essential for farmers
who have as their only source of income their agricultural crops.

A challenge faced by the agricultural sector is the climate conditions which
affect production and cause environmental changes. To monitor environmental
variables and create large database is of paramount importance for producers
to make assertive decisions. In this sense, Smart Farming (SF) is considered by
several authors to be the best solution for data-driven monitoring and decision-
making issues. It is the use of information and communication technologies to
identify, monitor, analyse and represent the characteristics of agricultural production and support decision-making [3,4].

Wolfert et al. [5] proposes a flexible architecture for the management of agricultural chains. Popović et al. [6] presents a private platform for IoT which meets
different stakeholders. Colezea et al. [7] feature a cloud web service platform

© IFIP International Federation for Information Processing 2022
Published by Springer Nature Switzerland AG 2022
D. Y. Kim et al. (Eds.): APMS 2022, IFIP AICT 664, pp. 66–73, 2022.
https://doi.org/10.1007/978-3-031-16411-8_9

which improves product quality and stimulates agricultural business development.

In the coffee sector, there is an effort to monitor climatic conditions which affect harvesting. The grain harvest is done in months of drought, preferably not on rainy days. Excess water can deteriorate the grain. In Brazil, it is common to use adapted technologies which help small producers during plantations and crops. Large producers, who are in the minority, have access and structure to use specific machinery.

Another point is the use of technologies aimed at grain processing. The processing phase consists of sorting and separation for transfering to the coffee industry afterwords. At this stage, the grains will be prepared for roasting in the industry. Grain roasting guarantees all grain qualities. There are not many reports on the use of available technologies in this segment.

To fill this gap, this article aims to investigate the use of technologies in the coffee sector. It is recognized the need for a concise and accessible source of literature to disseminate the findings about the growing knowledge in the coffee sector according to new technologies. This review brings together abstracts of articles from different sources in a systematic way, and presents the chosen ones as having relevance in the coffee technology sector.

2   Methodology

This review was provided as follows using articles between the years 2017 and 2022:

1. Literature Search: Indexed databases were used as Science Direct, Emerald, Web of Science, Taylor and Francis and others. Articles were selected in English. Terms such as drones, IoT, Big Data, Blockchain, artificial intelligence, Cloud and cloud computing associated with agribusiness were used;
2. Article screening: The titles and abstracts of the articles selected were based on their relevance to the subject and technological innovations used. Articles related to the studied pillars were included to show the scenario. Therefore articles dealing only with technologies were excluded;
3. Full article review: The articles chosen were summarized, highlighting the main findings and strengths of each one, so that it was possible to present an overview of the sector.

3   Literature Review

3.1   Smart Farming

Smart farming or precision agriculture covers the use of new agricultural technologies which emerged at the beginning of the fourth industrial revolution to increase quantity and quality of production, minimizing environmental impact and increasing food safety [3, 4, 8].

It consists of applying personalized treatments to each portion of production area to get the most out of it. Some technologies stand out : drones, IoT, Big Data, Blockchain, artificial intelligence (AI), Cloud and cloud computing [8].

Drones are remotely commanded aircrafts of various sizes. They are used for image capture, image transmissions, object delivery and fun [9]. In the agricultural environment, they facilitate the supervision of farms, can cover hundreds of hectares in a single flight, gather images from different angles and collect a wide variety of information of land conditions, need to irrigation, crop growth and possible pathogens [10].

Big Data is a huge collection of online databases, to be used anywhere in the world and for different purposes [11]. Farmers can manage the information obtained by drones, IoT and other measurement instruments and integrate them with historical farm information and weather data in order to optimize production steps [12].

Blockchain is a network of distributed information records that change through encryption-protected transaction blocks and cannot be changed or deleted after their verification [13]. Technology makes it possible to monitor growth crops delivery to suppliers, improving supply chain traceability [14].

Artificial intelligence has potential to modify the way organizations operate. It goes beyond mechanical automation, encompassing cognitive processes which generate learning capacity. This system is capable of performing repetitive, numerous and manual activities and also performs activities that require analysis and decision making [15,16]. In agriculture, artificial intelligence and robotization are used in interpretation of field images and in application of fertilizers and pesticides with surgical precision or to deal with weeds [15].

Cloud transforms the IT framework into software which performs tasks on the computer. It is possible to connect it to a structure over Internet and use its resources without having to install resources on physical equipment [17,18].

3.2   State of the Art Smart Farming in Agricultural Sector

Here, some papers on the technologies used in the agro-industrial sector which are considered part of Industry 4.0 are presented.

A field-focused study on Agro-gain brings an end-to-end platform for data-driven agriculture, collecting data from different sources such as drones, cameras, and sensors. It uses weather forecasts to click work of different components of base station [19].

Another point is the study on the implementation of industry 4.0 strategies in companies, enabling them to improve efficiency and keep growing in face of international competition. It was a survey via mail to collect information about people's knowledge about technologies in the primary products industry in the case of wood. The knowledge of technologies is low. The main limiting factor for implementation of technologies is lack of skilled workers, outdated facilities and unclear financial benefits [20].

Use of smart farming for sustainable agricultural systems is a competitive advantage for farmers, extension services, agribusiness, and policymakers. Other authors claim to be the best solution, but do not bring recommendations on how to elect the best and most appropriate IoT technology and do not provide options for managing IoT. This study brings the implementation of a Smart Farming System based on three layers (Agriculture Perception, Edge Computing and Data Analytics). SF increases farmers' profits by improving product quality; coffee value chain model provides usability and farm management; data analysis flavors implementation of machine learning algorithms; Edge Layer is able to detect discrepancies by avoiding use of unreliable data; Perception Layer compares technologies by performance, usability and price [2].

Carraro et al. [21] bring a study on the applicability of terms of industry 4.0 in Brazilian agribusiness, ascertaining whether its use can be a mechanism for reducing production costs.

This review shows the trajectory of industrial and agricultural revolution, analysing challenges faced by agriculture along supply chain, to allow implementation of industry guidelines 4.0 and how to improve these techniques to be relevant to agricultural sector [22].

The article brings a systemic vision on how to learn to manage all processes that characterize agricultural chain from production to sale to the final consumer. It investigates the use of digital technologies to boost agribusiness supply chain [23].

Colezea et al. [7] comes up a web service platform based on cloud. It increases quality of products and supports development of agricultural businesses. It is related to providing detailed information to elect the most appropriate IoT technology, IoT infrastructure management and agricultural production estimation.

Strozzi et al. [24] puts on scene an overview of scientific literature on the concept of smart farming, which remains in focus in academic and professional environment due to innovations in manufacturing sector.

Rodríguez et al. [25] bring an estimate of coffee production based on computer vision techniques that deal with rust, a disease that affects plants, but smart farming techniques are not implemented because there are few sample data.

Kouadio et al. [26] proposes an extreme learning machine model to analyze soil and its fertility properties with the intention of generating an accurate estimate of robust coffee production based on environmental, climatic and soil fertility conditions.

Bergier et al. [17] bring the use of a cloud mobile app. This connects landowners and slaughterhouses; it is a point-to-point network. They bring the perspective that livestock farming is associated with unsustainable land use and climate change. Moreover, the use of geolocation and traceability can promote sustainable meat markets. A digital market has been designed to produce reliable data, generating big data. This big data analysis has potential sustainability compliance.

Debauche et al. [27] bring the perspective that smart farming is at the origin of producing a large amount of data that must be collected, stored, and processed quickly. For processing to be performed, a specific infrastructure *which uses adapted IoT is needed. They offer a comparison of Central Cloud, Distributed

Cloud Architectures, Collaborative Computing Strategies, and new trends used in the context of Agriculture 4.0.

Guo [28] understands that knowledge of agricultural cycle of current agribusiness is concerned with information, veracity, and perspectives. With the use of IoT, innovations quickly overhauled all sectors, including smart agribusiness, transforming their business. It provides the description of remote sensor and functions of Horticulture IoT and how to handle applications related to remote sensors experienced in agriculture.

Sreeja et al. [29] show that IoT is moving forward with various technologies to renew agriculture and increase crop efficiency and yields. They focus on an IoT-based crop monitoring system with three sensors, a WiFi module and a DC engine that measure and display the different parameters for the crop, promote intelligent agricultural monitoring by providing water and air to the system. It provides real-time assistance to farmers using an IoT platform.

Relf-Eckstein et al. [30] have the prospect that a new smart agricultural future is created as digital technologies meet with agriculture. It's a case study on an intelligent agricultural innovation of machines used in conservation crops. They find that knowledge and experiences of agriculture, coding skills and robotics generate innovations in problem solving. However, there is still a lack of evidence, mechanisms for assessing environmental and social benefits/risks.

4   Results and Discussion

Figure 1 presents an overview of the scenario of the coffee bean production, industrialization and commercialization.

In Fig. 1 it is possible to observe that in the first phase of production, the "Farm", the agricultural sector is influenced by Artificial Inteligence, Blockchain, Big Data and Cloud technologies. The same influence is perceived in the third phase "Market" of marketing. It is noted that the processing in the "Industry" phase is not influenced by the technologies used by the sector. However, these technologies could be used to increase the competitiveness of the sector.

The use of technologies significantly impacts the agricultural sector [28,29]. It allows a controlled and monitored production, with correct use of pesticides and quality assurance. Consumers are increasingly concerned about environment. One way to minimize impacts and optimize results is to worry about shape of the planting and how this production was cultivated. In this sense, technologies such as drones, cameras and sensors which monitor and collect data for upcoming plantations stand out [2,7,19,26–29]. A different view is brought to this study. It uses computational techniques to predict coffee production and possible pests but reinforces that these techniques are not used because there are few sample data [2]. The producer who perceives this new niche stands out and has advantage over others.

Investment in technologies is still an obstacle for small producers and beneficiaries. In general, coffee sector is made up of family producers and for producers to invest a large amount is not always an option. Public policies are necessary

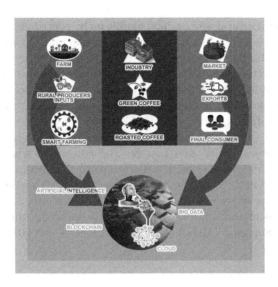

Fig. 1. Technologies that may influence the coffee bean production, industrialization and commercialization

for agro-industrial coffee sector to transform Industry 4.0 and improve its competitiveness in the sector. A study shows that the applicability of Industry 4.0 can be a cost reduction mechanism [21].

Another important issue in the coffee segment is the scarcity of labor due to seasonal production and poor qualification of workers. A differential in the sector would be the use of technologies to monitor coffee production together with other crops for better utilization and adequacy of soil nutrients. In addition to investments in new technologies, producers should also qualify professionals who will make use of these technologies.

It was observed that most of the studies found are related to the use of technologies in the field and that the industry which benefits coffee beans do not suffer the same influence. Few works address Industry 4.0 technologies in the primary products industry. Legg et al. [20] brings a study on the subject and finds that about 77% of the surveyed group does not recognize the terms Industry 4.0 or Smart Manufacturing. Another review presents considerations on how technological development affects industry and agriculture in different ways but does not bring recommendations on how to apply such resources in practice [22].

5   Final Remarks and Outlook

This work aimed to explore how technologies that are part of Industry 4.0 work in coffee agro-industrial sector. A literature review showed an overview of the sector and brought important issues that inspire further studies.

The coffee agricultural sector has significantly contributed for studies. It brings some proposals on which technologies could be used and how each of them could help during plantations and crops. The coffee industry has a gap for studies. The sector that emphasizes the qualities of grains does not present studies to improve its competitiveness and keeps doing its work without major innovations. One exception is the coffee industry in capsules, which is a specific market and differs from the proposal of this study.

Investments in the agro-industrial sector are needed in order to the sector to be competitive worldwide and to offer the consumer, who is increasingly demanding, a quality product with a better price. For future work, technical visits are suggested in the coffee bean processing industry to score the key points and propose the use of technologies that meet Industry 4.0.

This study was financed in part by the Coordenação de Aperfeiçoamento de Pessoal de Nível Superior - Brasil (CAPES). Finance Code 001.

References

1. Nations, U.: 2019 Revision of World Population Prospects-World Population Prospects - Population Division - United Nations (2019). https://population.un.org/wpp/

2. Rodríguez, J.P., Montoya-Munoz, A.I., Rodriguez-Pabon, C., Hoyos, J., Corrales, J.C.: IoT-Agro: a smart farming system to Colombian coffee farms. Comput. Electron. Agric. **190**, 106442 (2021)

3. Glaroudis, D., Iossifides, A., Chatzimisios, P.: Survey, comparison and research challenges of IoT application protocols for smart farming. Comput. Netw. **168**, 107037 (2020)

4. Ryu, M., Yun, J., Miao, T., Ahn, I.Y., Choi, S.C., Kim, J.: Design and implementation of a connected farm for smart farming system. In: 2015 IEEE Sensors, pp. 1–4. IEEE, Busan (2015)

5. Wolfert, S., Ge, L., Verdouw, C., Bogaardt, M.J.: Big data in smart farming - a review. Agric. Syst. **153**, 69–80 (2017)

6. Popović, T., Latinović, N., Pešić, A., Zečević, Krstajić, B., Djukanović, S.: Architecting an IoT-enabled platform for precision agriculture and ecological monitoring: a case study. Comput. Electron. Agric. **140**, 255–265 (2017)

7. Colezea, M., Musat, G., Pop, F., Negru, C., Dumitrascu, A., Mocanu, M.: CLUe-FARM: integrated web-service platform for smart farms. Comput. Electron. Agric. **154**, 134–154 (2018)

8. Alwis, S.D., Hou, Z., Zhang, Y., Na, M.H., Ofoghi, B., Sajjanhar, A.: A survey on smart farming data, applications and techniques. Comput. Ind. **138**, 103624 (2022)

9. Chinthi-Reddy, S.R., Lim, S., Choi, G.S., Chae, J., Pu, C.: DarkSky: privacy-preserving target tracking strategies using a flying drone. Veh. Commun. **35**, 100459 (2022)

10. Hafeez, A., et al.: Implementation of drone technology for farm monitoring & pesticide spraying: a review. Inf. Process. Agric. (2022)

11. Oracle: O Que é Big Data?—Oracle Brasil (2022). https://www.oracle.com/br/big-data/what-is-big-data/

12. Zhang, A., et al.: Who will benefit from big data? farmers' perspective on willingness to share farm data. J. Rural Stud. **88**, 346–353 (2021)

13. Paul, T., Islam, N., Mondal, S., Rakshit, S.: RFID-integrated blockchain-driven circular supply chain management: A system architecture for B2B tea industry. Ind. Mark. Manag. **101**, 238–257 (2022)

14. Hu, S., Huang, S., Huang, J., Su, J.: Blockchain and edge computing technology enabling organic agricultural supply chain: a framework solution to trust crisis. Comput. Ind. Eng. **153**, 107079 (2021)

15. Albiero, D., Garcia, A.P., Umezu, C.K., de Paulo, R.L.: Swarm robots in mechanized agricultural operations: a review about challenges for research. Comput. Electron. Agric. **193**, 106608 (2022)

16. Mark, R.: Ethics of using AI and big data in agriculture: the case of a large agriculture multinational. ORBIT J. **2**(2), 1–27 (2019)

17. Bergier, I., Papa, M., Silva, R., Santos, P.M.: Cloud/edge computing for compliance in the Brazilian livestock supply chain. Sci. Total Environ. **761**, 143276 (2021)

18. IBM: O que é Cloud? - IBM Brasil (2020). https://www.ibm.com/br-pt/cloud/learn/cloud-computing

19. Manikandan, D., Skl, A.M., Sethukarasi, T.: Agro-Gain - an absolute agriculture by sensing and data-driven through IOT platform. Procedia Comput. Sci. **172**, 534–539 (2020)

20. Legg, B., Dorfner, B., Leavengood, S., Hansen, E.: Industry 4.0 implementation in us primary wood products industry. Drvna industrija **72**(2), 143–153 (2021)

21. Carraro, N.C., Filho, M.G., Oliveira, E.C.D.: Technologies of the Industry 4.0: perspectives of application in the Brazilian agribusiness. Int. J. Adv. Eng. Res. Sci. **6**(7), 319–330 (2019)

22. Zambon, I., Cecchini, M., Egidi, G., Saporito, M.G., Colantoni, A.: Revolution 4.0: Industry vs. agriculture in a future development for SMEs. Processes **7**(1), 36 (2019)

23. Rangone, A.: Innovative agribusiness: which strategy for a dynamic development? Agribus. Inf. Manag. **11**(2), 5–15 (2019)

24. Strozzi, F., Colicchia, C., Creazza, A., Noé, C.: Literature review on the 'Smart Factory' concept using bibliometric tools. Int. J. Prod. Res. **55**(22), 6572–6591 (2017). https://doi.org/10.1080/00207543.2017.1326643

25. Rodríguez, J.P., Girón, E.J., Corrales, D.C., Corrales, J.C.: A guideline for building large coffee rust samples applying machine learning methods. In: Angelov, P., Iglesias, J.A., Corrales, J.C. (eds.) AACC'17 2017. AISC, vol. 687, pp. 97–110. Springer, Cham (2018). https://doi.org/10.1007/978-3-319-70187-5_8

26. Kouadio, L., Deo, R.C., Byrareddy, V., Adamowski, J.F., Mushtaq, S., Phuong Nguyen, V.: Artificial intelligence approach for the prediction of Robusta coffee yield using soil fertility properties. Comput. Electron. Agric. **155**, 324–338 (2018)

27. Debauche, O., Mahmoudi, S., Manneback, P., Lebeau, F.: Cloud and distributed architectures for data management in agriculture 4.0: review and future trends. J. King Saud Univ. - Comput. Inf. Sci. (2021)

28. Guo, X.: Application of agricultural IoT technology based on 5 G network and FPGA. Microprocess. Microsyst. **80**, 103597 (2021)

29. Sreeja, B., Manoj Kumar, S., Sherubha, P., Sasirekha, S.: Crop monitoring using wireless sensor networks. Mater. Today: Proc. (2020)

30. Relf-Eckstein, J., Ballantyne, A.T., Phillips, P.W.: Farming Reimagined: a case study of autonomous farm equipment and creating an innovation opportunity space for broadacre smart farming. NJAS - Wageningen J. Life Sci., 90–91 (2019)

Value Chain of Edible Insect Production: A Bibliometric Study

Jaqueline Geisa Cunha Gomes[2] ⓘ, Marcelo Tsuguio Okano[1,2(✉)] ⓘ, and Oduvaldo Vendrametto[2] ⓘ

[1] CEETEPS, São Paulo, Brazil
marcelo.okano@unip.br
[2] PPGEP-UNIP, São Paulo, Brazil

Abstract. Projections by the Food and Agriculture Organization of the United Nations (FAO) of a significant increase in protein production by 2050 to feed an estimated 9 billion people raise concerns about healthiness and sustainability, as this growth is linked to the challenges non-increase in land use, decrease in energy and water consumption and reduction of CO_2 emissions. This scenario makes the food and food ingredients industry look for innovative ways of producing proteins. The production of edible insects is part of this quest. The objective of this article is to analyze the evolution of the scientific field of the role of insects in human food in a sustainable way, considering the state-of-the-art study (reference to the current state of knowledge about a particular topic being study) as a tool to analyze the value chain of edible insects. The bibliometric results show the evolution of publications referring to the term "edible insects", which were qualitatively categorized into three main topics: 15 articles about insects as food and feed, 34 articles about food science, and 1 article about veterinary humanities and social sciences. This article may be useful for researchers interested in the topic, especially those who wish to respond to the challenges imposed to meet the global demand for sustainable protein.

Keywords: Edible insects · Insect cultivation · Sustainability · Value chain

1 Introduction

According to updated projections from the Food and Agriculture Organization of the United Nations (FAO), a 60% increase in protein production will be needed by 2050 to feed a world population that will reach around 9 billion people [1]. A major challenge to meet this demand is related to how to do it without increasing the use of resources such as land, consuming less energy and water, and reducing CO 2 emissions. To meet this challenge, FAO points out the need to use alternative sources of proteins. An alternative to keep up with the increase in this demand is the production of edible insects as a sustainable proposal for human consumption [2].

D. Y. Kim et al. (Eds.): APMS 2022, IFIP AICT 664, pp. 74–82, 2022.
https://doi.org/10.1007/978-3-031-16411-8_10

Despite the worldwide attention on the topic, a bibliometric review on the Web of Science on the term "edible insects" resulted in only 50 articles, demonstrating a research gap. The objective of this article is to analyze the evolution of scientific articles on the role of insects for human food in a sustainable way. In this article the study of art will be considered to analyze the value chain of edible insect production.

2 Literature Review

2.1 Climate and Environmental Changes and the Cultivation of Insects

Global warming has become a problem, mainly due to the great impact it has on agriculture and consequently on food security, triggering climatic events that have affected food sustainability [3]. In this way, it has become a focus of interest for researchers from different areas, who strive to solve its negative and often irreversible effects [4].

As adaptation and mitigation strategies to combat the effects of climate change in 2015, 195 countries and the European Union (EU) signed the first universal global climate agreement, pledging to stop the rise in the planet's temperature below 2 °C above pre-industrial levels, significantly reducing the impacts of climate change.

According to Huis and Oonincx [5] to reduce such impacts, some measures can be taken, such as reducing demand for livestock products, reducing manure emissions, and increasing carbon sequestration in pastures. As a quarter of all anthropogenic greenhouse gas emissions from global food production, insect consumption has been suggested as a sustainable and healthier route to animal protein consumption [6].

Climate and environmental changes have contributed to the increasing popularity of this consumption. Thus, it has become increasingly important to protect traditional practices of harvesting edible insects, especially in countries where the practice is already a daily habit, as in several parts of Africa, and thus guarantee the availability of these resources for future generations [7].

2.2 Food Safety and Consumption of Edible Insects

According to the Committee on World Security, food security exists when all people always have access to sufficient food to meet their needs, considering four pillars: availability, access, use and stability, in which the nutritional dimension is considered a part. Integral to food security [8].

Simion et al. [4] consider the risks are global and access to food has become a challenge not only for developing countries, but an economic priority around the world, as many causes have contributed to the increase in food insecurity, such as: increasing population growth, global warming, use of food resources, natural disasters, and armed conflict. According to FAO data (2018), 60% of people who suffer from hunger are in countries affected by conflict and 40% are in countries that suffer from drought.

According to Van Huis [2], edible insects can contribute to food security and be the solution to the lack of nutrients, especially as a source of protein. In addition, the production of edible insects emits low greenhouse gas emissions, requires reduced land, and has high conversion efficiency, and insects can partially replace ingredients in compound feed for livestock and aquaculture, allowing cereals used as animal feed will be used for human consumption.

Countries such as Belgium, Switzerland and the Netherlands have shown favorability for the production and consumption of insects. Switzerland has supported the sale of crickets, locusts, and mealworms since 2015, while Belgium in 2014 concluded that it seems highly unlikely that insects raised in controlled and hygienic circumstances will become infected, although the heating step is essential before being infected. Available for consumption [8].

2.3   Edible Insect Value Chain

The topic of edible insects involves several areas of research, such as: nature conservation, food, feed, organic waste recycling, poverty reduction, business development, food and agricultural policy and legislation, involving many stakeholders who meet at different operational levels of the value chain [9].

Research on the consumption of edible insects has grown over the last few years, bringing together international scientists to present their analyzes and findings related to the applicability of consumption as a new source of protein, both for human food and for animal feed, in addition to considering the different stages of the value chain. An example of this scientific interest and commitment was the symposium held in 2018 in the Netherlands, which marked 10 years of research in this area [10].

Odongo et al. [11] investigated the commercialization of edible insects in Uganda and Burandi, describing the value chain and market opportunities, revealing results in which the edible insect trade presents an alternative source of livelihood from collectors, street vendors and traders alike of rural and urban areas. Research data showed that a specific kilo of edible insect cost US$3.00, while beef and fish cost US$3.50 and US$1.95 respectively.

Considering that insect value chains can suffer structural differences according to the analyzed country, Mermúdez-Serrano [12] elaborated a value chain of edible insects, considering an overview of the main actors involved, showing in Fig. 1.

The value chain of edible insects is composed of the main actors involved in production, processing, and international marketing, but does not consider the interrelationships between the different actors, since these relationships depend on the context in which they are inserted [12].

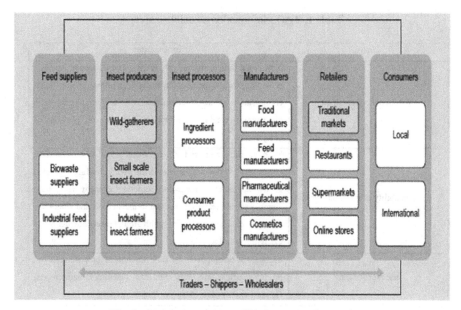

Fig. 1. Main actors in the edible insects' value chain

2.4 Regulation of Edible Insects

Since November 25, 2015, the EU, through Regulation 2015/2283, considers insects as a novel food, subjecting them to a simpler, clearer, and more efficient authorization procedure, in which insect-based foods can be marketed in throughout the territory, explicitly clarifying that insects can be consumed whole or in parts [12, 13].

However, this type of regulation does not occur in most countries, in which the lack of regulation is caused. Decision makers interpret insects as pests and not as potential food, directly affecting entrepreneurs as the challenges in marketing and product development increase, in addition to generating irrational exploitation, ineffective collections, promotion of monopolies, over-intermediation and poor conservation of the animals. Resources [12, 14].

According to Vantomme [9], FAO can help member countries by gathering and comprehensively disseminating the following information on edible insects, showing in Table 1.

Table 1. FAO - information on edible insects

Topics	Information
Nutritional composition	Nutritional composition tables for more insect species, promoting similar methodologies across countries on nutritional compositions of insect consumption, easily comparable with other major protein sources such as fish, chicken, pork, beans and pulses
Bioavailability of micronutrients	Such as iron, zinc and others, mainly due to the massive occurrence of these deficiencies in the tropics, leading to stunted growth in children. This is very important in many developing countries characterized by protein-deficient diets and where, for example, mixing cassava flour with ground insect powder could easily improve local diets.
insect processing	Extracts in recomposed foods: extraction of proteins and by-products such as fats, chitin, minerals, vitamins in hamburgers, spreads, energy bars, etc.
Legal and regulatory frameworks	Support inclusive legal and regulatory frameworks for insect consumption, such as novel foods, Codex Alimentarius, food safety standards, and healthy food regulations

3 Methodology

Considering the study of art to analyze the consumption of insects for human consumption in a sustainable way, the qualitative approach was adopted. This article was prepared through bibliographic research. Bibliometric analysis emerged with the aim of studying and evaluating scientific production activities in the early 19th century. Its development took place having as main landmark the studies from empirical laws on the behavior of literature [15].

The study used Thomson Reuters' Web of Science database, the former ISI Web of Knowledge, which is an online scientific information wizard. This database allows scholars access to journal articles, books, and other scholarly documents in all fields of science. In addition, Thomson Reuters Web of Science journals have impact factors in the Journal Citation Report (JCR).

To answer the research objective the search string "edible insects" was defined. After using the search string in the Web of Science database, the following criteria were used to select the articles included in this systematic review: Articles published in peer-reviewed journals or conferences that answer questions and research:

Articles published in the last 16 years, from 2006 to 2021;

- Studies available for download in the defined search bases.
- Duplicate studies were excluded from the sample.
- Articles that did not answer the research question were excluded.

Bibliometrics was carried out with the purpose of gathering knowledge about edible insects and other areas of knowledge, aiming to find primary studies on the subject and the solutions pointed out in the literature.

4   Analysis and Discussion of Results

The research examined articles published from 2006 to 2021 in the Web of Science database, focused on insect consumption, totaling a sample of 50 articles. The bibliometric indicators used considered: research publications on insect consumption; number of research papers on insect consumption published between 2006 and 2021; areas of knowledge in which the authors have published research on insect consumption and the authors published: insects as food and feed, food science and veterinary humanities, and social sciences. Food insects being the most studied topic with 34 articles. Bibliometric indicators are shown in Fig. 2.

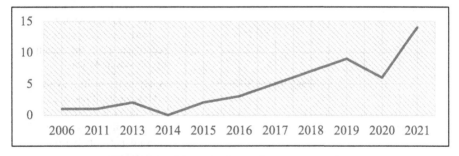

Fig. 2. Scientific production on insect consumption.

The period from 2006 to 2015 has an average of 1.5 articles per year. From 2016 to 2019, there was a linear growth of 2 articles per year, representing an annual average of 6 articles. After a decrease in 2020, it is possible to observe a significant increase in 2021 with the publication of 14 articles, demonstrating the evolution of research in the analyzed period. Based on the selected articles, the scientific journals were qualitatively categorized as follows: insects as food and feed, food science, and veterinary humanities and social sciences. The main contributions of the most recent publications are shown in Table 2.

Table 2. Categorization of selected surveys

Categorization	Authors	Main Contributions
Insects as food and feed	Mermúdez- Serrano (2020) [12]	It analyzes the potential for cultivation and processing of edible insects in Latin America, using the systemic competitiveness approach to list the main opportunities and challenges for the development of the sector in the region, considering the coordinated efforts between all the actors involved in the different systemic levels: entrepreneurs, research institutions, government, and society
	Niassy et al. (2018) [16]	Organization of the 22nd meeting of the Association of African Insect Scientists (AAIS) in Wad Medani, Sudan, in 2017, aiming to support impactful research that will produce genuine edible insect products, sustain value chains that improve food and nutrition security, and support sustainable livelihoods in Africa
	Vantomme (2015) [9]	Analyzes the main activities and achievements of insect recognition as a contribution to food security, suggesting ways forward, particularly from the FAO perspective
Food science	Ayieko et al. (2021) [17]	Selectively summarizes current trends related to the consumption of edible insects among residents, consumers in the food and beverage industry, and its prospects as a major draw in tourist destinations

(continued)

Table 2. (*continued*)

Categorization	Authors	Main Contributions
	Nyangena et al. (2021) [9]	Reviews the discussion of how climate change has affected food production and cash crops, along with animal production, the resulting human nutritional imbalances, and the impact of climate change on edible insects
	Kyung Kim et al. (2019) [18]	It summarizes current trends related to insects as food resources among consumers, industry, and academia, revealing that entomophagy is experiencing a steady increase worldwide, despite its unfamiliarity to consumers influenced by western eating habits
Veterinary humanities and social sciences	Musundire et al. (2021) [7]	It proposes a path that can accelerate the recognition and appreciation of edible insects as important food and feed resources in Sub-Saharan Africa, including improved policies to support good stewardship of these resources for sustainability

5 Conclusion

The objective of this article was to analyze the evolution of scientific articles and the role of insects for human food in a sustainable way. To achieve this objective, a bibliometric analysis was carried out in the Web of Science database. A list containing 50 articles published between 2006 and 2021 was diligently extracted and analyzed.

The bibliometric results of the term "edible insects" showed the evolution of publications. The period from 2006 to 2015 has an average of 1.5 articles per year. From 2016 to 2019, there was a linear growth of 2 articles per year, representing an annual average of 6 articles. After a decrease in 2020, it is possible to observe a significant increase in 2021 with the publication of 14 articles, demonstrating the evolution of research in the analyzed period. The content of scientific journals was qualitatively categorized into three main topics: insects as food and feed, food science, and veterinary humanities and social sciences.

From the analysis of scientific productions, it was possible to identify an increasing number of publications about edible insects, especially from 2017, strengthening the expansion of the field.

This article may be useful to researchers interested in the topic, especially those who wish to respond to the challenges imposed to meet the world demand for protein without increasing land use, consuming less energy and water, and reducing CO_2 emissions by 2050.

References

1. UN. Global perspective human stories (2015). https://news.un.org/en/story/2015/01/488592#. VL6UBEfF8kR
2. Van Huis, A., et al.: Edible insects: future prospects for food and feed security. In: FAO Forestry paper 171 (2013)
3. Nyangena, D.N., Kinyuru, J., Imathiu, S.: Climate change: a natural streamliner towards entomophagy? Int. J. Trop. Insect Sci. **41**(3), 2133–2147 (2020). https://doi.org/10.1007/s42 690-020-00292-8
4. Simion, V.E., Ţoniş, B.-M.R., Amfim, A., Dourado, O.M., Sekovska, B., Dijmărescu, I.: Entomofagy - a viable solution for supporting food security. Amfiteatru Econ. **21**(51), 462–479 (2019)
5. Van Huis, A., Oonincx, D.G.A.B.: The environmental sustainability of insects as food and feed. A review. Agron. Sustain. Dev. **37**, 43 (2017)
6. Miglietta, P., De Leo, F., Ruberti, M., Massari, S.: Mealworms for food: a water footprint perspective. Water **7**, 6190–6203 (2015)
7. Musundire, R., et al.: Stewardship of wild and farmed edible insects as food and feed in Sub-Saharan Africa: a perspective (2021)
8. Van Huis, A.: Edible insects contributing to food security? Agric. Food Secur. **4**, 1–9 (2015)
9. Vantomme, P.: Way forward to bring insects in the human food chain. J. Insects Food Feed **1**, 121–129 (2015)
10. Lakemond, C.M.M., Veldkamp, T., Van Huis, A.: Edible insects: the value chain. J. Insects Food Feed **5**(4), 245–246 (2019)
11. Odongo, W., Okia, C.A., Nalika, N., Nzabamwita, P.H., Ndimubando, J., Nyeko, P.: Marketing of edible insects in Lake Victoria basin: the case of Uganda and Burundi. J. Insects Food Feed **4**(4), 285–293 (2018)
12. Bermúdez-Serrano, I.M.: Challenges and opportunities for the development of an edible insect food industry in Latin America. J. Insects Food Feed **6**, 537–556 (2020)
13. Van Huis, A.: Edible insects are the future? Proc. Nutr. Soc. **75**(3), 294–305 (2016)
14. Ramos-Elorduy, J.: Threatened edible insects in Hidalgo, Mexico and some measures to preserve them. J. Ethnobiol. Ethnomed. **2**, 51 (2006)
15. Araújo, C.A.A.: Bibliometria: evolução histórica e questões atuais. Em Questão, pp. 11–32 (2006). https://seer.ufrgs.br/index.php/EmQuestao/article/view/16
16. Niassy, S., Musundire, S., Ekesi, S., Van Huis, A.: Edible insect value chains in Africa. J. Insects Food Feed **4**(4), 199–201 (2018)
17. Magara, H.J., et al.: Edible crickets (Orthoptera) around the world: distribution, nutritional value, and other benefits—a review. Front. Nutr. **7**, 257 (2021)
18. Kim, T.K., Yong, H.I., Kim, Y.B., Kim, H.W., Choi, Y.S.: Edible insects as a protein source: a review of public perception, processing technology, and research trends. Food Sci. Anim. Resour. **39**(4), 521 (2019)

Digital Transformation in the Milk Production Chain

Marcelo T. Okano[1,2,3](✉) [iD], Oduvaldo Vendrametto[1] [iD], and Celi Langhi[1,2] [iD]

[1] Universidade Paulista UNIP, São Paulo, SP, Brazil
marcelo.okano@unip.br
[2] CEETEPS, São Paulo, SP, Brazil
[3] FT-UNICAMP, Limeira, SP, Brazil

Abstract. The use of digital technologies has spread to areas other than industry and has given rise to new areas such as smart cities, smart health, and education 4.0. The milk production chain is also benefiting from these digital innovations, but due to their characteristics, in a gradual and focused way. The objective of this research is to verify the use of digital technologies through digital transformation to improve the dairy production chain in the last 14 years. The methodology consisted of a longitudinal survey between 2008 and 2022. In 2008, we analyzed the digital technologies used in 3 large Brazilian dairy farms. In 2022, we look at the digital technologies that the XPTO company offers to dairy farms. We were able to verify that the use of digital technologies through digital transformation improved the production of the dairy chain. We can highlight that the main advances were in the automation of production with intelligent sensors such as IOT and digital platforms for online data processing with the use of AI, the evolution of computer network technologies and farm management systems.

Keywords: Digital transformation · Digital technologies · AI · Dairy chain

1 Introduction

Currently, there is a lot of discussion about the application of new digital technologies in the industrial production chain, the so-called Industry 4.0. It is also known as the Fourth Industrial Revolution. Strictly speaking, Industry 4.0 is a technological concept based on cyber-physical systems, the Internet of Things (IoT), which enables the factory of the future [1].

According to Portal da Industria [2], examples of technologies used in industry 4.0 are: artificial intelligence, cloud computing, big data, cyber security, internet of things, advanced robotics, digital manufacturing, additive manufacturing, systems integration, simulation and digitization systems.

The use of these digital technologies has spread to other areas and given rise to new areas like smart cities, smart health, education 4.0, etc. The milk production chain is also benefiting from these digital innovations, but due to its characteristics, in a gradual and focused way.

Published by Springer Nature Switzerland AG 2022
D. Y. Kim et al. (Eds.): APMS 2022, IFIP AICT 664, pp. 83–91, 2022.
https://doi.org/10.1007/978-3-031-16411-8_11

According to Pezzuolo et al. [3], dairy production is rapidly shifting in recent years towards intelligent livestock systems, driven by the rapid pace of technological advances such as the Internet of Things, big data, machine learning, augmented reality and robotics. These technologies are driving the collection, implementation, transmission and widespread use of digitized information on livestock farms.

In other areas, Creedon et al. [4] consider that new digital technologies providing veterinarians with immediate on-farm test results will allow for early clinical interventions, thus ensuring food safety and reducing losses.

Kochetkova and Shiryaeva [5] define that main reason for the low rate of dairy farming digitalization is that enterprise top executives are lacking clear understanding of how their organization should be transformed using modern information technologies.

Milk production in Brazil is an important activity of the agricultural sector has a vital role in the process of economic and social development of the country [6]. Digital technologies have contributed to improving dairy production in terms of control, measurement, analysis and cost reduction, in addition to making the entire chain reliable and safe.

The objective is to verify the use of digital technologies through digital transformation to improve the dairy production chain in the last 14 years.

2 Literature Review

2.1 Digital Transformation

According to Schwertner [7], digital transformation mainly involves production processes. This is particularly typical for manufacturing companies. Reducing costs by digitizing the development, testing and production processes of new products is of paramount importance. Mobile applications are most important for improving production processes and internal communications for employees who interact with customers that are mostly unusual. Large databases and information processing are more production focused. The digitalization of production processes opens opportunities to expand business and for its great internationalization/globalization.

Digital Transformation can be defined, according to Ebert and Duarte [8], as the adoption of disruptive technologies to increase productivity, value creation and social well-being. In this sense, Digital Transformation is enabling the development of the following types of technologies: collaborative equipment (drones and robots), 3D printing, digital interconnection of objects (IoT - Internet of Things), agile development, blockchain (trust protocol), APIs and Artificial Intelligence (AI). Finally, the authors highlight, in Table 1, that this Digital Transformation has objectives both in the social and economic fields.

In this scenario, Bharadwaj et al. [9] highlight that, during the last decade, impressive improvements in information, communication and connectivity technologies have triggered new functionalities. Thus, the following external digital trends provided the foundation for the new business infrastructure in the digital age: pervasive connectivity, information abundance, global supply chains, better IT price/performance, growth of cloud computing, and the emergence of Big Data. Therefore, the expanded scope

Table 1. Objectives of digital transformation

Perspective	Objective
Social	Promote the development of a more innovative and collaborative culture in industry and society
	Change the education system to provide new skills and future guidance to people so that they can achieve excellence in digital work and society
	Create and maintain digital communication infrastructures and ensure their governance, accessibility, quality of service and accessibility
	Strengthen digital data protection, transparency, autonomy and trust
	Improve the accessibility and quality of digital services offered to the population
Economic	Implement innovative business models
	Increase income generation, productivity and added value
	Improve the regulatory framework and technical standards.1 Introduction

Source: Adapted from Ebert and Duarte [8].

and scale of digital business can assist in executing the digital business strategy to create business differential and value creation, as the speed of decisions and actions are aligned with the speed of market conditions.

2.2 Milk Production Chains

The dairy chain is one of the most important activity of the agricultural sector and it plays a vital important role in the process of economic and social development of the country. After half a century of little change, largely explained by strong government intervention in the market sector, the milk production chain begins in the early 90s to experience profound changes as genetic control, artificial insemination, endemic controls, improvement of feeding and grazing, establishment of strict criteria for inspection, treatment, and sanitation, technological advances and product quality. These changes helped to increase the productivity of farms that were able to invest and to plan but impaired the dairy farms which were not able to keep up with changes, thus leading to dissatisfaction producers [10].

The milk production chain is one of the main economic activities in Brazil, with a strong effect on the generation of employment and income. Present in almost all Brazilian municipalities, milk production involves more than one million producers in the field, in addition to generating millions of jobs in other segments of the chain. In 2019, the gross value of primary milk production reached almost R$35 billion and the net sales of dairy products reached R$70.9 billion [11].

There is no consensus on the answer to the question whether technology adoption increases the cost of milk production. This question can be asked another way: Do more technical milk production systems have a higher average cost? Some think so, others, no. Those who think so argue that the adoption of technology implies the use of more of this food, medicines, fertilizers, correctives, mineral salt and other inputs from nature. Thus, higher technological level implies higher average cost [12].

According to de Rocha et al. [11], due to the adoption of new technologies, it was possible to significantly increase the productivity of animals, land and labor and consequently the scale of production of farms. Thus, Brazil has become the third largest milk producer in the world, but still has great potential to be explored, mainly in terms of productivity gains, in order to also become one of the main players in the global milk market and derivatives.

On the other hand, those who don't argue that the main purpose of technology is to increase productivity and, by extension, reduce average cost. In addition, the more technified production systems, the production grows, or are the most technified, which have greater power of competition either because of the lower average cost [12].

3   Methodology

The methodology consisted of a longitudinal survey between 2008 and 2022, where the following variables were studied, according to Table 2, related to digital technologies used in dairy production.

Table 2. Variables and descriptions.

Variable	Description
Automation and robotics systems	Applied at different levels of livestock production systems, for example Automatic Milking Systems (AMS), Automatic Feeding Systems (AFS) and Automatic Robotic Systems (ARS)
Digital and precision livestock farming sensors/tools	To increase the number of correct decisions per animal or per unit time. For example, the use of accelerometers for the monitoring, classification of behavior's, the use of NIR (Near-Infrared spectroscopy) technology during the preparation, mixing and distribution phases of the feed-ration
Farm management systems	Such as tools for data collection, processing, storing and disseminating data in specific form to carry out livestock operations, analysis and functions. Although the development of Farm Management Systems able to manage data deriving from multiple sources is in strong growth, today there are difficulties at farm level in the compatibility and data management between different technologies

(continued)

Table 2. (*continued*)

Variable	Description
Data sources	Represent the "sites" where the data are originally produced, stored or computed. For example: sensors technology for animals or livestock environment (dairy barn), remote animal monitoring (cow feeding, standing behavioral activities), feed ration analysis and monitoring of milking efficiency/parameters (e.g. Near Infrared Spectroscopy - NIR)
Data users	As the devices which receive data and provide a representation (results) or decision, such as management software's, plant/machine terminals (e.g. Automatic Milking Systems, mixer wagon, …), smart devices (smartphones, tablet, etc.)
Data repositories	As the "places" where historical/new data or synthesis parameters and processed data are stored. Technologies for the storage of such data are represented by hard drive (conventional), farm server but the "Cloud" technology is increasingly widespread to facilitate access and sharing of data with other support figures for the livestock activity (e.g. veterinarian, agronomist, nutritionist)
Transmission systems	Constitute an enabling technology supporting data transfers

Source: Pezzuolo et al. [3].

In 2008, we analyzed the digital technologies used in 3 large Brazilian dairy farms. In 2022, we look at the digital technologies that the company XPTO offers to dairy farms.

4   Results and Analysis

Table 3 shows the results:

Table 3. Results

Variable	2008	2022
Automation and robotics systems	The three farms were the most modern in the country, the main systems Automatic Milking Systems (AMS), Automatic Feeding Systems (AFS) and Automatic Robotic Systems (ARS)	XPTO has not developed a solution for AMS, but according to the Milkpoint website [13], Automatic Milking Systems simply have been present in the dairy industry for two decades. Currently more than 40,000 units are ordering cows and buffaloes in different production systems around the world
Digital and precision livestock farming sensors/tools	The three farms used sensors for identification and traceability of cows, such as: the most used identification in dairy herds, kept in an intensive production system, was the use of electronic collars. Another type of electronic animal identification was microchip identification, also known as transponder and bar codes and RFID allow the automatic capture of the animal's identity Another sensor used was the pedometer, which is an electronic equipment that continuously records the movement of animals by counting steps, is used for their identification and evaluation of their movement and the application is the detection of heat, as cows with hormonal changes, characteristic of the estrus period, walk more	The sensors attached to the animals monitor temperature, steps, rumination, estrus potential and send the information to an artificial intelligence platform that indicates, according to XPTO, clearly and easily accessible information, reproductive cycles, health problems or any nonconformity in behavior. of the animal. This data helps prevent possible diseases, with a direct impact on farm productivity The tool makes it possible to follow the entire route, monitoring the temperature, number of times the tank was opened and if the milk was removed without authorization The sensors located in the cooling tanks indicate if the product temperature is adequate to market standards or if it has undergone any variation above what is allowed. The technology also ensures that the volume sold with the dairy is the same as indicated in the tanks, ensuring operational efficiency and avoiding losses or contamination at the time of collection The sensors also guarantee cheaper maintenance and less technical unavailability, as they follow the usage time and useful life of the tank cooling motors, predicting with the help of artificial intelligence, the need for replacement, repair and root cause of the problem

(*continued*)

Table 3. (*continued*)

Variable	2008	2022
Farm management systems	The existing systems in 2008 were very precarious compared to the current ones, the data was not collected online as they did not have networks or technologies that allowed covering the entire dairy farm, the data generated by the systems and sensors were manually updated on the farm's server. There were several types of data analysis for decision making, but only with manually collected data and this system helped the property management	Currently, XPTO has created a system that combines the use of Artificial Intelligence, an Internet of Things network and monitoring and tracking sensors for monitoring the milk production chain, generating indicators for quality assurance, operational efficiency gains and agility in all the stages of the production process
Data sources	In 2008, data was not shared	In 2022, XPTO uses a digital platform that integrates IoT solutions
Data users	In 2008, it was not available	In 2022, several devices, mainly mobile
Data repositories	In 2008, on server disks and backups	In 2022, in the clouds
Transmission systems	The existing systems in 2008 were very precarious compared to the current ones, the data was not collected online as they did not have networks or technologies that allowed covering the entire dairy farm	According to XPTO, application eliminates the need for a robust technological infrastructure, such as connectivity and energy on the farms. Batteries with an average lifespan of ten years and specific communication networks for IoT are used, in addition to enabling a simple implementation, in a plug-and-play model "Through Wi-Fi coverage, or other similar technology, the information captured is sent to the cloud, where software can intelligently process and generate the data on screen", Words from XPTO's CTO.

In 2008, automation represented the main advances in digital technologies applied in dairy production, the farms surveyed already used the AMS, AFS and ARS systems, but it was not the reality of most dairy farms. According to Pezzuolo et al. [3], automation has historically represented the first line of development in the livestock sector and is currently successfully developed for various commercial applications. XPTO chose not to develop a solution for automation, as competition is high in this area, and they preferred to focus on an area with fewer competitors.

The evolution of these automatic systems has shown an important reduction in the necessary manpower but, thanks to the growing equipment of sensors and intelligent technologies [3], in 2008, the sensors were already being used in a timid way and in 2022, we could verify that sensors are being used in all areas of dairy production, mainly for data collection for decision making.

The systems or programs used to manage the farms have evolved a lot in 14 years. In 2008, the systems were used for controls with little data collected online, because, due to the large extensions of the properties, there were no systems, sensors and networks that allowed the coverage of the entire area. In 2022, systems and programs are considered digital platforms that receive data instantly from an Internet of Things network and monitoring and tracking sensors and process with the use of Artificial Intelligence allowing to monitor the milk production chain.

The evolution of data, users and network are linked to advances in digital technologies that have provided new network technologies such as wireless networks and devices for the use of the internet in mobile devices such as cell phones, tablets and sensors and also the emergence of cloud computing. In 2008, networks were non-existent for dairy production areas, only the headquarters and some parts of the farm had quality internet, which had an impact on not having online data in real time. The advancement of digital technologies has allowed technological advances such as mobile applications that have improved production processes and internal employee communications [7], the use of IoT sensors in various parts of the dairy farm to collect data and have the data stored in the clouds (cloud computing).

5 Conclusion

The objective was achieved, we were able to verify that the use of digital technologies through digital transformation improved the production of the dairy chain. We can highlight that the main advances were in production automation because despite being the pioneer and the main focus in 2008, the AMS, AFS and ARS systems received several updates such as intelligent sensors such as IOT and digital platforms for online data processing. Line with the use of AI, the evolution of computer networking technologies such as wireless networking, cloud computing and the Internet itself to obtain data anywhere in dairy production and farm management systems that with online data line allow for better property management.

As future studies, research with production and economic indicators is suggested to measure the benefits obtained from the use of digital technologies and digital transformation.

References

1. Haddara, M., Elragal, A.: The readiness of ERP systems for the factory of the future. Procedia Comput. Sci. **64**, 721–728 (2015)
2. Portal da Industria. Industria 4.0. https://www.portaldaindustria.com.br/industria-de-a-z/ind ustria-4-0/. Accessed 21 Feb 2022
3. Pezzuolo, A., Guo, H., Marchesini, G., Brscic, M., Guercini, S., Marinello, F.: Digital technologies and automation in livestock production systems: a digital footprint from multi-source data. In: 2021 IEEE International Workshop on Metrology for Agriculture and Forestry (MetroAgriFor), pp. 258–262, November 2021 IEEE
4. Creedon, N., Robinson, C., Kennedy, E., Riordan, A.O.: Agriculture 4.0: development of seriological on-farm immunosensor for animal health applications. In: 2019 IEEE Sensors, pp. 1–4, October 2019. IEEE

5. Kochetkova, O.V., Shiryaeva, E.V.: Perspective architecture of dairy farming enterprises, using modern digital technologies for sustainable development. In: IOP Conference Series: Earth and Environmental Science, vol. 965, no. 1, p. 012062. IOP Publishing (2022)

6. Vendrametto, O., Mollo Neto, M., Okano, M.T.: Indicators innovations for productivity gains of milk chain. Revista Brasileira de Engenharia de Biossistemas, Tupã, São Paulo, Brazil, **4**(3), 223–232 (2010)

7. Schwertner, K.: Digital transformation of business. Trakia J. Sci. **15**(1), 388–393 (2017)

8. Ebert, C., Duarte, C.H.C.: Digital transformation. IEEE Softw. **35**(4), 16–21 (2018). https://doi.org/10.1109/MS.2018.2801537

9. Bharadwaj, A., et al.: Digital business strategy: toward a next generation of insights. MIS Q . **37**(2), 471–482 (2013)

10. Okano, M.T.: Improving productivity of dairy chain through the development of indicators and classification of milk producers. Thesis (Ph. D. in Production Engineering) - Instituto de Ciências Exatas e Tecnológicas, Universidade Paulista (2010)

11. da Rocha, D.T., Carvalho, G.R., de Resende, J.C.: Cadeia produtiva do leite no Brasil: produção primária. Embrapa Gado de Leite-Circular Técnica (INFOTECA-E) (2020)

12. Gomes, S.T.: Evolução recente e perspectivas da produção de leite no Brasil. O agronegócio do leite no Brasil, pp. 207–240. EMBRAPA/CNPGL, Juiz de Fora (2001)

13. Milkpoint: Utilização de robôs de ordenha em sistemas de produção de leite à pasto (2018). https://www.milkpoint.com.br/canais-empresariais/delaval/utilizacao-de-robos-de-ordenha-em-sistemas-de-producao-de-leite-a-pasto-207741/. Accessed 26 Mar 2022

Supplying School Canteens with Organic and Local Products: Comparative Analysis

Laura Palacios-Argüello[1], João Gilberto Mendes dos Reis[2,3]([✉]),
and João Roberto Maiellaro[2,4]

[1] Luxembourg Centre for Logistics and Supply Chain Management (LCL),
MIT University of Luxembourg, Luxembourg, Luxembourg
laura.palacios@uni.lu
[2] RESUP - Research Group in Supply Chain Management - Postgraduate Program
in Production Engineering, Universidade Paulista, São Paulo, Brazil
joao.reis@docente.unip.br
[3] Centro de Ciências Sociais Aplicadas, Mackenzie Presbyterian University,
São Paulo, Brazil
joao.reis@mackenzie.br
[4] Faculdade de Tecnologia da Zona Leste, Centro Paula Souza, São Paulo, Brazil
joao.maiellaro@fatec.sp.gov.br

Abstract. Governments are facing the challenge of feeding students in
schools in a city environment in a process that revolves around the coordination of multiple producers, distributors, logistics operators and traders
of perishable foods. This paper aims to analyse food collection and distribution to assess the potential of urban food systems regarding school feeding. To do so, we compared school feeding distribution systems in Brazil
and France to identify the main issues and investigate the role of local
food systems. Our results showed that all cities are concerned about the
involvement of short food supply chains to provide vegetables and fruits
for schools to promote small local farming but there are cultural characteristics that require the use of different approaches.

Keywords: School canteens · Local production · Organic food
production · Short food supply chains

1 Introduction

Nowadays, the governments are facing the challenge of feeding cities, involving the
coordination of multiple producers, distributors, logistics operators and traders
of perishable foods. Because the increasing of population, more food and better
freight transport systems are required [1–3]. In the last 10 years, the demand for
locally grown food has dramatically increased in countries [4] and due to the concentration of the population in the cities and urban areas, the task of feeding has
taken great attention since the growing population needs to be fed.

Food supply brings several implications such as sustainability, social equity and economic development, and they are key in different policy discussions and must be considered in the food transportation strategy. In fact, aiming to decrease the transport nuisances and to improve the quality and sustainability of the food supply systems, several cities have started to think on how to outperform their local supply systems by combining proximity producers' supply with advanced city logistics systems.

To deal with the food supply requirements, several control entities and supply chain stakeholders have promoted local food production and consumption [5]. Compared to conventional channels, they propose to reduce the distance that food travels to reach the consumer [6], becoming easier to access to freshest and better quality foods [1]. In fact, local authorities have introduced a requirement for short circuits and local products in institutional catering [7].

A well planned food supply system is key to ensure the distribution of food in an efficient way both time and quality wise [6]. However, according to Barham et al. [8], one of the challenges faced by food producers is the lack of a distribution infrastructure that can allow them to respond against the increasing demand of local products in large markets. This added to the fact that food distribution system seeks to capture the growing demand at lower prices, but they do not always share the localization and distribution infrastructure strategies [9].

Despite the concept of food supply chain deal with the idea of 'farm to fork', in which raw material is transformed as it goes through multiple stages and agents [10] some researchers point to the shortening of these food supply chains [11].

Short food supply chains involve direct purchases of local food from familiar farmers with smaller distances between the production and consumption [12]. It contains the idea of local food, which means distinguishing product features, natural raw materials and methods, and direct incomes for families [13].

In this sense, some initiatives are gaining core around the world. French cities, for instance, are nowadays organizing collective restauration under unified structures that allow initiatives like consolidation and food hub (FHs) deployment. The local authorities has been promoted two main sustainable food policies: (i) to deploy organic and local supply strategies (fruits and vegetables); (ii) to make opportunities such as grouping local producers into urban food hubs. And this is not only a case for developed countries, Brazil, for example, include in law the obligation of municipalities spends at least 30% of resources destined for school feeding to purchase products coming from family farms.

With these ideas in mind, the aim of this paper is to analyse food collection and distribution to assess the potential of urban food systems for collective uses revolving around school feeding. To do so, we compare schools feeding distribution systems, one in Brazil and one in France to identify the main issues and investigate the role of local farm systems.

2   Methodology

The methodology proposed here is that of case study research [14] but will include both a quantitative assessment and a qualitative analysis. The construction of the case study and its consequent analyses is organized in the following phases:

1. Data collection: mainly based on a documentary analysis (with both scientific and technical/legislation documents) [15, 16], this phase consists on collecting the main information to describe the case and the context that explain how the meals distribution works.
2. Data analysis for food distribution system comparison: after having described the case qualification, a comparison between two distribution systems for school canteens is performed.

   – Data is analysed with two objectives: the first is to define the current context by addressing the main issues of the distribution services; and
   – The second is to examine data to propose practical implications and proposals of actions for the municipality.

3   Results and Discussion

3.1   French Case

The case study is that of two French cities. The geographical scope of the study focuses in two urban area that has about 160 school canteens, that represents 28,000 meals per day and works 140 days per year. The main families of products distributed are groceries, fresh and frozen products (for this study it will be only considered the fruits and vegetables supply). In France, the percentage of students eating at the school canteen was set to 40%–60% of the students registered.

Aiming to allow all children to have equal access to food, the meal prices vary between French municipalities. The meal cost is defined by the city, the department, or the region according to the school level. The parents pay part of this cost considers the income and family size. The average price per meal paid by parents is between 3 and 3.50 euros, but wealthiest families pay 7 euros, and the lowest-income families pay 20 cents per meal.

The school canteens is used to be supplied mainly on semi-manufactured and frozen products coming from platforms at different locations of the urban area. The aim of the municipality is to substitute some of those industrial distribution chains by short circuits of small local and organic producers.

The menu for school canteen is planned for the year and adjusted monthly. This means that the producer knows in advance the approximately amount of food that will be requested by the central kitchen (where the food is cooked) via the Food Hub (FH), nevertheless, the central kitchen confirms two days before the right amount of food that will request. Also, institutional catering is not the only customer of the FH, they also served other establishments from HORECA sector. The FHs are in charge of collecting, storing and distributing the products from the producers to the customers.

By using FHs enable short supply chains and allow an increase in the share of local and organic products available for institutional catering [17]. Nevertheless, the main issues of the distribution system founded are:

1. The producers allocation related to an administrative subdivision or a geographical proximity allocation; and
2. The impacts on the transportation collaboration policy related to food delivery directly by the producers or food collected from the FHs.

3.2 Brazilian Case

The Brazilian city is located in the metropolitan area of Sao Paulo, in Sao Paulo state, southeast region in Brazil. The municipality has 28.7% of urban areas and 71.3% of rural areas. There are 203 schools that provide meals 200 days per year for more than 55 thousand students (2017 number). In this study, we considered only vegetables supply by 58 local family farmers. Each school has a kitchen and cooker to prepare meals. Before being dispatched to the schools, products are stored in cooperative deposits or sometimes collected directly from the field and delivered to the logistics operator.

Vegetables are acquired for three local cooperatives of farms that gather the items in a central deposit and the vegetables are distributed twice a week per school using a third party logistics provider. The aim of the municipality is to guarantee at least 30% of financial resources obtained from the Federal Government are used to purchase products from small family farm producers (Brazilian law 11,947/2009).

The local government based on the immense rural area of the municipality and agriculture cluster area seeks to promote short supply chains assuring that federal government investments in school feeding add-value to the municipality. The main issues in the distribution system are:

- Food menu - (a) schools can choose items in a list of secretary of education - there is no obligation of purchase all items, (b) farmers offer vegetables according to the seasonality and their production;
- Transportation - (a) there are many schools in rural areas that difficult the access and distribution, (b) there is no pattern of vegetables, it difficulties the logistics operation;
- Budget restrains - the value per student is less than 0.20 US$ per student/day;
- Storage: the area in schools for is storage items are insufficient and there are deficiencies in refrigeration systems.

3.3 Case Comparison

Figure 1 presents the comparison of both cases.

All cities are concerned about the involvement of short food supply chains to provide vegetables and fruits for schools to promote small local farming, however, there is a difference in the production of these items. In France, there is a concern to use organic items, and in Brazil, the challenge is one step behind, the idea is offered to students more vegetables in the menus but the use of agricultural pesticides is permitted.

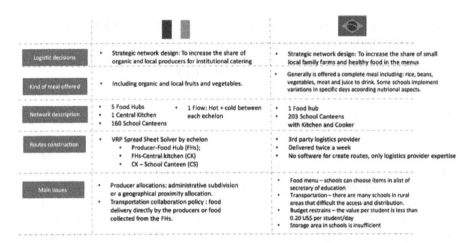

Logistic decisions	• Strategic network design: To increase the share of organic and local producers for institutional catering	• Strategic network design: To increase the share of small local family farms and healthy food in the menus
Kind of meal offered	• Including organic and local fruits and vegetables.	• Generally is offered a complete meal including: rice, beans, vegetables, meat and juice to drink. Some schools implement variations in specific days acoording nutrional aspects.
Network description	• 5 Food Hubs • 1 Flow: Hot + cold between • 1 Central Kitchen each echelon • 160 School Canteens	• 1 Food hub • 203 School Canteens with Kitchen and Cooker

Routes construction	• VRP Spread Sheet Solver by echelon
	   • Producer-Food Hub (FHs);
	   • FHs-Central kitchen (CK)
	   • CK – School Canteen (CS)
		• 3rd party logistics provider
		• Delivered twice a week
		• No software for create routes, only logistics provider expertise

Main issues	• Producer allocations: administrative subdivision or a geographical proximity allocation. • Transportation collaboration policy : food delivery directly by the producers or food collected from the FHs.	• Food menu – schools can choose items in alist of secretary of education • Transportation – there are many schools in rural areas that difficult the access and distribution. • Budget restrains – the value per student is less than 0.20 US$ per student/day • Storage area in schools is insufficient

Fig. 1. Case comparison

Regarding the approach of distribution while in France the meals are prepared in a central kitchen in Brazil the operation is decentralized and each school has a kitchen and cooker.

For logistics distribution in Brazil, a 3rd party logistics has a contract with the city hall and is responsible to distribute the items from a central deposit managed by cooperatives of farmers to the schools while in France the food is delivery directly by the producers to FHs or it is food collected from the FHs. Then, the food is distributed to a central kitchen where the food is cooked. The last mile distribution is performed by a 3rd party logistics who has a contract with the city hall, who supplies the school canteens.

Finally, in order to identify a policy, practical implications and proposals of actions for the municipality, the proposed systems imply a consequent modification of supply chain and transport practices. Indeed, those changes impact different stakeholders in the distribution chain, who have different objectives, issues, and perspectives. A particular focus will be made on the comparison between two different context and how those food supply systems impact current practices considering the risks related to their development.

4   Conclusions

This paper analysis local food distribution to school canteens in two cities in France and one in Brazil and compare challenges and logistics distribution.

Our results showed that in both countries there is the use of short food supply chains to provide vegetables and fruits for schools to promote small local farming. However, we observed the existence of different approaches. In France, is adopted organic items and ready-to-eat meals using a central kitchen delivered by producers. While in Brazil the canteens are centralized in schools and vegetables and fruits are conventional - the use of pesticides is allowed - delivered by a 3PL partner contracted by the city government.

The limitation of this study is the sample size, and the results need to be viewed in an exploratory manner. However, this fact does not invalidate the importance of this comparison using two different countries - developed and underdeveloped - but with the same objectives to ensure that students of school age could receive assistance to focus on their studies development.

As further research is an analysis using more delivered systems in the same and other countries to identify similar and different approaches that can be used in a future model of distribution of food for school canteens, considering short food supply chains.

References

1. Cretella, A., Buenger, M.S.: Food as creative city politics in the city of Rotterdam. Cities **51**, 1–10 (2016). https://www.sciencedirect.com/science/article/pii/S026427511530024X
2. Pisano, U., Lepuschitz, K., Berger, G.: Framing urban sustainable development: features, challenges and potentials of urban SD from a multi-level governance perspective. Technical report, European Sustainable Development Network: Institute for Managing Sustainability (2014)
3. Heilig, J.K.: World urbanization prospects the 2011 revision. Technical report, United Nations, New York (2012)
4. Jablonski, B.B.R., Schmit, T.M., Kay, D.: Assessing the economic impacts of food hubs on regional economies: a framework that includes opportunity cost. Agric. Resour. Econ. Rev. **45**(1), 143–172 (2016). https://www.cambridge.org/core/product/identifier/S2372261416000096/type/journal_article
5. Stroink, M.L., Nelson, C.H.: Complexity and food hubs: five case studies from Northern Ontario. Local Environ. **18**(5), 620–635 (2013). https://doi.org/10.1080/13549839.2013.798635
6. Severson, R.M., Schmit, T.M.: Building success of food hubs through the cooperative experience - a case study perspective. Report, Cornell University (2015). https://ecommons.cornell.edu/handle/1813/66064
7. Lessirard, J., Patier, C., Perret, A., Richard, M.A.: Sociétés de restauration collective en gestion concédée, en restauration commerciale et approvisionnements de proximité. Technical report, CGAAER (2017)
8. Barham, J., Tropp, D.: Regional food hub resource guide. Technical report, United States Department of Agriculture: Agricultural Marketing Service (2012)
9. Cleveland, D.A., Müller, N.M., Tranovich, A.C., Mazaroli, D.N., Hinson, K.: Local food hubs for alternative food systems: a case study from Santa Barbara County, California. J. Rural Stud. **35**, 26–36 (2014). https://www.sciencedirect.com/science/article/pii/S0743016714000436
10. Dani, S.: Food Supply Chain Management and Logistics: From Farm to Fork. Kogan Page, London (2015)
11. Aggestam, V., Fleiß, E., Posch, A.: Scaling-up short food supply chains? A survey study on the drivers behind the intention of food producers. J. Rural Stud. **51**, 64–72 (2017). https://linkinghub.elsevier.com/retrieve/pii/S0743016717301006

12. Mundler, P., Laughrea, S.: The contributions of short food supply chains to territorial development: a study of three Quebec territories. J. Rural Stud. **45**, 218–229 (2016). https://linkinghub.elsevier.com/retrieve/pii/S0743016716300547

13. Sage, C.: Social embeddedness and relations of regard. J. Rural Stud. **19**(1), 47–60 (2003). https://linkinghub.elsevier.com/retrieve/pii/S074301670200044X

14. Eisenhardt, K.M.: Making fast strategic decisions in high-velocity environments. Acad. Manag. J. **32**(3), 543–576 (1989)

15. Palacios-Argüello, L.: Characterization and assessment of distribution schemes for food supply and distribution systems considering environmentally sensitive demand. Ph.D. thesis, Lyon (2019)

16. Maiellaro, J.R.: Cadeia de suprimentos do Programa Nacional de Alimentação Escolar na cidade de Mogi das Cruzes SP. Ph.D. thesis, Universidade Paulista, São Paulo (2019)

17. Palacios-Argüello, L., Sanchez-Diaz, I., Gonzalez-Feliu, J., Gondran, N.: The role of food hubs in enabling local sourcing for school canteens. In: Aktas, E., Bourlakis, M. (eds.) Food Supply Chains in Cities, pp. 233–263. Springer, Cham (2020). https://doi.org/10.1007/978-3-030-34065-0_8

School Feeding and Family Farming: Partnership for the Generation of Employment and Income

Antonio Carlos Estender$^{(\boxtimes)}$ ⓘ, Luciana de Melo Costa$^{(\boxtimes)}$ ⓘ, and Oduvaldo Vendrametto$^{(\boxtimes)}$ ⓘ

Graduate Studies in Production Engineering, Paulista University - UNIP, PPGEP, São Paulo, Brazil

{estender,oduvaldo}@uol.com.br, lueducita@yahoo.com.br

Abstract. School meals made in partnership with family farmers tend to foster local economies, driving productive diversification and increasing the income of family farmers. Through the Brazilian School Meals Program, purchases of family farming products are encouraged, under special conditions of at least 30% of the resources transferred by the Brazilian Fund for Education Development. This incentive allows better marketing alternatives and valorization of the local farmer. The municipality has a significant return on its economy when these resources are added to those spent by the municipality itself. Numerous benefits would be generated for family farmers, shop- keepers, industrialists, and local service providers, as well as the return of revenue in the form of consumption taxes. This paper describes financial and social gains in the presence of municipal policies that induce the food acquisition process.

Keywords: Family farming · School feeding · Food bank · Micro-economy

1 Introduction

School feeding in partnership with family farming tends to foster local economies, enabling actions that generate employment and income. The National School Feeding Program of Brazil (PNAE), among its competencies, should also stimulate local economies and enable productive diversification and income increase of family farmers, offering more and better-marketing alternatives and valorization of the local farmer [1].

The program advocates legally the purchase of food produced by family farmers, be at least 30% of the resource transfer, favoring the generation of income, causing a greater impact on small and medium-sized cities, while promoting citizenship and food security, encouraging education in the communities through a comprehensive feeding system in public schools [2].

The effectiveness of school feeding will be expressive the greater the involvement of the community, public management, and inspection. The objective of this article is to evaluate how the resources used in school feeding can contribute to the local economy,

D. Y. Kim et al. (Eds.): APMS 2022, IFIP AICT 664, pp. 99–106, 2022.
https://doi.org/10.1007/978-3-031-16411-8_13

adding income to family farmers and the community, and bringing social returns to the municipality. In May 2020, a governmental resolution made clear the understanding of all the eligibility criteria for family farmers and forcefully addresses considerations of the Food Guide for the Brazilian Population and the Food Guide for Brazilian Children recommending the purchase of fresh or minimally processed foods [3].

PNAE is an important tool for partnerships between the executing units, to provide opportunities for the generation of employment and income, because it recognizes, stimulates, and values the local agricultural family production, and the cultural specificities of food consumption, resulting in the construction of a healthy school menu and the movement of the financial wheel that provides all the access and consumption of the participating community. This includes all sorts of services involved in the smooth running of the school kitchen, such as maintenance, logistics, and other necessary inputs, as well as goods and services accessible to family farmers with their new income possibilities.

2 Literature Review

Initiatives around the world to meet food needs in schools reveal the concern with the school environment, including factors such as childhood obesity and the counterpoint to large-scale consumption of industrialized products. This premise brings benefits such as the correction of poor food environments, improvement in the nutritional quality of students, and revitalization of local agriculture [4].

In Brazil, public policies have been implemented to ensure nutritional food security as a human right to healthy food and in adequate quantities. As part of its historical landmarks, it instituted the Federal Law n° 5.537 in 1968, establishing the Brazilian Fund for Education Development (FNDE), whose function is to elaborate educational policies and provide resources for school feeding [1].

The National School Feeding Program of Brazil was created to elaborate policies on school feeding and is managed by the FNDE. PNAE is responsible for technical assistance and supports the states and municipalities, to contribute to the implementation of educational actions [5].

For the food to arrive on the table of the school canteen, the capillarity was promoted, transferring the execution to the municipalities, which must complement the financial resources passed by FNDE, set up and manage the whole infrastructure, from the purchase of food, its transport, organization, and preparation of the menus with the assistance of nutritionists [1].

To meet the requirement of spending a minimum of 30% of school feeding expenses on in-nature products, the process favors the elimination of intermediaries and the exemption of bidding processes based on the lowest price. It will be up to each executing entity to publish this demand through a public call, at fair prices, publicizing it widely in newspapers, electronic media, or in other ways, prioritizing family entrepreneurs or organizations of agrarian reform settlements, and indigenous people [6].

The respect for food culture and seasonality of production are also beneficial effects in this construction so that the preparation of this menu following these premises can positively affect the field and the student's plate [5]. The increasing use of quality and fiber-rich foods, and the strengthening of the micro-economy for food production and food delivery should be a systematic search to guarantee this public policy [3].

The menu should be prepared by a nutritionist who is registered in PNAE, and it should respect the local food culture, and specify the variety of products and quantity, with high nutritional content so that it can base the list of products for the acquisition. The nutritionist must be aware of the local production to compose the menu. In this way, the public call, the modality that governs this acquisition will be compatible to meet the intended demand. The production of healthier food for students reinforces the local economy, as it proposes a guaranteed fixed income to the family farmer [7].

The supply chains should be short to preserve the freshness and quality of food, respect regional eating habits, and generate a supply of products that can even promote food education and change eating habits. The economic, social, and local development effects of school feeding influence the performance of the local economy, the National School Feeding Program of Brazil helps in the economic capillarity of the municipalities because the amount received by farmers will also reverberate in small businesses and the increase of tax collection in the municipality [8].

PNAE grants election criteria to suppliers of the short chain that produce organic and ecological food, because the resolution allows that in these cases the price is increased by 30% valuing the responsible cultivation and aligned to the Sustainable Development Goals (SDG) of the UN agenda 2030 [9].

The construction of a sustainable development mechanism for family farmers must be a systematic and holistic project, so that the support can be continued and translated into the inclusion of family farming, especially in the attention to their needs and future projects [10].

For the farmer to participate in the public call, it is necessary to follow and be up to date with the documentary requirements qualifying them as suppliers. The reference prices should be parameters so that the products can have a fair and balanced price. In this document, the producer will indicate which products and quantities will be made available, compatible with its production and limits of individual resource contracting/year, established by Resolution N° 21, of November 16, 2021 [6].

The most important resource of income comes from the PNAE, that despite prioritizing local producers, the same producers can access several municipalities where surpluses are available, accumulating in the same year several sales projects and multiplying its income [11].

In Brazil apart from PNAE there are other school feeding programs and modalities that aid small producers such as PAA - Food Acquisition Program, the modality CONAB - National Supply Company and the modality Term of Adhesion (municipal and state). The creation of a partnership among economic agents that encourages networking to strengthen management and promote exchange within the region itself is necessary since the work of social policies presents different realities and capabilities but is complementary and essential for sustainable rural development [12].

3 Methods

The research was carried out with family farmers, members of the Association of Rural Producers of the Rio Branco Basin, Artisanal Fishermen, and Indigenous People of Itanhaém/SP-Brazil and Region - AMIBRA, the main suppliers who deliver foodstuffs to the city government. In the first stage of the research, visits were made to understand how producers in the region have increased food production with the help of PNAE, PAA, and local companies, to make a diagnosis. Data collection was carried out at the Food Bank of Itanhaém, to assess how the resources employed in school feeding can contribute to the local economy, adding income to family farmers and the community, and bringing social returns to the municipality. The data collected was compiled in an electronic database of the Microsoft Excel program, and from there it was possible to structure and understand the income generation model of the farmers.

4 Result and Discussion

Itanhaém was based on local food characteristics, with banana cultivation as its main crop, but the new perspective of access to commercialization, such as the PNAE and institutional support, have changed the production dynamics, posing the challenge to the producers' associations of changing and diversifying the plantation to meet the demands of school meals.

According to the farmers' reports, the first participation in sales was only bananas, and when the diversification occurred the number of products grown from 1 to 10. Table 1, data from the public call 001/2021 demonstrates this alignment, in addition to the respect for the cultivars of traditional communities [13].

Table 1. Public call 001/2021 - Itanhaém/SP-Brazil

Product	Unit	Quantity	Price unitary USD	Total USD
Banana silver	kg	50.000	0.673	33.674.99
Dwarf banana	kg	60.167	0.631	37.989.81
Lettuce	kg	24.104	21.047	50.731.37
Processed manioc	kg	11.000	14.733	16.206.09
Organic Cabbage	kg	10.000	11.576	55.000.00
Organic beet	kg	10.100	10.944	11.575.77
Sweet potato	kg	10.000	0.758	7.576.87
Yam	kg	10.000	0.842	8.418.74
Guarani sweet potato	kg	300	18.521	555.63
Guarani corn	kg	60	1.869	168.20

Source: Prepared by the authors

In 2009/2010, the municipality of Itanhaém published the public call for proposals, quickly complying with the new legislation, on the back of the positive experience of the implementation of the Food Bank (2007) and the Food Purchase Program - Purchase for Simultaneous Donation.

The coincidence of the Food Bank is in the same organizational chart as the School Feeding Department, both in the Municipal Education Secretariat, provided the articulation of a socio-technical network beneficial to the PNAE and especially to the group of farmers who were assisted in the field extension, strategic planning, formalization, and document updating, in addition to the defense of seasonality and delivery logistics.

The agriculture department aligned itself with the Food Bank and it was decisive for the productive group to change the banana monoculture characteristic in the following years, besides the revival of local culture products and the valorization of the Guarani ethnic group. In the same way, together they have elaborated the routes to facilitate point-to-point delivery as required by the public call: Center/East (Beach) and Center-West (Hill) distributing in a logical line about 62 schools including 8 state schools that are annually agreed in the municipal school feeding.

With Resolution N. 21, November 2021, the bill that can be glimpsed is the same one that transformed the lives of farmers in Itanhaém and made sustainable rural development move forward, consolidating the real short chain around local products and above all returning the socio-political visibility of the right. The resolution changes the value of the individual sales limit of the family farmer and the rural family entrepreneur for school meals, establishing a new maximum value to be respected, setting it to USD 8,500.00.

Table 2 shows the real gain for producers, adding the maximum values of the family farm in Itanhaém/SP-Brazil from 2009 to 2021.

Table 2. Income Generation USD - Public Policies - Food Purchase Program

Year	PNAE income/year	PAA CDS income/year	Income total/year	Income/month
2009		1.000.00	1.000.00	80.00
2011	1.800.00	1.000.00	2.800.00	237.00
2013	4.200.00	1.000.00	5.200.00	430.00
2015	4.200.00	1.400.00	26.500,00	465.00
2017	4.200.00	1.400.00	26.500,00	465.00
2019	4.200.00	1.400.00	26.500,00	465.00
2021	8.500.00	2.500.00	11.000.00	920.00

Source: Prepared by the authors from various reports on the operationalization of food acquisition programs

One of the most successful actions of the whole process was the inclusion of the indigenous family farmer as a priority beneficiary of these programs. The joint work between the Brazilian Indian Foundation - Southern Coast Regional Coordination and the Food Bank revitalized the planting of Guarani corn, soon introduced in school meals for consumption in indigenous schools, as sacred food for the ethnic group [14]. This initiative pushed the inclusion of other products from the villages, meeting the criteria of prioritization of traditional peoples and communities, specificities that are foreseen in the guiding Resolution of PNAE [7].

The collaboration between the government and farmers promoted food security and income generation, through the implementation of these programs. It is known that the benefits of school meals vary according to the economic needs of the region, in the richest and most developed regions school meals are a source of nutritious meals that complement the food offered by the family, in the poorest regions and countries is an incentive to send children to school and continue their education, being, therefore, a relevant factor to ensure food security and attention to children in vulnerable situations [8].

5 Conclusion

The results observed point out that the purchase of family farming through the PNAE can contribute to the local economy, adding income to family farmers and the community, and bringing social returns to the municipality. According to the association of farmers of Itanhaém, promoting food production and local supply systems operated by short production and supply chains are instruments for generating income and promoting citizenship.

The access to public purchases, besides revitalizing the rural area, served to strengthen the associative arrangement of small local producers, reflecting on the quality and freshness of the school feeding supply, and providing social and economic visibility for each producer in the community [14].

The supply of food for PNAE, with the support of the city hall, helps local farmers employing direct purchase, promoting the improvement of their incomes that are guaranteed for a certain time, giving rise to situational diagnoses such as higher generation of jobs; increase of the portion of re- sources destined to the remuneration of labor and the increase of the economic movement in the whole region, reorganization in the food production process, increase of the productive volume, the incentive to the consumption of fresher and healthier products by the students. The development of family farming to improve school meals, the central pillar of PNAE, can also eliminate the intermediary agent, allowing a direct connection between the field and the table, generating a fairer income for farmers. Other modalities of food acquisition programs also provide opportunities for diversification and direct commercialization of Family Farming [15].

Given this, the Itanhaém Food Bank, as executor of the purchase modality has been the guiding thread of the connection between family farming production, menu formulation, and preparation of the school feeding public call, establishing healthy management in the municipality, presenting itself as a viable alternative for the success of food systems around school feeding and the processes that culminate in the restructuring of short production and supply chains. Because of the impression that there are opportunities optimized by partner actions in the execution of the PNAE, it is understood that by force of law there is a preexisting demand to be met and important socio-economic gains. The Itanhaém Food Bank in a collaborative role appears as a viable alternative for the success of food systems around school meals. The technical interventions have formalized an expressive number of small producers that were irregular, from 28 to 61, an increase of 117% [16].

However, weaknesses such as the different productive stages may respond with little supply in local agriculture. It was found that knowing the reality of local rural production and intersectional strategic planning can in-cite and produce short-term changes and real impacts on the local economy.

Acknowledgment. This study was financed in part by the Coordenação de Aperfeiçoamento de Pessoal de Nível Superior - Brasil (CAPES) - Finance Code 001".

References

1. FNDE N.E.D.F.: National school feeding program – PNAE. https://www.fnde.gov.br/progra mas/pnae. Accessed 21 Apr 2022
2. Lopes, S.R.S., Diniz, P.R.: Boas práticas de agricultura familiar para a alimentação escolar/Programa Nacional de Alimentação Escolar, 182. FNDE, Brasília (2017) http://www.com unidade.diaadia.pr.gov.br/arquivos/File/agricultura_familiar/caderno_boas_praticas.pdf
3. Brasil: FNDE. Ministério da Educação. Resolução no 6, de 08 de maio 2020. https://www.fnde.gov.br/index.php/acesso-a-informacao/institucional/legislacao. Accessed 21 Apr 2022
4. Bagdonis, J.M., Hinrichs, C.C., Schafft, K.A.: The emergence and framing of farm-to-school initiatives: civic engagement, health and local agriculture. Agric. Hum. Values **26**(1), 107–119 (2009). https://doi.org/10.1007/s10460-008-9173-6. http://link.springer.com/10.1007/s10460-008-9173-6
5. Brasil: L11947. http://www.planalto.gov.br/ccivil_03/_Ato2007-2010/2009/Lei/L11947.htm. Accessed 22 Mar 2022
6. FNDE B: https://www.fnde.gov.br. Resolução n° 21, de 16 de novembro de 2021. https://www.fnde.gov.br/index.php/programas/pnae/pnae-sobre-o-programa/pnae-leg islacao. Accessed 21 Apr 2021
7. Brasil: Decreto N° 10.880, de 2 de dezembro. Regulamenta o Programa Alimenta Brasil, instituído pela Medida Provisória n° 1061, de 9 de agosto de 2021. https://www.in.gov.br/en/web/dou/-/decreto-n-10.880-de-2-de-dezembro-de-2021-364265206. Accessed 22 Apr 2022
8. de Souza, A.E., et al.: Short agri-food supply chains: a proposal in a food bank. In: Lalic, B., Majstorovic, V., Marjanovic, U., von Cieminski, G., Romero, D. (eds.) APMS 2020. IFIP AICT, vol. 592, pp. 601–608. Springer, Cham (2020). https://doi.org/10.1007/978-3-030-57997-5_69
9. United Nations Organization U: Sustainable Development Goal 2: Fome zero e agricultura sustentável. https://nacoesunidas.org/pos2015/ods2/2019. Accessed 10 Mar 2022
10. WFP, W.F.P.: The state of school feeding (2015). https://www.wfp.org/content/state-school-feeding-worldwide. Accessed 20 Apr 2021
11. Brasil.: L11947, 8, Brasil. L11947 (2009). http://www.planalto.gov.br/ccivil_03/_Ato200 72010/2009/Lei/L11947.htm. Accessed 11 Apr 2022
12. WWP: Asseismodalidadesdopaa. https://wwp.org.br/wp-content/up-loads/2017/02/PAA__PT.pdf. Accessed 11 Apr 2022
13. PMI-Administration Secretary Supplies Department, Itanhaém City Hall (2021). http://www2.itanhaem.sp.gov.br/wp-content/uploads/2021/04/01-21-Edital-ChamadaP%C3%BAblica-Aquisi%C3%A7%C3%A3o-de-G%C3%AAneros-Aliment%C3%ACios-Pnae-1.pdf. Accessed 17 June 2022
14. PMI: Food Bank, Itanhaém City Hall. http://www2.itanhaem.sp.gov.br/2018/08/06/banco-de-alimentos-municipal-apresentara-iniciativa-inovadora-no-projeto-bota-na-mesa2018/. Accessed 17 June 2022

15. Estender A. C.; Vendrametto, O.; Melo, L. Strengthening the local economy through school meals. Res. Soc. Dev. **10**(15), e270101522863 (2021). https://doi.org/10.33448/rsd-v10i15.22863. Disponível em: https://rsdjournal.org/index.php/rsd/article/view/22863. Accessed 7 Mar 2022

16. PMI-Food Bank, Itanhaém City Hall (2017). http://arquivos.ambiente.sp.gov.br/municipio verdeazul/2016/07/rs3-nao-geracao_itanhaem.pdf. Accessed 18 June 2022

Simulation-Based Game Theoretical Analysis of Japanese Milk Supply Chain for Food Waste Reduction

Hajime Mizuyama[1]([✉]) [iD], Sota Yamaguchi[1], Shota Suginouchi[1] [iD], and Mizuho Sato[2] [iD]

[1] Aoyama Gakuin University, 5-10-1 Fuchinobe, Chuoku 252-5258, Sagamihara, Japan
mizuyama@ise.aoyama.ac.jp
[2] Tokyo University of Agriculture, 1-1-1, Sakuragaoka, Setagayaku 156-0054, Tokyo, Japan

Abstract. The one-third rule, which sets tight wholesale and retail limits for food products, is arguably a primary cause of huge food waste in Japan. However, the effect of relaxing the limits was found to vary depending on some conditions. Thus, to further understand how these limits affect food wastage, we take a game-theoretical analysis approach. In this approach, we formulate a normal-form game played by a manufacturer and a retailer in a milk supply chain, develop a simulation model of the chain, and use the simulator to obtain sample values of the players' payoffs earned under every pair of their strategies. We then apply a statistical multiple comparison test to the data to identify the *statistical best responses* of a player to each opponent strategy, derive *statistical Nash equilibriums*, and compare the equilibriums obtained under different limits and consumers' preferences. Consequently, it is confirmed that relaxing the limits may undesirably impact food waste.

Keywords: Food supply chain · Food waste · Normal-form game

1 Introduction

The Sustainable Development Goals (SDGs) adopted at the United Nations Summit in 2015 aim to reduce by half the per capita global food waste at the retail and consumer levels and the food losses along the production and supply chains [1]. Reportedly, about 25.31 million tons of food waste was caused in FY 2018 in Japan [2]. Further, the waste is estimated to include six million tons of food that were still edible, of which 3.24 million tons were generated from businesses, including the food manufacturing, wholesale, retail, and restaurant industry, and 2.76 million tons were generated from households. Thus, it is crucial to mitigate food waste across the whole supply chain [3,4].

It is argued that the one-third rule [5] is a primary cause of the significant food waste. This rule is a commercial custom that is widely followed in the Japanese food industry. It divides the time between production and expiration dates of a food product

D. Y. Kim et al. (Eds.): APMS 2022, IFIP AICT 664, pp. 107–115, 2022.
https://doi.org/10.1007/978-3-031-16411-8_14

into three equal length intervals and sets the wholesale and retail limits of the food at the end of the first interval and the second interval, respectively. Such limits are also imposed in some other countries; however, they tend to be more relaxed than those in Japan are. Furthermore, social experiments conducted in 2013 observed the effect of relaxing the wholesale limit to one-half to be bidirectional [6]. While, relaxing the limit reduced the amount of waste in some food categories, the waste caused by retailers in other categories slightly increased. This suggests the complexity of the relation between the limits and food waste, mediated by various decisions made by the different players in the food supply chain, such as manufacturers, wholesalers, retailers, and consumers. Therefore, deepening the understanding of the mechanism of how the limits affect food wastage is required to devise effective means for food waste reduction.

To address this challenge, we take a game-theoretical analysis approach in this paper. Since most supply chains are composed of several self-centered business entities, game theoretical models have become a standard approach for analyzing supply chains [7–9]. When using a game-theoretical model, we usually simplify the supply chain considerably to make it straightforward to calculate the payoffs that each player earns in the game. However, such simplification makes it difficult to investigate the complex mechanism that we are interested in, here. Thus, in this paper, we rely on the numerical simulation instead, to obtain sample values of the players' payoffs and utilize statistical techniques to analyze the data.

In the remainder of this paper, after introducing the supply chain simulation model and statistical game-theoretical analysis approach, we present numerical experiments, their results, and discuss their implications. Finally, we conclude this paper by providing some future research directions.

2 Supply Chain Simulation Model

2.1 Model Outline

Our milk supply chain model comprises a manufacturer, a retailer, and anonymous consumers. The manufacturer produces particular milk packages from raw milk and holds them in their warehouse. The retailer buys the packages from the manufacturer and takes them to their warehouse. They then move packages to their shelf and sell them to consumers. The number of consumers visiting the retailer each day d is a random variable following a normal distribution $n_d \sim N\left(\bar{n}, \sigma_n^2\right) (= N(100, 100)$ in the numerical experiments below). Each consumer may choose a candidate package on the shelf and buy it or leave the store without buying the milk package. This decision is affected by the remaining days to expiration and the price of the milk packages on the shelf. That is, they prefer fresher and cheaper milk packages.

The time to expiration of the milk packages is L^C days, including the date of production as the first day ($L^C = 12$ in the numerical experiments). Thus, if the one-third rule is applied, the wholesale limit L^M and the retail limit L^R are set at $\lceil L^C/3 \rceil$ th day and $\lceil 2 \cdot L^C/3 \rceil$ th day respectively ($L^M = 4, L^R = 8$). Otherwise, both are regarded as equal to L^C ($L^M = L^R = 12$).

The number of milk packages whose *days-from-production* (DFP) is δ held in the manufacturer's warehouse is denoted by s_δ^M, and the total number of packages in the warehouse is given by $s^M = \sum_\delta s_\delta^M$. This inventory is controlled by determining the production order quantity o_d^M placed on day d according to a standard periodical ordering policy. A fixed lead time $lt^M (= 1)$ is necessary between planning and completing production. Raw milk is assumed to be always available as much as required at a fixed cost per unit. Its storage is outside the scope of the model, and no other costs related to production are considered.

The numbers of milk packages whose DFP is δ held in the retailer's warehouse and on-shelf are denoted by s_δ^R and s_δ^S, respectively, and the total numbers of packages in the warehouse and on the shelf are given by $s^R = \sum_\delta s_\delta^R$ and $s^S = \sum_\delta s_\delta^S$, respectively. The total inventory of the retailer $s^R + s^S$ is controlled by determining the purchase order quantity o_d^R placed on day d according to a standard periodical ordering policy. A fixed lead time $lt^R (= 1)$ is necessary between placing an order and replenishment. The capacity of the shelf is limited to $c^S (= 50)$; no capacity limit is imposed on the warehouses of the manufacturer and the retailer.

2.2 Operational Flow of Manufacturer

At the beginning of each day d, the manufacturer determines the order quantity:

$$
o_d^M = \sum_{t=d-lt^R}^{d-1} o_t^R + b_{d-1}^R + \left(lt^M - lt^R + 2 \right) \cdot \bar{n} - \sum_{t=d-lt^M}^{d-1} o_t^M - s^M + ss^M \tag{1}
$$

where b_{d-1}^R specifies the number of stockout milk packages remaining unshipped on the day before, and ss^M denotes the safety stock level:

$$
ss^M = k^M \cdot \sqrt{\max(0, lt^M - lt^R + 2)} \cdot \sigma_n \tag{2}
$$

where k^M is the manufacturer's safety stock coefficient.

Then, it ships out milk packages to the retailer. The total number to be shipped is:

$$
f_d^M = \min(s^M, o_{d-lt^R}^R + b_{d-1}^R) \tag{3}
$$

The manufacturer chooses the order in which the packages are shipped between FIFO (from old to new) or LIFO (from new to old). In the case of FIFO, the number of milk packages shipped whose DFP is δ is given recursively by:

$$
f_{d,\delta}^M = \min\left(s_\delta^M, f_d^M - \sum_{\tau=\delta+1}^{L^M} f_{d,\tau}^M \right) \quad (\delta = L^M, L^M - 1, \cdots) \tag{4}
$$

Otherwise, it is given by:

$$
f_{d,\delta}^M = \min\left(s_\delta^M, f_d^M - \sum_{\tau=1}^{\delta-1} f_{d,\tau}^M \right) \quad (\delta = 1, 2, \cdots) \tag{5}
$$

After shipping out, the manufacturer's inventory is updated as $s_\delta^M = s_\delta^M - f_{d,\delta}^M$ ($\forall\delta$) and the stockout is given by $b_d^R = o_{d-lt^R}^R + b_{d-1}^R - f_d^M$.

When the production of the day is completed, the produced milk packages are replenished in the warehouse as $s_1^M = o_{d-lt^M}^M$.

At the end of the day, the milk packages whose DFP has reached the limit L^M are wasted as $(w_d^M, s_{L^M}^M) = (s_{L^M}^M, 0)$, where w_d^M is the number of milk packages wasted by the manufacturer on day d. Further, the reward of the manufacturer is updated:

$$r^M = r^M + \sum_{\delta=1}^{L^M} p_\delta^R \cdot f_{d,\delta}^M - p^M \cdot s_1^M - p^B \cdot b_d^R - p^W \cdot w_d^M \tag{6}$$

where p_δ^R is the wholesale price of a milk package whose DFP is δ, $p^M (= 100)$ is the unitary price of raw milk, and $p^B (= 5)$ and $p^W (= 0)$ are the penalty of stockout and wastage, respectively. The wholesale price is given by:

$$p_\delta^R = 150 - \Delta^M (\delta - 1) \tag{7}$$

where Δ^M is the discount rate of the wholesale price determined by the manufacturer.

Finally, when the next day starts, the DFP of the milk packages in the warehouse is updated:

$$s_\delta^M = \begin{cases} 0 & (\delta = 1) \\ s_{\delta-1}^M & (1 < \delta \le L^M) \end{cases} \tag{8}$$

2.3 Operational Flow of Retailer

At the beginning of each day d, the retailer determines the order quantity:

$$o_d^R = \left(lt^R + 2\right) \cdot \bar{n} - \sum_{t=d-lt^R}^{d-1} o_t^R - b_{d-1}^R - s^R - s^S + ss^R \tag{9}$$

where ss^R denotes the safety stock level:

$$ss^R = k^R \cdot \sqrt{lt^R + 2} \cdot \sigma_n \tag{10}$$

where k^R is the retailer's safety stock coefficient.

At the beginning of the day as well as, at most, twice during the day when s^S reaches the ordering point $op(= 10)$, the retailer moves milk packages from the warehouse to the shelf. The number of packages to be moved at $i (\le 3)$ th occasion of day d is given by:

$$f_{d,i}^R = \min(s^R, c^S - s^S) \tag{11}$$

The retailer chooses the order in which the packages are moved between FIFO or LIFO. In the case of FIFO, the number of milk packages moved on this occasion whose DFP is δ is given recursively by:

$$f^R_{d,i,\delta} = \min\left(s^R_\delta, f^R_{d,i} - \sum_{\tau=\delta+1}^{L^R} f^R_{d,i,\tau}\right) \quad (\delta = L^R, L^R - 1, \cdots) \tag{12}$$

Otherwise, it is given by:

$$f^R_{d,i,\delta} = \min\left(s^R_\delta, f^R_{d,i} - \sum_{\tau=1}^{\delta-1} f^R_{d,i,\tau}\right) \quad (\delta = 1, 2, \cdots) \tag{13}$$

After moving them to the shelf, the retailer's inventory is updated:

$$\left(s^R_\delta, s^S_\delta\right) = (s^R_\delta - f^R_{d,i,\delta} \cdot s^S_\delta + f^R_{d,i,\delta}) \quad (\forall \delta) \tag{14}$$

The number of milk packages on the shelf s^S_δ decreases when a consumer buys one.

At the end of the day, the packages shipped from the manufacturer arrive, and they are replenished in the warehouse as $s^R_\delta = s^R_\delta + f^M_{d,\delta}$ ($\forall \delta$). Then, the milk packages whose DFP has reached the limit L^R are wasted as $(w^R_d, s^R_{L^R}, s^S_{L^R}) = (s^R_{L^R} + s^S_{L^R}, 0, 0)$, where w^R_d is the number of milk packages wasted by the retailer on day d. Further, the reward of the retailer is updated:

$$r^R = r^R + \sum_{\delta=1}^{L^R} p^S_\delta \cdot f^S_{d,\delta} + p^B \cdot b^R_d - \sum_{\delta=1}^{L^M} p^R_\delta v f^M_{d,\delta} - p^W \cdot w^R_d \tag{15}$$

where $f^S_{d,\delta}$ is the number of milk packages, whose DFP is δ, sold to consumers on day d, and p^S_δ is the retail price of those packages:

$$p^S_\delta = 200 - \Delta^R(\delta - 1) \tag{16}$$

where Δ^R is the discount rate of the retail price determined by the retailer.

Finally, when the next day starts, the DFP of the milk packages in the warehouse and on the shelf is updated:

$$(s^R_\delta, s^S_\delta) = \begin{cases} (0, 0) & (\delta = 1) \\ (s^R_{\delta-1}, s^S_{\delta-1}) & (1 < \delta \le L^R) \end{cases} \tag{17}$$

2.4 Consumers' Behavior

The number of milk packages $f_{d,\delta}^S$ bought by consumers each day d is determined by their behavior. On day d, in total, n_d consumers arrive at the store one by one. Each first chooses a candidate milk ('s DFP δ) if the shelf is not empty ($\{\delta | s_\delta^S > 0\} \equiv D \neq \varnothing$) when they arrive at the store. If the shelf is empty ($D = \varnothing$), they leave the store without buying a package. This decision is made according to the nested logit choice model [10], whose first step specifies the probability of choosing δ:

$$prob_1(\delta) = \frac{\exp(u_\delta)}{\sum_{\tau \in D} \exp(u_\tau)} \tag{18}$$

where u_δ specifies the utility of buying a milk package of δ:

$$u_\delta = 0.6789 \cdot (12 - \delta) + 0.1356 \cdot (200 - p_\delta^S) \tag{19}$$

The values of the utility model's coefficients are determined according to a conjoint analysis study conducted earlier in Japan [11]. Then, the second step decides whether they buy the candidate milk or not according to:

$$prob_2(\delta) = \frac{\exp(u_\delta)}{\exp(u_\delta) + \exp(u_\varnothing)} \tag{20}$$

where $u_\varnothing$ denotes the utility of buying no milk, which is assumed to be:

$$u_\varnothing = 0.6789 \cdot \left(12 - \delta_\varnothing\right) \tag{21}$$

In this equation, $\delta_\varnothing$ can be regarded as a parameter expressing the consumers' preference for freshness. The higher this value, the looser the preference.

3   Statistical Game Theoretical Analysis

The performance of the supply chain is determined by a strategic interaction between the manufacturer and retailer. We capture this interaction as a normal-form game.

The set of the manufacturer's strategy is given by $A^M = \{FRL, FRH, FDL, FDH, LRL, LRH, LDL, LDH\}$. The first alphabet specifies whether the shipping order is FIFO (F) or LIFO (L), which we expect to be a primary determinant of food waste. The second shows whether old milk packages are discounted, which may have an interaction with the shipping order. Regular price policy (R) does not discount old packages ($\Delta^M = 0$), and discounted price policy (D) discounts them ($\Delta^M = 3$). The last one concerns the safety stock level, which will also affect food waste. Low level (L) sets the service level at 90% ($k^M = 1.29$), and high level (H) sets it at 99% ($k^M = 2.33$).

Similarly, the set of the retailer's strategy is given by $A^R = \{FRL, FRH, FDL, FDH, LRL, LRH, LDL, LDH\}$. The first alphabet denotes whether milk packages are moved from the warehouse to the shelf in FIFO (F) or LIFO (L), which we envisage as another determinant of food waste. The second specifies the pricing policy. In the case of R, old packages are not discounted ($\Delta^R = 0$), and L, they are discounted so that they should seem approximately equally preferable to consumers as a new one ($\Delta^R = 4$). The last is the safety stock policy. L sets the service level at 90% ($k^R = 1.29$), and H sets it at 99% ($k^R = 2.33$).

Since the payoff matrix is not given a priori, we derive the equilibriums of this game using the supply chain simulation model introduced above and a statistical technique. Specifically, we follow the steps below to identify the equilibriums.

Step 1: If all the strategy pairs in $A^M \otimes A^R$ have been investigated, go to **Step 3**. Otherwise, choose a strategy pair to investigate next and move to **Step 2**.

Step 2: Run the simulation model 10 times under the specified strategy pair for 365 days (after 100 days of dry run) and obtain 10 sample values of the two players' rewards. Go back to **Step 1**.

Step 3: Apply a statistical multiple comparison test to the data of sample reward values obtained by each of the eight strategies of one player against the other and identify the *statistical best responses* of the former player to each strategy of the latter.

Step 4: Identify *statistical Nash equilibriums*, the set of strategy pairs that are *statistical best responses* to each other.

4 Numerical Experiments

We verify the proposed approach and assess the effect of the one-third rule on food waste and consumers' satisfaction by carrying out numerical experiments with and without the rule under different values of $\delta_\varnothing (\in \{12, 8, 7\})$, a parameter representing the consumers' preference for freshness. Figure 1 shows the statistical Nash equilibriums obtained in each case. We can see that equilibriums depend on both whether the one-third rule is imposed and the consumers' preference ($\delta_\varnothing$).

The amount of waste depends primarily on the shipping order policy of the manufacturer and secondarily on the moving order policy of the retailer. For reducing food waste, both are preferred to be FIFO. Interestingly, the results show that the one-third rule has an effect of eliminating equilibriums, including the LIFO policy of the manufacturer. It will positively impact food waste reduction. This effect may be because imposing the wholesale limit will make it unnecessary for the retailer to insist on the LIFO policy (of the manufacturer) to avoid buying very old milk packages. On the other hand, the one-third rule does not affect the retailer's moving order policy.

The average consumers' satisfaction (or the utility) mainly depends on whether the retailer takes the discounted price policy. This policy is favorable to consumers. However, it appears in equilibriums only when the preference is tight ($\delta_\varnothing = 7$). It may be because consumers buy old milk packages even without a discount in the other cases. It suggests that the linear discounting policy can rarely be economically justified, and other ways of discounting should be tried out.

	FRL	FRH	FDL	FDH	LRL	LRH	LDL	LDH
FRL			★	★			★	
FRH			★	★			★	
FDL								
FDH								
LRL	★							
LRH								
LDL								
LDH								

(a) With the one-third rule & $\delta_\emptyset = 7$

	FRL	FRH	FDL	FDH	LRL	LRH	LDL	LDH
FRL			★				★	
FRH			★				★	
FDL								
FDH								
LRL	★	★						
LRH	★	★						
LDL	★	★						
LDH		★						

(d) Without the one-third rule & $\delta_\emptyset = 7$

	FRL	FRH	FDL	FDH	LRL	LRH	LDL	LDH
FRL	★	★						
FRH	★							
FDL								
FDH								
LRL								
LRH								
LDL								
LDH								

(b) With the one-third rule & $\delta_\emptyset = 8$

	FRL	FRH	FDL	FDH	LRL	LRH	LDL	LDH
FRL	★							
FRH	★	★						
FDL								
FDH								
LRL			★					
LRH								
LDL								
LDH								

(e) Without the one-third rule & $\delta_\emptyset = 8$

	FRL	FRH	FDL	FDH	LRL	LRH	LDL	LDH
FRL	★	★						
FRH	★	★			★			
FDL								
FDH								
LRL								
LRH								
LDL								
LDH								

(c) With the one-third rule & $\delta_\emptyset = 12$

	FRL	FRH	FDL	FDH	LRL	LRH	LDL	LDH
FRL	★	★			★			
FRH	★	★						
FDL								
FDH								
LRL	★	★						
LRH								
LDL								
LDH								

(f) Without the one-third rule & $\delta_\emptyset = 12$

Fig. 1. Statistical Nash equilibriums obtained in each case, where the row player is the manufacturer, and the column player is the retailer.

5   Conclusions

To investigate how the one-third rule affects food wastage, we formulated and analyzed a normal-form game played by a manufacturer and a retailer in a milk supply chain. During this study, we also developed a simulation model of the chain and proposed a statistical analysis approach for the game whose payoff matrix needs to be evaluated through simulation. As a result of numerical experiments using the simulator, statistical Nash equilibriums can be identified by the proposed approach. Thus, the approach is expected to be effective also for other complex games defined using a simulator. We further confirmed that, in some conditions, imposing the one-third rule eliminates undesirable equilibriums, including the LIFO policy of the manufacturer, and thus reduces the food waste contrary to ordinary expectations. This provides a possible explanation for the bidirectional effects observed in the social experiments [6]. Since we have conducted experiments only under limited settings, it is necessary to investigate a wider range of conditions. Extending the game model will be the next step. For example, it is an interesting extension to consider the effect of competition among multiple manufacturers and multiple retailers. Verifying the results using human subjects, for example, on a serious game like [12], is also important.

References

1. Transforming our world: The 2030 agenda for sustainable development. https://sdgs.un.org/2030agenda. (Accessed 6 April 2021)
2. Usage status of food waste, etc. (Estimated in FY 2018). http://www.maff.go.jp/j/shokusan/recycle/syoku_loss/attach/pdf/161227_4-118.pdf. (Accessed 6 April 2021) (in Japanese)
3. Lemma, Y., Kitaw, D., Gatew, G.: Loss in perishable food supply chain: An optimization approach literature review. Int. J. Sci. Eng. Res. 5(5), 302–311 (2014)
4. Luo, N., Olsen, T, Liu, Y., Zhang, A.: Reducing food loss and waste in supply chain operations. Transp. Res. Part E Logist. Transp. Rev, 162, 102730 (2022)
5. Parry, A., Bleazard, P., Okawa, K.: Preventing food waste: Case studies of Japan and the United Kingdom. OECD Food, Agriculture and Fisheries Papers, vol. 76 (2015)
6. Working team for reviewing commercial custom for food waste reduction, FY (2013). https://www.jora.jp/support_business/5271/. (Accessed 6 Apr 2021) (in Japanese)
7. Cachon, G.P., Netessine, S.: Game theory in supply chain analysis. Tutor. Operat. Res. 200–233 (2006)
8. Behzadi, G., O'Sullivan, M.J., Olsen, T.L., Zhang, A.: Agribusiness supply chain risk management: a review of quantitative decision models. Omega 79, 21–42 (2018)
9. Agi, M.A.N., Faramarzi-Oghani, S., Hazir, O.: Game theory-based models in green supply chain management: A review of the literature. Int. J. Prod. Res. 59(15), 4736–4755 (2021)
10. Carrasco, J.A., Ortúzar, J.D.: Review and assessment of the nested logit model. Transp. Rev. 22(2), 197–218 (2002)
11. Iwamoto, H.: Consumers' willingness-to-pay for HACCP and eco labeled milk. HUSCAP 11(2), 48–60 (2004) (in Japanese)
12. Sato, M., Tsunoda, M., Imamura, H., Mizuyama, H., Nakano, M.: The design and evaluation of a multi-player milk supply chain management game. In: Lukosch, H.K., Bekebrede, G., Kortmann, R. (eds.) ISAGA 2017. LNCS, vol. 10825, pp. 110–118. Springer, Cham (2018). https://doi.org/10.1007/978-3-319-91902-7_11

Assessing Energy Efficiency in Processes of the Agri-Food Sector: From Delivery of Natural Resources to Finished Products

M. T. Alvela Nieto[(✉)] [iD] and K.-D. Thoben[iD]

Faculty of Production Engineering, BIK-Institute for Integrated Product
Development, University of Bremen, 28359 Bremen, Germany
{malvela,thoben}@uni-bremen.de

Abstract. The agri-food sector accounts for 26% of the EU energy consumption, where 28% of this energy belongs to natural resource processing. As multiple products are produced on the same line and numerous process steps are interrelated, the energy use in this industry is complex in general. Moreover, bottom-up data analysis of how much energy processes are used, and furthermore, why and where opportunities for improvements exist, are less prevalent. This paper proposes a methodology for estimating the energy consumption of the agri-food processing. The collection of real data from several industrial enterprises in Germany as part of research programs enabled an accurate assessment of energy consumption and savings.

Keywords: Energy efficiency · Agri-food sector · Product

1 Introduction

Efficient energy use is one of the basic requirements for the future of the agri-food sector, more so since, with the recent increase in energy prices, it is important to boost global food production, which is highly dependent on the use of energy, mainly electrical and fuel energy [5]. Energy is used throughout the agri-food supply chain, starting from the production and use of agricultural inputs and then moving to processing, packaging, and distribution to the customer. In the EU, alone the natural resource processing accounts for 28% of the total agri-food sector energy [3]. Small and medium-sized companies (SME) allocate the majority of the fuel energy, namely natural gas, across production processes in the food processing phase (up to 85%) [9]. On the other side, the energy percentage of auxiliary processes (also called support processes) is typically assumed to be lower and mainly electric [7,9]. On average, the use of lighting, compressed air production and cooling is pure electric [9]. A production process, such as grinding and mixing, is more heterogeneous across companies than auxiliary processes,

© IFIP International Federation for Information Processing 2022
Published by Springer Nature Switzerland AG 2022
D. Y. Kim et al. (Eds.): APMS 2022, IFIP AICT 664, pp. 116–123, 2022.
https://doi.org/10.1007/978-3-031-16411-8_15

directly related to the core business, and managed mainly by production managers [2]. Auxiliary processes, on the other hand, are those which maintain the manufacturing activities but do not result in products as such (e.g., ventilation, pumping). Food is typically produced in batches (product lots) in this sector, and each batch's energy requirements for bringing it "from natural resource to fork" varies greatly from the next. Even when analyzing the same product type, its energy "cost" can differ notably, reflecting the low efficiency of production processes as a result of changing resource properties (owing to cultivation, farming practices, etc.) [10]. The overall goal of this study is to enable companies to make a robust statement about the specific energy consumption (SEC) of each individual batch. Key process parameters are frequently not paired with the properties of food resources due to their stochastic character. Incorporating these key batch characteristics into the energy analysis can allow for a precise evaluation of the product quality in terms of energy consumption. In line with authors' previous works and research projects [1, 2], production processes were examined using a methodology based on machine learning (ML) and historical data about process conditions, product characteristics and energy values, without any investments in (new) efficient equipment. Unless stated otherwise, the estimation of energy consumed by a batch in this work includes the required process energy from the delivery of natural resources (raw material) until the production of a finished product, excluding logistic and auxiliary systems. On the project experiences and results, this study contributes to developing a methodology for estimating energy consumption through a validation of process operating conditions as a means of product quality improvements.

2   Methodology for Estimating the Energy Consumption of Agri-Food Processes

Energy efficient improvements are defined as increasing the output per unit of energy used, resulting in energy savings if the output does not change [4]. In the industrial sector, it can mean getting the most out of every unit of energy it is bought [4]. Therefore, an increase in energy efficiency (EE) can be realized by actions, e.g., technical or technological actions, seeking to save energy without altering the product quality. In the agri-food sector, particularly, processes that are energy-intensive vary by sub-sector (e.g., cereals, sugar, coffee, etc.). For instance, milling and centrifuges in sugar processing and grain milling in the ingredients sector use the most electrical energy [3]. Most of these processes rely on electric motor systems, including steam systems, pumps and compressors, and also heating, cooling and refrigeration systems. While not exclusively, most opportunities to EE in this segment of the food sector come from measuring the demand for electrical and thermal energy [8].

Previous studies use different accounting methods, and system boundary conditions which result in a large range of specific values where steps, processes and product properties were mostly unknown [5]. Equipment details were rarely provided, and the processes included were often not mentioned. These unaccountable factors could have a large impact on the values of the process energy obtained. A complete energy evaluation of the processing stage should start with the delivery of resources, including pre-storing, and should finalize by wrapping and post-storing. However, data at high granularity are not overall acquired. The focus of this study thus lies on the processing line, excluding wrapping, storing, and auxiliary processes. Any variations of a production process line are costly and not as easily accomplished as it is, e.g., changing the lighting in an industrial facility. To make it apparent, which processes are being studied, the entire agri-food processing segment can be split into three stages (see Fig. 1):

S0: Storing and preparation of raw materials according to the production requirements before the production line.
S1: Processing of raw materials on the production line.
S2: Product wrapping and storing before shipment.

Stage 1 (S1) has indeed the most significant impact on specific energy consumption because they are usually connected to thermal processes [5]. Stages 0 and 2 thus are out of the scope of this study. It is convenient to use a methodology that comprises the natural resource processing (e.g. one or more machines or production lines) for an accurate calculation of the required energy to a certain products batch, as well as it is applicable to various sub-sectors and batch qualities (e.g. multiple products passing through the same line or single machine). The assessment of energy efficiency is to be understood as the ratio of batch size out to the energy input. From these settings, energy efficiency can be achieved with the help of data-driven models based on ML methods [1]. Then a view of the process design and data sources related to the production process and batch characteristics (raw materials) is of importance. In addition, the term SEC defined by [6] is required as an instrument to capture the amount of energy used by an (intermediate) product at each process step. Hence, the successful application of the methodology depends on the continuous measurability and availability of SEC ($e_1, .. \ e_n$) in a timely manner. The allocation and aggregation of SEC ($e = e_1 + .. + e_n$) along a production process ($p_1 .. p_n$) expresses the embodied energy of a finished product quantity e_{emb} associated with the processing phase S1 (see Fig. 1).

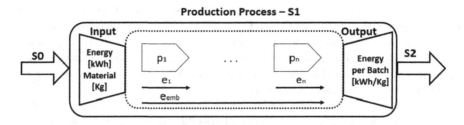

Fig. 1. Energy analysis of a production process at S1.

The proposed methodology for estimating the embodied energy is derived from works on research projects within the food segment. As visualized in Fig. 2, the methodology is characterized by two parallel processes, which interact with each other during the entire development period. The design process focuses on determining the specific energy by following a predefined series of necessary steps. Specific energy data can be collected based on process-based metrics, where energy input in kilowatt per hour (kWh) is divided by product output quantity, e.g., in tonnes (t). Energy values expressed in different units are to be converted when possible. This format provides a consistent (and comparative) basis. Simultaneously, the data sourcing process consider the analysis of data with regards to availability, collection and storage. Indeed, data collections are categorized depending on the aim of the process. For example, data about conveyor systems are, as mentioned before, not included in the energy analysis. Each of the production process steps in S1 has to be connected to meter units. To reduce inaccuracies on energy values, unit conversions of raw data, such as process data, should be manipulated as little as possible.

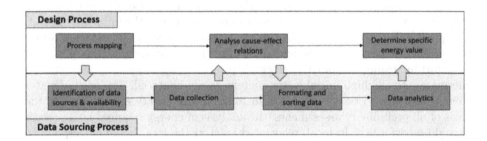

Fig. 2. Methodology.

Hence, the first step contains the analysis of system boundaries, which processes are support processes and which are not. For example, support processes can be divided into ten categories, including ventilation, internal transport and cooling [9]. However, the array of processes under the term support processes has to be carefully examined. Then, for instance, pumping and compressed air are difficult to exclude from production processes in some industries. Further, this study corresponds to the individual industrial sites of SMEs, and thus transport and logistics across different company facilities are not applicable. Next, objectives concerning energy efficiency and current operating conditions, such as reducing thermal energy values, are to be defined. Most of the requirements to product and process quality can be identified and better understood through interviews with plant-side experts. In the next step, it is crucial to analyze and understand the underlying cause-effect relationships as well as interdependencies between process steps and their effects on energy consumption. Many factors that can happen during a production process have to be taken into account, e.g. fluctuating quality resources and/or operating conditions. For instance, when a cheese type repines longer than 14 days, the specific energy demand can increase up to 65% [5]. Therefore, process variables need to be defined and measured (i.e. room temperature, humidity), representing key process parameters and reflecting the cause and effect relations of the cheese quality. A close look into the data sourcing is essential as data availability and measurability for such parameters are prerequisites. As mentioned, processes depend on many factors, and even under the same conditions, the energy consumption can differ from product to product because of the changing properties of natural resources. In our studies, the estimation of consumed energy of the part of the product life cycle from the crops delivery to the shipment as flour (as a finished product) was compared. In early summer, a product was produced in a certain production line. Three months later, the same product with the same predefined quality was made in the same production line; only the time frame of crop harvesting differed. Flour belonging to earlier summer consumed 6,5% (91,41 kWh/t) lower energy than flour from later summer (102,11 kWh/t). Considering these data and the fact that the flour was produced in the same way regardless of the date of harvesting (or time of storing), it can be said that the time of harvesting (due to weather events) or storage significantly affects the intrinsic properties of the cereal and thus the consumed energy of a process. In order to include the influence of product quality characteristics on the process consumed energy, information about the product properties is to be added into the energy analysis. Drying potatoes, as a further example from the research projects, consumes large amounts of energy due to the high initial water content as raw material. The level of water content are thus to be captured and included in the energy estimation. On the basis of all preliminary assessments, the analysis of energy required by a process should be performed. In total, relevant characteristic data should correspond to the production processes that are stored in the databases, e.g., motor speed rates, etc. But also key characteristic data of the product, which are not changeable, such as moisture or starch. The latter are uncontrollable and product-specific variables whose values have to be considered for precise energy estimation. It is evident that methodologies that deal with the complexity and wide range of unstructured data, and their volume, synergistically benefiting from them, are required. Data of process and product can contain valuable insights on where, how and why along process energy values from batch to batch fluctuate. Moving from pure quantitative models to ML, that can limit energy values and maximize quality, can support manufacturers in estimating their specific energy demands for particular resource characteristics and quality specifications. Particularly, the modeling of physical correlations between process settings and quality criteria can be used to characterize and thus optimize the impact of operational decisions on energy consumption, on the one hand. On the other hand, the influence of changing material quality characteristics on the quality of the finished products batch can be better understood in terms of process consumed energy.

3   Discussion

The methodology of this paper was evaluated in multiple settings and sub-sectors of the agri-food segment [1]. Hence, it is not tailored to specific sub-sectors or production processes. Nevertheless, the identification of energy consumption trends was difficult, as the agri-food processing industry is very fragmented, products are processed to varying degrees, and production is not always continuous.

Allocation of Energy Consumption: The data collections showed that, notably in the ingredients sector, the production processes accounted for the majority of the consumed energy, with thermal processes alone accounting for about 60–70% percent of spent energy. From the study, it was also noted that fossil fuels (gas) are the primary source of thermal energy, which is mostly used for drying or sterilizing. Further, the data across sub-sectors demonstrated that the more energy-intensive and smaller a company is, the more difficult it is to distinguish the energy values from production and auxiliary operations. From the SMEs case studies [1], results revealed that auxiliary processes consume up to 40% energy on average. This figure outweights what has been previously calculated by previous research (i.e. [9]), what may pose unexploited potential in energy-intensive SMEs.

Energy Efficiency Potential: From the literature, the majority of the energy-efficient measures for SMEs are proposed for generic auxiliary processes. These measures are mainly related to replacing ventilation, reducing space heating, etc. [9]. Our findings across sub-sectors suggested that production processes can lower their consumed energy by 30–35%. This is reasonable, especially in case of no "state of the art" equipment. Further, a factor which seemed to affect positively the energy efficiency of a process is the level of capacity (as total mass): The more natural resources are processed at once, the less embodied energy is allocated to a batch. Moreover, this study only addressed the theoretical energy-efficient potential of production processes in terms of operating conditions through historical product and process data. The real potential is only achieved if 1) Data quality and granularity are sufficient, 2) All measures derived from the data analysis with ML are implemented. Derived measures can be, for instance, an adjustment of process operating conditions under changing resource characteristics. Further, auxiliary processes should also be considered in the embodied energy calculation with a factor of 0.4. However, the calculation of this factor should be further investigated, as it might vary up to the sub-sector.

Limitations of Methodology: This study only accounted for the electrical and thermal energy use of production processes. Many feed and food products have a processing phase that involves energy use at specific processing stages (e.g., grinding) plus energy usage related to intensive internal transportation or other intermediate inputs that ultimately go into a finished product. The additional consumed energy values should be added to the embodied energy of a product batch. Due to factors such as low diary orders or maintenance breaks, production is not always continuous, therefore idle modes still utilize energy and should be factored into the assessment of embodied energy. Results also showed that the estimates of energy consumption for the same batch qualities across different seasons revealed significant variances. Consequently, the energy values can only be assigned to individual product batches rather than general feed or food groups.

Measurable Product Properties Data: The supply of data, particularly key product characteristics at each process step at high granularity, can become challenging. At least food processing industries are interested in intrinsic or geometric (so-called physio-chemical) product properties as continuous measurements. Nevertheless, these systems, including cameras, are susceptible to surrounding environments and material flow rates. For instance, sensor calibrations to each (new) product require a unique calibration pattern. Other sensors are not highly sensitive to the product properties, e.g., particle size distribution for flour production. These examples of data acquisition to critical quality attributes prevent obtaining valuable (qualitative and/or quantitative) information from the product, and therefore, data quality can become insufficient.

Machine Learning to Data Analysis: ML analysis often has more difficult meeting data challenges rather than conventional methods. Data challenges include the amount, quality, and types of data required, among others. Aside from the expert knowledge needed to build these models, the most challenging tasks in realizing successful production data analysis were at the start of the data pipeline, namely, the data acquisition.

4   Conclusions

The assessment of energy efficiency can, of course, not substitute an energy label on a product, such as a carbon footprint label or an energy audit. Still it can act as a preliminary company-internal audit, indicating where a company should focus its efforts. Some methodological improvements, such as the significance of taking into account the consumed energy by auxiliary operations from the implementation, were found to be necessary. Furthermore, this research suggested to incorporate a division between production processes and auxiliary processes. However, a general energy-use taxonomy and standardization would greatly enhance the knowledge of data across the sector. A similar approach to the Nutri-Score could allow customers to compare energy values along the same product qualities, promoting energy efficiency in the agri-food sector. In a long-term scenario, a greater collaborative effort is required to report consumed energy data not only at the processing stage but throughout the food chain.

Acknowledgments. The authors would like to thank the Federal Ministry for Economic Affairs and Energy (BMWi) and the Project Management Juelich (PtJ) for funding the projects "Increasing energy efficiency in production through digitization and AI" - ecoKI (funding code 03EN2047A) and "AI-supported platform for the assistance of production control for improving energy efficiency" - KIPro (funding code 03ET1265A).

References

1. Alvela Nieto, M.T., Nabati, E.G., Bode, D., Redecker, M.A., Decker, A., Thoben, K.-D.: Enabling energy efficiency in manufacturing environments through deep learning approaches: lessons learned. In: Ameri, F., Stecke, K.E., von Cieminski, G., Kiritsis, D. (eds.) APMS 2019. IAICT, vol. 567, pp. 567–574. Springer, Cham (2019). https://doi.org/10.1007/978-3-030-29996-5_65
2. Alvela Nieto, M.T., Nabati, E.G., Thoben, K.-D.: Energy transparency in compound feed production. In: Dolgui, A., Bernard, A., Lemoine, D., von Cieminski, G., Romero, D. (eds.) APMS 2021. IAICT, vol. 634, pp. 496–503. Springer, Cham (2021). https://doi.org/10.1007/978-3-030-85914-5_53
3. European Commission. Joint Research Centre: Energy use in the EU food sector: state of play and opportunities for improvement. Publications Office (2015). https://doi.org/10.2790/158316
4. Herring, H.: Energy efficiency–a critical view. Energy **31**(1), 10–20 (2006). https://doi.org/10.1016/j.energy.2004.04.055
5. Ladha-Sabur, A., Bakalis, S., Fryer, P.J., Lopez-Quiroga, E.: Mapping energy consumption in food manufacturing. Trends Food Sci. Technol. **86**, 270–280 (2019). https://doi.org/10.1016/j.tifs.2019.02.034, https://www.sciencedirect.com/science/article/pii/S0924224417303394
6. Lawrence, A., Thollander, P., Andrei, M., Karlsson, M.: Specific energy consumption/use (SEC) in energy management for improving energy efficiency in industry: meaning, usage and differences. Energies **12**(2), 247 (2019). https://doi.org/10.3390/en12020247
7. Paramonova, S., Thollander, P.: Ex-post impact and process evaluation of the Swedish energy audit policy programme for small and medium-sized enterprises. J. Clean. Prod. **135**, 932–949 (2016). https://doi.org/10.1016/j.jclepro.2016.06.139
8. Santos, H.C.M., Maranduba, H.L., de Almeida Neto, J.A., Rodrigues, L.B.: Life cycle assessment of cheese production process in a small-sized dairy industry in Brazil. Environ. Sci. Pollut. Res. **24**(4), 3470–3482 (2016). https://doi.org/10.1007/s11356-016-8084-0
9. Thollander, P., et al.: International study on energy end-use data among industrial SMEs (small and medium-sized enterprises) and energy end-use efficiency improvement opportunities. J. Clean. Prod. **104**, 282–296 (2015). https://doi.org/10.1016/j.jclepro.2015.04.073
10. Vermeulen, S.J., Campbell, B.M., Ingram, J.S.: Climate change and food systems. Annu. Rev. Environ. Resour. **37**(1), 195–222 (2012). https://doi.org/10.1146/annurev-environ-020411-130608

Technologies Used for Animal Welfare Monitoring

Jonatas Santos de Souza[1]([✉])(iD) and João Gilberto Mendes dos Reis[1,2](iD)

[1] RESUP - Research Group in Supply Chain Management,
Postgraduate Program in Production Engineering, Universidade Paulista - UNIP,
R. Dr. Bacelar, 1212-4fl, São Paulo 04026002, Brazil
jonatas1516@gmail.com, joao.reis@docente.unip.br
[2] Centro de Ciências Sociais Aplicadas, Mackenzie Presbyterian University,
São Paulo, Brazil
joao.reis@mackenzie.br

Abstract. With the use of technology in the livestock sector, it has been allowed an increase in animal production and reduction of waste with more precision. The use of these technological resources in the sector gave rise to Precision Cattle Raising, which makes use of information and communication technology to extract the best from animal production with more precision. Studies show the use of te-lemetry to measure the state of animal welfare. However, during transportation from the farm to the slaughterhouse there is no specific way to check animal wel-fare, this can affect meat quality and the livestock economic sector and animal production. This study aims to identify the variables that can be read through sen-sors or biomarkers for monitoring animal welfare.

Keywords: Telemetry · Precision livestock · Animal welfare · Monitoring

1 Introduction

Animal welfare is associated with the comfort that the individual feels in relation to his environment and his harmonious behavior with it [1]. It relates to stress, health, and the physiological and psychological needs of the animal [1,2].

The environment in which the animal is inserted also contributes to welfare, and is related to the interaction of the animal with the environment and its fellows [3]. This presents variables that can be controlled and that influence positively or not in the production [1].

During the transport of animals to the slaughterhouse, there are several variables that bring discomfort to the animal, such as environment temperature, relative humidity, space, the balance of transport during the journey, thirst, and hunger.

Several studies discuss animal welfare in long-distance transport and how this affects meat production and quality due to a high level of stress on the animal during the long journey.

Published by Springer Nature Switzerland AG 2022
D. Y. Kim et al. (Eds.): APMS 2022, IFIP AICT 664, pp. 124–130, 2022.
https://doi.org/10.1007/978-3-031-16411-8_16

The objective of this study is to identify which variables can be read by sensors to bring thermal comfort to the animal and to monitor the animal's stress level.

1.1   Animal Welfare

According to the user's guide to animal welfare, it is described that animal welfare is related to the physical health and physiological conditions experienced by the animal [4].

Broom [2,5] describes that inability and difficulty in dealing with problems cause feelings of fear and anger, generate stress levels that alter an individual's well-being [5].

According to the Terrestrial Animal Health Code (Terrestrial Code) of the World Organization for Animal Health (OiE) [4] defines animal welfare as the behavior and conditions in which the animal lives, that is, an animal that is well nourished, able to perform innate behavior, healthy, and is not in distress, pain, and fear, is considered to be in a good state of welfare [4].

For an animal to be in a good state of well-being, it is necessary for the animal to have veterinary treatment to treat and prevent disease, proper shelter, good food, and an environment that brings comfort [2–7].

In order for farms to be able to guarantee a good welfare state for the animal, they use tools that make it possible to measure variables about the animal and the internal environment.

1.2   Telemetry

With the advancement of information and communication technology (ICT), farms make use of telemetry to take measurements of the indoor environment and the animal [8–10].

Telemetry allows measurement of the environment through sensors that take real-time readings on relative humidity, ambient temperature, water temperature, and recognition of stress level through the sound emitted by the animal [11,12].

This insertion of telemetry in the livestock sector is known as precision livestock, or Precision Animal Science [13,14], which makes use of technological resources to more accurately assess and monitor the conditions of the areas of animal production activities, measuring and analyzing the data of each animal.

Precision livestock presents similar objectives to precision agriculture [15], to follow the technological advances to automate animal production, and can assist in increasing production [13], saving water and energy, reducing costs and waste, and detecting pests and caring for the animal's health.

According to Dawkins [3], measuring animal welfare is not an easy task, just as measuring the height of a five-story building is, and it is complex due to the many variables that can be presented during the measurement. However, highlighted some activities that can be observed to analyze and measure animal welfare [3]: (1) Natural Animal Behavior; (2) Fitness and Longevity; (3) Stress and Physiological Symptoms.

In observing these activities it is possible to perform tests to generate behavioral indicators [3], for example, cutting off the water supply for a long period and analyzing the behavior and measuring body temperature and the sound emitted by the animal. In this way it allows a better analysis to measure the state of animal welfare.

2   Materials and Methods

In this study, a literature review was conducted [16,17], in order to identify related work on the use of technologies to measure animal welfare and stress levels.

It was established that to avoid duplicate work and because it is one of the largest databases, the Scopus database, the Scopus database was used to identify, evaluate, and interpret the results relevant to the scope of this research.

The expression used was 'animal transport for slaughter', papers were selected that contained the keywords 'animal transport', 'animal welfare', 'slaughter' and 'monitor animal' (Table 1).

3   Results and Discussion

After an analysis of the literature found in the scopus database, it was noted that the studies are related to the use of telemetry in farms where the environment can be controlled and automated. And they follow the guidelines established by Farm Animal Welfare Committee (FAWC) [6,7] for production on farms, known as the five animal freedoms (Fig. 1).

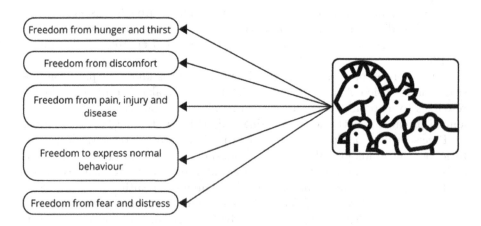

Fig. 1. Five freedoms of animals.

Table 1. Selected papers

Title	Objective	Method	Reference
Automatic prediction of stress in piglets (Sus Scrofa) using infrared skin temperature	Development of a model to predict stress in piglets using an infrared sensor	Thermal image analysis detects stressful conditions in piglets	[8]
Classification of piglet (Sus Scrofa) stress conditions using vocalization pattern and applying paraconsistent logic Eτ	Analysis to automatically classify stressful conditions in piglets using vocalization	Animal sound analysis detects stressful conditions in piglets	[9]
Use of Temperature, Humidity, and Slaughter Condemnation Data to Predict Increases in Transport Losses in Three Classes of Swine and Resulting Foregone Revenue	Analysis of the effects of temperature and humidity on pig deaths during transport	Analysis of meteorological data and temperature sensors	[10]
Transforming the Adaptation Physiology of Farm Animals through Sensors	Review of technologies for evaluating the adaptation of farm animals	Analysis of sensor technologies used on farms	[11]
Precision animal production: image analysis to study broiler's behavior under stress conditions	Evaluation of broiler behavior by analyzing images	Use of images to analyze behavior under heat stress	[14]
Welfare of lambs subjected to road transport and assessment of carcasses and meat	Evaluation of the welfare status of lambs in road transport and the impact of stress on meat	Evaluation of carcasses and meat	[18]
Temperature conditions during commercial transportation of cull sows to slaughter	Describing temperature changes and variations within trucks transporting sows to slaughter	Analysis of the temperature inside the trucks depending on the stop/movement	[19]

The five animal freedoms present guidelines for the animal to have access to water, nutritious food to maintain vigor and health, provide an appropriate and comfortable environment that allows the animal to express its natural behavior [6,7]. Veterinary care is also included presenting techniques and procedures for prevention, rapid diagnosis and treatment ensuring conditions that avoid suffering such as disease, injury and pain [6,7].

In order to achieve these guidelines, the farms make use of ICT to analyze and automate processes, and in this way can ensure a good state of animal welfare.

The study by da Fonseca et al. [8], used infrared imaging to measure temperature and identify thirst and stress conditions with high accuracy, thus presenting a non-invasive method to identify the level of stress.

With the use of a software that analyzes the vocal signals of piglets, obtained 93% (percent) accuracy for identification of pain condition [9], the vocal signals of 40 readers were analyzed through a scenario with stressful conditions of thirst, pain, hunger, cold and heat [9].

Researchers Peterson et al. [10], conducted an observational study, where he used temperature and relative humidity data to predict increases in pig losses and the impacts on lost revenue [8,20].

Peterson et al. [10], analyzed data from weather stations that are located near slaughterhouses in the United States from 2010 to 2015, to identify the high and low temperature periods. And during the study period, it was noted that a loss of USD $18.6 million due to condemnations of pigs that were not fit for trade because of injuries to the meat caused by high and low temperatures [10].

Neethirajan [11], presented some Sensors and biomarkers that can be used for welfare monitoring used in farms (Fig. 2), thus bringing advantages and disadvantages in adopting sensor technologies in farms [11].

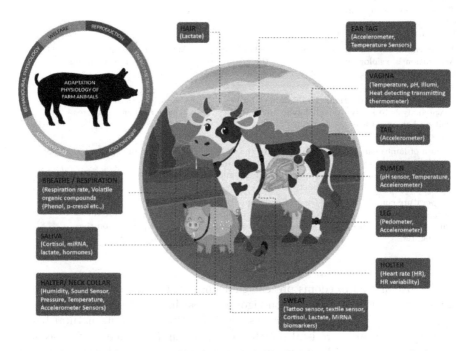

Fig. 2. Wearable sensors and biomarkers for animal welfare monitoring [11].

Sevegnani et al. [14], analyzed the behavior of chickens through images under heat stress conditions, the results indicated that the chickens ingested more water and less feed at high temperatures. This implies a decrease in live weight in longer transport.

The study by Silva et al. [18], analyzed images of lambs' behavior for slaughter, on trips between 7H30 to 10H30, the lambs ruminated more often than on shorter trips due to the stress conditions of hunger and thirst on long trips and shows that there is a greater chance of tissue injury [18,21].

Thodberg et al. [19], analyzed the internal temperature of the truck to know in which period there is an increase in temperature during movement or when the truck is stopped. Data from 39 commercial trips were analyzed and it was noted that there was an increase in temperature when the vehicle is stopped thus leaving the thermal comfort zone of the nuts [19].

4   Conclusion

Through this study it was possible to identify the telemetry technologies that are used on farms to measure and achieve good animal welfare status.

Monitoring the animal makes it possible to perform operations that can improve the animal's welfare by decreasing discomfort due to stress conditions from hunger, thirst, and pain, thus reducing losses due to confusion or injuries to the meat.

Studies show concerns with animal welfare and how much this impacts the livestock economic sector. Through this study, the cattle breeder can identify which sensor technologies for monitoring can be used on the farm, thus reducing eventual risks and losses.

Another study is needed to analyze the factors that make the implementation of these technologies feasible. The prices and maintenance costs are factors that can make the use of monitoring technologies unviable.

As a complement to this study, research is being carried out that will make it possible to develop a low-cost prototype to monitor animal welfare in transports that travel long distances in Brazil.

Acknowledgments. This study was financed in part by the Coordenação de Aperfeiçoamento de Pessoal de Nível Superior - Brasil (CAPES) - Finance Code 001.

References

1. Machado, S.T., Santos, R.C.: O papel do bem-estar animal e as tendências de ambiência animal. In: dos Reis, J.G.M., de Oliveira Costa Neto, P.L. (eds.) Engenharia de produção aplicada ao agronegócio, pp. 263–290. Blucher, São Paulo (2018)
2. Broom, D.M.: Animal welfare: concepts and measurements. J. Anim. Sci. **69**(10), 4167–4175 (1991)
3. Dawkins, M.S.: Evolution and animal welfare. Q. Rev. Biol. **73**(3), 305–328 (1998)
4. International Office of Epizootics: Terrestrial animal health code (2021). OCLC: 1308956605. https://doc.woah.org/dyn/portal/index.xhtml?page=alo&aloId=41548&req=103&cid=a95aa508-fdf8-4dcb-b0c9-eecf3224ab68
5. Broom, D.M.: Welfare concepts. In: Encyclopedia of Animal Behavior, pp. 80–83. Elsevier (2019). https://doi.org/10.1016/B978-0-12-809633-8.01321-2
6. Farm animal welfare committee (FAWC). www.gov.uk/government/groups/farm-animal-welfare-committee-fawc
7. Animal welfare committee (AWC). www.gov.uk/government/groups/animal-welfare-committee-awc

8. da Fonseca, F.N., Abe, J.M., de Alencar Nääs, I., da Silva Cordeiro, A.F., do Amaral, F.V., Ungaro, H.C.: Automatic prediction of stress in piglets (Sus Scrofa) using infrared skin temperature. Comput. Electron. Agric. **168**, 105148 (2020). https://doi.org/10.1016/j.compag.2019.105148

9. da Silva, J.P., de Alencar Nääs, I., Abe, J.M., da Silva Cordeiro, A.F.: Classification of piglet (Sus Scrofa) stress conditions using vocalization pattern and applying paraconsistent logic Et. Comput. Electron. Agric. **166**, 105020 (2019). https://doi.org/10.1016/j.compag.2019.105020

10. Peterson, E., Remmenga, M., Hagerman, A.D., Akkina, J.E.: Use of temperature, humidity, and slaughter condemnation data to predict increases in transport losses in three classes of swine and resulting foregone revenue. Front. Vet. Sci. **4**, 67 (2017). https://doi.org/10.3389/fvets.2017.00067

11. Neethirajan, S.: Transforming the adaptation physiology of farm animals through sensors. Animals **10**, 1512 (2020). https://doi.org/10.3390/ani10091512

12. Stephen, B., Michie, C., Andonovic, I.: Remote sensing in agricultural livestock welfare monitoring: practical considerations. In: Mukhopadhyay, S., Jiang, J.A. (eds.) Wireless Sensor Networks and Ecological Monitoring. Smart Sensors, Measurement and Instrumentation, vol. 3, pp. 179–193. Springer, Berlin, Heidelberg (2013). https://doi.org/10.1007/978-3-642-36365-8_7

13. Pandorfi, H., Almeida, G.L.P., Guiselini, C.: Precision animal production: basic principles and news in the swine production **13**, 558–568. UFBA - Universidade Federal da Bahia. www.scielo.br/j/rbspa/a/zrsddbNQGp5mTkDLnRGmFLm/?lang=pt

14. Sevegnani, K.B., Caror, I.W., Pandorfi, H., da Silva, I.J.O., de Moura, D.J.: Precision animal production: image analysis to study broiler's behavior under stress conditions. Rev. Bras. Eng. Agríc. Ambient. **9**, 115–119 (2005). https://doi.org/10.1590/S1415-43662005000100017

15. Pierce, F.J., Nowak, P.: Aspects of precision agriculture. Adv. Agron. **67**, 1–85. Elsevier (1999). https://doi.org/10.1016/S0065-2113(08)60513-1

16. Esquirol-Caussa, J., Sanchez-Aldeguer, J., Santamaria, I.: A bibliographical review: the basis of our research. Physiotherapy Updates, 33–36 (2017)

17. Pautasso, M.: Ten simple rules for writing a literature review. PLoS Comput. Biol. **9**, e1003149 (2013). https://doi.org/10.1371/journal.pcbi.1003149

18. Silva, F.V., et al.: Welfare of lambs subjected to road transport and assessment of carcasses and meat. Pesquisa Vet. Bras. **37**, 630–636 (2017). https://doi.org/10.1590/S0100-736X2017000600017

19. Thodberg, K., Foldager, L., Fogsgaard, K.K., Gaillard, C., Herskin, M.S.: Temperature conditions during commercial transportation of cull sows to slaughter. Comput. Electron. Agric. **192**, 106626 (2022). https://doi.org/10.1016/j.compag.2021.106626

20. Lana, R.F., da Cunha, A.F., Lana, R.F., Santos, L.F., Araújo, F.R., da Silva, M.D.: Influence of feed withdrawal on mortality, body weight loss, fractures, bruises and contamination of carcasses in poultry slaughterhouse. Arch. Vet. Sci. **23**, 24–32 (2018). https://doi.org/10.5380/avs.v23i1.44731

21. Sousa, R.S., Nunes, E.D.S.C.L., Neto, M.S.D., Cardoso, G.V.F.: Occurrence of contusions in bovine carcasses in the state of Pará due to transport. Med. Vet. (Brazil) **15**, 70–74 (2021). https://doi.org/10.26605/medvet-v15n1-2268

Digital Transformation Approaches in Production Management

Managing Technological Obsolescence in a Digitally Transformed SME

Aylin Ates[1]([✉]) [iD] and Nuran Acur[2] [iD]

[1] University of Strathclyde Business School, Glasgow G4 0QU, UK
aylin.ates@strath.ac.uk
[2] University of Glasgow, Glasgow, UK

Abstract. We seek to enrich the literature by investigating the digitalization journey of a high-tech, manufacturing small and medium-sized enterprise (SME) to shed light on the topic. We undertook an interpretive longitudinal study between 2009 and 2020, capturing the transformation journey of an award-winning high-tech SME that is designing and manufacturing high-end home entertainment systems including digital streaming products, music players, and speakers. This study offers important contributions to theory and practice. We conceptualize and define the link between technological obsolescence and the digital transformation process. We offer a conceptual framework to explain the interplay of the adaptive capabilities namely empirical sensitivities and habitus in the context of digital transformation in SMEs. In addition, our study has important implications for practice. SME managers should pay attention to developing non-cognitive dynamic capabilities to effectively respond to digitalization trends by orienting their employees toward careful management of technology obsolescence in a manner unique to the firm's history and experiences.

Keywords: Dynamic capabilities · Small and medium-sized enterprises-SME · Obsolescence management · Consumer electronics · Digitalization

1 Introduction

There are several technological dependencies in complex products as firms increasingly work with various partners in the ecosystem. Moreover, the fast pace of change in technology and innovation creates waves of disruption across various industries as the obsolescence puzzle has become a focal issue for firms [11]. Obsolescence arises when a new service, product, or technology replaces an older one [14] such as the introduction of digital music downloads, which replaced compact discs (CDs) [3]. Obsolescence hinders a firm's ability to adapt to the unprecedented changes in the environment, which may lead to deteriorating performance and viability [8, 15] and makes firms slowly lose dynamic capabilities due to the obsolescence of technologies and knowledge [8, 26]. As such, the capacity to manage technological obsolescence is becoming strategically important for firms to survive and thrive in today's rapidly changing environment. However, there is a

© IFIP International Federation for Information Processing 2022
Published by Springer Nature Switzerland AG 2022
D. Y. Kim et al. (Eds.): APMS 2022, IFIP AICT 664, pp. 133–139, 2022.
https://doi.org/10.1007/978-3-031-16411-8_17

lack of conceptual clarity on the underlying design logic of digitally transformed firms [4].

We seek to enrich the literature by investigating the digitalization journey of a high-tech, manufacturing small and medium-sized enterprise (SME) to shed light on the topic. Our research question is: *How do high-tech manufacturing SMEs execute digital transformations to avoid technological obsolescence?* To address these issues, we develop a framework for managing technological obsolescence in the context of digital transformation.

We proceed by first exploring the relevant literature. We then provide an overview of our case study and qualitative methods before presenting our empirical findings structured as a conceptual model that illustrates the management of obsolescence in SMEs. We then discuss our conceptual model and implications for theory and practice.

2 Literature Review

2.1 Technology Obsolescence

The rapid technology changes coupled with short product life cycles create both challenges and opportunities for organizations [20]. Advances in technology lead to obsolescence in older versions of the products. Product obsolescence usually occurs due to technological obsolescence [3, 20] caused by customers being attracted to newer functions in products. Moreover, some parts incorporated in particularly electronics products have their own life cycles, which must be taken into account when examining technology obsolescence [6]. These electronic parts may have a shorter lifespan than the product they support [5]. Therefore, due to technological products getting more complex and modular, it is essential to think about the system holistically to manage obsolescence [10].

Many authors have come up with different methods and tools to manage obsolescence that unfolds over time. For example, Hurst [13] explains that during the renewal cycle, managers can not directly manage change. They can only manage the organization's ability to change that is to prevent obsolescence. Besides, Rojo et al. [21] point out that planning and managing the firm responses are the only ways to mitigate the risk and minimize the impact of obsolescence. So, it is necessary for organizations to have processes and capabilities to manage obsolescence proactively [19]. As Adetunji et al. (2018) [1,] pointed out obsolescence is here to stay as digitalization and technological turbulence continue to rise. Therefore, it is important to develop necessary organizational capabilities to manage the risk of obsolescence [2, 24, 25].

2.2 Dynamic Capabilities Perspective

To appreciate the firm-environment nexus and explain how firms execute digital transformation, we focus on dynamic capabilities theory [23]. Teece and his colleagues define dynamic capabilities as 'the firm's ability to integrate, build and reconfigure internal and external competencies to address rapidly changing environments [23: p. 516]. In fact, dynamic capabilities are said to allow better decision-making in an environment that is volatile but attractive [16].

Recent research by Nayak et al. [18, p. 284] suggests that it is important to go beyond the concepts of analytical best practices and routines [12] and focus on 'a firm's collectively shared, historically shaped practices and predispositions' to understand tacit, noncognitive aspects of dynamic capabilities. Hence, they suggest that 'empirical sensitivity' and 'habitus' are the two key concepts to study the underpinnings of tacit dynamic capabilities [18, p. 288]. Nayak et al. [18, p. 282] argue that 'a finely honed sensitivity to changing environmental conditions and the corresponding development of a set of generic coping skills are what underpins dynamic capabilities.' They suggest that we need to investigate firms' empirical sensitivities that reflect its distinctive collective history and experiences in order to explain noncognitive aspects of dynamic capabilities.

Consequently, our theoretical approach goes beyond best practices and reflects how dynamic capabilities needed to manage the digital transformation to avoid obsolescence originate from the accumulation of everyday actions [9].

3 Methodology

This study is based on deep collaboration with a UK-based high-tech SME that manufactures high-end home entertainment and music systems. Our case study's history is characterized by multiple efforts at major digital transformations. Conducting rigorous longitudinal studies demands considerable time and effort to collect and interpret data over a long period of time. Therefore, having access to and long-term relationships with the firm was an important asset. Besides, we focused on a technology-intensive manufacturing SME as the rate of change is high in the context of Industry 4.0 [17]. Indeed, the electronics and audio industry has undergone significant change over the past years, driven largely by the advancements in digital technologies [22].

Qualitative data were obtained through studies of internal and public documents, a total of 22 semi-structured face-to-face interviews, discussions, and observations. As the last step of data collection, secondary sources such as the company website (i.e. our story section), archival information, and publicly available written documents from media (e.g. magazine and newspaper articles), as well as recent podcasts about the firm, were collected. All primary and secondary data were uploaded to a database using NVivo 11 Pro software for coding purposes.

Data analysis occurred by way of an open coding process using thematic analysis. The thematic analysis offers effective identification of patterns in a large and complex dataset, as well as links within analytical themes (Braun and Clarke, 2006).

4 Findings and Discussions

We found that the high-tech SME went through three phases of digital transformation (See Fig. 1): phase 1 in converting analog to digital technology in order to tighten IT alignment with obsolescence, phase 2 in building the foundation for both obtaining non-cognitive capabilities and continuing alignment to avoid technological obsolescence, and phase 3 infusing business and technology to avoid obsolescence by company-wide change, implementing and constantly revising non-cognitive dynamic capabilities [18].

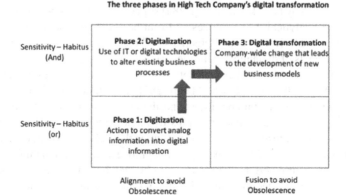

Fig. 1. The conceptual model

This high-tech SME's digital transformation journey is still continuing today but tracking it through the different phases of transformation shows us an insight into how non-cognitive capabilities development help to counter obsolescence. Two key non-cognitive capabilities motives stand out: First, enterprise-wide, empirical sensitivities and habitus of the firm have created the foundation for an enterprise to move through different phases of digital transformation.

In terms of digital technology, this is manifested in a technology development exploration and exploitation activity. This comprises the operational pillar where exploration and exploitation of digital streaming technology and the use of Industry 4.0 technologies are developed and deployed at the ecosystem level. In terms of business, non-cognitive capabilities are manifested in the concurrent but mutually reinforcing efforts within each digital transformation phase to drive the exploitation of existing business via repositioning and exploration of new growth opportunities.

We realize a conscious shift toward the exploitation of technological and environmental certainties to counter the competence or failure trap and the exploration of new possibilities to counter the obsolescence trap. These include the development of new non-cognitive capabilities for "search, refinement, selection, re-focus, network connectivity," on the one hand, and "variation, modularity, strategic alignment, grassroots involvement in innovation, flexibility, upgradability" on the other hand. As such, there is a mutual influence between empirical sensitivity and the habitus of the firm (i.e., empirical sensitivity generates habitus, and habitus constrains empirical sensitivity). The observation is consistent with current literature that highlights reciprocal interactions between empirical sensitivities and habitus that have been conceptually discussed before [e.g., 7, 18]. These qualities, which often complement one another, are fundamental indicators of the challenging demands for SMEs.

The second motive of a digitally transformed SME to avoid the obsolescence trap is to bridge the hidden split between the social side of business and technology. This statement is, again, in line with current practitioner literature that searches to evaluate the digital transformation corresponding to tightening IT alignment with business or reorganization around business capabilities (i.e., sensing, seizing, and transforming)

[23, 25]. The treatment is often a development to a higher level of digital superiority (e.g., from an IT alignment to becoming a digital leader) via the development of dynamic capabilities. But what is stimulating with the case of our high-tech SME is the extent of penetration required in business-digital technology integration at the ecosystem level.

4.1 Conceptualizing "Obsolescence"

The insights derived from the transformation journey of our high-tech SME company support the conceptual framework in Fig. 1 in unpacking the non-cognitive dynamic capabilities development logic of a digitally transformed SME. The greater the extent of non-cognitive capabilities namely environmental sensitivity and habitus that an SME can develop in moving digital transformation phases, the more alert it will be in adapting to counter obsolescence trap. The more continuous the business-digital technology fusion SME can achieve, the more it is able to adjust digital ubiquitously to counter obsolescence in all aspects of its business.

The ideal level of non-cognitive capabilities and business-digital technology fusion may differ in different digital transformation phases. For example, in a less complex environment, or in an industry that has less competition a lesser degree of IT alignment or business-digital technology fusion may suffice to avert technological obsolescence. Most digital transformations are likely to be at the first phase of the digital transformation process, largely taking efforts focusing on environmental sensitivity to reposition existing businesses or habitus to seek new growth opportunities, with strong support from digital technology. The second and third phase of digital transformation tends to be more pervasive in driving both environmental sensitivity (e.g., select, refocus processing-acquired intelligence - a finely honed attunement to environmental solicitations and the discernment of obsolescence) and habitus (e.g., internal responsiveness nurtured through the collective complex history of an SME—its tacitly acquired/transmitted outlooks, social predispositions, and internalized practices). An additional level of complexity in digital transformation comes from the fusion between business and digital technology— that is, such sensitivity and habitus efforts are motivated by Industry 4.0 technologies where business and technologies are effortlessly integrated. The fusion provides a greater skill to counter the technology obsolescence trap. Mere digital technology alignment is insufficient to avert obsolescence demanded in the digital future.

5   Conclusions

Based on the findings from the review of literature and empirical research, we presented the relationships between the key theoretical constructs emerging from our study in a model for digital transformation in Fig. 1. As with all research, the current study is not without its limitations. First, the conceptual clarity of obsolescence, non-cognitive capabilities, and digital transformation link consequently help to bridge the gap between academic research and what SMEs are doing. Practitioners' understanding of the term digitally transformed enterprise can thus be linked conceptually to the research. The 2 × 2 matrix (as shown in Fig. 1) also provides a way to outline conceptually the level of complexity for different digital transformation phases' efforts to counter obsolescence.

In conclusion, making obsolescence obsolete has become increasingly a key organizational capability for SMEs in a technology-driven environment to stay viable. We offer a novel conceptual framework to explain the interplay of these empirical sensitivities and habitus, that collectively shape the noncognitive DCs, in the context of digital transformation in SMEs. Finally, continued study of making obsolescence obsolete capability in firms operating in technology-driven environments will serve to improve our understanding of firm survival and viability in a world with rapid and unprecedented change.

References

1. Adetunji, O., Bischoff, J., Willy, C.J.: Managing system obsolescence via multicriteria decision making. Syst. Eng. **21**(4), 307–321 (2018)
2. Agarwal, R., Helfat, C.E.: Strategic renewal of organizations. Organ. Sci. **20**(2), 281–293 (2009)
3. Amankwah-Amoah, J.: Integrated vs. add-on: a multidimensional conceptualisation of technology obsolescence. Technol. Forecast. Soc. Chang. **116**, 299–307 (2017)
4. Ates, A., Acur, N.: Making obsolescence obsolete: Execution of digital transformation in a high-tech manufacturing SME. J. Bus. Res. **152**, 336–348 (2022)
5. Bartels, B., Ermel, U., Sandborn, P., Pecht, M.G.: Strategies to the Prediction, Mitigation, and Management of Product Obsolescence, vol. 87. John Wiley & Sons, Hoboken (2012)
6. Bradley, J.R., Guerrero, H.H.: Lifetime buy decisions with multiple obsolete parts. Prod. Oper. Manag. **18**(1), 114–126 (2009)
7. Bruineberg, J., Rietveld, E.: Self-organization, free energy minimization, and optimal grip on a field of affordances. Front. Hum. Neurosci. **8**(599), 1–14 (2014)
8. Chen, S., Yu, D.: The impacts of ambidextrous innovation on organizational obsolescence in turbulent environments. Kybernetes (2021). https://doi.org/10.1108/K-08-2020-0514
9. Chia, R., Holt, R.: Strategy as practical coping: a heideggerian perspective. Organ. Stud. **27**, 635–655 (2006)
10. Chung, S.W., Han, J.K., Sohn, Y.S.: Technological expectation and consumer preferences for product form. J. Bus. Res. **65**(9), 1290–1294 (2012)
11. Del Giudice, M., Scuotto, V., Papa, A., Tarba, S.Y., Bresciani, S., Warkentin, M.: A self-tuning model for smart manufacturing SMEs: effects on digital innovation. J. Prod. Innov. Manag. **38**(1), 68–89 (2021)
12. Eisenhardt, K.M., Martin, J.A.: Dynamic capabilities: what are they? Strateg. Manag. J. **21**(10–11), 1105–1121 (2000)
13. Hurst, D.K.: Crisis & Renewal: Meeting the Challenge of Organizational Change, pp. 120–123. Harvard Business School Press, Boston (1995)
14. Jain, A.: Learning by hiring and change to organizational knowledge: countering obsolescence as organizations age. Strateg. Manag. J. **37**(8), 1667–1687 (2016)
15. Le Mens, G., Hannan, M., Polos, L.: Organizational obsolescence, drifting tastes and age dependence in organizational life chances. Organ. Sci. **26**(2), 550–570 (2015)
16. Li, D.Y., Liu, J.: Dynamic capabilities, environmental dynamism, and competitive advantage: evidence from China. J. Bus. Res. **67**(1), 2793–2799 (2014)
17. Müller, J.M., Buliga, O., Voigt, K.-I.: Fortune favors the prepared: how SMEs approach business model innovations in Industry 4.0. Technol. Forecast. Soc. Chang. **132**, 2–17 (2018)
18. Nayak, A., Chia, R., Canales, J.I.: Noncognitive microfoundations: understanding dynamic capabilities as idiosyncratically refined sensitivities and predispositions. Acad. Manag. Rev. **45**(2), 280–303 (2020)

19. Pobiak, T.G., Mazzuchi, T.A., Sarkani, S.: Creating a proactive obsolescence management system framework through the systems engineering continuum. Syst. Eng. **17**(2), 125–139 (2014)
20. Rai, R., Terpenny, J.: Principles for managing technological product obsolescence. IEEE Trans. Compon. Pack. Technol. **31**(4), 880–889 (2008)
21. Rojo, F.J.R., Roy, R., Shehab, E., Wardle, P.J.: Obsolescence challenges for Product-service systems in aerospace and defense industry. In: The 1st CIRP Industrial Product-Service Systems (IPS2) Conference, Cranfield University, p. 255 (2009)
22. Shen, X., Williams, R., Zheng, S., Liu, Y., Li, Y., Gerst, M.: Digital online music in China – a "laboratory" for business experiment. Technol. Forecast. Soc. Chang. **139**, 235–249 (2019)
23. Teece, D.J., Pisano, G., Shuen, A.: Dynamic capabilities and strategic management. Strateg. Manag. J. **18**(7), 509–533 (1997)
24. Vial, G.: Understanding digital transformation: a review and a research agenda. J. Strateg. Inf. Syst. **28**(2), 118–144 (2019)
25. Warner, K.S., Wäger, M.: Building dynamic capabilities for digital transformation: an ongoing process of strategic renewal. Long Range Plan. **52**(3), 326–349 (2019)
26. Westerman, G., Bonnet, D.: Revamping your business through digital transformation. MIT Sloan Manag. Rev. **56**(3), 10 (2015)

Expense and Revenue Factors of Smart Factories: Analysis of the Economic Effects of Condition Monitoring

Moritz Spatz[1]([⊠]) [iD] and Ralph Riedel[2] [iD]

[1] ZF Friedrichshafen AG, Graf-Zeppelin-Straße 1, 94136 Thyrnau, Germany
moritz.spatz@zf.com
[2] Westsächsische Hochschule Zwickau, Kornmarkt 1, 08056 Zwickau, Germany
ralph.riedel@fh-zwickau.de

Abstract. Numerous approaches for assisting Smart Factory implementations in production companies have been published over the last few years. However, guidelines for calculating the profitability of these efforts have barely been addressed by scientific approaches so far. This paper aims to close this research gap using the Smart Factory application Condition Monitoring as an example. Therefore, a framework of the expense structure, as well as a framework of accompanying effects on business processes and resources, are presented. Based on these frameworks a procedure to support the financial assessment prior to the actual implementation is proposed. This procedure enables decision-makers to follow a deductive approach when identifying the economic relevant factors of smart factory applications. The authors argue that the shift towards a descriptive character of effect assessment simplifies and precises the profitability calculation. The construct validity of the frameworks and the usability of the proposed approach are confirmed in two case studies in separate production plants of ZF Friedrichshafen AG.

Keywords: Smart factory · Condition monitoring · Economic assessment

1 Introduction

Smart Factories are enabled by the evolution of Industry 4.0 and integrate the associated technologies within a production plant. Information and communications technology make it possible for employees, products and assets to exchange information in real-time. [1] Technology is used within the production processes which thereby are enabled to act context-aware and partly autonomous. [2] Production management is supported by enhanced data availability and decision-making assistance tools. The goal is to exploit the capabilities of digitalization in order to generate insights into business processes or to optimize them. [3] Since previous studies already determined purposeful measure identification and implementation approaches [4, 5] this paper addresses their vulnerability. Existing approaches and maturity models were investigated and a lack of assistance

© IFIP International Federation for Information Processing 2022
Published by Springer Nature Switzerland AG 2022
D. Y. Kim et al. (Eds.): APMS 2022, IFIP AICT 664, pp. 140–147, 2022.
https://doi.org/10.1007/978-3-031-16411-8_18

tools for performing an economical ex-ante evaluation was identified. The few existing guidelines follow an inductive approach to determine cost-effectiveness. [6, 7] As a basis for a deductive approach, the following research question must be answered: "What are the expense and revenue drivers of Smart Factory applications?" Due to the large scope of this research question, the subject of this paper is reduced to the economic impact factors of one specific Smart Factory application, namely Condition Monitoring (hereafter CM).

In order to implement a Smart Factory, actions can be taken in six consecutive categories. These are Computerization, Connectivity, Visibility, Transparency, Predictability and Adaptability. [8] CM can be assigned to multiple of these categories. Schuh et al. classify the application as a measure to gain transparency [8] whereas Fleischer et al. categorize CM into Computerization, Connectivity or Visibility depending on the setup in the specific use case. [9] Since CM covers a wide range of Smart Factory categories focusing on this application appears to be reasonable. An analysis of the verifiable expenses and revenues might reveal extensive insights into the economic impact factors of Smart Factories.

Choosing CM for the exemplary analysis is also justifiable by a practical approach. Service, maintenance and repair of production machines are essential activities in order to keep a manufacturing business running. [10] As the main goal of CM is to optimize the efficiency of these measures, this Smart Factory application might be beneficial to a brought range of enterprises. Furthermore, CM is a prerequisite for the AI application Predictive Maintenance [11] which is currently researched intensively by computer science studies. Therefore, it is likely that the importance of CM will be maintained in the future. This suggests that from a practical perspective, comprehensive knowledge of the economic impact of CM adds value.

2 Calculation Approaches

One barrier to Smart Factory investments in enterprises is the difficulty in calculating the profitability of single applications. [12] Orzes et al. explain this observation by lack of experience with the upcoming technologies, large sums of initial expenditures and uncertain cash returns [13].

Existing guidelines for Smart Factory implementation mostly address methodical, technological and chronological aspects. Applicable methods regarding measure identification focus on how to pick suitable applications based on qualitative factors. [6, 11] Quantitative impact determination methods rely on an inductive analysis of the expected effort and benefit. [7] Performing such estimations is hard for inexperienced companies as expertise in smart factory implementation is required. [13] Multiple guidelines recommend using the Net Present Value calculation method [14] without providing further information. It can be stated that the calculation of Smart Factory applications is barely addressed by scientific approaches.

In this paper, a framework of categorized expense and revenue drivers is introduced. The framework represents the cost structure of a CM investment as well as its conceivable effect on business processes and resources. The authors took into account that intended as well as unwanted effects might occur. In contrast to the existing methods, the provided framework enables a deductive approach for effort and benefit determination. Users are guided through the relevant economic factors when considering an investment in CM systems. The explorative character of impact assessments changes towards a descriptive character.

The holistic listing of economically relevant factors reduces the need for prior experience in Smart Factory implementations. Detailed knowledge about the possible effects of an application is not necessary. Using the framework, it must be determined whether certain effects will have an impact in the specific setting of implementation. The authors state that this procedure simplifies the effect identification and therefore reduces hurdles to implement Smart Factory applications. The evaluation precision might also be optimized since relevant factors will not be disregarded. A reasonable investment calculation can be derived. Following the recommendation of Issa et al., it is suggested that a small heterogenous group of shopfloor employers and management members perform the proposed procedure [7].

3   Method

The databases ScienceDirect, Web of Science, and EbscoHost are consulted for identifying the expense and revenue structure of CM use cases. The search terms are combinations of the words "Condition Monitoring" and "impact", "cost", "expense", "benefit", "revenue" or "calculation". 30 relevant papers are identified. In addition, documentation of actual use cases and their effects provided by the database of "Plattform Industrie 4.0" are considered. The search term "Condition Monitoring" returns eight listings in the manufacturing industry. Based on the obtained material, expense and revenue drivers of CM are determined. Therefore inductive category formation according to Mayring is carried out. [15] The obtained categories and the assignments have been modified within qualitative, partial-narrative, semi-structured expert interviews and two frameworks were compiled.

Verifying the determined expense and revenue factors as well as the suggested framework usage two case studies have been performed. Elaborating a structured procedure for the case studies the proposed procedure for effect identification was applied. Thereby functionality and applicability of the approach were evaluated. The case studies cover already implemented CM applications in different production departments of ZF Friedrichshafen AG. Accompanying economic effects of the considered CM application are analyzed retrospectively. The internal validity of the frameworks is assessed by the comparison of listed factors and observed effects.

4   Condition Monitoring

4.1   Types of Condition Monitoring

The literature differentiates two relevant types of CM. Solutions based on machine control signals as well as sensor-based signals can be identified. Machine state and processing data are available from the PLC. Further data might also be available on the machine depending on the initial setup of the control unit. For data gathering, a collaboration with the machine vendor or PLC and communication protocol experts is carried out. Other relevant information can be obtained by attaching appropriate sensors. For this, ready-to-use solutions are available on the market. All incoming signals are getting processed by the CM system. Based on the connected data sources relevant insights can be generated. Feasible evaluations are trend detection, timer and counter implementation and are based on the definition of optimal operating modes deviation detection. Insights can be visualized or responsible employees can be alerted. Condition-based maintenance for the monitored assets is enabled. Typically monitored data points are listed in Table 1 [16, 17].

Table 1. Typical data points of Condition Monitoring

Signal source	Data points
PLC	currents, forces, machine states, pressures, positions, process parameters, speed, torques
External sensor	acoustic emissions, flow rate, geometries, material alteration, material stress, optical alteration vibrations
Possibly both signal sources	consumptions, temperatures, timestamps

4.2 Economic Effects of Condition Monitoring

One framework lists all identified kinds of potential project expenses while the second framework is dedicated to possible effects on business processes and resources. The authors ensured that the Smart Factory application is considered both a conventional asset investment and an IT project. Both perspectives provide insights about possible expenses and revenues. Depending on the type and environment of the application some of the factors might not be relevant in specific settings. Figure 1 and Fig. 2 represent the frameworks.

Factor	Type	Expenses
Asset connection	Hardware	additional sensors, PLC upgrade
	Workload	installation, PLC parameterization, signal interpretation, testing
Infrastructure	Hardware	infrastructure components, network components
	Workload	installation
More one-off expenses		false alarms, licenses, efficiency losses due to the learning curve, traveling expenses, training
Project efforts		project management, ramp-up
Recurring expenses		licenses, internal support efforts, energy consumption
Software		data integration, programming, testing

Fig. 1. Possible expenses of Condition Monitoring

Factor	Lever	Effect
Cost	Consumed goods	consumption of air pressure, consumables, energy, equipment, oil, tools, water
	Inventory	need for consumables, equipment, production assets, spare parts, tools
	Manpower	effort in maintenance processes, planning and scheduling, quality processes, operator waiting for machine
	Quality	amount of rework, scrap
	Services	need for external or maintenance services
Leadtime	Operations	availability, duration of documentations
	Quality	grade of automatization, duration of documentation, information availability
Output	Machine capabilities	processing speed, amount of rework and scrap
	Scheduled downtime	amount and duration of planned maintenance
	Unscheduled downtime	amount and duration of breakdowns, waiting / searching for information, waiting / searching for spare parts

Fig. 2. Possible effects of Condition Monitoring on processes and resources

With the established frameworks, the prerequisite for the deductive determination of relevant economic factors of CM is given. The practical relevance of the determined factors as well as the feasibility of the framework usage has to be validated.

5 Validation and Evaluation

Use cases where several signals are monitored, a group of multiple production assets is connected, the responsible employees are amenable and actual measures have already been derived from the gathered information were considered for the case studies. Furthermore, a prerequisite for the quantitative analysis of the profitability is that the required data is available for periods prior to implementation.

In order to show the construct validity two use cases have been chosen. Both types of CM applications are represented. While the sensor-based solution is analyzed in the heat treatment department of a European site, a manufacturing plant in Asia provides a PLC-based solution. The solutions have been fully integrated into the business processes. A total of nineteen production assets are part of the observation.

The case studies started with a narrative interview with the respective project leads. The authors determined the initial cause of the CM implementation, the organizational and technical realization, the integration into daily business processes and the achieved effects. Factors known to affect the economic viability of CM have been recorded and quantified as far as data was available. A second interview was structured based on the introduced frameworks. The appearance of the listings was assessed by the project leads and one production manager. The qualitative validation was completed by a process chain analysis based on data logs and documentation.

The quantification of the expenses was carried out based on statements from the interviews, archival materials and additional documentation. For the quantification of the effects on business processes and resources, a time series analysis of descriptive KPIs was performed. The impact on the retrievals and the lifecycle of spare parts, the uptime of production machines and the occurrence of maintenance tasks were observed. Significant results ($\alpha \leq 0,06$) are shown in the following figure (Fig. 3).

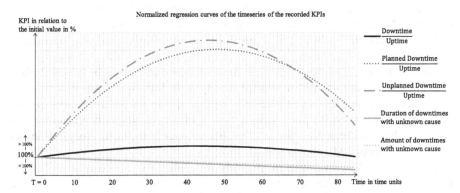

Fig. 3. Significant regression curves of the evolution of relevant KPIs (Axes are unlabeled for reasons of confidentiality)

A correlation between the implementation of the CM application and the observed KPIs is evident. The analysis reveals that after the completion of the CM implementation downtime in relation to the uptime rises at first. As the usage of the system is established, a decline in downtime due to maintenance reasons is determined. After 85 time units, the initial ratio of down-to uptime is restored. The extrapolation of the regression curve shows for future time units that further optimization is likely.

At the beginning of the CM usage more planned stoppages occur due to misinterpretations of the gathered data and wrong intervention limits. Unplanned stoppages rise due to the same reasons. Not having all the relevant information to derive proper actions also leads to unplanned stoppages. False-positive and false-negative alarms can be observed. A high trust level in the system operationalizes these false alarms into downtimes. Knowing the characteristics of the monitored asset and the CM system itself, the usage is adjusted. From a certain date on, a decrease in downtimes results. In contrast, the amount and duration of machine stops with unknown causes decrease from the beginning on. The derived measures act preventively. Additionally, the causes can now be determined by the available data and are not unknown.[1]

The obtained results from the quantitative analysis can be comprehended relying on the experts' statements. Although other optimization measures took place at the same time, none of them were focusing on key maintenance performance indicators as CM did. The observed KPI evolution can at least partly be led back to the implementation of CM. Based on the consistent observations the authors consider their methodological approach to identify the relevant expense and revenue factors and the derived frameworks as justified.

---

[1] The given explanations for the KPI evolution are derived from the expert interviews.

6 Conclusion

The performed approach allows the following conclusions to be drawn. It was determined that the initial decisions to introduce CM were made based on quantitative, qualitative and strategic considerations. Neither of the two use cases were calculated with the inclusion of all relevant economic factors. Incomplete consideration of effects can lead to biased decisions. The need for well-founded calculation guidelines has been confirmed. Based on the shown evidence in Sect. 5, it is reasonable to integrate the concept of experience curves [18] in the calculations.

The economic factors identified in the considered case studies can be fully described by the presented frameworks. The internal validity of the frameworks was strengthened. The chosen conceptual approach for determining the expense and revenue factors appears to be appropriate. Factors that were derived from the literature and which were not evident in the cases have not been discarded from the frameworks. These factors may be relevant for other settings of CM implementations.

In the case studies, the proposed approach was applied for the ex-post identification of economic effects originating from CM applications. The applicability as well as the functionality of the approach were shown. According to the authors, this conclusion is transferable to ex-ante analyses.

Expenses and payment arrangements for the most common variants of the considered Smart Factory application have been recorded. The authors conclude that the supposed approach based on the presented frameworks is suitable for supporting an analysis of CM applications. According to the provided justification, CM is considered a representative of Smart Factory applications in this paper. Nevertheless, the external validity of the approach cannot be fully argued. The constraints are determined based on the categorization of Smart Factory applications according to Fleischer et al. [8]. Due to the similar purpose of applications within one Smart Factory category, the validity of the framework for other applications associated with Computerization, Connectivity Visibility or Transparency is likely. Limitations regarding the transferability to other Smart Factory categories cannot be specified.

The observed effects also depend on the business environment. Liebrecht argues that a correct classification of the observations is achieved by considering production type and level of automation. [11] The provided results were generated in production processes which can be assigned to a small-batch production of industrial gear units. Compared to the KPIs of the automotive industry the cycle time of the products is large, the number of produced units and the number of produced variants is low. The production type can be identified as balanced between quantities and variants. The production is organized with a balanced level of automatization. The transferability of the frameworks to other business environments is not readily possible.

The frameworks focus on monetizable factors of a Smart Factory application. According to Hoitsch, the goal of productions might also include social or environmental goals. [8] Exclusively qualitative determinable effects of CM have not been analyzed in the case studies and are not yet included in the frameworks.

Further research is necessary to meet the identified constraints and extend the applicability of the frameworks.

References

1. Kaufmann, T., Forstner, L.: Horizontale Integration der Wertschöpfungskette in der Halbleiterindustrie, 1st edn. In: ten Hompel, M. (eds.) Handbuch-Industrie 4.0: Produktion, 2nd edn. pp. 95–103. Springer, Cham (2017). https://doi.org/10.1007/978-3-662-45279-0_31
2. Rüb, J., Bahemia, H.: A review of the literature on smart factory implementation. In: 2019 IEEE International Conference on Engineering, Technology and Innovation, pp. 1–9 (2019)
3. Kleinemeier, M.: Von der Automatisierungspyramide zu Unternehmenssteuerungs-Netzwerken, 1st edn. In: ten Hompel, M. (eds.) Handbuch-Industrie 4.0: Produktion, 2nd edn, pp. 219–226. Springer, Cham (2017)
4. Verhulst, E., Brenden, S.F.: Strategic roadmapping towards Industry 4.0 for manufacturing SMEs. In: Dolgui, A., Bernard, A., Lemoine, D., von Cieminski, G., Romero, D. (eds.) APMS 2021. IAICT, vol. 631, pp. 3–12. Springer, Cham (2021). https://doi.org/10.1007/978-3-030-85902-2_1
5. Terstegen, S., Hennegriff, S., Dander, H., Adler, P.: Vergleichsstudie über Vorgehensmodelle zur Einführung und Umsetzung von Digitalisierungsmaßnahmen in der produzierenden Industrie. In: Frühjahrskongress 2019, pp. 3–13 (2019)
6. Leone, D., Barni, A.: Industry 4.0 on demand. In: APMS. The Path to Digital Transformation and Innovation of Production Management Systems 2020, vol. 2(12) (2020)
7. Issa, A., Hatiboglu, B., Bildstein, A., Bauernhansl, T.: Industrie 4.0 roadmap. In: 51st CIRP Conference on Manufacturing Systems, vol. 72, pp. 985–988 (2018)
8. Schuh, G., Anderl, R., Dumitrescu, R., Krüger, A., ten Hompel, M.: Industrie 4.0 Maturity Index. Acatech STUDY, München (2020)
9. Fleischer, J., Lanza, G., Schulze, V.: Erfassung von Prozessdaten (u.a.) durch Maschinen und Werkzeuge. http://www.intro40-webtools.de/dl/15_Erfassung_von_Prozessdaten.pdf. Accessed 28 Feb 2022
10. Schuh, P., Schneider, D., Funke, L., Tracht, K.: Cost-optimal spare parts inventory planning for wind energy systems. Logist. Res. 8(1), 1–8 (2015). https://doi.org/10.1007/s12159-015-0122-7
11. Liebrecht, C.: Entscheidungsunterstützung für den Industrie 4.0-Methodeneinsatz. Shaker Verlag, Herzogenrath (2020)
12. Glass, R., Meissner, A., Gebauer, C., Stürmer, S., Metternich, J.: Identifying the barriers to Industrie 4.0. In: 51st CIRP Conference on Manufacturing Systems, vol. 72, pp. 985–988 (2018)
13. Orzes, G., Rauch, E., Bednar, S., Poklemba, R.: Industry 4.0 implementation barriers in small and medium sized enterprises. In: 2018 IEEE International Conference on Industrial Engineering and Engineering Management, pp. 1348–1352 (2018)
14. Liebrecht, C., Schaumann, S., Daniel, Z., Alica, A., Gisela, L.: Analysis of interactions and support of decision making for the implementation of manufacturing systems 4.0 methods. In: 10th CIRP Conference on Industrial Product-Service Systems, vol. 73, pp. 161–166 (2018)
15. Mayring, P.: Qualitative Inhaltsanalyse, 11th edn. Beltz Verlag, Weinheim (2010)
16. Nath, C.: Integrated tool condition monitoring systems and their applications. In: 48th SME North American Manufacturing Research Conference, vol. 48, pp. 852–863 (2020)
17. Schuh, G., Kampker, A., Odak, R.: Verfügbarkeitsorientierte Instandhaltung, 1st edn. Apprimus Verlag, Aachen (2009)
18. Henderson, B.: Die Erfahrungskurve in der Unternehmensstrategie, 2nd edn. Campus Verlag, Frankfurt am Main (1974)

Procurement 4.0: A Systematic Review of Its Technological Evolution

Robson Elias Bueno$^{(\boxtimes)}$ (ID), Helton Almeida dos Santos$^{(\boxtimes)}$ (ID),
Moacir de Junior Freitas$^{(\boxtimes)}$ (ID), Rodrigo Carlo Toloi$^{(\boxtimes)}$ (ID),
and Rodrigo Franco Gonçalves$^{(\boxtimes)}$ (ID)

Graduate Studies in Production Engineering, University Paulista, Sao Paulo, Brazil
robsonebueno@gmail.com, heltonalmeidasantos@gmail.com,
bicimo@uol.com.br, toloirodrigo@gmail.com, rofranco212@gmail.com

Abstract. Industry 4.0 is significantly transforming the traditional way of managing supply chains. However, Industry 4.0 tools can be expensive and not affordable and can be implemented in a variety of ways. Therefore, the benefits of implementing these tools should be clarified before investing in digitizing the Procurement process. The objective of the work is to present the dimensions (Competencies, Management, Partnerships, Processes, Systems/Technologies, and Sustainability) and the tools of Ind4.0 motivating the trends of evolution in the procurement area in the face of these changes in technologies and digital transformation. Despite the importance of this issue, few studies have attempted to address the effects of Ind4.0, technologies, and intelligent systems in procurement. To fill this gap, in the applications of Ind4.0 tools a conceptual model was developed to classify different value propositions provided by the different applications of Ind4.0 tools in the internal and external processes of the area. Finally, the results conclude that the six dimensions proposed in the conceptual model can provide a better understanding of the Procurement area, demonstrating the trends of the implementation of Ind4.0 tools related to different activities, presented by the literature authors.

Keywords: Industry 4.0 · Procurement 4.0 · Value proposition · Supply chain · Digitization

1 Introduction

The new industrial revolution is beginning and is changing the way we live, work and relate to each other [1]. To meet this new requirement, manufacturing and all processes of companies will need to adapt [2]. The importance of developing and managing innovative procurement *strategies is* clear [3]. From a historical perspective, procurement has undergone major transitions, especially in recent decades, in the sense that organizations have had to deal with pressures related to cost reduction and increased profits [4].

© IFIP International Federation for Information Processing 2022
Published by Springer Nature Switzerland AG 2022
D. Y. Kim et al. (Eds.): APMS 2022, IFIP AICT 664, pp. 148–156, 2022.
https://doi.org/10.1007/978-3-031-16411-8_19

According to Batran et al. (2017) [5], the reality is that the pace of change and the scale of challenges we face require a new approach to how we do business. Change is continuous: Procurement 4.0 must be able to easily adapt and take advantage of emerging opportunities. It is also an integral and essential component of a larger system within a given organization. Procurement 4.0 can improve supply chain performance by adding values and improving visibility and resiliency. The idea of Procurement 4.0 and the values aggregated by this concept is a new subject that is rarely addressed and suffers from great uncertainty due to the involvement of complex supply chain activities and multicriteria decision-making [6]. In terms of processes, problems, and solutions in defining how procurement can add value to customers, inside and outside an organization; and how it can help manage relationships, improve processes, and better resource management, both internally and with partners [7]. In this sense, the research questions are: How will the process be different from the current Procurement system to Procurement 4.0? What technologies can be used? What is the tendency of Procurement evolution?

The paper is conceptual to achieve the goal of organizing the literature through a systematic review and evaluating the process, technologies, and trends of the evolution of Procurement to Procurement 4.0.

For this, we carried out a systematic review of the literature and established a conceptual frame (table 1) of Procurement evolution, technologies, and tendencies of Procurement 4.0.

The paper is organized as follows: Sect. 2 presents the background of the review of Industry 4.0 and Procurement concepts; Sect. 3 presents the systematic review method, used to organize and classify the literature into six dimensions; Sect. 4 presents the results of literature research on Procurement, technologies of industry 4.0 and the respective references; Sect. 5 presents the discussion and conclusions about the evolution of Procurement to Procurement 4.0, emphasizing process improvements.

2 Theoretical Review

2.1 Industry 4.0

As a way to contextualize the *Procurement 4.0 scenario*, we raise information about industry 4.0, digital technologies, and the structure of procurement. Germany brings a new paradigm of industrial production to the world, with the appropriation of digital technology disseminated on the Internet and executed by the Elements Internet of Things [8]. Bonilla et al. (2018) [9], common that due to its unique characteristics, the goal of Industry 4.0 is to increase productivity and customization that are achieved through the flexibilization of manufacturing and decentralization through the digitization and integration of the information network, allowing the real-time monitoring and control.

2.2 Procurement and Procurement 4.0

Procurement can be defined as the "business management function that ensures the identification, supply, access, and management of external resources that an organization needs or may need to meet its strategic objectives" [10]. Procurement is a function of procurement of products and services, especially for commercial purposes. Among them are supplier selection, payment terms, contract negotiation, regulatory compliance, analysis, and outsourcing [11]. This is possible because Procurement has strategic know-how about suppliers and their markets, deep expertise in the products and services purchased, and the alternatives on offer, including emerging innovations [12].

Procurement 4.0 connects the organization with its suppliers and enables dynamic cooperation and coordination of the procurement process [13]. Procurement 4.0 includes a range of processes and changes within a company as they work to develop new procurement value propositions and incorporate supplier management into purchasing software [14]. According to current literature, Procurement 4.0 can be understood as an intelligent system capable of autonomously detecting material demand, generating your order, and even transmitting the order to the supplier without the need for human involvement [15]. Procurement 4.0 aims to optimize the value provided by the purchasing function [3].

3   Method

First, we selected the Google Scholar, Scopus, and Web of Science databases. In the second step, we select the keyword applied to collect related articles. The keyword "procurement 4.0" is new to academic literature and the resulting terminology for the new synonym for I4.0 and Supply Chain 4.0. The illustration presents the methodology in Fig. 1.

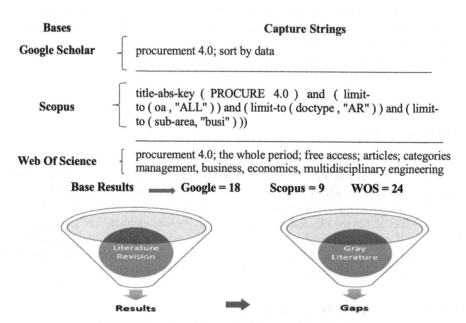

Fig. 1. Illustration of the methodology used in this article.

Instead of covering a rigid systematic review, we conducted a review at different levels, looking for text representative of technologies within the Procurement approach, showing a current or potential use in the construction of Procurement 4.0. After the analysis of the articles, a gap was presented in the literature presented, of the term Procurement 4.0 for still being reduced publications, to repair it was used an approach in the gray literature [34], specialized scientific journals and management reports were used to extract technologies applied in various forms and levels of intervention that help to manage this change. Public Procurement cases were discarded because they did not belong to the scope of the search.

For example, Henke and Schulte [16] argue that the acquisition of partners and the interface layer of production solutions offer the opportunity to position itself as a key factor for the development of industry 4.0, postulating several opportunities. Contributing to this reasoning, Bueno et al. [17] present six essential dimensions for the implementation of Procurement 4.0 that will require a mutation in companies, and their Strategic, Tactical, and Operational planning: Competencies, Management, Partnerships, Processes, Systems/Technologies, and Sustainability. Figure 2 Illustrates the established dimensions of Procurement 4.0.

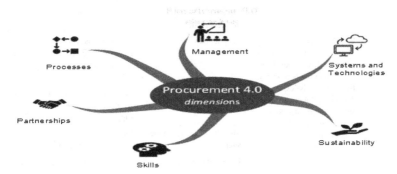

Fig. 2. Dimensions for Procurement 4.0, based on Bueno et al. [17]

4   Results

The intention advocated in this article was to address the six dimensions and technologies of industry 4.0, to present the due rupture [3] of Procurement for Procurement 4.0. The introduction of 4.0 technologies will mean developing new value propositions, meeting new business needs, and integrating data between roles and value chains. Procurement 4.0 include forming service level agreements with suppliers, maintaining the procurement intranet site, frequent design reviews and stakeholder satisfaction surveys, and identifying and implementing opportunities for improvement [15]. Table 1 presents the procurement break for version 4.0.

Table 1. Evolution of procurement technologies

Dimensions	Industry 4.0 technologies	Transition in procurement operations	Tendencies	Authors
Skills	Cloud Computing, Internet of Things (IoT), Blockchain Technology, Cybersecurity, Big Data Analytics, Advanced Robotics, Virtual/Augmented Reality, 3D Printing, and Additive Manufacturing	Reduced team workload	Multi talent profiles	[18]
			Consultants	[19]
		Creating synergies	Data analysts (descriptive analytics to cognitive analytics)	[20]
			Strategic with the business	[21]
		Communication	Relationship management and strategic thinking	[22]
Management	Cloud Computing, Internet of Things (IoT), Blockchain Technology, Cybersecurity, Big Data Analytics, Advanced Robotics, Virtual/Augmented Reality, 3D Printing, and Additive Manufacturing	Strategic positioning	Mastery of proprietary technology	[18]
		Creation of new business networks	Third party independence	[19]
			Process and data integration	[5]
		Cost reduction	Cost of acquisition and supplier selection	[24]
			Higher profits	[20]
		More customer-oriented business models	Greater autonomy	[21]
Partnerships	Cloud Computing, Internet of Things (IoT), Internet of Services (Ios), Blockchain Technology, Cybersecurity, Big Data Analytics, Advanced Robotics, Virtual/Augmented Reality, 3D Printing, and Additive Manufacturing	Supplier administration	Creation of new business networks. Use of blockchains for contract validation	[18]
			More agile communication with customers and suppliers	[19]
		More transparency in the supply chain	Increased transparency of data and information	[20]
		Proactive response	Early issuance of outage notices	[23]
		Risk management	Strategic partners	[5]
			Improved evaluation of customer and supplier data	[21]
Processes	Cloud Computing, Internet of Things (IoT), Internet of Services (Ios), Artificial Intelligence, Simulation, Blockchain Technology, Cybersecurity, Cyber Physical Systems, Big Data Analytics, Advanced Robotics, Virtual/Augmented Reality, 3D Printing, and Additive Manufacturing	Demand analysis	Digitization of processes and procedures	[18]

(*continued*)

Table 1. (*continued*)

Dimensions	Industry 4.0 technologies	Transition in procurement operations	Tendencies	Authors
			Greater efficiency, flexibility and fast reaction time	[19]
		Information flow	Automated allows perfect coordination, saving coordination costs	[13]
		Process standardization	Decreased travel costs and increased speed in decision making	[20]
		Fast reaction times	Better connections with global supplier network	[21]
Systems and Technologies	Cloud Computing, Internet of Things (IoT), Internet of Services (IoS), Blockchain Technology, Simulation, Cyber Security, Big Data Analytics, Advanced Robotics, Virtual/Augmented Reality, 3D Printing, Additive Manufacturing, and Artificial Intelligence	Improved data quality (greater significance due to information and not just data)	Real-time availability of data and information	[18]
		Real-time availability of data and information	Improved data availability, fully computerized	[19]
			Increased transparency of data and information	
		Intelligent behavior	Autonomous vehicle routing, locating potential suppliers, order scaling, and lot storage	[25, 26]
		Database security	Data sharing, visibility and transparency promotes trust	[15]
		Fully automated information flow	Improved evaluation of customer and supplier data	[21]
Sustainability	Cloud Computing, Internet of Things (IoT), Blockchain Technology, Cybersecurity, Big Data Analytics, Advanced Robotics, Virtual/Augmented Reality, 3D Printing, and Additive Manufacturing	Reduction of costs associated with waste management	Socially responsible shopping	[27]
		Sustainable shopping	Cloud data associated with sustainability, such as carbon footprint (environmental) and waste disposal costs (economic) and social aspects	[28]
		Corporative image	Economic, environmental and social behavior depends heavily on your supply chain	[29]
		Sustainable production	Flexibility in production volumes	[19]
		Facilitates compliance with legal requirements	Acquisitions covering environmental, economic and social (TBL) elements	[29]

(*continued*)

Table 1. (*continued*)

Dimensions	Industry 4.0 technologies	Transition in procurement operations	Tendencies	Authors
			Incorporation of new technologies	[20]
		It demonstrates the organization's commitment to a sustainability and social responsibility policy	Perceived costs/benefits: sustainable products play a prominent role in sustainable procurement	[30]

5   Discussion and Conclusions

Despite the emerging literature on this subject, it is notorious that there is a lack of comprehensive and systematic structures, strategies, and approaches for the implementation of Industry 4.0 concepts in the Procurement processes. The literature has in common that the described procurement process was initiated not by a single technology, but by the interaction of various technologies and solutions whose effects created new modes of production, but also influenced organizations, the environment, and social functions, in accordance with [31].

Procurement is no longer a personality-centered function, where professionals in the area manage everything on their own, using only the knowledge they have acquired over time. Based on the research of the literature presented, the table presented how Industry 4.0 technologies will change the way the Procurement process works and what are the trends of this evolution. Procurement 4.0 will transform the operation of the Supply Chain. Applicable technologies represented substantial values and aggregated values consist of improving performance in operations associated with purchasing management in supply chains, such as pricing, supplier selection, evaluation, cost-benefit, data collection, and analysis. The presence of digital integration is transforming business processes, both internal and external, with the implementation of Ind.4.0 technologies. Processes and data are increasingly transparent and accessible, intelligence in Procurement 4.0 requires a transformation in the organization in the six dimensions presented.

The adoption of Procurement 4.0 results in autonomy, flexibility, and transparency of operations associated with purchasing management to optimize pricing decisions, supplier management, and purchasing management, or to develop sustainability and data sharing security [32, 33]. Given the issues related to the application of Industry 4.0 technologies in Procurement and compared with the existing literature in the area, this article focuses not only on technological trends but proposes a vision of Procurement evolution and tendencies. However, our reviewed literature does not find a clear concept of Procurement 4.0. Future studies can focus on a conceptual model of Procurement 4.0.

References

1. Kagermann, H., Anderl, R., Gausemeier, J., Schuh, G., Wahlster, W. (eds.): ("the digital world") Industrie 4.0 in a Global Context: Strategies for Cooperating with International Partners. Herbert Utz Verlag, Munich (2016)

2. Chiang, W.C.: Development of a lean non-adjusting setup system – a case study of Aluminum rims production. Christian University, Chung Yuan, Taiwan, 104p. (2016)
3. Nicoletti, B.: Procurement 4.0 and the Fourth Industrial Revolution. Palgrave Macmillan, Cham (2020). https://doi.org/10.1007/978-3-030-35979-9_1
4. Uusitalo, J.: Strategic acquisitions in the face of uncertainty. Master's thesis. University of Jyväskylä, Finland (2019)
5. Batran, A., et al.: A survival guide in a digital, disruptive world. Campus, Frankfurt (2017)
6. Bag, S., Wood, L.C., Mangla, S.K., Luthra, S.: Procurement 4.0 and its implications for business process performance in an economy circular. Resour. Conserv. Recycl. **152**, 104502 (2020)
7. Nicoletti, B.: Agile Acquisitions. Volume II: Designing and Implementing a Digital Transformation. Springer, London (2017). https://doi.org/10.1007/978-3-319-61085-6ISBN 978-3-319-61085-6
8. Kagermann, H., Wahlster, W., Helbig, J.B.: Securing the future of German manufacturing industry: recommendations for implementing the strategic initiative INDUSTRIE 4.0. German National Academy of Science and Engineering (ACAT- ECH) Technical Report (2013)
9. Bonilla, S.H., Silva, H.R.O., Terra da Silva, M., Franco Gonçalves, R., Sacomano, J.B: Industry 4.0 and implications of sustainability: a scenario-based analysis of impacts and challenges. Sustainability **10**, 3740 (2018). https://doi.org/10.3390/su10103740
10. Andrew, K.: The definition of acquisitions, pp. 1–7. Chartered Institute of Purchasing and Supply, Australia (2005)
11. Chakravarty, S.: What is the difference between procurement and sourcing? (2017). www.ten dersinfo.com/blogs/what-is-the-difference-between-procurement-purchasing-and-sourcing
12. Weissbarth, R., Geissbauer, R., Wetzstein, J.: Procurement 4.0: are you ready for the digital revolution? (2016). https://www.strategyand.pwc.com/report/procurement-4-digital-rev olution. Accessed 20 Apr 2020
13. Glas, A.H., Kleemann, P.F.C.: The impact of Industry 4.0 on procurement and supply management: a conceptual and qualitative analysis. Int. J. Bus. Manag. Invent. **5**(6), 55–66 (2016)
14. PWC Report: Procurement 4.0: Are You Ready for Digital Revolution? (2016). https://www.strategyand.pwc.com/report/procurement-4-digital-revolution. Accessed on June 25, 2020
15. Bienhaus, F., Haddud, A., Bienhaus, F., Haddud, A.: Procurement 4. 0: factors influencing the digitization of procurement and supply chains. Bus. Process. Manag. J. **24**(4), 965–984 (2018)
16. Henke, M., Schulte, A.T.: Einkauf und die 4. Industrielle Revolution. Beschaffung Aktuell **62**(3), 20–21 (2015)
17. Bueno, R.E., Freitas Junior, M.D, da Silva, M.A., Lombardi, I., Bueno, J.V.: The evolution of logistics: Procurement 4.0. In: Martinsm E.R. (Organizer) Production Engineering [Electronic Book]: Quality Management, Production, and Operations, vol. 2. Scientific Digital, Guarujá (2021). https://doi.org/10.37885/978-65-5360-036-2. ISBN 978-65-5360-036-2
18. Burton, N.: Procurement 2025: 10 Challenges that Will Transform Global Sourcing (2015). Disponível em www.industryweek.com/global-sourcing. Acesso em 20/04/2021
19. Fraunhofer, IML: The Digitalization of Procurement. Pilot Study Procurement 4.0 Fraunhofer IML BME (2016). Disponível em: https://www.iml.fraunhofer.de/content/dam/iml/en/documents/OE260/Pilot%20Study_Procurement%204-0_Fraunhofer%20IML_BME.pdf. Acesso em 20/04/2021
20. Biazzin, C.: Inteligência em Compras. GV executivo, vol. 16, no. 6. Supply Chain, Operações e Logística inteligência em compras, nov/dez 2017. Disponível em. https://bibliotecadigital.fgv.br/ojs/index.php/gvexecutivo/article/view/73256
21. CIPS: Digitalization in Procurement and Supply (2019). Disponível em: https://www.cips.org/PageFiles/138071/CIPS_Digitalisation_of_Procurement_WEB.pdf. Accessed 02 July 2021

22. Bals, L., Schulze, H., Kelly, S., Stek, K.: Journal of Purchasing and supply management purchasing and supply management (PSM) competencies: current and future requirements. J. Purch. Supply Manag. **25**(5), 100572 (2019)

23. Tripathi, S., Gupta, M.: A framework for procurement process re-engineering in Industry 4.0. Bus. Process Manag. J. (2020, ahead-of-print). https://doi.org/10.1108/BPMJ-07-2020-0321

24. Klunder, T., Niklas, J., Steven, M.:. Procurement 4.0: how the digital disruption supports cost-reduction in Procurement. Production **29** (2019). https://doi.org/10.1590/0103-6513.201 80104

25. Pomerleau, D.: Neural Network Perception for Mobile Robot Guidance, p. 239. Springer, Heidelberg, Volume (2012)

26. Ciula, G., D'Amico, A., Brano, V.L., Traverso, M.: Application of an optimized artificial intelligence algorithm to assess the heating energy demand of non-residential buildings at a European level. Energy **176**, 380–391 (2019)

27. Park, H., Stoel, L.: A model of socially responsible purchasing/supply decision-making processes. Int. J. Retail Distrib. Manag. **33**(4), 235–248 (2005)

28. Singh, A., Kumari, S., Malekpour, H., Mishra, N.: Big data cloud computing framework for selecting low carbon suppliers in the supply chain beef supply. J. Clean. Product **202**, 139–149 (2018)

29. Meehan, J., Bryd, D.: Sustainable procurement practice. Bus. Strat. Environ. **20**, 94–106 (2011). https://doi.org/10.1002/bse.678

30. Brammer, S., Walker, H.: Sustainable procurement in the public sector: an international comparative study. Int. J. Oper. Prod. Manag. **31**(4), 452–476 (2011)

31. Schmidt, R., Möhring, M., Härting, R.-C., Reichstein, C., Neumaier, P., Jozinović, P.: Industry 4.0 - potentials for creating smart products: empirical research results. In: Abramowicz, W. (ed.) BIS 2015. LNBIP, vol. 208, pp. 16–27. Springer, Cham (2015). https://doi.org/10.1007/978-3-319-19027-3_2

32. Babiceanu, R.F., Seker, R.: Big data and virtualization for the fabrication of cyber-physical systems: a survey of current status and future perspectives. Comput. Ind. **81**, 128–137 (2016)

33. Fatorachian, H., Kazemi, H.: Impact of Industry 4.0 on supply chain performance. Product Plann. Control **32**, 63–81 (2021)

34. Côrtes, P.L.: The importance of the grey literature available on the internet for the areas of accounting and business administration. Braz. J. Bus. Manag. **8**(20), 13–22 (2006). Álvares Penteado School of Commerce Foundation São Paulo, Brazil

Introducing a Fast Lane to Multi-Project Environments in Factories to Focus on Digital Transformation

Justin Hook[1(✉)], Lars Nielsen[2], and Peter Nyhuis[1]

[1] Institute of Production Systems and Logistics, Leibniz University Hannover, 30823 Garbsen, Germany
hook@ifa.uni-hannover.de
[2] Bahlsen GmbH & Co. KG, Hanover, Germany

Abstract. In today's highly dynamic and volatile market, the need for change increases steadily in companies induced by megatrends like globalisation or digitalisation. To keep up with current developments and to meet ever higher customer demands ensuring their satisfaction many companies initiate a digital transformation process. Digital Transformation (DT) processes might change products, processes or entire business models in an organisation, to ensure staying competitive. For realising constant adaptation and change, companies are forced to initiate projects in their factories on a regular basis. Multi-project management (MPM) models are used to plan and control projects efficiently. In this article, digital transformation projects are described, an approach for multi-project planning and control (MPPC) in the factory is presented and a way of categorising projects is shown. By combining knowledge from those segments, a fast lane for MPPC is introduced that enables companies to standardise certain tasks in project management to focus on disruptive digital transformation projects.

Keywords: Multi-project management · Fast lane · Factory planning

1 Introduction

Manufacturing companies are confronted with a constant need for change, which is progressing at an increasingly rapid pace in times of globalisation. This development is reflected in ever shorter product life cycles [1]. In a market, characterised by growing competition and correspondingly higher expectations and requirements, products have to be developed, manufactured and marketed in a shorter time by initiating projects [2]. Megatrends such as digitalisation or urbanisation reinforce the changes that need to be continuously mastered [3]. Digitalisation is not only considered a megatrend but can be also seen as a chance for improving efficiency in internal organisational processes, or for creating opportunities like developing new services to customers [4].

Transforming a company's products, processes or the entire business model regarding their level of digitalisation has become such a major movement that the term digital

© IFIP International Federation for Information Processing 2022
Published by Springer Nature Switzerland AG 2022
D. Y. Kim et al. (Eds.): APMS 2022, IFIP AICT 664, pp. 157–164, 2022.
https://doi.org/10.1007/978-3-031-16411-8_20

transformation is commonly used. The basic prerequisite for a successful digital transformation (DT) of a company is a corresponding digitalisation strategy. In addition, the processes, products and business models must be developed digitally and the transformational skills to initiate the change processes in the company must exist [5]. Change processes usually derive from adaptation needs, which are primarily realised through projects in factories [6–8]. Implementing digital capacities to enable a transformation process of the business model is usually part of a DT project or programme. Throughout the entire organisation existing habits and modes of operation may be questioned regarding processes and resources as well as employees and customers [9].

A project describes an "initiative that is essentially characterised by the uniqueness of the conditions in their entirety" [10]. As examples of such conditions, DIN 69901–5 mentions objectives, limitations, e.g. in terms of time, finances or personnel, the possibility of differentiation from other projects and a project-specific organisation [10]. An increasing project orientation results in a highly complex and dynamic project landscape. Project management at individual project level cannot sufficiently guarantee the application of strategies especially because of interdependencies between projects regarding resources, technical intermediate results and others. A complementary multi-project management (MPM) is needed that enables companies to systematically design and steer the project landscape in line with the strategy [6]. To ensure a company has the capacities needed for major change initiatives like the digital transformation, projects of less disruptive character should be managed as efficiently as possible allowing to focus on the digital transformation. Being able to determine projects of less innovative character gives the chance of standardising certain steps in their planning and control. A concept for this procedure is introduced in this paper, referred to as a fast lane. A fast lane leaves more resources in project management and enables companies to focus on pioneer projects. Pioneer projects can relate to a wide range of topics but definitely include digital transformation. The following chapters give insight to digital transformation projects, planning and controlling of multi-project environments and project categorisation to then propose a fast lane for multi-project environments dealing with projects with high standardisation potential.

2 Need for Research

The following chapter aims at giving a short introduction to the characteristics of digital transformation projects and project management in general. It is then explained why a new approach to implementing digital transformation projects into existing multi-project management approaches is needed.

2.1 Digital Transformation Projects and Programmes

Anshin and Bobyleva describe digital transformation as a logical and content wise adjustment of processes [11]. The underlying strategies of a DT process must be in accordance to other strategies already implemented in a company. The demand for a high level of coordination also comes from digital transformation being a cross functional topic regarding several if not all areas of a company [11, 12]. Digital transformation must therefore be approached following established rules for implementing new projects taking into account their potential for being integrated into programmes [11]. Matt et al. state that research must provide guidelines for structuring processes enabling companies to align their strategies, set their goals accordingly and manage collaboration throughout the organisation [12]. This collaboration is managed in projects to enable the desired changes in the organisation.

In project management, the term programme stands for the "parallel and sequential networking of individual projects and tasks that in their entirety implement a strategic corporate goal" [2]. A programme can contain part of the entirety of projects or all of them [13]. Implementing a suitable programme organisation serves the purpose of reaching the superordinate target effectively and as efficiently as possible. The foundation of realising such target is set by the outcome of the individual projects [14]. A DT process should therefore be implemented as a programme in order to manage several individual projects with their clearly defined scopes aligned to the direction of objectives formulated in a programme. An adjustment of programmes is sometimes necessary after the first definition, as usually not all measures and individual projects are defined at the same time. This inaccuracy can be counteracted by initiating new projects or tasks [2]. The focus of a DT project can lie on implementing different technologies, e.g. cyber-physical systems, automated robotics, Big Data analytics, and cloud computing [15]. Gertzen et al. state that DT projects aim for changing a company's identity, develop a new business strategy or even restructure the whole idea of value creation [16].

2.2 Planning and Controlling Multi-Project Environments in Factories

Managing multi-project environments is a topic not only relevant for factories but all kinds of companies and business units. Approaches to MPM have therefore been around for a long time. Examples include Seidl or DIN 69909–2 [17, 18]. Managing projects is a process that can be divided into the project management phases 'Initialisation', 'Definition', 'Planning', 'Control' and 'Closure' [19]. The tasks in multi-project management are usually clearly assigned to such phases and are linked semantically. While regarding a factory setting the management of multi-project environments can still be described and managed through models like the above mentioned, special requirements and targets demanded by production environments and their factories are not considered. Previous approaches lacked decision making support regarding the possibility of a conflict of objectives. At the Institute of Production Systems and Logistics (IFA) the combination of insights from the fields of production planning and control (PPC) and MPM has been investigated [20, 21]. This approach enables the development of a concept of multi-project planning and control (MPPC) with a focus on factories, which offers a holistic view of relevant tasks and links them via interrelationships [20, 21]. Task profiles are part of the MPPC model and have already been created [20] Currently interrelationships of the model in terms of target fulfilment are being investigated. The main tasks of MPPC are generate project proposal, release project proposals, define project, define portfolio, determine project structure and make or buy shares, plan and assign make or buy shares, appoint project, control and monitor project, control and monitor programme and portfolio, close project [21]. These main tasks are to be taken step after step following the project management phases. The measures and activities that shall be implemented over the course of a change process in order to achieve the desired change are described as the project design [22]. A suitable project design can help to relieve the workload on organisations. Regarding digital transformation, this represents a great opportunity, as these projects require a great share of attention in the company due to their enormous importance for its success. If intelligent project design is used to reduce the workload in the organisation, more resources are left for the crucial DT projects. Standardised procedural models can help to define the processes, phases, tasks and roles in projects more quickly and with less use of resources by exchanging experience and knowledge across projects. For the use of standardised process models tailoring may sometimes be necessary, which describes the adaptation and individualisation of process models and their elements in the form of additions, changes or reductions. In some cases, process models can also be used without tailoring [22]. An important factor regarding project design and the degree of standardisation is the type of project [22]. It is therefore necessary to categorise the projects.

2.3 Project Categorisation

Projects can be categorised according to various criteria. A differentiation according to the type of project makes it possible to use commonalities in the sense of efficient project management [2]. Patzak and Rattay mention the project content, the client position or the degree of repetition as classification criteria [2]. In addition to this form of classification, there are other criteria to determine the type of project and might also serve as an aid to project organisation. Kuster et al. distinguish between open and closed tasks and high and low complexity [13]. Numerous models can be used to categorise projects accordingly, but they are not fundamentally differentiated according to type of project [23]. Wheelwright and Clark have developed a distinction of project type for development projects, which is based on the changes in processes and products that accompany them [24]. For the context of manufacturing companies and digital transformation this represents an ideal base. The project matrix can be seen in Fig.1.

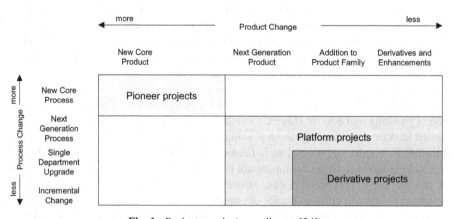

Fig. 1. Project matrix (according to [24])

A distinction is originally made between 'Breakthrough projects', 'Platform projects' and 'Derivative projects' with decreasing intensity of change [24]. Projects called 'breakthrough projects' use or generate revolutionary and new technologies [24]. For the purpose of this work, regarding the whole factory environment and especially digital transformation as a continuous process, the term 'pioneer project' is introduced as the category with the highest degree of change instead. This includes all projects that have no usable analogies or similarities to past or current projects.

3   Introducing a Fast Lane to MPPC

Similarities between project contents can influence the design and scope of individual project management tasks. The platform concept from production can be mentioned here as an analogy. In vehicle construction, this method was developed to build different types of vehicles on the same platform and thus to use synergies [1]. Transferred to projects, a platform concept reveals potentials for the standardisation of documents and processes, e.g. in the determination of project requirements or the development of project structures. These documents and processes are summarised in the following under the term standardised process models. For a project platform concept, referred to as a fast lane in the context of this paper, the project differentiation after Wheelwright and Clark offers a suitable starting point [24]. Figure 2 shows the three project types and their potentials along the project management phases in terms of a fast lane.

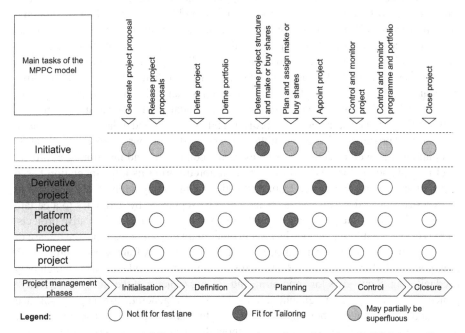

Fig. 2. Fast lane potential of different project types along the main tasks of MPPC (according to [21, 24])

Including a task in the fast lane does not mean that it is completely autonomous or standardised. Instead, synergies with similar projects might increase efficiency through standardised process models or template use [2]. Templates provide guidelines for realisation or set necessary framework conditions and come from the database of a holistic knowledge management. Templates are not meant to solely copy past project data. For this paper a distinction is made between two degrees of standardisation. The first degree is projects being able to use standardised process models after being tailored. Templates might be used in a modified way, standardised process models might be slightly reduced or added to. The second kind of project is able to make use of standardised process models without the need for tailoring. This requires greater similarities to other projects. The term 'fit for fast lane' sums up the potential use of standardised process models either with or without the need for tailoring in the sense of the fast lane so projects can generate an increase in efficiency at a certain main task of MPPC. The term initiative serves to clarify that a complete use of standardised process models does not lead to an ideal fast lane, but instead prevents a classification as a project. This fact can be attributed to the unique character of a project (see Sect. 1). If an initiative can be supported in every aspect with templates, this contradicts the definition of a project. The pioneer project cannot be supported in any of the main tasks through the use of standardised process models. This means that highly innovative projects like those pursuing digital transformation cannot be managed using a fast lane. The benefit of the fast lane for those projects lies in designing less innovative projects in such a way that resources and capacities can be concentrated on digital transformation. An example of a pioneer project is the development of an application for integrating big data from different sources within the company, since technical problems are still often encountered in such process [15]. Platform projects have potential for standardisation in the tasks generate project proposal', 'define project', determine project structure and make or buy shares' plan and assign make or buy shares' as well as 'control and monitor project'. All of these tasks are fit for fast lane with the constraint that tailoring is needed first. An example of a platform project is the execution of an audit. As an essential part of any internal quality management, audits can be standardised to a certain extent [25]. Still, audits are to be characterised as projects and do not fall under day-to-day business. Standardised process models and templates can be used at various points of initialisation and planning, as well as control. As an example, controlling and monitoring at project level is explained below. An audit can be monitored during its implementation based on existing data and experience from past audits by including templates. Compared to platform concepts, derivative projects may also be supported by templates to a certain degree. While all of the potentials of platform projects also exist for derivative projects, there is even potential for standardisation in other main tasks. For example the release of project proposals might be standardised to a certain degree. A framework contract with a supplier could for example set the base for cooperation in similar projects which only need tailoring. Same goes for appointing and closing projects of the category derivative project. There is also greater potential in the main tasks 'generate project proposal' and 'plan and assign make or buy shares' compared to platform projects. These tasks may have the potential of being standardised without the need for tailoring regarding derivative projects. An example is the setup of a new machine in production where a high number of identical or similar machines have already been installed. That experience can be expected to support generating the project proposal and assigning make or buy shares to commission a contractor. The chosen examples show how much the fitness for fast lane increases from pioneer projects over platform projects to derivative projects. Depending on the level of innovativeness projects might not be fit for fast lane, fit for tailoring or might even be partially superfluous. Minimising the capacities for setting up a machine or executing an audit could therefore improve the situation for the pioneer project on big data by releasing more staff capacity.

4 Conclusion and Outlook

In the last chapters of this paper it could be shown that MPPC offers a chance of supporting the digital transformation in organisations. Since projects dealing with digital transformation are usually highly innovative and complex, a high degree of attention, focus and resources is needed. Due to these high requirements for the organisation, every action that enables project management to focus more on such projects should be taken. Defining project types with regard to their innovativeness allows for a distinction between pioneer projects, platform projects and derivative projects. Based on this categorisation the project design can be chosen, giving options to include standardised process models along the project management phases to enable projects for a so called fast lane. In future research criteria for defining project types could be established and further investigation regarding the impact on resources and capacities resulting from implementing a fast lane could be carried out.

Acknowledgements. The authors kindly thank the German Research Foundation (DFG) for the financial support to accomplish the research project "Entwicklung eines Prozessmodells der Multiprojektplanung und-steuerung in der Fabrik (MPPS-Fabrik)" (project number NY 4/72–1).

References

1. Wiendahl, H.-P., Reichardt, J., Nyhuis, P.: Handbuch Fabrikplanung: Konzept, Gestaltung und Umsetzung wandlungsfähiger Produktionsstätten, 2., überarb. und erw. Aufl. ed. Carl Hanser Verlag, München Wien, pp. 35469 (2014)
2. Patzak, G., Rattay, G.: Projektmanagement: Projekte, Projektportfolios, Programme und projektorientierte Unternehmen, 7, aktualisierte, Auflage, p. 791. Linde Verlag Ges.m.b.H, Wien (2018)
3. Hingst, L., Wecken, L., Brunotte, E., Nyhuis, P.: Einordnung der Robustheit und Resilienz in die Veränderungsfähigkeit (2022)
4. Parviainen, P., Tihinen, M., Kääriäinen, J., Teppola, S.: Tackling the digitalization challenge: how to benefit from digitalization in practice. IJISPM 5(1), 63–77 (2017)
5. Obermaier, R.: Handbuch Industrie 4.0 und Digitale Transformation. Springer, Wiesbaden (2019). https://doi.org/10.1007/978-3-658-24576-4
6. Aurich, J.C., Barbian, P., Naab, C.: Multiprojektmanagement in der projektorientierten Produktion: Gestaltung und Lenkung der Projektlandschaft in der Produktion. wt Werkstattstechnik online 95 (1/2), 19–24 (2005)

7. VDI: Fabrikplanung Planungsvorgehen. Beuth Verlag, Berlin (2011)
8. Wiendahl, H.-P.: Betriebsorganisation für Ingenieure. Carl Hanser Verlag GmbH & Co, KG, München (2019)
9. Henriette, E., Feki, M., Boughzala, I.: The shape of digital transformation: a systematic literature review
10. Bierhoff, H.-W., et al.: Begriffe. In: Bohlken, E., Thies, C. (eds.) Handbuch Anthropologie, pp. 283–445. J.B. Metzler, Stuttgart (2009). https://doi.org/10.1007/978-3-476-05218-6_4
11. Anshin, V., Bobyleva, A.: The digital transformation program management in medium-sized businesses: a network approach. Serb J Management **16**(1), 147–159 (2021)
12. Matt, C., Hess, T., Benlian, A.: Digital transformation strategies. Bus. Inf. Syst. Eng. **57**(5), 339–343 (2015). https://doi.org/10.1007/s12599-015-0401-5
13. Kuster, J., et al.: Handbuch Projektmanagement, 3, Auflage, p. 460. Springer-Verlag, Berlin Heidelberg, Heidelberg, Dordrecht, London, New York (2011)
14. Rhodius, O., Lofing, J.: Grundlagen. In: Kapitalertragsteuer Und Abgeltungsteuer Verstehen, pp. 17–40. Springer, Wiesbaden (2013). https://doi.org/10.1007/978-3-658-00404-0_1
15. Xu, L.D., Xu, E.L., Li, L.: Industry 4.0: state of the art and future trends. Int. J. Prod. Res. **56**(8), 2941–2962 (2018)
16. Gertzen, W.M., van der Lingen, E., Steyn, H.: Goals and benefits of digital transformation projects: Insights into project selection criteria. SAJEMS 25(1) (2022)
17. DIN: Multiprojektmanagement–Management von Projektportfolios, Programmen und Projekten-Teil 2: Prozesse. Beuth Verlag, Berlin, Prozessmodell (2013)
18. Seidl, J.: Multiprojektmanagement: Übergreifende Steuerung von Mehrprojektsituationen durch Projektportfolio- und Programmmanagement. Springer-Verlag, Berlin, Heidelberg (2011)
19. DIN: Projektmanagement–Projektmanagementsysteme-Teil 2: Prozesse. Beuth Verlag, Berlin, Prozessmodell (2009)
20. Hook, J., Nielsen, L., Nyhuis, P.: Introduction of a concept for planning and controlling multi-project environments in factories (2021)
21. Nielsen, L.: Prozessmodell für Multiprojektmanagement in der Fabrik. Dissertation, pp. 231 (2020)
22. G.D.G.f.P.e.M., V.: Kompetenzbasiertes Projektmanagement (PM4): Handbuch für Praxis und Weiterbildung im Projektmanagement, 1st edn., p. 11701. Buch & media, München (2019)
23. Kunz, C.: Strategisches Multiprojektmanagement: Konzeption, Methoden und Strukturen, 2nd edn., p. 312. Deutscher Universitäts-Verlag GWV Fachverlage GmbH, Wiesbaden (2007)
24. Wheelwright, S., Clark, K.: Creating project plans to focus product development. Harvard Business Review, pp. 1–14 (2003)
25. Foster, S.T.: Managing Quality: Integrating the Supply Chain, 5th ed. ed. Pearson, Boston, xxiv, p. 453 (2013)

Business Process Digitalization Tracking and Monitoring: An Heuristic Software-Based Approach

Selver Softic[1(✉)] ⓘ, Daniel Resanovic[1], and Egon Lüftenegger[2] ⓘ

[1] CAMPUS 02 University of Applied Sciences, Graz, Austria
{selver.softic,daniel.resanovic}@campus02.at
[2] Salzburg University of Applied Sciences, Salzburg, Austria
egon.lueftenegger@fh-salzburg.ac.at

Abstract. In this paper, we introduce a software-based heuristic approach for scoring the grade of digitalization for business processes modeled in BPMN: The DigiTrack tool. Our tool enables the measurement of the digitalization maturity of a business process by calculating scores for each task. This new method is shown though a case study with a simplified check in process at airport.

Keywords: Heuristic model · Digitalization · BPMN

1 Motivation and Introduction

The importance of digitization has just become apparent in the current COVID crisis. Conventional business models of companies were suddenly difficult or even impossible to implement in many industries - the internal organization also had to react flexibly. Companies that successfully master the digital transformation of business processes are twice as successful as laggards. This shows that companies without digital business models have lost customers and were hit harder by the crisis [1].

The world we live in is changing faster than ever. Some technologies and trends are already outdated before they can establish themselves on the market. Digitization in particular has further strengthened this trend - the circulation speed in our economy and in social coexistence has increased dramatically. With all the adjustment needs associated with the digital transformation, the opportunities and potential of new technologies are enormous. At the same time, customers are putting more pressure on companies to push ahead with digitalization. Customers already expect mature digital offers from companies.

Therefore there is a gap for approaches to track and monitor the digitalization level of companies down to the business process level.

© IFIP International Federation for Information Processing 2022
Published by Springer Nature Switzerland AG 2022
D. Y. Kim et al. (Eds.): APMS 2022, IFIP AICT 664, pp. 165–170, 2022.
https://doi.org/10.1007/978-3-031-16411-8_21

2 Related Work

In this section we will elaborate some important definition, standards, aspects and works that help us address the problem of tracking the level of digitalization in the approach we are proposing in this paper.

2.1 Digitization, Digitalization and Digital Transformation

Digitization involves converting information from a physical format (analogue) to a digital one. This very often leads to digitization being perceived as digitalization, which results in a false perception of one's own degree of digitalization.

In digitalization, digitization is used to improve business processes. In its simplest form, this is a digital image of the analog processes. However, that should not be the ultimate goal.

Finally, the digital transformation is the transformation of business activities, processes, products and models in order to fully exploit the opportunities of digital technologies (change management). Digital transformation is more about people than digital technology.

2.2 Business Process Modeling

The overall goal of Business Process Modeling is to establish a common perspective and understanding for a business process within an enterprise between the relevant stakeholders involved. Hereby, the most common graphical representation such as flowchart [2] or similar serves as base to show the process steps and workflows. This approach is widely used to recognize and prevent potential weaknesses and implement improvements in companies processes as well as to offer a good base for comprehensive understanding of a processes in general.

2.3 BPMN

The BPMN 2.0[1] is a new standard for business process specification developed by a variety of Business Process Modeling (BPM) tool vendors. This standard is one of the most important forms of representing business process models, offering clear and simple semantics to describe the business process of a business [3,4]. This language was developed with the intention of modeling typical business modeling activities [5,6].

2.4 BPM Lifecycle

BPM lifecycle described in [7] represents different phases of the process beginning by analysis and ending by process monitoring and controlling and process discovery. Our usage scenario in this lifecycle is placed in process monitoring part.

---

[1] https://www.omg.org/bpmn/.

3   Tracking Digitalization Level in a Business Process

Tracking and measuring business processes have been implemented in [8,9]. However, these approaches do not cover digitalization maturity aproaches.

As possible heuristic approach to track the digitalization in business processes we defined a set of metrics and maturity levels that will be assigned to the BPMN models of these processes.

3.1   Metrics and Maturity Levels

The metrics we are using to calculate the **digitalization level score** (DLS) expressed in percent and reflected through maturity levels: explorer, beginner, advanced, expert; considers three main aspects:

– **Digital Tool Existence (DTE)** - whether the task is operated manually or with tool (either 0 or 1)
– **Digital Tool Integration Level (DTIL)** - how far is the digitization tool integrated for specific task regarding precending and ascending tasks, with possible values: 1 (no integration) - 5 (full integration)
– **Data Automation Grade (DAG)** - telling us how far the data processing for current task is automated, as scale with possible values: 1 (no automation/manual), 5 (fully automated data processing)

All the aspects are related into following formula

$$DLS = (DTE * (DTIL + DAG)/10) * 100 \tag{1}$$

In order to distinguish the maturity level of the digitalization for a certain BPMN modeled process we also defined intervals for overall DLS.

Overall DLS of a Process in a BPMN diagram is calculated average of task-wise DLS.

– 0% - 25% - Explorer
– 26% - 50% - Beginner
– 51% - 75% - Advanced
– 76% - 100% - Expert

3.2   Application Use Case

As use case we introduce an experimental desktop tool called DigiTrack developed by our institution(s) which allows us to manage, search and tag the BPMN modeled processes. Application based approach has been also approved in other phases of Business-Process Lifecycle as well e.g. by analysis and redesign [10].

Operating BPMN Files. At the current state of implementation the Digi-Track tool allows import of an BPMN file (accepted format: *.bpmn) into local repository (see Fig. 1), search for processes using name of processes, name of tasks and wildcards and loading into main view for labeling the process steps with task-wise DLS scores.

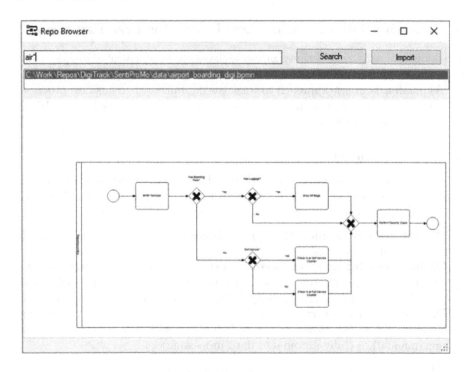

Fig. 1. BPMN process repository.

Entering DLS for Process Tasks. After the project is loaded from repository the tool allows entering and editing the DLS over separate user interface. Currently the calculation of DLS happens manually and only the final score is entered. In the future we will support entering the metrics over the same window. Additionally the name of the tool can be specified. This process is depicted in Fig. 2 where a calculated value for DLS expressed in percent is entered for the task "Check-in at Self Service Counter" in the Airport Boarding process.

Presenting Digitalisation Level Score. Depending what is the average DLS value and to which maturity interval it belongs the value is depicted as chart in red (Explorer), yellow (Beginner), orange or green (Expert) color (see Fig. 3). This chart is placed in the lower left corner of the DigiTrack application.

4   Discussion and Outlook

Within this paper we introduced a small use case based upon an application called DigiTrack and a heuristic approach including corresponding metrics such as Digital Tool Existence (DTE), Digital Tool Integration Level (DTIL) and Data Automation Grade (DAG) for calculating the digitalization level score (DLS) task-wise in a BPMN presentation of a business process. We also presented

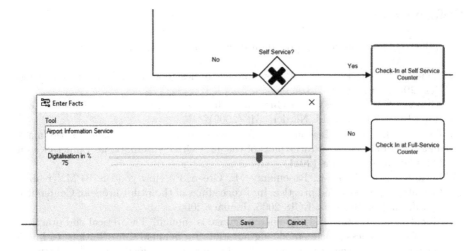

Fig. 2. Entering calculated DLS for a single task.

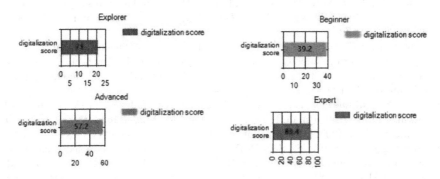

Fig. 3. Average DLS over all tasks in process with maturity level coloring. (Color figure online)

how calculated average DLS is assigned to the one of four digital maturity levels we defined. First results are showing the potential on how simple ideas can allow us to rise the awareness of digitalization at process and task level in an very universal manner. As next steps in the future we are planning to implement the selection of calculation metrics within the user interface and further analytic charts for better monitoring. We will also integrate and adapt already existing digital maturity levels to our approach to check whether they can offer better overview and tracking of digitalization. Also as one of the potential application scenarios of our heuristic approach along with DigiTrack tool would be testing different digitalization strategies with different tools.

References

1. Holger, S.: So verändert sich die digitale wirtschaft durch corona. Handelsblatt, 15 May 2020
2. Wynn, D.C., Clarkson, P.J.: Process models in design and development. Res. Eng. Des. **29**(2), 161–202 (2018)
3. Allweyer, T.: BPMN 2.0: Introduction to the Standard for Business Process Modeling. Books on Demand, Norderstedt (2009)
4. Zor, S., Schumm, D., Leymann, F.: A proposal of BPMN extensions for the manufacturing domain. In: Proceedings of the 44th CIRP International Conference on Manufacturing Systems (2011)
5. Recker, J., Indulska, M., Rosemann, M., Green, P.: How good is BPMN really? Insights from theory and practice. In: Proceedings of the 14th European Conference on Information Systems, ECIS 2006, January 2006
6. Muehlen, M., Recker, J.: How much language is enough? Theoretical and practical use of the business process modeling notation. In: Seminal Contributions to Information Systems Engineering, pp. 429–443. Springer, Heidelberg (2013). https://doi.org/10.1007/978-3-642-36926-1_35
7. Dumas, M., Rosa, M.L., Mendling, J., Reijers, H.A.: Fundamentals of Business Process Management. Springer, Berlin, Heidelberg (2018). https://doi.org/10.1007/978-3-662-56509-4
8. Lüftenegger, E., Softic, S., Hatzl, S., Pergler, E.: A management tool for business process performance tracking in smart production. In: Dachselt, R., Weber, G. (eds.) Mensch und Computer 2018 - Workshopband, Bonn, Gesellschaft für Informatik e.V. (2018)
9. Softic, S., Lüftenegger, E., Turcin, I.: Tracking and analyzing processes in smart production. In: Al-Turjman, F. (ed.) Trends in Cloud-based IoT. EICC, pp. 37–50. Springer, Cham (2020). https://doi.org/10.1007/978-3-030-40037-8_3
10. Lüftenegger, E., Softic, S.: SentiProMo: a sentiment analysis-enabled social business process modeling tool. In: Del Río Ortega, A., Leopold, H., Santoro, F.M. (eds.) BPM 2020. LNBIP, vol. 397, pp. 83–89. Springer, Cham (2020). https://doi.org/10.1007/978-3-030-66498-5_7

Crowdsourced Sentiment-Driven Process Re-design with SentiProMoWeb: Towards Enterprise Social Information Systems

Egon Lüftenegger[1]([⊠]) [iD] and Selver Softic[2] [iD]

[1] Salzburg University of Applied Sciences, Salzburg, Austria
egon.lueftenegger@fh-salzburg.ac.at
[2] CAMPUS 02 University of Applied Sciences, Graz, Austria
selver.softic@campus02.at

Abstract. Due to the new remote working conditions driven by the consequences of the Covid-19 pandemic, we extend our previous work on sentiment-enabled business process modeling by including crowdsourcing capabilities with a web interface: SentiProMoWeb. These capabilities enable us to perform sentiment-driven business process re-design method with remote stakeholders from different locations. SentiProMoWeb implements an enterprise social information system to capture the feedback from stakeholders in a crowdsourced manner. We demonstrate the crowdsourcing capabilities of our approach with an illustrative scenario by using our SentiProMoWeb software.

Keywords: Social information systems · Business process re-design · Crowdsourcing

1 Introduction

Social information systems (IS) are different from traditional business information systems. Social IS shifts the core system function from work support to online social interaction (e.g., the system allows commenting and similar feedback mechanisms) or open collaboration (i.e., the number of contributors or participants in the system is not predefined). Hence, we can reach a significant amount of feedback and comments from social interactions into a Social IS.

Firms increasingly use open and social processes for their value-creation activities and communication between users (consumers) and employees. One key area of social information systems research focuses on using Social IS within the firm. Industry often labels these supporting social technologies as social enterprise software or enterprise 2.0. Firms embracing social technologies for internal use are constantly increasing. Due to the social distancing measures triggered by the Covid-19 pandemic, social interaction through technology has become key in performing daily work within companies. Social software such as Slack and Microsoft teams are driving social interactions in companies. In today's working environment, driven by the increase of remote working at home, the

D. Y. Kim et al. (Eds.): APMS 2022, IFIP AICT 664, pp. 171–178, 2022.
https://doi.org/10.1007/978-3-031-16411-8_22

adoption of such social applications is expanding from start-ups worldwide to traditional companies such as airlines [1].

One area that combines social IS with business process management is social BPM, which combines social IS concepts with BPM. Embracing and modifying business processes is crucial for companies to cope with growing competition and customer expectations in a digital-driven business landscape [2]. Many methods and techniques support the systematic redesign of processes defined as a logical sequence of steps [3]. However, it often happens in a black box because creating to-be process designs primarily results from a creative process [4]. In particular, the discussion on business process redesign has shifted from physical to remote work. Hence, we need methods and tools for performing business process redesign initiatives in the home office. This paper presents a software-supported method to assist business process analysts in performing business process redesign initiatives. In this research paper, we extend the current capabilities of our sentiment-enabled business process modeling (SentiProMo) software to capture the voice of users regarding a business process task following social information systems aspects: SentiProMoWeb.

The structure of this paper is as follows: First, in Sect. 2, we present the result of following the aspects of social information systems in our sentiment-driven business process modeling approach. Next, Sect. 3 presents our crowdsourced sentiment-driven business process re-redesign method with a running example within SentiPro-MoWeb. Finally, we end this paper with discussions and the next steps.

2   Social Information System and Crowdsourced Business Process Re-design

Due to social distancing, we encounter home-working issues during our preliminary tests with Senti-ProMo as a desktop software tool with an airline company. As a requirement, we need to obtain the crowdsourced customer feedback in a contactless manner for redesigning customer-focused airline processes. Furthermore, social BPM scholars identify the enhancement of business processes with annotations from different sources as a relevant problem to solve [5]. By following design science research [10], we formulate the following research question: How to conduct sentiment-driven business process redesign in home-office during the Covid-19 pan-demic with social information systems? In our previous work, we presented SeniProMo as a tool for business process redesign to assist business process analysts. Senti-ProMo uses the stakeholders' comments on a business process task to guide the analyst in the business process redesign with positive and negative aspects. A business analyst can use the negative aspects to improve a business process. However, due to the limitations driven by working at home, we need to adopt the guidelines of a social information system for capturing stakeholders' feedback through crowdsourcing [6]. In this work, we aim to solve our research question by adopting the unique features of social information systems such as sociality, openness, contributions, content, technology, and location [7]. We explain each term briefly and how we apply it to our approach as follows:

Sociality. The sociality aspect of Social IS focuses on information exchange rather than solely on information processing. The system is open to a broad range of participants/contributors: The crowd. Usually, the decision to participate is voluntary. This aspect of traditional IS represents a shift from solely focusing on information processing to communication and information exchange. Hence, we embrace this aspect as an easy mechanism to capture stakeholders' opinions.

Openness. This aspect of Social IS focuses on including many users that can contribute voluntarily. Enterprise social information systems limit their access to the firm's stakeholders rather than publicly open to anyone. However, it should be open enough to let different stakeholders participate inclusively and voluntarily. Concerning traditional IS, this aspect represents a shift from limited and mandatory use toward an inclusive and voluntary contribution. In our approach, we implement this feature with a web commenting user interface that is available to all users related to the business processes. We enabled the access as a web link generated by the business analyst. The business analysist could share this link within social enterprise tools such as Slack and Microsoft Teams (See Fig. 1).

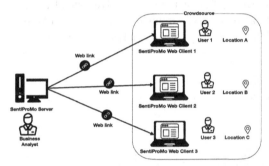

Fig. 1. In SeniProMo, the business analysist can reach users' opinions from different location with a web link that opens a web form for inserting comments regarding a business process.

Contributions. This aspect calls for various forms of user co-creation to emerge on the Internet, effectively constituting a new production method. In our approach, the users make comments as a Crowd-sourcing mechanism for gathering comments (See Fig. 2).

Content. The content aspect aims to facilitate user-created content as a co-production mechanism with the contributors. Concerning traditional IS, this aspect represents a shift from professionally created content to user-generated content. In our approach, we transform the user-generated opinions into a positive and negative sentiment that guides the business analyst into the business process re-design. The content as options is crowdsourced and then transformed into positive and negative feedback with our tool.

Technology. Social computing tools are the technology core of social information systems. The technology aspect aims to include social technologies such as wikis, social

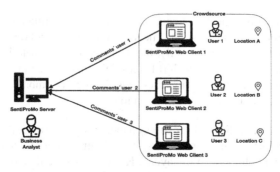

Fig. 2. In our approach, the users contribute with comments as content.

networking sites, collaboration platforms, blogs, and similar social (media) tools. Concerning traditional IS, this aspect represents a shift from complex software to lightweight tools [8]. Our focus relies on enabling crowdsourcing capabilities for conducting remote business process re-design sessions asynchronous rather than physical and synchronic. These capabilities enable the business analyst to perform process re-design initiatives in remote locations with different time zones. We extend our previous SentiProMo architecture [6] into a client-server architecture by adding a Web layer that consumes SenitProMo's modules, such as sentiment analysis as web services.

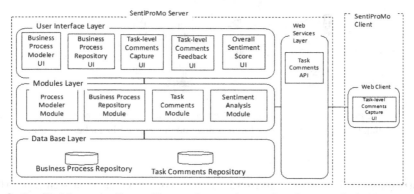

Fig. 3. SentiProMo server-client architecture for crowdsourced sentiment-analysis driven process redesign.

In Fig. 3, we present the architecture of SentiPromo as an enterprise social IS. As the first step, we modified SentiProMo's architecture into a client and server by adding a Web services layer that acts as a bridge between the modules and software clients.

This software extends our previous work by bringing a service interface for connecting to remote applications such as web applications. In this way, we are extending sentiment-analysis-driven process redesign from an isolated software tool and a method to a crowdsourcing tool that enables to co-creation of process improvement among different stakeholders.

Location. Usually, social information systems are online Web-based systems hosted as a server with Web browser access. Concerning traditional IS, this aspect represents a shift from offline and local IS towards online and networked IS [8]. In our approach, we reach stakeholders not present in a single physical space by using a server with Web browser access to crowdsourcing users to capture their feedback on the business process.

3 Using Crowdsourced Business Process Re-design with SentiProMo: Use Case and Method

An airline company wanted to test its check-in process's workflow, as presented in Fig. 4. Due to the home-office constraints, the company shifted its workforce from the physical workplace to the home office. Moreover, getting feedback face-to-face from customers during the Covid-19 pandemic presents a risk. Resulting in a change to test remote crowdsourced feedback with our sentiment-driven business process re-design approach. We present the steps of the crowdsourced sentiment-driven process re-design method with our web-enabled SentiProMo software by using the check-in process running example as follows:

1. First, the business analyst designs the as-is process within SentiProMoWeb to be re-designed. For instance, in Fig. 5, we present the check-in process from our case study.

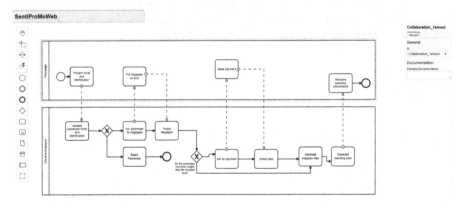

Fig. 4. Check-in process at the airport with the airline employee

2. The business analyst selects the process to be redesigned and submits web links to the involved stakeholders for crowdsourcing of comments.
3. The stakeholders comment on the business process tasks within the business process with SentiPromoWeb. In this way, we can share the link with many customers to capture feedback for business process re-design. The resulting web interface captures comments at the task level for a defined swim lane (See Fig. 2.)

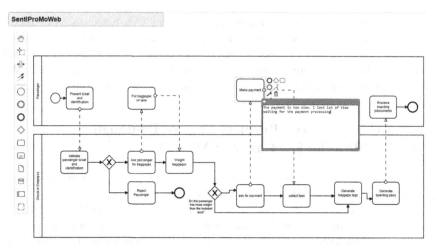

Fig. 5. SentiProMoWeb offers access to business process stakeholders to capture their comments on the business process tasks

4. SentiProMoWeb performs comment analysis to calculate the sentient of each comment (For more profound information on how we implemented and applied the sentiment analysis module, please refer to our previous research work [9, 11, 12]). As shown in Fig. 2, a customer introduced the comment "the payment is too slow. I lost lot of time waiting for the payment processing" into SentiProMoWeb. As shown in Fig. 3, this comment on the is identified as a negative one by the server-side of SentiProMoWeb with a sentiment score of −5,439894.

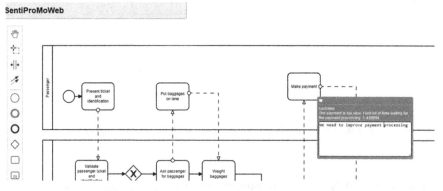

Fig. 6. SentiProMo sentiment-analysis feedback

5. The business analyst performs business process re-design with the crowd's voice as negative or positive aspects of each task. In our case study, reducing the time in payment processing is one aspect to improve.
6. If needed, repeat the process until the business analyst is satisfied with the level of acceptance of the business process with the stakeholders. In our case study, this business process is continuously improving until we reduce the negative sentiments from the business process. Hence, we can constantly improve the business process by monitoring the negative sentiments.

4 Discussion and Next Steps

Our research paper contributes to the advancement of social information systems by presenting a software-supported method for crowdsourced business process re-design with SentiProMoWeb. We developed this approach by following design science research for implementing critical aspects of social information systems regarding sociality, openness, contributions, content, and technology into SentiProMoWeb. The result is a server-client implementation that uses a lightweight Web user interface to reach the crowd's opinion. Our software tool processes the comments into negative and positive ones. In this way, we can assist the business analyst in re-designing the business process's negative aspects by reaching stakeholders in different places and time zones. This time difference is especially important in our case study with the airline company's customers in different countries and regions.

References

1. McAfee, A.P.: How a Connected Workforce Innovates. In: Harvard Business Review. pp. 80–81 (2009)
2. Beverungen, D., et al.: Seven paradoxes of business process management in a hyper-connected world. Bus. Inf. Syst. Eng. 63, 145–156 (2020). https://doi.org/10.1007/s12533-020-00646-z
3. Dumas, M., La Rose, M., Mendling, J., Reijers, H.A.: Fundamentals of Business Process Management. Springer Berlin Heidelberg, Berlin, Heidelberg (2018). https://doi.org/10.1007/978-3-662-56509-4
4. Vanwersch, R.J.B., Vanderfeesten, I., Rietzschel, E., Reijers, H.A.: Improving Business Processes: Does Anybody have an Idea? In: Motahari-Nezhad, H.R., Recker, J., Weidlich, M. (eds.) BPM 2015. LNCS, vol. 9253, pp. 3–18. Springer, Cham (2015). https://doi.org/10.1007/978-3-319-23063-4_1
5. Nurcan, S., Schmidt, R.: Special section of BPMDS'2017: enabling business transformation by business process modeling, development and support. Softw. Syst. Model. 19(3), 529–530 (2019). https://doi.org/10.1007/s10270-019-00771-8
6. Lüftenegger, E., Softic, S.: SentiProMo: A Sentiment Analysis-Enabled Social Business Process Modeling Tool. In: Del Río Ortega, A., Leopold, H., Santoro, F.M. (eds.) BPM 2020. LNBIP, vol. 397, pp. 83–89. Springer, Cham (2020). https://doi.org/10.1007/978-3-030-66498-5_7
7. Schlagwein, D., Schoder, D., Fischbach, K.: Social information systems: review, framework, and research agenda. In: Proceedings of the 32nd International Conference on Information Systems. Shanghai, China (2011)

8. Kaplan, A., Haenlein, M.: Users of the world, unite! the challenges and opportunities of social media. Bus. Horiz. **53**(1), 59–68 (2010)
9. Softic, S., Lüftenegger, E.: Towards Empowering Business Process Redesign with Sentiment Analysis. In: Yang, X.-S., Sherratt, S., Dey, N., Joshi, A. (eds.) Proceedings of Sixth International Congress on Information and Communication Technology. LNNS, vol. 236, pp. 119–126. Springer, Singapore (2022). https://doi.org/10.1007/978-981-16-2380-6_10
10. Peffers, K., Tuunanen, T., Rothenberger, M.A., Chatterjee, S.: A design science research methodology for information systems research. J. Manag. Inf. Syst. **24**(3), 45–77 (2007)
11. Lüftenegger, E., Softic, S.: Supporting Manufacturing Processes Design Using Stakeholder Opinions and Sentiment Analysis. In: Dolgui, A., Bernard, A., Lemoine, D., von Cieminski, G., Romero, D. (eds.) APMS 2021. IAICT, vol. 632, pp. 112–117. Springer, Cham (2021). https://doi.org/10.1007/978-3-030-85906-0_13
12. Softic, S., Lüftenegger, E., Stojic, A.: Collaborative manufacturing process redesign using sentiment analysis. In: Wienrich, C., Wintersberger, P. & Weyers, B. (Hrsg.), Mensch und Computer 2021 - Workshopband. Bonn: Gesellschaft für Informatik e.V. (2021). https://doi.org/10.18420/muc2021-mci-ws04-380

Digital Technologies as an Essential Part of Smart Factories and Their Impact on Productivity

Maja Miloradov[1]([✉]) [ID], Slavko Rakic[1] [ID], Danijela Ciric Lalic[1] [ID],
Milena Savkovic[1] [ID], Selver Softic[2] [ID], and Ugljesa Marjanovic[1] [ID]

[1] Faculty of Technical Sciences, University of Novi Sad, Novi Sad, Serbia
maja.miloradov@uns.ac.rs
[2] IT and Business Informatics, CAMPUS 02 University of Applied Sciences, 8010 Graz, Austria

Abstract. Industry 4.0 has led to the emergence of various digital technologies. To keep pace with the digital transformation, manufacturing companies must adapt to the new conditions imposed by the business market and increasingly strive to implement so-called smart factories. This paper points out the most common digital technologies related to the management of manufacturing systems. In addition to identification, a systematic literature review was conducted to investigate their impact on increasing productivity. Results indicate that a significant increase in the number of research began in 2015 and is experiencing its greatest expansion in 2018. Important methodologies observed during the literature analysis are a systematic review of the literature for the largest number of theoretically oriented papers, and case studies, practical models for the minority that make up the practice-oriented papers. Also, 68 percent of papers focus more on the theoretical than on the practical implications, and 72 papers indicate a direct link between productivity and digital technologies used in the digital transformation and implementation of smart factories.

Keywords: Industry 4.0 · Digital technologies · Smart factory · Productivity

1 Introduction

In today's manufacturing landscape, traditionally oriented companies are facing numerous challenges like high competition and globalization. These challenges are forcing companies to constantly change, innovate, and digitize. What is driving companies into the so-called Fourth Industrial Revolution, known as Industry 4.0, is the need for automated, more efficient processes, as well as faster delivery times [1]. Identification of trends that are current in industrial automation and include new production technologies that increase productivity and production quality is attributed to Industry 4.0.

The widespread use of interdependent digital technologies and the rise of cyberphysical spaces or smart factories are common to Industry 4.0. [2]. To achieve sustainability and further develop their businesses, manufacturing companies need to find an

D. Y. Kim et al. (Eds.): APMS 2022, IFIP AICT 664, pp. 179–187, 2022.
https://doi.org/10.1007/978-3-031-16411-8_23

appropriate response to the frequent changes in customer demands, development of new technologies, and dynamic competition [3]. To prepare for the decline in added value in the manufacturing industry and improve productivity, the manufacturing sector is now working on process innovation, i.e. smart factories [4, 5].

Given that digital technologies are an integral part of smart factories and are increasingly represented, this paper intends to shed the light on their domain by answering the following research questions:

1. What are the key technologies in the digital transformation of manufacturing companies?
2. What impact do digital technologies have on the productivity of smart factories?

The paper's structure is as follows: section two describes the methodology in detail, followed by the description of identified digital technologies. Section four presents their impact on the productivity of smart factories, followed by a discussion in section five. Finally, the paper is concluded in section six.

2 Research Methodology

A characteristic that is the essence of academic research is the review of literature because knowledge is improved and built on previously existing work. Insight into previously existing work helps us to move the border of knowledge, pointing out where that border is. To understand the true breadth and depth of existing work and be able to identify shortcomings that need to be explored, a systematic literature review of the relevant literature is needed. By analyzing and grouping related literature, we can find answers to the above-stated two research questions. In addition, there is an opportunity to use the criteria to identify certain weaknesses and inconsistencies of existing work, as well as its quality [6]. Some of the perceived advantages of the systematic literature review method are reflected in the summarization of previous work, identifying what has been achieved and gaps if any, and avoiding duplication [7]. A successful systematic literature review includes three main phases: review planning, review implementation, and review reporting [8]. Given this, a systematic literature review was conducted by identifying and selecting primary studies, extracting, analyzing, and synthesizing data. The systematic literature review presented in this article follows the principles of deductive reasoning and aims to answer a particular research question. When analyzing the literature, it was noticed that significant growth of research conducted on this topic began in 2015, and the greatest expansion is experienced in 2018.

Online databases, Scopus and Web of Science were used to find and analyze the literature, these specific index bases were selected because of their reliability and a large number of papers for analysis. The keyword string and the systematic review process are presented in Fig. 1. By the initial search, 171 articles were obtained, while after the abstract analysis, this number was reduced to 136. After noticing repetitions and overlaps, relating to the occurrence of the same papers on both bases, 87 articles were selected for the final analysis.

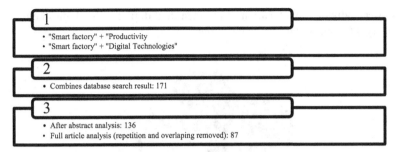

Fig. 1. Overview of the systematic literature review process

3 Digital Transformation Technologies

Industry 4.0 implies the transformation of industrial production into smart production. What has been considered the driving force of this transformation is the advanced development of digital technologies that make up the trend of Industry 4.0. What is crucial about these digital technologies is their integration and efficient use in data-driven production in such a way as to create value and meaningful information [9, 10]. The ubiquitous, massive use of interdependent digital technologies forms the basis of Industry 4.0. In this sense, smart factories represent a cyber-physical space in which production processes involve machine-machine and human-machine interactions and in which various objects are transformed into mutually communicating intelligent systems [2, 11]. The use of digital technologies enables companies to save costs by helping them optimize the waste of materials and inventory. Thanks to remote cooperation, the cooperation of employees who are on the spot and outside are significantly facilitated. Digital technologies help them keep up to date with information and reduce communication gaps. The merging of information and operational technology has brought new digital solutions such as additive manufacturing, advanced robotics, augmented and virtual reality, big data, cloud computing, and the Internet of Things (IoT) creating a cyber-physical environment. Figure 2 shows the previously listed digital technologies identified during the literature review, related to production management. By applying the mentioned additive manufacturing, significant progress is made in processes such as research and development. Industry 4.0 with its rapid advances in digital transformation and digital technologies can make an impact on entire manufacturing systems, through technologies such as IoT and Artificial Intelligence (AI). The digital transformation in the manufacturing sector is caused precisely by the integration of these technologies with previous processes and systems across the value chain [12, 13].

By a detailed analysis of 87 papers, it is possible to see what is the trend in digital technology research in the context of the smart factory. A significant increase in the number of research began in 2015 and is experiencing its greatest expansion in 2018. The largest percentage of papers (68%) focus more on the theoretical than on the practical implications of this topic. What they have in common is that they point out the possibilities provided by the above-mentioned digital technologies. What is also noticeable are the dominant areas that deal with this topic, and those are Engineering and Computer Science.

A closer, individual explanation of the identified digital technologies belonging to the Industry 4.0 concept will be given below.

Fig. 2. Digital technologies related to manufacturing system management

3.1 Additive Manufacturing

Additive Manufacturing is a process used for creating complex structures using Computer-Aided Design (CAD) data. It has caused the time and expense of design to decrease. With this 3-D printing process, items can be personalized to a broader degree. Additive Manufacturing's worldwide, industry revenue is continuously increasing. It provides major advancements in the research and development process [1, 12].

3.2 Advanced Robotics

Robots have been an essential part of the manufacturing sector for a very long time. In Industry 4.0, robots are no longer tools that were used by humans. Instead, they are independent, self-governing, and intelligent machines integral to work units. There have been numerous improvements compared to traditional robots. Due to these improvements, the tasks have become much more economical than earlier [12].

3.3 Augmented Virtual and Mixed Reality

These technologies have made it possible for the business to provide personalized product design, a dedicated manufacturing process, and individual after-sales service. Augmented Reality: Instead of fully providing a virtual experience, this technology enhances the real-world experience with pictures, text, and other virtual data with smartphones, smart lenses, AR glasses, etc. Virtual Reality: This technology enables the user to feel that they are moving in a virtual surrounding. It uses a VR headset that is connected to a PC or a console. Mixed Reality: This technology is a step beyond AR. The user needs to wear an MR headset to experience mixed reality, which offers a holographic experience through the translucent glass. Using MR, virtual objects placed in the real world respond like real objects. To be summed up, it is a combination of gesture, gaze, and voice recognition technology with a motion controller that helps deliver the MR experience [12, 14].

3.4 Big Data

The advanced sensors, actuators, and processes produce a large amount of industrial data [14]. As the word says, big data means a massive amount of data increasing exponentially with time. It uses software that consolidates data mining, data storage, and data visualization. The comprehensive term embraces data, and data framework, including tools and techniques used to investigate and transform data [12, 15].

3.5 Cloud Computing

Cloud Computing (CC) is revolutionizing IT environments in most fields of the economy. Its service-based approach enables collaboration and data exchange on a higher level, with better efficiency and parallel decreasing costs. Also, manufacturing environments can benefit from cloud technology and better fulfill fast changes in market demands, by applying diverse cloud deployment models and by virtualizing manufacturing processes and assets into services [12]. CC is in general an IT architectural model where computing services (both hardware and software) are abstracted and delivered to customers over the Internet, on-demand, in a self-service fashion, independent of device and location. The Cloud model embodies unique characteristics and can have various service and deployment models: while service models are typically an end-user's perspective in the CC industry, different delivery models refer to different layers of the CC architecture [16]. For example, Kehoe [17] pointed out how CC influences system improvement by providing access to datasets, models, publications, simulation tools and benchmarks, public calls for projects and systems, and open-source software.

3.6 Internet of Things

The Internet of Things is a network of physical objects that use sensors, software, and other smart devices to transfer and receive data from other systems over the internet. It has endless business or personal possibilities. Industrial applications of IoT are extensible and customizable. It has various prebuilt applications for fraud detection, predictive maintenance, and Supply network optimization. Advanced analytics platforms such as IoT platforms can extract data from multiple types of sources such as applications, sensors, devices, files, etc. via connectors and facilitate complex analysis including what-if analysis. This in turn provides valuable insights that help improve efficiency, reduce costs and achieve optimization [12, 18, 19].

4 Impact of Digital Technologies on Smart Factory Productivity

Mechanization, electricity, and information technology have caused a large increase in productivity during the previous three industrial revolutions. The core technology for Industry 4.0 consists of Cyber-Physical Systems (CPS), which by making production systems changeable and modular enable mass production of highly customized products. Communicating over the IoT, CPS connects goals, machines, infrastructure, processes, and people, enabling the integration of the physical and virtual worlds [1]. The very concept of CPS is shown in Fig. 3. Technological revolutions, such as Industry 4.0, which include new paradigms of IoT and CPS for analysis, monitoring, and overall process automation, are transforming production and logistics processes by creating smart factories, intending to increase efficiency and productivity. In this context, the basis of industrial IoT consists of wireless sensors that are used to detect irregularities such as downtime, optimize efficiency and increase productivity in real-time. These wireless sensor networks are much more flexible and cost-effective to install and allow faster integration into existing industrial production networks [20]. New digital technologies, as part of the Industry 4.0 concept, point to the possibility of achieving flexibility and superior productivity at the same time [21].

Authors such as Wang [22] present a framework that includes three elements, industrial wireless networks, CC, and fixed or mobile terminals with smart artifacts such as products, machines, and conveyors. Such ecosystems can self-organize with the help of feedback from the big data analytics blocks working in the cloud. Based on this, it was concluded that self-organization, coordination, and feedback are what provide communication between products and smart machines to be tuned for flexible and productive production of multiple product types.

The largest number of analyzed papers, as many as 72 papers, indicate a direct link between productivity and digital technologies used in the digital transformation and implementation of smart factories. Almost all of these isolated studies imply that digital technologies have a positive impact on the productivity of manufacturing companies. The productivity of smart manufacturing systems is undoubtedly very closely related to the application of digital technologies shown in Fig. 2.

Fig. 3. The concept of cyber-physical systems

5 Discussion

An analysis of the existing literature has identified that certain digital technologies have a positive impact on the productivity of smart factories. Such a positive impact is made possible by the realization of the benefits of implementing digital technologies, and they are directly related to productivity. This means that the connection between these two variables is still of the indirect type. That is, some of the main advantages of the application of digital technologies are the reduction of labor costs, energy and time savings, better health and safety of employees, big data management, and more efficient supply chains. All of the above further leads to increased productivity as well as increased revenue and profits.

What is important is the role of man in such a system. Certain mistakes as a result of the human factor can lead to impaired productivity, while on the other hand, a quality operator can significantly contribute to that productivity. Therefore, the issue of training and retraining employees in smart factories arises. For digital technologies to reach their full potential and full impact on productivity, in addition to their introduction, it is necessary to pay attention to people, not just technology.

Although it may be a risky and difficult undertaking, the development and transition to smart factories bring many benefits. If the company successfully implements a smart factory, it will achieve significant savings, while increasing the quality of the product, shortening its market entry, and increasing sales. The implementation of a smart factory enables significant growth in flexibility, productivity, and profitability. To reap all these benefits of a smart factory, companies must adhere to three basic principles: cultivate digital people, introduce agile processes, and configure digital, modular technologies for production optimization [5, 18]. These three principles represent the challenges that manufacturing companies face when they decide to implement the smart factory concept.

However, when analyzing the literature, a large omission was noticed, which exists and is not negligible, and that is that the works mostly deal only with theoretical knowledge, while the great lack of application of this knowledge in practice, on real examples, which needs to change in the future for as much knowledge as possible to be supported by facts and therefore relevant.

6 Conclusion

This paper identifies digital technologies that are applied in smart factories and have an impact on productivity. These technologies are presented individually and their positive impact on productivity is explained, through the action on various business indicators, which achieved an answer to research questions but also identified research directions that are not covered. Results indicate that a significant increase in the number of research began in 2015 and is experiencing its greatest expansion in 2018. Also, 68 percent of papers focus more on the theoretical than on the practical implications, and 72 papers indicate a direct link between productivity and digital technologies used in the digital transformation and implementation of smart factories.

The limitation of this paper is related to the principles listed in the previous chapter and first refers to the potential problems in the acceptance of digital technologies by employees in manufacturing companies. Digital technologies, although to some extent autonomous, require the presence of humans, so it is very important to observe this factor as well. The second limitation concerns the possible mismatch of infrastructure, machinery, and process structure, which requires adaptation and also like the previous limitation, maybe the direction of future research. The third limitation, which is perhaps the biggest problem in the implementation of digital technologies, is data protection. This paper does not cover measures implemented to enable data protection and should be included in research in the future.

References

1. Zheng, T., Ardolino, M., Bacchetti, A., Perona, M.: The applications of Industry 4.0 technologies in manufacturing context: a systematic literature review. Int. J. Prod. Res. **59**(6), 1922–1954 (2021). https://doi.org/10.1080/00207543.2020.1824085
2. Muscio, A., Ciffolilli, A.: What drives the capacity to integrate industry 4.0 technologies? evidence from European R&D projects. Econ. Innov. New Technol. **29**(2), 169–183 (2020). https://doi.org/10.1080/10438599.2019.1597413
3. Rakic, S., Pavlovic, M., Marjanovic, U.: A precondition of sustainability: industry 4.0 readiness. Sustainability **13**(12), 6641 (2021). https://doi.org/10.3390/su13126641
4. Kim, D.-H., et al.: Smart machining process using machine learning: a review and perspective on machining industry. Int. J. of Precis. Eng. Manuf.-Green Technol. **5**(4), 555–568 (2018). https://doi.org/10.1007/s40684-018-0057-y
5. Sjödin, D.R., Parida, V., Leksell, M., Petrovic, A.: Smart Factory Implementation and Process Innovation: a preliminary maturity model for leveraging digitalization in manufacturing moving to smart factories presents specific challenges that can be addressed through a structured approach focused on people, p. Res. Technol. Manag. **61**(5), 22–31 (2018). https://doi.org/10.1080/08956308.2018.1471277
6. Templier, M., Paré, G.: A framework for guiding and evaluating literature reviews. Commun. Assoc. Inf. Syst. **37**(August), 112–137 (2015). https://doi.org/10.17705/1cais.03706
7. Grant, M.J., Booth, A.: A typology of reviews: an analysis of 14 review types and associated methodologies. Health Info. Libr. J. **26**(2), 91–108 (2009). https://doi.org/10.1111/j.1471-1842.2009.00848.x
8. Xiao, Y., Watson, M.: Guidance on conducting a systematic literature review. J. Plan. Educ. Res. **39**(1), 93–112 (2019). https://doi.org/10.1177/0739456X17723971
9. Sufian, A.T., Abdullah, B.M., Ateeq, M., Wah, R., Clements, D.: Six-gear roadmap towards the smart factory. Appl. Sci. **11**(8), 3568 (2021). https://doi.org/10.3390/app11083568
10. Shahatha Al-Mashhadani, A.F., Qureshi, M.I., Hishan, S.S., Md Saad, M.S., Vaicondam, Y., Khan, N.: Towards the development of digital manufacturing ecosystems for sustainable performance: learning from the past two decades of research. Energies **14**(10), pp. 1–17 (2021). https://doi.org/10.3390/en14102945
11. Spasojevic, I., Havzi, S., Stefanovic, D., Ristic, S., Marjanovic, U.: Research trends and topics in IJIEM from 2010 to 2020: a statistical history. Int. J. Ind. Eng. Manag. **12**(4), 228–242 (2021). https://doi.org/10.24867/IJIEM-2021-4-290
12. Ammar, M., Haleem, A., Javaid, M., Walia, R., Bahl, S.: Improving material quality management and manufacturing organizations system through Industry 4.0 technologies. Mater. Today Proc. **45**, 5089–5096 (2021). https://doi.org/10.1016/j.matpr.2021.01.585
13. Zivlak, N., Rakic, S., Marjanovic, U., Ciric, D., Bogojevic, B.: The role of digital servitization in transition economy: An SNA approach. Teh. Vjesn. **28**(6), 1912–1919 (2021). https://doi.org/10.17559/TV-20210325083229

14. Salunkhe, O., Berglund, F.: Industry 4.0 enabling technologies for increasing operational flexibility in final assembly. Int. J. Ind. Eng. Manag. **13**(1), 38–48 (2022). https://doi.org/10.24867/IJIEM-2022-1-299
15. Pavlović, M., Marjanović, U., Rakić, S., Tasić, N., Lalić, B.: The big potential of big data in Manufacturing: evidence from emerging economies. In: Lalic, B., Majstorovic, V., Marjanovic, U., von Cieminski, G., Romero, D. (eds.) Advances in Production Management Systems. Towards Smart and Digital Manufacturing. IFIP Advances in Information and Communication Technology, vol. 592, pp. 100–107. Springer, Cham (2020). https://doi.org/10.1007/978-3-030-57997-5_12
16. Pedone, G., Mezgár, I.: Model similarity evidence and interoperability affinity in cloud-ready Industry 4.0 technologies. Comput. Ind. **100**(February), 278–286 (2018). https://doi.org/10.1016/j.compind.2018.05.003
17. Kehoe, B., Patil, S., Abbeel, P., Goldberg, K.: A survey of research on cloud robotics and automation. IEEE Trans. Autom. Sci. Eng. **12**(2), 398–409 (2015). https://doi.org/10.1109/TASE.2014.2376492
18. Illa, P.K., Padhi, N.: Practical guide to smart factory transition using IoT, big data and edge analytics. IEEE Access **6**, 55162–55170 (2018). https://doi.org/10.1109/ACCESS.2018.2872799
19. Lalic, B., Marjanovic, U., Rakic, S., Pavlovic, M., Todorovic, T., Medic, N.: Big Data Analysis as a Digital Service: Evidence Form Manufacturing Firms. In: Wang, L., Majstorovic, V.D., Mourtzis, D., Carpanzano, E., Moroni, G., Galantucci, L.M. (eds.) Proceedings of 5th International Conference on the Industry 4.0 Model for Advanced Manufacturing. Lecture Notes in Mechanical Engineering, pp. 263–269. Springer, Cham (2020). https://doi.org/10.1007/978-3-030-46212-3_19
20. Preuveneers, D., Ilie-Zudor, E.: The intelligent industry of the future: a survey on emerging trends, research challenges and opportunities in Industry 4.0. J. Ambient Intell. Smart Environ. **9**(3), 287–298 (2017). https://doi.org/10.3233/AIS-170432
21. Miqueo, A., Torralba, M., Yagüe-Fabra, J.A.: Lean manual assembly 4.0: a systematic review. Appl. Sci. **10**(23), 1–37 (2020). https://doi.org/10.3390/app10238555
22. Wang, S., Wan, J., Li, D., Zhang, C.: Implementing Smart Factory of Industrie 4.0: an Outlook. Int. J. Distrib. Sens. Netw. **12**(1), 3159805 (2016). https://doi.org/10.1155/2016/3159805

KNOWO: A Tool for Generation of Semantic Knowledge Graphs from Maintenance Workorders Data

Farhad Ameri[✉] and Renita Tahsin

Engineering Informatics Lab, Texas State University, San Marcos, USA
{ameri,r_t298}@txstate.edu

Abstract. A major portion of industrial maintenance data is in unstructured form, which makes its organization, search, and reuse very challenging. For this reason, the knowledge embedded in historical maintenance data is seldom analyzed or reused for purposes such as root cause analysis, failure prevention, and maintenance diagnostics. If the valuable knowledge patterns nested in maintenance data are identified, liberated, and formalized, they can significantly improve the intelligence of maintenance management systems by providing actionable insights. The objective of this research is to help advance the progression from data to information and knowledge through data-driven creation of a public and open-source knowledge graphs built from the textual data available in maintenance workorders. A SKOS-based thesaurus is used to support automated entity extraction from the text. A formal OWL-based ontology provides the semantic schema of the knowledge graph. A software tool (KnoWo) is developed to streamline the text-to-graph translation process. It was observed that the proposed text-to-graph tool chain improves knowledge discovery by analyzing maintenance logs.

Keywords: Knowledge graph · Maintenance workorder · Ontology · Thesaurus

1 Introduction

Maintenance is defined as the actions intended to retain an asset or to restore it to a state in which it can perform a required function [1]. In order to minimize machine downtime and maximize the availability of critical assets and equipment uptime, manufacturers use a wide range of maintenance management tools and technologies with varying levels of automation. In particular, Computerized Maintenance Management Systems (CMMS) are widely used in most industries to manage, plan, and execute preventive and planned maintenance activities [2]. Despite widespread adoption of maintenance automation solutions in industry, maintenance management is still a highly human-centric process since efficient acquisition, formalization, and reuse of maintenance knowledge is a major challenge [3].

© IFIP International Federation for Information Processing 2022
Published by Springer Nature Switzerland AG 2022
D. Y. Kim et al. (Eds.): APMS 2022, IFIP AICT 664, pp. 188–195, 2022.
https://doi.org/10.1007/978-3-031-16411-8_24

The data generated during maintenance management activities (including identification, planning, scheduling, and execution) is often stored in Maintenance Work Orders (MWO). MWO records are often generated by maintenance technicians and stored in the database of CMMS packages for archiving, reporting, or analysis purposes [4]. Enormous collections of historical maintenance logs, representing a wealth of diagnostic knowledge, can be found in most industries. The knowledge embedded in MWOs can be used to inform the maintenance diagnosis process. However, the unstructured data provided by MWOs are often under-used since it is not presented in a computable form [1, 5]. Additionally, the data is often flooded with misspellings, jargons, abbreviations, and contradictory statements since they are prepared by multiple technicians with varying levels of experience and background knowledge. There is a need for developing formal methods and models for data cleaning and knowledge extraction and formalization to improve the reusability and findability of the knowledge embedded in MWOs. As the size and number of MWO records increases, manual search and analysis of those records becomes more cumbersome and less efficient. Without proper tools and techniques for analyzing, mining, and contextualizing that knowledge, the usefulness of these maintenance logs is severely limited.

Advanced techniques supported by Natural Language Processing (NLP) and Machine Learning (ML) can be applied to extract useful patterns and rules from the raw text that are otherwise hidden in the historical maintenance work order data [6]. These techniques are particularly useful for cleaning maintenance logs, extracting important terms, classifying, and clustering similar workorders, and identifying associativity relationships between the extracted terms. One difficulty in effective analysis of MWO data using NLP is that the size of MWO data is often smaller than what is needed by most NLP/ML tools for training purposes [7]. A major of the existing data-driven methods is that they take the semantics of data for granted which results in with working with semantically fractured and low-quality data that is not properly contextualized.

An alternative solution for learning from MWO data is to convert the raw text into knowledge graphs. A knowledge graph represents data as a collection of nodes (concepts) connected through edges (relationships). Knowledge graphs are quickly becoming the preferred models for data representation since they promise to bridge the gap between the data and its meaning, and they serve as the natural model for data integration thanks to their flexibility and extensibility. There have been some efforts for automated generation of knowledge graphs from MWO data supported by deep learning and the NLP pipeline [8]. Such works are significant achievements in this field, but they still need to be further developed to address some shortcomings, including a lack of alignment with formal ontologies.

The underlying research challenge that motivates this work is to generate more structured and formal knowledge models, including ontologies and knowledge graphs. Addressing this challenge will require using a hybrid approach that incorporates top-down methods for generation and curation of knowledge models by domain experts as well as bottom-up methods for data-driven extension and validation of knowledge models. This work reports the preliminary results of an ongoing research project.

2 Research Method

The proposed approach for the generation of a knowledge graph uses two semantic models, namely, a thesaurus and an ontology. The thesaurus provides lexical semantics, whereas the ontology provides logical semantics. The thesaurus concepts are mapped to the ontology classes to enable semi-automated text translation into knowledge graphs. Description Logic (DL) is used as the knowledge representation formalism in ontology modeling. The generated knowledge graph is more available computationally compared to natural language text and can be queried or reasoned over to detect latent or recurring patterns in the data. The proposed approach adopts a human-in-the-loop (HITL) strategy since some contextual and common-sense knowledge is needed for workorder text disambiguation and decomposition into a set of interrelated concepts with well-defined semantics. The level of involvement of human experts gradually diminishes as the thesaurus and the ontology becomes more mature and stable.

3 Maintenance Diagnostics Thesaurus (MDT)

The Maintenance Diagnosis Thesaurus (MDT) is a controlled vocabulary for maintenance terms that uses the Simple Knowledge Organization System (SKOS) for its syntax and semantics. The thesaurus is used to facilitate automatic extraction of key maintenance concepts from the workorder text. SKOS is a standard published by World Wide Web Consortium (W3C) that provides a structured framework for building controlled vocabularies such as thesauri, concept schemes, and taxonomies to be used and understood by both human and machine agents. SKOS models are considered to be lightweight ontologies as they do not have the expressivity of heavyweight, axiomatic ontologies such as OWL models. For this reason, their development cost is relatively low, and they can be quickly expanded in a decentralized fashion by various user communities. The MD Thesaurus provides a set of vocabulary often used by technicians when documenting their observations when diagnosing functional failures and maintenance issues. MD Thesaurus concepts are categorized under seven concept groups or schemes, namely, Action, Artifact, Condition, Event, Function, Material Substance, and Property. The lower-level concepts under each scheme are collected through tagging relevant terms in an experimental dataset. The development and curation of the thesaurus in supported by a web-based tool (SKOS Tool) that enables the user to upload the text, tag and classify the terms under appropriate broader concepts in an interactive fashion. The MD Thesaurus can be exported in the RDF-JSON data interchange standard and shared across multiple platforms that are compatible with Semantic Web standards [6]. Figure 1 shows examples of the concepts under the Condition concept scheme. These concepts are often used by maintenance technicians to describe the observed condition of a maintainable item (machine or equipment). Another utility of the MD thesaurus is to capture the alternative terms that are often used to refer to the same concept. For example, as shown in Fig. 2, *hydraulic leak, lube leak, hyd leak,* and *oil leak* are synonym terms that are used for labeling the same concept. Using SKOS annotation property, it is possible to select one preferred label for a given concept and assign multiple alternative labels as needed.

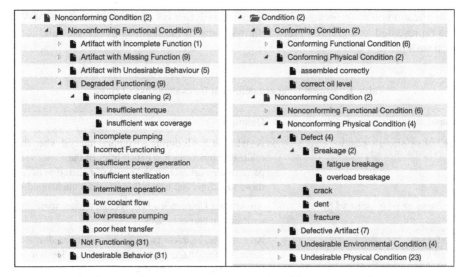

Fig. 1. Examples of concepts under the "Condition" concept scheme.

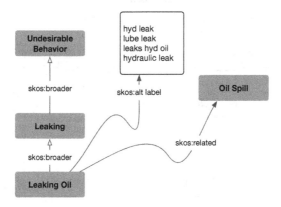

Fig. 2. Broader and Related concepts for Leaking Oil along with its alternative labels

4   Workorder Ontology (WOO)

Workorder Ontology (WOO) is a formal OWL-based ontology that can be used for the formal representation of entities and their relationships in the maintenance domain. WOO uses Basic Formal Ontology (BFO) as its top-level, or foundational, ontology. However, WOO only uses a sub-set of BFO terms and, therefore, it does not import BFO entirely. Using a top-level ontology facilitates ontology reuse and also provides a logical framework for ontology development that is consistent with established philosophical theories. Each class in WOO has a natural language and formal definition to enable unambiguous human-to-human and machine-to-machine communication. Table 1 Shows natural language definitions for some of the key classes in WOO. It should be noted that the WOO is not intended to serve as a reference ontology for the maintenance domain. Rather, it is an application ontology designed for a specific task that is to provide meaning to MWO data represented as a graph. Figure 3 shows some of the main WOO classes and their relationships.

Table 1. Natural language definition for example WOO classes

Class	Definition
Maintenance state	A state that holds during a temporal interval when the realizable functions and capabilities of the participating artifact, or the grade of realization of those functions and capabilities, remain unchanged
Undesirable behavior	An Artifact Unintended Process that causes some undesirable consequences
Defect	An attribute, characteristics, or feature inhered in some Artifact that does not conform to the Design Specifications of the Artifact
Artifact with degraded functionality	An Artifact that realizes its primary functions at a degraded level

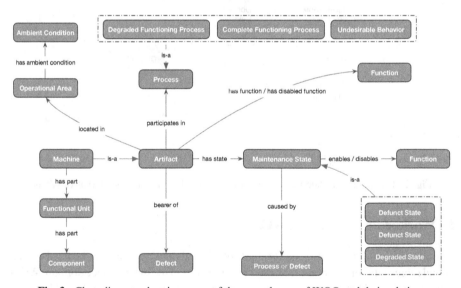

Fig. 3. Class diagram showing some of the core classes of WOO and their relations

5   Workorder Knowledge Graph Generator Tool (KNOWO)

KNOWO is a java-based tool for the automated creation of knowledge graphs from maintenance workorders. The user first enters the text for a single workorder, and then the tool analyzes the text and automatically extracts the thesaurus concepts that appear in the text either through their preferred label or their alternative label. The concept extractor also provides a list of the concepts that are *related* to primary concepts (the second table in Fig. 4 - left). The user has the option of introducing new concepts that are not available in the thesaurus, but they are needed to build a complete graph for the selected workorder (the third table in Fig. 4- left: user-defined concepts). All concepts in the thesaurus are mapped to ontological classes. Therefore, each detected or user-defined concept represents an instantiation of a class in WOO ontology. For example, *blown o-ring* is an instance of `Defective Artifact` class, and *leaking oil* is an instance of `Undesirable Behavior` class. The user can select the individuals that need to be transferred to the next step, which is about connecting the selected individuals using ontological relationships.

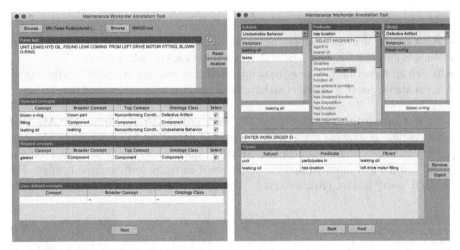

Fig. 4. KNOWO interface for the first step: concept extraction and ontology instantiation (left), KNOWO interface for the second step: connecting the generated individuals using ontological classes (right)

As can be seen in Fig. 4 - right, the user can select the instances in the domain and range (subject and object) of each RDF triples and connect them using the appropriate property.

For example, the user can specify that leaking oil *is caused by* blown o-ring. Once all necessary triples are built, the tool exports the final set of triples in turtle (.ttl) format, a file format for expressing data in the Resource Description Framework (RDF) data model. The.ttl file can then be visualized using general-purpose RDF visualizers such as RDF Grapher. The output of the RDF Grapher for the selected example is shown in Fig. 5.

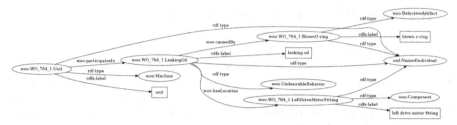

Fig. 5. The final knowledge graph generated automatically based on the exported triples

6 Validation

The standard method for validating ontologies and knowledge graphs is to test them with respect to their ability in responding to a set of competency questions. These questions are often determined at the early stages of the ontology development process to serve as a set of requirements for the ontology. Some of the competency questions for WOO ontology are listed below:

- What are the causes of different undesirable behaviors of given equipment?
- What are the observed maintenance states of a given machine?
- What is the most frequent type of defect that has caused failure events?
- Which artifacts (machine or equipment) have demonstrated degraded functioning?
- What are the functional units that have been in a defunct state at some time?

A test knowledge graph based on 100 work orders extracted from the CMMS of a construction equipment manufacturer was used during the validation step. All competency questions were formulated as SPARQL queries and executed against the test graph, and it was confirmed that the graph could correctly resolve those queries. The SPARQL query and the retrieved results related to the last query are provided in Fig. 6.

```
PREFIX rdf: <http://www.w3.org/1999/02/22-rdf-syntax-ns#>
PREFIX owl: <http://www.w3.org/2002/07/owl#>
PREFIX rdfs: <http://www.w3.org/2000/01/rdf-schema#>
PREFIX xsd: <http://www.w3.org/2001/XMLSchema#>
PREFIX woo: <http://infoneer.txstate.edu/ontology/MWOO/>

SELECT ?item ?state
WHERE {
    ?item woo:hasState ?state.
    ?state a woo:DefunctState.
    ?item a woo:FunctionalUnit.
}
```

Functional Unit	Defunct State
Winch	Not Holding Load
Generator	Not Working
Pump	Not Functioning
Fuel Pump	Inoperative
Engine	Not Functioning
Elect Motor	Not Turning On
Control Box	Not Operating
Seat Belt	Not Latching
ECM	Not Displaying

Fig. 6. The example SPARQL query that returns all Functional Units that have participated in some Defunct State at some time

7   Conclusion

In this paper, a human-assisted method for the creation of RDF knowledge graphs from MWO data was proposed. A java-based tool called KnoWo, was developed to facilitate the knowledge graph generation process. The main functions of KnoWo include extracting key concepts from MWO text (based on a list of known terms provided by a SKOS thesaurus), instantiating ontology classes according to the extracted concepts, and relating the generated instances using ontological relationships.

This work particularly focused on formalizing the data related to observed symptoms and probable causes at the time of failure. However, a major component of MWO data is related to the action taken to restore an asset. In the future, the ontology and thesaurus will be extended to capture the maintenance treatment and link them to the failures and symptoms. In this way, the graph can be searched to retrieve potential solutions for different types of failures.

References:

1. Melinda, H., Mark Tien-Wei, H.: Cleaning historical maintenance work order data for reliability analysis. J. Qual. Maint. Eng. **22**(2), 146–163 (2016)
2. Wienker, M., Henderson, K., Volkerts, J.: The computerized maintenance management system an essential tool for world class maintenance. Procedia Eng. **138**(Supplement C), 413–420 (2016)
3. Sharp, M., Sexton, T., Brundage, M.P.: Toward semi-autonomous information. In: Lödding, H., Riedel, R., Thoben, K.-D., von Cieminski, G., Kiritsis, D. (eds.) APMS 2017. IAICT, vol. 513, pp. 425–432. Springer, Cham (2017). https://doi.org/10.1007/978-3-319-66923-6_50
4. Lopes, I., et al.: Requirements specification of a computerized maintenance management system – a case study. Procedia CIRP **52**(Supplement C), 268–273 (2016)
5. Data-driven methods for predictive maintenance of industrial equipment: a survey. IEEE J. Maga. IEEE Xplore. https://ieeexplore.ieee.org/abstract/document/8707108?casa_token=_Z-I6jlA8M8AAAAA:sebswuj-64yjhVqWv4yLEWGJHpJJZkd9kcCwOhh0r_z4Y6A2tjrCTO jajJDr8KkQZJLcF1ntkkA. Accessed 26 June 2022
6. Lukens, S., Naik, M., Saetia, K., Hu, X.: Best practices framework for improving maintenance data quality to enable asset performance analytics. In: Annual Conference of the Phm Society (2019)
7. Sexton, T., Hodkiewicz, M., Brundage, M. P., and Smoker, T.: Benchmarking for keyword extraction methodologies in maintenance work orders (2018)
8. Stewart, M., Liu, W.: Seq2KG: an end-to-end neural model for domain agnostic knowledge graph (not text graph) construction from text. KR **17**(1), 748–757 (2020)

Digital Transformation in the Engineering Research Area: Scientific Performance and Strategic Themes

Danijela Ciric Lalic$^{(\boxtimes)}$ ⓘ, Danijela Gracanin ⓘ, Teodora Lolic ⓘ, Bojan Lalic ⓘ, and Nenad Simeunovic ⓘ

Faculty of Technical Sciences, University of Novi Sad, 21000 Novi Sad, Serbia
danijela.ciric@uns.ac.rs

Abstract. In recent years, digital transformation has gained increasing interest from researchers and practitioners, putting efforts towards developing a better understanding, resulting in emerging independent research areas. Consequently, the research under the digital transformation, even though becoming a hotspot, remains very fragmented. This study has tried to provide a quick overview of the scientific output in this field, recognizing prolific authors, most productive countries and most relevant and influential journals in the DT field by using bibliometric analysis on 946 publications published during the timespan 2001:2022, retrieved from Thompson Reuters Web of Science. Also, this study presented the thematic analysis and provided insights to researchers and scholars in the field of DT regarding the current research landscape and prospects. The resulting knowledge will help scholars and researchers detect research opportunities and gaps for future works and contribute to continuing research in this area.

Keywords: Digital transformation · Engineering research · Bibliometric analysis · Bibliometrix

1 Introduction

Digital technologies are disrupting the way we connect and create value for users, by transforming business models and how businesses introduce innovations and sustain their competitive advantages, enabling manifold benefits [1–4]. Digitization and digital transformation (DT) have been occurring in organizations since the 1950s [5]. However, it has been 342 years since Gottfried Wilhelm Leibniz developed the binary system in 1679 and 75 years since ENAIK (ENIAC-Electronic Numerical Integrator and Calculator), the first computer to start its use was built in 1946 at the University of Pennsylvania. From them, and especially in recent years, the concept of digital transformation has gained increasing interest from both researchers and practitioners, putting efforts towards developing a better understanding, resulting in emerging independent research areas [6].

© IFIP International Federation for Information Processing 2022
Published by Springer Nature Switzerland AG 2022
D. Y. Kim et al. (Eds.): APMS 2022, IFIP AICT 664, pp. 196–204, 2022.
https://doi.org/10.1007/978-3-031-16411-8_25

Many authors have used bibliometric analysis to identify aspects of science that receive the most contributions from authors, journals, countries, and the collaborative and co-occurrence networks among them [7–12]. To contribute to a better understanding of DT performance in the scientific literature, including its intellectual and social structure, several studies performed a bibliometric analysis of the DT literature [6, 13–16]. Unlike the previously mentioned studies, by using a bibliometric analysis we wanted to focus on an in-depth analysis of DT in the engineering research area.

The primary purpose of this study was to investigate DT scientific performance and strategic themes landscape in the engineering research area. The resulting knowledge will help scholars and researchers detect research opportunities and gaps for future works and contribute to continuing research in this area [17, 18].

2 Research Methodology and Dataset

The search and data collection was conducted on the 1st of February 2022 in the online bibliographic database Clarivate Analytics Web of Science (WoS) Core Collection. We used the search string: "Digital transformation" in the Topic field (including title, abstract and keywords) for the period 2001 till 2022 (inclusive). 2001 was taken as the starting year, as no publication matching the search criteria had been identified before that year. From the retrieved database under the category Document types, we excluded: editorial materials, corrections, additions, book reviews, retracted publications, biographical items and reprints. Furthermore, the search was restricted to the Engineering research area and English language articles. We exported the Full record with cited references (all article information available, including the authors' name, abstract, keywords, editors, references etc.) in plaintext format; A total of 946 documents and 2,958 keywords were included for analysis.

Query link: https://www.webofscience.com/wos/woscc/summary/f5aed942-add3-43f8-8da3-f7702c9f84b5-3371e9b5/relevance/1.

Finally, we used the "bibliometrix" R-package software for quantitative research in bibliometrics and scientometrics developed by Aria and Cuccurallo and written in the R language [19]. Specifically, we used a web interface Biblioshiny aimed at users without coding skills.

3 Performance Analysis

Before moving forward with the analysis, the following section provides the descriptive characteristics of DT literature. The final dataset consisted of 946 publications published during the timespan 2001:2022. There were 506 articles (including early access) comprising 53.5% of total production, followed by 440 proceedings papers. These publications were produced by 3034 authors (93 authors of single-authored documents and 2941 authors of multi-authored documents) with 3341 author appearances and 0.312 documents per author. In addition, there were 97 single-authored and 849 multi-authored articles with 3.53 co-authors per document and a collaboration index of 3.46 (calculated as Total Authors of Multi-Authored Articles/Total Multi-Authored Articles.

Publications Scientific Production Over Time. Figure 1 graphically represents the dynamic of the scientific production over time. It is possible to observe in Fig. 1 the appearance of the first publication in 2001. Until 2015 publications related to DT were circumstantial, and the number of publications published per year stagnated. There was limited production at the start, but literature production grew exponentially from 2017 until today. Total citations per year increased exponentially from 2017, with the maximum number of citations reached in 2021 (3,313). In total, 6,309 citations, 5,863 without self-citations with 6.67 citations average per item and the h-index 36. The h-index value is based on a list of publications ranked in descending order by the times cited count. It looks like publications and citations are decreasing after 2021, but it must be noted that Fig. 1 doesn't present all data for 2022 but only until April.

The Performance Analysis of Countries. Research contribution to the collection of 946 publications originated from 81 countries. Table 2 shows two sets of data, summarizing the top 10 contributing countries with the highest scientific production frequency in the publications collection (left side) and the total citations (TC) of publications (right side). The most productive country by far is the Germany (n = 249), followed by China (n = 141), the USA (n = 138), the Russia (n = 130), the Italy (n = 127), UK (n = 103), Spain (n = 94), Brazil (n = 77), Portugal (n = 60) and India (n = 56). Ten most productive countries have more than 57.8% of all countries' frequency in publications collection, while Germany solely has more than 12.25%. Germany comes in first place in TC as well (Table 1).

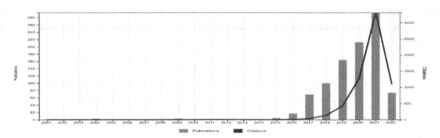

Fig. 1. Citations and publications over time.

Table 1. Most productive/cited countries.

Country	Frequency	Country	TC
Germany	249	Germany	953
China	141	Brazil	743
USA	138	UK	526
Russia	130	Italy	380
Italy	127	China	310
UK	103	Spain	307
Spain	94	USA	293
Brazil	77	Iran	272
Portugal	60	Austria	200
India	56	Canada	180

The Performance Analysis of Journals. Table 2 ranks the journals based on number of publications per source (No. A) with their source impact indicators (h-index and TC). These are the core sources for publishing DT related research in engineering research area. The most relevant source is the IEEE Access, followed by the Applied Sciences-Basel and Sensors.

Table 2. Most productive journals

Sources	No. A	H-index
IEEE Access	37	8
Applied Sciences-Basel	35	7
Sensors	23	8
IEEE Transactions on Engineering Management	18	3
Journal of Manufacturing Technology Management	17	6
Electronics	14	3
Production Planning & Control	13	8
Advanced Engineering Informatics	12	5
International Journal of Production Economics	11	7
Automation in Construction	9	4

The Performance Analysis of Authors. Table 3 shows the top 10 most cited and productive authors, based on the number of published articles (No. A) and TC. It is possible to observe that Leitao, P. is the most productive author, followed by Romero, D. and Stjepandic, J. However, Ayala, N.F., Dalenogare, L.S. and Frank. A.G. are the most cited. A.G. Their contribution is concentrated in one joint article, 'Industry 4.0 technologies: Implementation patterns in manufacturing companies' [20] which is also the most cited publication in the database. In this article, the authors aimed to analyze the adoption patterns of Industry 4.0 technologies in manufacturing firms. These authors are followed by Ghobakhloo, M., whose main contribution is concentrated in two articles: 'Industry 4.0, digitization, and opportunities for sustainability [22] which contributes to the sustainability literature by systematically identifying the sustainability functions of Industry 4.0, and 'Corporate survival in Industry 4.0 era: the enabling role of lean-digitized manufacturing ' [23] demonstrating how small manufacturing firms can leverage their Information Technology (IT) resources to develop the lean-digitized manufacturing system that offers sustained competitiveness in the Industry 4.0 era.

Table 3. Most cited/productive authors.

Most cited authors	No. A	TC	Most productive authors	No. A
Ayala, NF	1	505	Leitao, P	10
Dalenogare, LS	1	505	Romero, D	8
Frank, AG	1	505	Stjepandic, J	8
Ghobakhloo, M	4	298	Pfouga, A	7
Mangla, SK	2	133	Deschamps, F	6
Li, J	5	125	Li, J	5
Kassem, M	1	119	Moller, DPF	5
Greenwood, M	1	115	Wuest, T	5
Macchi, M	4	112	Barata, J	4
Fathi, M	2	110	Barbosa, J	4

Also, the author that appears on both sides is Li, J. It must be highlighted here that Barata, J and Barbosa, J, with four publications, are on this list because the order of the authors is listed alphabetically. Apart from them, several other authors have published four publications, which are not listed in the table among the most productive authors but are among the most cited authors. The most productive authors Leitao, P. (No., A = 10), has 59 citations, Romero, D. (No. A = 8) has 43 citations and Stjepandic, J. (No. A = 8) has 65 citations.

4   Mapping Strategic Themes

A thematic map is constructed based on a full-time span from 2001 to 2022 by employing co-word analysis. We have used the top 400 keywords, and the minimum cluster frequency was set to 5 per thousand documents. First, co-word analysis allowed us to discover the clusters of closely tied keywords (and their interconnections) [21].Then, these clusters were considered as themes and analyzed according to their relevance and level of development [22]. According to the semantic strength of their density (y-axis) and centrality (x-axis), themes were classified and mapped in a two-dimensional space or thematic map. The centrality measures the importance of the selected theme by the degree of collaboration among different topics (external associations), and density measures the development of the chosen theme by the cohesiveness among the keywords (internal associations). Thus, in the high-density and high-centrality quadrant (Q1), we would find the primary research themes that attract the most scientific output and citations related to this topic: the "motor themes." Conversely, we see emerging themes or those fading out in the low-density, low-centrality quadrant (Q3). The upper left-hand quadrant, representing high density and low centrality, refers to those highly developed themes internally but isolated—unconnected to other networks (Q2). Finally, in the lower right-hand quadrant (Q4) (low density and high centrality), we find those essential or core themes that cut across various areas of knowledge [11, 21, 23]. The number of representative labels in each theme is set to 3. The most central keyword (with the highest value) is used to label each thematic network.

Notable, from the Fig. 2 clusters such as "manufacturing" and "sustainability" are central and intensively discussed in relation to DT in engineering research area. We could call them a mainstream theme. It could be noted that "manufacturing" is sandwiched between Q1 and Q4, is well developed and capable of structuring the research field and it remains the leading theme in the field due to its centrality. The theme "sustainability"' lies in the border of the Q1 and Q2 on and may thence be described as having a modest external connection. This theme is central to the research area but requires more focus. Clusters in Q2 such as "sustainable development" and "change management" with their subtopics have developed internal bonds, may be considered as specialized but still underrepresented with marginal contribution the development of the field. These findings suggested that themes need to be more connected to DT.

Researchers in this field can expand these concepts and explore their potential interconnections with other topics in the field. When we look at the "big data" cluster in Q3 with its sub-topics it appears that it is emerging and transverses to Q4. These themes converge on "digital twin" cluster in Q4 and are very important for the further development and maturing of the manufacturing and DT research field [24, 25]. On the contrary, it could be assumed that "digitalization" cluster with sub-topics related to the Covid-19 and the pandemic are declining themes since more than two years have passed since the beginning of the pandemic and the intensity of research is declining. Clusters "digital transformation", "Industry 4.0", "digital twin" in Q4 are the basics, general, and transversal themes with high external associations, and are very important for DT field's development in engineering research. They may correspond to the mainstream themes in the future.

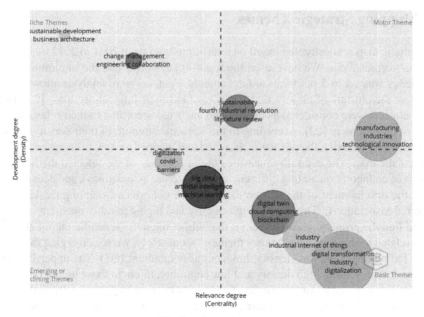

Fig. 2. Thematic map.

5 Conclusion

This study has tried to provide a quick overview of the scientific output in this field, recognizing prolific authors, most productive countries and most relevant and influential journals in the DT field by using bibliometric analysis. This study revealed that the first publication on DT in the engineering research area was published in 2001, but until 2015 publications were circumstantial and stagnated. Literature production grew exponentially from 2017 until today. Foremost among the publishing journals revealed by the study is the "IEEE Access." This result provides an important guide to scholars regarding the suitable publishing outlet for their research papers. Also, this study presented the thematic analysis and provided insights to researchers and scholars in the field of DT regarding the current research landscape and prospects. New and emerging technologies connected with the "big data" cluster theme are significant for the further development and maturing of the research field. The study's weakness is the sample data collection. The analysis was limited to articles and proceeding papers in English, collected only from WoS. Collecting bibliographic data from multiple databases with expanded keywords would improve the study significantly. Future studies should include intellectual, conceptual and social structure and more in-depth co-word, co-citations and collaboration networks. Also, studies should be performed to explore the DT thematic evolution structure in the engineering area over time and investigate each thematic cluster in more depth to identify perspectives of the research field.

References

1. LNCS Homepage. http://www.springer.com/lncs, Accessed 21 Nov 2016
2. Rakic, S., Visnjic, I., Gaiardelli, P., Romero, D., Marjanovic, U.: Transformation of manufacturing firms: towards digital servitization. In: Dolgui, A., Bernard, A., Lemoine, D., von Cieminski, G., Romero, D. (eds.) APMS 2021. IAICT, vol. 631, pp. 153–161. Springer, Cham (2021). https://doi.org/10.1007/978-3-030-85902-2_17
3. Rakic, S., Pavlovic, M., Marjanovic, U.: A precondition of sustainability: Industry 4.0 readiness. Sustainability **13**(12), 6641 (2021)
4. Ciric, D., Lolic, T., Gracanin, D., Stefanovic, D., Lalic, B.: The application of ICT solutions in manufacturing companies in Serbia. In: Lalic, B., Majstorovic, V., Marjanovic, U., von Cieminski, G., Romero, D. (eds.) APMS 2020. IAICT, vol. 592, pp. 122–129. Springer, Cham (2020). https://doi.org/10.1007/978-3-030-57997-5_15
5. Dukić Mijatović, M., Uzelac, O., Stoiljković, A.: Effects of human resources management on the manufacturing firm performance: sustainable development approach. Int. J. Ind. Eng. Manag. **11**(3), 205–212 (2021)
6. Heavin, C., Power, D.J.: Challenges for digital transformation–towards a conceptual decision support guide for managers. J. Decis. Syst. **27**(May), 38–45 (2018)
7. Chinotaikul, P., Vinayavekhin, S.: Digital transformation in business and management research: bibliometric and co-word network analysis. In: 1st International Conference on Big Data Analytics and Practices, IBDAP 2020, pp. 1–5 (2020)
8. Echchakoui, S., Barka, N.: Industry 4.0 and its impact in plastics industry: a literature review. J. Ind. Inf. Integr. **20**(September), 100172 (2020)
9. Bashir, M.F.: Analysis of environmental taxes publications: a bibliometric and systematic literature review. Environ. Sci. Pollut. Res. **28**, 20700–20716 (2021)
10. Ciric, D., Lalic, B., Marjanovic, U., Savkovic, M., Rakic, S.: A bibliometric analysis approach to review mass customization scientific production. In: Dolgui, A., Bernard, A., Lemoine, D., von Cieminski, G., Romero, D. (eds.) APMS 2021. IAICT, vol. 634, pp. 328–338. Springer, Cham (2021). https://doi.org/10.1007/978-3-030-85914-5_35
11. Agbo, F.J., Oyelere, S.S., Suhonen, J., Tukiainen, M.: Scientific production and thematic breakthroughs in smart learning environments: a bibliometric analysis. Smart Learn. Environ. **8**(1), 1–25 (2021). https://doi.org/10.1186/s40561-020-00145-4
12. Rojas-Lamorena, Á.J., Del Barrio-García, S., Alcántara-Pilar, J.M.: A review of three decades of academic research on brand equity: a bibliometric approach using co-word analysis and bibliographic coupling. J. Bus. Res. **139**, 1067–1083 (2022)
13. Spasojević, I., Havzi, S., Stefanović, D., Ristić, S., Marjanović, U.: Research trends and topics in IJIEM from 2010 to 2020: a statistical history. Int. J. Ind. Eng. Manag. **12**(4), 228–242 (2021)
14. Chawla, R.N., Goyal, P.: Emerging trends in digital transformation: a bibliometric analysis. Benchmarking **29**(4), 1069–1113 (2021)
15. Pizzi, S., Venturelli, A., Variale, M., Macario, G.P.: Assessing the impacts of digital transformation on internal auditing: a bibliometric analysis. Technol. Soc. **67**(September), 101738 (2021)
16. Adekunle, S.A., Aigbavboa, C.O., Ejohwomu, O., Adekunle, E.A., Thwala, W.D.: Digital transformation in the construction industry: a bibliometric review. J. Eng. Des. Technol. (2021)
17. Lee, C.H., Liu, C.L., Trappey, A.J.C., Mo, J.P.T., Desouza, K.C.: Understanding digital transformation in advanced manufacturing and engineering: a bibliometric analysis, topic modeling and research trend discovery. Adv. Eng. Inf. **50**(October), 101428 (2021)

18. López-Robles, J.R., Otegi-Olaso, J.R., Porto Gómez, I., Cobo, M.J.: 30 years of intelligence models in management and business: a bibliometric review. Int. J. Inf. Manag. **48**, 22–38 (2019)
19. Furstenau, L.B., et al.: An overview of 42 years of lean production: applying bibliometric analysis to investigate strategic themes and scientific evolution structure. Technol. Anal. Strat. Manag. **33**(9), 1068–1087 (2021)
20. Aria, M., Cuccurullo, C.: bibliometrix: an R-tool for comprehensive science mapping analysis. J. Informet. **11**(4), 959–975 (2017)
21. Frank, A., Dalenogare, L., Ayala, N.: Industry 4.0 technologies: implementation patterns in manufacturing companies. Int. J. Prod. Econ. **210**, 15–26 (2019)
22. Cobo, M.J., Herrera, F.: An approach for detecting, quantifying, and visualizing the evolution of a research field: a practical application to the fuzzy sets theory field. J. Informet. **5**(1), 146–166 (2011)
23. Callon, M., Courtial, J., Laville, F.: Co-word analysis as a tool for describing the network of interactions between basic and technological research: the case of polymer chemistry. Scientometrics **22**(1), 155–205 (1991)
24. Nasir, A., Shaukat, K., Hameed, I.A., Luo, S., Alam, T.M., Iqbal, F.: A bibliometric analysis of corona pandemic in social sciences: a review of influential aspects and conceptual structure. IEEE Access **8**, 133377–133402 (2020)
25. Pavlović, M., Marjanović, U., Rakić, S., Tasić, N., Lalić, B.: The big potential of big data in manufacturing: evidence from emerging economies. In: Lalic, B., Majstorovic, V., Marjanovic, U., von Cieminski, G., Romero, D. (eds.) APMS 2020. IAICT, vol. 592, pp. 100–107. Springer, Cham (2020). https://doi.org/10.1007/978-3-030-57997-5_12
26. Zivlak, N., Rakic, S., Marjanovic, U., Ciric, D., Bogojevic, B.: The role of digital servitization in transition economy: an SNA approach. Tech. Gazette **28**(6), 1912–1919 (2021)

Smart Supply Chain and Production in Society 5.0 Era

A Proposal of Data-Driven and Multi-scale Modeling Approach for Material Flow Simulation

Satoshi Nagahara[1,2](✉), Toshiya Kaihara[2] (iD), Nobutada Fujii[2],
and Daisuke Kokuryo[2] (iD)

[1] Industry Automation Research Department, Hitachi, Ltd., Yokohama-shi, Kanagawa, Japan
`satoshi.nagahara.eb@hitachi.com`
[2] Graduate School of System Informatics, Kobe University, 1-1 Rokkodai-cho, Nada-ku,
Kobe-shi 657-8501, Hyogo, Japan

Abstract. Material flow simulation is a powerful tool to realize efficient operation in complicated production systems such as high-mix and low-volume production. However, it takes great efforts and expertise to construct accurate simulation models. On the other hand, in recent years, IoT and machine learning techniques that collect and utilize field data are advancing rapidly. In this research, we propose a data-driven and multi-scale modeling approach which constructs accurate simulation models semi-automatically. The proposed approach aims to optimize the configuration of simulation model by combining deductive models such as queue model and inductive model such as machine learning model to maximize accuracy. In this article, we introduce the concept of the proposed method and experimental results on a simple production system.

Keywords: Material flow simulation · Queueing system · Machine learning

1 Introduction

In recent years, the diversification of market needs makes production systems more complicated such as high-mix low-volume production. In this situation, Cyber-Physical Production System (CPPS) and Digital Twin are attracting attention as concepts that realize efficient operation in such complicated systems [1]. In these concepts, material flow simulation has an important role to predict the future behavior of production systems [2]. However, it takes a lot of efforts and expertise to make accurate simulation models. This difficulty is one of the barriers to realize CPPS/Digital Twin concept in practice. On the other hand, in recent years, more data can be obtained from production system thanks to the advance of IoT devices. In addition, Machine Learning (ML) techniques are remarkably advancing. These technologies enable us to automatically identify system behavior from data. Additionally, ML techniques are capable to make models with different scales such as production process and whole system. This capability will be useful because it is difficult to completely mimic real system and we need to abstract

© IFIP International Federation for Information Processing 2022
Published by Springer Nature Switzerland AG 2022
D. Y. Kim et al. (Eds.): APMS 2022, IFIP AICT 664, pp. 207–215, 2022.
https://doi.org/10.1007/978-3-031-16411-8_26

the system according to the available data. Therefore, in this research, we propose a data-driven and multi-scale modeling approach which semi-automatically constructs simulation models by utilizing the data in production system and ML.

2 Challenges in Material Flow Simulation Modeling

2.1 General Modeling Process for Material Flow Simulation

A general modeling process for material flow simulation is as follows:

Step 1: Modelers define the scope and granularity of simulation model based on their experience and knowledge so that the purpose of simulation use is achieved.

Step 2: Many types of data required to express the system behavior are collected and created. Data such as Bill of Materials and process routing often can be obtained from IT systems such as ERP and MES. However, data rarely managed in ERP/MES such as operational control rules need to be defined through analysis and interview.

Step 3: The developed model is implemented on simulation software using the data.

Step 4: The simulation accuracy is evaluated by the comparison of simulation results with production log. The model is reviewed mostly by trial and error until the required accuracy is archived. The parameters and such as operation time and dispatching rules are mainly adjusted, but the model configuration is also changed if necessary.

2.2 Related Works and Challenge

Most research for automatic modeling regards to data models and system architectures to generate simulation program from data in IT systems [3]. For instance, Kirchhof et al. proposed a method in which simulation objects representing production process are defined in advance, then a simulation program is generated by combining the objects based on MES data [4]. These studies contribute to automate Step 3 in Sect. 2.1.

In addition, there are some researches about the improvement of simulation accuracy. For example, Karnok et al. proposed a method which estimates process route and operation time from production log [5]. Popovics et al. proposed a method to construct the response model of equipment in a conveyor system from PLC program [6]. In addition, Nagahara et al. proposed a method which identifies dispatching rules from production log by ML techniques [7]. They also proposed a method which adjusts parameters in simulation model to improve accuracy [8]. These studies aim to extract the information required for simulation from the data. They contribute to automate the data collection process and improve simulation accuracy.

Furthermore, ML-based methods which directly express the input-output relationship of the system from production log have been proposed. For example, Lingitz et al. proposed a method that predicts production lead time in semiconductor production systems using ANN (Artificial Neural Network), Random Forest, and so on [9].

The above modeling methods enable us to express production system by various scales of model such as each process and whole system. However, it is not clear what kind of model configuration and modeling method are suitable for a specific system. Thus, the automation and optimization of model configuration is still a challenging issue. Therefore, in this research, we propose a novel modeling approach that optimizes model configuration to improve simulation accuracy. The proposed method aims to automatically generate various model configurations by combining multiple models with different scale and modeling method and derive the optimal one.

3 Proposed Method

3.1 Classification of Modeling Methods

Priori to the explanation of the proposed method, we first summarize and classify various modeling methods. Most of production systems consists of multiple production processes, and production process consists of various activities such as setup, machining, resource allocation, and so on. In this research, therefore, we classify modeling methods in three scales: activity scale, process scale and system scale.

In the activity scale, we consider two types of models: "Activity White Box Model (WBM)" and "Activity Black Box Model (BBM)". Activity WBM is a model in which the activity behavior is explicitly and deductively described based on the background knowledge. On the other hand, Activity BBM is a ML based model which inductively expresses the input-output relationship of the activity from activity log.

In the process scale, we consider "Process WBM" and "Process BBM" as well as the activity level. The former is a kind of queue model in which all activities is expressed by WBM and the connection between activities is also explicitly and deductively described. The latter is a ML based model that predicts the process output from the input. In addition, we can consider "Process Gray Box Model (GBM)" as a kind of queue model in which some or all activities are expressed by BBM.

In the system scale, we consider "System WBM", "System BBM" and "System GBM". System WBM is a model in which all process is expressed by WBM. Most of conventional models constructed using commercial software corresponds to System WBM. System BBM is a ML model that predicts system output from system input such as the method by Lingitz et al.[9]. Furthermore, we consider two types of models as System GBM. One is a model in which some or all processes is expressed by GBM or BBM. Another is a model that any sub-system, which is composed with some processes, in the entire system is expressed by System BBM.

3.2 Data-Driven and Multi-scale Modeling for Material Flow Simulation

Based on the classification in Sect. 3.1, we propose a novel modeling approach called as data-driven and multi-scale simulation modeling. Figure 1 shows a schematic view of the proposed method. The proposed method aims to derive an accurate simulation model by combining various modeling methods. W/G/B in Fig. 1 represent WBM/GBM/BBM in arbitrary scale (activity/process/system) respectively. As shown in Model (a), (b) and (c) in Fig. 1, we can consider various configurations of simulation model for a certain target system. In this method, multiple model configurations are generated by integrating and dividing the processes and activities in target system (Fig. 1(1)). As an example, Model (a), (b) and (c) represent System WBM, GBM and BBM respectively. System

WBM is generated from data in ERP/MES using appropriate data interface of simulation software. The data representing background knowledge such as activity information is also utilized for model generation. On the other hand, Activity/Process/System BBM in Model (b) and (c) are generated from production activity logs by ML techniques. Then, according to the input-output requirements for the simulation use, the parameters in each model are calibrated to accurately predict changes in the output with respect to changes in the input (Fig. 1(2)). Let us consider a case that the requirement for simulation is to predict job completion time from job arrival time in the system. In this case, for instance, we can consider a simulation model in which each process is described by Process WBM, GBM or BBM and they predict process completion time of each job in their corresponding process from completion time in the previous processes. Then, the parameters in each model can be calibrated by optimization techniques to minimize the prediction error on job completion time of the overall model. Finally, the most accurate model is selected (Fig. 1(3)). This method is a data-driven method that selects the optimal model configuration based on the prediction accuracy to the target system. Furthermore, this method is a multi-scale modeling method that combines models with different scale (activity, process and system level) and modeling method (white/black/gray box model) to express the entire system.

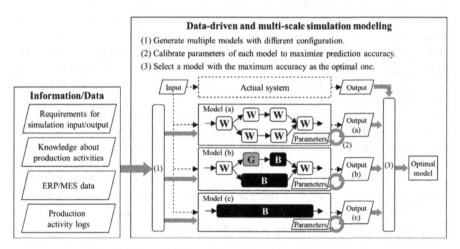

Fig. 1. Schematic view of the proposed modeling approach.

4   Computational Experiments

4.1   Purpose of Experiments

The proposed method combines WBM/BBM/GBM to achieve high accuracy. In other words, the proposed method assumes that a certain modeling method is not always the best and the superiority of modeling method depends on the target system. The superiority of modeling method is closely related to the available data and background knowledge. For example, if we know all activities in the target system and the behavior of them, System WBM will achieve high accuracy. If the activities and/or their activity are partially unknown, the accuracy of the System WBM would be low. On the other hand, if the activity log of some activities is available, it is possible to construct Activity BBM of them. From this point of view, we conducted a computational experiment to compare multiple modeling methods and find out the relationship between the availability of data and the superiority of those modeling methods.

4.2 Experimental Conditions

In this experiment, the virtual production systems A and B in Fig. 2 are considered as target production systems. Both systems A and B are one-equipment and mixed flow systems. The system A has dispatching and machining activities, and the system B has transportation and sequence-dependent setup activities in addition. The dispatching rule is first-in first-out (FIFO), and the transportation time l_p and machining time d_p differ for product type p. The setup time $s_{p,q}$ differs for the combination of previous product type p and successive product type q. The values of $l_p, d_p, s_{p,q}$ are randomly set, and the number of product types M is 5 and the number of jobs N is 50 in each scenario. We created 1,000 scenarios, in which the arrival date-time t_i^{in} and product type index pt_i of job i are randomly set, for model construction and evaluation respectively. The completion date-time t_i^{out} and lead time lt_i of job i are calculated for each scenario from the simulation results of the Process WBMs of system A and B.

In this experiment, Process WBMs of system A and B are assumed as actual systems, and the simulation results of the Process WBMs are assumed as actual activity log. In this experiment, it is assumed that the purpose of simulation use is to predict the lead time of each job from the arrival date-time and product type of each job.

Here, since the systems A and B are deterministic systems, it is obvious that Process WBM is the same as the target system if the activities and their behavior are known. In addition, even in the case that the behavior of each activity is unknown, if the activity log, i.e., start and completion date-time of transportation, setup and machining activities, is available, we can obtain accurate Process GBM by constructing Activity BBM for each activity. In this experiment, therefore, we consider the case in which the behavior of some activities is unknown and the activity log of them is unavailable. Specifically, the time information $l_p, s_{p,q}, d_p$ is unknown, and only the information described in "Input" and "Output" part in Fig. 1 is available as the activity log.

In the above problem setting, Process GBM and Process BBM are compared. For Process GBM, we build a queue model and calibrate the time information parameters to minimize the prediction error. Particle Swarm Optimization (PSO) is used to calibrate parameters. As Process GBM, we consider two models, GBM-A and GBM-B. GBM-A and GBM-B consists of the same activities with system A and system B respectively. As Process BBM, we build a ML model which predicts the lead time of each job from the product type and arrival date-time of each job. ANN is used for the ML model.

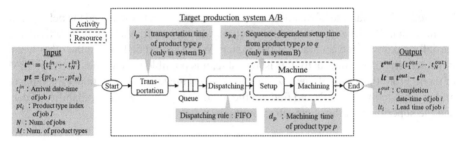

Fig. 2. Experimental conditions: target production system.

4.3 Parameter Calibration in Process GBM by PSO

In the parameter calibration in GBM, the parameters that minimize the objective function J^{GBM} in Eq. (1) are searched.

$$J^{GBM} = \|lt^{ref} - lt^{GBM}\| \tag{1}$$

Here, lt^{ref} and lt^{GBM} are vectors of the lead time in the target system and GBM respectively. Let X be a vector whose elements are the values of the parameters $(l_p, s_{p,q}, d_p)$. lt^{GBM} is the simulation result by GBM with X.

In this experiment, PSO with R-best Model proposed by Choi et al. is used for parameter calibration [10]. In general, the vector representing the solution is called as position vector, and its value is updated by Eq. (2) and (3).

$$X_i^{k+1} = X_i^k + V_i^{k+1} \tag{2}$$

$$V_i^{k+1} = w \times V_i^k + c_1 \times rand() \times \left(gbest - X_i^k\right) + c_2 \times rand() \times \left(pbest_i - X_i^k\right) \tag{3}$$

Here, X_i^k and V_i^k are the position vector and velocity vector of the individual i at the k-th generation, respectively, *gbest* is the position vector of the best solution during the search process, and *pbest_i* is the position vector of the best solution of the individual i during the search process. w, c_1, c_2 are weight coefficients.

4.4 ANN Model for Process BBM

For a Process BBM, we use an ANN model with N inputs and 1 output. The inputs of the ANN are the features related to an arbitrary job, and the output of it is the predicted lead time of that job. The loss function J^{BBM} is shown in Eq. (4).

$$J^{BBM} = \|lt^{ref} - lt^{BBM}\| \tag{4}$$

Here, lt^{BBM} is a vector of the predicted lead time by BBM. Since the lead time of job i depends on not only the product type and arrival date-time of job i but also the jobs which arrive before and after job i, the inputs of ANN should be designed to include such information. Therefore, we define the features of job i by Eq. (5), (6), and (7).

$$x_l = \begin{cases} 1 \ \textit{if } pt_i = l \\ 0 \ \textit{otherwise} \end{cases} (l = 1, \dots, M) \tag{5}$$

$$y_{d,l} = \sum_j \delta_{j,d,l} (j = 1, \dots, N, d = -D, \dots, D-1, l = 1, \dots, M) \tag{6}$$

where

$$\delta_{j,d,l} = \begin{cases} 0 \ \textit{if } j \neq i \textit{ and } t_i^{in} + d \cdot \Delta D \leq t_j^{in} < t_i^{in} + (d+1) \cdot \Delta D \textit{ and } pt_j = l \\ 0 \ \textit{otherwise} \end{cases} \tag{7}$$

Here, M, N is the number of product types and jobs respectively. $y_{d,l}$ is the number of arrival jobs of product type l in a certain period determined by the arrival date-time of job i and parameters D and ΔD. D indicates how long the number of arrival jobs before and after job i is considered, and ΔD is the unit length of the above period.

4.5 Experimental Result

The experimental results are shown in Fig. 3. The horizontal and vertical axes of each plot in Fig. 3 are the normalized lead time in the target system and GBM/BBM respectively, and each point represents each job. (a), (b) and (c) in Fig. 3 are the results of the target system A, and (d), (e), and (f) are the results of the target system B. (a) and (e) are the results when the activity configuration in GBM is the same as that of the target system, and (b) and (d) are the results when the activity configuration is different.

From the results shown in Fig. 3, the most accurate model for system A and system B is GBM-A and GBM-B respectively. It means that GBM could be superior to BBM if the activity configuration of the target system is known. Additionally, the accuracy of (b) and (d) is lower than that of (a) and (e) respectively. (d) is a result of GBM-A in which some activities are lacked compared to system B. Therefore, there is not the solution of parameters that completely matches GBM-A with system B. (b) is a result of GBM-B in which some activities are excessive compared to system A. Although there is the solution that completely matches GBM-B with system A, the parameter search by PSO fell into a local optimal. This indicates that if a model is too complicated, the parameter calibration may become difficult. BBM shows high accuracy for system A (Fig. 3(c)) and more accurate than GBM-B (Fig. 3(b)). It means that BBM may be superior if the background knowledge about activity configuration of the target system is insufficient. On the other hand, BBM shows less accuracy than GBM-A and GBM-B for system B (Fig. 3(f)). This result indicates that it is difficult for ANN to express a system that includes activities strongly affected by the processing order of jobs such as sequence-dependent setup.

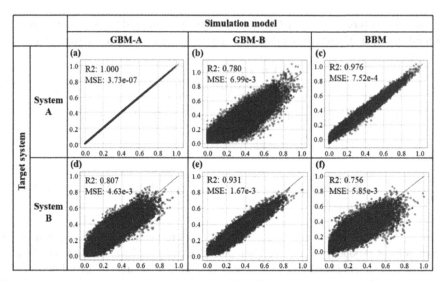

Fig. 3. Experimental results: comparison of prediction accuracy for job lead time. (Horizontal axis: job lead time in target system, Vertical axis: job lead time in simulation model)

5 Conclusion

In this research, we proposed a novel modeling approach for material flow simulation called as data-driven and multi-scale simulation modeling. We classified the existing modeling methods from the perspective of activity, process and system scale and White, Black and Gray Box modeling. Then, we introduced a modeling approach that optimizes model configuration by combining those modeling methods. It has been confirmed that the proposed method is expected to contribute to automate the design phase of model configuration and execute simulation more accurate. In addition, we verified the effects of differences in available data on the superiority of modeling methods through computational experiments.

As future works, the comparison of WBM/GBM/BBM for more complicated system will be conducted. Additionally, we should consider the parameter calibration method for GBM and the design of feature variables and model structure for BBM suitable to express production system. Furthermore, we'll develop methods which automatically generate multiple configurations of simulation model to realize the proposed concept.

References

1. Monostori, L.: Cyber-physical production systems: roots, expectations and R&D challenges. Procedia CIRP **17**, 9–13 (2014)
2. Rosen, R., Wichert, G., Lo, G., Betternhausen, K.D.: About the importance of autonomy and digital twins for the future of manufacturing. IFAC-PapersOnLine **48**(3), 567–572 (2015)
3. Kirchhof, P.: Automatically generation flow shop simulation models from SAP data. In: Proceedings of the 2016 Winter Simulation Conference, pp. 3588–3589 (2016)

4. Barlas, P. and Heavey C.: Automation of input data to discrete event simulation for manufacturing: a review. Int. J. Model. Simul. Sci. Comput. 7, 1630001 (2016)
5. Karnok, D., Monostori, L.: Determination of routings and process time information from event logs. In: Preprints of the 18th IFAC World Congress, pp. 14055–14060 (2011)
6. Popovics, G., Monostori, L.: ISA standard simulation model generation supported by data stored in low level controllers. Procedia CIRP 12, 432–437 (2013)
7. Nagahara, S., Sprock, T.A., Helu, M.M.: Toward data-driven production simulation modeling: dispatching rule identification by machine learning techniques. Procedia CIRP 81, 222–227 (2019)
8. Nagahara, S., et al.: Toward data-driven modeling of material flow simulation: automatic parameter calibration of multiple agents from sparse production log. In: 16th IEEE International Conference on Automation Science and Engineering, pp. 1096–1101 (2020)
9. Lingitz, L., et al.: Lead time prediction using machine learning algorithms: a case study by a semiconductor manufacturer. Procedia CIRP 72, 1051–1056 (2018)
10. Choi, H., Ohmori, S., Yoshimoto, K.: Improvement of particle swarm optimization: Proposal of R-best model and parameter adjustment with consideration to searching phase and state. In: 21st International Conference on Production Research, pp. 2079–2083 (2011)

Distributed Optimization for Supply Chain Planning for Multiple Companies Using Subgradient Method and Consensus Control

Naoto Debuchi, Tatsushi Nishi$^{(\boxtimes)}$, and Ziang Liu

Graduate School of Natural Science and Technology, Okayama University, 3-1-1
Tsushima-naka, Kita-ku, Okayama City 700-8530, Japan
nishi.tatsushi@okayama-u.ac.jp

Abstract. With recent liberalization and enlarging of trade among companies, it is necessary to generate an optimal supply chain planning by cooperation and coordination of supply chain planning for multiple companies without sharing sensitive information such as costs and profit among competitive companies. A distributed optimization can solve the optimization problems with limited information. A distributed optimization method using subgradient and consensus control methods has been proposed to solve continuous optimization problems. However, conventional distributed optimization methods using subgradient and consensus control methods cannot be applied to the supply chain planning for multiple companies including 0–1 decision variables. In this paper, we propose a new distributed optimization method for solving the supply chain planning problem for multiple companies by subgradient method and consensus control. By branching the cases 0–1 variables, an optimal solution can be obtained by the enumeration. A method to reduce the computational effort has been developed in the proposed method. From numerical experiments, it is confirmed that we can obtain an optimal solution by the reduction of the computation.

Keywords: Distributed optimization · Supply chain planning · Subgradient method · Consensus control

1 Introduction

With liberalization and enlarging of trade among companies, coordination of supply chain planning becomes more complex. Therefore, it is necessary to create optimal supply chain planning by cooperation and coordination of supply chain planning for multiple companies. In the optimization processes, companies should share their sensitive information to optimize a supply chain planning. However, it is desirable to create a supply chain planning without sharing sensitive information such as costs and profit among competitive companies. Therefore, in this study, we propose a distributed optimization method that can solve the optimization problems with limited information. Distributed

© IFIP International Federation for Information Processing 2022
Published by Springer Nature Switzerland AG 2022
D. Y. Kim et al. (Eds.): APMS 2022, IFIP AICT 664, pp. 216–223, 2022.
https://doi.org/10.1007/978-3-031-16411-8_27

optimization methods have been studied widely. In the conventional distributed optimization methods, the subgradient method [1, 2] and the consensus control [3] have been used. Subgradient method is one of the optimization methods, which obtain a better solution by moving a decision variable towards the direction of subgradient. Consensus control is that all decision variables agree with the same state by sharing information [4–6]. In recent study, the method using both subgradient method and consensus control [7–9] has been proposed. An optimization model of supply chain planning for multiple companies is proposed in [10]. In [10], an augmented Lagrangian decomposition method is used to solve the problem. The performance of the algorithm is compared with that of Lagrangian relaxation and the penalty function method. These methods can obtain an approximate solution of optimization problems. On the other hand, the distributed optimization method in [7] can obtain an optimal solution of convex continuous optimization problems. In this study, we solve supply chain planning for multiple companies based on the method in [7]. Since the method in [7] cannot be applied to an optimization problem including 0–1 decision variables, we propose a new method which can obtain an optimal solution by branching the cases of 0–1 variables. The proposed method can obtain an optimal solution of optimization problems by the enumerations without using a commercial solver.

2   Supply Chain Planning for Multiple Companies

Supply chain planning for multiple companies is explained in this section. The objective of this problem is to determine the daily trade volume of multiple arrival companies and shipping companies. Each company has a preferred trade volume of each product each day, and it costs a shortage and excess cost when a trade volume has shortage or excess towards preferred trade volume. If the trade volume differs in consecutive days, it costs a trade dividing cost. When each company carries out a trade, it costs a trade implementation cost. This problem needs to meet four constraints: an arrival volume and a shipping volume of products must be equal, prescribed trade volume must be traded, they cannot trade over the upper limit per day, and they can trade only one type or fewer types in each day. We formulate this problem in two ways. The one is formulation including only continuous variables by omitted 0–1 variables. The another is the formulation as 0–1 mixed integer programming problem, including 0–1 variables as an original supply chain planning for multiple companies.

Figure 1 shows an example of supply chain planning for multiple companies. In this example, there are two arrival companies A, B and two shipping companies C, D. Products are two types, the one is blue and the another is yellow. Time period is ten days. The numbers in Fig. 1 indicate each company's trade volume in each day. This supply chain planning meets a constraint which an arrival volume and a shipping volume of products must be an equal and a constraint which companies can trade only one type or fewer types in each day. Trade dividing cost is incurred when the trade volume differs in consecutive days, for example days 1–2 of company D.

Company A	50	50		10	10					30
Company B	20			40	40	40			60	30
Company C				20	20	20			60	60
Company D	70	50		30	30	20				
Time Period	1	2	3	4	5	6	7	8	9	10

Fig. 1. An example of supply chain planning for multiple companies

We define sets, constants, and variables of supply chain planning for multiple companies for formulation.

Sets

Z_d: A set of arrival companies
Z_s: A set of shipping companies
P: A set of products

Constants

s_i^{max}: An upper limit of product i's trade volume
m_i: A product i's prescribed trade volume
$D_{i,t}^c$: A company c's preferred trade volume of product i on day t
$\beta_{i,t}^c$: A company c's coefficient of a shortage and excess cost of product i on day t
e_i^c: A company c's coefficient of a trade dividing cost of product i
$d_{i,t}^c$: A company c's coefficient of a trade implementation cost of product i on day t

Variables

$S_{i,t}^c$: A company c's trade volume of product i on day t
$X_{i,t}^c$: A 0–1 variable indicates company c's trade dividing of product i on day t
$Y_{i,t}^c$: A 0–1 variable indicates company c's presence or absence of trade of product i on day t

2.1 Formulation Including Only Continuous Variables

$$min \sum_{c \in Z_d \cup Z_s} \sum_{i \in P} \sum_t \left\{ \beta_{i,t}^c \left| D_{i,t}^c - S_{i,t}^c \right| \right\} \qquad (2.1)$$

subject to

$$\sum_{c \in Z_d} S_{i,t}^c = \sum_{c \in Z_s} S_{i,t}^c \qquad (2.2)$$

$$\sum_t S_{i,t}^c = m_i \qquad (2.3)$$

$$S_{i,t}^c \leq s_i^{max} \qquad (2.4)$$

(2.1) is an objective function that minimizes the total trade costs. Trade dividing costs and trade implementation costs are not considered in this formulation. (2.2) is a constraint ensuring that an arrival volume and a shipping volume of products must be equal. (2.3) is a constraint which state that the trade volume must be traded. (2.4) is a constraint which companies cannot trade over the upper limit per day. A constraint that companies can trade only one type or fewer types in each day is not considered in this formulation.

2.2 Formulation Including 0–1 Variables

$$min \sum_{c \in Z_d \cup Z_s} \sum_{i \in P} \sum_t \left\{ \beta_{i,t}^c \left| D_{i,t}^c - S_{i,t}^c \right| + e_i^c X_{i,t}^c + d_{i,t}^c Y_{i,t}^c \right\} \tag{2.5}$$

subject to

$$\sum_{c \in Z_d} S_{i,t}^c = \sum_{c \in Z_s} S_{i,t}^c \tag{2.6}$$

$$\sum_t S_{i,t}^c = m_i \tag{2.7}$$

$$S_{i,t}^c \leq s_i^{max} \tag{2.8}$$

$$\sum_{i \in P} Y_{i,t}^c \leq 1 \tag{2.9}$$

$$X_{i,t}^c = \begin{cases} 1 \left(S_{i,t}^c \neq S_{i,t-1}^c \right) \\ 0 \left(S_{i,t}^c = S_{i,t-1}^c \right) \end{cases} \tag{2.10}$$

$$Y_{i,t}^c = \begin{cases} 1 \left(S_{i,t}^c > 0 \right) \\ 0 \left(S_{i,t}^c = 0 \right) \end{cases} \tag{2.11}$$

(2.5) is an objective function that minimizes the total trade costs. (2.6) is a constraint which an arrival volume and a shipping volume of products must be equal. (2.7) is a constraint ensuring that prescribed trade volume must be traded. (2.8) is a constraint which companies cannot trade over the upper limit per day. (2.9) is a constraint which companies can trade only one type or fewer types in each day. (2.10) is a 0–1 variable which shows the dividing of trade. (2.11) is a 0–1 variable which shows the implementation of trade.

3 Solution of the Optimization Problems Including Only Continuous Variables

We use the distributed penalty primal-dual subgradient algorithm (DPPDS algorithm) proposed in [7]. Algorithm 1 shows the DPPDS algorithm.

$$v_x^i(k) = \sum_{j=1}^N a_j^i x^j(k) \tag{3.1}$$

$$v^i_\mu(k) = \sum_{j=1}^{N} a^i_j \mu^j(k) \tag{3.2}$$

$$v^i_\lambda(k) = \sum_{j=1}^{N} a^i_j \lambda^j(k) \tag{3.3}$$

$$x^i(k+1) = P_X\left[v^i_x(k) - \alpha(k)S^i_x(k)\right] \tag{3.4}$$

$$\mu^i(k+1) = v^i_\mu(k) + \alpha(k)\left[g\left(v^i_x(k)\right)\right]^+ \tag{3.5}$$

$$\lambda^i(k+1) = v^i_\lambda(k) + \alpha(k)\left|h\left(v^i_x(k)\right)\right| \tag{3.6}$$

$$S^i_x(k) = D_{f^i}\left(v^i_x(k)\right) + \sum_{\ell=1}^{m} v^i_\mu(k)\left[D_{g_\ell}\left(v^i_x(k)\right)\right]^+ + \sum_{s=1}^{v} v^i_\lambda(k)\left|D_{h_s}\left(v^i_x(k)\right)\right| \tag{3.7}$$

Algorithm1 DPPDS algorithm

1: **Given** initial variables $x^i(0), \mu^i(0), \lambda^i(0)$ for each agent $i, i = 1, \cdots, N$; set $k = 1$
2: **repeat**
3:   For $i = 1, \cdots, N$, each agent i computes (3.1) ~ (3.3)
4:   For $i = 1, \cdots, N$, each agent i computes (3.4) ~ (3.7)
5:   **Set** $k = k + 1$
6: **until** a predefined stopping criterion (e.g., $k = 1000$) is satisfied.
7: computes $z = f(x(k))$

(3.1)–(3.3) indicate consensus control. Each company updates the variables by sharing variables with other companies. (3.4)–(3.7) are the updating equations of variables to optimal solution by subgradient method. An optimal solution can be obtained by enough times of updates of variables by consensus control and subgradient method.

4 Applying to the Optimization Problems Including 0–1 Variables

In this study, we apply the DPPDS algorithm to supply chain planning for multiple companies by branching the cases 0–1 variables and regarding them as continuous variables. There are two 0–1 variables which must be considered in this problem, $X^c_{i,t}$ and $Y^c_{i,t}$. For branching $X^c_{i,t}$ value, we add a constraint which the trade volume $S^c_{i,t}$ must be equal to $S^c_{i,t-1}$ when $X^c_{i,t} = 0$. For branching $Y^c_{i,t}$ value, we add a constraint which the trade volume $S^c_{i,t}$ must be zero when $Y^c_{i,t} = 0$. We don't add a constraint when $X^c_{i,t} = 1$ or $Y^c_{i,t} = 1$. We obtain an optimal solution by obtaining the solution of the optimization problems of each case and comparing the value of the objective function. However, in some cases branched by $Y^c_{i,t}$ value does not satisfy the constraint that can trade only one type or fewer types in each day. To satisfy this constraint, we choose a type of products which can be traded in each day. Algorithm 2 shows the exhaustive search algorithm of a supply chain planning for multiple companies by using the DPPDS algorithm.

Algorithm2 Exhaustive search algorithm

1: **Given** initial variables $X_{i,t}^c = 1, Y_{i,t}^c = 1$; for $c = 1, \cdots, n$, $i = 1, \cdots, p$, $t = 1, \cdots, h$
2: **repeat**
3: $flg = 0$
4: computes $Z_{i,t} = Y_{i,t}^1 + \cdots + Y_{i,t}^n$; for $i = 1, \cdots, p$, $t = 1, \cdots, h$
5: **if** more than two of $Z_{p,t} \geq 1$; for $t = 1, \cdots, h$ **then** $flg = 1$
6: **if** $flg = 0$
7:   **if** $X_{i,t}^c = 0$; for $c = 1, \cdots, n$, $i = 1, \cdots, p$, $t = 1, \cdots, h$
8:    adds constrains $S_{i,t}^c = S_{i,t-1}^c$
9:   **if** $Y_{i,t}^c = 0$; for $c = 1, \cdots, n$, $i = 1, \cdots, p$, $t = 1, \cdots, h$
10:    adds constrains $S_{i,t}^c = 0$
11:   computes z by **Algorithm1**
12:   **if** $z <$ total cost
13:    total cost $\leftarrow z$
14:    $S_{i,t}^{*c} \leftarrow S_{i,t}^c(k)$; for $c = 1, \cdots, n$, $i = 1, \cdots, p$, $t = 1, \cdots, h$
15: changes value of $X_{i,t}^c, Y_{i,t}^c$ one by one; for $i = 1, \cdots, p$, $t = 1, \cdots, h$
16: **until** $X_{i,t}^c = 0, Y_{i,t}^c = 0$; for $c = 1, \cdots, n$, $i = 1, \cdots, p$, $t = 1, \cdots, h$

$Z_{i,t}$ indicates product i which can be traded on day t and product i can be traded when $Z_{i,t} \geq 1$. $S_{i,t}^{*c}$ is a tentative optimal solution and *totalcost* is a value of the objective function by $S_{i,t}^{*c}$ value. We omit the cases not satisfying the constraint which companies can trade only one type or fewer types in each day in line 4, 5. Tentative optimal solution is updated if we obtain a better solution in line 12 ~ 14. We compute the cases from all $X_{i,t}^c$ and $Y_{i,t}^c$ are 1 to all $X_{i,t}^c$ and $Y_{i,t}^c$ are 0.

In this algorithm, we confirm that an optimal solution is derived. However, the number of computations becomes much larger. Therefore, we have to omit the computation of the cases overlapping constraints with other cases or not being able to obtain a feasible solution.

As the cases overlapping constraints with other cases, there are the cases which the trade volume on day t and day $t - 1$ are equal depending on the values of $Y_{i,t}^c$ and $Y_{i,t-1}^c$. For example, if we solve the case which $Y_{i,t}^c = 0$, $Y_{i,t-1}^c = 0$, $X_{i,t}^c = 1$, then we do not have to solve the cases which either $Y_{i,t}^c$ or $Y_{i,t-1}^c$ is zero and $X_{i,t}^c = 0$. When $Y_{i,t}^c = 0$, $Y_{i,t-1}^c = 0$, $X_{i,t}^c = 1$, the trade volume $S_{i,t}^c$ and $S_{i,t-1}^c$ are zero by a constraint which the trade volume $S_{i,t}^c$ must be zero when $Y_{i,t}^c = 0$. If either $Y_{i,t}^c$ or $Y_{i,t-1}^c$ is zero and $X_{i,t}^c = 0$, the trade volume $S_{i,t}^c$ and $S_{i,t-1}^c$ must be zero by a constraint which the trade volume $S_{i,t}^c$ must be equal to $S_{i,t-1}^c$ when $X_{i,t}^c = 0$. Therefore, solving this case is same as solving the case which $Y_{i,t}^c = 0$, $Y_{i,t-1}^c = 0$, $X_{i,t}^c = 1$.

As the cases not being able to obtain a feasible solution, there are the cases which do not satisfy a constraint ensuring that prescribed trade volume must be traded depending on the values of $Y_{i,t}^c$. To satisfy the constraint that can trade only one type or fewer types in each day, we choose a type of products which can be traded in each day. We define the number of days which can trade product i is N_i, then $N_i \times s_i^{max}$ is max trade volume of product i, s_i^{max} is an upper limit of product i's trade volume in each day. If $N_i \times s_i^{max}$ is less than m_i, a constraint ensuring that prescribed trade volume must be traded is not satisfied, m_i is A product i's prescribed trade volume. We omit the cases like this before the computations.

5 Computational Experiments

To confirm the effectiveness of the proposed method, we obtain an optimal solution by using CPLEX. In optimization by CPLEX, not using a distributed optimization, we solve a supply chain planning for multiple companies as a total optimization problem. By numeral experiments, it is confirmed that we can obtain an optimal solution of a supply chain planning for multiple companies by the proposed method. Also, we compare the number of computations between exhaustive search algorithm and the proposed algorithm with the reduction of the computations. Table 1 shows the comparison of the number of computations between exhaustive search algorithm and the proposed algorithm. From the result, it is confirmed that the number of computations is significantly reduced, more than 99 percent in all cases. As the size of problem is larger, the reduction rate is higher. It is because that as the size of problem is larger, the proportion of the cases overlapping constraints with other cases is higher.

Table 1. The comparison of the number of computations between exhaustive search algorithm and algorithm reducing the computation.

	Exhaustive search	Reduction of the computation	Reduction rate [%]
case1	784	2	99.744898
case2	87,808	9	99.989750
case3	1,101,453,552	193	99.999982
case4	123,363,917,824	6,548	99.999994
case5	13,824,000	540	99.996093
case6	1,952,382,976	6,561	99.999664
case7	13,271,040,000	11,898	99.999910
case8	4,096,000	6	99.999854
case9	2,621,440,000	114	99.999996
case10	2,791,309,312	162	99.999994

It is confirmed that our proposed distributed optimization method can reduce the number of computations, however it is not enough to solve much larger problems. Therefore, we need to continue to find the way to reduce the number of computations. The values of constants influence on the number of computations, so we have to continue to consider the influence of the value of constants on the optimality.

6 Conclusion

In this study, we examine the solution of optimization problems by the DPPDS algorithm and propose the solution using an exhaustive search algorithm to solve a supply chain planning for multiple companies including 0–1 variables. Also, we examine the method reducing the computation while retaining optimality. As a result, we confirm that we can obtain an optimal solution of the supply chain planning for multiple companies by proposed method. Also, we confirm that the number of computations in the proposed method can be reduced by the examined method. As a future work, we need to examine the method to reduce the number of computations more while retaining optimality. We also need to examine the influence on calculation time or optimality by assessing the influence on the value of the objective function before computation and omitting the case which cannot be expected an optimal solution.

References

1. Nishi, T.: Distributed optimization technique for supply chain management. Jpa. Soc. Artif. Intell. **19**(5), 571–578 (2004)
2. Sakurama, K.: Networked distributed optimization of massive systems. J. Soc. Instr. Control Eng. **56**(12), 949–954 (2017)
3. Hatanaka, T.: Control of multi-agent systems – VI distributed optimization. Syst. Control Inf. **58**(3), 124–131 (2014)
4. Sakurama, K.: Control of multi-agent systems – III consensus control (1). Syst. Control Inf. **57**(9), 386–396 (2013)
5. Sakurama, K.: Control of multi-agent systems – IV consensus control (2). Syst. Control Inf. **57**(11), 470–479 (2013)
6. Hayashi, N., Nagahara, M.: Control of multi-agent systems – II algebraic graph theory. Syst. Control Inf. **57**(7), 283–292 (2013)
7. Zhu, M., Martínez, S.: On distributed convex optimization under inequality and equality constraints via primal-dual subgradient methods. IEEE Trans. Autom. Control **57**, 151–164 (2012)
8. Chang, T., Nedić, A., Scaglione, A.: Distributed constrained optimization by consensus-based primal-dual perturbation method. IEEE Trans. Autom. Control **59**, 1524–1538 (2014)
9. Nedić, A., Ozdaglar, A., Parrilo, P.A.: Constrained consensus and optimization in multi-agent networks. IEEE Trans. Autom. Control **55**, 922–938 (2010)
10. Nishi, T., Shinozaki, R., Konishi, M.: A distributed optimization system for supply chain planning among multi-companies using an augmented Lagrangian decomposition method. Soc. Instr. Control Eng. **40**(5), 582–589 (2004)

An Ant Colony Optimization with Turn-Around-Time Reduction Mechanism for the Robust Aircraft Maintenance Routing Problem

Abdelrahman E. E. Eltoukhy[1]([⊠]) [ID] and Noha Mostafa[2,3] [ID]

[1] Department of Industrial and Systems Engineering, The Hong Kong Polytechnic University, Hung Hum, Hong Kong
abdelrahman.eltoukhy@polyu.edu.hk
[2] Mechanical Engineering Department, Faculty of Engineering, The British University in Egypt, Shorouk 11837, Egypt
noha.mostafa@bue.edu.eg, namostafa@eng.zu.edu.eg
[3] Industrial Engineering Department, Faculty of Engineering, Zagazig University, Zagazig 44519, Egypt

Abstract. The robust aircraft maintenance routing problem (RAMRP) is adopted by airlines to determine aircraft routes with better withstanding for possible disruptions. This can be achieved using a common approach called the buffer time insertion approach (BT). From the literature, it was observed that this approach has a pitfall of reducing the fleet productivity while inserting long buffer times. Besides, it cannot accommodate flight delays while inserting short buffer times. These disadvantages were the motivation to conduct this study to propose a RAMRP solution that incorporates a novel robustness approach, called turn-around-time reduction (TR), in which all the previous drawbacks are avoided. An ant colony-based algorithm (AC) was developed to solve the proposed RAMRP. To demonstrate the viability and effectiveness of the proposed approach, experiments are conducted based on real data obtained from a major airline company located in the Middle East. The results show that the proposed TR outperforms the existing BT in terms of fleet productivity and delay accommodation.

Keywords: Aircraft maintenance routing problem · Airline operations · Robustness · Ant Colony optimization

1 Introduction

The aircraft maintenance routing problem (AMRP) is essential for airlines because it constructs the aircraft routes and schedules the aircraft maintenance visits. The AMRP has been addressed in the literature through three different variants: tactical (TAMRP) [1, 2], operational (OAMRP) [3–7], and robust (RAMRP) [8–11]. The focus of this research

© IFIP International Federation for Information Processing 2022
Published by Springer Nature Switzerland AG 2022
D. Y. Kim et al. (Eds.): APMS 2022, IFIP AICT 664, pp. 224–231, 2022.
https://doi.org/10.1007/978-3-031-16411-8_28

is the RAMRP, which adopts the robustness idea to create flexible routes that can withstand unpredictable events [8–11]. In RAMRP, the flight delays are considered besides the operational maintenance requirements. Usually, the robustness can be achieved using an approach, called the buffer time insertion approach (BT). This approach is used to insert buffer or slack time between flight legs to deal with the expected flight delays. Indeed, the BT approach was widely adopted in the literature [12, 13]. However, there are significant drawbacks of the BT approach. On the one hand, imposing a large buffer time among flight legs reduces the number of flight legs covered by each aircraft, henceforth reducing fleet productivity, mainly when covering many flight legs. On the other hand, inserting a short buffer time may not be enough to absorb the expected delays. The recent survey in [14] provides further details about the AMRP.

This study makes the following contributions; first, in contrast to the BT robustness approach, we propose a novel robustness approach, called the TR. Before proposing this approach, it is essential to define the turn-around time (TRT) as the time required by the airlines, or other service companies, to help the aircraft complete the operations related to the last covered flight legs and to finalize the operations associated with the next flight legs. These operations are called ground handling operations and include unloading the luggage of the previously covered flight leg, loading the luggage for the next flight leg, moving the aircraft between gates, and fueling the aircraft. The main idea of the TR is to speed up or to reduce the normal TRT by allocating more ground resources (i.e., workforce and facilities) while observing any delay. Consequently, the accumulated propagated delay can be mitigated, avoiding the delay propagation for the downstream flight legs, leading to significant recovery cost savings for the airlines company. Before designing the TR, several interviews were made with experts in a major Middle Eastern airlines company, they mentioned that allocating more ground resources can contribute to speeding up some ground operations, resulting in a 30–50% reduction in the normal TRT. Based on this remark, three types of TRT were addressed: the normal TRT, the reduced TRT (i.e., 30% reduction of the normal TRT), and the extra-reduced TRT (i.e., 50% reduction of the normal TRT). The first TRT is applied when the accumulated propagated delay does not appear, whereas the rest of the TRTs are used when the delay appears.

The remainder of this paper is organized as follows. In Sect. 2, the model formulation is presented. The solution method for the RAMRP and the computational experiments are provided in Sect. 3. Finally, Sect. 4 gives the conclusions of the study.

2 Model Formulation

The RAMRP is formulated based on the connection network [3]. The node sets of the network include the flight legs set (I) and the maintenance stations set (MT), whereas the arc sets of the network include the normal TRT coverage arc set $(COVN)$, the reduced TRT coverage arc set $(COVR)$, the extra-reduced TRT coverage set $(COVE)$, the visiting maintenance arc set (VMA), and the leaving maintenance arc set (LMA). The normal TRT coverage arc $covn(i, j) \in COVN$ is used to link two consecutive flight legs, such that the TRT is normal, i.e. when there is no accumulated propagated delay. On the other hand, when the accumulated propagated delay appears, $covr(i, j) \in COVR$ and $cove(i, j) \in$

COVE, are used, depending on the severity of the accumulated propagated delay. The visiting maintenance arc $vma(i, m) \in VMA$ is designed to prepare maintenance visits for the aircraft, whereas the leaving maintenance arc $lma(m, j) \in LMA$ is incorporated in the network to let the aircraft leave the maintenance stations and resume covering the subsequent flight legs.

Notations used throughout the model are given as follows:

Sets and indices:

A	Set of airports, indexed by a
MT	Set of maintenance stations, indexed by m
I	Set of flight legs, indexed by i or j
K	Set of aircraft, indexed by k
$t \in T$	Turn-around time (TRT) types $\{n, r, e\}$, such that n, r, and e represent the normal TRT, the reduced TRT, and the extra-reduced TRT, respectively
$v \in \{1, 2, \ldots, \Psi\}$	The average number of maintenance checks that each aircraft should receive during the planning horizon
$\{o, s\}$	Starting and ending node of the modified connection network

Parameters:

DT_i	Flight leg i departure time
O_{ia}	Binary integer. It takes a value of 1 if the origin airport of flight leg i is airport a and 0 otherwise
AT_i	Flight leg i arrival time
D_{ia}	Binary integer. It takes a value of 1 if the destination airport of flight leg i is airport a and 0 otherwise
FT_i	Duration of flight leg i
TRT^t	Turn-around time of type t. It is noteworthy that TRT is the time consumed in unloading and loading the luggage, and fueling the aircraft
$E(NPD_i)$	The expected value of the non-propagated delay of flight leg i.
Mb_{ma}	Binary indicator. It takes a value of 1 if maintenance station m is located at airport a and 0 otherwise
MAT	Time required to complete Type A maintenance check
FS	Fleet size
Ψ	The maximum average number of maintenance checks should be received by each aircraft. The value of Ψ can be achieved through $\Psi = \sum_{i \in NF} FT_i / (T_{max} FS)$
M	A big number
PD^t_{ijkv}	The propagated delay value appears when flight leg i and j are consecutively flown by aircraft k, while using turn-around time of type t, before receiving the maintenance check number v
PD_{ikv}	The accumulated propagated delay value appears before covering flight leg i by aircraft k, before receiving the maintenance check number v
SEV	Severity threshold for the accumulated propagated delay such that going beyond it causes sever delays for the downstream flights

C_{pD} Expected cost incurred by the airline for each minute of propagated delay

Decision variables:

$x_{ijkv}^t \in \{0, 1\}$ It takes a value of 1 if aircraft k covers two consecutive flight legs i and j using turn-around time of type t, before receiving the maintenance check number v, and 0 otherwise

$y_{imkv} \in \{0, 1\}$ It takes a value of 1 if flight leg i is covered by aircraft k, then the aircraft proceeds to maintenance station m to receive the maintenance check number v, and 0 otherwise

$z_{mjkv} \in \{0, 1\}$ It takes a value of 1 if aircraft k leaves maintenance station m to cover flight leg j, after receiving the maintenance check number v, and 0 otherwise

$RT_{kvm} > 0$ The ready time when aircraft k completes receiving the maintenance check number v at maintenance station m, and can fly the next scheduled flight legs

Based on the previous defined notations, the formulation of the RAMRP can be represented as follows:

$$\min \sum_{v=1,\ldots,\Psi} C_{pD}\left(\sum_{k\in K}\sum_{i\in I}\sum_{j\in I}\sum_{t\in T} PD_{ijkv}^t x_{ijkv}^t\right) \tag{1}$$

Subject to

$$PD_{ijkv}^t = (PD_{ikv} + E(NPD_i) - (DT_j - AT_i - TRT^t))^+ \quad \begin{matrix} \forall i,j \in I, \forall t \in T, \forall k \in K, \\ \forall v = 1,\ldots,\Psi \end{matrix} \tag{2}$$

$$\sum_{k\in K}\left(\sum_{j\in I\cup\{s\}}\sum_{t\in T}\sum_{v\in\Psi} x_{ijkv}^t + \sum_{m\in MT}\sum_{v\in\Psi} y_{imkv}\right) = 1 \; \forall i \in I \tag{3}$$

$$\sum_{j\in I\cup\{o\}}\sum_{t\in T} x_{jikv}^t + \sum_{m\in MT} z_{mikv} = \sum_{j\in I\cup\{s\}}\sum_{t\in T} x_{ijkv}^t + \sum_{m\in MT} y_{imkv} \quad \begin{matrix} \forall i \in I, \forall k \in K, \\ \forall v = 1,\ldots,\Psi \end{matrix}$$
$$\tag{4}$$

$$\sum_{j\in I}\sum_{v=1,\ldots,\Psi} y_{jmkv} = \sum_{j\in I\cup\{t\}}\sum_{v=1,\ldots,\Psi} z_{mjkv} \; \forall m \in MT, \forall k \in K \tag{5}$$

$$AT_i + TRT^t - DT_j \le M\left(1 - x_{ijkv}^t\right) \forall i,j \in I, \forall t \in T, \forall k \in K, \forall v = 1,\ldots,\Psi \tag{6}$$

$$\sum_{k\in K} x_{ijkv}^t \le \sum_{a\in A} D_{ia}O_{ja} \; \forall i,j \in I, \forall v = 1,\ldots,\Psi \tag{7}$$

$$x_{ijkv}^n + x_{ijkv}^r + x_{ijkv}^e \le 1 \; \forall i,j \in I, \forall k \in K, \forall v = 1,\ldots,\Psi \tag{8}$$

$$1 - PD_{ikv} \le M\left(1 - x_{ijkv}^n\right) \forall i,j \in I, \forall k \in K, \forall v = 1,\ldots,\Psi \tag{9}$$

$$PD_{ikv} - SEV \le M\left(1 - x_{ijkv}^r\right) \forall i,j \in I, \forall k \in K, \forall v = 1,\ldots,\Psi \tag{10}$$

$$SEV - PD_{ikv} \le M\left(1 - x^e_{ijkv}\right) \; \forall i,j \in I, \forall k \in K, \forall v = 1, \ldots, \Psi \tag{11}$$

$$\sum_{k \in K} y_{imkv} \le \sum_{a \in A} D_{ia} Mb_{ma} \; \forall i \in I, \forall m \in MT, \forall v = 1, \ldots, \Psi \tag{12}$$

$$\sum_{k \in K} z_{mjkv} \le \sum_{a \in A} Mb_{ma} O_{ja} \; \forall m \in MT, \forall j \in I, \forall v = 1, \ldots, \Psi \tag{13}$$

$$RT_{kvm} - DT_j \le M\left(1 - z_{mjkv}\right) \; \forall m \in MT, \forall j \in I, \forall k \in K, \forall v = 1, \ldots, \Psi \tag{14}$$

$$RT_{kvm} \ge \sum_{i \in I \cup \{o\}} \sum_{j \in I \cup \{t\}} \sum_{m \in MT} (AT_i + MAT) z_{mjkv} \; \begin{matrix} \forall k \in K, \forall v = 1, \ldots, \Psi, \\ \forall m \in MT \end{matrix} \tag{15}$$

The objective function stated in (1) is to minimize the expected propagated delay cost over the planning horizon. Constraints (2) express the propagated delay calculations. Constraints (3) are cast to cover all the flight legs, which indicates covering each flight leg strictly by one aircraft. Balance constraints (4) and (5) are formulated to keep the aircraft's circulation throughout the network. To connect two flight legs by using the same aircraft, that connection should be feasible in terms of time and space considerations, as described by constraints (6) and (7). As mentioned earlier, one of the distinctive features of the proposed model is using the TR as a robustness approach. This approach is indicated in constraints (8)–(11). To prepare a maintenance visit for the aircraft, constraints (12) are formulated to consider the locations of the maintenance stations. After finishing the maintenance operation, the aircraft should resume covering its route. For this purpose, constraints (13)–(15) are developed.

3   Solution Method and Computational Experiments

Since the RAMRP is modeled as a network-based problem, the ACO has been selected as it has been successfully applied in solving large and complex network-based problems [15–18]. The ACO based-algorithm proposed by Eltoukhy, et al. [5] was used to solve the RAMRP model. In addition, this algorithm employs a neural network algorithm for flight delay prediction [19]. The adopted ACO algorithm has two main parts; route construction with the help of an ant that simulates an aircraft moving throughout the network, and updating the pheromone trail to improve the solution quality through several iterations.

To demonstrate the effectiveness of the proposed TR approach, computational experiments were conducted based on real data obtained from a major Middle Eastern airline. A summary of the data is given in Table 1.

Table 1. Features of the collected test cases

Test cases	Number of flight legs	Fleet size	Maximum number of take-offs	Number of airports	Maintenance Stations
Case 1	400	65	15	28	18
Case 2	2040	332	15	35	24
Case 3	4080	664	15	35	24

3.1 Performance Analysis

To test the superiority of the proposed TR over the BT approach, our experiments are conducted to compare the performance of the TR with the BT approach proposed by Liang, et al. [12]. The performance of the robustness approaches is shown in Table 2.

Table 2. Performance characteristics of the two robustness approaches

Test case	No. of flight legs	BT approach		TR approach		$\%(\overline{Z})_{BT}$	$\%(FP)_{BT}$
		$\overline{Z}$	FP	$\overline{Z}$	FP		
Case 1	400	6849	365	6,325	400	7.65	8.75
Case 2	2040	53,308	1802	47,754	2040	10.42	11.67
Case 3	4080	154,501	3526	135,652	4080	12.20	13.58

Regarding the TR and the BT, Table 2 shows that the structure of the TR enables it to outperform the BT by about 7.65–12.20% and 8.75–13.58% while handling the propagated delay costs and fleet productivity, respectively. The proposed approach was able to reduce the TRT times by allocating more ground resources when the propagated delay appears. This results in accommodating the propagated delay, leading to significant savings in the propagated delay costs. In contrast to the TR, the BT sometimes inserts short buffer times, which may not be enough to absorb the propagated delays, increasing the propagated delay costs. Moving to the reason for the outperformance in terms of fleet productivity. Indeed, the BT sometimes imposes a long buffer time between the flight legs, which reduces the number of flight legs that should be covered by each aircraft. Consequently, the BT suffers from reduced fleet productivity, mainly when covering many flight legs. Opposite to the BT, the TR does not include those large-time slots, so the fleet productivity reduction can be easily avoided.

4   Conclusions

This study investigates the RAMRP and sought to propose a novel robust approach, called the TR. The effectiveness of the proposed TR approach is demonstrated through computational experiments using real data acquired from a major Middle Eastern airline. In our computational experiments, we demonstrate the importance of the TR, which is included in the RAMRP, by making a comparison with the BT approach. The results reveal an outperformance of the TR over the BT by about 7.65–12.20% and 8.75–13.58% while handling the propagated delay costs and fleet productivity, respectively. The results of this study indicate that the novel TR has excellent potential for implementation in the airline industry. Since the airlines have high uncertainty levels, it could be fruitful to develop an AMRP model while considering stochastic parameters such as arrival and departure times [20–22]. For future research, it is recommended to carry out further tests to assess the superiority of the new approach over the existing ones, particularly in different real-life scenarios. Besides, the sensitivity of the obtained results against changes in external parameters might be another avenue for future research.

Acknowledgments. The study presented in this article was mainly supported by a grant from the Research Committee of The Hong Kong Polytechnic University under project code P0036181and RGC (Hong Kong).

References

1. Gopalan, R., Talluri, K.T.: The aircraft maintenance routing problem. Oper. Res. **46**(2), 260–271 (1998)
2. Liang, Z., Chaovalitwongse, W.A., Huang, H.C., Johnson, E.L.: On a new rotation tour network model for aircraft maintenance routing problem. Transp. Sci. **45**(1), 109–120 (2011)
3. Eltoukhy, A.E.E., Chan, F.T.S., Chung, S.H., Niu, B.: A model with a solution algorithm for the operational aircraft maintenance routing problem. Comput. Ind. Eng. **120**, 346–359 (2018)
4. Eltoukhy, A.E.E., Chan, F.T.S., Chung, S.H., Niu, B., Wang, X.P.: Heuristic approaches for operational aircraft maintenance routing problem with maximum flying hours and man-power availability considerations. Ind. Manag. Data Syst. **117**(10), 2142–2170 (2017)
5. Eltoukhy, A.E.E., Wang, Z.X., Chan, F.T.S., Chung, S.H.: Joint optimization using a leader–follower Stackelberg game for coordinated configuration of stochastic operational aircraft maintenance routing and maintenance staffing. Comput. Ind. Eng. **125**, 46–68 (2018)
6. Eltoukhy, A.E.E., Wang, Z.X., Chan, F.T.S., Fu, X.: Data analytics in managing aircraft routing and maintenance staffing with price competition by a Stackelberg-Nash game model. Transp. Res. Part E: Logist. Transp. Rev. **122**, 143–168 (2019)
7. Eltoukhy, A.E.E., Wang, Z.X., Shaban, I.A., Chan, F.T.S.: Coordinating aircraft maintenance routing and integrated maintenance staffing and rostering: a Stackelberg game theoretical model. Int. J. Prod. Res., 1–25 (2022)
8. Hashim, H.A., Eltoukhy, A.E.E.: Landmark and IMU data fusion: systematic convergence geometric nonlinear observer for SLAM and velocity bias. IEEE Trans. Intell. Transp. Syst. **23**(4), 3292–3301 (2022)
9. Hashim, H.A., Eltoukhy, A.E.E.: Nonlinear filter for simultaneous localization and mapping on a matrix lie group using IMU and feature measurements. IEEE Trans. Syst. Man Cybern. Syst. **52**(4), 2098–2109 (2022)
10. Hashim, H.A.: guaranteed performance nonlinear observer for simultaneous localization and mapping. IEEE Control Syst. Lett. **5**(1), 91–96 (2021)
11. Hashim, H.A., Abouheaf, M., Vamvoudakis, K.G.: Neural-adaptive stochastic attitude filter on SO(3). IEEE Control Syst. Lett. **6**, 1549–1554 (2022)

12. Liang, Z., Feng, Y., Zhang, X., Wu, T., Chaovalitwongse, W.A.: Robust weekly aircraft maintenance routing problem and the extension to the tail assignment problem. Transp. Res. Part B: Methodol. **78**, 238–259 (2015)
13. Jamili, A.: A robust mathematical model and heuristic algorithms for integrated aircraft routing and scheduling, with consideration of fleet assignment problem. J. Air Transp. Manag. **58**, 21–30 (2017)
14. Eltoukhy, A.E.E., Chan, F.T.S., Chung, S.H.: Airline schedule planning: a review and future directions. Ind. Manag. Data Syst. **117**(6), 1201–1243 (2017)
15. Huang, S.-H., Huang, Y.-H., Blazquez, C.A., Paredes-Belmar, G.: Application of the ant colony optimization in the resolution of the bridge inspection routing problem. Appl. Soft Comput. **65**, 443–461 (2018)
16. Mahato, D.P., Singh, R.S., Tripathi, A.K., Maurya, A.K.: On scheduling transactions in a grid processing system considering load through Ant Colony Optimization. Appl. Soft Comput. **61**, 875–891 (2017)
17. Skinderowicz, R.: An improved ant colony system for the sequential ordering problem. Comput. Oper. Res. **86**, 1–17 (2017)
18. Balseiro, S.R., Loiseau, I., Ramonet, J.: An ant colony algorithm hybridized with insertion heuristics for the time dependent vehicle routing problem with time windows. Comput. Oper. Res. **38**(6), 954–966 (2011)
19. Eltoukhy, A.E.E., Shaban, I.A., Chan, F.T.S., Abdel-Aal, M.A.M.: Data analytics for predicting COVID-19 cases in top affected countries: observations and recommendations. Int. J. Environ. Res. Public Health **17**(19), 7080 (2020)
20. Hashim, H.A.: A geometric nonlinear stochastic filter for simultaneous localization and mapping. Aerosp. Sci. Technol. **111**, 106569 (2021)
21. Hashim, H.A.: Exponentially stable observer-based controller for VTOL-UAVs without velocity measurements. Int. J. Control, 1–15 (2022)
22. Hashim, H.A., Abouheaf, M., Abido, M.A.: Geometric stochastic filter with guaranteed performance for autonomous navigation based on IMU and feature sensor fusion. Control. Eng. Pract. **116**, 104926 (2021)

Exploring a Commercial Game for Adoption to Logistics Training

Matthias Kalverkamp[1]([✉]) [iD], Jannicke Baalsrud Hauge[2] [iD], and Theodore Lim[3] [iD]

[1] Wiesbaden Business School, RheinMain University of Applied Sciences, 65183 Wiesbaden, Germany
matthias.kalverkamp@hs-rm.de
[2] KTH Stockholm, Södertälje, Sweden
jmbh@kth.se
[3] School of Engineering and Physical Sciences, Hariot-Watt University, Edinburgh, UK
T.Lim@hw.ac.uk

Abstract. Supply Chain & logistics as a subject lends itself readily to game-based learning. SCM subject learning is primarily about decision making, logistics and strategic management of resources. Most of the serious games designed for SCM are used in a workshop setting, and much of the learning outcome is achieved through the debriefing part of the workshop, i.e., not as an integrated part of the game. However, many such serious games expose their internal mechanics too easily. This side effect coupled with high development costs and limited and often constrained assessment schemas are reasons for low uptake. Another aspect is that games age and thus can often not be used for a long period. The usage of commercial off the shelf games might be a solution, but it requires that the game can be modded to fit the intended learning outcomes in the course it should be used. This article reports on the work carried out to identify if such a game, not specifically designed for the specific curriculum of SCM, can be used or not.

Keywords: Serious games · Commercial games · Logistics training

1 Introduction

1.1 Serious Games in Education

In higher education, logistics courses and programs differ primarily in their area of emphasis and program degree. In a general business degree, courses typically cover a mix of finance, accounting, operations management, and economics. A more specialized degree in logistics management would have a curriculum focused, for example, on supply chain management, transportation, manufacturing, warehousing, or procurement; logistics courses relevant in engineering programs focus more on system thinking and the implementation of suitable systems and equipment. Despite the need to examine logistics as a complete system, logistics courses are still mostly addressed at a theoretical level. Thus, a graduate's perspective remains narrow around logistic functions and

© IFIP International Federation for Information Processing 2022
Published by Springer Nature Switzerland AG 2022
D. Y. Kim et al. (Eds.): APMS 2022, IFIP AICT 664, pp. 232–239, 2022.
https://doi.org/10.1007/978-3-031-16411-8_29

their interactions that affect system performance. With respect to preparing a career in logistics, graduates face a steep learning curve to anticipate the impact of their decisions in a real-world environment.

This paper is to review a management-strategy simulation game for the purpose of Game-based learning (GBL) in logistics. While game-based approaches are not new, they offer a way to deliver an otherwise difficult subject. The gaming environment offers simultaneous problem- and practice-based instructional methods to create learning situations that further promote and develop critical thinking, where learning is extended from theoretical models as such, to their application in realistic settings. Reflection upon the appropriateness of the models then becomes essential [1–3].

For the subject on logistics, it is important for students to know how performance attributes and metrics [4] like the attributes SC reliability and flexibility and corresponding metrics [5] are defined and measured. Still, it is necessary to understand how these are generated in a process and how they can be monitored and controlled. The latter is difficult to grasp from a textbook, and thus more practical experiences in a course setting might be more appropriate [6–9].

The authors have experience in using serious games in higher education, such as the MIT-born beer game (and adoptions thereof), individual developments such as Sumaga—a beer game [10], Beware a SCRM game [11], Seconds—a game for understanding the interactions in supply network and distributed production [12] (no longer usable due to too old data in the processes) as well as other solutions (e.g., the SHORTFALL game, no longer playable because based on Flash technology). Ageing of games [13] as well as the need to facilitate courses on logistics and process management in (industrial) engineering and business administration motivates the authors to identify new serious games for their teaching environments.

1.2 Problem and Approach

Although solutions developed at and maintained by universities and research institutions are regularly a good choice due to their focus on specific educational objectives, these solutions may be lacking latest features and graphics as well as long-term technical support. In addition, most serious games for logistics and SCM are round based instead of a real-time simulation. Due to these challenges, the authors aimed to identify a commercial solution that can be used for their respective courses considering the defined learning objectives and the intended learning outcomes (ILOs).

Initially, the authors reviewed their courses' ILOs to ensure a necessary degree of consistency. In the next step, they explored different potential sources of both serious and commercial games left mainly with serious games and simulations that are text-based and where the simulation of production processes is left to a 'black box' and is not part of the actual game play; i.e., round-based games with simulation results being calculated between rounds vs. a building simulation (city-building style, not round-based) where the actual simulation is constantly running. The game Production Line offered the latter option and was therefore selected for further analysis against the ILOs. The analysis outlined in the following is also intended to support others that consider COTS games for teaching purposes and to contribute to respective discussions in the community.

This paper explores the game Production Line (Sect. 2) and presents the analysis whether the game can facilitate those ILOs the authors share between their respective university courses on logistics (Sect. 3). The paper concludes with a discussion on how to adopt the game (Sect. 4) and the next steps (Sect. 5).

2 Background and Game

Several serious games are available to teach SCM and logistics. To the knowledge of the authors, most solutions draw a broader picture at a higher level of business, e.g., focusing on functions such as SCM, Finance, Marketing/Sales, limiting the way how production and processes are managed at a technical and operational level. In addition, simulations are often round based, i.e., in between rounds decisions are prepared by the player(s). Therein different approaches exist, either running over a defined period (e.g., SHORTFALL or The Fresh Connection [14]) or providing a result of a somewhat steady state as basis for the next round (e.g., The Blue Connection [15]). Solutions based upon the idea of a building simulation such as the popular SimCity game or similar were more difficult to identify. In such simulations, time is constantly running, and decisions must often be made under time pressure inherent to the game itself rather than being imposed externally by a facilitator.

The authors identified the simulation game Production Line© by Positech Games as a promising solution. Production Line resembles the design and development of a modern car factory. The game is designed as a single-player simulation game that provides a factory environment to build a production line. The underlying objective of the game is to constantly increase the efficiency of the production line to increase turnover, profits (to reinvest in research and technology) and ultimately gain more market share. However, different playing options such as sandbox or scenarios are available and may steer the player towards specific strategies. Scenarios are defined around a defined number of vehicles of specific car body types (sedan, SUV, etc.) that must be built within a given time frame and starting with a specific budget. Cars that are produced are to be sold at the market and revenues are used to finance running production, investments in the production itself as well as research and development for new vehicle technologies (e.g., new vehicle functions such as air conditioning) and improved production process (e.g., specialized operations in the paint shop and new robots). Figure 1 shows a screenshot of the game during a virtual session with the building elements menu on the left and the actual car factory in the centre, in this case a simple production line set by the authors to test some of the functionalities and effects of player's decisions.

As stated on the game developer's website: "This game is designed to appeal to the efficiency geek in all of us, the person who cannot help but organize things for maximum performance" [https://www.positech.co.uk/productionline/]. Organizing and designing the factory (layout), assessing its (lack of) performance, designing and researching potential solutions, and eventually adopting strategies to overcome bottlenecks and improve performance are not only tasks inherent to the game but also main tasks related to the authors ILOs as will be explained in the following.

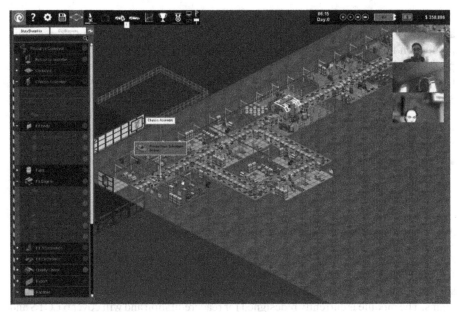

Fig. 1. A screenshot from Production Line by Positech played by the authors during a test session in April 2022.

3   Educational Setting and Learning Objectives

The authors represent three different European institutions of higher education where they are teaching courses on logistics in either engineering-oriented or business administration undergrad programs (amongst others). The authors have all long experience in using different games as an integrated part of specific courses. So far both commercial-on-the-shelf (COTS), as well as serious games, have been used in both courses designed for game-based learning as well as in courses which have had the most lectures. In two of the institutions, Production Line will replace a serious game that is no longer maintained and thus cannot be used [16]. The integration of Production Line will vary both within an institution as well as from one institution to another. The usage depends very much on the topic and the flexibility of the curriculum. Therefore, in a first step, we need to investigate if the game will help the students in achieving the intended learning outcomes and if the play can be sufficiently flexible. It is our aim that we will use the game already in the upcoming academic year.

3.1   An Introductory Course on Production Logistics at the Royal Institute of Technology (KTH)

At KTH the game will be used in a course on production logistics (6 ECTS) [17] in the 3rd semester of the degree program (5 years) in industrial technology and sustainability and is mandatory. The game will be used as an examination moment with 1,5 ECTS and will address two out of six ILOs. It is one of 4 examinations. In previous years, two different games were used (shortfall and a beer game). Yet a game is needed that supports all aspects of ILO4 and 5. The intention is that the practical experiment of making a production line will better visualise all elements that play a role in the performance of production logistics as well as to let the students experience how different designs and the planning of a production line are affected by early decisions taken at the planning stage.

- (ILO1) Explain how materials and information management technologies are structured and how they can help optimise production logistics.
- (ILO2) Apply methods and calculation methods for controlling production, inventory, and order logistics, including forecasts, order point security inventory, and order quantity.

3.2   Course on Logistics and Operations at Wiesbaden Business School

At the Wiesbaden Business School (WBS), the game will be used in a 5 ECTS course from an elective module on supply chain and operations to 4/5th semester undergrad students from both the business administration and the international management programs. The module is currently redesigned for reaccreditation and will cover 6 ECTS and host students from the digital business management program in the future. The relevant ILOs from the future course are equal or close to the current ILOs.

- (ILO3) Analyze business processes using respective tools such as activity-based costing/process cost accounting and benchmarking and identify improvement potentials in operations.
- (ILO4) Review for digital and/or process solutions to improve process efficiency.
- (ILO5) Make decisions on process improvement measures, apply solutions, and critically evaluate the results.

3.3   Heriot-Watt University Engineering and Manufacturing Course

At Heriot-Watt production and operations management is covered under the engineering and manufacturing course. This semester two course has the equivalent of 7.5 ECTS and is mandatory for all final year mechanical engineering students. The primary ILOs are:

- (ILO6) Capacity resource planning and materials requirements planning. Apply methods and calculation methods for controlling production, inventory, and order logistics, including forecasts, order point security inventory, and order quantity
- (ILO7) Another related LO is how factory layout affects shop-floor logistics and production.
- (ILO8) Digital manufacturing. This applies to digitalisation of shopfloor logistics and production workflow automation.

3.4 Intended Learning Outcomes and Production Line

After having collected the ILOs and identified common ground between the courses, it is necessary to understand which of the ILOs are in line with the functionalities of Production Line. Although each course has some unique directions resulting from their respective study programs' contexts, some commonalities related to production logistics and operations management were identified. The ILOs on process management and controlling are reflected in all three courses (see ILO2 at KTH, ILO 6 at Heriot-Watt, and ILO3 and partly ILO5 at WBS). In addition, the courses aim to teach students on technologies used to improve processes and operations management (ILO1 at KTH; ILO4 and ILO5 at WBS; ILO8 at Heriot-Watt).

4 Discussion of Game Adoption

In reviewing whether the game could be used to meet the different ILOs, the authors experimented with the game set-up while discussing in more detail how the game can best be integrated in a learning environment and what needs to be considered by a facilitator's as well as from a teacher's point of view (see Fig. 1). This includes considerations related to the introduction of the game and explaining its functionalities, and tasks the students are supposed to perform prior to, during and after gameplay. Hence the analysis is evocative of some general considerations that are relevant when applying a COTS game.

As previously mentioned, Production Line is a COTS single player game. The manual and tutorial are built in the game play, which often give a more immersive experience. However, used in a learning context, it is important that both learning objectives and gameplay are understood. The easiest way of ensuring this, is to add a briefing phase in which the facilitator explains the game elements, the objective of both the game and the expected learning. This will also allow an experienced facilitator to adapt the game play to the right level for the students and to suggest variations in the game play in case the game is played several times or with the objective to trigger and investigate a specific problem.

A limitation the authors have seen in their own play experience is the need of proper instruction to achieve a common base for all players, e.g., on the type of factory size and scenario to be played as well as a detailed overview of all possible variables. The authors consider starting with a small factory and a pre-defined scenario rather than a sandbox (e.g., with unlimited resources) to have goals the students would need to work towards. This also allows adding a competitive element outside the game in the classroom comparing players or teams of players in a high score.

In the current analysis of possible ways of using the game in the different courses, we have identified several possibilities to use the same game scenario to address different challenges and different learning goals. These findings and reviewing the ILOs discussed here may also help other teachers to evaluate whether Production Line may be appropriate for their syllabus. However, so far only the authors have played the game in such a setting. To evaluate the ease of use as well as the immersiveness among students, we need to test the game with the target group to see whether the game can be played in the given timeframe with the expected learning outcomes per student. Applying the game in different study programs will allow the authors to better understand differences due to students' backgrounds and skills. This can support the authors to optimize the delivery of a good learning experience.

5 Conclusion and Next Steps

According to our analysis, the COTS game Production Line seems to fulfil our requirements to be implemented and used in different ways in the envisage courses.

Regarding the flexibility of the gameplay, we see that the game has the potential for being used to:

- Explore shop floor design and factory layout and investigate the impact on the production capacity and throughput time
- Experience resource management
- Investigate the role of technology development and research (qualification)
- Apply different strategies on the operational level, depending on pre-defined criteria as goals.

In the next step, the author will develop the supporting material and define test-scenarios that can be used to evaluate how well the game supports the learning process. It is our intention to implement the game in the upcoming academic year. Based on the evaluation results and students' feedback the authors will adapt both supportive material and, if required, the description on how to develop the sandbox game.

References

1. Tehran, B.P., Oliveira, M.F., Taisch, M., et al.: Status and trends of serious game application in engineering and manufacturing education. In: International Simulation and Gaming Association Conference, pp. 77–84 (2013)
2. Duin, H., Hauge, J.B., Hunecker, F., et al.: Application of serious games in industrial contexts. In: Business, Technological, and Social Dimensions of Computer Games: Multidisciplinary Developments, pp. 331–347. IGI Global (2013)
3. Wood, L., Reiners, T.: Gamification in logistics and supply chain education: extending active learning. Internet Technol. Soc. **2012**, 101–108 (2012)
4. Supply Chain Process Improvement, Inc. SCOR Metrics. https://scpiteam.com/SCOR%20M etrics.htm?msclkid=5fcc50abc86b11ec8eeaab90d845cbeb. Accessed 30 Apr 2022
5. Dissanayake, C.K., Cross, J.A.: Systematic mechanism for identifying the relative impact of supply chain performance areas on the overall supply chain performance using SCOR model and SEM. Int. J. Prod. Econ. **201**, 102–115 (2018). https://doi.org/10.1016/j.ijpe.2018.04.027
6. Despeisse, M.: GAMES and simulations in industrial engineering education: a review of the cognitive and affective learning outcomeS. In: 2018 Winter Simulation Conference (WSC), pp. 4046–4057. IEEE (2018)
7. Woschank, M., Pacher, C.: A holistic didactical approach for industrial logistics engineering education in the LOGILAB at the Montanuniversitaet Leoben. Procedia Manuf. **51**, 1814–1818 (2020). https://doi.org/10.1016/j.promfg.2020.10.252
8. Ştefan, I.A., Hauge, J.B., Hasse, F., et al.: Using serious games and simulations for teaching co-operative decision-making. Procedia Comput. Sci. **162**, 745–753 (2019). https://doi.org/10.1016/j.procs.2019.12.046

9. Karl, C.K., Lokosch, H.: Increasing decision making competencies by applying simulation and gaming in technology and engineering education. In: Vries M de, Fletcher, S., Kruse, S., et al. (eds.) The impact of technology education: International insights, Waxmann, Münster, New York, p. 63 (2020)

10. Hauge, J.B., Stefan, I.A., Sallinen, N., et al.: Accessibility considerations in the design of serious games for production and logistics. In: Dolgui, A., Bernard, A., Lemoine, D., et al. (eds) Advances in production Management Systems. Artificial Intelligence For, vol. 633, pp. 510–519. Springer, Heidelberg (2021). https://doi.org/10.1007/978-3-030-85910-7_54

11. Hauge, J.M.B., Pourabdollahian, B., Riedel, J.C.K.H.: The use of serious games in the education of engineers, pp. 622–629. Springer, Heidelberg (2013). https://doi.org/10.1007/978-3-642-40352-1_78

12. Riedel, J.C.K.H., Hauge, J.B.: State of the art of serious games for business and industry. In: 2011 17th International Conference on Concurrent Enterprising, pp. 1–8 (2011)

13. Arnold, U., Söbke, H., Reichelt, M.: SimCity in infrastructure management education. Educ. Sci. **9**, 209 (2019). https://doi.org/10.3390/educsci9030209

14. Inchainge B.V. Discover The Fresh Connection. https://inchainge.com/business-games/tfc/. Accessed 30 Apr 2022

15. Inchainge B.V. Discover The Blue Connection: From Linear to Circular. https://inchainge. com/business-games/tbc/. Accessed 30 Apr 2022

16. Hauge, J.B., Kalverkamp, M., Bellotti, F., et al.: Requirements on learning analytics for facilitated and non facilitated games. In: 2014 IEEE Global Engineering Education Conference (EDUCON), pp. 1126–1132. IEEE (2014)

17. KTH ML1504 Produktionslogistik: 6, 0 hp. Logistics in Production. https://www.kth.se/student/kurser/kurs/kursplan/ML1504-20192.pdf?lang=sv. Accessed 30 Apr 2022

Service and Operations Management in the Context of Digitally-Enabled Product-Service Systems

Commercialization of Digitally-Enabled Products and Services: Overcoming the Barriers by Applying Action Learning

Thomas Sautter[1], Shaun West[2](✉) (iD), David Harrison[1](✉), and Paolo Gaiardelli[3](✉) (iD)

[1] Glasgow Caledonian University, Glasgow G4 0BA, Scotland, UK
thomas.sautter@voith.com, D.K.Harrison@gcu.ac.uk
[2] School of Technology and Architecture, Lucerne University of Applied Sciences and Arts, Lucerne, Switzerland
shaun.west@hslu.ch
[3] University of Bergamo, via Pasubio 7, Dalmine, Italy
paolo.gaiardelli@unibg.it

Abstract. This paper describes and analyses the application of Demings PDCA circle in combination with action learning methods to support the commercialization of digitally-enabled products and services. It does this through a single use case where one of the authors was embedded. The paper considers the challenges for a traditional firm selling solutions based on digital technology and how this is then converted into a value proposition. PDCA provided a change management framework that supported the action learning that was taking place by providing iterations with refection phases. This allowed the firm to proactively identify the barriers that it had to overcome and then to understand how it overcame these barriers. In doing so, it built new knowledge within the firm that could be standardized. This is an initial study, and additional studies should be made of alternative cases to allow for a deeper comparison.

Keywords: Commercialization · Digitally-enabled · PSS · PDCA · Action learning

1 Introduction

The motivation for this paper is to understand how a German capital equipment manufacturer used its performance improvement process to help to commercialize its digital solutions. Commercializing digital solutions within a Product-Service System (PSS) context has been challenging for many firms [1]. Traditional firms often find selling digital-enabled solutions challenging, not realizing that in many cases, "digital products" are in fact "services" [2]. They also miss the interplay between digitally enabled and traditional offerings [3]. The digitally-enabled solutions force an adaption to the firm's underpinning business model and lead to challenges internally with the delivery of digitally-enabled solutions and externally in terms of the sales processes.

© IFIP International Federation for Information Processing 2022
Published by Springer Nature Switzerland AG 2022
D. Y. Kim et al. (Eds.): APMS 2022, IFIP AICT 664, pp. 243–252, 2022.
https://doi.org/10.1007/978-3-031-16411-8_30

This study follows a German-based manufacturing firm that designs and manufactures equipment for drive lines in commercial vehicles, rail applications, and marine propulsion. The digital business developed a solution to monitor bus performance. The firm applied its PDCA (Plan-Do-Check-Act) improvement process to overcome the barriers to commercialization with the new digitally-enabled value proposition. Based on this, the research question for this paper is: *"How did the PDCA process help the management to overcome the barriers to the successful commercialization of the new digital solution?"*.

2 Literature Review

The literature review focuses on the three aspects that were considered important from the research question, namely the challenges of the commercialization of "digital solutions", understanding the value proposition being solid, and the PDCA of Deming process approach [4] process used in operations management to improve performance.

2.1 Challenges for Traditional Manufacturing Firms of Selling Digital Offerings

The integration of digital solutions into the market offering affects the business model [3] and its configuration. This is because the addition of digital solutions enables the creation of new value propositions, transforming the product by means of the servitization process [3]. Transforming a traditional manufacturing firm to one that sells digital offerings based on Industry 4.0 technologies is not without its challenges [5]. As confirmed by Pasupuleti & Adusumalli [6] challenges concern both traditional manufacturing and high technology-based firms and also apply to SMEs [7]. In this regard, the taxonomy of barriers [8] provides a set of dimensions with questions to understand the challenges that a specific firm faces when making the transition to digitally-enabled solutions from more traditional offerings. This can be translated into a solution (or value proposition) that customers are willing to buy. The integration of digital solutions into the firm's offerings also affects the business model [3]. Adopting a lean approach has been recognized in the literature as an effective way firms can overcome barriers that slow or prevent the commercialization of new business opportunities [9]. Based on the idea of action learning, lean management promotes the innovation process through the diffusion of knowledge fostered by information sharing and people commitment [10].

2.2 Understanding Value and the Value Proposition

The literature describes the importance of understanding what customers value in B2B environments and confirms that customers do not buy "features" but generally purchase a solution that delivers a value proposition that supports the purchaser's value creation process [11]. This confirms the need to describe the points of difference between alternative solutions, not by comparing features but rather by estimating the value creation potential.

By leveraging the experience of early adopters, new technologies can be used to help firms develop alternative value propositions [12]. This requires linking the (digital) strategy to the value proposition and then to its commercialization [13]. Nussipova [14] describes the challenges in adapting the existing value propositions with new digital technologies to enhance the value creation process.

2.3 Improving Performance in a Firm

The use of lean principles has been used in many manufacturing firms to improve operational performance. Among others, A3 sheets are adopted to help describe a problem and its root cause, prior to taking any corrective action [15]. A3 sheets force analysis of the problem step by step and avoid jumping to a solution. The approach taken follows the PDCA cycle, [16] based on Deming:

i.   Plan – identify and analyze the problem;
ii. Do – develop solutions, implement the solutions;
iii. Check – evaluate the results to identify if the desired goal was achieved;
iv. Act – standardize the solution.

The benefit of using the PDCA cycle lies in the creation of an environment for continuous learning [17] based on a structured standardized approach [18]. The result is a marked improvement of the firm's long-term performance [19]. A PDCA cycle can be used in any improvement project based on lean thinking principles, including the development, design and delivery of digital solutions [20].

3   Methodology

A single case study was considered appropriate to answer the research question of this study [21]. The action research during the execution of the change management process was based on the PDCA approach [17]. One of the authors was embedded within the case, and an action research approach was used [22], to limit the observational bias that is a risk of embedded qualitative research [23].

The approach taken is (PDCA circle with elements of action learning) in this study is described in Fig. 1. Each of the action research phases is based around the four stages of the PDCA improvement process. Each of these was assessed in terms of the planning (or inputs), the action (or transformation) and the results (or outputs) achieved. The assessment of the reflections from each phase was described by the embedded researcher, evidence was shared with the other authors and jointly reviewed to reduce researcher bias. The final phase of the methodology was a reflection of the whole change management process. As with action research the four phases can be further analyzed down as [24]:

i.   Planning (or input);
ii. Action (or transformation);
iii. Results (or outputs);
iv. Reflection (or feedback).

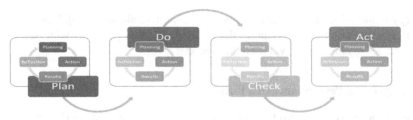

Fig. 1. Action research methodology that supported the analysis of the PDCA improvement processes applied in the case

4   Results

The case is based on the products of a start-up company integrated into a firm, as it is the main shareholder. The start-up company has developed a data transfer solution with a gateway for public transport in buses and a fuel economy software solution using the gateway plus an information screen for drivers. By taking a major share of the start-up company, the firm was willing to support global sales and marketing with resources and structures from its existing setup. The firm has a global and local presence in all relevant markets for public transport in the sectors of rail, buses, and ferries. The start-up company has 25 employees – mostly in development areas and only 1.5 sales employees. The start-up has only 5 customers in the Nordic region. Two big contracts have been lost due to bad performance. The main task of the sales initiative was to put the startup company's business on a larger foundation with more customers.

4.1   Plan

In the "Plan" phase a study and workshops with the existing board and sales forces of the startup were executed. Added to this are customer interviews offering insights into the business model and the product base. Different organization models for additional sales resources have been evaluated. The chosen model – to use existing salespeople – who know the bus market – as multipliers in their regions for the new product was worked out in detail, including face-to-face training. In Table 1 the Plan phase scores are shown with the main results.

Table 1. Action research main outcomes: plan phase

Step	Findings
Input/planning	- Salesforce available - Market know-how is present - Motivation for selling a new product must be created

(continued)

Table 1. (*continued*)

Step	Findings
Transformation/action	- Giving a defined team a sales task - Create a training plan - Run a workshop to define blocking points – based on first sales experience
Output/results	- Understanding the blocking points - Definition for added value is needed - Training of the multipliers
Reflections	- Motivation of the team was positive – a clear willingness to provide something "new" - Sizing of the selected team sounds right - Understanding the value of the offering was the biggest challenge

4.2 Do

The "Do" phase was dominated by an intense training workshop at the startup's premises, followed by customer interviews in a limited promotional tour for the data transmission and fuel economy solution. The criteria for the first customer meetings were an existing business relationship and good personal relationships with members of the customers' organization as shown in Table 2.

Table 2. Action research main outcomes: do phase

Step	Findings
Input/planning	- Planning of a training session - Starting with different skill levels - Ensure the general motivation level is high and stays at the high level
Transformation/action	- Execute the training in theory - Additionally, to show use-cases from different markets - Share experience with salespeople who already sold the digital products successfully
Output/results	- Trained sales staff - Availability to answer a customer's initial questions - Knowing when to integrate the technical experts into a customer discussion
Reflections	- Training sessions should be very detailed – adapted to different skill and experience levels of the participants - Real use cases are help create confidence - Sales force needs to be able to answer – on a professional level – at least the first 3 detailed questions of a potential customer

4.3 Check

The main results during the "Do" phase have been revised in the "Check" phase. The team arranged bi-weekly online meetings to share experience and identify potential blocks to sales. Business market management is the process of understanding, creating, and delivering value to targeted business markets and customers [11]. The value description of the data transfer is lacking, though the value for the fuel economy solution has been clear and obvious (Table 3).

Table 3. Action research main outcomes: check phase

Step	Findings
Input/planning	- Slow sales success - Customers do not show serious interest in the products - Added value of the products is not clear
Transformation/action	- The product management of the startup will define added values - Sharpen the market needs – as an input from the sales teams - Have an intense discussion – learn where the value is (hidden)
Output/results	- Data has no value – unless they lead to an information level helping customer's business case - USPs to be defined - Positive input needed on cost, cash, safety or "go-green" on customer side
Reflections	- Even after first successes, clear product values are needed - Added values must be presented to the sales force - Marketing material must focus on customer benefits

4.4 Act

The "Act" phase concentrated on both products – knowing that the added value for a customer with the fuel economy solution was always transferred first in the sales process. The possibilities for data transfer and looking for customer specific needs were added later. Table 4 shows the general findings of the act phase.

5 Discussion

Returning to the research question of this paper, the PDCA approach was familiar to the staff within the firm. However, the authors confirm that it was generally applied within the production environment rather than in commercial or sales related fields. PDCA is an action learning approach to problem solving [19], and the commercialization of digital offerings is one such example of problem solving. The firm did not apply the Lean Startup approach, which is closely related to PDCA and again is an action learning tool, as it was not an approach that was known within the firm and the main result – quick prototyping – does not apply for this case. Nevertheless, PDCA provided a known framework to structure the commercialization of the offering and to overcome the barriers to change. In other cases, the application of Lean Start-up may have been considered, yet here the management would have only focused on two, or at maximum three of the blocks, and so it is hypothesized that PDCA provided a sufficient framework to allow the sales team to overcome the barriers they were facing.

Next to Lean Start up the firm applied action learning approach of Deming (i.e., PCDA). Action learning shows its greatest strength in learning and adapting new processes and way of acting, where in the case of overcoming the barriers, a wider range had to be considered. Action research follows a guided structure as the PDCA circle as well and it was found to combine the action research tools into the phases of Demings PDCA logic.

Table 4. Action research main outcomes: Act phase

Step	Findings
Input/planning	- Plan to run sales activities in different countries - Create a structured plan on customer view - Prepare sales and marketing material
Transformation/action	- Organize and execute customer visits or calls - Combine – if necessary – a technical specialist with an experienced salesperson - Share the experience on the sales journey in bi-weekly calls with a clear leadership
Output/results	- Provide - during the common calls - decisions to reach the next level in the sales process - Find the right product for entering each customer discussion - Celebrate sales successes
Reflections	- A sales execution plan is the base for a successful market roll-out - Regular reviews to share experience within the team are essential - Highlighting even small successes supports motivation

The "Plan" phase allowed the team to identify the barriers that they needed to overcome and to identify the tools that they needed (or thought they might need). The barriers have been: (i) mental barriers to sell an unknown product, (ii) missing added value proposition to the customers, (iii) market barriers, as the products have not been promoted in a bigger area, (iv) financial barriers as missing customer values meant market-driven pricing was not installed or available, (v) barriers on the product because it was not developed for a global or defined market, (vi) know how and information barriers hindered a quick global roll-out and entering new markets. This led to the need to motivate the (sales) team and to develop the desire/motivation to offer something new. This was important, as change requires the team to identify the barriers that exist and then be able to overcome them [8]. This requires change in the mindset of the sales team and the ability to demonstrate value to the potential buyer of their new offer [11]. The "Plan" phase of PDCA is based on the understanding that planning can only support the "Do" phase and that the plan must be adaptable to overcome unforeseen challenges 5).

The "Do" phase was supported by the development of the sales training to change to a consultative selling approach [11]. Not all sales managers could do this without first being trained. Part of this needed a move to using real cases to help describe where value could (and would) be created with the new offering, often using example cases. This also provides the opportunity to understand the customer's problems and needs from their perspectives [10].

The "Check" phase allowed the adaptation of the process, this was necessary as even after the initial successes, updates were needed, based on the findings, as not everything followed the plan as expected. For example, even after training the sale managers could not describe the solutions fully and some fell back to pushing the features rather than focusing on the value creation and points of difference [11].

The final "Act" phase within PDCA provides a mechanism to standardize the approach. Based on the reflections from the prior phases a sales execution plan for the wider rollout was developed, including support with consultative value-based selling. As part of the process, it was found that the sales managers need regular reviews to share their experience of selling. This was necessary even for experienced sales managers.

The main barriers in the commercialization of digitally-enabled products and services have been identified as: missing an experienced and trained team, dealing with a product missing value adds for the customers and a non-existing sales organization and leadership with targets and timelines. These barriers were successful solved especially with the findings in the act phase.

5.1 Managerial Relevance

The PDCA approach from Lean can be used to support action learning in the development of a sales approach for digital-enabled services. Often the approach is used within a production environment, yet there is evidence here that it supports the changes needed to develop a sales approach. Having a look into the lean Sensei philosophy, which describes a management system and mindset, Ballé et al. [25] find there as well the base of lean and PDCA. There is some evidence that supports the application of PDCA as a change management tool and this is in line with Pietrzak & Paliszkiewicz [17]. The basis was the marketing approach of Anderson & Narus [11].

5.2 Academic Implications

PDCA is a form of action learning [20], that helped the firm to identify and overcome the barriers for selling digitally enabled services. Typically, it is generally confined to the production environment [15], yet in this example it has been used to guide the change management process for the commercialization of digital offerings within a manufacturing firm. The firm did not consider Lean Start-up as an approach, because the main positive effect of this method is rapid prototyping and the dominating question for this firm has been the analysis and the structured review. The PDCA method leads to a structured way of thinking and developing that is understood and followed by all the people and organizations involved.

6 Conclusions and Future Research

PDCA provided a structured framework, with reflection, that supported the development of the commercialization of the digitally-enabled solutions. The use of the action learning approach was supportive and made the team consider the actual barriers that they faced with this change. It provided the structure to allow the team to overcome emerging barriers that were not initially anticipated, it also provided the team with an approach to embed the lessons learned into the standard business processes.

This is an initial study and further analysis is needed around the categorization of the barriers identified and actions to overcome them. Also, the link with Lean Start-up approaches could be further examined.

References

1. Stoll, O., West, S., Gaiardelli, P., Harrison, D., Corcoran, F.J.: The successful commercialization of a digital twin in an industrial product service system. In: Lalic, B., Majstorovic, V., Marjanovic, U., von Cieminski, G., Romero, D. (eds.) APMS 2020. IAICT, vol. 592, pp. 275–282. Springer, Cham (2020). https://doi.org/10.1007/978-3-030-57997-5_32
2. Anderson, M., West, S., Harrison, D.: Exploring accidental digital servitization in an industrial context. In: Dolgui, A., Bernard, A., Lemoine, D., von Cieminski, G., Romero, D. (eds.) APMS 2021. IAICT, vol. 632, pp. 126–135. Springer, Cham (2021). https://doi.org/10.1007/978-3-030-85906-0_15
3. Gebauer, H., et al.: How to convert digital offerings into revenue enhancement-conceptualizing business model dynamics through explorative case studies. Ind. Market. Manag. **91**, 429–441 (2020). https://doi.org/10.1016/j.indmarman.2020.10.006
4. Tranfield, D., Denyer, D., Smart, P.: Towards a methodology for developing evidence-informed management knowledge by means of systematic review. Br. J. Manag. **14**(3), 207–222 (2003). https://doi.org/10.1111/1467-8551.00375
5. Petrillo, A., De Felice, F., Cioffi, R., Zomparelli, F.: Fourth industrial revolution: current practices, challenges, and opportunities. In Petrillo, A., Cioffi, R., De Felice, F. (eds.) Digital Transformation in Smart Manufacturing, pp. 1–20. InTech, Rijeka (2018)
6. Pasupuleti, M.B., Adusumalli, H.P.: Digital transformation of the high-technology manufacturing: an overview of main blockades. Am. J. Trade Policy **5**(3), 139–142 (2018). https://doi.org/10.18034/ajtp.v5i3.599

7. Stentoft, J., Adsbøll Wickstrøm, K., Philipsen, K., Haug, A.: Drivers and barriers for Industry 4.0 readiness and practice: empirical evidence from small and medium-sized manufacturers. Prod. Plan. Control **32**(10), 811–828 (2021). https://doi.org/10.1080/09537287.2020.176 8318

8. Vogelsang, K., Liere-Netheler, K., Packmohr, S., Hoppe, U.: A taxonomy of barriers to digital transformation. In: 14th International Conference on Wirtschaftsinformatik, Siegen, Germany, pp. 736–750 (2019)

9. Silva, D.S., Ghezzi, A., de Aguiar, R.B., Cortimiglia, M.N., ten Caten, C.S.: Lean startup, agile methodologies and customer development for business model innovation: a systematic review and research agenda. Int. J. Entrepreneurial Behav. Res. **26**(4), 595–628 (2020). https://doi.org/10.1108/IJEBR-07-2019-0425

10. Powell, D., Oliveira, M.: Insights from a digital lean startup: co-creating digital tools for cognitive augmentation of the worker. Proc. CIRP **104**, 1384–1388 (2021). https://doi.org/10.1016/j.procir.2021.11.233

11. Anderson, J.C., Narus, J.A.: Business marketing: understand what customers value. Harvard Bus. Rev. **76**, 53–67 (1998)

12. Wouters, M., Anderson, J.C., Kirchberger, M.: New-technology startups seeking pilot customers: crafting a pair of value propositions. Calif. Manage. Rev. **60**(4), 101–124 (2018). https://doi.org/10.1177/0008125618778855

13. Payne, A., Frow, P., Steinhoff, L., Eggert, A.: Toward a comprehensive framework of value proposition development: from strategy to implementation. Ind. Market. Manag. **87**, 244–255 (2020). https://doi.org/10.1016/j.indmarman.2020.02.015

14. Nussipova, G.: Framing changes of the value proposition of emerging technologies in a B2B context. J. Bus-Bus. Mark. **29**(2), 99–118 (2022). https://doi.org/10.1080/1051712X.2022.2051833

15. Shook, J.: Toyota's secret. MIT Sloan Manage. Rev. **50**(4), 30–33 (2009)

16. Johnson, C.N.: The benefits of PDCA. Qual. Progr. **49**(1), 45 (2016)

17. Pietrzak, M., Paliszkiewicz, J.: Framework of strategic learning: the PDCA cycle. Management **10**(2), 149–161 (2015)

18. Holweg, M., Davies, J., De Meyer, A., Lawson, B., Schmenner, R.W.: Process Theory: The Principles of Operations Management. Oxford University Press, Oxford (2018)

19. Lodgaard, E., Gamme, I., Aasland, K.E.: Success factors for PDCA as continuous improvement method in product development. In: Emmanouilidis, C., Taisch, M., Kiritsis, D. (eds.) APMS 2012. IAICT, vol. 397, pp. 645–652. Springer, Heidelberg (2013). https://doi.org/10.1007/978-3-642-40352-1_81

20. Santhiapillai, F.P., Ratnayake, R.M.C.: Utilizing lean thinking as a means to digital transformation in service organizations. In: Lalic, B., Majstorovic, V., Marjanovic, U., von Cieminski, G., Romero, D. (eds.) APMS 2020. IAICT, vol. 592, pp. 371–378. Springer, Cham (2020). https://doi.org/10.1007/978-3-030-57997-5_43

21. Bryman, A., Bell, E.: Business Research Methods, 2nd edn. Oxford University Press, New York (2007)

22. Bradbury, H.: The SAGE Handbook of Action Research. SAGE Publications, Thousand Oaks (2015)

23. Bryman, A., Bell, E., Mills, A.J., Yue, A.R.: Business research strategies, 2nd edn. In: Bryman, A., Bell, E. (eds.) Business Research Methods, pp 226–238 Oxford University Press, New York (2007)

24. Lewin, K.: Group decision and social change. Read. Soc. Psychol. **3**(1), 197–211 (1947)

25. Ballé, M., Chartier, N., Coignet, P., Olivencia, S., Powell, D., Reke, E.: The Lean Sensei. Go, See, Challenge. Lean Enterprise Institute, Boston (2019)

The Significance and Barriers to Organizational Interoperability in Smart Service Ecosystems: A Socio-technical Systems Approach

Godfrey Mugurusi[1](✉) (iD), Jurga Vesterté[2], David Asamoah[3] (iD), Pankaj Khatiwada[4],
Christina Marie Mitcheltree[1], Halvor Holtskog[1], and Stian Underbekken[5]

[1] Department of Industrial Economics and Technology Management in Gjøvik, Norwegian
University of Science and Technology, Trondheim, Norway
godfrey.mugurusi@ntnu.no
[2] Department of Management, Faculty of Business Management, Vilnius Gediminas Technical
University, Vilnius, Lithuania
[3] KNUST School of Business, Kwame Nkrumah University of Science and Technology,
Kumasi, Ghana
[4] Department of Information Security and Communication Technology, Norwegian University
of Science and Technology, Trondheim, Norway
[5] Ikomm AS, Lillehammer, Norway

Abstract. Smart service ecosystems (SSEs) struggle a lot with interoperability. Interoperability consists of many types but two are of interest in this paper: - (1) syntactic and semantic interoperability, and (2) organizational interoperability. While both have received a fair amount of attention in the literature, there's little discussion on the alignment between (1) and (2), which we argue, is a key enabler of dynamic service integration in SSEs.

This paper explores the significance of (mis)alignment between (1) and (2), and the barriers to organizational interoperability in smart service ecosystems. The empirical data for the paper comes from an ongoing innovation project in Norway that aims to develop a smart, secure, and cost-effective home access solution for senior care homes in the municipality of Lillehammer. The empirical findings emphasize the significance of organizational contexts, and demonstrate in part, the theoretical limitations of the socio-technical systems approach when applied to the SSE perspective.

Keywords: Smart services · Smart service ecosystems · Ecosystems · Organizational interoperability · Socio-technical systems approach

1 Introduction

Advances in information technology particularly in industry 4.0, ubiquitous computing, and device miniaturization have led to rapid innovation in services. As a result, smart service innovations have emerged to address some of society's complex challenges [1].

© IFIP International Federation for Information Processing 2022
Published by Springer Nature Switzerland AG 2022
D. Y. Kim et al. (Eds.): APMS 2022, IFIP AICT 664, pp. 253–261, 2022.
https://doi.org/10.1007/978-3-031-16411-8_31

The term smart service means "a service delivered through intelligent products that feature awareness and connectivity" [2]. The nature of value creation of smart services is built around product or service platforms that leverage resources and technologies of hundreds of value chain actors (suppliers, competitors, etc.) hence the concept of smart service ecosystems [3, 4].

An ecosystem can be defined as a community of loose but interdependent actors that engage in complementary value co-creation [2, 5]. Ecosystems "enable intensive data and information interactions among people and organizations to improve their decision making and operations" [2, 6]: and have self-configuration and regulation capabilities. By this characterization, smart service ecosystems (SSEs) infer technology-mediated service systems where value co-creation occurs by mutual cooperation and resource sharing across different actors, each with their own value/service offerings [1, 3, 7].

The development (and co-production) of a smart service in an SSE environment requires multiple organizations to interact at two layers of interoperability. The technical layer, i.e., syntactic and semantic interoperability, and the organizational layer, i.e., organizational interoperability [8, 9]. Technical interoperability involves machine-to-machine interactions whose standards such as TCP/IP, HTML, SOAP, etc. are relatively well developed both in the information systems (IS) literature [6, 7] and in the ISO standards. In this paper, we specifically focus on ISO9241 and ISO23903. Organizational interoperability however largely depends on generic frameworks such as the European interoperability framework (EIF), e-government Interoperability Framework (eGIF), Level of Information System Interoperability System (LISI), etc. [10]. This paper shall specifically focus on the more comprehensive EIF.

While the two interoperability layers demonstrate a comprehensive backbone for value co-creation in most SSE, they are domain-specific and rarely linked [9, 11]. SSE attributes demand that individual actors cope with the interaction complexity that comes with the multiple actors, different technology platforms, and their different data and information exchange models – often involving heterogeneous user devices, protocols, and system architectures [1, 2, 6]. Some level of alignment of both technical and organizational layers is expected, yet this has gone unnoticed in the organizational sciences (OS) literature [8, 12].

In this paper, we want to argue for the significance of alignment of the technical and the organizational interoperability layers, and then outline some of the barriers to organizational interoperability in the design and production of smart services. The significance of such an alignment in the development of smart service ecosystems is twofold. First, the additional cost of attracting new, innovative actors to participate in the further development of platform-interdependent services will be considerably low due to the ease of fit amongst all actors at the two interoperability levels layers [13]. And second, the quality of service (QoS) improves due to the ease of the available actionable data and information that is negotiated consistently across each actor's organizational boundaries in the entire SSE [2].

The aim and contribution of the paper are to advance new knowledge about the significance and the challenges of translating technical standards and frameworks into inter-organizational interoperability in SSEs. According to Kosanke [11], new frameworks and standards are needed to address interoperability beyond data syntaxes and more as the basis for cross-enterprise decision support in order to increase information usability and the quality of decisions at the operational level. This is precisely what organizational interoperability aims to address.

This paper is organized as follows. First, we briefly review relevant literature on interoperability challenges in SSE environments; second, we describe the methods used; third, we discuss the findings from a project which aims to design and deploy an IoT-based solution for home care services, and finally, we present the synthesis and key learning points including theoretical implications.

2 The Significance and Challenges of Interoperability in SSEs

The concept of "interoperability" has long been associated with the ability of systems to provide and exchange services with other systems and can accept services from other systems based on agreed operational semantics [12, 14]. However, in the OS literature, the human-technology-organization interface is usually the focal point, where interoperability is seen as the "ability of an enterprise to cooperate with its business partners and to efficiently establish, conduct, and develop IT-supported business relationships with the objective of creating value" [10, p. 3].

Several studies [3, 9, 14] suggest that ecosystems, in general, depend on inter-organizational cooperation as a basic building block for human-technology cooperation even at the enterprise systems architectural level. Broy et al. [15] show how cyber-plant systems increase user value because of a better connection between things and people and between things and providers. Weichhart et al. [13] maintain that enterprise integration supports informational and knowledge exchange which in turn supports interoperability of IT applications. Heiler [14] provides some useful examples of the significance of human-system cooperation enabling better interoperability, i.e., that human intelligence is needed to resolve mismatches in semantic information, while the documentation of semantics of legacy systems requires human interventions.

In sum, technical (machine, syntactic and semantic) interoperability levels require context which resides at the organizational level. Organizational contexts provide resources, workflow mechanisms, and processes that allow data and information sharing across different organizational boundaries [12]. SSEs that appropriate the most value tend to be those that efficiently integrate both technical (syntactic and semantic) and organization interoperability at both the enterprise level and the ecosystem level.

While the linkage between technical and organizational interoperability is notably challenging in practice [7], we have argued that the feasibility of such a linkage is critical for the viability and deployment of SSEs and other similar digital service solutions. In a study of cyber plant systems, Broy et al. [15] classify interoperability challenges into two groups: social challenges and technological/engineering challenges. Examples of social challenges cited include i) the design of suitable human-system cooperation, (ii) suitability of the system to task, and (iii) explainability and fault tolerance of the system. Technological challenges cited include, (i) integrating different domains into the system, (ii) interoperation of infrastructures or reference architectures, and (iii) modeling non-functional requirements and privacy aspects.

To conclude, there exists an admissible link between technical and organizational interoperability despite the idiosyncratic challenges each from their knowledge domain.

Most importantly, the blurred line between the IS and OS literature on interoperability barriers provides reason to adopt the socio-technical systems (STS) lens going forward.

3 Research Setting, Methods, and Empirics

3.1 Conceptual Framework

Building further on the literature, we adopt the STS approach to frame the forthcoming analysis and discussion. The STS approach offers the view of organizations through the social (people, processes, and relationships) and technical (equipment and technology) subsystems [9]. We contextualize the development of interoperable SSEs as environments that demand a holistic lens across both the technical areas such as data, security, platforms, etc. and the non-technical areas such as culture, organizational policies, local coalitions, business models, etc. [9]. The STS approach strongly emphasizes interaction and communication, and collective action in the development of technical artifacts as a system of work [16]. Our departure point is the principle of interdependence and contextual understanding of information acquisition, analysis, and diagnosis (e.g., of actors, roles and interests, and interfaces). This aligns nicely with the multilayer framework for service system analysis of Frost et al. [6].

3.2 Methods and Material

The paper is a qualitative inquiry based on the case study method [17]. It draws empirical data from an ongoing innovation project called "internet of my things" (https://www.int ernetofmythings.no/) (the IoMt project). The IoMt project aims to develop a proof of concept (POC) for a load-bearing structure of an internet of things (IoT)-based system where elderly inhabitants in Lillehammer municipality can use their privately owned devices to access home care services offered by the municipality.

While the scope of the project is much wider than what we can present in this paper, we specifically focus on the processes involving the development of the POC for a smart-door lock solution. In this regard, the municipality hopes it will replace the mechanical "key and key box" located at the door of each home care service receiver in the municipality. More details of the case are presented in the next section. However, the central idea behind the project is to develop a robust, well-integrated IoT-based architecture using the smart-doorlock solution as the starting point. Such systems do exist already in Norway and abroad, but most are not well integrated between users and homecare workers. Besides the proposed solution shall give more power to users to be able to digitally give and withdraw consent/and access to their homes as they wish.

In this case study, several organizations are involved in the POC development, but we focus on 5 as the main source of data for the paper. This excludes 2 R&D partners. The 5 actors include a platform owner, a hardware supplier, the service owner, a solution support company, and an internet infrastructure service company. The empirical data sources included: 4 in-person interviews, 6 stakeholder workshops, 5 focus group discussion (FGD) workshops, 2 internal project meetings, and numerous secondary data that have been collected into *Miro,* a data visualization and collaboration tool. This data is sufficient for case research whose aim is theory generation [17].

3.3 A Brief Case Description and the Empirical Basis for Discussion

Homecare services in Norway are regulated by the *Health and Care Services Act* which gives municipalities the overall responsibility to ensure that all inhabitants have comprehensive access to health and home care services (*Health and Care Services Act §3–1*). Some of these services, such as home care visits, user-managed personal assistance (BPA) services, occupational therapy, drug-assisted rehabilitation services, etc. are offered at the home of a patient by home care nurses and BPA assistants. 24-h/7day access to patient homes is available through physical keys located in "key boxes" at the patients' homes where care nurses or BPA assistants follow a defined schedule for home visits. Currently, the key handling and administration procedures are far too complex, inefficient, not user-centered, and can involve several security risks. The municipality wants to overhaul the entire "key and key box" system hence the ioMt project.

The project was a result of a need by the municipality of Lillehammer to digitalize the key handling procedures thus the proposed smart-doorlock solution. Compared to the traditional "keys and key box", the benefit of the proposed smart-door lock solution would give the care-receiver ownership and control of the access rights to their home. This involves giving and withdrawing permission of access for planned visits by the municipality and unplanned visits when the patient needs emergency help. The municipality believes the new service will reduce cost and inefficiency in the "keys and key box" system. The unit purchase cost of the "keys and keybox" solution is about 1650 NOK (≈$165 or €155). The new solution will be economically cheaper in the long run.

What are the Main Interests? Benefits aside, the development of the smart doorlock solution (i.e., the POC) highlights several emergent technical and organizational issues and interests that we emphasize in Fig. 1. The most important ones identified in FGD workshops were reliability, trust, and data privacy of the solution. The municipality's home care services department needs to trust that the smart doorlock can be opened whenever they have service needs based on the agreed day's plan and that the patient can trust that the digital technology and data that are logged with the municipality's homecare service is used according to the inhabitant's individual privacy preferences.

Who are the Key Actors? For this paper, we chose to limit the ecosystem to the actors directly involved in the POC development as presented in a simplified SSE structure in Fig. 1. The patient or inhabitant (*In*) "purchases" home care services from the municipality (*Mc*) and is given access to the solution by *Mc*. The homecare personnel (*Hp*) have access to all patient data (EPJ) through a *Mobile Lifecare Pleie* app (LMP). *Ci* is a 3rd party supplier that provides technical support to *Mc* in healthcare. In this SSE, *Ci* works to develop data trust systems as a service to the municipality. Another company *Cii* provides an application programming interface (API) in which the hardware (the smart doorlock) and the IoT gateway speak to each other. Software for the IoT gateway is provided by another company *Ciii* which owns a robust IoT business platform on which the smart doorlock solution is to be hosted. *Ciii*'s IoT platform already hosts numerous applications for other companies involved in energy-loss monitoring, fire protection, moisture monitoring, air-quality monitoring, etc.

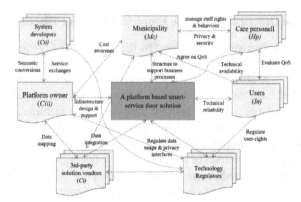

Fig. 1. A simplified service development ecosystem for the smart door solution

What are the Key Interfaces in this SSE? In Fig. 1, we identified several interfaces, but we grouped all the SSE actors into 3 main schemas based on the strength of the interaction intensity in their interests' using data from the FGDs. From these schemas, we identified overlap areas across 3 schemas shown in Table 1. These overlaps are the most convergent interoperability dimensions that we discuss further in Sect. 4.

a) In *the solution–Mc–Hp–In interface*, the primary beneficiary *In* is interested in trust and privacy (e.g., data protection), the QoS, and reliability of the service. *Hp* is largely interested in the technical availability and reliability of the service. *Mc* is interested in ensuring consistency of the solution and coherence with the existing "key and key box" processes, role and policy clarity, the cost-effectiveness of the solution, and alignment with organizational strategy and vision.

b) In *the solution–Ci–Cii–Ciii interface*, the platform owner *Ciii* is interested in the alignment of data semantics, and the platform deployment model with *Cii*, while the vendor *Ci* who represents *MC's* technical interests seeks to ensure that platform's information exchange models, schemas, and interfaces are aligned with *Mc's* infrastructure, data policies, business processes, and resources.

c) In *the solution–In–regulators interface*, the interest of regulators (*reg.*) is that solution does not breach the national data protection laws and the EU's General Data Protection Regulations laws concerning the rights of *In*, and *Hp*. *Mc* and *Ci* work to embed these legal requirements in their data governance policies.

4   Discussion, Conclusions, and Further Research

Getting back to the significance of alignment of the technical and organizational interoperability layers, our findings show us that alignment is possible because all actors that participate in service ecosystems tend to have common methods and routines of organizing work and interactions. At an abstract level, most organizations are similarly structured [9]. Table 1 highlights these overlapping themes such as strategy and

Table 1. Identifying the most aligned interoperability dimensions.

Schema	Mc	Hp	In	Reg	Ci	Cii	Ciii	Overlapping interests
Solution–Mc–Hp–In interface	–	–	–	✓	✓		✓	Business processes: organizational policies & strategy: cost
Solution–Ci–Cii–Ciii interface	✓		✓	–	–	–		Data integration standards: semantic matching
Solution–In–regulators' interface	✓		–	–	✓	✓	✓	Common understanding of legislation: internal policies and rules

business process alignment, and organizational design comparability. The OS literature would suggest that organizations are by nature social structures whose governance and work routines tend to have similar patterns [2, 9]. These characterizations are partly consistent with Liu et al. [18] however a notable distinction of our study from Liu et al. is the significance of organizational contexts which in this case, appears to limit alignment and integration when more specific themes such as business model designs, ethics and cultures, and idiosyncratic knowledge are considered – c.f. [9, 12, 14].

We found similar evidence across the technological layer. As one moved away from the general themes to more specific dimensions, SSE actors' interests differed significantly, especially in their infrastructure models and how they applied the different technical standards. While all actors agreed that trust and privacy were important themes of the project, each actor's knowledge of trust and privacy for the doorlock solution varied. The reason for this variation was the ever-changing standards and interests within each organization. Even in the adoption of standards frameworks, domain-specific extensions and ontologies exist and are not covered comprehensively by standards [7, 8].

With regard to the challenges to organizational interoperability in the design and co-production of smart services, SSEs appear to present unique barriers that are unknown in practice and theory. We found several barriers mainly as a result of ecosystem heterogeneity. The common barriers included varied data semantics and representations, different data, and information exchange models, as well how each actor sought to deploy resources in the POC or the solution. Perhaps the biggest barrier as also noted by [8, 12] was the different competence levels among SSE actors, which increases the complexity as new platforms and new devices emerge.

In short, attaining full-scale social and technological interoperability in projects involving the design and deployment of smart services is near impossible – particularly in SSE environments. This study highlights some factors which support this position. Conversely, there are also overarching factors that can support successful interoperation. These include the existence of (1) enterprise interoperability frameworks and (2) global standards. The most used framework is the EIF, and two International Organization for Standardization (ISO) standards, i.e., ISO9241 (human-centered design principles and activities for computer-based interactive systems, 2020) and ISO23903 (interoperability and integration reference architecture for Health informatics, 2021). Our main take-away is that familiar interoperability frameworks and standards will tend to "enforce" organizational interoperability, but shared interests enable it – c.f. [9, 18].

4.1 Towards Refinement of the Socio-technical Systems Approach

We attempted to frame the interoperability problem in the development of smart services using the STS approach. However, the criticism of STS theory that's emerged out of this paper is the overall abstractness of the approach which makes it difficult for empirical testing. The other challenge emerges from the limited constructs available within STS to enable detailed deconstruction of social and organizational complexity in SSEs (e.g., reconciling different technical interests). Therefore, to refine the STS perspective we propose expanding the STS lexicon. The other approach proposed by [16] seeks to combine STS thinking with the socio-technical systems engineering (STSE) perspective to change mindsets and convince engineers of the STS's value.

Acknowledgment. The ioMt project is funded by the Regional Research Fund (RFF) Innlandet of Norway. Special thanks to the RFF Innlandet and the consortium working on the project including IKOMM AS, Eidsiva Bredbånd, KeyFree AS, Safe4 Security Group AS, HelseInn, Lillehammer Kommune, NTNU and Høgskolen i Innlandet.

References

1. Zheng, M., Ming, X., Wang, L., Yin, D., Zhang, X.: Status review and future perspectives on the framework of smart product service ecosystem. Procedia CIRP **64**, 181–186 (2017)
2. Lim, C., Maglio, P.P.: Data-driven understanding of smart service systems through text mining. Serv. Sci. **10**(2), 154–180 (2018)
3. Rabe, M., Asmar, L., Kühn, A., Dumitrescu, R.: Planning of smart services based on a reference architecture. In: DS 92: Proceedings of the 15th International Design Conference, pp. 2949–2960 (2018)
4. West, S., Gaiardelli, P., Rapaccini, M.: Exploring technology-driven service innovation in manufacturing firms through the lens of Service Dominant logic. IFAC-Papersonline **51**(11), 1317–1322 (2018)
5. Mugurusi, G.: Supply chains must evolve into supply chain ecosystems: why, and lessons from the COVID-19 pandemic. In: Proceedings of 30th Annual IPSERA Conference 2021, Knoxville, USA (2021)
6. Frost, R.B., Cheng, M., Lyons, K.: A multilayer framework for service system analysis. In: Maglio, P.P., et al. (eds.) Handbook of Service Science. Research and Innovations in the Service Economy, Springer, Cham (2019). https://doi.org/10.1007/978-3-319-98512-1_13
7. Burzlaff, F., Wilken, N., Bartelt, C., Stuckenschmidt, H.: Semantic interoperability methods for smart service systems: a survey. IEEE Trans. Eng. Manag., 1–15 (2019). https://doi.org/10.1109/TEM.2019.2922103
8. Zarko, I.P., et al.: Towards an IoT framework for semantic and organizational interoperability. In: 2017 GIoTS, pp. 1–6. IEEE (2017)
9. Rohatgi, M., Friedman, G.: A structured approach for assessing & analyzing technical & nontechnical interoperability in socio-technical systems. In: 2010 IEEE International Systems Conference, pp. 581–586. IEEE (2010)

10. Legner, C., Wende, K.: Towards an excellence framework for business interoperability. In: Proceedings of the 19th Bled eConference eValues, Bled, Slovenia (2006)
11. Kosanke, K.: ISO standards for interoperability: a comparison. In: Konstantas, D., Bourrières, J.P., Léonard, M., Boudjlida, N. (eds.) Interoperability of Enterprise Software and Applications, pp. 55–64. Springer, London (2006). https://doi.org/10.1007/1-84628-152-0_6
12. Lewis, G.A., Morris, E., Simanta, S., Wrage, L.: Why standards are not enough to guarantee end-to-end interoperability. In: 7th International Conference on Composition-Based Software Systems, pp. 164–173. IEEE (2008)
13. Weichhart, G., Feiner, T., Stary, C.: Implementing organizational interoperability—the SUddEN approach. Comput. Ind. **61**(2), 152–160 (2010)
14. Heiler, S.: Semantic interoperability. ACM Comput. Surv. (CSUR) **27**(2), 271–273 (1995)
15. Broy, M., Cengarle, M.V., Geisberger, E.: Cyber-physical systems: imminent challenges. In: Calinescu, R., Garlan, D. (eds.) Monterey Workshop 2012. LNCS, vol. 7539, pp. 1–28. Springer, Heidelberg (2012). https://doi.org/10.1007/978-3-642-34059-8_1
16. Alter, S.: STS through a work system lens: a possible path for reconciling system conceptualizations, business realities, and humanist values in IS development. In: 1st STPIS, Stockholm, Sweden, June 2015
17. Ketokivi, M., Choi, T.: Renaissance of case research as a scientific method. JOM **32**(5), 232–240 (2014)
18. Liu, L., Li, W., Aljohani, N.R., Lytras, M.D., Hassan, S.U., Nawaz, R.: A framework to evaluate the interoperability of information systems–measuring the maturity of the business process alignment. Int. J. Inf. Manage. **54**, 102153 (2020)

A Framework for Asset Centered Servitization Based on Micro-services

Alessandro Ruberti[✉][iD], Adalberto Polenghi[✉][iD], and Marco Macchi[✉][iD]

Department of Management, Economics and Industrial Engineering, Politecnico di Milano,
Piazza Leonardo da Vinci 32, 20133 Milan, Italy
{alessandro.ruberti,adalberto.polenghi,marco.macchi}@polimi.it

Abstract. This paper focuses on the proposal of a framework for a servitization model applied on an asset centered environment – including production machines as the physical assets – and populated by micro-services as the means to deliver the asset-related services. The asset centered servitization is, for many production machines manufacturers, a core value proposition. As a matter of fact, servitization represents a business-model change, with companies moving from selling goods to selling an integrated combination of goods and services. Competitive advantage is an outcome of this shift. This research proposes an evolution from the traditional, monolithic approach of servitization, often materialized in the concept of "platform/catalogue of services" to choose from, towards a modern view of "environment of micro-services" in which the physical assets are immersed. In the proposed framework, micro-services are summoned and function depending on the operating conditions and the actual usage, so to achieve a flexible and dynamic environment by design.

Keywords: Micro-services · Data-driven product service systems · Physical assets

1 Introduction

From the moment it was first spotted in academic literature [4], the "Servitization of Business" was defined as the tendency of adding value to products through service. This concept sparked radical business transformations by expanding the offer to customers and by creating new revenue streams. One of the core aspects is how to deliver the servitization while maintaining sustainable performance levels for the industry; hence, being scalable, robust, effective, and providing high and consistent performance, is fundamental for the success of the business transformations. However, many are the challenges (data not available, restrictions in accessing the internet, etc.) to build an effective and efficient service delivery architecture, in case of technical services such as maintenance which requires a range of activities, from the collection of data, through the application of advanced data analytics, to the engagement of all the decision-makers [2]. This is especially true when the service is extended from operational to tactical and strategic decisions, which compel the discipline of Asset Management (AM), Furthermore, it

© IFIP International Federation for Information Processing 2022
Published by Springer Nature Switzerland AG 2022
D. Y. Kim et al. (Eds.): APMS 2022, IFIP AICT 664, pp. 262–269, 2022.
https://doi.org/10.1007/978-3-031-16411-8_32

has been pointed out how the adoption of AM grants a better inclusion of stakeholders affected by the service of the asset(s). It is at this juncture that the concept of micro-services falls into place, as a way to evolve from monolithic approaches in offering services to a flexible solution more adaptable to customer needs and requirements.

The notion of delivering services with micro adaptive containment - that is: micro-services - was originally defined and developed for ICT applications [5], with the main idea to split software and applications into smaller "functions" working together to deliver the same, original intended result. These functions could be shared between multiple applications, thus increasing the effectiveness of each micro-service and also favoring a modular approach for services offering. Due to the inherited flexible nature of micro-services, computer scientists developed "Kubernetes" as an open-source container-orchestration system for automating computer application deployment, scaling, and management of micro-services. It was thanks to Kubernetes that micro-services were perceived as a real "way to go" in programming complex applications.

Building on the potential provided by micro-services, this paper postulates that AM needs a framework to configure and manage services in order to benefit from micro-services key features and advantages for asset operations management and governance. Furthermore, considering that the theory of data-driven PSS is at an early stage [6], the proposed framework aims to bring a contribution to such theory as a concrete concept linking information and data flows due to the digital transformation, to a flexible and dynamic capability to configure and manage services delivered to support the AM.

2 Literature Review

The literature review was carried out to understand the current state at the interception of the three areas this research revolves on, which are servitization, AM and micro-services. The review, based on a combination of open web search, Google Scholar and Scopus, is composed by three phases: (1) the topic and the scope perimeter definition; (2) the documents selection and (3) the value extraction.

Phase 1 consisted of the definition of the topics and keywords to properly direct the literature search (see Table 1). The keywords definition is influenced by business needs and strategy of the case company where this research is placed; thus, the scope definition should be considered coherent with the company business value proposition.

Table 1. Keywords selected

Macro-topic	Main keyword	Alternative keywords
Servitization	Servitization	Service, product-service system
Asset	Asset operations	Asset management, fleet management
Micro-services	Micro-services	Containers, kubernetes, componentization via services

Phase 2 consisted in the selection process, built on the document metadata, tags, title and abstracts, and the following inclusion criteria: (1) English-written documents only; (2) Peer-reviewed papers and conference papers, also extending the review to "grey" literature; (3) Publication year as the research was limited to documents published starting from 2005 (included) onwards (year of introduction of the modern definition of micro-services).

Phase 3 consisted of a full-body critical analysis of each relevant paper selected in the previous phase, to extract the key take-aways from which this work extends from.

From the literature findings it is possible to see that the trends about servitization and micro-services (two main keywords connected with this research) show a growing interest (Fig. 1). These signals are coherent between themselves (similar increase) even if – by analysing the sources – the trend of servitization relates a community interested in business topics, whereas the trend of micro-services is mostly confined to the technological (IT-related) topics.

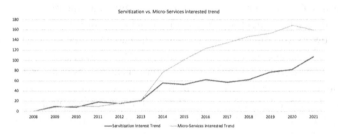

Fig. 1. "Servitization" and "Micro-Service" keyword trend

Focusing on the trends of asset operations (the third main keyword), this is also growing: the major share of the upsurge in interest is fueled by a managerial attention of asset operations (Fig. 2).

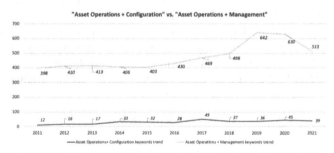

Fig. 2. "Asset Operations" keyword trend with 2 research attributes [Configuration and Management]

The following Table 2 provides a summary of the distribution of the literature findings, with information about the percentage relevance to the research scope, the subject area (Computer Science vs. Industrial Engineering), the language (English) and the exclusion of conference papers.

Table 2. Distribution of literature findings

Keywords	No. Of Results Total papers found on Platform	Relevance (ratio: interesting papers vs total papers)	No. Of papers studied and in scope of analysis	Subject Area
"Servitization"	745	8%	58	Engineering + Computer Science
"Asset Operations"	2114	7%	148	Engineering
"Computing Environment"	578	2%	11	Computer Science
"Micro-Services"	143	7%	10	Engineering + Computer Science
"Asset Operations" + "Configuration"	219	4%	8	Mostly Engineering
"Asset Operations" + "Management"	1431	11%	158	Mostly Engineering
"Asset Operations" + "Micro-Services"	89	10%	8	Engineering + Computer Science

With a specific insight on the servitization-related findings, customization, by adapting to the needs of each customer, is fundamental to provide services responsive to the needs. The proposed framework then considers a servitization with high level of customization in asset operations, with the micro-services as technological enablers to grant the realization of a cost-effective data-driven PSS (Product Service System).

3   The Framework

3.1   Overview of the Framework

The proposed framework is illustrated as three connected blocks which function in synergy as Fig. 3 shows.

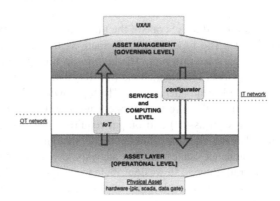

Fig. 3. High level schema of the framework

The schema connects the UX/UI (User Experience/User Interface) block with the physical asset so to consider a flow starting from the user and ending with the production machine, i.e. the physical asset. The generic term user, can be embodied by different figures in a company: a company manager, a workshop coordinator, a production planner, etc. In general, the stance taken is of a manager with a significant responsibility and the ability to configure production machines so that they achieve their productions goals. The production asset/machine itself, is not intended only as a physical artifact; it also includes the automation and digitization components, local to the machine, such as PLCs (Programmable Logic Controllers), SCADA (Supervisory Control And Data Acquisition), data gates and brokers.

Three levels then connect the user and the physical asset. Each of these three levels performs specific transformations, by enriching and providing new inputs to the data so that the operations management and governance system is flexible and dynamic, thus adapting to the various conditions that can arise from business and operational needs.

The Asset Management level is the 1st level where – starting from business needs – the strategic decisions take place and governance is established. Here, the physical assets are governed with a specific strategy aligned with company values. This AM level concretizes in user profiles, thus translating the user needs in lieu of the original specification and features defined and planned.

The Services and Computing Level (2nd level) processes the rules, the settings, the inputs provided by the 1st level, via a configurator (in a nutshell, a 'mapping service' between existing micro-services and business needs) which seamlessly builds and recalls the necessary micro-services into newly assembled service(s). Besides, this level runs the information management from the production floor: via the IoT devices, the level processes the information coming from the physical asset itself back up the 1st level: this is the basis to create a virtuous loop for keeping the information updated.

The Asset Level is the 3rd level where the machines/production assets operate. This is the arrival point for configurations, strategic inputs, planning and deliverables coming from the above levels. It's also the most *raw*-data rich as the IoT devices and the sensors collect a variety of data related to any event happening on the production floor. Raw data will be sent back to the above levels to become information to finally leverage on asset intelligence.

The flow of information and data is one of the most important exchanges that occur across the different levels. The types of transformations through which these flows of information and data pass are different. The bottom-up flow matures raw-data into information and then into asset intelligence via (mostly) data-driven analysis, experts' interpretation and machine learning deep dives. The top-down flow starts with business needs and value propositions that are transformed into governing principles (how to conduct properly the physical assets) and output requirements (what to expect from the assets utilization). This block of information finally becomes a delivery of services such as predictive maintenance, state machine analysis, performance self-assessment and correction, etc. Overall, the two flows contribute to the creation of a PSS, which is of a data-driven type, through the adoption of micro-services to guarantee customization of the service delivery.

3.2   The Role of Micro-services and of the Configurator of Services

Micro-services are at the heart of the conversion of AM guidelines into asset operations, and the configurator – a tool that allows users to customize the components and features of a product/service so that the final configured product/service meets their expectations as much as possible – is a key function to this end.

The popularity of configurators for engineering products is increasing as the number of products is also increasing and different components/sub-products can be assembled to create customized products. Likewise, a configurator of services is also perceived as an interesting method to govern service and product-service systems. Typically, to develop a configurator of services is required a two-stage approach: (1) developing/activating the enabling technology [3] and (2) decoding business goals into the technological design [1]. Micro-services are considered as the chosen technology in this research, and a configurator of (macro) services (i.e., those delivered to the customers) is a relevant function to adjust the delivered services to the customer.

The micro-services – micro adaptive containment – enable to think on the possibility to move from the traditional, monolithic approach of servitization, which is often materialized in the concept of "platform/catalogue of services" to choose from, towards a modern view of "environment of micro-services" in which physical assets are immersed and (micro-) services activated upon requests. In this view, micro-services are summoned, and function based on the conditions and the actual usage, creating a flexible and dynamic environment by design.

To fully enable the configurator of services, the 2nd level of the framework requires that the business goals are decoded into the technological medium: micro-services need to represent atomic, micro-needs that implement the high-level business goals. This 2nd level demands the development of a catalogue of services, in which the intended services to be provided to answer the business needs of the market are built through correctly structured micro-services. These micro-services altogether – as assembly of micro-services – then determine the (macro) services associated to the physical asset and delivered to support asset-related decisions.

Depending on the complexity and the correlation among the services, the creation of the catalogue requires to split each of the services to be delivered into small functions so that their sum, as adaptive integration, returns the intended result(s) of the originating service as required. As a result, a complex web of micro-services is expected, and the catalogue itself can be understood more as a honeycomb structure, rather than a hierarchical tree structure.

3.3 Exemplar of Micro-services Architecture for Prognostics and Health Management Within Asset Management

Even though services may be of multiple nature, predictive maintenance is one of the current hot services required by customers. For this reason, a first schema on how to structure micro-services so to provide prognostic capabilities is realized, grounded on the ISO 13334-1. This standard, also called OSA-CBM (Open Standard Architecture – Condition Based Maintenance) is useful as it is technology independent and could hence be established through monolithic as well as micro-services architecture. Figure 4 shows an abstract case that considers the micro-services designed to realize the catalogue of predictive maintenance services to be delivered on the physical asset, classified in: Data Treatment micro-services, Anomaly Detection micro-services, Diagnosis/Prognosis micro-services, and Decision-making micro-services.

When the micro-services are implemented and the business goals (like 'risk minimization' in the specific case of predictive maintenance) decoded onto the catalogue, the configurator works as the engine which pairs a business need (or multiple business needs) with interconnected micro-services taken from the catalogue designed by the provider. Figure 4 offers insight on the way the configurator selects the micro-services from the catalogue to provide human support in a predictive maintenance strategy. All the micro-services are assembled together in order to finally achieve the intended/demanded (macro) services to be provided, as it is a notification about the Remaining Useful Life of a component and an Advisory generation on the maintenance action to be executed.

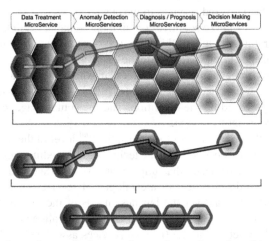

Fig. 4. From the catalogue of micro-services to the configuration of (macro) services

On the one hand, the customer/user sees the offered (macro) services as a result of customization; on the other hand, the provider manages multiple, interconnected, enabling micro-services, to finally achieve efficiency by design to deliver the customized services. In particular, in the definition of the micro-services as small functions, it is possible to find similarities among the functions themselves and thus utilize a single one for multiple purposes. For example, an anomaly detection service can be described as the interaction of 4 micro-services [A-B-C-D] while a diagnosis service by [A-B-E-F] which shares A and B as micro-services because A executes certain data cleaning tasks and B performs a regression analysis. The services are made unique by the [C-D] and [E-F] not-shared micro-services, which then specifically lead to deliver the customized service, e.g. an alerting procedure for the anomaly detection or a failure mode isolation algorithm for the diagnosis, both of them built on the common ground brough by the coupling [A-B].

4   Conclusions

This paper presented a first concept of a framework that connects the capabilities due to a key enabling technology leading to micro-services, with the business interest of servitization and, in particular, the development of a data-driven PSS on physical assets.

The concept considered the benefit by design achieved with the adoption of micro-services, while revealing the need for a proper management of the complexity of micro-services to finally obtain an efficient method for delivering customized services according to their intended use for the customer/user and operational features of the physical asset. The framework has been realized looking at AM and, particularly, to the Prognostics and Health Management, as a set of exemplar services that are highly requirements by industrial customers in the current contexts.

In future works, we expect to develop the concept further, while being driven by the business requirements derived from the value proposition of the case company and to analyze the limits of the framework, such as the need of data and their availability in the network (internal and external). The specific interest will be devoted to demonstrating that the micro-services features help achieve an efficient delivery of customized services for physical asset management.

Different abilities should be under scrutiny to evaluate the benefits of the proposed framework. Amongst them: i) the ability to re-use micro-services in multiple industrial contexts, to enable maintainability and resilience over the asset lifecycle; ii) the ability to meet remotization requirements due to specific operational conditions where the physical asset is not connected to the network and the micro-services can operate on-edge; iii) the data share-ability, considering the possibility to have different policies of access to data produced by the physical assets in their standard operations environment.

Overall, the provider is expected to not only achieve an efficient way to customize services, but also an effective capability to make a continuous improvement from the application of the same micro-services in different contexts, which grants its result(s) in different scenarios and eventually a learning experience from data in different industries.

References

1. Düllmann, T.F., van Hoorn, A.: Model-driven generation of microservice architectures for benchmarking performance & resilience engineering approaches. In: ICPE 2017 - Companion of the 2017 ACM/SPEC International Conference on Performance Engineering, pp. 171–172 (2017). https://doi.org/10.1145/3053600.3053627
2. Sala, R., Bertoni, M., Pirola, F., Pezzotta, G.: Data-based decision-making in maintenance service delivery: the D3M framework. J. Manuf. Technol. Manag. **32**(9), 122–141 (2021). https://doi.org/10.1108/JMTM-08-2020-0301
3. Schäffer, E., Penczek, L.N., Bartelt, M., Brossog, M., Kuhlenkötter, B., Franke, J.: A microservice- And AutomationML-based reference architecture for an engineering config-urator web platform. Procedia CIRP **103**, 274–279 (2021). https://doi.org/10.1016/j.procir.2021.10.044
4. Vandermerwe, S., Rada, J.: Servitization of business: adding value by adding services. Eur. Manag. J. **6**(4), 314–324 (1988). https://doi.org/10.1016/0263-2373(88)90033-3
5. Wilde, N., Gonen, B., El-Sheikh, E., Zimmermann, A.: Approaches to the evolution of SOA systems. In: El-Sheikh, E., Zimmermann, A., Jain, L.C. (eds.) Emerging Trends in the Evolution of Service-Oriented and Enterprise Architectures. ISRL, vol. 111, pp. 5–21. Springer, Cham (2016). https://doi.org/10.1007/978-3-319-40564-3_2
6. Zambetti, M., Pezzotta, G., Pinto, R., Rapaccini, M., Barbieri, C., Adrodegari, F.: From data to value: conceptualizing data-driven product service system. Prod. Plann. Control (2021). https://doi.org/10.1080/09537287.2021.1903113

Interactions in the Multi-level Distribution Management of Data-Driven Services for Manufacturing Companies

Marcel Faulhaber[(⊠)], Volker Stich, Günther Schuh, and Lennard Holst

Institute for Industrial Management (FIR), RWTH Aachen University, Campus-Boulevard 55, 52074 Aachen, Germany
marcel.faulhaber@fir.rwth-aachen.de

Abstract. Manufacturing companies (MFRs) are increasingly extending their portfolios with services and data-driven services (DDS) to differentiate themselves from competitors, tap new revenue potential, and gain competitive advantages through digitization and the subsequently generated data. Nonetheless, DDS fail more often than traditional industrial services and products within the first year on the market. Particularly, companies are failing to sell DDS successfully and efficiently with their existing (multi-level) distribution structures. Surprisingly, there is a lack of scientific research addressing this issue. Since there are currently no holistic models for an end-to-end description of distribution-tasks for DDS in the manufacturing industry, this paper contributes to a task-oriented reference model for mapping interactions in the multi-level distribution management. Therefore, a case study research approach is used, to identify and describe the interactions in the multi-level distribution management of DDS, as well as to develop a regulatory framework for MFRs and their multi-level distribution management. This research uses the established theoretical framework of Service-Dominant-Logic to address the co-creation in multi-level distribution management of DDS. As a result, this paper identifies different interaction variants as well as the need for a new management function with 4 main and 14 basic tasks.

Keywords: Distribution management · Data-driven services · Case study research · Manufacturing · Regulatory framework · Reference model

1 Introduction

Against the backdrop of the fourth industrial revolution, the manufacturing sector is on the verge of a transformation from purely manufacturing to equally service-providing companies. Leading industrial companies are already extending their offerings with data-driven services (DDS) and thereby creating new revenue streams. The possibilities offered by Industry 4.0 for generating, storing, transmitting, and processing large volumes of data in real time will drive this trend. With the advancement of digital technologies, the decreasing cost of sensors, and their connectivity via increasingly powerful,

© IFIP International Federation for Information Processing 2022
Published by Springer Nature Switzerland AG 2022
D. Y. Kim et al. (Eds.): APMS 2022, IFIP AICT 664, pp. 270–282, 2022.
https://doi.org/10.1007/978-3-031-16411-8_33

Internet-enabled networks known as the Industrial Internet of Things (IIoT), more and more companies are adding DDS to their existing portfolios of products and accompanying services (Product Service Systems, or PSS) [1]. DDS in combination with digital business models represent promising new growth areas in MFRs. MFRs are not only pursuing the development of new revenue streams, but also the strengthening of their product business by offering DDS. Against the backdrop of stagnating technical product innovations and the fundamental expectation of a good product with high quality on the part of customers, the importance of (data-driven) services as a means of differentiation from the competition is increasing significantly [2]. Furthermore, the data derived from DDS is of great strategic and operative importance for MFRs. Historically, data was mainly generated alongside the transactional business processes and managed individually by the respective intra-divisional silos, such as Marketing, Sales, Service, Production, R&D, etc. DDS on the other hand enable MFRs for the first time to get a data-based insight in the usage phase of their products and services. By combining data from various sources, companies can create valuable customer insights for improving business processes, as well as their offerings, all in all to become more customer centric. The thus improved customer experience is the main area where 89% of companies believe they will be competing with each other in the future [3]. Customer centricity not only benefits the customer, but also the MFRs. Customer centric firms not only are up to 60% more profitable compared to their peers [4], but also their business is more resilient [5]. Consequently, being able to develop, sell and operate data-driven services become indispensable skills for future success of MFRs.

In order to ensure customer proximity and support while at the same time minimize their financial invest, MFRs often make use of and rely on downstream channel partners to market, sell, distribute and service their products [6]. Additionally, distribution partners play a key role for the business internationalization of MFRs [7]. While these partners are central to the MFRs' product business, they present a number of challenges for the distribution of services and DDS in particular [2]. Depending on the partner as well as the DDS, the challenges lie in the marketing (e.g. explanation of benefits), billing (e.g. recurring payments) as well as support during the usage phase of DDS (e.g. technical support). OEMs have to reevaluate central aspects of their current business models and processes, when it comes to selling DDS [8]. In addition to find answers to the challenges mentioned above, companies also must find a way to actively manage and steer the sales of data-driven services, without causing great negative effects on the existing business model [7, 9]. In typical organizational structures of MFRs, the tasks to be performed are located in different areas of responsibility. In addition to internal departments such as sales, digital product management and service, external partners are also involved, which in turn increases the complexity.

In the literature, different aspects have been addressed in different research fields (e.g. channel management, customer relationship management, key account management, customer success management, etc.). So far, there is no consolidated and application-oriented approach to the topic [2, 10].

For this reason, in successful companies, those responsible for the digital business also take on tasks to coordinate the core business to centrally coordinate and solve the challenges described above. These sales management functions operate at the interface of internal and external stakeholders and coordinate short- and long-term success for both, product- and DDS-business. Their central task and challenge is, to successfully build up the digital business of MFRs within organizational setups for product and service business. Since this is uncharted territory for practitioners as well as for researchers, a regulatory framework is needed to structure and define the global area of responsibility. Furthermore, a task-oriented reference model enables a more detailed description of the process steps to be completed and thus supports the development and professionalization of the new function.

As a first step, we studied MFRs in their efforts to sell their DDS in established structures, using a case study approach. Our aim in this paper is to identify and describe the interactions in the multi-level distribution management of data-driven services, as well as to develop a regulatory framework for MFRs and their multi-level distribution management.

2 State of Research

2.1 Data-Driven Services

Data-driven services (DDS) comprise service offerings based on data and ICT, which are provided on demand via electronic interfaces. Data-driven services are services that are linked to physical products as data suppliers (Smart PSS) and meaningfully supplement or extend them (Fig. 1).

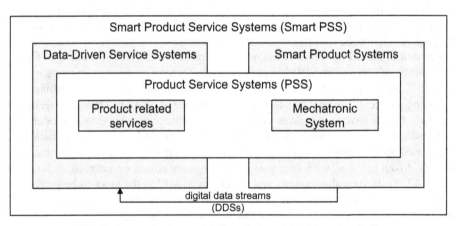

Fig. 1. Categorization and differentiation of DDS based on [11]

Although academic literature and research is frequently addressing DDS, they focus mainly on descriptive approaches of their characteristics and procedures and methods for the development of DDS [12]. Only very limited approaches address the marketing and sales of DDS, let alone multi-level distribution management.

While physical products can be described and compared largely by **search properties** (e.g. price, weight, size, type of material), buyers of services and especially of DDS have to evaluate them by **experience properties** (e.g. repaired machine) and **trust properties** (e.g. prevented failures of a machine) [13]. Due to the novelty of its performance scope, it is a challenge for MFRs and especially for their distribution partners to sell DDS. Not only the performance scope of DDS is new within multi-level business relationships, but also the respective **revenue** and **billing models**. In an industry characterized by mostly high one-time transactions with established margins, MFRs and their distribution partners reach limits with their processes and IT systems when it comes to billing flat rates (price per available time unit), pay-per use (price per used time unit), pay per output (price per unit produced), pay per success (price per performance increase). In addition to the technical possibility of mapping these billing models, they are also more difficult to explain to the customer.

2.2 Multi-level Distribution Management

"Distribution covers all decisions that affect the path of a product from the provider to the final customer" [14]. Today, distributors have more complex relationships and act as self-reliant retail enterprises with their own market power. Distributors are of great importance to the core business of MFRs, as they are responsible for sales activities towards customers [15].

Distribution channels can be distinguished in **direct distribution** (no independent trading company between the manufacturer and the final customer) and **indirect distribution** (at least one independent trading company between the manufacturer and the final customer). Indirect distribution channels can further be described by their **width** (number of distribution partners used in parallel) and their **length** (number of intermediate distribution partners in one channel) [16, 17].

Recent scientific literature in the fields of B2B Marketing does focus on aspects of digitalization of sales, multi-channel management and solution sales. Existing literature in these fields can be used to lay the groundwork of this paper, but neither multi-level distribution management tasks are described for the sales of DDS. As such, the work of Husmann [18] can be mentioned here, in which he examined "Success Factors in the Market Launch of DDS for Equipment Manufactures". However, there is a lack of research regarding the topics of multi-level distribution management, the sale of DDS as well as managing multi-level distribution of DDS. Regarding the scientific literature in the field of reference modelling, to this date no explicit models for mapping the interactions between, manufacturer, partner and customer in the multi-level distribution management of data-driven services can be found. This is especially surprising, since MFRs face the challenge, of identifying new ways of collaborating with distribution partners in order to market and sell DDS.

The SDL is a conceptual framework introduced by Vargo and Lusch (2004). In this framework, all economic exchanges are carried out by service, which they defined as "the application of specialized competences through deeds, processes, and performances for the benefit of another entity or the entity itself" [19]. One of the corner pillars of their framework is value co-creation. Creating shared value is a collaborative and two-way process in which actors and entities interact independently to integrate resources for mutual benefit. We use the concept of co-creation to address the interaction between manufacturer, distributors and customers in the multi-level distribution management of DDS.

3   Research Process

In order to initially develop a regulatory framework for mapping the interactions in the multi-level distribution management of digital products for MFRs a case-based research method according to Eisenhardt was chosen [20]. This method allows for a practical research process consisting of eight steps, which are listed in Table 1.

Table 1.   Case study process and implemented research activities, based on [20]

Process step	Activities	Realization within the research process
I. Getting started	Define the research question(s)	How can the interactions in the multi-level distribution management of DDS be described? How does a regulatory framework for multi-level distribution management of DDS look like?
II. Selecting cases	Specify population	Examination of 13 MFRs and 5 distributors between 2019 and 2022 with an established product and service business as well as with DDS in the branches printing, industrial tools & equipment, medical devices, industrial & automotive supplier, intralogistics, agriculture, cleaning equipment, food industry equipment, heating products & industrial cooling systems, electrical connection technology
III. Crafting instruments	Combine data collection methods	Telephone and in-person interviews, workshops, internal documents, secondary source documents
IV. Entering the field	Overlap data collection and analysis	Two iterations: 1. Deriving conceptual interactions. 2. Transferring results into a regulatory framework

(continued)

Table 1. (*continued*)

Process step	Activities	Realization within the research process
V. Analyzing data	Identify cross-case patterns	Comparing distribution approaches and tasks performed by MFRs
VI. Shaping hypotheses	Confirm, extend, and sharpen theory	Conclusion after two iterations: Two major interaction approaches, 4 order-giving dimensions and 14 basic tasks were identified
VII. Enfolding literature	Compare with conflicting and similar literature	Comparison with existing literature, regulatory frameworks and task-oriented reference models presented in Sect. 2
VIII. Reaching closure	Observe theo. Saturation (when possible)	Observed flattening curve regarding knowledge improvement

4   Results

The following Sects. 4.1 and 4.2 present the results of the first and second iterations of the conducted case study research. As a result of the first iteration, the different types of interactions were identified. Building up on the first iteration, the result of the second iteration in combination with the conducted literature review presented in Sect. 2, the regulatory framework was derived.

4.1   Types of Interactions for Manufacturing Companies and Distribution Partners

In order to describe the interactions between MFRs and distributors, **exchange objects** are used as the level of consideration. They are at the center of the business relationship and include products and services, financial flows as well as information and data [21]. They build the basis for the cooperation between manufacturer and sales partner, because only through them the sales partner can take over the sales task. The special characteristics of the exchange objects generally include the scope, quality and time, e.g. the attractiveness of the financial conditions, the timing of the information or the quantity of the services provided.

Financial flows (funds) are the counterpart of commodity flows (products and services) because they express the value of the commodity flows and can be used to measure the contribution to the monetary targets of the manufacturer. Since a payment flow from the sales partner to the manufacturer means a positive target contribution for the latter, quite in contrast to the sales partner, a conflict of interest arises. The desire for better conditions is therefore more or less inherent in the system.

In this context, **information** is understood to mean verbal and numerical content of the most varied nature. In particular, information on customer contact data, inquiries, orders, customer statements, customer requests, etc., but also reminders, invoices, statistics, etc. is exchanged between the manufacturer and the distributor. Against the background of DDS, these mainly focus on the valuable DDSs from the customer usage phase described in Sect. 1 and 2.

Finally, the actual **products and services (offerings)** that are sold to the customer are to be included to describe the business interactions. Depending on the individual scenario, products and services can be offered to the customer by the different players (manufacturer and distributor). Products and services can either get passed on along the distribution levels, with each individual level being remunerated for its contribution (e.g. commission model) or levels can be skipped and a competitive situation between manufacturer and distributors can arise.

The following Fig. 2 illustrates the basic interactions between the key actor's manufacturer, distributor, and customers in a typical multi-level product distribution setup. The manufacturer sells the product to the distributor, who then sells it to the customer. Based on the individual situation, distributors keep a margin (y), when compensating the manufacturer. Within the manufacturing sector, distributors often have information on their customers, which they do not share with the manufacturer, because of the fear to lose their business to them.

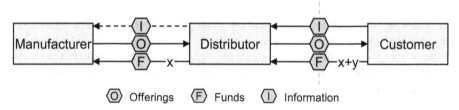

Fig. 2. Interactions for a multi-level product distribution

However, when it comes to the multi-level distribution of DDS, different approaches for the interactions between MFRs and distributors can be observed. MFRs either integrate their distributors in the sale of DDS (indirect distribution of DDS), or they build up capacities on their own to sell DDS by themselves (direct distribution of DDS).

Figure 3 illustrates two different variants (variant A and variant B) for the **integration of distributors** by MFRs. In both variants, MFRs are using the active salesforce of their distributors to market and sell DDS to their customers. Distributors in the variant A receive a margin (y) based on the sold DDS and its respective generated revenue. Although the margins of DDS are very attractive compared with services and especially compared with product business, the overall revenue is rather small compared. Due this reason, distributors are often not incentivized to offer DDS to their customers, which is why MFRs integrate distributors into the generated information flow and let them participate on insights regarding customer needs and behaviors. Depending on the individual setup, as well as the digital maturity of the distributors, they either receive processed data and information from the manufacturer (solid line from manufacturer to the distributor) or they receive the raw data (dashed line from customer to the distributor). Depending on who is the contracting partner for the customer (legal setup for DDS), funds can also go directly from the customer to the manufacturer, who then compensates the distributor.

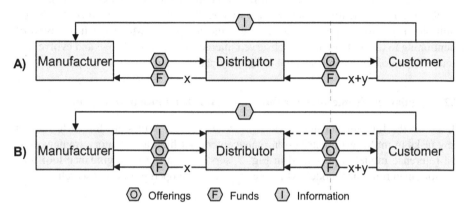

Fig. 3. Interaction variants for a multi-level DDS distribution while integrating distributors

Finally, Fig. 4 illustrates two different variants for the interactions when MFRs follow a direct approach for the distribution of their DDS. In these cases, manufacturer decide to use their own salesforces (if already present) or build up new salesforces in order to directly sell DDS to the customers. In practice, companies decide in favor of this variant if they have already failed with the distribution of DDS via their partners, or if they do not view the distribution of DDS via their partners as being very successful due to the need for explanation and the low sales volume of DDS transactions. However, the direct approach of customers by MFRs puts a strain on the relationship between MFRs and distributors,

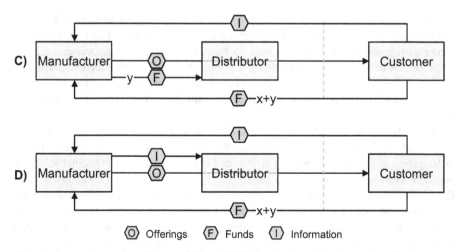

Fig. 4. Interaction variants for a multi-level DDS distribution while integrating distributors

as they get the impression of becoming obsolete. Since the MFRs need the partners in the future for the success and efficiency of their core business, they compensate the distributors responsible for the customers. This is analogous to direct sales, either via the provision of information to strengthen the product and service business (variant C), via a revenue share from DDS (variant D), or a combination of the two variants.

Regarding the identified interaction variants, the authors did not expect to observe multiple interaction variants at once in use at the companies. Moreover, it seems worth mentioning to the authors that the observed interaction variants change and evolve over time. The ongoing research sets out to identify patterns and development paths.

4.2   Regulatory Framework for the Multi-level Distribution Management

Based on the fundamental interactions described above, MFRs are forced to take on new tasks in multi-level distribution management. At first, a regulatory framework of the reference model is presented in Fig. 5, serving as a top-level guidance tool for a task-oriented reference model, which needs to be developed in future research.

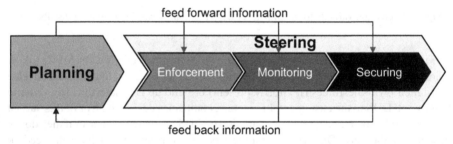

Fig. 5. Regulatory framework of the task-oriented reference model for multi-level distribution management of DDS based on [22].

The illustrated regulatory framework consists of four consecutive main tasks, which can be differentiated in the two levels "planning" and "steering". The four main tasks (order-giving dimensions) are not only to be run through and interconnected in the sense of a waterfall logic, but furthermore, with the connections "feed forward" and "feed back" to the planning level, they have an exchange of information for the constant regulation and continuous improvement of the multi-level distribution management of DSS.

In the following, the currently identified basic and elementary tasks are assigned to the four main tasks shown in the regulatory framework, see Table 2. Within the first order-giving dimension (**Planning**) MFRs need to derive operational (attainable, action-oriented, short-term) objectives for their DDS, based on the overall company strategy. Based on this, companies need to derive a sales strategy for their DDS that pursues the operational objectives. This in turn serves as the basis for the organizational and resource planning of multi-level distribution management. Essential for this basic task is the correct analysis and evaluation of the existing sales channels, the DDS distribution-relevant characteristics, as well as the customer segments to be served. The tasks within the first order-giving dimension are performed by the MFRs and their distribution or partner managers. The second order-giving dimension (**Enforcement**) copes the actual sale of the DDS to the customer and user. Based on the individual sales channel setup, the competences, and capacities of channel partners the basic tasks identified here can be performed by either the manufacturing company or their service and distribution partners (compare interaction variants described in Sect. 4.1). Starting with identifying potential customers for the DDS in the prospect management, the actual transaction and sale of the DDS, as well as supporting the customers and users with their needs after buying the DDS. In contrast to the one-off, transactional product business, the monitoring of customer loyalty and the tasks of customer churn prevention and customer recovery based on this are key to the long-term success of the companies in the sale of DDS. The third order-giving dimension (**Monitoring**) contains the tasks determining deviations from the derived sales plan and strategy, as well as identifying the root causes for these deviations. Compared to long-term sales goals for product and service business, MFRs must monitor the sales success of DDS more frequently. Within the fourth order-giving dimension (**Securing**) the MFRs act upon identified deviations and their sources of interference. By deriving countermeasures, implementing them and checking up on their effect, MFRs have to deep understanding of their customer and partner needs, as well as of their DDS performance.

Table 2. Basic tasks assigned to the main tasks of the regulatory framework for multi-level distribution management of DDS

Main task	Basic task
1 Planning	1.1 Operationalize objectives
	1.2 Definition of the sales strategy
	1.3 Organization and resource planning
2 Enforcement	2.1 Prospect management
	2.2 Sales
	2.3 After-sales support
	2.4 Customer loyalty
	2.5 Customer churn prevention
	2.6 Customer recovery
3 Monitoring	3.1 Determine sales plan deviations
	3.2 Identify sources of interference
4 Securing	4.1 Derivation of countermeasures

(continued)

Table 2. (*continued*)

Main task	Basic task
	4.2 Ensuring the implementation of measures
	4.3 Ensuring of the measure's success

5 Conclusion and Further Research

In this paper, a research process was described for deriving a regulatory framework for the multi-level distribution management of MFRs. The purpose of this work was to identify and describe the interactions of MFRs and their distributors with their customers in regards of DDS. Based on the identified conceptual interactions identified in the practice-oriented case study research process, the need for a new management function was identified. Considering the needs in practice as well as existing research regarding sales steering concepts a regulatory framework with 4 main tasks was defined. The 4 main tasks were further detailed by describing 14 basic tasks.

As for future research, further investigations are required focusing developing a task-oriented reference model. This reference model should describe on a functional layer, what the reference functions for MFRs look like. By further adding the layer of a data model and creating a combined process view in order to support MFRs with a complete reference model for the setup of their new sales function. As this research process is in process, the final testing and validation of the currently identified (basic and elementary) tasks is ongoing. Additionally, there is a need for further research regarding the measurement of quantitative effects of the sales management function in order to capture and prove its long-term benefits. Finally, recommendations for the implementation of the reference model need to be derived to support companies in a successful adaptation of the new management function.

Acknowledgement. The research project that forms the basis for this report is funded through an industry consortium of MFRs. This project is managed by the Institute for Industrial Management (FIR) at RWTH Aachen University and the Center Smart Services (CSS). The authors are responsible for the content of this publication.

References

1. Chowdhury, S., Haftor, D., Pashkevich, N.: Smart product-service systems (Smart PSS) in industrial firms: a literature review. Procedia CIRP **73**, 26–31 (2018)
2. Kampker, A., Husmann, M., Jussen, P., Schwerdt, L.: Market launch process of data-driven services for manufacturers: a qualitative guideline. In: Satzger, G., Patrício, L., Zaki, M., Kühl, N., Hottum, P. (eds.) IESS 2018. LNBIP, vol. 331, pp. 177–189. Springer, Cham (2018). https://doi.org/10.1007/978-3-030-00713-3_14
3. Gartner: Customer Experience Is the New Competitive Battlefield. Publisher Gartner. https://www.gartner.com/en/documents/3069817/customer-experience-is-the-new-competitive-battlefield. Accessed 21 Apr 2012

4. Deloitte: Wealth Management Digitalization changes client advisory more than ever before. Publisher Deloitte (2017). https://www2.deloitte.com/content/dam/Deloitte/de/Documents/financial-services/Wealth%20Management%20Digitalization.pdf. Accessed 21 Apr 2012
5. BCG: The Digital Path to Business Resilience. Publisher The Boston Consulting Group (2020). https://web-assets.bcg.com/af/28/359647864f67a53a16ec1e5200cc/bcg-the-digital-path-to-business-resilience-jul-2020.pdf. Accessed 21 Apr 2012
6. Homburg, C., Schäfer, H., Schneider, J.: Sales Excellence. Systematic Sales Management. Management for Professionals. Springer, Heidelberg (2012). https://doi.org/10.1007/978-3-642-29169-2
7. Homburg, C.: Marketingmanagement. Strategie - Instrumente - Umsetzung - Unternehmensführung. 7., überarbeitete und erweiterte Auflage (2020)
8. Buchholz, B.; Ferdinand, J.; Gieschen, J.; Seidel, U.: Digitalisierung industrieller Wertschöpfung – Transformationsansätze für KMU. Publisher Begleitforschung AUTONOMIK für Industrie 4.0iit-Institut für Innovation und Technik in der VDI/VDE Innovation + Technik GmbH. BMWI (2017). https://www.digitale-technologien.de/DT/Redaktion/DE/Downloads/Publikation/2017-04-27_AUT%20Studie%20Wertsch%C3%B6pfungsketten.pdf?__blob=publicationFile&v=2. Accessed 22 Apr 2012
9. TSIA: The State of Subscription Sales 2019/2020. Publisher TSIA. Technology & Services Industry Association. San Diego (TSIA-05536), June 2019, https://www.tsia.com/resources/the-state-of-subscription-sales-2019-2020. Accessed 21 Apr 2012
10. Scheed, B., Scherer, P.: Strategisches Vertriebsmanagement: B2B-Vertrieb im digitalen Zeitalter. Springer Fachmedien Wiesbaden, Wiesbaden (2019). https://doi.org/10.1007/978-3-658-22201-7
11. Holst, L., Stich, V., Schuh, G., Frank, J.: Towards a comparative data value assessment framework for smart product service systems. In: Lalic, B., Majstorovic, V., Marjanovic, U., von Cieminski, G., Romero, D. (eds.) APMS 2020. IAICT, vol. 592, pp. 330–337. Springer, Cham (2020). https://doi.org/10.1007/978-3-030-57997-5_39
12. Schuh, G., Kolz, D.: Morphology of strategic components for data-driven industrial services. In: Lödding, H., Riedel, R., Thoben, K.-D., von Cieminski, G., Kiritsis, D. (eds.) APMS 2017. IAICT, vol. 514, pp. 214–221. Springer, Cham (2017). https://doi.org/10.1007/978-3-319-66926-7_25
13. Zeithaml, V.: How Consumer Evaluation Processes Differ Between Goods and Services, pp. 186–190. Publisher J. Donnelly & W. George, Marketing of Services, Chicago (1981)
14. Tomczak, T., Reinecke, S., Kuss, A.: Strategic Marketing: Market-Oriented Corporate and Business Unit Planning. Springer Gabler imprint is published by Springer Nature (2018). https://doi.org/10.1007/978-3-658-18417-9
15. Webster, F.E.: The role of the industrial distributor in marketing strategy: the industrial distributor and his role in the manufacturer's marketing strategy are changing—slowly. J. Mark. **40**(3), 10–16 (1976)
16. Homburg, C., Kuester, S., Krohmer, H.: Marketing Management: A Contemporary Perspective. McGraw-Hill Higher Education (2009)
17. Moriarty, R.T., Moran, U.: Managing hybrid marketing systems. Harvard (1990). https://hbr.org/1990/11/managing-hybrid-marketing-systems. Accessed 26 Apr 2012
18. Husmann, M.: Erfolgsfaktoren bei der Markteinführung von datenbasierten Dienstleistungen im Maschinen- und Anlagenbau, Apprimus Verlag, Aachen (2020)
19. Vargo, S.L., Lusch, R.F.: Service-dominant logic: continuing the evolution. J. Acad. Mark. Sci. **36**(1), 1–10 (2008)
20. Eisenhardt, K.M.: Building theories from case study research. Acad. Manag. Rev. **14**, 532 (1989)

21. Schmitz, C.: Internationales Vertriebsmanagement für Industriegüter. 1. Aufl. s.l.: DUV Deutscher Universitäts-Verlag (Marketing-Management) (2006). http://gbv.eblib.com/patron/ FullRecord.aspx?p=751287

22. Wüller, F.: Kundenwertorientierte Vertriebssteuerung im Firmenkundengeschaeft der Kreditgenossenschaften. Kundenwertmodellierung, -Operationalisierung und konzeptionelle Gestaltungsempfehlungen. Frankfurt: Lang (Beiträge zum Controlling, 17) (2012). http:// gbv.eblib.com/patron/FullRecord.aspx?p=1129308

Breaking Transactional Sales: Towards an Acquisition Cycle in Subscription Business of Manufacturing Companies

Calvin Rix[✉], Günther Schuh, Volker Stich, and Lennard Holst

Institute for Industrial Management (FIR) at RWTH Aachen University, Campus-Boulevard 55, 52074 Aachen, Germany
calvin.rix@fir.rwth-aachen.de

Abstract. More and more manufacturing companies are starting to transform the transaction-based business model into a customer value-based subscription business to monetize the potential of digitization in times of saturated markets. However, historically evolved, linear acquisition processes, focusing the transaction-oriented product sales, prevent this development substantially. Elemental features of the subscription business such as recurring payments, short-term release cycles, data-driven learning, and a focus on customer success are not considered in this approach. Since existing transactional-driven acquisition approaches are not successfully applicable to the subscription business, a systematic approach to an acquisition cycle of the subscription business in the manufacturing industry is presented, aiming at a long-term participative business. Applying a grounded theory approach, a task-oriented model for the manufacturing industry was developed. The model consisting of five main tasks and 14 basis tasks serves as best practice to support manufacturing companies in adapting or redesigning acquisition activities for their subscription business models.

Keywords: Acquisition cycle · Subscription business · Manufacturing companies · Task model

1 Introduction

In order to achieve significant economic success with digitization in industrial practice a sustainable innovation of the business model is necessary, which requires a rethinking of previous value creation processes [1, 2]. Thus, in recent years manufacturing companies started to transform the transaction-based business model into a customer value-based subscription business model aiming to monetize the potential of digitization in times of saturated markets and increasing competitive pressure [1–3]. Through developing machines into "smart connected products" a permanent, data-based learning process with continuous releases is aspired to increase customer success and unleash the digital servitization paradigm [4–6]. Provider and customer enter into a long-term business relationship to strive for customer-oriented solutions and align their interests [7].

© IFIP International Federation for Information Processing 2022
Published by Springer Nature Switzerland AG 2022
D. Y. Kim et al. (Eds.): APMS 2022, IFIP AICT 664, pp. 283–293, 2022.
https://doi.org/10.1007/978-3-031-16411-8_34

However, manufacturing companies face numerous hurdles in establishing subscription businesses. One central challenge represents the acquisition of potential new and existing customers for innovative subscription models [8–10]. Currently, the customer acquisition of most manufacturing companies is based on static, intra-functional marketing and sales activities along the classic sales funnel [11, 12]. Here, the company's activities focus on the value that is captured transactionally in the sale of machines and services, ignoring the value that is created during the customer's usage phase [12]. Hence, facing the premises of subscription business, traditional marketing and sales approaches can no longer lead to success [13, 14]. The joint transition to a participatory subscription business requires collaborative solution design and delivery with a high demand for coordination, information, security and trust, which has not been necessary until now [14]. This goes hand in hand with high expectations regarding the trustworthiness, fairness and competence of the supplier, who must be able to conduct an explorative, realistic needs assessment during the acquisition process and build up an understanding of the entire value creation process on the customer side [14]. To meet these challenges, manufacturing companies must strive to move from the previous serial, intra-functional approach to a cross-functional and cross-organizational holistic acquisition process that consistently focuses on optimizing customer success before, during and after the purchasing process [10, 14, 15]. To create the basis for and build on a lasting win-win situation, a task-oriented, continuous acquisition cycle should be aimed for with product management, marketing, sales, service and customer success experts working closely together to enable the best possible customer journey [16, 17].

To move from transactional to a subscription-compliant acquisition cycle, practitioners need to obtain a holistic overview of the respective tasks and their requirements. Since there are currently no holistic models describing the acquisition tasks of subscription business in the manufacturing industry, the following research question is addressed: *How should a task-oriented model for acquiring subscription business in manufacturing companies be designed?* Based on a systematic literature review, empirical data were aggregated to develop the model through a grounded theory approach.

The article is structured as follows: After the introduction, the state of research on an acquisition cycle for subscription business models is discussed. Subsequently, the research methodology and the result of the task-oriented model of the subscription acquisition cycle is described. Lastly, we briefly discuss the implications of this paper, as well as its limitations and future research.

2 State of Research

Since subscription business has attracted lot of attention in industrial practice, there has been an increase in recent publications. Nevertheless, research around acquisition tasks for this business model area is still in its infancy.

First of all, acquisition is understood as winning prospects (new potential customers), whereby the customers can be either new to the product category (subscription business) or to the company [18]. Models and definitions in the literature which describe the acquisition process in detail - even if terms such as "cycle" are used - describe a linear sequence which ends with the purchase or the conclusion of the contract [19–22].

Relevant publications from the field of subscription research, however, show that the transformation to a subscription provider must inevitably be accompanied by a change to a cyclic acquisition process [7, 23]. However, the works do not provide usable models for manufacturing companies to design a new acquisition approach.

One of the most important areas of research for the acquisition of subscription business models is the field of value-based selling, which has recently come to the fore in scientific publications due to the increased interest in the transformation from product to solution provider [9, 10]. Existing works deal with the basic dimensions of value-based selling [24], selling-process model for plant engineering [10], differentiation of collaborative and supplier/customer activities [12], as well as the legal and contractual particularities [25]. Even though the specifics and tasks of value-based sales are comprehensively described in the existing literature, the usage phase is not sufficiently considered for a subscription acquisition approach. Following the idea of a transactional sale of a value-based solution, activities in the post-sales phase are hardly explored.

In contrast Edelmann and Singer [26] pursue the approach of a continuous and holistic "loop" process. The authors imply the elimination of a lengthy consideration and evaluation process and instead the transition of the customer into a perpetual customer loyalty loop. Even if the work is B2C-oriented and in the first place leaves out subscription models for manufacturing companies, the innovative approach is adaptable for our research and represents a fundamental pillar of our considerations.

Another relevant area of research is account-based marketing, which, in contrast to traditional lead and campaign management, addresses all key stakeholders involved in the customers' decision-making process. Even though some works can be found in the literature [27–29] that pursue the goal of a long-term, participatory partnership and an orientation towards customer benefits, the works do not sufficiently consider the usage phase in particular, which is essential for the subscription business. Nonetheless, the publications provide a promising foundation for early stages of the acquisition cycle.

Even though the state of research provides building blocks to answer the research question, there is currently no holistic approach, which can be used as a task-oriented guideline for an acquisition cycle of subscription business in manufacturing companies.

3   Methodology

To develop a new approach for the acquisition of subscription models, a qualitative empirical research approach was used. This was chosen because qualitative research has a constructivist and exploratory research character [30, 31]. Thus, it is suitable for opening up unexplored facts in a structured and holistic way [32]. Furthermore, it is widely accepted in research of subscription and solution sales [10, 25, 33–35].

Data was systematically collected according to Glaser and Strauss' grounded theory [36] to identify recurring elements and derive a theoretical task-oriented model. For this the general process of grounded theory [31, 36] have been followed: (1) deciding on a research problem, (2) framing the research question, (3) data collection, (4) data coding and analysis and (5) theory development. We combined different research methods to collect and analyze primary data, such as expert interviews and observations. In addition, the results of the literature review are used to enrich the model with secondary data. Table 1 provides an overview of the collected data for the research.

Table 1. Overview of the qualitative data collection types with company and participants.

Company	Data collection type[a]		Role of participants
Compressor manufacturer	Interview	Focus group	Subscription Product Manager, Head of Service Sales, Head of Marketing
Bearing manufacturer 1	Interview	One-on-one	Subscription Sales, Product Manager
Bearing manufacturer 2	Interview	Focus group	Sales Engineer, Subscription Manager
	Interview	One-on-one	Product Manager Subscription
Plant manufacturer	Observation	Participants	Business Development Manager, Subscription Product Manager, Sales Engineer
Packaging machine manufacturer	Interview	Focus group	Head of Sales, Market Intelligence Manager
Cutting machine manufacturer	Interview	One-on-one	Head of Product Management
Printing machine manufacturer 1	Interview	One-on-one	Head of Digital Business
Printing machine manufacturer 2	Interview	One-on-one	Head of Subscription
Industrial software provider	Interview	One-on-one	Director Marketing & Sales
Risk consultancy	Interview	One-on-one	Business Development Manager

[a] According to types of qualitative data collection [30]

4 Results

In this section, the results of the research are presented. Figure 1 presents the task-oriented model, which shows five main and 14 basis tasks.

To develop the superior structure of the model the Plan Do Check Act (PDCA) cycle was used to consider the continuous improvement of the provider-customer service system as a premise of the subscription business. Another fundamental success factor for the acquisition of subscription customers is the holistic design of the process considering provider and customer activities and interactions. Therefore, in combination with the PDCA cycle [37], the three phases (pre-purchase, purchase and post-purchase) of customer interaction according to Lemon and Verhoef [38] were used as a framework for designing the continuous process. In the following subchapters the main and associated basis tasks that were derived and detailed through the iterative qualitative research process are described.

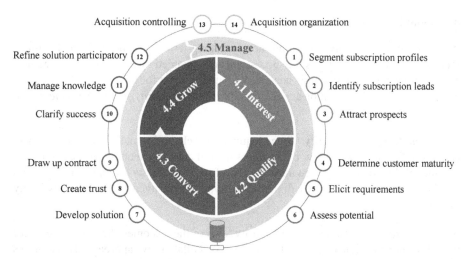

Fig. 1. Task-oriented model of the subscription acquisition cycle

4.1 Interest

For the subscription business it is crucial that the right customers are addressed and interested with whom customer success can be guaranteed and in the best case continuously increased. The main task *Interest* is subordinate to the basis tasks *segment subscription profiles*, *identify subscription leads* and *attract prospects*.

Segment Subscription Profiles: In addition to strategic criteria (e.g., relevant target industries) and formal aspects (e.g., size, customer competencies, openness for solution business), needs-based criteria (e.g., striving for flexibility, efficiency or security) must be taken into account for segmenting subscription customer profiles [9, 14].

Identify Subscription Leads: To establish a fit with the subscription profiles and to identify potential subscription leads operational and service data of existing customers should be aggregated in a customer data cloud to derive the potential for subscription business via a lead algorithm. To attract new customers, potential contacts should be directed to subscription-relevant content (webinars, whitepapers, etc.) via optimized UX design. Subscription content becomes available through a registration barrier and enables automatic evaluation of contact forms and chats to identify subscription leads.

Attract Prospects: Since buying centers sometimes lack structure for buying sub-subscription models, it is important to find the right prospect for initial contact [14]. In contrast to the product business, this often requires communication at the decision-maker level. Even at this early stage, it is necessary to communicate the value of the potential solution [39]. To overcome objections, business model-specific arguments should be used to convince the customer of the added value (e.g., security of supply, elimination of operating obligations and cost predictability) [14].

4.2 Qualify

As the subscription involves a commitment with long-term consequences, and the fulfill-ment and associated prospects for success are accompanied by a wide range of require-ments on the customer side, it is necessary to qualify them for the new business model. The basis tasks of qualification are *determine customer maturity*, *elicit requirements* and *assess potential*.

Determine Customer Maturity: Since requirements elicitation and potential assessment are high-effort activities, a low-effort assessment of customer maturity for the subscrip-tion model should be completed initially. Therefore, e. g. affinity for innovative business models, operator competencies, digital maturity, risk aversion and service accessibility play a key role.

Elicit Requirements: Based on the maturity level of the customer, the requirements for the subscription design are realized in an iterative, collaborative approach. This requires an exploratory process in which provider and customer gradually identify specifics for implementing the solution. This requires extended understanding of the customer's value creation process (e.g., energy costs, service deliverability, value creation interfaces, finance and tax) not taken into account in traditional product business [14].

Assess Potential: In order to identify the potential and ultimately the improvement opportunities of the customers, it is necessary to gain deep insights into the customer's production and value creation processes [9]. Providers must be able to identify which processes could be made more efficient and how much value could be added with sub-scription solutions. Routines and templates for conducting and reporting asset audits are to be established. Service personnel should also perform routine audits on an ongoing basis to identify business opportunities (see *Identify subscription leads*). Collecting and analyzing customer data to gain assessable insights, while time-consuming and difficult, is essential to value-based pricing and the subscription acquisition cycle [10].

4.3 Convert

As soon as a high potential customer has been identified, the conversion from a transaction-based to a subscription customer must be carried out. The focus lies on creat-ing trust in the provider, the solution and ultimately the new partnership. The conversion involves the tasks *develop solution*, *create trust* and *draw up contract*.

Develop Solution: The conception of the subscription model is cooperative and inte-grates an extended buying center, which is composed of more roles (e.g. IT, law, con-trolling, management, production) and hierarchies compared to traditional product sales. The reason is higher, perceived risk and the more extensive participation in the develop-ment of the solution. A decisive success factor for solution development is the consistent focus on the possible customer benefits and the intelligent orchestration of the services, considering the customer's existing resources, while at the same time critically reflect-ing on the capabilities and risks taken by the provider. The holistic view of the value creation process (e.g., knowledge of existing usable resources, partially utilized compressors) or incorrectly dimensioned systems (e.g., too high energy consumption) should be considered and are crowned with high customer appreciation.

Create Trust: The trustworthiness and reputation of the company is particularly important to gain the necessary access to information of the customer processes and to promote the perception of fairness [9]. Trust and credibility are especially solidified with long-term partners who have already demonstrated outstanding performance in transactional business. Here, trust in the capabilities of service plays a special role, as maintenance delivery is strongly emphasized for subscription capability. Confidence-building measures represent systematic risk assessment and prevention. By analyzing the existing operational/production liability, necessary supplementary warranty risks are identified, and the contractual, technical, and insurance-related preventive measures are derived. Transparent communication with the customer is to be aimed for and additional trust may be built up via third parties (e.g., reinsurers).

Draw Up Contract: The drafting of subscription contracts is an unavoidable, but difficult and expensive challenge that correlates with the complexity of customers' value functions [25]. Contract design requires proactive and cross-functional integration of legal, sales and product development functions. Raising awareness of contract and legal issues among executives and acquisition staff and carefully designing business processes that engage legal departments at the right time are critical [25]. A fundamental problem with existing subscription agreements is that they often focus solely on protecting self-interest. As a result, contracts tend to be used defensively, leading to extremely complicated contractual arrangements that hinder mutual welfare. In the long term sustainable and lean contractual models should be aimed for, which enable a quick start and joint further development steps based on trust.

4.4 Grow

Finally, Subscription is about developing the ability to grow with customers beyond the initial contract as they gradually gain more experience. Via a data-driven learning approach and proactive dialogs the continuous customer-oriented evolution and extension of the subscription contract is targeted. Customers increasingly understand how they can benefit, which expands the scope for potential agreements to better and better meet customers' needs and creates further barriers for competitors. *Clarify success, manage knowledge,* and *refine offer participatory* are basis tasks for the continuous growth.

Clarify Success: The mere fulfillment of contractual obligations is not sufficient in a subscription business. Since subscription offers run over a longer period, it is necessary to demonstrate value creation at regular intervals. Customers tend to quickly forget the benefits of what is delivered, such as the cost savings from reduced effort and resources [10]. In addition, during the contract period, it is important to maintain the feeling that the value created is distributed fairly. Only in this way it is possible to contribute capabilities and resources in a value-oriented manner [9, 40].

Manage Knowledge: The knowledge that is gathered during the subscription about the provision of the solution and the fulfillment of customer needs must be systematically collected and processed in order to be able to use it for further development [10]. In addition to aggregation via software tools, the exchange between employees on site represents a valuable source of information. Factors such as silo mentality on the customer and supplier side can hinder the exchange of knowledge and should therefore be taken into account [10].

Refine Offer Participatory: In summary, subscriptions must aim to satisfy customers' business needs at profitable prices [33]. Long-term management of the customer relationship with participatory recurring development of the offering is therefore an important part of the subscription capabilities and tasks. Standardized routines, protocols, and the use of information systems must be employed to capture subscription relationship information for shared growth. Despite possible concerns about sharing value and cost information, providers and customers must recognize the great potential for shared learning in the partnership to refine the offer continuously.

4.5 Manage

Assembling, managing and motivating employees for the acquisition cycle is a major task, as extensive demands are placed on employees and new metrics are required to measure the attractiveness of a business compared to the product business. The basis tasks *acquisition controlling* and *acquisition organization* are necessary for this.

Acquisition Controlling: Firstly, success should no longer be measured by revenue-driven metrics, but e. g. by customer lifetime value. To escape commission-oriented key figures, a more attractive base salary must be introduced to take account of the business model-inherent characteristics (extensive, demanding acquisition phases, irregular conclusion of contracts). Additional monetary incentives can be measured via bonuses (usually for entire acquisition team) based on leads generated, contract duration or realized return on investment. However, non-monetary motivation concepts are particularly important for subscriptions. Purposeful target agreements should be defined jointly between the executive and the acquisition team (e.g., number of offers placed). The recognition for the work is also a significant stimulus for the employees.

Acquisition Organization: Subscription implementation requires the establishment of a specific acquisition organization unit. To gain access to the relevant market, experienced sales and key account staff should be trained and deployed to identify potential customers. In addition, the organizational unit should consist of subscription experts who are able to evaluate the specifics of the business model and the feasibility, as a broader knowledge is required compared to product sales.

5   Conclusion and Outlook

In this article, the tasks of a reference model for the acquisition of subscription customers were shown, which either represent new customers or want to switch from the classic transactional business to the subscription business.

Considering the identified research gap, five main tasks with 14 basis tasks of the acquisition cycle in the manufacturing context were derived based on a grounded theory approach. The main and basis tasks were detailed and show a guideline for practitioners. The model shown in this paper represents the overarching regulatory framework for the acquisition cycle of subscription businesses. For the further development into a reference model applicable in practice, the tasks shown will be further detailed and elementary tasks derived in further research activities. These will provide even more precise guidelines for the user. Furthermore, the addition of a data model is aimed at, which describes the necessary data points in the process steps to meet the requirement of data-driven action and learning capability during the acquisition. This is aimed at the basic subscription requirement that activities are based on the analysis of usage data in order to exploit the optimum potential for the provider on the one hand and to create the best possible business added value for the customer [6, 23]. Furthermore, a continuous development and evaluation of the model must be carried out by the application in practice to meet a high-quality standard.

References

1. Mansard, M., Cagin, J.-M.: Reaping the Recurring Benefits of Industry 4.0: a manufacturing executive playbook for business model transformation towards new revenue streams. In: Berger, R. (eds.) Zuora, Inc. (2019)
2. Seebacher, U.: Praxishandbuch B2B-Marketing: Neueste Konzepte, Strategien und Technologien sowie praxiserprobte Vorgehensmodelle – mit 11 Fallstudien. Springer, Wiesbaden (2021). https://doi.org/10.1007/978-3-658-31651-8
3. Schuh, G., Frank, J., Jussen, P., Rix, C., Harland, T.: Monetizing Industry 4.0: design principles for subscription business in the manufacturing industry. In: IEEE (ed.) 2019 IEEE International Conference on Engineering, Technology and Innovation (ICE/ITMC), pp. 1–9. IEEE (2019)
4. Porter, M.E., Heppelmann, J.E.: How Smart, Connected Products Are Transforming Companies (2015). https://hbr.org/2015/10/how-smart-connected-products-are-transforming-com panies. Accessed 20 July 2022
5. Paschou, T., Rapaccini, M., Adrodegari, F., Saccani, N.: Digital servitization in manufacturing: a systematic literature review and research agenda. Ind. Mark. Manag. **89**, 278–292 (2020)
6. Schuh, G., Wenger, L., Stich, V., Hicking, J., Gailus, J.: Outcome economy: subscription business models in machinery and plant engineering. Procedia CIRP **93**, 599–604 (2020)
7. Tzuo, T., Weisert, G.: Subscribed: Why the Subscription Model Will Be Your Company's Future – and What to Do About It. Portfolio/Penguin, New York (2018)
8. Reiterer, J., Scheiber, E.-M.: Die Bedeutung von Value Based Selling im Vermarktungsprozess der Anlagenplanung. E-conom **10**(1), 16–33 (2021)
9. Töytäri, P., Rajala, R.: Value-based selling: An organizational capability perspective. Ind. Mark. Manag. **45**(1), 101–112 (2015)

10. Raja, J.Z., Frandsen, T., Kowalkowski, C., Jarmatz, M.: Learning to discover value: value-based pricing and selling capabilities for services and solutions. J. Bus. Res. **114k.H.**, 142–159 (2020)
11. Homburg, C.: Marketingmanagement. Springer, Wiesbaden (2020). https://doi.org/10.1007/978-3-658-29636-0
12. Luotola, H., Hellström, M., Gustafsson, M., Perminova-Harikoski, O.: Embracing uncertainty in value-based selling by means of design thinking. Ind. Mark. Manag. **65**, 59–75 (2017)
13. Belz, C., Dannenberg, H., Redemann, M., Weibel, M.: Value Selling: Kundennutzen sichtbar machen, Interaktion gestalten, Wertschöpfung optimieren. Schäffer-Poeschel Verlag, Stuttgart (2016)
14. Ruffer, S.: Vertriebsseitige Herausforderungen bei industriellen Betreibermodellen: Eine integrierte Betrachtung der Anbieter- und Nachfragerperspektive: Dissertation, Technische Universität Dortmund (2018)
15. Jacob, F.: Solutions Buying – Herausforderungen für die Kaufverhaltensanalyse in Industriegütermärkten. Mark. Rev. St. Gallen **41**(4), 26–35 (2013)
16. Gartner: Strategic Roadmap for Accelerating Revenue Growth (2021). https://www.gartner.com/en/sales/trends/accelerating-revenue-growth. Accessed 20 July 2022
17. Sassanelli, C., Da Costa Fernandes, S., Rozenfeld, H., Mascarenhas, J., Terzi, S.: Enhancing knowledge management in the PSS detailed design: a case study in a food and bakery machinery company. Concurr. Eng. **29**(4), 295–308 (2021)
18. Buttle, F.: Customer Relationship Management: Concepts and Tools. Elsevier Butterworth-Heinemann, Amsterdam, Heidelberg (2004)
19. D'Haen, J., van den Poel, D.: Model-supported business-to-business prospect prediction based on an iterative customer acquisition framework. Ind. Mark. Manag. **42**(4), 544–551 (2013)
20. Yu, Y.-P., Cai, S.-Q.: A new approach to customer targeting under conditions of information shortage. Mark. Intell. Plann. **25**(4), 343–359 (2007)
21. Lippold, D.: Akquisitionsgrundlagen im B2B-Bereich. Springer, Wiesbaden (2019). https://doi.org/10.1007/978-3-658-25937-2
22. Ang, L., Buttle, F.: Managing for successful customer acquisition: an exploration. J. Mark. Manag. **223–4**, 295–317 (2006)
23. Lah, T., Wood, J.B.: Technology-as-a-Service Playbook: How to Grow a Profitable Subscription Business. Point B Inc, s.l. (2016)
24. Eggert, A., Haas, A., Ulaga, W., Terho, H.: Wertbasiertes Verkaufen auf Industriegütermärkten. In: Backhaus, K., Voeth, M. (eds.) Handbuch Business-to-Business-Marketing, pp. 483–495. Springer, Wiesbaden (2015). https://doi.org/10.1007/978-3-8349-4681-2_23
25. Liinamaa, J., Viljanen, M., Hurmerinta, A., Ivanova-Gongne, M., Luotola, H., Gustafsson, M.: Performance-based and functional contracting in value-based solution selling. Ind. Mark. Manag. **59**, 37–49 (2016)
26. Edelmann, D.C., Singer, M.: Competing on customer journeys. Harv. Bus. Rev. **93**(11), 88–98 (2015)
27. Golec, C., Isaacson, P., Fewless, J.: Account-Based Marketing, 1st edn. Wiley, New York (2019)
28. Burgess, B., Munn, D.: A Practitioner's Guide to Account-Based Marketing: Accelerating Growth in Strategic Accounts, 1st edn. Kogan Page, London (2017)
29. Kumar, G.P., Rajasekhar, K.: Account based Marketing in B2B industry. J. Interdiscip. Cycl. Res. **7**(2), 1154–1161 (2020)
30. Creswell, J.W., Poth, C.N.: Qualitative Inquiry & Research Design: Choosing Among Five Approaches. Sage, Thousand Oaks (2018)
31. Strauss, A., Corbin, J.M.: Grounded Theory in Practice. Sage, Thousand Oaks (1997)
32. Edmondson, A.C., Mcmanus, S.E.: Methodological fit in management field research. AMR **32**(4), 1246–1264 (2007)

33. Tuli, K.R., Kohli, A.K., Bharadwaj, S.G.: Rethinking customer solutions: from product bundles to relational processes. J. Mark. **71**(3), 1–17 (2007)
34. Macdonald, E.K., Kleinaltenkamp, M., Wilson, H.N.: How business customers judge solutions: solution quality and value in use. J. Mark. **80**(3), 96–120 (2016)
35. Lay, G., Schroeter, M., Biege, S.: Service-based business concepts: a typology for business-to-business markets. Eur. Manag. J. **27**(6), 442–455 (2009)
36. Glaser, B.G., Strauss, A.L.: The Discovery of Grounded Theory: Strategies for Qualitative Research. Aldine, New York (1967)
37. Pietrzak, M., Paliszkiewicz, J.: Framework of strategic learning: PDCA cycle. Manag. Univ. Primorska **10**(2), 149–161 (2015)
38. Lemon, K.N., Verhoef, P.C.: Understanding customer experience throughout the customer journey. J. Mark. **80**(6), 69–96 (2016)
39. Töytäri, P., Keränen, J., Rajala, R.: Barriers to implementing value-based pricing in industrial markets: A micro-foundations perspective. J. Bus. Res. **76**, 237–246 (2017)
40. Terho, H., Haas, A., Eggert, A., Ulaga, W.: 'It's almost like taking the sales out of selling': towards a conceptualization of value-based selling in business markets. Ind. Mark. Manag. **41**(1), 174–185 (2012)

Using Operational Data to Represent Machine Components Health and Derive Data-Driven Services

Stefan Wiesner[1]([✉]) [iD], Lukas Egbert[2] [iD], and Anton Zitnikov[2] [iD]

[1] BIBA - Bremer Institut für Produktion und Logistik GmbH at the University of Bremen, Hochschulring 20, 28359 Bremen, Germany
wie@biba.uni-bremen.de

[2] Faculty of Production Engineering, University of Bremen, Badgasteiner Strasse 1, 28359 Bremen, Germany
{egb,zit}@biba.uni-bremen.de

Abstract. A highly competitive global market and rapid technological changes have induced a transformation in the manufacturing industry. In order to stay competitive, companies are intensifying the collection of life cycle data from their products in order to add customized digital services. The resulting digitally-enabled Product-Service Systems (PSS) can boost differentiation, but concrete business opportunities and their implementation often remain vague. An example is the data-driven assessment of machine components health status. While such information could be used to generate services like predictive maintenance or remanufacturing, the necessary data and algorithms to predict the remaining useful life and ways to convey the value to the customer are often unclear. This paper illustrates the engineering of a predictive maintenance service base on operational machine data. Furthermore, possible PSS offerings and the related business models are analysed. The results are tested in a use case from the manufacturing industry and finally implications for digitally-enabled PSS are discussed.

Keywords: Product-service system · Engineering of data-driven services · Digital twin · Industrial case study

1 Introduction

A highly competitive global market and rapid technological changes have induced a transformation in the manufacturing industry. In order to stay competitive, companies are intensifying the collection of life cycle data from their products in order to add customized digital services that customers increasingly demand [1, 2]. This has led to the introduction of digitally-enabled Product-Service Systems (PSS), describing the integrated development, realization and offering of specific data-driven product-service bundles as a solution for the customer. Such PSS can boost differentiation, but concrete business opportunities and their implementation often remain vague [3].

© IFIP International Federation for Information Processing 2022
Published by Springer Nature Switzerland AG 2022
D. Y. Kim et al. (Eds.): APMS 2022, IFIP AICT 664, pp. 294–301, 2022.
https://doi.org/10.1007/978-3-031-16411-8_35

An example is the data-driven assessment of machine components health status. System components experience wear and tear over their period of use and their service life is designed based on the operational loads. Each component has certain functional capabilities that usually decrease during operations, this is referred to as the wear reserve [4]. Before usage, a component has a wear reserve of 100%, which decreases with the duration, frequency and strength of the occurring loads. This wear reserve can, however, be restored or delayed by maintenance measures [5]. General conditions and disturbances in the utilisation phase often lead to unplannable wear and tear of components, leading to machine failures. In order to make this behaviour predictable, machine and plant construction is increasingly relying on proactive action through monitoring. Suitable sensor technology in combination with IT infrastructure monitors system components during operation and under the name of predictive maintenance, systems are used today whose goal is to maximise the service life of technical systems. Individual component conditions are recorded and evaluated here, which means that maintenance measures can be planned at an early stage and components can be replaced in good time before they fail. As the system complexity and uncertainties increase, knowledge-driven approaches based on expertise on failure modes and physics are replaced by data-driven approaches applying machine learning algorithms on operational data [6].

However the necessary data and algorithms to predict the remaining useful life and ways to convey the value to the customer are often unclear [7]. When monitoring a technical system, the focus should be on the function-critical and failure-critical components. A prediction of their remaining service life requires the determination of their current condition, applied loads and prevailing environmental influences [8]. Therefore, an approach is needed to assess the initial service life of a component, a classification of the relevant types of wear, the identification of impact factors for wear, suitable sensors to detect such impacts and a prognosis model for the remaining service life [9]. Thus, the aim of this paper is to develop an indirect condition description via component loads, types of wear and the identification and monitoring of relevant parameters. The approach is applied in a reaction casting unit use case. The resulting information enables engineering a predictive maintenance service base on operational machine data. Possible digitally-enabled PSS and related Business Models are discussed.

2 Approach for Machine Component Health Assessment

The challenge to determine a machine components health, with a prognosis of the remaining service life, shall be achieved with a temporary recording of special condition data of the component. The process of a prognosis always consists of different work steps that can be arranged chronologically. Basically, it is always a target/actual comparison within the framework of a condition diagnosis. Design data and knowledge about operational use are compared with information derived from condition monitoring and condition analysis [10].

Loads on components in operation are usually dynamic and time-dependent. If the loads are determined by measurements or calculations, they can be represented as a function over time. When considering service life, load collectives can be included via the damage accumulation theory, which states that load levels that are higher than the fatigue strength lead to wear of the component [11]. At the beginning of its service life, a component has a certain performance related to its condition, which in turn is based on physical, chemical and other characteristics. These are influenced by process conditions, environmental influences and extraordinary impacts, and this is referred to as technical wear and tear [12]. A classification can be made according to the different wear mechanisms:

Abrasion means the progressive loss of material on the surface of a solid body, caused by mechanical causes. *Corrosion* means the destruction of the material surface by chemical or electrochemical reaction with its environment. *Material fatigue* describes the reduction of material strength depending on the magnitude and direction of constantly changing stress. The internal processes in the material structure of a component, which occur independently of its stress and lead to wear, fall under the term *ageing*. The determination of the actual condition of a component that has already been subjected to load cycles results from the as-new condition minus any technical wear that may have occurred. For each of the types of wear presented, different influencing variables can be identified that contribute to component wear. During tests, the question is answered as to what type and level of effect the influencing variables have on the component service life. It makes sense to consider the influencing variables that make the greatest contribution to wear. It must also be possible to measure the selected influencing variables in a targeted and reproducible manner, as the extent of their influence depends on their intensity [13].

Suitable sensor technology can help to monitor the operating condition of components during operation. The characteristics of the previously identified influencing factors are recorded as measured variables. The changes in the measured variables can be directly or indirectly attributed to wear of the components. For example, the increasing intensity of a measured variable (e.g. temperature) can indicate increasing wear (e.g. material removal through friction) on a component. However, the collection of corresponding measurement data is not sufficient for a service life prediction. In order to determine the degree of wear and thus the remaining service life of the components from the recorded measured variables, the application of a prognosis model is necessary [14].

The determination of the remaining service life of the components is to be carried out with the help of a prognosis model, which predicts potential wear processes on the basis of determined component data and known correlations. The characteristics for the wear of the components and the influencing variables responsible for this are recorded in a time-discrete manner with the selected sensor technology. For the implementation of this requirement, the monitoring of the components and the automated analysis and evaluation of the recorded data are necessary. For prognosis, the supervised machine learning approach can be used to determine the remaining useful life of critical components [15, 16]. The selected sensors provide the data for learning the model. The algorithms used identify correlations and unknown patterns from the available data. The model is able to evaluate the recorded condition of the components and to predict a remaining service life.

3   Use Case: Spindle Bearing of a Reaction Casting Unit

The approach for assessing machine component health is tested on a reaction casting unit, which includes a mixing screw with spindle and associated bearing (see Fig. 1). Within the unit, polyol is mixed with isocyanate in a chamber with the aid of the screw in order to obtain a reactive mixture that foams up within a mould. The spindle bearing was identified as a critical component, as its failure or impairment of its original function causes machine downtimes. Currently, the machine condition is qualitatively assessed and communicated by the operator. In particular, the expertise of the operating personnel is used to document whether, for example, unusual behaviour such as vibrations and disturbance variables have been detected.

Fig. 1. Housing with the spindle bearing and the mixing screw of the injection unit

In general, the service life of a spindle is determined by the number of injection processes. Furthermore, the service life depends on the additional loads to which the components have been subjected and the prevailing environmental conditions. Therefore, these conditions as well as operating data such as speed, operating hours and load variables must be compiled. The spindle itself can be described as fatigue resistant, while the bearings are designed for approx. 5,000 operating hours. An average duration for one injection cycle is 18 s, which means the rolling bearings must withstand $\approx 1,000,000$ load cycles.

Based on knowledge from construction and operation, damage descriptions, damage patterns, damage mechanisms and characteristics were identified for the bearings. This forms the basis for deriving the required sensor technology and calculating the factors for determining the remaining useful life of the bearing. The disturbance influences acting on the reaction casting unit can have different causes and dependencies. This is illustrated by an exemplary damage chain (see Fig. 2):

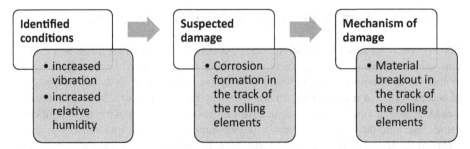

Fig. 2. Example of a damage chain for bearings

The sensors for recording the measured values were selected on the basis of the expected types of wear. Furthermore, a constructive implementation must be possible. For the bearing, it is expected that characteristic values change with increasing material removal due to corrosion, as the track of the rolling elements becomes more irregular, resulting in increased friction and imbalance due to the rolling over of unevenness. Sensors for vibration and acoustics can provide physically measurable results that indicate such a change. Since the humidity in the environment is of great importance for the formation of corrosion, an air humidity sensor is included.

Thus, a sensor box has been developed accordingly (see Fig. 3). Ethernet (industrial standard) is used for the connectivity of the sensor box. This interface enables the box to be connected to a network that is usually available and already transmits operating data from the shop floor system.

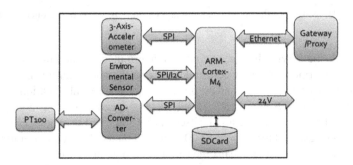

Fig. 3. Sensor implementation

The collected data, sensor box and operating data, are transferred to a cloud as JSON files. An NTP server provides the current time stamps so that the recorded data can be synchronised. For data exchange, REST interfaces were defined and implemented according to the OpenAPI standard. An engine receives the data stream and performs the analysis of the data and the enrichment of the data stream with derived forecasts.

The mathematical approach for quantifying component wear combines data-driven and physical models into a hybrid modelling approach. It relies on a target-performance comparison of relevant measured process parameters. For the use case, those input parameters consist of reliable component condition indicators for abrasion, i.e. load cycles and vibration. Through test runs and historical data of the use case processes, empirical courses of the parameters were identified and linked to the wear and condition of the spindle bearing. For the lifetime prognosis, a Bayesian network assesses the difference between the empirical and the actual course of the parameters, identifies the potential deviation (whether the wear is proceeding faster or slower than expected) as a conditional probability and predicts the remaining time to failure based on this gap.

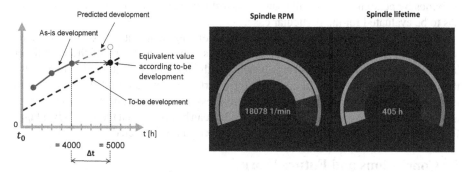

Fig. 4. Spindle wear quantification and lifetime visualization

The application visualises the evaluation (see Fig. 4), i.e. the detection of events on the basis of the forecasts. This can mean, for example, that a threshold value for the expected remaining useful life of a component has been undershot. It can also indicate that the remaining useful life can be extended if the machine utilisation is reduced. When stating the remaining service life, it is important to note that the result is subject to certain uncertainties and cannot be absolutely reliable. This is due to the fact that both the correction factors and the designed load cycle number are statistical values that are subject to certain probability distributions.

4 Discussion

For a practical lifetime prediction, a proven relationship between field tests, test bench tests and calculations is required. Likewise, the evaluation and assessment of recorded data in order to ultimately be able to represent an effective tool is important. The aim of product development is to develop products in such a way that they achieve the required service life under specified loads. Wear and tear lead to shortened service life expectations, which must be countered with suitable strategies. An option is the integration of data-driven services to create a digitally-enabled PSS. These can be service life calculations, as well as maintenance measures and sensor-based monitoring of operating conditions. Based on this, maintenance measures can be derived as well as new business models, as a service offer can be improved with a prognosis system and, in addition, new opportunities can be opened up.

The presented approach requires the provision of data for model development and to provide the service of prognosis. Since some enterprises are reluctant regarding the provision of data, reference business models are required to reduce this reluctance. Theoretically it is possible to save data that enables conclusions regarding the productivity of the operator of the machine. Hence, such data should be anonymised (hide time stamp for a data set or use decoding methods). The effort to gather data that is required for the later application of the prognosis service depends on the technical realisation of the measuring device. The effort can be low, if the device and the sensors are already integrated in the system and can be accessed automatically. But the measurement can also require activities by personnel for installation of the test bed and the actual measurement. This has to be evaluated for the particular case.

The main sources of benefits and the corresponding recipients are on the one hand avoidance of unplanned downtimes that are caused by breakdowns of the module or late availability of spare parts brings benefit for the machine operators and thereby for the enterprise. On the other hand, input for a further optimisation of the machines to increase customer satisfaction and competitiveness. Today, new business models must also be viewed in the context of sustainability. If it can be proven that there are advantages for all partners involved, a high level of acceptance can be expected.

5   Conclusions and Future Work

The collection of operational, machine and environmental data offers new possibilities for improved maintenance planning, which enables more reliable processes. By determining the remaining service life, the functionality of components can be better utilised, which saves resources and costs. The created database in connection with a continuous recording of component conditions can also be used to predict preventive maintenance and, if necessary, replacement measures more accurately, to deliver necessary replacement components to the place of use in good time and to plan the service deployment. Replaced components can then be checked to see whether they can be used again in less demanding applications and/or within the framework of other legal requirements for the installation of new components. In this way, it should also be possible to determine a useful life that can be reliably predicted for used components.

For the approach presented here, detailed knowledge of the wear processes in the affected components is necessary. This can be used to determine a suitable sensor system with which the relevant or correlating measured values that indicate wear can be recorded directly or indirectly. In addition, system configurations are required for each application, as the systems to be monitored each have specific characteristics and features that make it necessary to adapt the model presented. For example, the probabilistic influence model used in the form of a Bayesian network must be adapted depending on the sensor data required in the application. In addition, a technical data connection, historical measurement data and a quantification of wear processes are required in order to be able to create the most accurate remaining service life forecast possible.

Acknowledgements. This research has been funded by the German Federal Ministry of Education and Research (BMBF) through the project "LongLife" (033R246A) and the German Federal Ministry for Economic Affairs and Climate Action (BMWK) through the project "Mittelstand 4.0 – Kompetenzzentrum Bremen" (01MF17004B). The authors wish to acknowledge the funding agency and all project partners for their contribution.

References

1. Kagermann, H., Helbig, J., Hellinger, A., Wahlster, W.: Umsetzungsempfehlungen für das Zukunftsprojekt Industrie 4.0. Deutschlands Zukunft als Produktionsstandort sichern; Abschlussbericht des Arbeitskreises Industrie 4.0. Forschungsunion; Geschäftsstelle der Plattform Industrie 4.0, Berlin, Frankfurt/Main (2013)
2. Kaihara, T., et al.: Value creation in production: reconsideration from interdisciplinary approaches. CIRP Ann. **67**, 791–813 (2018). https://doi.org/10.1016/j.cirp.2018.05.002
3. Baines, T., Ziaee Bigdeli, A., Bustinza, O.F., Shi, V.G., Baldwin, J., Ridgway, K.: Servitization: revisiting the state-of-the-art and research priorities. Int. J. Op. Prod. Manage. **37**, 256–278 (2017). https://doi.org/10.1108/IJOPM-06-2015-0312
4. Ritter, F.: Lebensdauer von Bauteilen und Bauelementen - Modellierung und praxisnahe Prognose. Darmstadt
5. DIN 31051:2019-06, Grundlagen der Instandhaltung. Beuth Verlag GmbH, Berlin
6. Calabrese, M., et al.: SOPHIA: an event-based IoT and machine learning architecture for predictive maintenance in Industry 4.0. Information **11**, 202 (2020). https://doi.org/10.3390/info11040202
7. Jimenez-Cortadi, A., Irigoien, I., Boto, F., Sierra, B., Rodriguez, G.: Predictive maintenance on the machining process and machine tool. Appl. Sci. **10**, 224 (2020). https://doi.org/10.3390/app10010224
8. Guo, L., Li, N., Jia, F., Lei, Y., Lin, J.: A recurrent neural network based health indicator for remaining useful life prediction of bearings. Neurocomputing **240**, 98–109 (2017). https://doi.org/10.1016/j.neucom.2017.02.045
9. Modoni, G.E., Trombetta, A., Veniero, M., Sacco, M., Mourtzis, D.: An event-driven integrative framework enabling information notification among manufacturing resources. Int. J. Comput. Integr. Manuf. **32**, 241–252 (2019). https://doi.org/10.1080/0951192X.2019.1571232
10. Sakib, N., Wuest, T.: Challenges and opportunities of condition-based predictive maintenance: a review. Procedia CIRP **78**, 267–272 (2018). https://doi.org/10.1016/j.procir.2018.08.318
11. Steinhilper, W., Sauer, B.: Grundlagen der Berechnung und Gestaltung von Maschinenelementen. Springer, Berlin (2008)
12. Zhang, S.: Instandhaltung und Anlagenkosten. Deutscher Universitätsverlag, Wiesbaden, s.l. (1990)
13. Schiefer, H., Schiefer, F.: Statistische Versuchsplanung, Design of Experiments (DoE). In: Statistik für Ingenieure. Springer Vieweg, Wiesbaden (2010). https://doi.org/10.1007/978-3-658-20640-6_1
14. Bender, A., Kaul, T., Sextro, W.: Entwicklung eines Condition Monitoring Systems für Gummi-Metall-Elemente. In: Verlagsschriftenreihe des Heinz Nixdorf Instituts Band 369, Paderborn, pp. 347–358 (2017)
15. Ray, S.: A quick review of machine learning algorithms. In: Proceedings of the International Conference on Machine Learning, Big Data, Cloud and Parallel Computing: Trends, Prespectives and Prospects. COMITCon 2019: 14th–16th February 2019, pp. 35–39. IEEE, Piscataway (2019). https://doi.org/10.1109/COMITCon.2019.8862451
16. Wuest, T., Weimer, D., Irgens, C., Thoben, K.-D.: Machine learning in manufacturing: advantages, challenges, and applications. Prod. Manuf. Res. **4**, 23–45 (2016). https://doi.org/10.1080/21693277.2016.1192517

From Product to Service Ramp-Up Management

Juliette Héraud[1], Shervin Kadkhoda Ahmadi[2], and Khaled Medini[2(✉)]

[1] Mines Saint-Etienne, F-42023 Saint-Etienne, France
[2] Henri Fayol Institute, Mines Saint-Etienne, Univ Clermont Auvergne, CNRS, UMR 6158 LIMOS, F-42023 Saint-Etienne, France
khaled.medini@emse.fr

Abstract. Ramp-up often requires the implementation of a new production system and some adaptations for the entire supply chain. It is also a major issue for service companies in both secondary and tertiary sectors. Although some of these companies are not confronted with the management of a new production system, they also have to face many difficulties during ramp-up. These difficulties are amplified by the growing uncertainties on the markets and the volatility of the customer demand. The current paper sheds light on common and diverging aspects of product and service ramp-ups as well as on solution approaches for service ramp-up management. As such, current research provides foundation for future research dealing specifically with service ramp-up.

Keywords: Ramp-up · Service · Stakeholders · Collaboration · Agility · Project

1 Introduction

Ramp-up is a challenging phase in product and service life cycles. It corresponds to the period when companies progressively deploy their new products or their new services to their customers. Numerous articles in the literature have studied ramp-up, but most of them have focused on companies in the secondary sector [1–3]. Indeed, ramp-up is extremely important for manufacturing companies, and often requires the implementation of a new production system and some adaptations for the entire supply chain. Ramp-up is also a major issue for service companies in both secondary and tertiary sectors. Although some of these companies are not confronted with the management of a new production system, they also have to face many difficulties during ramp-up which are amplified by the growing uncertainties on the markets and the volatility of the customer demand [4].

The current study contributes to building knowledge about service ramp-up by exploring related research works and by identifying common and diverging aspects of product and service ramp-up as well as solution approaches to deal with service ramp-up. The remainder of the paper is organized as follows; Sect. 2 provides a background on the topic. Section 3 briefly reports on the research method. Sections 4 and 5 report respectively on common and diverging aspects of product and service ramp-up. Section 6 presents solution approaches for service ramp-up. The paper ends with concluding remarks in Sect. 7.

© IFIP International Federation for Information Processing 2022
Published by Springer Nature Switzerland AG 2022
D. Y. Kim et al. (Eds.): APMS 2022, IFIP AICT 664, pp. 302–309, 2022.
https://doi.org/10.1007/978-3-031-16411-8_36

2 Background

Companies are increasingly confronted with issues during ramp-up of products and services, which is partly due to growing market pressure [5]. For manufacturing companies, Bergs et al. [6] underline that product lifetime tends to decrease with a more rapid evolution of customer requirements. This is also true for service companies, as Akkermans et al. [5] explain in their research about ramp-up and ramp-down dynamics. Indeed, it is shown that market pressures lead to accelerate the design of new services and their deployment. Among the other causes explaining the growing importance of service ramp-up, Akkermans et al. [5] argue that digitalization is progressing in different sectors, such as banking, media, or insurance. This development entails profound changes in the service offer of companies, and notably requires some improvements or adjustments. This compels many companies to carefully address service ramp-up phase. The progress of servitization also contributes to explaining the recent emergence of service ramp-up, in particular for industrial companies. For these cases, service ramp-up is often a more crucial issue since these companies are not necessarily used to propose services [7].

According to Akkermans et al. [5], service ramp-up is defined as a "process of rapidly increasing the delivery of a service to meet the demand". However, ramp-up leads usually to many problems about delivering newly designed services. For instance, companies need to deal with the satisfaction of customer demands and internal upheavals due to process changes and increase in capacity. These two main issues often have opposing goals, so that reconciling them is not an easy task for companies [5]. Ramp-up is particularly crucial since it highly impacts the deployment of a new service, and it partly conditions the success of the new service. Akkermans et al. [5] report that the ramp-up difficulties are actually one of the main reasons that can explain the failure of a new product or a new service deployed by companies. A service ramp-up entails changes in the supply chain and in process. In a ramp-up context, difficulties are inevitable: many experts notice that problems are inherent to ramp-up. Backlogs, high costs or lack of resources are regarded as the main problems encountered by companies [5].

3 Method

In order to investigate the scientific literature and address the research problem, a three-step method is used (see Fig. 1). First step aims to collect articles about service ramp-up including case studies and applications of ramp-up in manufacturing and service sectors. Main used keywords are "service ramp-up", "service supply chain", "new service development", "demand", and "change management". Additional keywords were used to expand the research such as "ramp-up", "learning curve", "new product development", and "production planning". Second step consists of selecting and classifying the most relevant studies using the following criteria: context and nature of the phenomenon studied, research method used (e.g. survey, simulation, etc.), scope (e.g. large scale, medium scale, case study), and key performance indicators (KPI). This step is not described in this paper because of page limit. The third step consists of a comparative analysis of product and service ramp-ups (Sects. 4 and 5) based on the selected articles. A focus is put on service ramp-up management by exploring main solution approaches to deal with its underlying challenges (Sect. 6).

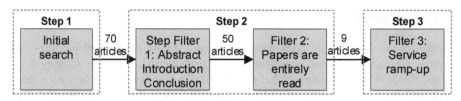

Fig. 1. Paper selection process

4   Converging Aspects of Product and Service Ramp-Up

4.1   Context

Product ramp-up and service ramp-up share common aspects related to ramp-up context. Akkermans et al. [8] highlight that the novelty of the product or of the service requires an increase in supply chain resources and capacities. The ramp-up in both contexts also creates impacts on the entire supply chain (e.g. involvement of all the supply chain actors). Besides, the context in which the ramp-up takes place is dynamic, whether it is for product or for service. This uncertain context explains the need of flexibility for companies dealing with ramp-up [9].

4.2   Challenges

Similarly to product ramp-up, Akkermans et al. [5] identified several issues faced by companies delivering services, namely time issues (observation of deadlines and back-log risk), quality issues (ensuring an acceptable level of quality for newly developed services), volume issues (managing deployment capacity), cost issues (avoiding over-runs and financial losses). Several studies addressed the same issues in product domain [10–12]. Both service and product companies are confronted with change management during ramp-up. Indeed, they need to face a moving situation, as process have to change and operators have to address these changes [5, 12], which requires in turn a suitable strategy for change management.

4.3   Learning

Scientific literature puts forth the importance of learning during the ramp-up for product and service domains alike. This phase is devoted in both cases to the acquisition of knowledge about the new offer proposed by companies and the process necessary to deliver it. Akkermans et al. [5, 8, 13] investigate three different case studies in the telecommunication sector and argue that learning is a key in service ramp-up. Bergs et al. [14] explain that acquiring knowledge is a crucial process during ramp-up. Von Cube and Schmitt [15] underline the importance of knowledge management. Several experts argue that ramp-up requires an important preparation, and this is often done by giving some time for operators testing and experimentation [16–18]. In these different studies, it has been clearly indicated that the ramp-up curve, which represents the progress of the ramp-up over time, is closely related to the learning ability of the operators, as well as their attitude towards change and their capacity to adapt.

5 Diverging Aspects of Product and Service Ramp-Up

5.1 Speed

One of the most striking differences between service and product ramp-ups is the speed at which ramp-up can be carried out. As Akkermans et al. [5] explain, ramp-up can be quicker in the case of services compared to product context. Indeed, product ramp-up is often a quite long process which stretches over several months at least. Most of the time, this important duration can be explained by the deep changes entailed by the ramp-up of production lines as well as operators. These deep changes can notably affect process and methods followed or the equipment used.

On the contrary, lead times may be particularly short for services, and more specifically for IT services. These short lead times explain that service ramp-up can be conducted very fast. Therefore ramp-up curve is often much steeper during service ramp-up [5, 12]. The authors clearly highlight that a too fast ramp-up is very risky for companies so that a violent ramp-up is likely to worsen the difficulties encountered by companies, whether it is with their customers, with their suppliers or within their own departments.

5.2 Ramp-Up Syndrome

The particularities of service ramp-up entail a specific phenomenon called ramp-up syndrome [8]. This syndrome is characterized by a too fast ramp-up at the beginning which leads many companies to temporarily stop the ramp-up and move to a ramp-down phase. All the more so since numerous companies suffer from the optimism bias. This bias, which is quite widespread, means that companies are overly optimistic about their capacity and their schedules, and entices them to neglect some risks. This too high optimism may also be worsened by a lack of visibility from which many companies suffer. On the other hand, the lack of mastery of the services delivered also contributes to aggravating the ramp-up syndrome. Indeed, that entails high rework levels for operations and highly affects internal workloads and reaction capacities of companies [8].

5.3 Link with the Customer

As far as services are concerned, production and consumption are simultaneous. This means that the problems faced during service ramp-up are very often visible for customers. Thus, these customers are directly impacted by the difficulties that companies encounter during the ramp-up and suffer from the lack of mastery faced by most companies, which is likely to entail quality problems [5]. Akkermans et al. [8] report that these problems especially affect the digital services. On the contrary, as far as products are concerned, production and consumption do not take place at the same time: most often, they are separated at least by delivery time. The problems faced by industrial companies during product ramp-up may be numerous and difficult to solve, but they have most of the time a rather small impact on the customers. They can only see, most often, longer delays before being delivered. The time interval between the production and the consumption of a product gives in a way an opportunity for industrial companies to identify problems and solve them before they directly impact their customers. That offers also more time for companies to correct mistakes and continue the learning phase. These consequences should not be underestimated, indeed, the customer relationship is an important issue for service companies, and such difficulties for delivering the expected services are likely to deeply deteriorate the relations between the two sides. That represents a cost for companies, in particular for their brand image and their reputation but also for their market value.

6 Solution Approaches to Service Ramp-Up Management

6.1 Internal Cooperation Between Marketing and Production

Several articles highlight that one of the main causes of the problems encountered during service ramp-up is related to the lack of information. That also echoes the learning issue, whose importance was underlined in numerous articles related to ramp-up [5, 6, 8]. This problem is partly related to difficulties in sharing the information between companies departments [5]. The importance of coordination between sales and operations has been underlined by setting a multidisciplinary ramp up team including sales, planning, logistics and operations, etc. [5]. The idea of improving cooperation between different departments during ramp-up has been highlighted in several other studies putting the focus on one or several aspects e.g. value chain perspective, customer focus, stakeholders' needs [15]. It is argued that marketing department is focused on sales improvement without necessarily taking into consideration technical and operational issues (they are unware of real production capacities). Similarly, operations department has difficulties to align with sales needs. Akkermans et al. [5] used several models for showing how these departments could coordinate their activities. The results obtained by simulating these models, showed that coordination between sales and operations reduces negative fallouts entailed by ramp-up (e.g. delays, quality defects, costs…).

6.2 Forecasting

Sperry and Dye [19] considered forecasting issues by investigating a case study about the opening of a new rail station. They have highlighted that the demand ramp-up is a long process (3 years). They argue that forecasts are useful with respect to the passenger profiles change, to secure the project and its financing and to calibrate the ramp-up. However, these forecasts are not sufficient, and it is necessary for companies to collect real data, through frequent traveler surveys.

Forecast quality has also been underlined in another article about toll road [20]. This study shows that most of the current models fail in taking into consideration the effects of the ramp-up, which leads to a global overestimation of the traffic, at least during the first years after the opening of the toll road. The authors highlighted the same phenomenon that Sperry & Dye [19] addressed: there is a ramp-up period after the opening of a new transport infrastructure before it is possible to reach its planned full potential demand. That is mainly due to the time, which is necessary for customers to change their behaviors, as Sperry & Dye explained [19], but the authors also enhanced that some operational teething disturbances, that are quite common for this kind of projects, are likely to penalize the new infrastructure at its opening and contributes to extending the duration of the demand ramp-up. To improve the forecast quality, Dharmawan et al. [20] used a stochastic method, based on Monte-Carlo simulation. That aimed at successfully modeling the demand evolution due to the ramp-up, with the learning phenomenon. Forecasting is also very useful in other service sectors, such as the hotel industry. Enz et al. [21], have underlined that the performance of new hotels which evolves during the ramp-up period can be improved by an adaptation and quality forecasting. More generally, forecasting importance echoes the essential need for companies to anticipate the ramp-up and prepare it.

6.3 Knowledge Management

Knowledge management is regarded as one of the substantial factors for successful ramp-up particularly for service companies [22]. Knowledge and information sharing have a major impact on the speed of adjustments and key decisions in ramp-up [23]. The exploitation of information and a corporate knowledge management can greatly and positively impact on value chain processes efficiency. This can be achieved through an organized coordination and collaborative learning between several stakeholders within and beyond the company, e.g. suppliers, logistic, human resources, process integration and customer [22]. Therefore, collaboration and corporate knowledge transfer among these stakeholders can have significant effects on the ramp-up performance and ramp-up targets. Several solutions based on the knowledge management concept such as Agile knowledge transfer framework [24], Multi-disciplinary Knowledge base [25] and dynamic management techniques like rolling wave planning [26] can be proposed in order to enhance the effectiveness of a service ramp-up process. Quirchmayr et al. [24] described an agile process to transfer knowledge in the context of software development. This work provided recommendations, especially in relation to human resource management with team building, motivation methods and commitment of the management. Moreover, it has underlined that knowledge transfer is essential and truly complementary to software development.

7 Conclusion

Companies suffer from a lack of knowledge and experience about newly designed services. These deficiencies create a climate of uncertainty and accentuate the different risks that companies are confronted with. Therefore, companies have to develop a know-how about new services particularly during the ramp-up phase. This is likely to support enlightened decisions for ramp-up management. Among these, the following can be cited: identifying the stage of service development at which ramp-up can/should be launched, while balancing uncertainty/risks inherent to ramp-up and the imperative need to deploy the new service; determining the speed at which the ramp-up (which is inherently a gradual process) is conducted, considering company's goals and available/allocated resources. Each of the challenges represents a potential perspective for further investigation in a relatively under-explored field.

Acknowledgement. This work is partly supported by Auvergne Rhône Alpes (AURA) Region through VARIETY project (https://variety.wp.imt.fr/).

References

1. Surbier, L., Alpan, G., Blanco, E.: A comparative study on production ramp-up: state-of-the-art and new challenges. Prod. Planning Control **25**(15), 1264–1286 (2014)
2. Glock, C.H., Grosse, E.H.: Decision support models for production ramp-up: a systematic literature review. Int. J. Prod. Res. **53**(21), 6637–6651 (2015)
3. Winkler, H., Heins, M., Nyhuis, P.: A controlling system based on cause–effect relationships for the ramp-up of production systems. Prod. Eng. Res. Devel. **1**(1), 103–111 (2007)
4. Lu, Q., Wu, J., Goh, M., De Souza, R.: Agility and resource dependency in ramp-up process of humanitarian organizations. The Int. J. Logistics Manage. **30**(3), 845–862 (2019)
5. Akkermans, H., Voss, C., Van Oers, R.: Ramp up and ramp down dynamics in digital services. J. Supply Chain Manag. **55**(3), 3–23 (2019)
6. Bergs, T., Apelt, S., Beckers, A., Barth, S.: Agile ramp-up production as an advantage of highly iterative product development. Manufacturing Letters **27**, 4–7 (2021)
7. Baines, T.: Exploring service innovation and the servitization of the manufacturing firm. Res. Technol. Manag. **58**(5), 9–11 (2015)
8. Akkermans, H., Voss, C., van Oers, R., Zhu, Q.: Never the twain shall meet? simulating sales & operations planning ramp-up dynamics in IT-enabled service supply chains. In: Proceedings International System Dynamics Conference, TU Delft, p. 1314 (2016)
9. Sampson, S.E., Spring, M.: Service supply chains: introducing the special topic forum. J. Supply Chain Manag. **48**(4), 3–7 (2012)
10. Medini, K., Romero, D., Wuest, T.: Developing a multi-agent system to support multi-variant production ramp-up management. Smart Sustainable Manufactur. Syst. **5**(1), 20200082 (2021)
11. Meiscl, F., Glock, C.H.: Self-induced learning vs. project-based supplier development for production ramp-up with two supply options. Int. J. Prod. Econ. **198**, 60–69 (2018)
12. Christensen, I., Rymaszewska, A.: Lean application to manufacturing ramp-up: A conceptual approach. Qual. Manag. J. **23**(1), 45–54 (2016)
13. Akkermans, H., Vos, B.: Amplification in service supply chains: an exploratory case study from the telecom industry. Prod. Oper. Manag. **12**(2), 204–223 (2003)
14. Berg, M., Säfsten, K.: Managing Production Ramp-up: Requirement on strategy content, Proceedings of POMS International 2006 (2006)
15. von Cube, J.P., Schmitt, R.: Execution of ramp-up projects in day-to-day operations through a quantitative risk management approach. Procedia CIRP **20**, 26–31 (2014)
16. Hansen, K.R., Grunow, M.: Modelling ramp-up curves to reflect learning: improving capacity planning in secondary pharmaceutical production. Int. J. Prod. Res. **53**(18), 5399–5417 (2015)
17. Bultó, R., Viles, E., Mateo, R.: Overview of ramp-up curves: a literature review and new challenges. Proceedings of the Institution of Mechanical Engineers, Part B: J. Eng. Manufacture **232**(5), 755–765 (2018)
18. Kwon, Y., Schoenherr, T., Kim, T., Lee, K.: Production resource planning for product transition considering learning effects. Appl. Math. Model. **98**, 207–228 (2021)
19. Sperry, B.R., Dye, T.: Impact of new passenger rail stations on ridership demand and passenger characteristics: Hiawatha service case study. Case Studies on Transport Policy **8**(4), 1158–1169 (2020)
20. Dharmawan, W.I., Sjafruddin, A., Frazila, R.B., Zukhruf, F.: Developing model of toll road traffic forecasting during ramp-up period. In: MATEC Web of Conferences, p. 270 (2019)

21. Enz, C., Peiró-Signes, A., Segarra-Oña, M.: How fast do new hotels ramp up performance? Cornell Hospitality Quaterly **55**(2), 141–151 (2014)
22. Yeleneva, J.Y., Kharin, A.A., Yelenev, K.S., Andreev, V.N., Kharina, O.S., Kruchkova, E.V.: Corporate knowledge management in Ramp-up conditions: The stakeholder interests account, the responsibility centers allocation. CIRP J. Manuf. Sci. Technol. **23**, 207–216 (2018)
23. Bußwolder, P., Burgahn, F., Hübner, M., Werker, M.: Classification of company-specific influence factors as part of a knowledge management system for ramp-up projects. Procedia CIRP **51**, 44–50 (2016)
24. Porrawatpreyakorn, N., Chutimaskul, W., Quirchmayr, G., Sodanil, M.: A knowledge transfer framework for supporting the transition to agile development of web application in the thai telecommunications industry. In: Proceedings of International Conference on Information Integration and Web-based Applications & Services, pp. 140–148 (2013)
25. Willmann, R., Kastner, W.: A deterministic product ramp-up process: how to integrate a multi-disciplinary knowledge base. In: Multi-Disciplinary Engineering for Cyber-Physical Production Systems, pp. 399–431 (2017)
26. Collyer, S., Warren, C., Hemsley, B., Stevens, C.: Aim, fire, aim—project planning styles in dynamic environments. Proj. Manag. J. **41**(4), 108–121 (2010)

Digital Servitization in the Manufacturing Sector: Survey Preliminary Results

Giuditta Pezzotta[1,11]([✉]) [ID], Veronica Arioli[1,11] [ID], Federico Adrodegari[2,11] [ID],
Mario Rapaccini[3,11] [ID], Nicola Saccani[2,11] [ID], Slavko Rakic[4] [ID],
Ugljesa Marjanovic[4] [ID], Shaun West[5] [ID], Oliver Stoll[5] [ID], Jürg Meierhofer[6] [ID],
Lennard Holst[7] [ID], Stefan A. Wiesner[8] [ID], Marco Bertoni[9] [ID], David Romero[10] [ID],
Fabiana Pirola[1] [ID], Roberto Sala[1] [ID], and Paolo Gaiardelli[1,11] [ID]

[1] University of Bergamo, Bergamo, Italy
{giuditta.pezzotta,veronica.arioli,fabiana.pirola,roberto.sala,
paolo.gaiardelli}@unibg.it
[2] University of Brescia, Brescia, Italy
{federico.adrodegari,nicola.saccani}@unibs.it
[3] University of Florence, Florence, Italy
mario.rapaccini@unifi.it
[4] Faculty of Technical Sciences, University of Novi Sad, Novi Sad, Serbia
{slavkorakic,umarjano}@uns.ac.rs
[5] Lucerne University of Applied Sciences and Arts, Luzern, Switzerland
{shaun.west,oliver.stoll}@hslu.ch
[6] ZHAW School of Engineering, Winterthur, Switzerland
meeo@zhaw.ch
[7] RWTH Aachen University, Aachen, Germany
lennard.holst@fir.rwth-aachen.de
[8] BIBA - Bremer Institut Für Produktion Und Logistik GmbH, Bremen, Germany
wie@biba.uni-bremen.de
[9] Blekinge Institute of Technology, Karlskrona, Sweden
marco.bertoni@bth.se
[10] Tecnológico de Monterrey, Mexico City, Mexico
[11] Research Center On Innovation and Service Management in Industrial Firms (ASAP),
Florence, Italy

Abstract. In the contention of the current industrial landscape, an increasing number of manufacturing firms are experimenting with the transition from product-centric offerings to service-based value concepts and product-service bundles as high-value integrated customer solutions to increase their revenues and build sustainable competitive advantages; a phenomenon known as the "servitization" of manufacturing. Nowadays, consistently with the Industry 4.0 paradigm, these companies have therefore started a process of integrating their traditional value offerings with digital services. This recent strategy is known as "Digital Servitization" and consists of developing new services and/or improving existing ones through digital technologies. However, this transformation is challenging, and companies often struggle to achieve their expectations. Thus, this study aims

D. Y. Kim et al. (Eds.): APMS 2022, IFIP AICT 664, pp. 310–320, 2022.
https://doi.org/10.1007/978-3-031-16411-8_37

to shed light on the current state of Digital Servitization strategies in the manufacturing sector based on a survey addressed to the top and middle management. The results obtained by the analysis of the data collected from the survey show an increasing trend towards the adoption of digital technologies for enabling innovation and differentiation in service delivery processes.

Keywords: Digitalization · Servitization · Digital servitization · Industry 4.0 · Product-service systems · Survey

1 Introduction

Over the past 20 years, the term "servitization" has been used to describe the phenomenon of manufacturing firms increasingly moving toward offering integrated product-service solutions to achieve growth and competitive advantages [1] and reduce the environmental impact [2].

The phenomenon of *servitization* was initially identified by [3] in the late 80s. The recent debate on *Digital Servitization* highlights the increasing attention given to the convergence of two important research and business trends, namely "servitization" and "digitization" [4]. Recently, the growing interest in the *digital transformation* of manufacturing firms, particularly for those technologies that have seen significant growth driven by the Fourth Industrial Revolution (or Industry 4.0) has favoured manufacturing firms in their servitization process by accelerating the deployment and adoption of product-service offerings [5–7]. Today, traditional service offerings, although still preponderant, make it increasingly challenging to be highly competitive in an Industry 4.0 context and growing digital economy [8], leading companies to "digitalize" their value offerings increasingly and thus change their organizational, tactical, and strategic value creation and delivery processes [9]. This process, journey, and phenomenon of manufacturing firms increasingly moving towards offering integrated product-service solutions, using digital technologies to achieve growth and competitive advantages is defined as "Digital Servitization".

Although literature agrees that the emergence of new digital and analytical technologies such as the (Industrial) Internet of Things (IIoT), cloud computing, and big data analytics have fostered and it is still fostering the adoption of innovative services by manufacturing firms (e.g. digital services, smart services), to date, this process still poses multiple challenges to firms, such as financial ones, lack of competences and experiences, and difficulties in creating a collaborative ecosystem of partners and customers [10]. Moreover, there is little evidence on how companies implement *servitization* and more specifically *Digital Servitization* [11].

It is noticeable how many manufacturing firms have spotted the opportunity of exploiting a *servitization strategy in manufacturing,* from Alstom to Thales [12], to ABB to Ericson, and from IBM [13] to Xerox [14]. However, Neely et al. [15], while conducting an extensive analysis of 12,521 companies, found out that many have suffered poor revenues and scarce return on their investments moving towards "servitized business models". What is happening here? Companies that invest heavily in extending their service business, increase their service offerings and incur higher costs, but this does not result in the expected correspondingly higher returns. Because of increasing costs and a lack of corresponding returns, the growth in service revenue fails to meet its intended objectives. This phenomenon is termed the *"service paradox in manufacturing firms"* [16, 17]. Instead of achieving a transition from products to servitized solutions, manufacturers leave the transition line and move into the *"service paradox"*.

Starting from these considerations and this paradox, the Special Interest Group (SIG) on "Service Systems Design, Engineering and Management" of the International Federation of Information Processing (IFIP), Working Group (WG) 5.7 on Advances in Production Management Systems (APMS) has launched a survey to answer the following research questions of academic and industrial interest:

- What is the actual service offering of manufacturing firms?
- How do companies envision the transformation of their service offerings?
- What digital technologies are mainly adopted by manufacturing firms in their service offerings?

The paper is structured as follows: Sect. 2 reports the methodology used to develop the survey and collect data, in Sect. 3 the main results related to the service offering and the adoption of digital technologies in service provision are described, while Sect. 4 concludes the paper summarizing the main lessons learned.

2 Survey Methodology

An exploratory survey was conducted to understand the current state of manufacturing firms in implementing a *Digital Servitization transformation*. Data was collected through the dissemination of a questionnaire, specifically designed for the research, and spread at the European level among the network of manufacturing firms.

The questionnaire itself was designed by a group of international experts involved in *Digital Servitization research* to provide a clear picture of the actual service offering and an understanding of how companies are implementing *Digital Servitization strategies* starting from the main research trends highlighted in the literature. The survey is made of two main sections:

- Section I is dedicated to the collection of data about the respondent (position, business function), the company (name, industry, number of employees, gross annual turnover, market, and sales), the service offering structure, and the level of utilization of digital technologies in service delivery processes, and
- Section II is dedicated to a deeper evaluation of actions at strategic, tactical, and operational levels that companies adopt to comply with their *Digital Servitization transformation process*. Five main areas of investigation, namely: (i) Product-Service System (PSS) design, (ii) Digital Servitization strategy, (iii) Assessing tool for PSS decisions, (iv) Knowledge management along the lifecycle, and (v) Sustainable business models, are analysed based on the primary research trends in "Digital Servitization" as identified by Pirola et al. [11].

The questionnaire was developed in English, translated into Italian, German and Spanish languages, and then disseminated to manufacturing firms by e-mailing lists and social media. It was disseminated at the end of January 2022 and, as a result, it has collected 142 responses until June of the same year. The answers collected were gathered into a comprehensive database to perform the analysis. This study is focused on providing a preliminary description of the current state of *Digital Servitization* in the manufacturing industry. Therefore, only the first part of the survey results is reported and discussed in this paper.

3 Main Findings

The respondents are mainly directors, managers and staff, with 20 years of experience on average and with very heterogeneous business functions (see Table 1).

Table 1. Number of respondents divided into business functions.

Business function	N° of respondents	Business function	N° of respondents
Service/After sales	35 (25%)	Sales	11 (8%)
General Management	20 (14%)	R&D/Engineering	10 (7%)
Production & Quality	19 (13%)	Supply Chain	2 (1%)
IT	11 (8%)	Other	26 (18%)

Tables 2 and 3 summarize the main characteristics of the sample. The sample is characterized by a more significant share of medium- and large-sized enterprises compared with the European Union population, where SMEs are mainly predominant. This may be due to large companies' greater awareness and interest in the "servitization" phenomenon, while SMEs are expected to have a lower degree of maturity in service-related aspects.

Table 2. Classification of the respondents based on companies' industry sectors.

Industry	N° of respondents
Capital goods (Aerospace and Defense, Construction, Machinery, Medical, Electronics)	42 (30%)
Oil and Gas, Energy, Chemicals and Materials (Plastics, Metals, Mining, Paper)	24 (17%)
Consumer (non-durable) goods (food, beverage, tobacco, household products)	14 (10%)
Consumer (durable) goods (consumer electronics, domestic appliances)	11 (8%)
Other	51 (36%)

Table 3. Classification of the respondents based on companies' size.

Company's size	N° of respondents
Large	31 (22%)
Medium	78 (55%)
Small	33 (23%)

The main findings resulting from the analysis of the data collected have been described in this order: firstly, focusing on the service offers provided by the responding companies to identify the current state and future trends; then, focusing on the digitalization of these services, to understand the level of adoption of digital technologies in the service delivery processes.

3.1 Service Offering: Current State and Future Trends

More and more manufacturing firms are interested in new business solutions-oriented to services. In particular, from the data analysis, it emerged that traditional product-oriented services [18], such as Spare parts delivery, are already in the portfolio of 68% of the respondents, as well as Repairs, Warranties, Maintenance, Retrofit, and Upgrading. These are followed by Training, Consultancy, and Engineering, which are present in 64% of the companies, and Maintenance long-term contracts, Pay-per-use, Full-Service contracts, and Outcome-based contracts in 55%. To a lesser extent, use-oriented services such as Leasing, Renting, Sharing, and Pooling are active only in 28% of the companies (see Fig. 1).

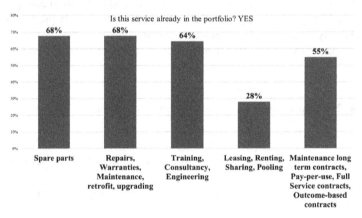

Fig. 1. Current service provision of the responding companies.

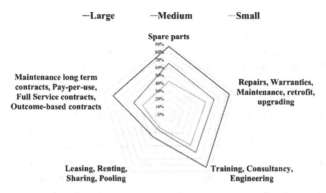

Fig. 2. Adoption of services by company size.

As shown in Fig. 2, almost all large companies provide a broad and multifaceted service offering that includes, on average, many services that have been developed to meet different end-customer needs. On average, the service portfolio of SMEs is more limited in terms of service quantity and type. Nevertheless, the study highlights an increasing interest, even among small companies, to offer more advanced services by expanding the traditional transactional service offerings based on the provision of spare parts, maintenance, and repair.

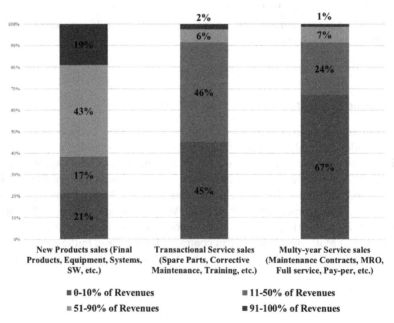

Fig. 3. Revenues share among new products, transactional service and multi-year service sales.

As expected, the highest source of revenue in the sample still corresponds to the sale of new products (see Fig. 3). Indeed, in most responding companies, the revenues deriving from the sales of service-related offers are no more than half of the total revenue. It has been observed that "transactional" services account for 0–10% of the total revenues in 45% of the responding companies, 11–50% of the revenues in 46% of the respondents, while 51–90% of the revenues in only 6% of them, and 91–100% in the 2%. Similar results have been obtained for multi-year services, in which sales still generate low revenues, which is not surprising, given that they are not fully present in companies' portfolios and even when they are present they are not yet particularly pervasive among customers. However, revenue from the sale of both "transactional" and "relational" services has grown for a large part of the sample in the past two years, and firms companies also expect revenue from service sales to increase in the coming years as they are becoming increasingly interested in providing more advanced services than standard services (see Fig. 4).

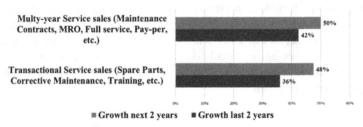

Fig. 4. Growing business trends among transactional service and multi-year service sales in the next two years and the last two years.

3.2 Technology Adoption in the Service Offering

Since the survey has been disseminated to understand the current state of *Digital Servitization,* the following analysis properly focuses on the digital technologies that companies are adopting to offer their service solutions. Firstly, the authors have explored the level of utilization of technology (no/partially/yes) for service delivery (see Fig. 5). It has been observed that digital technologies are mainly utilized for (i) Spare parts provision (in 53% of the companies), (ii) Repairs, Warranties, Maintenance, Retrofit, and Upgrading (52%), and (iii) Training, Consultancy, and Engineering (52%). These are followed by (iv) Maintenance long-term contracts, Pay-per-use, Full-Service contracts, and Outcome-based contracts (46%), and finally, (v) Leasing, Renting, Sharing, and Pooling (only 20%).

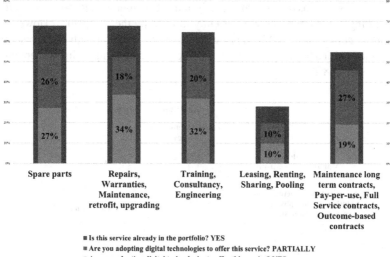

Fig. 5. Level of utilization (yes and partially) of digital technologies for providing related service offers.

Among the digital technologies [7, 19] that companies are currently adopting in their service offerings (see Fig. 6), the (Industrial) Internet of Things (IIoT) is the most utilized, followed by Cyber Security and Cloud Computing. Instead, Big Data Analytics, Simulation of Connected Machines (e.g., Digital Twin), and Mixed Reality (Virtual and Augmented Reality) are still characterized by a low utilization level, but they are expected to be further adopted in service delivery, meaning they are very attractive for manufacturing firms. Artificial Intelligence (AI)/Machine Learning (ML), Advanced

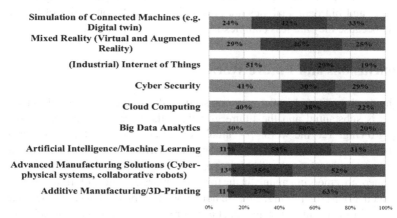

Fig. 6. Level of adoption of digital technologies.

Manufacturing Solutions (Cyber-Physical Systems, Collaborative Robots), and Additive Manufacturing/3D-Printing are not currently utilized by the companies. However, it is interesting to notice that AR/ML represents the digital solution with more potential of being adopted, with a higher percentage of companies evaluating its implementation for service delivery (58%).

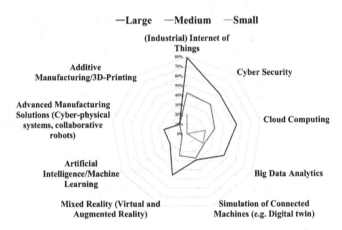

Fig. 7. Digital technologies adopted about the companies' size.

In addition, it has been observed that the companies already adopting these digital technologies are mainly large-sized enterprises (see Fig. 7), although medium-sized enterprises also appear to have a good level of implementation of the same technologies. On the contrary, small-sized enterprises have a low adoption level of such technologies, which may be explained by the limited financial resources, a lack of digital skills and resources, and the challenges of networking with other companies. Only IIoT, cloud computing, and big data analytics are present in the small companies of the sample, probably because they are less complex to implement and manage.

4   Conclusions and Future Work

From the results reported in the previous section, the service business of manufacturing firms is substantial and the future growth of their service offerings is estimated to keep growing. Yet, the word "potential" is used here because there remains a very product-centric view of the offering, although an increasing number of companies are offering "transactional services". Multi-year services, in particular the ones related to maintenance, are emerging mainly in the form of contacts. While, unfortunately, business models such as leasing, renting, etc., are not yet widely spread. However, these services generate still low revenues for manufacturing firms that have already introduced them in their portfolio. Thus, the data shows that although the service offering is there, it is not yet possible for most companies to achieve enough revenues to enable a paradigm shift.

Digital technologies, although more slowly than the literature often points out, are pushing companies toward a "service-oriented offering". Technologies turn out to be an effective enabler: they have already become an indispensable element characterizing the offering and are helping companies propose an increasingly broad and articulated service offering. The most adopted technologies to date are related to IIoT, followed by Cyber Security and Cloud computing, which are increasingly interesting when linked to XaaS (Everything-as-a-Service) service offerings. Finally, a high interest emerges, although still exploratory, in technologies such as Mixed Reality and AI/ML, technologies undoubtedly more complex to implement and manage, where the need for in-house expertise becomes a distinguishing factor. Moreover, it emerges that SMEs are focusing only on a few technologies such as IIoT, cloud computing, and big data analytics.

Future work should address the extension of the responding sample. Then, it would be particularly interesting to investigate the actions taken by manufacturing firms at operational, tactical, and strategic levels to implement a *Digital Servitization transition,* as well as to study their impacts on the entire supply chain ecosystem.

References

1. Baines, T., et al.: Servitization: revisiting the state-of-the-art and research priorities. Int. J. Oper. Prod. Manag. **37**(2), 256–278 (2017)
2. Mont, O.K.: Clarifying the concept of product-service system. J. Cleaner Prod., Clean Prod. **10**(3), 237–245 (2002)
3. Vandermerwe, S., Rada, J.: Servitization of business: adding value by adding services. Eur. Manag. J. **6**(4), 314–324 (1998)
4. Vendrell-Herrero, F., Wilson, J.R.: Servitization for territorial competitiveness: taxonomy and research agenda. Compet. Rev. **27**, 2–11 (2017)
5. Brax, S.A., Jonsson, K.: Developing integrated solution offerings for remote diagnostics: a comparative case study of two manufacturers. Int. J. Oper. Prod. Manag. **29**(5), 539–560 (2009)
6. Nylén, D., Holmström, J.: Digital innovation strategy: a framework for diagnosing and improving digital product and service innovation. Bus. Horiz. **58**(1), 57–67 (2015)
7. Romero, D., Gaiardelli, P., Pezzotta, G., Cavalieri, S.: The impact of digital technologies on services characteristics: towards digital servitization. In: Ameri, F., Stecke, K.E., von Cieminski, G., Kiritsis, D. (eds.) APMS 2019. IAICT, vol. 566, pp. 493–501. Springer, Cham (2019). https://doi.org/10.1007/978-3-030-30000-5_61
8. Liu, Z., Ming, X.: A methodological framework with rough-entropy-ELECTRE TRI to classify failure modes for co-implementation of smart PSS. Adv. Eng. Inform. **42**, 100968 (2019)
9. Gaiardelli, P., Pezzotta, G., Rondini, A., Romero, D., et al.: Product-service systems evolution in the era of industry 4.0. Services Bus. **15**, 177–207 (2021)
10. Paiola, M.: Digitalization and servitization: opportunities and challenges for Italian SMES. Sinergie Italian J. Manage. **36**(107), 11–22 (2018)
11. Pirola, F., Boucher, X., Wiesner, S., Pezzotta, G.: Digital technologies in product-service systems: a literature review and a research agenda. Comput. Ind. **123**, 103301 (2020)
12. Davies, A., Brady, T., Hobday, M.: Charting a path toward integrated solutions. Sloan Manage. Review **47**, 39–48 (2006)
13. Miller, D., Hope, Q., Eisenstat, R., et al.: The problem of solutions: balancing clients and capabilities. Bus. Horiz. **45**(2), 3–12 (2002)

14. Baines, T., Lightfoot, H.W.: Servitization of the manufacturing firm: exploring the operations practices and technologies that deliver advanced services. Int. J. Oper. Prod. Manag. **34**, 2–35 (2014)
15. Neely, A., Benedettini, O., Visnjic, I.: The servitization of manufacturing: further evidence. In: 18th European Operations Management Association Conference, Cambridge (2011)
16. Gebauer, H., Fleisch, E., Friedli, T.: Overcoming the service paradox in manufacturing companies. Eur. Manag. J. **23**(1), 14–26 (2005)
17. Kuijken, B., Gemser, G., Wijnberg, N.M.: Categorization and willingness to pay for new products: the role of category cues as value anchors. J. Prod. Innov. Manag. **34**(6), 757–771 (2017)
18. Gaiardelli, P., Resta, B., Martinez, V., Pinto, R., Albores, P.: A classification model for product-service offerings. J. Clean. Prod. **66**, 507–519 (2014)
19. Frank, A.G., Dalenogare, L.S., Ayala, N.F.: Industry 4.0 technologies: implementation patterns in manufacturing companies. Int. J. Prod. Economics **210**, 15–26 (2019)

Sales and Operations Planning for Delivery Date Setting in Engineer-to-Order Maritime Equipment Manufacturing: Insights from Two Case Studies

Swapnil Bhalla[1]([✉]) [iD], Erlend Alfnes[1] [iD], and Hans-Henrik Hvolby[2] [iD]

[1] Norwegian University of Science and Technology, Trondheim, Norway
swapnil.bhalla@ntnu.no
[2] Aalborg University, Aalborg, Denmark

Abstract. Delivery date setting (DDS) is a challenging and competitively critical tactical decision in engineer-to-order (ETO) environments, which requires integrated planning for effective decision-making. Despite the variety of industrial contexts in DDS literature, the maritime equipment industry has been an unexplored context vis-à-vis planning needs for effective DDS. This study uses a sales and operations planning (S&OP) framework to investigate the current state of the DDS process of two maritime equipment suppliers. Findings indicate that the low market demand over the last few years has influenced the DDS process design in the companies, suggesting that the process should be reconfigured to remain effective under periods of high demand. More cases from the maritime equipment industry are needed to assess if the findings are valid across the industry.

Keywords: Tactical sales and operations planning · Delivery date setting · Engineer-to-order

1 Introduction

Maritime equipment such as engines, propellers, thrusters, cranes, winches, etc., for ships are complex, high-value, electromechanical products that are often customized according to the requirements of ship owners, designers, and engineers. Adopting such an engineer-to-order (ETO) strategy for delivering customized equipment allows maritime equipment suppliers to deliver technologically competitive and innovative solutions to their customers [1]. However, operating with an ETO strategy also creates substantial uncertainty in product specifications, process specifications, and delivery lead times, making delivery date setting (DDS) a complex and challenging task [1, 2]. The DDS process and effectiveness can be competitively critical for winning orders in ETO contexts [3, 4]. The planning needs for effective DDS vary across ETO companies and industry sectors [2, 5], and case studies from various ETO contexts can be found in the extant DDS literature, e.g., industrial machinery production [2, 6, 7], boiler and reactor

© IFIP International Federation for Information Processing 2022
Published by Springer Nature Switzerland AG 2022
D. Y. Kim et al. (Eds.): APMS 2022, IFIP AICT 664, pp. 321–328, 2022.
https://doi.org/10.1007/978-3-031-16411-8_38

manufacturing [8], engineered wood production [9], industrial electrical and electronic equipment [10], etc. However, there are no case studies on the DDS practices of maritime equipment suppliers in the extant literature, and studying these practices in unexplored industrial contexts is one of the main research needs for establishing a common reference framework for tactical planning activities across ETO contexts [5]. This paper aims to contribute to this research need by investigating the DDS practices in the maritime equipment industry using the case research approach. The paper studies these practices based on a modest case sample of two case companies to ensure greater detail for the studied cases and the contextual factors affecting DDS practices in the cases. The paper investigates the two equipment suppliers' DDS practices using a tactical sales and operations planning (S&OP) theoretical framework presented in Sect. 2. Section 3 presents findings from the case studies. Section 4 concludes the paper by summarizing the implications of the main findings.

2 Theoretical Framework

The ETO strategy has been widely adopted by companies producing complex, big-sized, industrial products that are often too high-value and customer-specific to be mass-produced [11]. The order-winning process in ETO environments usually entails a tendering or customer enquiry stage, where a customer's technical and commercial requirements are translated to preliminary specifications of the product and estimated commercial characteristics of order-fulfillment such as price and delivery dates [1, 12]. Setting these delivery dates is usually a tactical planning decision in ETO environments, which entails creating preliminary aggregate plans and roughly estimating quantities, flow times, and resource requirements [8, 9, 13].

DDS is a complex decision since there are various order-fulfillment activities, e.g., design, engineering, procurement, fabrication, assembly, testing, etc., whose lead times should be considered while setting delivery dates in ETO environments [9, 14, 15]. Furthermore, due to varying levels of customer-specificity of these order-fulfillment activities, variables affecting the activity lead times, i.e., product specifications, material requirements, resource requirements, etc., are often uncertain [1, 2, 4]. These characteristics of DDS in ETO companies create a uniquely complex and uncertain context for tactical planning. Extant research on DDS in ETO environments suggests formalization of the tactical planning process and integrated planning across functions as best practices for managing the complexity and uncertainty of DDS [2, 7, 9, 14, 16]. Integrated planning across functions enables cross-functional information sharing and coordination and ensures that relevant factors are considered in the planning process. Formalizing the planning process standardizes or systematizes planning and decision-making with pre-defined rules and procedures that ensure the involvement of relevant actors in planning and decision-making based on explicitly stated objectives or priorities.

While previous DDS research emphasizes the importance of formalizing and integrating the tactical planning process for effective DDS, the extant literature has lacked frameworks that can support companies in adopting these practices [5]. Meanwhile, sales and operations planning (S&OP) has emerged as an approach for integrated tactical planning, whose applications in ETO environments have been essentially overlooked in the extant research, despite its potential to address the complexity and uncertainty characterizing tactical planning and DDS in ETO environments [17]. S&OP integrates tactical planning across functions and supply chains, effectively balancing demand and supply while aligning plans for operational activities with strategic objectives and constraints [18]. Linking S&OP with DDS in ETO environments, **Table 1** shows a framework of the main S&OP activities for DDS, clustered under four main planning functions for sales, engineering, procurement, and production, which also correspond to the four main supply chain functions in ETO environments [19].

Table 1. The theoretical framework of S&OP activities for DDS in ETO environments

Planning function	Planning activities	Ref
Sales planning	Selecting customer enquiries	[2]
	Prioritizing customer enquiries	[12]
	Determining delivery lead time, date, and price	[20]
Engineering planning	Defining preliminary product specifications	[1, 12]
	Determining detailed engineering activities and resources	[1, 12]
	Estimating lead times and costs and setting due dates	[9, 10]
	Identifying external capability and additional capacity needs	[1, 9]
Procurement planning	Identifying critical items	[7, 14]
	Selecting potential suppliers	[7, 14]
	Determining procurement lead times and prices	[14, 21]
Production planning	Identifying main production activities & resource requirements	[8, 12]
	Identifying feasible production start and end dates	[8, 9]
	Estimating production costs & non-regular capacity requirements	[8]

3   Case Studies

The Norwegian shipbuilding and maritime equipment industries are known for their high-quality, highly customized, and innovative products [22–24], with the widespread adoption of the ETO strategy [1, 21, 25]. Maritime equipment suppliers base the fundamental designs of their products on the targeted customer segments (i.e., ship types) and the requirements imposed by the codes, standards, and rules specified by ship classification societies such as DNV (Det Norske Veritas) and Lloyd's Register. Relevant systems and sub-systems can be selected from these basic designs, and their specifications may be modified and combined in different configurations to address specific customers' requirements. The level of customization offered by equipment suppliers may vary across market segments and companies [1].

The operating profits of Norwegian maritime equipment suppliers have dropped historically over the last decade [24], following the dramatic effects of the decline of oil prices in 2014–15 on the global shipbuilding industry [23, 24, 26, 27]. Demand from the higher-margin oil and gas segment has decreased, while sales and delivery of equipment to other segments, e.g., cruise ships, ferries, fisheries, aquaculture, etc., have increased significantly [24].

Maritime equipment suppliers are essential parts of shipbuilding supply chains [21, 27], whose contextual characteristics and planning needs have not received much attention in extant ETO planning and control literature, especially within DDS and tactical planning. To address this gap, this section presents the case studies of the DDS process of two Norwegian ETO maritime equipment suppliers operating in the global shipbuilding market. The first case company is a supplier of propulsion and maneuvering systems for various types of ships and is referred to as ProCo (fictitious name – short for propulsion equipment company). The second case company is a supplier of handling equipment and structures such as cranes, winches, gangways, etc., and is referred to as HanCo (fictitious name – short for handling equipment company).

3.1 Description of Cases

The first case company, ProCo, supplies propulsion and maneuvering systems for various types of ships, e.g., fishing vessels, aquaculture or fish farming vessels, shuttle tankers, ferries, cruise ships, offshore vessels, etc. Their product portfolio includes various standard propellers, thrusters, gearboxes, control systems, etc., that can be configured and customized according to customer requirements. ProCo has a strong strategic focus on localized manufacturing in Norway and is characterized by a high degree of vertical integration with primarily in-house engineering and production, supported by a few strategic suppliers. The second case company, HanCo, supplies specialized handling equipment such as cranes, winches, gangways, etc., for ships used in fishing, aquaculture, offshore oil and gas, offshore wind, etc. The company focuses on the engineering and development of hardware and software technology, and most of the production is outsourced to suppliers, mainly in Europe and some in Asia. HanCo's portfolio of existing product designs has continually expanded since the company was founded ten years ago, with customer requirements often driving the expansion.

In both case companies, tenders and customer enquiries are primarily managed by the sales department without much involvement from the other functions. After identifying potential customers' requirements from tender invitations, sales leads, customer enquiries, etc., engineers in the sales department prepare technical proposals with preliminary product specifications describing how the company's product technology can address the customer's requirements. In most instances, the engineering, procurement, and production departments are first involved in a customer order after contract signing or order confirmation, when the delivery date and price have already been committed using estimates based on historical data on lead times and costs from completed orders. In ProCo's case, the company's planning department, which is responsible for production and inventory planning, may be contacted by sales personnel before contract signing in some cases if the customer-imposed delivery dates are considered 'too tight'. In such cases, the master planner assesses the availability of relevant production resources and critical suppliers to meet the delivery date. For HanCo's case, many customer orders entail prototyping of newly designed modules. The sales department at HanCo estimates the workload for in-house engineering disciplines (mechanical, hydraulics, electrical and electronics, and software) as part of the DDS or S&OP process, and the need for hiring personnel with new competencies is also identified at this stage. However, these estimates are primarily used for estimating the quoted product price. Any capacity-oriented feasibility assessment of meeting the committed delivery dates is not undertaken until after order confirmation. Table 2 characterizes the DDS process of the two case companies using the S&OP framework of planning activities.

Table 2. Evidence of DDS/S&OP activities in the cases

	S1	S2	S3	E1	E2	E3	E4	Pc1	Pc2	Pc3	Pd1	Pd2	Pd3
ProCo	--	--	✓	✓*	--	--	--	✓#	✓#	✓#	✓#	✓#	--
HanCo	--	--	✓	✓*	✓*	--	✓*	--	--	--	--	--	--

Legend:

✓: evidence of activity found in the case   *: activities performed by the sales department
--: evidence of activity not found   #: activities performed for some orders only

S1: select enquiries; **S2**: prioritize enquiries; **S3**: determine delivery lead time/date & price; **E1**: define preliminary specs; **E2**: determine engineering activities & resources; **E3**: estimate engineering lead times & costs; **E4**: identify external capability & capacity needs; **Pc1**: identify critical items; **Pc2**: select potential suppliers; **Pc3**: determine procurement lead times & prices; **Pd1**: identify main production activities & resource requirements; **Pd2**: identify feasible production start & end dates; **Pd3**: estimate production costs & non-regular capacity req.

3.2 Analysis and Discussion

The analysis of the two case companies provides insights into the similarities and differences among their DDS processes, and the main contextual factors influencing their process designs. As Table 2 indicates, many of the S&OP activities in our theoretical framework (Table 1) are not performed in most instances for DDS in the companies. Neither case provides evidence for the sales planning activities of selecting and prioritizing customer enquiries (S1, S2). The estimation of overall lead time and prices (S3) is primarily based on historical data in both cases, usually without any planning inputs from the other functions. Specification of the preliminary product characteristics (E1) is also handled by engineers in the sales departments in both companies. Engineering activities, workload, and capability requirements (E2, E4) are estimated in HanCo's case but only used for cost and price estimation purposes, not for capacity planning before order confirmation. In ProCo's case, procurement- and production planning activities (Pc1–3, Pd1–2) are only performed for enquiries with short delivery times.

We find the characteristically low demand for the shipbuilding and maritime equipment industry as the main contextual factor explaining the lack of evidence for many of the planning activities – S1, S2, E3, Pc1, Pc2, Pc3, Pd1, Pd2, and Pd3, in most cases for both companies. Given the low demand, the companies have focused on maximizing sales, thus overlooking the selection and prioritization of enquiries. The perceived importance of supply planning issues before order confirmation, i.e., capacity planning for engineering and production functions and supplier lead times, has also diminished in recent years due to low demand, long durations of shipbuilding projects, and surplus capacity in the upstream supply chains. As a result, the case companies have focused on winning orders, and usually postpone planning for supply-related issues until after order confirmation in most instances.

The main observed differences between the companies' DDS processes can be explained based on the companies' vertical integration and sourcing strategies. ProCo's highly integrated production and diverse specialized in-house production equipment necessitate closer monitoring of workloads and capacity. Furthermore, their strategic focus on localized manufacturing constrains which suppliers can be used for sourcing components, necessitating closer monitoring of their availability under tight delivery schedules. In contrast, with low vertical integration and outsourced production, engineering is HanCo's core capability, and early identification of the need for new engineering capabilities and additional engineering personnel is essential for maintaining their competitive advantage. Furthermore, flexibility vis-à-vis supplier locations for outsourced production provide HanCo with higher flexibility in acquiring production capacity after order confirmation. This flexibility has possibly been amplified in recent years due to the low demand and surplus capacity in this industry, explaining the lack of HanCo's focus on procurement planning in DDS despite low vertical integration.

Experts within the maritime industry expect demand to increase in the coming years [28], which suggests that the effectiveness of the companies' DDS process could be vulnerable to these changes. With increased demand, engineering capacity planning could be challenging for HanCo, as the managers and planners report difficulties in engineering capacity planning and activity monitoring even in the current market environment. Production capacity planning is expected to be one of the main planning challenges for ProCo under increased demand since the existing backward loading-based planning functionality is inefficient for DDS, requiring multiple manual iterations. Procurement planning is expected to have higher importance for both cases in a high-demand market scenario due to increased competition for obtaining suppliers' capacities.

4   Conclusion

This study has provided some insights into the DDS processes of two ETO maritime equipment suppliers and the contextual factors influencing their process design. The overall market demand in the maritime industry, and the companies' vertical integration and sourcing strategies are found to be the most influential contextual factors for explaining the similarities and differences in DDS practices across the cases. While we consider the influence of the vertical integration and sourcing strategies on the DDS process design to be strategic choices, we believe that elements of the process design that the market demand has influenced should be reconsidered in the case companies for minimizing the vulnerability of their DDS processes to future demand growth expected in the maritime industry [28]. Such a reassessment of the process design can increase its robustness toward market changes. Since the paper investigates the current state of the DDS process of only two maritime equipment suppliers, it is premature to generalize the findings to other companies in this industry. However, previous findings from other industry sectors [2, 7] support the contextual factors identified in this paper, highlighting the potential for their broader relevance. The cases presented in this paper also provide empirical support for the research need to develop effective engineering and production capacity planning tools for addressing the industrial needs of ETO companies, as highlighted in the authors' recent state-of-the-art review on DDS [5].

References

1. Alfnes, E., Gosling, J., Naim, M., Dreyer, H.C.: Exploring systemic factors creating uncertainty in complex engineer-to-order supply chains: case studies from Norwegian shipbuilding first tier suppliers. Int. J. Prod. Economics **240**, 108211 (2021)
2. Zorzini, M., Hendry, L., Stevenson, M., Pozzetti, A.: Customer enquiry management and product customization: an empirical multi-case study analysis in the Italian capital goods sector. Int. J. Oper. Prod. Manag. **28**(12), 1186–1218 (2008)
3. Amaro, G., Hendry, L., Kingsman, B.: Competitive advantage, customisation and a new taxonomy for non make-to-stock companies. Int. J. Oper. Prod. Manag. **19**(4), 349–371 (1999)
4. Cannas, V.G., Gosling, J., Pero, M., Rossi, T.: Determinants for order-fulfilment strategies in engineer-to-order companies: insights from the machinery industry. Int. J. Prod. Econ. **228**, 107743 (2020)
5. Bhalla, S., E. Alfnes, and H.-H. Hvolby, Tools and practices for tactical delivery date setting in engineer-to-order environments: a systematic literature review. International Journal of Production Research, 2022: p. 1–33
6. Zorzini, M., Corti, D., Pozzetti, A.: Due date (DD) quotation and capacity planning in make-to-order companies: results from an empirical analysis. Int. J. Prod. Econ. **112**(2), 919–933 (2008)
7. Zorzini, M., Stevenson, M., Hendry, L.C.: Customer enquiry management in global supply chains: a comparative multi-case study analysis. Eur. Manag. J. **30**(2), 121–140 (2012)
8. Carvalho, A.N., Oliveira, F., Scavarda, L.F.: Tactical capacity planning in a real-world ETO industry case: an action research. Int. J. Prod. Econ. **167**, 187–203 (2015)
9. Ghiyasinasab, M., Lehoux, N., Ménard, S., Cloutier, C.: Production planning and project scheduling for engineer-to-order systems- case study for engineered wood production. Int. J. Prod. Res. **59**(4), 1068–1087 (2021)
10. Grabenstetter, D.H., Usher, J.M.: Developing due dates in an engineer-to-order engineering environment. Int. J. Prod. Res. **52**(21), 6349–6361 (2014)
11. Zennaro, I., Finco, S., Battini, D., Persona, A.: Big size highly customised product manufacturing systems: a literature review and future research agenda. Int. J. Prod. Res. **57**(15–16), 5362–5385 (2019)
12. Adrodegari, F., Bacchetti, A., Pinto, R., Pirola, F., Zanardini, M.: Engineer-to-order (ETO) production planning and control: an empirical framework for machinery-building companies. Production Planning and Control **26**(11), 910–932 (2015)
13. Hans, E.W., Herroelen, W., Leus, R., Wullink, G.: A hierarchical approach to multi-project planning under uncertainty. Omega **35**(5), 563–577 (2007)

14. Hicks, C., McGovern, T., Earl, C.F.: Supply chain management: a strategic issue in engineer to order manufacturing. Int. J. Prod. Econ. **65**(2), 179–190 (2000)
15. Shurrab, H., Jonsson, P., Johansson, M.I.: A tactical demand-supply planning framework to manage complexity in engineer-to-order environments: insights from an in-depth case study. Production Planning & Control **33**(5), 462–479 (2020)
16. Shurrab, H., Jonsson, P., Johansson, M.I.: Managing complexity through integrative tactical planning in engineer-to-order environments: insights from four case studies. Prod. Plann. Control **33**(9–10), 907–924 (2020)
17. Kreuter, T., Kalla, C., Scavarda, L.F., Thomé, A.M.T., Hellingrath, B.: Developing and implementing contextualised S&OP designs–an enterprise architecture management approach. Int. J. Phys. Distrib. Logist. Manag. **51**(6), 634–655 (2021)
18. Grimson, J.A., Pyke, D.F.: Sales and operations planning: an exploratory study and framework. Int. J. Logistics Manage. **18**(3), 322–346 (2007)
19. Nam, S., Shen, H., Ryu, C., Shin, J.G.: SCP-Matrix based shipyard APS design: application to long-term production plan. Int. J. Naval Architecture Ocean Eng. **10**(6), 741–761 (2018)
20. Kingsman, B., Hendry, L., Mercer, A., De Souza, A.: Responding to customer enquiries in make-to-order companies problems and solutions. Int. J. Prod. Econ. **46–47**, 219–231 (1996)
21. Mello, M.H., Gosling, J., Naim, M.M., Strandhagen, J.O., Brett, P.O.: Improving coordination in an engineer-to-order supply chain using a soft systems approach. Prod. Plann. Control **28**(2), 89–107 (2017)
22. Strandhagen, J.W., et al.: Factors affecting shipyard operations and logistics: a framework and comparison of shipbuilding approaches. In: IFIP International Conference on Advances in Production Management Systems, pp. 529–537. Springer (2020)
23. Steidl, C., Yildiran, L.D.C.: Peer Review of the Norwegian Shipbuilding Industry (2017)
24. Haugland, L.M., Abrahamoglu, S., Jakobsen, E.W.: Norwegian maritime equipment suppliers 2021: key performance indicators and future expectations. Menon Economics (2021)
25. Iakymenko, N., Romsdal, A., Alfnes, E., Semini, M., Strandhagen, J.O.: Status of engineering change management in the engineer-to-order production environment: insights from a multiple case study. Int. J. Prod. Res. **58**(15), 4506–4528 (2020)
26. Organisation for Economic Co-operation and Development (OECD), Shipbuilding Market Developments. 2018
27. Strandhagen, J.W., Buer, S.-V., Semini, M., Alfnes, E., Strandhagen, J.O.: Sustainability challenges and how Industry 4.0 technologies can address them: a case study of a shipbuilding supply chain. Prod. Plann. Control **33**(9–10), 995–1010 (2020)
28. Willmington, R.: Shipbuilding: full orderbooks but profits remain elusive. In: lloyd's list. Informa (2022)

Centralized vs Decentralized Production Planning in ETO Environments: A Theoretical Discussion

Bella B. Nujen[1](✉), Erlend Alfnes[2], Deodat Mwesiumo[3], Erik Gran[4],
and Tore Tomasgard[3]

[1] Department of International Business, Norwegian University of Science and Technology,
Trondheim, Norway
Bella.nujen@ntnu.no
[2] Department of Mechanical and Industrial Engineering, Norwegian University of Science and
Technology, Trondheim, Norway
[3] Møreforsking AS, Molde, Norway
[4] SINTEF Manufacturing, Raufoss, Norway

Abstract. The characteristics of ETO production call for further analysis to investigate the implications of traditional (deterministic) systems of planning i.e., centralized, and hierarchal, compared with decentralized systems. Accordingly, this study delineates the potential implications of centralized and decentralized planning approaches in the context of ETO. Hence, the contradictory pressure for either decentralized or centralized approaches promote one-sided solutions accentuating the crucial significance of a theoretical discussion. Our analysis suggests that implementing decentralized systems should engender flexibility, transparency and responsive, which in turn can strengthen the impact of production planning on project delivery. In contrast, implementing centralized systems is likely to stifle the impact of production planning due to the rigidity, sequential interdependence, and the top-down nature of this approach. As such, our study provides opportunities for extending extant theory on centralized and decentralized production planning within ETO contexts, while providing a tentative framework for ETO practitioners that can be applicable when decisions concerning an (re)evaluation of production planning systems are to be made.

Keywords: Engineer-to-order · Centralized production planning · Decentralized production planning

1 Introduction

The productivity of Engineer-to-Order (ETO) production can be improved by the restructuring of both the production process and production management. A vital point in the required development of such a restructuring lies within the area of production planning. With regards to production planning this restructuring should not merely focus on the planning and control activities and resources of manufacturing and assembly, but it

© IFIP International Federation for Information Processing 2022
Published by Springer Nature Switzerland AG 2022
D. Y. Kim et al. (Eds.): APMS 2022, IFIP AICT 664, pp. 329–338, 2022.
https://doi.org/10.1007/978-3-031-16411-8_39

should also take into account the planning requirements of activities in the fields of procurement, quality control, engineering and production, production facilities and plants involvement. This is because ETO is characterized by the strong influence of customer specification and by the continuous changes to the specification during the project; from design and engineering to time of delivery [1].

The large volume of engineering requires an equivalent effort by the ETO manufacturer and thus, also to their need for high production flexibility to handle unpredictability. Compared to traditional (serial) production, in ETO all production activities required for design and production must be synchronized, especially with respect to delivery time, something that indicates that many of the engineering and production processes needs to be executed in parallel. Hence, due to such complexities the planning of production can be affected by a disintegration from the overarching plan leading to problems of incomplete information sharing along different stages in the production. Such issues are probably more evident when operating with several production plants [2, 3]. This is because a multiple-plant context operates with a higher level of intra-and interorganizational interactions compared with a single plant (e.g., standalone business unit), and therefore exposed for more disturbance. Hence, a major difficulty in managing ETO is to integrate planning of different stages or production processes within a multiple project environment. Consequently, the characteristics of ETO production implies that there is a need for further emphasize to whether one should embrace and improve the traditional (deterministic) approach of planning i.e., centralized, and hierarchal systems, or if ETO firms operating with several production plants benefits from collaborative planning approaches, i.e., decentralized systems. Accordingly, there seem to be an inherent conflict in these two areas of production planning systems, which warrants further discussions – which this study aims to contribute with.

The rest of the composition of the study is as follows: An introduction to relevant centralized and decentralized production planning systems is provided in Sect. 2, while Sect. 3 conceptualize the ETO environment within the realm of those systems. In Sect. 4, we provide a discussion which also represent the frame of reference for the concluding remarks in Sect. 5.

2 Theoretical Background

2.1 Centralized vs Decentralized Production Planning

The tendencies in production planning can take different forms. At one extreme, production planning is almost exclusively centralized. That is, production is seen as a linear and predictable entity that can be planned by a central authority and then precisely implemented [4, p. 256]. Here the production plan follows a predetermined approach, where the demand planning for e.g., the next quarter is established only by one central level without involvement of others. As such, decision making (head/master planner) is often disconnected from where the production or service take place. It follows a superior-subordinate management philosophy where control decisions propagate in a top-down manner and the status is reported from a bottom-up fashion. At the other end of the spectrum, the production planning system is almost completely decentralized. Here each plant is operating as a stand-alone business, deploying a production planning approach for 'local' optimization. Compared to the centralized approach, the production plan is perceived as a resource for situated action where the involved actors can adapt plans to requirements of its enquiries. As such, neither the production nor the planning activity is adhered to as something predictable [5]. Consequently, decentralized production systems require control and autonomy to be distributed to more than one decision maker or level, to be able to react to local conditions in real time. As such, a decentralized production planning system is based on autonomous entities with enough decision space as its core.

Hence, production planning is a key mechanism in manufacturing, since planning puts the firm in a position to meet the production requirements as effectively as possible [6]. Supported by digitalized planning systems and solutions it can mitigate uncertainty by providing information for better decision-making [7]. For instance, in central production planning systems, such as MRP II (Manufacturing Resource Planning), every decision concerning all facilities is made at one central level, distant from other production plants. Likewise, ERP (Enterprise Resource Planning) which is a centralized software composed of a set of applications to manage vital functions of a firm (e.g., sales, inventory and planning). The strength of such systems is their power to integrate information in a streamlined manner which can ease the information flow enterprise wide. Hence, it helps in increasing transparency in workflows leading to better forecasting, as delivery dates can be planned in advanced to meet customer needs. As such, a centralized approach provides opportunities to create a big-picture information flow and consistency, overall risk management and coordination [4]. Especially, in contexts where work operations can be conducted independently and low levels of co-operation between plants is necessary. Other benefits with centralized planning systems when operating with multiple plants (that produce the same or rather similar projects) is that it allows for economies of scale for other firm functions such as procurement. However, in changeable environments with high variation in e.g., engineering and production, the applicability of centralized planning systems decreases. The same can be argued if the production processes are complex and interdependent; operating with multistage procedures that causes production processes to start and finalize at different plants. Thus, this type of system appears suitable particularly for firms operating in environments with high determinism [8]. As a result, scholars focusing on complex production environments [e.g., 9,10] have started to question the effectiveness of centralized production planning systems and thus shifted their focus towards more decentralized modes.

A decentralized system is claimed to be a key element in effective project and production management and is predominantly focusing on the social sides of the production planning processes in addition to technical results [4]. Decentralized systems are dynamic in nature and demonstrate a high level of adaptability to changes in production and are known to ease communication, increase flexibility and autonomy. Decentralization is hard though; one must be cautious so that it does not get too detached and hampers the overall goal. If not managed, it can result in unsystematized production with informal decentralized management and dependency of tacit knowledge [11]. Thus, to succeed, the production planning system must become more collaborative [12]. Collaborative planning is based on information exchange in support of joint strategic, tactical and operational planning, forecasting and demand fulfilment process [13, p. 74]. In complex project environments a frequently applied system supporting collaboration is the Last Planner System (LPS; a lean production approach) [14]. Here, manufacturers are operating with a close integration mode, where employees are part of the decision-making process, while the head planner/headquarter act as a facilitator more than as an authority [4].

LPS composes three levels. First, at an overarching level, where long-term planning goals are set. It is here one decides what aspects that need to be achieved during the execution of the project [14]. Secondly, at a medium-term planning level where obstacles are identified and detached, ensuring that the necessary resources, e.g., materials, information, and equipment, are made available. Thirdly, at the short-term planning level, the focus is turned towards production reliability and timely availability of needed resources. Thus, effort is put on shielding planned work from upstream variation and by encouraging and initiating conscious and reliable commitment of workers [14]. As such, an integrated approach is developed to support the decentralization of decisions to lower levels of operational responsibilities. In so doing, it enables for planning and control activities to not only start according to predetermined time schedules, but also accommodate for planning according to unforeseen events. For instance, when changes in customer orders or engineering changes occur after the production has started LPS enables a proactive approach to handle uncertainties [15]. This is because other levels than just the central decision-making level can exchange information on conditions in their own executions concurrently. As such, required information is more accurate because it is subjugated by the actual customer order and/or engineering changes. Hence, this helps bypassing the inability to secure delivery times as one manages to handle deviations from the original production plan in a collaborative manner. Accordingly, decentralized planning is more agile and responsive as it eases re-optimization which is hard to achieve in centralized production planning. Similar argumentation can be valid when considering variability and disturbances within the context of multiple-plants and production planning. For instance, if manufacturers are confronted with a high degree of complexity and uncertainties, autonomy should be assigned across plants in order to increase responsiveness and flexibility in the production [2, 5]. More so, when engineering and production is conducted at multiple plants, it is difficult to determine what and how much work will be available at a future state. It makes it a hurdle to arrange for specific resources requires, and thus it is impractical to develop predetermined and rigid plans [14] especially since it has a negative effect on the overall decision space (e.g., which adjustments can be accepted at which level and at which consequences).

As can be seen the most important differences between them seem to be the robustness in systems. In the following section, we conceptualize whether the characteristics of ETO and its environment fits with a production planning system following a centralized planning approach, adhering to a fully decentralized approach or benefit from a collaborative mode of organization.

3   Conceptualization

As stated earlier, ETO is characterized by an inherent uncertainty in product complexities and high levels of customer involvement, and hence interdependencies between plant functions and activities [16]. The aspects of interdependencies require extensive cross-functional integration [17] which induce additional complexity in planning processes and tools [16]. As such, it is important that ETO firms deploy a suitable planning approach that accommodates the embedded complexity in their environment [6]. Especially, since a lack of fit between the characteristics of the environment and the chosen planning approach can impose negative effects to the performance outcome [9]. This notion is particularly important to accentuate for ETO firms compared to e.g., Make-to-Stock (MTS). This is because the latter manufacturers often operate in an environment characterized with higher levels of predictabilities which reduce potential obstacles in planning and control issues and thus favors the universalistic 'one size fits all' planning approach [10]. Despite this being heightened, existing planning approaches applied to ETO are mostly based on a serial production type of thinking [18] which adheres to a 'linearism' way of thinking. A linear strategy implies dependent and sequential phases executed according to a plan established in the beginning of a project [19]. Hence, it does not accommodate the uncertainties that can be found in change operations regarding for instance, engineering after the entry of customer enquires [16] which are common, if not constant in ETO. For example, in MTS environments, engineering changes are actions that are planned priori production start (except for changes owing to safety issues). In this context, changes are implemented in the next product version or production run; updated design and engineering drawings are made, the inventories are gradually phased out, and new parts and components are ordered from suppliers [20, p. 2]. While in ETO, engineering changes must be instantly implemented and cannot be postponed until a new/next product version or production run, causing work in process being disposed and parts and components to be reworked or even scrapped. As such, the embedded variabilities in engineering work can have a huge impact on everything from ongoing production, assembly processes and inventory, leading to the need of immediate replanning [20].

More so, the obstacles regarding uncertainties accentuated with regards to linearism are similar to those aired in centralized production planning systems, such as MRP II and ERP which are dominating the current practice [4]. Despite their dominance both ERP and MRP II have been argued to lack an appropriate level of flexibility and responsiveness. For instance, it is rather challenging to accommodate changes in MRP II in ETO firms, as more often than not, the system relies on a predefined bill-of-materials (BOM) structure, which is not easily changed between projects [18]. Besides, the changes in BOMs are often made in engineering through an iterative process between customers, procurement and sometimes also suppliers, which reinforces the difficulties in changing predefined production plans. Furthermore, it is important to acknowledge the premises of MRP (II) systems, as they are based on two erratic assumptions. The first being the infinite capacity levels of production lines, and the second is based on constant lead-times [8]. While the former can create obstacles when capacity levels are reaching its limits, the latter is challenging when practicing with fixed values. With fixed values one tends to apply long lead-times in order to cope with uncertainty, which induces additional inventories [8]. Hence, in ETO this is problematic as one only operates with variabilities. Consequently, the changeable environment and variation in design and production in ETO environments may severely affect the applicability of such centralized systems [4]. Adding to this, are the issues of coordination in planning when operating with multiple production plants. Often, there is quite a bit of room for autonomy and local decision making for planners in their work, where the decision space depends in part on the amount of variability in orders and processes and on the knowledge and experiences of the planner. However, when operating with multiple production plants this can become a hurdle process [12]. Herein lies the vital differences in management characteristics, i.e., the degree of autonomy or decision space the plant/headquarter management has concerning different decisions such as capacity, facilities, organization, quality systems and hence, production planning and control systems [2, 3]. Thus, manufacturers that are encountered with a high level of complexity and uncertainties either due to e.g., internal miscalculations such as lack of capacities or due to external circumstances in e.g., change orders, should operate with autonomy among its plants in order to ease such unforeseen obstacles [5]. This does not mean that a full decentralized approach is the most appropriate one to adhere to. ETO firms can still accommodate some of these complexities and uncertainties through centralized determined software's, however, to achieve this, one requires some level of coordination at least. Thus, a suitable production planning approach is one that operates in an integrated manner in parallel with a e.g., ERP system as the main coordinator of the different planning processes among and between plants. According to [21] any mode of production planning and control holds elements of both centralized and decentralized features. Consequently, a planning system which assigns authority in the decision space primary on a centralized level is preferable only if the level of uncertainty and complexity of its production system is low [5], which hence does not fit within the context of an ETO environment.

The below framework (Fig. 1) depicts the implications of deploying centralized vs decentralized production planning within the context of ETO and multiple production plants.

As shown in Fig. 1, considering the characteristics of ETO, production planning that takes into account customer order and addresses it by involving all key functional areas such as design, engineering, procurement, production, and sales should lead to delivery of projects within agreed lead time along with the required quality standards. A critical aspect is the customer involvement throughout the process. However, implementing decentralized approach engenders flexibility, transparency and responsive, which in turn strengthen the impact of decentralized planning on project delivery. In contrast, implementing centralized approach is likely to stifle the impact of production planning due to the rigidity, sequential interdependence and the top-down nature of this approach. Accordingly, the implementation of digitalized planning solutions and collaborative approach can enhance the positive impact of decentralization and weaken the potential negative impact of centralization.

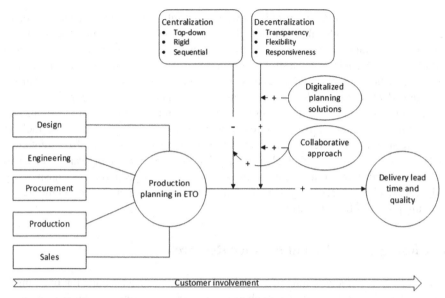

Fig. 1. Impact of centralized vs decentralized production planning in the context of ETO (+) indicates positive/strengthening impact; (-) indicates negative impact on project delivery

4 Discussion

What the best approach to the organization of production planning may be depends on the characteristics of the manufacturing system and its environment as well as the obstacles faced in the pursuit of achieving a delivery within the realm of its objectives. Nonetheless, the final choice of a production planning system eventually depend on how the production planning systems are managed, weighted and what is the nature of the tradeoffs between them. Clearly a decentralized planning approach may induce very different pros/cons compared to a centralized planning approach. For instance, decentralized planning often results in loss of efficiency with respect to centralized planning, while its pros often are recognized as increased agility in responsiveness to changes and customer demands, better commitment to goals, and increased motivation and well-being of employees [4, 14]. Thus, disagreement between different levels of coordination and autonomy between plants or quite different products require different attention. Looking at the organization of a planning system in isolation can yield counterproductive results, especially for ETO firms. Nevertheless, decision making and hence, planning is generally employed either centrally or decentralized where digital software solutions on a central level is deployed, while failing to integrate production planning in a collaborative manner. Unfortunately, firms often seem to make ill-informed production planning decision based on superficial software features rather than on a selection of features that are applicable for their production environment [10, p. 870]. This is rather interesting as the complexity embedded in ETO environments is omnipresent acknowledged yet – paradoxically – overlooked. Hence, many of todays' ETO firms still departure from a serial production planning philosophy [18], which might explain why the application of centralized and hierarchical production planning systems continue being the norm.

Based on extant literature and this discussion we claim that a decentralized production planning system is the most suitable when the level of uncertainties and complexities are high and thus requires continuous modes of organization, as is the case for ETO firms. Preferable deployed in a collaborative manner. If not, a decentralized approach can risk replicating some of the disadvantages that can be found in a fully centralized production planning system, as this too can result in obstacles in production progress tracking and coordination deficiencies along interdependent functions and thus also disentangle itself from the overarching plan. Nonetheless, its strengths in reducing variabilities and increase reliability in production planning systems due to aspects such as transparency and larger decision space, heightens its potential as a positive approach to embrace in planning practices for ETO firms.

5   Closing Remarks and Further Research

The recognition of the dilemma of centralized vs. decentralized production planning is not new. However, critical aspects such as engineering and customer changes and non-collocated production plants impose additional aspects which can hamper the effectiveness of hierarchal planning systems. This is because in ETO changes in engineering can propagate, as there is no next product run, instead production is discontinuing, requiring engineering and production processes to be executed in parallel. And when operating with multiple plants the decision space of planner/headquarter might require different modes of organization. Hence, both these aspects act as important boundary conditions to the universalistic 'one size fits all' planning system.

Based on extant theoretical and conceptual groundwork, the study delineated potential implications and opportunities with centralized and decentralized planning approaches within the context of ETO and multiple production plants. Hence, the contradictory pressure for either decentralized or centralized approaches promote one-sided solutions [4] accentuating the crucial significance of our theoretical discussion also for practitioners. As such, our study provides opportunities for extending extant theory on centralized and decentralized production planning within ETO contexts, while providing a tentative framework for ETO practitioners that can be applicable when decisions concerning an (re)evaluation of production planning systems are to be made.

Although the findings of this study are interesting and warrants further discussions, a limitation with the study is the difficulty to maintain a neutral perspective [22].

Furthermore, our discussion can be argued simplistic, especially since there are different forms of (de)centralized production planning systems, as well as new technological advancements e.g., Industry 4.0 applications. Yet we claim that the question at hand will still be heightened as a centralized vs decentralized approach also when accentuated by the means of Industry 4.0 applications. For example, in cloud-based solutions the reaction to engineering changes in ETO as well as the responsiveness to changes in local conditions at multiple plants will not diminish, and new technological systems will still be designed and used by people. Thus, we encourage future research to also investigate how production planning will be affected from such views. Especially since Industry

5.0 seem to reinforce the element of human participation, perceptions and hence input of information to such systems.

Acknowledgment. The authors acknowledge the support of the Research Council of Norway for the research project Respons.

References

1. Gosling, J., Naim, M.M.: Engineer-to-order supply chain management: a literature review and research agenda. Int. J. Prod. Econ. **2**, 741–754 (2009)
2. Chen, W.-L., Huang, C.-Y., Lai, Y.-C.: Multi-tier and multi-site collaborative production: illustrated by a case example of TFT-LCD manufacturing. Comput. Ind. Eng. **57**(1), 61–72 (2009)
3. Olhager, J., Feldmann, A.: Distribution of manufacturing strategy decision-making in multiplant networks. Int. J. Prod. Res. **56**(1–2), 692–708 (2018)
4. Lehtovaara, J., Seppänen, O., Peltokorpi, A.: Improving construction management with decentralised production planning and control: exploring the production crew and manager perspectives through a multi-method approach. Const. Manag. Economics **40**(4), 254–277 (2022)
5. Windischer, A., et al.: Characteristics and organizational constraints of collaborative planning. Cogni. Tech. Work. **11**(2), 87–101 (2009)
6. Bhalla, S., Alfnes, E., Hvolby, H.-H., Oluyisola, O.E.: Requirements for sales and operations planning in an engineer-to-order manufacturing environment. In: Dolgui, A., Bernard, A., Lemoine, D., von Cieminski, G., Romero, D. (eds.) APMS 2021. IAICT, vol. 633, pp. 371–380. Springer, Cham (2021). https://doi.org/10.1007/978-3-030-85910-7_39
7. Powell, D., Lodgaard, E., Dreyer, H.: Investigating the challenges and opportunities for production planning and control in digital lean manufacturing. In: Lalic, B., Majstorovic, V., Marjanovic, U., von Cieminski, G., Romero, D. (eds.) APMS 2020. IAICT, vol. 592, pp. 425–431. Springer, Cham (2020). https://doi.org/10.1007/978-3-030-57997-5_49
8. Alfnes, E., et al.: A concept for collaborative supply chain planning. In: Proceedings of the 3rd International Conference on Cognitive Infocommunications. IEEE (2012)
9. Jonsson, P., Mattsson, S.-A.: The implications of fit between planning environments and manufacturing planning and control methods. Int. J. Oper. Prod. Manag. (2003)
10. Stevenson, M., Hendry, L.C., Kingsman, B.G.: A review of production planning and control: the applicability of key concepts to the make-to-order industry. Int. J. Prod. Res. **43**(5), 869–898 (2005)
11. Parente, M., et al.: Production scheduling in the context of Industry 4.0: review and trends. Int. J. Prod. Res. **58**(17), 5401–5431 (2020)
12. Klein, J.A.: A reexamination of autonomy in light of new manufacturing practices. Hum. Rel. **44**(1), 21–38 (1991)
13. Barratt, M.: Unveiling enablers and inhibitors of collaborative planning. Int. J. Log. Manag. **15**(1), 73–90 (2004)
14. Ballard, G., Howell, G.: Shielding production: essential step in production control. J. Const. Eng. Manag. **124**(1), 11–17 (1998)
15. Kjersem, K.: Contributing to resolving a project planning paradox in ETO: from plan to planning (2020)
16. Shurrab, H., Jonsson, P., Johansson, M.I.: A tactical demand-supply planning framework to manage complexity in engineer-to-order environments: insights from an in-depth case study. Prod. Plan. Control. **33**(5), 1–18 (2020)

17. Mello, M.H., Strandhagen, J.O., Alfnes, E.: Analyzing the factors affecting coordination in engineer-to-order supply chain. Int. J. Oper. Prod. Manag. **35**, 1005–1031 (2015)
18. Kjersem, K., Giskeødegård, M.: Planning procurement activities in ETO projects. In: Lalic, B., Majstorovic, V., Marjanovic, U., von Cieminski, G., Romero, D. (eds.) APMS 2020. IAICT, vol. 592, pp. 565–572. Springer, Cham (2020). https://doi.org/10.1007/978-3-030-57997-5_65
19. Fernandez, D.J., Fernandez, J.D.: Agile project management—agilism versus traditional approaches. J. Comp. Inf. Systems. **49**(2), 10–17 (2008)
20. Iakymenko, N., et al.: Analyzing the factors affecting engineering change implementation performance in the engineer-to-order production environment: case studies from a Norwegian shipbuilding group. Prod. Plan. Control., 1–17 (2020)
21. de Haas, H., Riis, J.O., Hvolby, H.-H.: Centralized and decentralized control: finding the right combination. In: Okino, N., Tamura, H., Fujii, S. (eds.) Advances in Production Management Systems. ITIFIP, pp. 218–229. Springer, Boston, MA (1998). https://doi.org/10.1007/978-0-387-35304-3_20
22. Cooper, H.M.: Organizing knowledge syntheses: a taxonomy of literature reviews. Know. Society. **1**, 104–126 (1988)

Sustainable and Digital Servitization

Future Trends in Digital Services and Products: Evidence from Serbian Manufacturing Firms

Slavko Rakic[1]([✉]) [iD], Ugljesa Marjanovic[1] [iD], Giuditta Pezzotta[2] [iD],
Paolo Gaiardelli[2] [iD], Anja Jankovic[1], and Federico Adrodegari[3] [iD]

[1] Faculty of Technical Sciences, University of Novi Sad, Novi Sad, Serbia
`slavkorakic@uns.ac.rs`
[2] University of Bergamo, Bergamo, Italy
[3] University of Brescia, Brescia, Italy

Abstract. The concepts of Industry 4.0 trigger the transformation of manufacturing firms. Digital technologies upgrade traditional products and services to increase the satisfaction of customers. In this paper, the authors investigate digital products and services in manufacturing firms. Additionally, the authors challenge relations between digital products and services and their share in the gross annual turnover of manufacturing firms. The data for this research are obtained through the Digital Servitization Survey coordinated by the IFIP WG5.7 Special Interest group on Service Systems Design, Engineering, and Management. We used the Serbian dataset from 136 manufacturing firms. The results show that 68% and 42% of manufacturing firms use digital technologies for product creation and digital services, respectively. Moreover, results demonstrate products have the 90% of the share in gross annual turnover in manufacturing firms. However, the prediction of the production managers for the next two years shows that services will reach a 30% share in gross annual turnover of firms.

Keywords: Product-service systems · Servitization · Digital services · Digital products · Survey

1 Introduction

In the last decade, the research community has given significant attention to advanced services in manufacturing firms [1]. Furthermore, the employment of Industry 4.0 concepts and digital technologies in firms support the transformation of products and services [2, 3]. To further develop their business, manufacturing firms need to find an appropriate way to transform it from traditional to digital [4]. Therefore, Product-Service Systems (PSS) could help production to provide the sustainability of organizations by achieving economic, environmental, and social benefits [5]. The transformation from traditional PSS to smart PSS depends on organizational and technological changes [4]. From a technology perspective, manufacturing firms need to buy or develop technologies such as the Internet of Things, Big Data, Augmented or Virtual Reality, and others [6, 7].

D. Y. Kim et al. (Eds.): APMS 2022, IFIP AICT 664, pp. 341–350, 2022.
https://doi.org/10.1007/978-3-031-16411-8_40

Moreover, production need to make a strategy on how to employ these digital technologies in the products and services offered [8, 9]. The driving role of digital technologies for PSS is also a part of the organization's changes [10].

The main challenges from an organizational perspective could be divided into organizational structure and performance metrics, human resource requirements, and supply network relationships [11]. In product-centered organizations, a measure of the firm's success is represented through financial performance; on the other side, service-oriented soft performance indicators are difficult to measure [11]. In this way, the performance measurement in PSS is very difficult for production managers. Furthermore, communication and networking skills are required for frontline employees to facilitate or sell PSS to customers [10, 12]. Thus, production needs to make a set of training for their employees to understand the value of PSS and how to communicate them to customers. The shift to PSS challenges the organization of value and supply chains. Production needs to move the focus from stable intra-firm transactional flows of physical materials to multiple, dynamic relationships and dual-way flows of materials and information with their suppliers [13]. According to these challenges, the transformation from traditional to smart PSS represents a very difficult process for manufacturing firms [4]. Moreover, the research community gives an overview that firms from developed countries easier achieve the advanced level of PSS than firms from developing countries [14]. Along with the different organizational and technical capacities, previous research shows the different shares of industry sectors in developed and developing countries [15]. In the share of total industry, high-tech firms (i.e. electrical equipment, machinery, etc.) have a higher share in developed countries [15]. On the other hand, in the share of total industry, low-tech firms (i.e. food production, textile, etc.) have a higher share in developing countries [16]. However, the integration of digital products and services is a growing trend among manufacturing firms which could together provide value chains for firms from developed and developing countries [17]. Furthermore, manufacturing firms from developing countries need to prepare themself to become a part of the value chain of manufacturing firms from developed countries via smart PSS [11]. This paper has the aim to fill the literature gap on findings from the use of smart PSS in developing countries. Moreover, with these findings manufacturing firms from developed countries could achieve new insights into the digitalization level of their partners from developing countries. Based on the literature background, the authors proposed following research questions:

- *RQ1: What is the share of products and services of gross annual turnover in Serbian manufacturing firms?*
- *RQ2: What is the level of smart PSS in Serbian manufacturing firms?*

2   Literature Review

The term PSS could be defined as a combination of products and services capable of jointly fulfilling a customer need at the market [18]. Furthermore, it enables manufacturing firms to be more sustainable and to make a better impact on the environment [19]. Additionally, a PSS business model allows manufacturing firms to increase their competitiveness at the market with the creation of better relations with customers [20].

In accordance with Tukker's classification, PSSs can be divided in the three periods of transformation, from product-oriented to service-oriented business models [19]. Specifically, product-related services refer to solutions closely related to product characteristics (i.e. maintenance, spare-parts), use-oriented services include product renting or leasing, while results-oriented services concern services such as pay per service units or long-term maintenance contracts [19, 21]. For the transformation from traditional to smart PSS, manufacturing firms need to understand how digital technologies make an impact on the products and on all of these three groups of services [22]. In the study of smart PSS, Lerch describes three different roles of digital technologies on the transformation of PSS [23]. In the first period, manufacturing firms involve digital technologies in product creation, after that firms involve digital technologies in service creation and finally digital technologies become an intelligent component of smart PSS [23]. The rapidly changing global market supports the transformation from traditional to smart PSS [24].

Smart PSS is known as an intelligent-linked system, with a combination of smart products and internet-based services [25]. Furthermore, a previous study divided the smart PSS into four layers: smart devices, network, data management, and software [25]. Smart PSS enables better providing of solutions (i.e. smart products and services) based on the customer needs [25]. To achieve smart PSS manufacturing firms need to pass challenges in the application of digital technologies [26]. Also, firms need to understand technical competence of digital technologies, ability to use digital technologies in a meaningful way, ability to evaluate digital technologies critically, and motivation to participate and commit in the digital culture of the firm [27, 28]. Manufacturing firms use digital technologies for the creation of digital products and services to make environmental, social and economic benefits [29]. There are many benefits to the application of digital products and services such as: simplifying mechanical components or replacing them with software, developing remote services to supplement or replace traditional services performed on-site, reducing transport of physical products, optimizing service tasks and travel routes by applying apps, synchronizing the supply chain of product and services [30]. Furthermore, smart PSS easier connects all actors in the PSS environment including PSS providers and suppliers, PSS customers and end-users, and the broad society in which it operates at the same digital platforms [30]. Also, previous research from developed countries shows that IoT combined with Big Data and Analytics techniques overcomes the PSS challenges and make more financial benefits for manufacturing firms [31]. Additionally, research from developed countries shows that easy-to-implement digital technologies produce a direct effect on firm financial performance with a low cost of their deployment [32]. On the other hand, the high quality of digital technology with the high cost of investments should be supported by other organizational capabilities of firms to achieve positive financial performance [32]. According to the findings from developed countries, this study investigates the future trend of digital products and services in the creation of smart PSS in developing countries (i.e. Serbian manufacturing firms). Moreover, this study investigates technology challenges (implementation of digital technologies in product and service creation) and organizational challenges (share of the gross annual turnover from products and services, market share, and structure of the industry sector).

3 Methodology

This study was based on data from the Digital Servitization Survey, research conducted in Italy, Germany, Sweden, Mexico Switzerland, and Serbia, and structured in two main areas: (1)The first area is aimed at understanding the offering of service and digital services of the companies. After an introductory section on the firm's distinctive characteristics, several questions are proposed to analyze both the industry 4.0 and the digital service offerings, (2)The second area aims at understanding the dynamics behind the digital servitization path starting from the output of Pirola et al. [33]. In particular, for those firms that in the first part of the survey present a digital service offering, their approaches towards Digital Servitization strategy, PSS design methods, Knowledge management, Assessment tools, and Sustainability issues are investigated. In particular, this research used a Serbian data set from 136 manufacturing firms obtained in 2022, and it is focused on the first part of the survey. The research was based on the analysis of manufacturing firms (NACE Rev 2 codes from 10 to 33). The data sample for this research was obtained by the method of determining the stratified sample in relation to the industrial sector and the size of the company in Serbia. The research was conducted within manufacturing firms with at least 20 employees. The questionary was sent online via Survey Monkey. The response rate was 15%. The result of the sample depicts that about 39% of the manufacturing firms in the sample are small, having between 20 and 49 employees, another 40% of the manufacturing firms have between 50 and 249 employees, and 21%, have more than 250 employees. Table 1 reports the distribution of manufacturing firms by sector.

Table 1. Distribution of sample by industry

Manufacturing industry	Share on total sample
Food production	27%
Production of fabricated metal products, except machinery and equipment	10%
Production of machinery and equipment n.e.c	9%
Production of textile	7%
Production of rubber and plastics	7%
Production of electrical equipment	7%
Production of motor vehicles, trailers, and semi-trailers	6%
Others	27%

4   Results

According to the research question *What is the share of products and services of gross annual turnover in Serbian manufacturing firms?*, Figs. 1 and 2 through a frequency analysis show the share of the gross annual turnover from products and services in Serbian manufacturing firms. Specifically, Fig. 1 reports the current share of gross annual turnover, while the forecast of the share of gross annual turnover for the next two years is presented in Fig. 2.

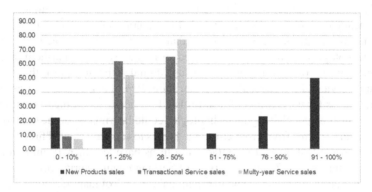

Fig. 1. The share of gross annual turnover in Serbian manufacturing firms

Figure 1 presented the share of gross annual turnover from products and services in 2022 in Serbian manufacturing firms. Results show that about 80 manufacturing firms have about 10% of the share in total gross annual turnover from services. On the other hand, about 50 manufacturing firms have about 90% of the share in total gross annual turnover from products. According to these findings, we demonstrate findings that Serbian manufacturing firms are more product-oriented than service-oriented.

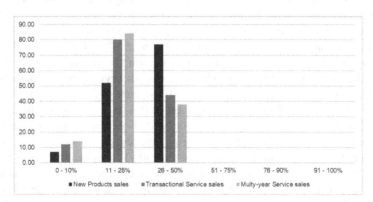

Fig. 2. The prediction of the share of gross annual turnover in Serbian manufacturing firms for 2024

Figure 2 presented the prediction of the share of gross annual turnover from products and services for 2024 in Serbian manufacturing firms. Results make the prediction that about 80 manufacturing firms will have about 40% of the share in total gross annual turnover from services. Additionally, predictions show that about 75 manufacturing firms will have about 50% of the share in total gross annual turnover from products. In comparison with results from the previous Fig. 1, we can demonstrate that Serbian manufacturing firms would like to transform their orientation from product to service-oriented business models. Moreover, according to the research question *What is the level of smart PSS in Serbian manufacturing firms?* results from the Survey show that about 60% of manufacturing firms use digital technologies for product creation. Also, only 10% of manufacturing firms don't use digital technologies for product creation. On the other hand, results from the Survey show that only 17% of manufacturing firms use digital technologies for the creation of product-related services. Furthermore, results show that only 6% of manufacturing firms use digital technologies for the creation of use-related services. Finally, results show that about 20% of manufacturing firms use digital technologies for the creation of result-related services. According to these findings, authors could conclude that digital technologies could be triggers for the transformation of manufacturing firms from product-oriented firms to service-oriented firms. Additionally, results show that 80% of manufacturing firms have less than 10 million euros in gross annual turnovers. The main markets of Serbian manufacturing firms are national for 48% of manufacturing firms and international for 41% of manufacturing firms. Only 11% of manufacturing firms have a local market as the main market.

5   Discussion and Conclusion

This study provides insights into the role of digital products and services in developing countries (i.e. Serbian manufacturing firms). Manufacturing firms from all 24 manufacturing sectors (NACE Rev 2 codes from 10 to 33) were assessed to answer the research question: *"What is the share of products and services of gross annual turnover in Serbian manufacturing firms?"*. Based on the research findings authors conclude that at this moment Serbian manufacturing firms are more product-oriented firms. The results show that 50 manufacturing firms from the sample generate 90% of gross annual turnover from products and 80 firms from the sample generate 10% of gross annual turnover from services. On the other hand, predictions of production managers for the next two years predict transformation from product-oriented to service-oriented manufacturing firms. Accordingly, they predict that 80 firms will generate 40% of gross annual turnover from services. Hence, authors give explanation on this transformation in the answer to research question 2: *"What is the level of smart PSS in Serbian manufacturing firms?"*. Findings show that about 60% of manufacturing firms use digital technologies for product creation. On the other hand, results show that only 17% of manufacturing firms use digital technologies for the creation of product-related services, 6% of manufacturing firms use digital technologies for the creation of use-related services, and that about 20% of manufacturing firms use digital technologies for the creation of result-related services. Based on this finding authors predict that with more employment of digital technologies in service creation manufacturing firms increase their share in gross annual turnover. Furthermore, according to the organizational challenges this research shows the trends in low-tech firms (i.e. food and textile production have 35% of share in total sample). According to this sample, authors could conclude that the process of digitization will enable low-tech firms from developing countries to become a part of the value chains of firms from developed countries. Additionally, for the transformation from product to service orientation manufacturing firms need to better understand the needs of their customers on the local, national and international levels. They need to develop different packages according to the market specification. From the theoretical implications, this research gives in-depth findings in the level of digitalization in products and service creation. Additionally, this research confirms previous studies which show that manufacturing firms easily transform services which are not closely related to product characteristics. Hence, research results show that training as a service is the most digitized service in the Serbian manufacturing firms. Also, findings confirm the important role of digital technologies in the creation of smart PSS. Future predictions in the share of services in gross annual turnover confirm trends of previous research which show the increasing trend in the use of smart PSS models in manufacturing firms. Also, this research confirms that low-tech firms have a lower level of possibility to employ digital technologies than high-tech firms.

The main contribution of this research from a theoretical perspective is to show how digital technologies could increase the role of services in the creation of gross annual turnover. Moreover, this research gives an overview of the market classification in the firms from developing countries. From the practical perspective, this research gives insights into the gross annual turnover in Serbian manufacturing firms. Moreover, with these findings manufacturing firms from developed countries could achieve new insights on how to make investments in developing countries to make value chains with manufacturing firms. Therefore, this finding shows a different perspective in the creation of gross annual turnover. At this moment results show the product-orientation of manufacturing firms in the process of digitization and in the share of profits generated from the products. In the future, they predict service-orientation of manufacturing firms which will achieve more profits from services with the employment of digital technologies in service creation. With this information, production managers could shape their business model to be more attractive for their customers with the creation of smart PSS. Smart PSS will provide more combinations of digital products and services which have a lower unit cost of creation than traditional products and services. Also, this research gives an overview of the market classification in Serbian manufacturing firms. With this information and with smart PSS manufacturing firms could make more B2B relations with international firms. In this way, manufacturing firms from Serbia could be more competitive in the international market. The major limitation of this paper is in the data set. This research uses the data set from Serbian manufacturing firms which have a high number of low-tech firms. Future research needs to use data sets from different countries which could better explain the general situation in future trends of digital products and services. Furthermore, this research uses more technology challenges in the offer of smart PSS. Future research needs to include more organizational challenges to better explain the creation process of smart PSS. With this information, research could measure the effect of the technological and organizational components on the financial benefits of smart PSS.

References

1. Baines, T., Ziaee Bigdeli, A., Bustinza, O.F., Shi, V.G., Baldwin, J., Ridgway, K.: Servitization: revisiting the state-of-the-art and research priorities. IJOPM 37(2), 256–278 (2017). https://doi.org/10.1108/IJOPM-06-2015-0312
2. Ardolino, M., Rapaccini, M., Saccani, N., Gaiardelli, P., Crespi, G., Ruggeri, C.: The role of digital technologies for the service transformation of industrial companies. Int. J. Prod. Res. 56(6), 2116–2132 (2018). https://doi.org/10.1080/00207543.2017.1324224
3. Rakic, S., Pavlovic, M., Marjanovic, U.: A precondition of sustainability: industry 4.0 readiness. Sustainability 13(12), 6641 (2021). https://doi.org/10.3390/su13126641
4. Kohtamäki, M., Parida, V., Oghazi, P., Gebauer, H., Baines, T.: Digital servitization business models in ecosystems: a theory of the firm. J. Bus. Res. 104, 380–392 (2019). https://doi.org/10.1016/j.jbusres.2019.06.027
5. Moro, S.R., Cauchick-Miguel, P.A., de Sousa Mendes, G.H.: Product-service systems benefits and barriers: an overview of literature review papers. Int. J. Ind. Eng. Manage. 11(1), 61–70 (2020). https://doi.org/10.24867/IJIEM-2020-1-25
6. Pavlović, M., Marjanović, U., Rakić, S., Tasić, N., Lalić, B.: The big potential of big data in manufacturing: evidence from emerging economies. In: Lalic, B., Majstorovic, V., Marjanovic, U., von Cieminski, G., Romero, D. (eds.) APMS 2020. IAICT, vol. 592, pp. 100–107. Springer, Cham (2020). https://doi.org/10.1007/978-3-030-57997-5_12
7. Lalic, B., Marjanovic, U., Rakic, S., Pavlovic, M., Todorovic, T., Medic, N.: Big data analysis as a digital service: evidence form manufacturing firms. In: Wang, L., Majstorovic, V.D., Mourtzis, D., Carpanzano, E., Moroni, G., Galantucci, L.M. (eds.) Proceedings of 5th International Conference on the Industry 4.0 Model for Advanced Manufacturing. LNME, pp. 263–269. Springer, Cham (2020). https://doi.org/10.1007/978-3-030-46212-3_19
8. Paul, M., et al.: Reconfigurable digitalized and servitized production systems: requirements and challenges. In: Lalic, B., Majstorovic, V., Marjanovic, U., von Cieminski, G., Romero, D. (eds.) APMS 2020. IAICT, vol. 592, pp. 501–508. Springer, Cham (2020). https://doi.org/10.1007/978-3-030-57997-5_58
9. Ciric, D., Lolic, T., Gracanin, D., Stefanovic, D., Lalic, B.: The application of ICT solutions in manufacturing companies in Serbia. In: Lalic, B., Majstorovic, V., Marjanovic, U., von Cieminski, G., Romero, D. (eds.) APMS 2020. IAICT, vol. 592, pp. 122–129. Springer, Cham (2020). https://doi.org/10.1007/978-3-030-57997-5_15
10. Li, A.Q., Rich, N., Found, P., Kumar, M., Brown, S.: Exploring product–service systems in the digital era: a socio-technical systems perspective. TQM 32(4), 897–913 (2020). https://doi.org/10.1108/TQM-11-2019-0272
11. Martinez, V., Bastl, M., Kingston, J., Evans, S.: Challenges in transforming manufacturing organisations into product-service providers. J. Manuf. Technol. Manag. 21(4), 449–469 (2010). https://doi.org/10.1108/17410381011046571
12. Ciric, D., Lalic, B., Marjanovic, U., Savkovic, M., Rakic, S.: A bibliometric analysis approach to review mass customization scientific production. In: Dolgui, A., Bernard, A., Lemoine, D., von Cieminski, G., Romero, D. (eds.) APMS 2021. IAICT, vol. 634, pp. 328–338. Springer, Cham (2021). https://doi.org/10.1007/978-3-030-85914-5_35
13. Spring, M., Araujo, L.: Service, services and products: rethinking operations strategy. Int. J. Oper. Prod. Manag. 29(5), 444–467 (2009). https://doi.org/10.1108/01443570910953586

14. Mastrogiacomo, L., Barravecchia, F., Franceschini, F.: A worldwide survey on manufacturing servitization. Int. J. Adv. Manufact. Technol. **103**(9–12), 3927–3942 (2019). https://doi.org/10.1007/s00170-019-03740-z

15. Bikfalvi, A., Lay, G., Maloca, S., Waser, B.R.: Servitization and networking: large-scale survey findings on product-related services. Serv. Bus. **7**(1), 61–82 (2013). https://doi.org/10.1007/s11628-012-0145-y

16. Rakic, S., Visnjic, I., Gaiardelli, P., Romero, D., Marjanovic, U.: Transformation of manufacturing firms: towards digital servitization. In: Dolgui, A., Bernard, A., Lemoine, D., von Cieminski, G., Romero, D. (eds.) APMS 2021. IAICT, vol. 631, pp. 153–161. Springer, Cham (2021). https://doi.org/10.1007/978-3-030-85902-2_17

17. Simonsson, J., Magnusson, M., Johanson, A.: Organizing the development of digital product-service platforms. Technol. Innov. Manage. Rev. **10**(3), 37–48 (2020). https://doi.org/10.22215/timreview/1335

18. Mont, O.K.: Clarifying the concept of product–service system. J. Clean. Prod. **10**(3), 237–245 (2002). https://doi.org/10.1016/S0959-6526(01)00039-7

19. Tukker, A.: Eight types of product–service system: eight ways to sustainability? experiences from SusProNet. Bus. Strat. Env. **13**(4), 246–260 (2004). https://doi.org/10.1002/bse.414

20. da Costa Fernandes, S., Pigosso, D.C.A., McAloone, T.C., Rozenfeld, H.: Towards product-service system oriented to circular economy: a systematic review of value proposition design approaches. J. Cleaner Prod. **257**, 120507 (2020). https://doi.org/10.1016/j.jclepro.2020.120507

21. Marjanovic, U., Lalic, B., Medic, N., Prester, J., Palcic, I.: Servitization in manufacturing: role of antecedents and firm characteristics. Int. J. Ind. Eng. Manag. **2**, 133–144 (2020). https://doi.org/10.24867/IJIEM-2020-2-259

22. Rapaccini, M., Adrodegari, F.: Conceptualizing customer value in data-driven services and smart PSS. Comput. Ind. **137**, 103607 (2022). https://doi.org/10.1016/j.compind.2022.103607

23. Lerch, C., Gotsch, M.: Digitalized product-service systems in manufacturing firms. Res. Technol. Manag. **58**(5), 45–52 (2015). https://doi.org/10.5437/08956308X5805357

24. Cong, J., Chen, C.-H., Zheng, P.: Design entropy theory: a new design methodology for smart PSS development. Adv. Eng. Inform. **45**, 101124 (2020). https://doi.org/10.1016/j.aei.2020.101124

25. Abdel-Basst, M., Mohamed, R., Elhoseny, M.: A novel framework to evaluate innovation value proposition for smart product–service systems. Environ. Technol. Innov. **20**, 101036 (2020). https://doi.org/10.1016/j.eti.2020.101036

26. Chowdhury, S., Haftor, D., Pashkevich, N.: Smart product-service systems (smart PSS) in industrial firms: a literature review. Procedia CIRP **73**, 26–31 (2018). https://doi.org/10.1016/j.procir.2018.03.333

27. Süße, T., Wilkens, U., Hohagen, S., Artinger, F.: Digital competence of stakeholders in product-service systems (PSS): conceptualization and empirical exploration. Procedia CIRP **73**, 197–202 (2018). https://doi.org/10.1016/j.procir.2018.03.297

28. Ciric, D., Delic, M., Lalic, B., Gracanin, D., Lolic, T.: Exploring the link between project management approach and project success dimensions: a structural model approach. Adv. Prod. Eng. Manag. **16**(1), 99–111 (2021). https://doi.org/10.14743/apem2021.1.387

29. Dakovic, M., Lalic, B., Delic, M., Tasic, N., Ciric, D.: Systematic mitigation of model sensitivity in the initiation phase of energy projects. Adv. Produc. Eng. Manag. **15**(2), 217–232 (2020). https://doi.org/10.14743/apem2020.2.360

30. Li, A.Q., Found, P.: Towards sustainability: PSS, digital technology and value co-creation. Procedia CIRP **64**, 79–84 (2017). https://doi.org/10.1016/j.procir.2017.05.002

31. Bressanelli, G., Adrodegari, F., Perona, M., Saccani, N.: The role of digital technologies to overcome circular economy challenges in PSS business models: an exploratory case study. Procedia CIRP **73**, 216–221 (2018). https://doi.org/10.1016/j.procir.2018.03.322

32. Kohtamäki, M., Parida, V., Patel, P.C., Gebauer, H.: The relationship between digitalization and servitization: the role of servitization in capturing the financial potential of digitalization. Technol. Forecast. Soc. Change **151**, 119804 (2020). https://doi.org/10.1016/j.techfore.2019.119804

33. Pirola, F., Boucher, X., Wiesner, S., Pezzotta, G.: Digital technologies in product-service systems: a literature review and a research agenda. Comput. Ind. **123**, 103301 (2020). https://doi.org/10.1016/j.compind.2020.103301

Environmental Assessment Methods of Smart PSS: Heating Appliance Case Study

Mariza Maliqi[1]([⊠]) [iD], Xavier Boucher[2] [iD], and Jonathan Villot[1] [iD]

[1] Mines Saint-Etienne, Univ Lyon, CNRS, Univ Jean Monnet, Univ Lumière Lyon 2, Lyon 3 Jean Moulin, ENS Lyon, ENTPE, ENSA Lyon, UMR 5600 EVS, Institut Henri Fayol, F – 42023 Saint-Etienne, France
{mariza.maliqi,villot}@emse.fr
[2] Mines Saint-Etienne, Univ Clermont Auvergne, CNRS, UMR 6158 LIMOS, CIS Center, 42023 Saint-Etienne, France
boucher@emse.fr

Abstract. At the heart of industry 4.0, industrials are developing integrated offers of "Smart Product-Service Systems". Many industrial firms are moving toward product-service systems (PSS) due to their capacity to involve value systems, business models, boundary spanning, dynamic capabilities, and other factors leading to reduced environmental impacts. In this paper, we introduce an easy-to-implement method to evaluate Smart PSSs applied to residential heating systems. Our approach is based on existing environmental assessment methods (focus on Life Cycle Assessment) and accounts for resource consumption, toxic and greenhouse gas emissions as well as waste generation. On the other hand, it also considers different features of the circular economy including the upgradability of Smart PSS offerings and end-of-life heating systems.

Keywords: Environmental assessment · Product-Service-Systems (PSS) · Life Cycle Assessment (LCA) · Upgradability (UP) · Heating systems

1 Introduction

The latest trends in industrial development show that firms are moving from product-driven businesses to service-oriented logic [1] through Product-Service systems (PSS). Doualle et al. [2] introduced PSS as one of the solutions for companies to maintain their competitiveness while overcoming the sustainability challenge. With the advancement of artificial intelligence (AI), and information and communication technologies (ICTs), items have grown more intelligent by adding smart components leading to the recent concept of smart PSS. The term smart PSS mainly refers to a PSS based on "networked smart products and service systems for providing new functionalities "[3] thus leveraging on digital infrastructures, the Internet of Things, cloud computing, and analytics [4] and making possible Digital Servitization strategies [5]. In recent years, public authorities, environmental experts and organizations, and other stakeholders have

© IFIP International Federation for Information Processing 2022
Published by Springer Nature Switzerland AG 2022
D. Y. Kim et al. (Eds.): APMS 2022, IFIP AICT 664, pp. 351–358, 2022.
https://doi.org/10.1007/978-3-031-16411-8_41

become increasingly interested in the environmental quality of industrial solutions. The PSS environmental assessment has a special interest because PSS are widely claimed to reduce environmental impacts while maintaining, transforming, or even adding to user satisfaction [6]. Consequently, this research aims to configure and adapt the predominant LCA method to make it applicable to smart PSS, then to test this proposal on an industrial case in the heating appliance field to study its limitations. The paper is structured as follows. Section 2 provides an investigation on similar methods used in the literature. Section 3 defined the method of LCA procedure configuration for smart PSS. Section 4 presents a case study in the field of heating appliances. Finally, the main findings of this paper and recommendations for future work are presented in Sect. 5.

2 Smart PSS Environmental Assessment: Literature Review

PSS is an interdisciplinary research field, which attracts many different points of view and contributions. The concepts, definitions and typologies come from distinct complementary areas. Typically, business management investigates the bundling of products and services to form solutions. A well-recognized definition in this area considers PSS as "a system of products, services, supporting networks and infrastructure that is designed to be: competitive, satisfy customer and needs while assuring lower environmental impact than traditional business models" [7]. The growing interest in the digital transformation of industrial firms has prompted academic interest in incorporating technology-based research into traditional PSS subjects of study [8]. Service propensity and digitalization are closely correlated and even mutually enhance each other. Accordingly, the notion of "Smart PSS" is presented as the accompanying digital technologies to provide new functionalities to meet individual customer needs successfully and in a sustainable manner. Examples include remote product monitoring, remote diagnostics, predictive maintenance, or equipment optimization based on operational data [5]. This leads to the concept of Upgradable PSS, which is introduced as 'an offer model providing an integrated mix of products and services that are together able to fulfill a particular customer demand, based on innovative interactions among the stakeholders of the value production system, where the economic and competitive interest of the providers continuously seeks environmentally and socio-ethically beneficial new solutions' [9].

2.1 Life Cycle Assessment for Smart PSS

Andersson et al. [10] compare 12 environmental methods and present LCA as one of the most relevant methods for service systems. In addition, LCA is structured by ISO standards and recognized by [11] as the key reference method to evaluate the environmental impact of PSS. With LCA, one can explore all of the many forms of environmental consequences of a system, with two primary applications: (i) analyzing the impact of several life cycle phases on overall environmental load in order to prioritize improvements on products or processes; and (ii) comparing the environmental impact of various product systems [12]. The LCA was not established for the PSS context, thus its application to this particular context requires an adaptation [13]. LCA is a tool for comparing the environmental impacts of systems that perform the same function. Thus, comparisons are made based on Functional Units (FU) within a specified scope. The definition of this functional unit is one illustration of this need for adaptation. Indeed, LCA was essentially designed for the assessment of the environmental impact of a product or service and not of a system comprising both products and services such as the PSS. It will then be necessary to be particularly vigilant in the definition of this FU. In addition, the definition of the FU is a crucial step because it is closely linked to the definition of the scope and therefore the result of the evaluation [2]. Other concerns encountered during the application of the LCA method in the PSS have been the level of uncertainty due to the hypotheses taken into account by the integration of services into the product system. Moreover, the smart concept of PSS also carries difficulties in the environmental evaluation of the ICT systems. This research focuses more on ICT environmental impacts, the need for upgradability, and uncertainty analysis.

2.2 Specificities of LCA for Smart PSS: ICT and Upgradability

The article focuses on Smart PSS where 'smart' dimension indicates the presence of a set of ICT systems. This leads to investigate more specifically the environmental impacts of the components integrated in a new model perimeter such as the ICT and UP modes. Literature sources indicate that ICT has both direct and indirect environmental impacts, including water, air, soil pollution, and natural resource. Berkhout and Hertin [14] have classified the environmental impacts of ICT into three main categories:

- (i) First order impacts (or direct impacts) on the environment caused by the production and use of ICTs on the environment.
- (ii) Second order impacts (or positive indirect impacts) which are concerned with the impact of ICTs on economy structure, production processes, and their associated distribution systems.
- (iii) Third order impacts (negative indirect impact) in which ICT plays the role in promoting structural change and economic growth [15].

Performing the LCA of an ICT network is very challenging. As a result of telecommunication and Internet services, which are globally connected and some national nodes are accessed by several operators, description of a national ICT network is complicated in terms of both scope and allocation. According to literature, due to study simplicity, effort, and relevance, more than half of all studies focused on only one or two impact types. Secondly, for ICT in particular, another reason for concentrating on just a few impact categories could be the limited access to relevant inventory data. The most typical impacts categories used to assess ICT environmental effect are global warming potential, energy or material demand/material depletion and cumulative energy demand [16]. Furthermore, the ReCiPe and CML methods were the most widely used throughout studies that investigated several impact categories. Another significant feature of Smart PSS is upgradability (functional improvements brought to a system over time) considered as the foundation of a new paradigm of consumption/production in order to satisfy at the same time the environmental sustainability notably due to the rationalization of materials use over time and the benefit of such systems for both clients and producers [17]. Khan et al., [18] defined upgradability as the potential aspect that might contribute to a product lifetime extension strategy, with an emphasis on PSS. Therefore, the term "upgradability" stands for an opportunity to provide an eco-design system, and this led to the eco-innovation methods identifying innovation axes to decrease radically the environmental impacts by considering stakeholder attractiveness criteria. In conclusion, LCA contains some limitations that require adapting its use to the design process. First, LCA focuses primarily upon quantitative environmental evaluation. Secondly, the functional unit reference does not efficiently deal with the user's needs. Thus, according to Trevisan, LCA should be coupled with eco-design approaches that are related to process planning or innovation methods [6].

3   Configuration of a LCA Procedure for Smart PSS

Specific recommendations for analyzing smart PSS environmental performance are still lacking in the literature and the limitations raised above remain uncovered. Life Cycle Assessment is a relatively new tool to analyze and assess the environmental impacts fully integrated systems embedding products, processes or services by multi-attribute systemic evaluations. This section aims to demonstrate how we configure the traditional LCA method to make it applicable to PSS: notably the capacity to represent a large variety of PSS added-values for any single PSS offering (by considering a notion of PSS scenarios); the ability to assess the impacts of upgradability; the consideration of ICT components; and the ability to check the uncertainty of assessment results. As described above, the LCA is a tool providing quantitative evaluation and consisting in different phases such as goal and scope definition, inventory analysis, impact assessment, and interpretation. Briefly, at the goal and scope definition stage, we seek to frame the life cycle analysis of the studied system. During the inventory phase, one must have a global vision of the resources used and the outgoing flows of products or services. In the impact assessment phase, the inventory of flows is translated into environmental impacts using modeling on LCA software. In the last phase, we interpret the results obtained in order to understand the multiple tables of figures and graphs that lead to the conclusions. It is sometimes necessary to carry out one or more sensitivity studies to refine its interpretation. One of the important questions of this research is whether it is possible to realize the adaptation of LCA to the PSS framework. According to us, the impacts of the PSS do not fundamentally dispute the methodology or LCA stages, but rather require more detailed work in configuring them to take into account the specificities. The life cycle analysis process consists of four main phases:

• **The Goal and Scope Definition:** this stage needs particular attention due to the structured mechanism for defining PSS scenarios. The mechanism that we propose is to define scenarios based on two criteria: Differentiating the economic models and differentiating the "service packages" of PSS result in the existence of more than one function of a system. In order to deal with the multifunctional system from the FU point of view, the main function of the PSS is taken into account and the other functions of the Smart system are considered as secondary (functions of comfort, maintenance, etc.,) and therefore ignored. In our case, the FU must be the same for all scenarios, and it results in heating the rooms included in the living area of the building.

• **Life Cycle Inventory:** First, during this phase, we must carefully choose the database and allocation method that will be used. In terms of database selection, it is performed based on the input and output typology flow criteria. Furthermore, it is critical to determine if there are recycling items in the materials inventory, which indicates the necessity to apply allocation techniques such as Apos that offer a perspective, in which waste producers are incentivized to assess recycling and reuse possibilities due to the partial allocation of impacts to useful treatment products. These materials are not present in the system under consideration. As a result, the Ecoinvent v3.8 database (which includes inventories of the materials we are looking for) and the cut-off allocation technique were chosen for use in the OpenLCA simulation. Secondly, the life-cycle inventory has to take into consideration the notion of the PSS Scenario introduced earlier. Each scenario requires a specific inventory, while all scenarios share common data. The variety of PSS offerings necessitates the incorporation of particular inventory types. For instance, considering the inventory of ICT materials for Smart PSS scenarios.

• **Impact Assessment:** specifically, this phase consists of defining the life cycle assessment approach and the characterization method. The attributional approach is therefore applied since the study focuses on comparisons of different PSS scenarios, each characterized by the same indicators. Our goal is to differentiate between the scenarios in order to determine which one has the best environmental characteristics, rather than to describe the effect of a change caused by a decision. Moreover, the ReCiPe characterization method is used in this study since it is a consistent method that meets the objectives and the perimeter of impact categories that must be analyzed. ReCiPe provides a harmonized implementation of cause-effect pathways for the calculation of both midpoint and endpoint characterization factors. The ReCipe focused on: (1) providing characterization factors that are representative for the global scale and (2) aims at simplifying the complexity of hundreds of flows into a few environmental areas of interest (it covers approximately 3000 substances and has 21 impact categories).

• **Interpretation of the Results:** At this point, it is necessary to consider: drawing conclusions; performing checks for completeness, sensitivity, consistency, data quality, and uncertainties; highlighting limitations, and making recommendations. During this phase, we are faced with the concept of uncertainty due to a lack of accurate data when constructing PSS scenarios. The uncertainty issues are more impactful since our approach requires a comparison between several scenarios. Thus, a sensitivity analysis becomes essential in order to determine which scenario dominates over another due to the uncertainties. In our analysis, uncertainty is related to the hypotheses considered for the Optibox Package and transport in Preventive and Curative Maintenance. For this reason, we propose to apply a simple sensitivity analysis that consists of a contribution and perturbation analysis. The goal of these analyses is to determine the effect of an arbitrary change in parameter values on the model's result. The variation of the result is calculated, and two ratios are particularly interesting to generate, such as the sensitivity coefficient (SC) and the sensitivity ratio (SR).

4 Case Study in the Field of Heating Appliances

4.1 Goal and Scope Study

The objective of this LCA is to carry out a comparative life cycle analysis between the traditional sales system and the new designed systems, and to develop suggestions for a better and broader use of the instrument. The context of the study is the industrial case proposed by elm. Leblanc (Bosch Group France): the analysis of a product-service system associated with the hybrid boiler, which the company already produces and offers for sale. We perform LCA analysis to examine the environmental impact at each stage of the life cycle, as well as the overall impact of each offer in particular, and to identify the categories of impact most influenced by our system, with a focus on global warming which provides data related to CO_2 emissions. Three different types of PSS scenarios based on economic models and service packages are being designed: the first one mainly provides a support on the purchase and financing phase; the second introduces the intelligent system, as it can remotely monitor different parameters by means of 18 a sensor and transmitter; and the last one, which includes upgradability service by integrating an Eco-design Balloon. The scenarios considered are listed in the Table 1.

Table 1. The characteristics of PSS scenarios.

Product-service-system scenarios			
Reference	PSS	Smart PSS	Upgradable PSS
−Basic system (10 years lifetime) −Regulatory maintenance (compulsory maintenance to ensure the proper functioning of the product system and its frequency is once a year)	−Basic system (10 years lifetime) −Transport + regulatory maintenance organization −Management and planning cost reduction in the maintenance phase	−Basic system (15 years lifetime) −Installation of OPTIBOX solution −Transport + Organization −Maintenance (regulatory, preventive and curative) −Gradually advancing in the cost reduction aspect of management & planning in the maintenance phase −Participation of ICT system	−Renewable system (20 years lifetime) −Transport + installation −Maintenance

4.2 Analysis of the Results

This section outlines PSS's potential to reduce environmental impact. The PSS offers are compared at this stage of the research using environmental effect indicators that are frequently generated during the project's goal and scope phase. Table 2 shows how the environmental impact is distributed in each phase of the entire lifecycle for different PSS scenarios. The interpretation of the results led to the following conclusions.

Firstly, PSS indicates the impact was diminished by 2–3% during the Utilization Phase due to the reduction in transportation. In the smart PSS, it is a result of reorganizing the transport services, implementing preventative maintenance, and optimizing energy use whereas, in the upgradable PSS, this is reflected by the general reduction of the system impact. Secondly, the categories with the highest impact in all PSS offers are human non-carcinogenic toxicity, terrestrial ecotoxicity, and water consumption. The human non-carcinogenic category has a high impact on the environment because it is related to the use of copper material, which has a significant percentage in the construction of the hybrid boiler, and the process associated with this effect is known as the treatment of sulfidic tailings from copper mine operations. The category of terrestrial ecotoxicity is linked to copper material manufacturing and waste plastic treatment operations. Furthermore, water consumption is affected by the use of electricity, and it is worth noting that energy consumption is the most impacting factor in the Utilization phase. Also, one of the most significant categories in our analysis is global warming (CO_2 emission) and it is worth mentioning that it is noticed environmental gains in Smart and Upgradable offers. Thirdly, in terms of an overall environmental and comparative analysis of the various scenarios evaluated, assume that Upgradable PSS has a 38% lower environmental impact than the Reference, Smart PSS at 18.6%, and the PSS at 0.3%. In this context, and with the hypotheses considered, PSS appears as a strong environmental driver.

Table 2. The environmental impact of each life cycle phase for PSSs offers.

Scenarios	Raw Materials	Assemblage	Installation	Utilization	End-of-life		Remanufacturing
					Package	Boiler	
Reference	5%	5–6%	6%	>65%	0.003%	18–18.5%	–
PSS	5%	5–6%	10%	62–63%	0.003%	18%	–
Smart PSS	7%	7.1%	7.2%	56–67%	0.003%	22.5%	–
UP PSS	1.5–3%	8.5–10%	11–12%	39–62%	0.003%	10–18%	0.001–0.15%

5 Conclusions and Perspectives

The findings of this research contribute to two main aspects. First, the approach provides an easy-to-implement method to evaluate a Smart PSS offering, which put forth the environmental added-value of PSS scenarios in this case study. Secondly, the approach makes an important contribution to the existing literature by bridging the gap between traditional products and smart PSS-LCA techniques. However, there are two main limitations related to this study: one is that due to the scope of the paper, the study was carried out by adjusting to the industrial case, leaving unresolved the issue of adaptation to various PSS systems, and so failing to provide a technique with "universal" use. Secondly, another further limitation is represented by the small size of the research. In fact, many other characteristic aspects of PSS have not been investigated, such as the multiplicity of life cycles and variety of UP modes, rigorous uncertainty, and eco-concept design analysis, which can certainly represent a prospect for future research.

References

1. Beuren, F.H., Gomes Ferreira, M.G., Cauchick Miguel, P.A.: Product-service systems: a literature review on integrated products and services. J. Clean. Prod. **47**, 222–231 (2013)
2. Doualle, B., Medini, K., Boucher, X., Laforest, V.: Investigating sustainability assessment methods of product-service systems. Procedia CIRP **30**, 161–166 (2015). https://doi.org/10.1016/j.procir.2015.03.008
3. Kuhlenköttera, B., et al.: New perspectives for generating smart pss solutions – life cycle, methodologies and transformation. Procedia CIRP **64**, 217–222 (2017)
4. Chowdhury, A., Rau, S.: A survey study on internet of things resource management. J. Netw. Comput. Appl. **120**, 42–60 (2018)
5. Pirola, F., Boucher, X., Wiesner, S., Pezzotta, G.: Digital technologies in product-service systems: a literature review and a research agenda. J. Comput. Ind. **123**, 103301 (2020). https://doi.org/10.1016/j.compind.2020.103301
6. Trevisan, L.: Conceptual Framework for the Integrated Eco-Design of Product-Service Systems. Doctoral dissertation, Université Grenoble Alpes (2016)
7. Mont, O.: Clarifying the concept of product-service system. J. Clean. Prod. **10**, 237–245 (2002)
8. Goedkoop, M.J., Van Halen, C.J., Te Riele, H.R., Rommens, P.J.: Product service systems, ecological and economic basics. Report for Dutch Ministries of environment and economic affairs (1999)
9. Vezzoli, C., Ceschin, F., Diehl, J.C., Kohtala, C.: New design challenges to widely implement 'sustainable product-service systems.' J. Clean. Prod. **97**, 1–12 (2015)
10. Andersson, K., Brynolf, S., Lindgren, J.F.: Shipping and the Environment. Springer (2016). https://doi.org/10.1007/978-3-662-49045-7_1
11. Lindahl, M., Sundin, E., Sakao, T.: Environmental and economic benefits of integrated product service offerings quantified with real business cases. J. Clean. Prod. **64**, 288–296 (2014)
12. Muralikrishna, I.V., Manickam, V.: Environmental Management (2017)
13. Dal Lago, M., Corti, D., Wellsandt, S.: Reinterpreting the LCA standard procedure for PSS. Procedia CIRP **64**, 73–78 (2017). https://doi.org/10.1016/j.procir.2017.03.017
14. Berkhout, F., Hertin, J.: De-materialising and re-materialising: digital technologies and the environment. Futures **36**(8), 903–920 (2004). https://doi.org/10.1016/j.futures.2004.01.003
15. Papanderou, M., Kor, A., Pattinson, C.: Evaluation of ICT environmental impact for an SME. In: Proceedings of the IEEE 14th International Conference on Dependable, Autonomic and Secure Computing, pp. 245–250 (2016)
16. Bonvoisin, J., Lelah, A., Mathieux, F.: An integrated method for environmental assessment and ecodesign of ICT-based optimization services. J. Clean. Prod. **68**, 144–154 (2014)
17. Pialot, O., Millet, D., Bisiaux, J.: "Upgradable PSS": clarifying a new concept of sustainable consumption/production based on upgradablility. J. Cleaner Prod. **141**, 538–550 (2017). https://doi.org/10.1016/j.jclepro.2016.08.161
18. Khan, M.A., Mittal, S., West, S., Wuest, T.: Review on upgradability – a product lifetime extension strategy in the context of product service systems. J. Cleaner Prod. **204**, 1154–1168 (2018). https://doi.org/10.1016/j.jclepro.2018.08.329

Subscription Business Models in the Manufacturing Field: Evidence from a Case Study

Veronica Arioli$^{(\boxtimes)}$ ⓘ, Roberto Sala ⓘ, Fabiana Pirola ⓘ, and Giuditta Pezzotta ⓘ

Department of Management, Information and Production Engineering, University of Bergamo, Viale Marconi, 5, 24044 Dalmine, BG, Italy
veronica.arioli@unibg.it

Abstract. Manufacturing companies operate in global environments where competition is increasingly aggressive. To remain competitive, they need to differentiate themselves by updating and expanding their offerings to customers, for instance through the digitalization and servitization phenomena, which allow companies to innovate business models in this direction. This paper deals with an analysis of the subscription business model, which has recently attracted the attention of manufacturing companies for the possibility to establish long-term partnerships with customers by providing services on a continuous basis in return of recurring payments. After a first analysis of the literature on this topic, the effective implementation of the subscription model in the manufacturing environment is analyzed through a case study. The analysis shows that the development of subscription models is strengthened by the utilization of digital tools since they enable processing customers' data for new service offering generation, leading companies to differentiate their business towards customer-centric solutions. In conjunction, the case study shows how barriers to the implementation of subscription models in the manufacturing sector are still present. Despite this, the Covid-19 pandemic has highlighted the potential of this offer, allowing companies to stay in touch with their customers, and to maintain, or even increase, the revenue streams.

Keywords: Subscription business models · Digitalization · Servitization · Covid-19 pandemic

1 Introduction

In the last years, companies in the manufacturing sector had faced an increasing competition which had negatively impacted their profits [1]. This competition had brought companies to constantly find new business models to adapt to different scenarios since it became clear that the traditional business models, based on transactional product sales, were no longer efficient [2]. The servitization phenomena helped companies in this direction, shifting the attention from products to services to generate new revenue streams and value for all the stakeholders. Moreover, the digitalization phenomena pointed out

© IFIP International Federation for Information Processing 2022
Published by Springer Nature Switzerland AG 2022
D. Y. Kim et al. (Eds.): APMS 2022, IFIP AICT 664, pp. 359–366, 2022.
https://doi.org/10.1007/978-3-031-16411-8_42

the potential of technologies to expand businesses towards new service solutions [2]. Despite this, for manufacturing companies, it has been difficult to adequately leverage the benefits of digitalization and servitization in providing new business models' solutions able to create added value to the entire supply chain [2]. In 2020, the Covid-19 pandemic hit hard all areas of the economy and society, dictating unprecedented new challenges [3, 4]. Sectors such as education, telemedicine, delivery of goods, have faced strong issues due to the pandemic, and they found in online platforms the solution to take one the new challenges [5]. In such a situation, where social distancing became a necessity, digitalization and adoption of Industry 4.0 technologies have seen exponential growth [5, 6], and similarly the development of new services accelerated [7]. Thus, the added value brought by these phenomena has finally emerged.

Nowadays, business model innovations can create stronger differentiation than product and process in the manufacturing industry [1]. In this context, subscription business model, that aims at exploiting the added value of services provided on the basis of customers' requests, for which they pay periodically [8], has been very successful in many industries and has begun to attract the attention of manufacturing companies.

In this context, the objective of this paper is to describe the state-of-the-art of subscription business models in the manufacturing sector to identify the main requirements for their implementation. Following, the application of a subscription model in a company is analyzed. The paper is structured as follow: Sect. 2 explains the methodology adopted to investigate the topic. Section 3 is focused on the literature review. Section 4 deals with the development of a subscription model in a company while Sect. 4.3 shows the results achieved. Eventually, Sect. 5 concludes the paper, also delineating future research directions.

2 Methodology

The methodology adopted in this study was split in two consecutive phases. Firstly, a literature review was conducted to define the state-of-the-art on the subscription models and identify the gaps. In particular, it was deemed appropriate to describe the context that led to their development. To run the search, SCOPUS has been utilized as research database. Keywords such as "Subscription business model", "business model", "servitization and digitalization", "customer-centricity", "remote assistance", and the related synonyms, were exploited to construct the queries, along with the operators "AND" and "OR". The obtained initial pool of articles has been filtered by reading the titles and the abstracts in order to eliminate all the papers not properly related to the topic of interest. Moreover, a final snowballing procedure identified other papers which have been added to the final pool. Table 1 shows the procedure that led to the identification of the pool of papers object of the analysis.

Then, to concretely understand the added value of subscription models, and the challenges of their implementation, a case study in the manufacturing sector has been explored. Participatory observation in company Alpha that was implementing a new remote assistance service and started to deliver it through different options of subscription business model (usage-based, tiered, and unlimited, according to [9]) has been employed to build the case study. The authors utilized interviews among the customer service department to collect data about the needs, and analysis of historical data about the service intervention, in order to, firstly, understand the as-is situation, followed by the definition of commercial proposal and the development of the supporting tools for the new service.

Table 1. Papers' numbers and filters.

	n. of documents
Initial pool	637
Title filtering	219 (−418)
Abstract filtering	88 (−131)
Content review	41 (−47)
Duplicate removal	36 (−5)
Snowballing	(+4)
Final set of papers	40

3 Literature Review

From the analysis of the literature, it clearly emerges that servitization and digitalization are increasing fields of discussion and research. The two phenomena are extremely interconnected and complementary [10]: on the one hand, digital technologies enable to structure new services, configuring themselves as the means to offer the service; on the other hand, they intrinsically provide functions and added values that can only reach the customer thanks to the services and, therefore, from this point of view, it is the service that acts as the means to make digital travel.

The predominant business models in the manufacturing sector are based on the sale of products and after-sales services [11]. The customers' requests, which are continuously changing, have brought to identify new ways to capture the values of products and services, through new business models which fully exploit the added value of services [12]. The industry mentality is shifting from models characterized by a "product centricity", where the product is the main revenue proposition, to ones where the business is oriented to customer satisfaction, namely "customer centric" models [13]. Industry 4.0 has helped in this innovation process of business models, since it allows information about the customers to be extracted from data analysis [1]. This is confirmed by authors such as [14] and [15], which show that the evolution of business models in the manufacturing field is oriented to offering digital solutions. In particular, with plant automation and interconnection, a positive impact could be achieved on both the technical, managerial, and communication aspects of the intervention [16]. However, companies do not necessarily need to use the most innovative smart technologies to be successful, but it is crucial to identify which digital features are right for them, allowing for improved customer engagement [7].

In this context, new forms of business models have been developed with the common purpose of recovering from the decline of "physical" sales, by shifting to services as sources of new profits [17]. Among these, Product-Service Systems are widely investigated in the manufacturing context, being new form of service-oriented business models [18]. More recently, a new method of business that focuses on access rather than ownership, has undergo an increasing trend within industries, the so-called Subscription business model. Despite this, today this is under investigated and, thus, it represents an interesting research field. The origin of the subscription models belongs to the XVI century, but they started to attract businesses only in the early 2000s with the development of streaming services such as Netflix and Spotify [19]. After their launch, other companies became interested in these business models, and the recent emerging popularity of subscription business models also drove the manufacturing sector to become interested. Different authors have studied the subscription business models in the manufacturing sector, providing the definition [8, 14, 20]. They agree when listing the main characteristics of a subscription business model, which can be summarized as follow: (i) the ability of meeting customers' needs and establishing long-term relationships with them; (ii) the ability of tailoring company offerings to current needs and predicting future ones, through the information on customers captured from the continuous analysis of the flow of data generated by subscriptions; (iii) greater financial predictability, and consequently, greater expenditures' flexibility for both the firm and the customer; (iv) the importance of digital technologies.

Subscription business models are widely used in other industries; concerning this, [21] revealed that following the outbreak of the Covid-19 pandemic, the subscription rate for services, in the delivery, gym, TV & film, and music industries, increased considerably. Nevertheless, their implementation in the manufacturing context faces different challenges. Firstly, the changing nature of customer requests which are difficult to be perceived in advance without recurring to data analysis, which forces the providers to continuously innovate the business model, and, mainly, the lack of references for introducing supporting tools enabling the new business solution at the operational level [20]. As highlighted by [1], mutual dependencies between the provider's business model, its organization and customers exist, but no management model is able to illustrate the complexity of these interdependencies in subscription models. However, as studied by [8], one of the most promising fields of application of subscription business models in manufacturing is related to maintenance activities.

4   Case Study

Company Alpha is an Italian manufacturing company that produces balancing machines, process control systems for machine tools and process monitoring systems for diagnostics. In recent years, the customer service of Alpha has assumed greater importance inside the company thanks to the servitization process that Alpha is undergoing, leading the company to consider the adoption of subscription models for the remote assistance service. The implementation of this subscription-based service has been analysed to gather the main characteristics and barriers highlighted by the literature on subscription models in the industrial field.

4.1 "Help Desk 24/7"

The transition from the traditional on-site assistance and maintenance services towards the remote assistance was trigged by the internal analysis within Service department of Alpha which showed that most of the problems were solved by telephone support. Thus, the company started considering the introduction of a new helpdesk service. Although the advantages of remote assistance were evident (i.e., reduced physical interventions, and reduced time of interventions given the possibility to avoid travels), multiple barriers for its implementation have been identified: (i) internal, due to the lack of resources and the absence of a revenue model for the remote service; (ii) external, due to the customers that did not recognize the necessity of the 24/7 assistance to justify an additional economic expenditure. The Covid-19 pandemic forced to overcome these barriers and both the company and its customers started recognizing the value of the remote assistance. Therefore, Alpha understood that the time was right for the implementation of the new remote assistance "Help Desk 24/7". Consequently, it invested in digitalization and innovated the business offer through the provision of subscription-based services to overcome the crisis.

The new Help Desk service aims to provide remote service support on company Alpha's equipment to all customers through dedicated service contracts in line with customer needs. This new service, which came into effect on September 1st, 2021, provided three types of remote assistance subscription contracts from the customers who could choose the one that best suits their needs, namely:

- Help Desk Time (HDT), a usage-based subscription model [9] where the support service is based on hourly billing (50 €/half an hour);
- Help Desk Limited (HDL), a tiered subscription associated with the serial number of the machines, that allows to use a fixed number of hours (20 h/machine) in a year for which the hourly billing can decrease based on the number of installed machines (from 500 € to 350 €/machine);
- Help Desk Open (HDO), an unlimited type of subscription associated with the customer, that allows to use the scheduled hours (20 h) on all the owned machines (1750 €/customer).

In all cases, only remotely managed interventions with a positive and out of warranty result were invoiced. The expected results were that customers owing higher number of machines started to subscribe for remote assistance, especially to HDO contracts, thus contributing to establish long-term relationships with customers and obtaining fixed additional incomes increasing the service company's profit.

4.2 Redesigned Process Flow

To comply with the main challenge related to the introduction of subscription models, which, as suggested by the literature, consists of the lack of management model supporting the transformation towards subscription-based services, lots of efforts have been employed to find the adequate way of managing the new remote assistance within the

Service department. It was necessary to create a computerized structure for the registration of service tickets, the selection of those to be invoiced, and the reporting of active subscriptions. Moreover, to have a general overview of the results achieved and analysed the performance of the Help Desk service, internal KPIs were selected and computed from the tickets database. The collection and analysis of data allows for a wider understanding of the customer requests, which is fundamental for adapting firm's business proposal to the actual needs and, also, predict the future ones.

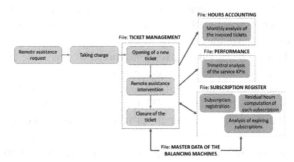

Fig. 1. Logical flow of the new service and the documents of interest. "Ticket management" contains the information about the remote assistance that are necessary to fill all the other files. It dialogues bidirectionally with "Subscription register" to verify the contracts and the residual hours. The master data of the balancing machines allows the automation of the two worksheets.

In Fig. 1 is represented the logical flow from the customer first contact to the opening and closure of the ticket for assistance, and all the documents of interest. Documentation for managing the service was made available in a shared folder on Google Drive, which allows technicians to work simultaneously and avoid additional capital expenditure for the company.

4.3 Results and Discussion

Following the case study presented in Sect. 4, the first results from the data analysis of the Help Desk Service of company Alpha are summarized in Fig. 2. The charts cover the period from the moment the Helpdesk 24/7 was launched, that is on 01/09/2021, to 01/12/2021. As shown in Fig. 2(a), a high percentage of remote interventions have a positive result, meaning the technicians have been successful in the remote assistance. The average time for the remote assistance has resulted to vary with respect to the different types of requests, Fig. 2(b). This information is helpful for the service department to identify the main issues, the average resolution time and, thus, the areas of future improvements to suit customers' requests. Figure 2(c) shows the distribution among types of customers, and these results are not surprising since the HDO subscription has been specifically designed for customers with a higher number of machines requiring assistance at global level and not just to solve issues of a fixed number of machines (for that the HDL is more appropriate). Thus, as emerged form literature, the predominant feature of this business model emerged, namely, the ability of customizing the offerings to best suit specific client requests.

Despite the literature does not provide a reference model for the management of subscription models in industry, company Alpha has demonstrated that there is no need for expensive investment in facilities to adopt this model, but more of an investment in digital tools, remarking their key role in the definition of subscription models. The company plans to redesign the business management system, because the proper management of data is vital, especially for these new business models. However, only around 3% of the machines in the registry resulted associated with a subscription contract when the results were collected, reflecting the external barrier related to the customers' perceived value which still exists. Therefore, marketing campaigns should be intensified to spread the potential of the new service among customers.

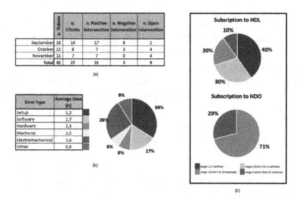

Fig. 2. Help Desk 24/7 implementation's results.

5 Conclusion

Subscription business models are becoming increasingly important in the manufacturing sector. More generally, it is possible to assess that the global pandemic of Covid-19 has triggered a series of innovations aimed at renewing business models in the perspective of servitization and digitalization, from which subscription-based business models can also benefit. The use of digital tools allows to better collect and process data that become essential for a company to generate new service solutions structured on the basis of the customer needs. From both the literature and the case study, service customization appears to be a key feature: specifically, standard subscriptions should be provided and then tailored to specific customer needs. Further knowledge about these service solutions should be shared by researchers, as well successful case studied to help companies aiming to implement a subscription model for differentiating their businesses.

References

1. Schuhs, G., Gützlaff, A., Cremer, S., Lammersmann, J., Liu, Y.: Business model and organization – interdependencies for customer-centric continuous innovation in subscription business. In: 2020 IEEE International Conference on Industrial Engineering and Engineering Management, pp. 260–264 (2020)

2. Chen, Y., Visnjic, I., Parida, V., Zhang, Z.: On the road to digital servitization – the (dis)continuous interplay between business model and digital technology. Int. J. Oper. Prod. Manag. **41**(5), 694–722 (2021)
3. Ivanov, D.: Viable supply chain model: integrating agility, resilience and sustainability perspectives - lessons from and thinking beyond the COVID-19 pandemic. Ann. Oper. Res. (2020)
4. Nicola, M., et al.: The socio-economic implications of the coronavirus pandemic (COVID-19): a review. Int. J. Surg. **78**, 185–193 (2020)
5. Jiang, X.: Digital economy in the post-pandemic era. J. Chin. Econ. Bus. Stud. **18**(4), 333–339 (2020)
6. Narayanamurthy, G., Tortorella, G.: Impact of COVID-19 outbreak on employee performance – moderating role of Industry 4.0 base technologies. Int. J. Prod. Econ. **234**, 108075 (2021)
7. Pezzotta, G., Saccani, N., Adrodegari, F., Rapaccini, M.: Digital servitization and smart services for the new normal. In: Dolgui, A., Bernard, A., Lemoine, D., von Cieminski, G., Romero, D. (eds.) APMS 2021. IAICT, vol. 631, pp. 192–201. Springer, Cham (2021). https://doi.org/10.1007/978-3-030-85902-2_21
8. Liu, Y., Gützlaff, A., Cremer, S., Grbev, T., Schuh, G.: Design of tailored subscription business models – a guide for machinery and equipment manufacturers. In: Behrens, B.-A., Brosius, A., Hintze, W., Ihlenfeldt, S., Wulfsberg, J.J. (eds.) WGP 2020. LNPE, pp. 717–727. Springer, Heidelberg (2021). https://doi.org/10.1007/978-3-662-62138-7_72
9. Suhr Hansen, M.: How to build a subscription business: 29 steps to subscription mastery (2014)
10. Kohtamäki, M., Rabetino, R., Einola, S., Parida, V., Patel, P.: Unfolding the digital servitization path from products to product-service-software systems: practicing change through intentional narratives. J. Bus. Res. **137**, 379–392 (2021)
11. Schuh, G., Frank, J., Jussen, P., Rix, C., Harland, T.: Monetizing Industry 4.0: design principles for subscription business in the manufacturing industry. In: 2019 IEEE International Conference on Engineering, Technology and Innovation, pp. 1–9 (2019)
12. Adrodegari, F., Pashou, T., Saccani, N.: Business model innovation: process and tools for service transformation of industrial firms. Proc. CIRP **64**, 103–108 (2017)
13. Aiyer, M., Panigrahi, J., Das, B.: Successful customer relationship management in business process integration and development of applications for project management. Int. J. Mech. Eng. Technol. **9**, 637–643 (2018)
14. Schuh, G., Wenger, L., Stich, V., Hicking, J., Gailus, J.: Outcome economy: subscription business models in machinery and plant engineering. Proc. CIRP **93**, 599–604 (2020)
15. Gebauer, H., et al.: How to convert digital offerings into revenue enhancement – conceptualizing business model dynamics through explorative case studies. Ind. Mark. Manag. **91**, 429–441 (2020)
16. Płaza, M., Pawlik, Ł.: Influence of the contact center systems development on key performance indicators. IEEE Access **9**, 44580–44591 (2021)
17. Monden, Y.: Risk spreading between the diversified subscription businesses and the existing business: focusing on the case of apple. Manag. Control Syst. Strat. Changes **17**, 1–18 (2020)
18. Tukker, A.: Eight types of product-service system: eight ways to sustainability? Experiences from susprone. Bus. Strategy Environ. **13**(4), 246–260 (2004)
19. Rudolph, T., Bischof, S., Boettger, T., Weiler, N.: Disruption at the door: a taxonomy on subscription models in retailing. Mark. Rev. St Gallen **34**, 18–25 (2017)
20. Riesener, M., Doelle, C., Ebi, M., Perau, S.: Methodology for the implementation of subscription models in machinery and plant engineering. Proc. CIRP **90**, 730–735 (2020)
21. Fosker, N., Cheung, B.: Pricing and proposition testing in subscription economies. Appl. Mark. Anal. **6**(3), 211–220 (2021)

Design and Engineer Data-Driven Product Service System: A Methodology Update

Fabiana Pirola$^{(\boxtimes)}$ (iD), Giuditta Pezzotta(iD), Veronica Arioli(iD), and Roberto Sala(iD)

Department of Management, Information and Production Engineering, University of Bergamo, Viale Marconi, 5, 24044 Dalmine, BG, Italy
fabiana.pirola@unibg.it

Abstract. Digitalization, sustainability, and servitization are transforming economy and society globally. Companies are increasingly changing their business model toward providing a data-driven Product Service System (PSS), namely bundles of products and services integrated with some digital technology. Different methods and tools have been proposed to design PSS and, more recently, smart PSS, but they still mainly focus on value propositions and do not address which kind of data can be collected from the operational stage. To overcome this gap, this paper proposes the Data-driven Service Engineering Methodology (D-SEEM) for the design and engineering of data-driven PSS, considering the tradeoff between customer satisfaction and internal efficiency and focusing on data and information. A case study in the professional appliances industry is then proposed to show the application of a part of the methodology in a real context.

Keywords: Data-driven product-service system · Data-driven PSS design and engineering · Operational data · Sustainability

1 Introduction and Literature Background

Nowadays, sustainability and digitalization are transforming economy and society at global level. Among the others, Internet of Things (IoT) and machine learning are the key components of industry transformation since they allow to collect and analyze large amounts of data retrieved from industrial assets to make processes more efficient and sustainable [1]. In this context, servitization (i.e., the phenomena leading manufacturing companies to offer services on top of physical products to cope with customers' requirements) is dramatically affected by digitalization, and more and more companies are leveraging on the opportunities offered by digital technologies changing their business model towards the provision of *data-driven Product Service System* (PSS), namely bundles of products and services integrated with some digital technology [2]. In particular, companies are increasingly developing services on top of IoT platforms (i.e., digital environments serving as an interface between the IoT devices and the users [3]) since IoT allows real-time monitoring of assets performance enabling data-driven decision-making related to asset management [4]. Furthermore, providing services, such

© IFIP International Federation for Information Processing 2022
Published by Springer Nature Switzerland AG 2022
D. Y. Kim et al. (Eds.): APMS 2022, IFIP AICT 664, pp. 367–375, 2022.
https://doi.org/10.1007/978-3-031-16411-8_43

as maintenance, repair, and remanufacturing, allows providers to reduce the environmental impacts and increase attractiveness and customer satisfaction [5]. Different methods and tools have been proposed to design PSS and smart PSS [2, 6, 7]. However, they still mainly focus on defining value propositions fulfilling customer needs, and do not address which kinds of data are needed and can be collected from the operational stage to make proper decisions enabling the new service offering [8]. Thus, new tools and approaches are required to design and engineer solutions that integrate digitalization and PSSs, using the sustainable dimension [9] and considering the data and information needed to provide PSSs. This paper goes in this direction and aims at integrating the SErvice Engineering Methodology (SEEM) developed by [10] to cover the design and engineering of data-driven PSS, with a focus on data and information. A case study in the professional appliances industry is then proposed to show the application of a part of the methodology in a real context. The SEEM has been selected since it has a double focus on customer satisfaction and internal company efficiency.

The paper is structured as follows: Sect. 2 describes the Data-driven SErvice Engineering Methodology (D-SEEM). Section 3 presents the case study while Sect. 4 provides conclusions and future development of the study.

2   Data-Driven SErvice Engineering Methodology (D-SEEM)

Considering PSS design methodologies available in literature, the SErvice Engineering Methodology (SEEM) [10, 11] does not address only customer needs, but try to balance the value perceived by customers with internal process efficiency. In doing so, the SEEM framework proposes 4 phases and related methods. The main drawback of such a methodology is that it does not specifically focus on data-driven PSS. The methodology has been updated to overcome this gap by integrating some steps (i.e., steps 2 and 4) more focused on data-driven services. The Data-driven SEEM (D-SEEM) shown in Fig. 1 is divided into four stages:

1. *Definition of PSS solution and related functionalities:* as in the original SEEM, the starting point of PSS (re)-engineering process is the customer, its behaviors and needs, and the critical analysis of the actual company service portfolio. Starting from the customer needs, the company should generate different PSS solutions and select the one (s) to be added to the value proposition. The main outcome of this phase is the PSS solution to be detailed and its main functionalities.
2. *Identification of data and information needed to enable the data-driven PSS provision:* since the methodology deals with data-driven service, an essential point of the methodology is related to the definition of data needed to provide the selected PSS solution and the information supporting the decision making and the service provision.
3. *Design and validation of internal and external PSS related processes:* as in the original SEEM, this phase is related to the (re)design and validation of the service provision processes, comprising both the external processes (towards the customers) and the internal processes (i.e., any processes affected by the new data and information available). The objective of this phase is to look for a tradeoff between the customer needs fulfillment and company efficiency.

4. *Creation and validation of the PSS proof of concept and the related infrastructure:* this phase deals with creating a proof of concept of the offer (e.g., dashboards of an IoT platform).

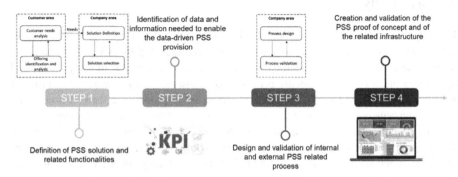

Fig. 1. Data-driven Service Engineering Methodology (D-SEEM)

For each phase, methods and tools are suggested to achieve the objectives proposed. In Step 1 the Persona Model (PM) is proposed to collect and present information about customers and define the needs used as the starting point of the Product Service Concept Tree (PSCT). This method, based on design thinking and functional design principles, aims to define possible PSS solutions to be provided to fulfill customers' needs and the related provider's resources. These solutions must then be assessed considering costs and benefits, and the one(s) to be engineered must be selected and the main functionalities defined. This solution and its functionalities are the input of the following step 2. The main data needed to provide the PSS must be defined in this step. For this purpose, classical methods from asset management manufacturing operations theories can be exploited. For example, in case of a solution dealing with the provision of condition-based and/or predictive maintenance, the Failure Mode, Effects, and Criticality Analysis (FMECA) [12] can be adopted to select the asset components to monitor and the data needed to implement status recognition and predictive algorithms. Indeed, FMECA allows to prioritize asset components based on frequency, criticality, and editability of failures and only the most critical components will be object of a condition-based and/or predictive maintenance policy. Once the PSS solution and the data and information needed to provide it are defined, the related internal process are (re)-designed. The method proposed to describe the service delivery process is BPMN2.0. Focus of the modeling activities are not only the processes towards the customers, but also the internal process that may be affected and improved by the PSS solution and the new information available. For example, if the solution is related to asset monitoring and predictive maintenance, the data retrieved by the field related to asset performance may be a relevant source of information to improve product design. This phase deals also with the validation of the process, and then the assessment of performance of alternative service provision processes, as well as the identification of the most suitable process and its best resource configuration. This phase can be performed leveraging on process simulation. The last step deals with creating a proof of concept of the selected solution, both in terms of data-driven services, the needed infrastructure to enable them and the final provision process.

3   Case Study

In this paper, a case study methodology has been applied to illustrate new and innovative practices that organizations are adopting, as suggested by [13]. The case study focuses on a medium Italian company (Alpha hereafter) working in the professional appliances industry and producing professional dishwashers and fryers. The company has always been strongly product-oriented and sells the products to the end users (e.g., bars, restaurants located all over the world) through distributors. These distributors provide after-sales assistance to the end users, but only corrective maintenance is in place. The main criticalities of the market are the following: i) Alpha company usually does not get in touch with the end users, and it does not even have visibility on the installed base; ii) the product is considered critical by end users, but they are not prone to invest in technology, iii) most of the distributors are micro-small companies (until 10 employees), well organized and recognizing the advantages coming from technology; iv) distributors usually have a high workload, tight timelines for interventions, limited competence on the product since they are multi-brands and have no time to follow training; v) in case of difficulties in problem diagnosis and resolution, or case of products under warranty, the distributors contact company Alpha asking for immediate support. Starting from these assumptions, Alpha, leveraging on digitalization and the increased connectivity available, is willing to move towards the provision of a data-driven PSS to better support the distributor during maintenance provision, increase final user loyalty and satisfaction, and gain more knowledge on the installed base. For this purpose, the company implemented the above-reported methodology. Hereafter, the implementation of the first three steps is described.

3.1   Definition of PSS Solution Functionalities

The starting point is the analysis of the customers and the definition of their needs. To this purpose, the customer identified is the distributor and its Persona Model has been developed thanks to interviews with the marketing & sales, and service managers (Fig. 2). Summarizing, while the distributor characteristics are summarized above, its needs have been defined as follows: enhance service interventions; know in advance the spare parts/products delivery times to inform end users; have good product knowledge for end user pre-sale support.

To identify possible PSS solutions the Product-Service Concept tree (PSCT) has been developed in a brainstorming session with the marketing & sales manager, the service manager, and the product designer. The PSCT (summarized in Table 1) is divided into 4 levels:

- *Needs* (N): main needs of the customers identified in the Persona Model;
- *Wishes* (W): how customers' wish to satisfy their needs;

Fig. 2. Persona Model of the distributor

- *Solutions* (S): possible PSS solutions (product, services or a bundle of them) that the company can identify to fulfil customers' wishes and needs;
- *Resources* (R): the main human/software resources and/or products to implement the solution.

Since the main issue related to the relationship with the distributors lies in the difficulty of managing maintenance and repair interventions, the company decided to focus on enhancing distributors' interventions by giving them a solution that would allow the rapid identification of faults, even in case they are not trained. Thus, after an internal and qualitative cost & benefits analysis of the PSS solutions identified, the company decided to focus on supporting distributors while delivering maintenance through a platform able to provide the following functionalities (derived from the solutions defined in the PSCT):

- Health status remote monitoring of the dishwashers connected through IoT, which allows to geolocalize the product and provide alerts when the health status of one of the components is deteriorating, suggesting the need for an intervention;
- Manual collection of data related to products identification and problem diagnosis;
- Guided diagnostic procedure: following a checklist, the distributor will be able to identify possible causes of the failure;
- Easy and fast retrieval of technical information related to the dishwasher.

This PSS solution is a data-driven solution since it is based on digital technologies (i.e., digital platform fed with data coming from the connected products, from distributors interventions and with applications supporting interventions).

Table 1. PSCT element description

PSCT element	Description
Needs	The main need of the distributor is: "enhance service interventions"
Whishes	To meet this need, four areas of intervention have been outlined: i) better planning of interventions; (ii) clear knowledge of the product; (iii) reduction of intervention time; (iv) clear and accessible service support
Solutions	Definition of a preventive maintenance contract to offer to end users; Creation of a system with alerts when preventive maintenance must be performed; Remote monitoring system with a guided diagnostic procedure, which allows to geolocalize the interventions and classifies them according to the severity of the alerts; Data collection system that is manually entered and stored with a guided diagnostic procedure; List of authorized installers; Easy visual instructions/manuals, via APP or PDF, of the product specifications, able to guide the interventions; Online system for spare parts and products purchase; Internal ticketing system for assistance, exploitable also for internal analysis of needs
Resources	Platform that allows both remote and manual data collection and that guides the diagnosis procedure; Company website with the list of authorized dealers and visual instructions; E-commerce platform with products and spare parts, simple and connected to the site; Internal ticketing system for collecting service information

3.2 Definition Data and Information Needed to Provide the PSS

Since the selected solution entails the remote monitoring of products through IoT for preventive maintenance purposes, it becomes relevant to understand the most critical components and the data needed to monitor the health status. Through interviews with the service manager and the product designer, a FMECA has been performed referring to a "standard model" of dishwasher representative of several models. This choice has been mainly supported by the structural, technological, and functional similarities that the models, although different, demonstrate. The FMECA is a reliability analysis at a different level of the decomposition of the product, and consists in the determination of modes, causes and effects of failures, to appropriately evaluate the criticality of the entity under analysis. The FMECA analysis carried (see an excerpt in Fig. 3), followed this procedure:

1. Functional breakdown of the product adopting a hierarchical-functional criterium that allowed to define 4 levels (group, system, equipment, sub-equipment);
2. Definition of criticality drivers to calculate the Risk Priority Number (RPN), that is the product of three drivers:

a. *Probability (P)* of occurrence of the failure.
b. *Severity (S)* of the failure. Two areas of severity have been identified, one related to the severity of the failure (i.e., the impact of the failure on the functioning of the machine) and the other associated with the repairability of the fault or the substitutability of the part. When calculating the RPN, it was decided to consider, for each mode of failure, the driver with the highest score.
c. *Detectability (D)* of the failure.

Four levels have been defined for each driver, from 1-low to 4–very high.
3. Analysis of modes, causes and effects of failures and calculation of RPN.

	Mode of failure	Cause of failure	Effect of failure	P	S1	S2	D	RPN
Group: Hydraulic part								
System: Rinsing circuit								
Equipment: Load solenoid valve	Clogs	Mains water is not clean (rare); Water goes back from the tub	Does not charge water or the flow rate is reduced	2	2	2	3	12
Equipment: Boiler Group								
Sub- equipment: Boiler resistors	Burn	The resistor loses insulation because it remains uncovered or because it is isolated	The machine does not start - The possibility of segregation of the resistance is activated	4	4	3	2	32

Fig. 3. Excerpt of the FMECA analysis of the dishwasher

After calculating the RPN indices for the different failure modes, several analyses were conducted to identify the most critical modes and causes. The FMECA shows that the most critical components are related to electronics, rinsing circuits, and opening systems. Furthermore, a deeper analysis showed that 8 out of 55 failure modes detected (or 14%) cover 50% of the criticality associated with the product. Based on these results, the following activity has identified improvement actions at the level of sensors installed (or installable) on the product. In particular, the focus was on the failure modes with higher criticality, especially in terms of detectability (that is the factor that mostly benefits from the introduction of new sensors on the machines). Thus, the analysis focuses on identifying elements and sensors contributing to the measurement of variables representing the health status of the machine. The analysis shows the need for sensors to detect door closing status and water leaks and measure water temperature, water level, and resistors power absorption.

3.3 Internal and External Process Design and Validation

The third step is the (re)design of service provision processes, referring to how the new solutions are delivered to customers and how the internal activities and decision-making will change given the information available by the PSS solution. For this purpose an analysis of actual criticalities through BPMN 2.0 has been performed through interviews with service manager and direct observation of service employees. The analysis showed the main criticalities (divided into internal and external) of actual processes and how the identified solution can help overcome them (Table 2).

Table 2. Analysis of actual process criticalities and definition of the improvements

Type	Criticality description	Improvement
Internal	Manual internal priority call management	The platform will provide an index of severity of the failure and a priority for the customer
Internal	No unique way to contact the service, but it can be reached by mobile phone or through the switchboard	The platform will be the main way to reach the service
Internal	The service department manually fills an excel file with customer and intervention details	The customers will fill in the needed information on the platform allowing the company service to save time
External	No support for the distributor and the internal service department to carry out fault analysis	The platform will have a guided checklist based on the FMECA analysis
External	Technical information on machines not easy to retrieve from the website or manuals	The platform will integrate a document management system to help distributors retrieve the information needed
External	The distributors do not have information about the return status	The platform will allow tracing the order status of the distributor, both related to spare parts and items returned

4 Conclusion

From a theoretical point of view, this paper, proposing the Data-driven Service Engineering Methodology (D-SEEM), aims at filling the gap in literature, namely the lack of methods and tools to design and engineer data-driven PSS balancing external and internal performance and specifically addressing the selection of data and information needed in the operational stage. Indeed, the proposed methodology has a strong focus on the definition of data, information and operational processes needed to deliver the selected solution. To demonstrate its applicability in industrial context, a case study in the professional appliances industry is proposed to show the application of the first three steps of the methodology in a real context. The case study demonstrates that the D-SEEM allows to achieve satisfactory results also with SMEs and could be applied in any sector since the steps and methods can be customized for different context. Further improvements are needed to improve the selection of PSS solutions in the first step and a complete implementation in more sectors and companies is required to validate it.

References

1. Watanabe, K., Okuma, T., Takenaka, T.: Evolutionary design framework for Smart PSS: service engineering approach. Adv. Eng. Inform. **45**, 101119 (2020)
2. Rapaccini, M., Adrodegari, F.: Conceptualizing customer value in data-driven services and smart PSS. Comput. Ind. **137**, 103607 (2022)

3. Asemani, M., Abdollahei, F., Jabbari, F.: Understanding IoT platforms: towards a comprehensive definition and main characteristic description. In: 2019 5th International Conference on Web Research (ICWR), pp. 172–177 (2019)
4. Syafrudin, M., Alfian, G., Fitriyani, N.L., Rhee, J.: Performance analysis of IoT-based sensor, big data processing, and machine learning model for real-time monitoring system in automotive manufacturing. Sensors **18**, 2946 (2018)
5. Sakao, T.T.: Increasing value capture by enhancing manufacturer commitment: Part 1 - designing a value co-creation system. IEEE Eng. Manag. Rev. **50**, 79–87 (2022)
6. Bu, L., Chen, C.-H., Ng, K.K.H., Zheng, P., Dong, G., Liu, H.: A user-centric design approach for smart product-service systems using virtual reality: a case study. J. Clean. Prod. **280**, 124413 (2021)
7. Ebel, M., Jaspert, D., Poeppelbuss, J.: Smart already at design time – pattern-based smart service innovation in manufacturing. Comput. Ind. **138**, 103625 (2022)
8. Machchhar, R.J., Toller, C.N.K., Bertoni, A., Bertoni, M.: Data-driven value creation in Smart Product-Service System design: state-of-the-art and research directions. Comput.
9. Lugnet, J., Ericson, Å., Larsson, T.: Design of product–service systems: toward an updated discourse. Systems **8**, 45 (2020)
10. Pezzotta, G., Pirola, F., Rondini, A., Pinto, R., Ouertani, M.-Z.: Towards a methodology to engineer industrial product-service system–evidence from power and automation industry. CIRP J. Manuf. Sci. Technol. **15**, 19–32 (2016)
11. Pirola, F., Pezzotta, G., Amlashi, D.M., Cavalieri, S.: Design and engineering of Product-Service Systems (PSS): TheSEEM methodology and modeling toolkit. In: Karagiannis, D., Lee, M., Hinkelmann, K., Utz, W. (eds.) Domain-Specific Conceptual Modeling: Concepts, Methods and ADOxx Tools, pp. 385–407. Springer, Cham (2022). https://doi.org/10.1007/978-3-030-93547-4_17
12. Carmignani, G.: An integrated structural framework to cost-based FMECA: the priority-cost FMECA. Reliab. Eng. Syst. Saf. **94**, 861–871 (2009)
13. Scapens, R.W.: Researching management accounting practice: the role of case study methods. Br. Account. Rev. **22**, 259–281 (1990)

Manufacturing Models and Practices for Eco-Efficient, Circular and Regenerative Industrial Systems

Thematic Research Framework for Eco-Efficient and Circular Industrial Systems

Mélanie Despeisse[1]([✉]) [iD], Federica Acerbi[2] [iD], Thorsten Wuest[3] [iD],
and David Romero[4] [iD]

[1] Chalmers University of Technology, Gothenburg, Sweden
melanie.despeisse@chalmers.se
[2] Politecnico di Milano, Milan, Italy
federica.acerbi@polimi.it
[3] West Virginia University, Morgantown, USA
thwuest@mail.wvu.edu
[4] Tecnológico de Monterrey, Mexico City, Mexico

Abstract. Global sustainability challenges are increasingly constraining and driving industrial development. Eco-efficiency and circular economy are powerful concepts providing guiding principles to achieve superior environmental performance. However, they are not systematically integrated into the design, planning, development, management and improvement of industrial systems, potentially resulting in increased environmental impacts and other unintended consequences. This paper presents a thematic research framework based on workshops with manufacturers and researchers in the field of production engineering and management. The framework aims to establish a stronger foundation to advance research and technological development for eco-efficient and circular industrial systems, embracing environmental sustainability as core operating principles.

Keywords: Circular economy · Eco-efficiency · Green manufacturing · Sustainable production · Research framework

1 Introduction

Addressing global and systemic environmental issues (e.g., climate change, accumulation or persistent pollutants, natural capital depletion) has been recognised as an imperative for decades to ensure a healthy future for our society and our planet. Industry is a key driver for sustainability transitions, especially since it has been a driving force for social and economic development, yet at a high environmental cost. Coordinated and systematic efforts are needed to accelerate actions if we are to mitigate and avoid the worst of the unintended consequences of industrial developments in the past centuries.

The United Nations created the Sustainable Development Goals (SDGs) in 2015 to establish an international agenda to assist such globally coordinated efforts. While the SDGs are high-level, many companies have translated them into ambitious strategic

D. Y. Kim et al. (Eds.): APMS 2022, IFIP AICT 664, pp. 379–389, 2022.
https://doi.org/10.1007/978-3-031-16411-8_44

goals and started to develop roadmaps to achieve them. Eco-efficiency and circular economy are powerful approaches to executing these strategies and roadmaps. Eco-efficiency is achieved "by the delivery of competitively priced goods and services that satisfy human needs and bring quality-of-life, while progressively reducing ecological impacts and resource intensity throughout the lifecycle to a level at least in line with the earth's estimated carrying capacity" [1]. Its guiding principles are: reduce material and energy intensity, reduce toxic dispersion (waste and pollution), enhance recyclability, maximise the sustainable use of renewable resources, extend product durability, and increase service intensity. These principles align with the circular economy principles as advocated by the Ellen MacArthur Foundation: eliminate waste and pollution, circulate products and materials at their highest value, and regenerate nature [2].

To support research in a more sustainable direction, the purpose of this paper is two-fold: (1) to provide priority areas and examples of research questions to advance production engineering and management research toward environmental sustainability; and (2) to propose a framework capturing different research themes to tackle environmental challenges meaningfully and realistically in industrial development.

2   Methods

A thematic analysis was used to identify common topics and patterns in production research towards eco-efficiency and circular industrial systems. The initial thematic research framework was developed based on a systematic review of the last ten years of research contributions from the International Federation for Information Processing Working Group 5.7 (IFIP WG5.7) on Advances in Production Management Systems (APMS) through its dedicated annual conference[1] [3]. Three workshops (see Table 1) were used to collect experts' inputs about research needs (challenges and opportunities) to transition to more eco-efficiency and circular industrial systems. The outputs from the workshops were analysed and clustered around similar research needs to create the initial priority areas. The thematic research framework was then iteratively refined by the authors and consolidated with research questions to reach a consensus about research priorities for more sustainable production systems.

Table 1. Workshop dates, topics, and number of participants.

Date	Workshop, No. of participants
29 April 2021	TRUST project[a], workshop on "Why is eco-efficiency so rare?", 21 participants from academia and industry
12 October 2021	Swedish Manufacturing R&D, Cluster on Production Management, workshop on "Sustainable production through eco-efficiency and circularity", 37 participants from academia and industry
23 March 2022	IFIP WG5.7, workshop for the Special Interest Group on Eco-efficient and Circular Industrial Systems, 20 participants from academia

[a]European project: Twinning foR indUstrial SustainabiliTy (TRUST)

---

[1] www.ifipwg57.org and www.apms-conference.org.

3 Results

This section summarises the results of the workshops with references to relevant work. For each priority area, we propose some research questions to guide future research and to track the impact of the research agenda on the community over time. The thematic framework is then presented to encourage researchers in the field of production research to (re)frame their contribution toward environmental sustainability.

3.1 Priority Areas and Research Questions

I. Redefining Success. Defining success metrics and strategic goals for organisations is a complex undertaking. This translates directly to the sustainability arena. When performance and success are defined with a narrow definition, it may limit the factors included in the design, planning, development, and management of manufacturing, service, and logistics operations. In the context of this thematic research framework, successful operations are considered *sustainable operations* [4] that follow eco-efficiency and circular principles. Moreover, the requirement to adopt a longer-time perspective can act as a barrier in many industries. Therefore, companies must deal with rebound effects [5] and the dilemma to balance short-term impact and long-term effectiveness [6] along their journey towards sustainable operations, accounting for the short-term successes that will make possible the long-term ones. Currently, decisions are often too short-sighted to deliver the desired sustainability benefits as they exceed the typical time horizon expected by some of the stakeholders (e.g., standard timeframe for return on investment). This requires a careful reframing of the purpose of industrial development to tackle environmental problems directly and prevent unintended consequences by design, and not as an afterthought (as predominantly done today); i.e., avoidance and direct reduction of detrimental impacts as part of industrial systems design (greenfield) and redesign (brownfield) requirements. If the technical and managerial solutions proposed do not contribute directly to sustainability, then we should question whether they are suitable options. If a "solution" creates more problems than it solves, then it should be redesigned or not be developed.

> *RQ1.1: What are the environmental sustainability implications of manufacturing, service, and logistics operations improvements in the short and long term for individual organisations and industry as a whole?*

> *RQ1.2: How can these environmental implications be measured and integrated into the definition of sustainable industrial performance and therefore success?*

II. Highlight Trade-Offs for Holistic, Evidence-Based Decisions. Beware of common sense and intuitive responses to *green options*. For example, circular and service-based solutions may only result in environmental benefits under specific conditions. Much of the data and evidence depends on the boundaries and characteristics of their providing system—a major hurdle in making scenarios truly comparable for objective decision making. The current gold standard is to adopt a holistic and lifecycle perspective as much as possible. For example, resource efficiency strategies are vulnerable to rebound effects when they lead to additional resource use via behavioural and systemic responses

[5]. If some negative impacts are unavoidable within current systems, they should be acknowledged and used as a learning opportunity to update the behavioural dynamics of the system modelled for future scenario simulations and assessments. These insights can help identify countermeasures to these unavoidable negative effects in the short term while developing options to eliminate them in the long term as the system moves towards a more sustainable state. Having the right measures and metrics available is the first step to making trade-offs visible, detecting and anticipating rebound effects, and understanding the underlying issues to solve present problems in the near future.

RQ2.1: What needs to be considered to enable holistic decision making from a lifecycle perspective for environmental sustainability?

RQ2.2: What are key variables to consider and appropriate simplifications to reduce complexity in decision-making processes for environmental sustainability?

III. Empowering People. For stakeholders, predominantly producers and consumers, to buy into the sustainability practices, they need to have sufficient control and the intrinsic motivation to do good. Given this assumption, understanding and putting sustainability principles into practice can better be achieved by empowering individuals throughout their organisation and personal life so their ideas can become actions. Hence, bottom-up initiatives can be more impactful than top-down approaches from the executive board. Achieving buy-in and the intrinsic desire to improve the current situation will avoid the 'it is not my job' attitude when it comes to proposing and promoting sustainable production and consumption practices and behaviours [7, 8]. While motivation and ideology may vary, (almost) everybody agrees that we need to conserve resources, avoid waste, and mitigate climate change. However, too few are ready and allowed to act within their current role (outside of their job description). To overcome this hurdle in the short term, creating incentives (e.g., gamify sustainable practices and behaviours) to involve all the stakeholders both internally and externally. This is particularly important for circular value chains in which producers, consumers; service providers (for maintenance, repair, remanufacturing, etc.) need to work together for product useful life extension and material recovery.

RQ3.1: What are the barriers preventing people from engaging directly (e.g., job description) and indirectly (e.g., motivation) in sustainable practices and behaviours?

RQ3.2: What are appropriate incentives to empower different stakeholders to transition towards environmentally sustainable practices and behaviours?

RQ3.3: How can employers and employees be actively involved in the transition towards environmentally sustainable operations?

IV. Continuous Improvement. A core aspect of industrial engineering is the continuous assessment and improvement of existing processes. Companies need to understand their current state and/or maturity, and the readiness level of their value chains when it comes to environmental sustainability, then identify what sustainability practices are already in place and why those were selected, e.g., lean, green, and circular manufacturing practices [9]. We should envision, design, and develop solutions building from where we are today through retrofits, upgrades, improvements, etc. Whenever possible, barriers to *change* should be removed or lowered significantly to increase buy-in from the stakeholders involved. Moreover, understanding that *change* takes time, it is important to create an environment to stimulate a learning curve and build momentum. No matter how small the incremental improvements are (short-term wins), they serve a purpose as long as they move us in the right direction (long-term gains). A roadmap and a strategic communication plan should inform stakeholders in an approachable way about the pathways and concrete benefits of continuous improvements towards sustainable operations at an individual organisation and value chain levels.

RQ4.1: How can manufacturing companies assess their current performance and identify potential for improvements towards environmental sustainability?

RQ4.2: What are the practices already in place to support environmentally sustainable activities? What improvements can be made to these practices/activities?

V. Disruptive Change. While continuous improvement is the dominant approach in most manufacturing environments, disruptive change can overcome hurdles that are tough to tackle in current systems. Regrouping and starting from a brand-new solution can enable leaps forward (e.g., replacing outdated machines with eco-efficient ones). Although it might slow down development, sustainability must be considered in the early planning stage to avoid falling back into the traditional 'first we build the system and then we make it sustainable'. In such a scenario, the system developed is initially unsustainable and achieving sustainability goals will take longer compared to considering it as an equal requirement integrated during the design and development stage. Getting it right on the first try is usually easier in the long run even if harder in the short term. This requires merging core business values with sustainability objectives in the overall Key Performance Indicators (KPIs) landscape and not viewing sustainability as an add-on or a stand-alone element to avoid conflict. Hence, all future industrial systems shall be 'Design for Sustainability' by default for the redesign of existing products, services, and systems, and the development of new ones [10], following an engineering approach that emphasizes the well-being of people and the environment as the outcome.

RQ5.1: How can sustainability be integrated and elevated as a core design principle for all products, services, and systems from their conception (and not as an add-on)?

VI. Dare to Fail and Share. In entrepreneurship, the 'fail fast' paradigm is considered an appropriate strategy towards success. As part of continuous improvement from a sustainability perspective, we need to embrace this design thinking mindset and methodology. Thus, we need to encourage and dare to experiment, fail, learn, and share both successes and failures. *Falsification* applied to qualitative research is a powerful way to advance our continuous improvement and innovation methods. Positive outcome bias in publishing results may prevent valuable lessons learnt to transfer to the rest of the research community. From a sustainability perspective, we are all working towards a common goal which is a significant pivot from our competitive driven mindset to a *coopetitive* one where 'competition' and 'cooperation' can go hand-to-hand since we all operate on one planet and a global market. *Coopetition* in the industrial ecosystem is the only sustainable way to face the challenges ahead in a volatile, uncertain, complex, and ambiguous environment. The triple bottom line of people, planet, and profit is under pressure to succeed before the time runs out for many organisations and value chains in face of new and stronger environmental regulations. Therefore, sharing the best environmental sustainability practices between organisations and value chains is the fastest track to sustainable industrial development [11].

> *RQ6.1: What are the best practices, tools, methods, and frameworks that ease the implementation of environmental solutions towards sustainable operations?*
>
> *RQ6.2: What are the pitfalls that hinder the implementation of environmental solutions towards sustainable operations?*
>
> *RQ6.3: How can falsification help to speed up the development of more effective, robust, and feasible environmental solutions, lowering the barriers to implementation and success in achieving sustainable operations?*

VII. Data-Driven Solutions. Digital transformation and smart manufacturing are inherently *data-driven*. Transparency, traceability, availability, accessibility, quality, usability, and standardisation of information and information models within and outside organisations (their value chains) are recurring challenges still unsolved today. This expands to sustainability KPIs, practices, and insights development. The objective is to have the right information (what) in the right format (how) for the right people (who) at the right time (when) for decision-making or action-taking on the shop floor and across value chains. This is even more challenging for environmental measures that require additional and costly infrastructure for data collection, processing, storage, and analysis solutions with potential outcomes that might be detrimental to the bottom line at first sight [12]. In addition, companies are often faced with the conundrum of having too much data but not in the right quality or state, or not the right data for environmental performance management and sustainability metrics. A lot of the data available are stored without the necessary context and represent data swamps that are hardly usable for informed decision making. The missing contextualization is partly traceable to a skills shortage, lack of awareness of the context for sustainability-related metrics among operators and data scientists, lack of standards to increase usability for different stakeholders, and a perceived lack of incentives to share data among stakeholders, within and outside the organisation. Moving forward, we need to create and use standards to facilitate collaboration (data integration, sharing, and usage) to achieve not only sustainable operations at individual organisations' level but also at the value chain level [13]. Using industry commons to design both products and processes in a sustainable manner (e.g., Design for Circularity) is essential for industrial development.

> *RQ7.1: What data/information needs to be shared, at which level of granularity, and amongst which stakeholder(s) to facilitate efficient, sustainable operations?*
>
> *RQ7.2: How to ensure information systems interoperability and avoid misinterpretation of data/information using standards for improved decision making?*

RQ7.3: How to facilitate communication and information exchange beyond organisational boundaries for more efficient, sustainable value chain operations?

VIII. Use Technology to Become the Ideal Partner for Sustainability. Take full advantage of the sustainability opportunities and new capabilities unlocked by the recent advances in operational and information technologies and systems, which companies are already investing in [12]; e.g., industrial digitalization, automation, and additive manufacturing. Digitalization has the potential to improve efficiency and the organisation's bottom line both directly and indirectly, but it would also lead to exacerbated ecological harm of industrialisation [14]. Technology development, selection and implementation should focus on sustainability as a primary goal (not secondary behind cost, quality, productivity, etc.). Direct gains include resource efficiency and pollution reduction. Indirect gains include the ability to manage sustainability-related data within companies and across value chains to coordinate sustainability efforts. The mechanisms through which technologies generate either negative or positive impacts should be characterised to ensure that additional impacts from producing, exploiting, and disposing of digital technologies are amortized [14].

RQ8.1: What are the environmental sustainability implications (positive and negative) when developing, selecting, and implementing advanced technologies?

RQ8.2: How can these implications be measured and integrated into technology development, selection, and implementation to ensure positive outcomes?

IX. Customer-Oriented Value Definition for Products and Services Design. Customers' choices (i.e., the voice of the customer) are fundamental for promoting sustainable business operations. Therefore, organisations' product and service portfolios must be sustainably improved by relying on what customers are willing to pay for. Customer orientation addresses the needs of the market by educating the consumer and promoting a sustainable consumption mindset (i.e., a healthier and more responsible consumption behaviour). Involving customers in the path towards circular and sustainable business models can be a competitive advantage since their consumption habits and attitudes are fundamental for sustainable consumer behaviours, which are based on four principles that encompass (i) selecting environmentally friendly products and services; (ii) minimising the range of consumption; (iii) maximising functionality and product life; and (iv) segregating waste to ease recycling or reuse [8] in the circular and sharing economies. Furthermore, taking customer requirements and needs as continuous improvement or innovation opportunities for sustainable business development.

RQ9.1: How to involve customers in the co-design of products and services to meet their needs in a more eco-efficient way?

RQ9.2: How to involve customers in extending the life of their products and increasing value co-creation during their usage phase?

RQ9.3: What type of product and service design standards facilitate the transition towards environmentally sustainable and circular business operations?

X. Doing Good. Can incremental improvements of non-sustainable processes eventually lead to sustainability? For example, time, efforts, and investment spent on improving a coal-fired power plant may seem necessary to reduce its environmental burden, but it may also distract from shifting to renewable energy systems. Sustainable alternatives should be the focus of industrial improvements to phase out as soon as possible non-sustainable activities and start new sustainable, environmentally positive ones [15]. However, regenerative sustainability is still rarely considered when planning, building and managing industrial systems. The traditional view that we are separate and independent from nature contributed to the disconnection of our human systems and the ecosystem services they rely on. Companies can move from doing *less bad* to doing *more good* and go beyond *zero impact* by understanding the mechanisms governing the well-functioning of the surrounding natural ecosystems and accounting for local renewal and assimilation rates [16]. Cumulating incremental and radical green improvements, production and consumption levels could pass the threshold for our society to operate within the planetary boundaries. First, specific vulnerabilities in damaged local ecosystems can be targeted to stop or remove the *bad* already done (passive regeneration and restoration). Then, more active measures can be adopted through bio-inspired innovations and technological developments to tackle the remaining negative impacts.

RQ10.1: How can companies operate within natural ecosystems' limits, accounting for their renewal and assimilation ability (eco-efficient and circular practices)?

RQ10.2: What are the mechanisms through which companies can contribute positively to ecosystems' health (regenerative and restorative practices)?

3.2 Thematic Research Framework

The thematic research framework (see Fig. 1) connects the priority areas to six dominant research themes or fields identified through a thematic analysis of the last ten years of APMS conference proceedings. Each theme captures a cluster of related topics:

1. **Operations management**—scheduling, production planning and control, lean and green, asset management, maintenance, quality management, risk management, etc.
2. **Business development**—strategic planning, organizational change, organizational learning, dynamic capabilities, innovative business models, servitization, etc.
3. **Value chain management**—product lifecycle, manufacturing strategy, green supply chains, industrial symbiosis, collaborative networks, transparency, etc.
4. **Technological development**—process and product design, novel applications of manufacturing technologies, ICT, automation, Industry 4.0, etc.
5. **Human factors**—health and safety, operator support, skills and knowledge, engineering education, professional training, continuous and life-long learning, etc.
6. **Performance management**—novel indicators, multi-criteria decision making, modelling and simulation, optimisation, machine learning, big data analytics, etc.

Some of these research themes already connect strongly to the priority areas. For example, the field of business development is challenging the definition of success and value (priority area I); e.g., corporate social responsibility, service-based business models, and sharing economy. A growing number of fields are taking advantage of data-driven solutions (priority area VII) with operations management and performance management leading the way. Research on human factors is developing better support systems to assist, inform and educate people to work more efficiently and safely, empowering them to make better decisions (priority area III); e.g., new and renewed occupational health and safety standards, modern worker assistance systems with augmented and collaborative technologies. Much can be learnt from the field of operations management regarding tools and methods for continuous improvement (priority area IV); e.g., lean-green and zero-defect paradigms to improve resource efficiency. However, regenerative sustainability (priority area X) is still rarely adopted in industrial research.

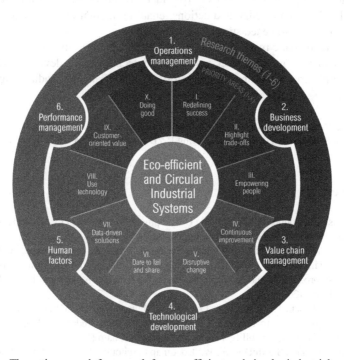

Fig. 1. Thematic research framework for eco-efficient and circular industrial systems.

Each research theme requires a different approach to tackle environmental sustainability meaningfully and realistically. The priority areas can be used to reframe the practical problems addressed and reflect on the conditions causing them. Then the proposed research questions can be used to prompt and guide the formulation of more specific research questions and research frameworks by individual researchers in their field. Ultimately, it is the responsibility of each researcher to scope and focus their contribution in the right direction, i.e., towards operating within the planetary boundaries.

4 Conclusions

This paper aims to stimulate discussions and encourage us all to address environmental sustainability more systematically and effectively in production engineering and management research. A thematic research framework for eco-efficient and circular industrial systems is presented to take advantage of the ongoing efforts on dominant research themes. With a clearer understanding of the research needs in the field of industrial sustainability, priority areas and research questions are proposed to guide ongoing and future research with a strong focus on environmental challenges to tackle them meaningfully in further industrial development. All stakeholders, from producers to consumers, need to embrace eco-efficiency and circular economy principles as the standard mode of operation for industry (production) and society (consumption), building on each other's knowledge and actions, enabling mutual learning, and eventually accelerating the much-needed sustainability transition.

Finally, the thematic research framework presents the priority areas along with six dominant themes to guide further research and technological development towards sustainable industrial solutions in the factory, supply chain, and industry as a whole level.

Acknowledgements. With thanks to the workshop participants, the European Research Council (grant no. 810764), the Swedish Manufacturing R&D, and the IFIP WG5.7.

References

1. World Business Council for Sustainable Development: Eco-efficient Leadership for Improved Economic and Environmental Performance (1996)
2. Ellen MacArthur Foundation. http://ellenmacarthurfoundation.org. Accessed 10 Apr 2022
3. Despeisse, M., Acerbi, F.: Toward eco-efficient and circular industrial systems: ten years of advances in production management systems and a thematic framework. Prod. Manuf. Res. **10**(1), 354–382 (2022)
4. Houman Andersen, P.: Sustainable Operations Management (SOM) strategy and management: an introduction to Part I. In: de Boer, L., Houman Andersen, P. (eds.) Operations Management and Sustainability. Palgrave Macmillan, Cham (2018)
5. Vivanco, D.F., Sala, S., McDowall, W.: Roadmap to rebound: how to address rebound effects from resource efficiency policy. Sustainability **10**(6), 2009 (2018)
6. Didonet, S.R., Fearne, A., Simmons, G.: Determining the presence of a long-term/short-term dilemma for SMEs when adopting strategic orientation to improve performance. Int. Small Bus. J. **38**(2), 90–110 (2020)
7. Alayón, C., Säfsten, K., Johansson, G.: Conceptual sustainable production principles in practice. J. Clean. Prod. **141**, 693–701 (2017)
8. Janikowski, R.: Imperative of a sustainable consumer: principles of a sustainable consumption. In: Pretterhofer, U. (ed.) Strategies of a Sustainable Policy, pp. 29–32. IFF/IFZ, Graz Austria (2000)
9. Powell, D.J., Romero, D., Gaiardelli, P.: New and renewed manufacturing paradigms for sustainable production. Sustainability **14**(3), 1279 (2022)
10. United Nations Environment Programme: Design for Sustainability: A Step-by-Step Approach (2009)

11. Moore, S.A.: The effect of knowledge sharing on the environmental performance of proactive environmental organisations. Ph.D. thesis. Southern Cross University (2010)
12. Wuest, T., Romero, D., Khan, M.A., Mittal, S.: The triple bottom line of smart manufacturing technologies: an economic, environmental, and social perspective. In: Kurz, H.D., et al. (eds.) The Routledge Handbook of Smart Technologies, pp. 310–330. Routledge (2022)
13. Acerbi, F., Sassanelli, C., Terzi, S., Taisch, M.: A systematic literature review on data and information required for circular manufacturing strategies adoption. Sustainability 13(4), 2047 (2021)
14. Kunkel, S., Tyfield, D.: Digitalisation, sustainable industrialisation and digital rebound – asking the right questions for a strategic research agenda. Energy Res. Soc. Sci. 82, 102295 (2021)
15. Rubio-Mozos, E., García-Muiña, F.E., Fuentes-Moraleda, L.: Rethinking 21st-century businesses: an approach to fourth sector SMEs in their transition to a sustainable model committed to SDGs. Sustainability 11(20), 5569 (2019)
16. Morseletto, P.: Restorative and regenerative: exploring the concepts in the circular economy. J. Ind. Ecol. 24, 763–773 (2020)

Ways to Circular and Transparent Value Chains

Maria Flavia Mogos[✉] [iD] and Giuseppe Fragapane [iD]

SINTEF Manufacturing, Grøndalsvegen 2, 2830 Raufoss, Norway
maria.flavia.mogos@sintef.no

Abstract. The purpose of this paper is to increase the knowledge about the implementation of circularity and other sustainability approaches in value chains. The objective is to develop roadmaps for the implementation of digital Circular manufacturing (CMA) and Social-life cycle (S-LCA) assessments in Textile and Clothing (TC) value chains. Implementing these digital assessments in TC value chains can increase their transparency, by validating that product manufacturing safeguards worker wellbeing and the environment. TC is one of the sectors with most critical social and environmental impacts. The roadmaps were developed through a Design Science methodology, combining: i) case studies to understand the practical problem, ii) literature study on CMA and S-LCA to develop the roadmaps, and iii) action research to iteratively apply the roadmaps to the cases and refine them with participants in an EU project, representing the entire TC value chain. The EU project is developing digital sustainability assessments with Blockchain functionality for increased data trustworthiness. This study aims to contribute to theory, practice, and public policies by providing a validated overview of the status, barriers, goals, and systematic activities for the implementation of CMA and S-LCA in TC value chains and for increased sustainability.

Keywords: Circular economy · Sustainability · Value chain transparency

1 Introduction

Nowadays, companies need to cope with increasing requirements of environmental and social sustainability from policymakers and customers, including requirements to increase the circularity and transparency of industrial value chains. However, the journey from linear value chains with a focus on economic sustainability, to circular value chains that also address environmental and social sustainability, is an exciting, yet tumultuous journey for many companies. This is also the case for the Textile and Clothing (TC) sector, the 4th highest 'pressure category' in the EU in terms of use of primary raw materials and water, while Food is the highest [1]. Unlike the food sector, most of the pressure and impact linked to TC occurs outside the EU, making the value chain circularity and transparency goals even more challenging. The TC production typically takes place in developing countries with lower production costs, but also lower environmental standards and working conditions. It is estimated that less than 1% of all textiles worldwide are recycled into new textiles [2]. Moreover, it is reported that nearly 10%

Published by Springer Nature Switzerland AG 2022
D. Y. Kim et al. (Eds.): APMS 2022, IFIP AICT 664, pp. 390–398, 2022.
https://doi.org/10.1007/978-3-031-16411-8_45

of the chemicals used in the TC sector are of potential concern to human health and that due to poor working conditions, almost 6% of the TC workers get injured every year [3]. As customer awareness about sustainability is growing, the TC sector is witnessing a plethora of companies claiming that they supply sustainable products. However, due to low-value chain transparency, the current anti-counterfeiting methods are suboptimal, thus enabling an unfair playing field for the suppliers that do comply with stricter sustainability requirements [4].

Roadmaps are acknowledged as important strategic planning methods that include the activities required to cope with challenges and achieve major advances in an area [5] such as the one of circular value chains. The circular economy is one of the concepts in the sustainability field that is truly embraced by the business community. In recent years, research studies provided more support to practitioners that are implementing circular strategies than earlier [6, 7]. Nevertheless, these studies have addressed the TC sector to a lesser extent, especially concerning the exploitation of methods and digital technologies for increased value chain transparency. Moreover, earlier studies have a limited focus on assessments as a point of departure for continuously improving value chain circularity and transparency [7]. Thus, the purpose of this study is to increase the knowledge about the implementation of digital sustainability assessments in the TC value chain, for increased circularity and transparency. To this end, the paper proposes two roadmaps that were developed in close collaboration with participants in the EU innovation project, TRICK [8], which represent the whole TC value chain. TRICK is developing five digital sustainability assessments, with Blockchain functionality for increased data trustworthiness. This paper addresses the CMA and S-LCA assessments.

2   Research Design

The research strategy has been Design Science, as described by Holmström et al. [9]. This strategy is recommended both for the development of methods with enhanced practical relevance—such as roadmaps, and for the development of the theory (e.g., [9, 10]). As Design science is a multi-method strategy, this study combined case studies, a systematic literature review and action research. First, to understand the practical problem of the case companies, we studied the industrial user needs, as well as barriers and enablers of these user needs. Second, a literature review was conducted, on the topics of CMA and S-LCA. Third, preliminary roadmaps were developed based on the literature. They were structured into common topics in the roadmap literature: current state, policies, barriers (to circular and transparent value chains), and goals and activities on the way towards the vision. Third, over a 6-month period, the roadmaps were iteratively applied to TC cases and refined together with the partners—through the action research method. To this end, workshops, semi-structured interviews, and a survey were conducted with project partners representing the TC value chain. The value chain actors included traditional and technical TC manufacturers, yarn and fibre producers, an online retailer of second-hand clothing, a platform provider for the sourcing of TC production, a recycling company, a customs agency, service and platform developers, and research partners.

3   Literature Background

3.1   Circular Manufacturing Assessment for the TC Sector

The Current State. Compared to linear manufacturing, circular manufacturing is a system of ideally, endless reutilization, remanufacturing and recycling of resources and goods. The 10R-framework (refuse, rethink, reduce, reuse, repair, refurbish, remanufacture, repurpose, recycle, recover) provides a basis for identifying manufacturing circularity [11]. The most common methodology to assess circularity is Life Cycle Assessment (LCA) [12]. While LCA shows great advantages in assessing the environmental impact, it has difficulties in capturing the variation of cycles and interplay of different lifespans [13]. The CMA is an assessment based on material flow and input-output analyses, which can address a wide array of environmental and economic variables through the product lifecycle [14]. CMA indicators for environmental and financial impact may include: air emissions, water and solid wastes, hazardous and toxic materials, environmental accidents, as well as the cost of materials, energy, waste, and environmental accidents [15]. However, the CMA analyses are still not commonly adopted by practitioners.

Policies. Relevant policies for CMA are the ISO 14040 and BS 8001 standards, Global Recycle Standard and the EU Ecolabel. ISO 14040 addresses environmental management and the LCA principles and framework, while BS 8001 provides a framework for implementing circular economy principles in organizations.

Barriers. The lack of a performance index is one of the main barriers to CMA implementation [16], as the method can only focus on a single or few performance indicators. The complexity of circular economy and manufacturing requires multi-dimensional indicators [17]. Moreover, the low CMA standardization makes it difficult to compare CMA results. There is also a lack of universal tracking and tracing technologies and the systems for monitoring circular indicators in the industry are immature or non-existent. Digital technologies are needed to aid manufacturers and recyclers in tracing and evaluating the lifespans of sold commodities, and in forecasting the collection frequency, and the quantity and value of returned merchandise [15].

Goals. The Sustainable Development Goals (SDG) that can support the development of specific KPIs for CMA are SDG 12—Target 12.5 and SDG 17—Target 17.16.

Research and Development (R&D) Activities. The latest literature reviews within circular manufacturing in TC emphasise that future research needs to [12, 14, 15]:

- Identify multi-dimensional performance indicators for CMA,
- Develop and standardize CMA methods, and
- Develop digital technologies to track and trace materials in the TC industry.

3.2   Social Life Cycle Assessment for the TC Sector

Current State. The TC actors may have social impacts, like poor rates of pay and working conditions, long working hours, child labour, frequent industrial accidents, and limitations to freedom of association [18]. However, consumers are increasingly aware of social impacts and are willing to pay more for sustainable TC products. S-LCA is the methodology recommended by the UN for the assessment of the social impacts of products and services across their life cycle [19]. Examples of S-LCA databases are PSILCA and SHDB.

Policies. Currently, there are more than 450 environmental and sustainability labels [20]. Relevant policies for the S-LCA that the UN recommends, include [19]: UN's Guiding Principles on Business and Human Rights from 2011, Good Weave label, Fairtrade, Rainforest Alliance label, SA8000 Standard, ISO 45001, Global Reporting Initiative, and the Accountability 1000 Assurance standard.

Barriers. Barriers to the implementation of digital S-LCA and social protection in the TC value chains may include [19, 21, 22]:

- Parts of the necessary data are not available.
- The S-LCA experts transform the data in a way that invalidates or distorts it.
- The data are not reliable because of human errors or bias during collection.
- Data do not relate well to the concept being measured, that is it is not valid.
- The study context has changed, limiting the validity of the collected data.

Moreover, it may be difficult and very costly to get site-specific social data about all actors in the value chains [19]. Finally, there might be a vested interest in value chain opacity, to defend local production—especially in developing countries [21].

Goals. The goals that UNEP recommends include the SDG Targets 1.1, 3.9, 4.7, 5.1, 5.5, 8.5, 8.7, 8.8, and 10.2 [23]. These goals/targets can inform the development of specific KPIs for the S-LCA implementation.

R&D Activities. Activities that can be relevant for the implementation of the digital S-LCA in TC value chains, include further research addressing the questions: What are the appropriate scope and the minimum data quality required to properly assess the social impacts from a life cycle perspective?; How to ensure that the assessment results are relevant in the local context and for the affected stakeholders?; What are the considerations for the integration of S-LCA results in a Life Cycle Sustainability Assessment?; How can the root causes of social impacts/performances be identified and addressed?; and How can S-LCA be considered for decision-making at the policy and industry sectors level? [19].

4 The Roadmaps from Linear to Circular Value Chains

Figure 1 presents the roadmaps for the implementation of the digital CMA and S-LCA in the TC sector, for increased value chain circularity and transparency. The roadmaps are based on results from the case studies, literature study, and action research, including short/mid/long-term goals and activities for the period between 2021 (first year of the

Current situation/ barriers	Activities/ goals by 2024	Activities/ goals by 2028	Activities/ goals by 2031
Circular development initiatives in the Textile & Clothing sector focus mainly on take-back management schemes and recycling, while the design for circularity has potentially the strongest impact in changing the TC sector from linear to circular. Manufacturing companies need support in automatically analyzing production data and life cycle data of products to evaluate circularity. *Policies:* ISO 14040, BS 8001 standards, Global Recycle Standard (GRS) and the EU Ecolabel.	- Develop methods to evaluate circular manufacturing and introduce multi-dimensional performance indicators - Develop methods and digital technologies to identify circular value chain and provide feedback on circular performance potentials - Develop methods and digital technologies (such as blockchain) to enable transparent value chains and traceability of materials	- Refine and standardize methods to assess manufacturing and the multi-dimensional performance indicators - Develop platforms to share securely material data between value chain actors - Support a wide range of Textile & Clothing companies to use the CMA as a strategic tool, to reach their circularity potential, and to form new and optimized value chain connections and business networks.	- Further research on integrating traceability and material circularity potential in the product design processes. - Further research on the implementation of customer awareness campaigns to promote Circular Economy goals and behavior for circularity.

CIRCULAR MANUFACTURING ASSESSMENT

Current situation/ barriers	Activities/ goals by 2024	Activities/ goals by 2028	Activities/ goals by 2031
Barriers: - Lack of a performance index is one of the main obstacles - Lack of standardization and acceptance of circular manufacturing assessment method - Lack of universal tracking and tracing technologies and immature or non-existent monitoring systems for assessment indicators for industry.	*Goals for environmental benefits:* >20% closed-loop recycling in Textile & Clothing. 25% open-loop recycling (e.g. composites) >5% materials recycled from other industries. 40% more end-of-life clothing collected for recycling 40% more sales of 2nd hand traditional clothing. >35% increase of reuse cycles for workwear	*Goals for environmental benefits:* Implement the legal obligation to separate the collection of waste textiles in the EU by 2025. 30% closed-loop recycling in Textile & Clothing. 30% open-loop recycling. 10% recycled materials from other industries. 60% more end-of-life clothing collected for recycling, and >50% more sales of 2nd hand traditional clothing.	*Goals for environmental benefits:* 40% closed-loop recycling. 50% increase of reuse cycles for workwear Substantially reduce waste generation through prevention, reduction, recycling, and reuse - by 2030. Enhance the multi-stakeholder partnerships that mobilize and share knowledge, expertise, technology, and financial resources e.g., in developing countries

Current situation/ barriers	Activities/ goals by 2024	Activities/ goals by 2028	Activities/ goals by 2031
Textile & Clothing actors may have impacts, like poor rates of pay and working conditions, long working hours, child labor, frequent industrial accidents, and limitations to freedom of association. However, consumers are increasingly aware of social impacts and are willing to pay more for sustainable products. *Policies:* UN's Guiding Principles on Business and Human Rights, UNEP S-LCA Guidelines, ISO 45001, SA8000 standard, Fairtrade, Global reporting initiative, Good Weave label, Rainforest Alliance.	- Define the specifications of the S-LCA software with the industrial users, addressing its scope and minimum data quality. - Develop the concept and pilot and iteratively validate and refine them with industrial users, addressing the software's integration with existing S-LCA databases, site-specific data, and the Blockchain-based traceability platform. - Publish the digital S-LCA on the marketplace.	- Effective methods for supplier selection, assessment, and development, including transparency, and worker inclusion. - New business models based on socially sustainable products, and public procurement of such products - Disseminate S-LCA results to consumers (e.g., on the labels) and other stakeholders. - Research addressing "How can S-LCA be considered for decision-making at the policy and industry sectors level?" and "What are the considerations for the integration of S-LCA results in a holistic Life Cycle Sustainability Assessment?"	- Further research addressing the question "How can the root causes of social impacts/ performances be identified and addressed?" - Include social sustainability in school education and workers' training. - Implement a holistic Life Cycle Sustainability Assessment. - Further dissemination of the S-LCA results to consumers and other stakeholders.

SOCIAL-LIFE CYCLE ASSESSMENT

Current situation/ barriers	Activities/ goals by 2024	Activities/ goals by 2028	Activities/ goals by 2031
Barriers: - Interest in value chain opacity, to de-fend local production. - Difficult to get site-specific social data about all value chain actors. - Lack of time or financial resources to collect necessary data. - Unreliable data because it is collected or transformed in a way that invalidates it.	*Goals for social and health benefits:* - The IT system provides 100% access to data to evaluate the Social and Ethical protection of workers in the traditional/ technical Textile & Clothing value chain, including recycling. - The value chain actors comply 100% with the UN's Guiding Principles on Business and Human Rights.	*Goals for social and health benefits:* - The labor rights are protected, and all workers have safe and secure working environments. - No child and forced labor, and no modern slavery and human trafficking in the value chain. - Ensure women's equal opportunities for leadership, at all decision-making levels.	*Goals for social and health benefits:* - Ensure that all workers acquire the knowledge and skills needed to promote sustainable development - Eradicate extreme poverty and achieve equal pay for work of equal value for all value chain workers.

Fig. 1. The roadmaps from linear to circular TC value chains

TRICK project) and 2031. The roadmaps' vision that the participants agreed on is: "A strong EU industrial ecosystem, by engaging all the smaller TC value chain actors in the evolution to circular and transparent value chains, and by enabling them to easily find the services and support needed for the adoption of the new production paradigms."

5 Discussion

This section discusses the roadmaps from Fig. 1 in light of the feedback from the value chain actors in the case studies, and the current literature.

CMA. The TC sector needs to shift toward a circular mindset, applying design for circularity, being transparent about the actual and potential circularity performance, and improving take-back and recycling schemes in its global, complex value chains. The acceptance of secondary product life cycles in terms of imperfections in recycled products, and consumers' perceptions of reduced hygiene need to increase according to the informants in the case studies. The barriers are social and cultural rather than technical, highlighting the importance of increasing consumer circularity-awareness and consumer education during the shift from linear to circular products. CMA is a needed tool both from a technical and a social perspective.

The roadmap illustrates steps towards reaching the 10-year goal of substantial reduction of waste generation and of increased use of secondary resources for material circularity, both textile to textile, and textile to other material. The short-term activities and goals focus on developing methods to evaluate circular manufacturing and introduce multi-dimensional performance indicators. Thereby, digital technologies such as Blockchain can enable transparent value chains and the traceability of materials. However, the methods and applications of Blockchain and tracing platforms are still in an immature development phase. Apart from the CMA, the roadmap KPIs are based on the SDG goals and the feedback from informants. By 2030, the TC value chain actors should substantially reduce waste generation through prevention, reduction, recycling, and reuse, thus facilitating and increase of closed-loop recycling to 40%, and an increase of reuse cycles for workwear to 50%. Moreover, the implementation of CMA into product development tools and processes, and the increase of consumer knowledge on circularity are listed as long-term R&D activities. These are pointing towards the awareness and circularity level needed to reach the chosen SDGs.

S-LCA. The goals and activities that the informants selected for the 2021–2024 period are those of the TRICK project, which is active in the same period. They are related to the development of the digital S-LCA, and its integration with existing databases, site-specific data, and the TRICK traceability platform. Moreover, they address the demonstration of the Digital S-LCA in TC value chains.

For 2024–2028, the goals are: i) the labor rights are protected, and all workers have safe and secure working environments, ii) no child and forced labor, and no modern slavery and human trafficking in the value chain, and iii) ensure women's equal opportunities for leadership, at all decision-making levels (based on SDGs 8.8, 8.7, 8.5, and 5.5). One of the mid-term activities is implementing effective methods for supplier selection, assessment, and development, including within social and ethical transparency. "The producers that intend to be transparent find the way to gather the necessary [assessment] data, typically by selecting the appropriate supplier", commented an informant from the fiber producer, thus acknowledging the importance of supplier selection. Other selected activities are developing new business models based on socially responsible products and disseminating S-LCA results to the consumer market and other stakeholders. The results can be displayed on the product labels, as recommended by the proposed policies. Moreover, as future R&D activities, the informants suggested identifying the considerations for the integration of S-LCA results in a holistic Life Cycle Sustainability Assessment. Through the digital CMA and S-LCA, TRICK addresses the environmental and social pillars of the sustainability concept. In the future, these can be integrated into a software for a holistic Life Cycle Sustainability Assessment, which should also include the Life Cycle Costing assessment, for the economical sustainability pillar [19].

Selected goals for 2028–2031 include achieving equal pay for work of equal value for all value chain workers, and eradicating extreme poverty, currently quantified as less than $1.25 a day (based on SDG 8.5 and 1.1) [23]. Another long-term goal is ensuring that all workers acquire the knowledge and skills needed to promote socially sustainable development (SDG 4.7). Thus, one of the selected activities for the producers is to continue developing their suppliers on a long-term basis, so that worker training and inclusion methods are implemented in the value chain wherever necessary. The TC actors and policymakers should increasingly include the social sustainability topic in school education, worker's training, and awareness-raising campaigns, along with ecological and economical sustainability [24]. This would facilitate a high consumer demand for socially and environmentally responsible products and would reinforce sustainable attitudes in producers. Policymakers can further encourage responsible business behaviour by providing financial and non-financial incentives for the procurement of socially and environmentally responsible goods (ibid.).

6   Concluding Remarks

The purpose of this study was to increase the knowledge about the implementation of digital sustainability assessments in the TC value chains, for increased circularity and transparency. The study proposes roadmaps for the implementation of digital CMA and S-LCA assessments. The roadmaps are based on a systematic literature study and are developed in close collaboration with the project participants in the EU project, TRICK [8], which represent the whole TC value chain. Implementing these digital assessments in TC value chains can increase their transparency by validating that product manufacturing safeguards worker wellbeing and the environment. This study aims to contribute to theory, practice, and public policies by providing a validated overview of the status, barriers, goals, and systematic activities for the implementation of CMA and S-LCA in TC value chains, and thereby for increased sustainability.

Acknowledgements. The authors would like to thank the European Commission and the TRICK (grant no. 958352) participants for their support and valuable contributions.

References

1. European environmental agency. https://www.eea.europa.eu/publications/textiles-in-eur opes-circular-economy/textiles-in-europe-s-circular-economy. Accessed 12 Apr 2022
2. Ellen Macarthur Foundation. https://ellenmacarthurfoundation.org/a-new-textiles-economy. Accessed 12 Apr 2022
3. Richero, R., Ferrigno, S.: A background analysis on transparency and traceability in the garment value chain. Directorate General for International Cooperation and Development, European Commission, Brussels (2016)
4. Wajsman, N., Burgos, C., Davies, C.: The economic cost of IPR infringement in the clothing, footwear and accessories sector. Office for Harmonisation in the Internal Market, Alicante, Spain (2015)
5. Camarinha-Matos, L.M., Afsarmanesh, H.: A roadmapping methodology for strategic research on VO. In: Camarinha-Matos, L.M., Afsarmanesh, H. (eds.) Collaborative Networked Organizations, pp. 275–288. Springer, Boston (2004). https://doi.org/10.1007/1-4020-7833-1_30
6. Jørgensen, M.S., Remmen, A.: A methodological approach to development of circular economy options in businesses. Procedia CIRP **69**, 816–821 (2018)
7. Frishammar, J., Parida, V.: Circular business model transformation: a roadmap for incumbent firms. Calif. Manage. Rev. **61**(2), 5–29 (2019)
8. TRICK. http://www.trick-project.eu/. Accessed 12 Apr 2022
9. Holmström, J., Ketokivi, M., Hameri, A.P.: Bridging practice and theory: a design science approach. Decis. Sci. **40**(1), 65–87 (2009)
10. Van Aken, J.E., Romme, G.: Reinventing the future: adding design science to the repertoire of organization and management studies. Organ. Manage. J. **6**(1), 5–12 (2009)
11. Potting, J., Hekkert, M. P., Worrell, E., Hanemaaijer, A.: Circular economy: measuring innovation in the product chain (No. 2544). PBL Publishers (2017)
12. Sassanelli, C., Rosa, P., Rocca, R., Terzi, S.: Circular economy performance assessment methods: a systematic literature review. J. Clean. Prod. **229**, 440–453 (2019)
13. van Stijn, A., Eberhardt, L.M., Jansen, B.W., Meijer, A.: A circular economy life cycle assessment (CE-LCA) model for building components. Resour. Conserv. Recycl. **174**, 105683 (2021)
14. Corona, B., Shen, L., Reike, D., Carreón, J.R., Worrell, E.: Towards sustainable development through the circular economy—A review and critical assessment on current circularity metrics. Resour. Conserv. Recycl. **151**, 104498 (2019)
15. Jia, F., Yin, S., Chen, L., Chen, X.: The circular economy in the textile and apparel industry: a systematic literature review. J. Clean. Prod. **259**, 120728 (2020)
16. De Jesus, A., Mendonça, S.: Lost in transition? Drivers and barriers in the eco-innovation road to the circular economy. Ecol. Econ. **145**, 75–89 (2018)
17. Rossi, E., Bertassini, A.C., dos Santos Ferreira, C., do Amaral, W.A.N., Ometto, A.R.: Circular economy indicators for organizations considering sustainability and business models. J. Clean. Prod. **247**, 119137 (2020)
18. European Environmental Agency. https://www.eea.europa.eu/publications/textiles-in-eur opes-circular-economy. Accessed 12 Apr 2022
19. Guidelines for Social Life Cycle Assessment of Products and Organisations. https://www.lif ecycleinitiative.org/library/guidelines-for-social-life-cycle-assessment-of-products-and-org anisations-2020/. Accessed 12 Apr 2022
20. Ecolabelindex. https://www.ecolabelindex.com/. Accessed 12 Apr 2022
21. Almanza, A.M.H., Corona, B.: Using Social Life Cycle Assessment to analyze the contribution of products to the Sustainable Development Goals: a case study in the textile sector. Int. J. Life Cycle Assess. **25**(9), 1833–1845 (2020)

22. Di Noi, C., Ciroth, A., Mancini, L., Eynard, U., Pennington, D., Blengini, G.A.: Can S-LCA methodology support responsible sourcing of raw materials in EU policy context? Int. J. Life Cycle Assess. **25**(2), 332–349 (2020)
23. United Nations - The 17 Goals. https://sdgs.un.org/goals. Accessed 12 Apr 2022
24. European Strategy for Sustainable Textile, Garments, Leather and Footwear. https://fairtr ade-advocacy.org/wp-content/uploads/2020/04/Civil-Society-European-Strategy-for-Sustai nable-Textiles.pdf. Accessed 12 Apr 2022

Lean & Green: Aligning Circular Economy and Kaizen Through Hoshin Kanri

Eivind Reke[1]([⊠]), Natalia Iakymenko[1], Kristina Kjersem[2], and Daryl Powell[3]

[1] SINTEF Manufacturing, Raufoss, Norway
eivind.reke@sintef.no
[2] Møreforsking, Molde, Norway
[3] Norwegian University of Technology and Science, Trondheim, Norway

Abstract. As organizations are moving towards a circular economy to enable a transition to more sustainable business practices, there is a need for knowledge on how companies can leverage the capabilities of the entire organization to reach this goal.

In this paper, we present some preliminary but promising results from a single company that has adapted the use of Hoshin Kanri—a strategic management method often associated with lean which seeks to engage the whole organization in breakthrough improvements in Safety, Quality, Delivery, and Cost. The case company has over the last year experimented with including Sustainability (the term the company uses internally) targets in their Hoshin, to develop circular capabilities within the organization. We present a literature study on Circular Economy, Sustainability, Kaizen and Hoshin Kanri, which formed the basis for Action Learning Research interventions. We then compare the results from these interventions with the findings from the review. Finally, we discuss the implications of the results and point to further research.

Keywords: Circular economy · Hoshin Kanri · Lean production · Sustainability

1 Introduction

The shift towards more sustainable products and manufacturing operations is pushing companies to improve their environmental performance and efficacy. The idea that lean production can support or facilitate this shift is not new. The underlying principles that they draw on are the same: Productivity improvements (more with less or same with less), quality, cost reduction, continuous improvement, and technology innovation [1]. As such, "lean production" (LP) is a promising approach for companies that wish to move towards sustainable business models that reduce waste, produce more with less, and improve material efficiency while minimizing costs. However, for many practitioners it remains unclear how exactly LP can contribute to a sustainable transformation of their organizations [2]. Building on [3], who suggests six different research questions to guide further research on lean and green, this paper explores the integration of lean and green as a consolidated approach.

© IFIP International Federation for Information Processing 2022
Published by Springer Nature Switzerland AG 2022
D. Y. Kim et al. (Eds.): APMS 2022, IFIP AICT 664, pp. 399–406, 2022.
https://doi.org/10.1007/978-3-031-16411-8_46

Circular Economy (CE), has recently emerged as a useful overarching framework for addressing the sustainability challenge, incorporating many previous environmental approaches [4]. However, as CE is a theoretical framework developed and popularized by the Ellen McArthur Foundation, there is a need for more research into the practical application of the framework. Several research papers [5–7] present result that show how different lean tools can be applied to support the implementation of the CE framework. Kaizen, a practical concept made popular through various books and case studies and closely associated with LP and Toyota Motor Company, is one such established practice that show promising results in aligning CE with front-line improvements [8].

Aligning front-line improvements with CE is only one part of the equation. A challenge already faced by companies is aligning and sustaining continuous improvement initiatives with the overall strategic direction of the company. I.e., that improvements are not just improvements for the sake of improving, but also contribute to improving the overall production, development, and delivery system of the company. Hoshin Kanri represents a method that can assist this alignment [9, 10]. Toyota, who has been practicing its version of Hoshin since 1961 [11], publicly present their own Hoshin on Sustainability as "Global 2050 Sustainability challenge—Going beyond Zero". In fact, Toyota have indeed been quite successful in addressing some of these challenges, expecting their production plants to be carbon net-zero by 2035 [12].

To better understand how companies can integrate lean and green by engaging the whole organization in improvements towards a CE, a study of the relevant literature was carried out. Based on this literature, action learning research interventions are ongoing in a single company. The rest of the paper is structured in the following manner: Sect. 2 present the literature study. Section 3, the action learning research methodology. Section 4 present the case company and the interventions, and Sect. 5 our preliminary observations and planned further research.

2 Literature Study

A considerable amount of literature has been published on the interplay between lean and green, sustainability, circularity/CE. It is important to understand the difference between the three terms. "Green" and "sustainable" terms both point to preservation of environment and natural resources. However, "green" is strictly about the environmental preservation, while "sustainable" includes environmental health, economic vitality, and social benefits. Similarities and difficulties between sustainability and CE are more ambiguous. [13] studied similarities and differences between sustainability and CE based on an extensive literature review. They define sustainability as "the balanced integration of economic performance, social inclusiveness, and environmental resilience, to the benefit of current and future generations" and CE as "a regenerative system in which resource input and waste, emission, and energy leakage are minimized by slowing, closing, and narrowing material and energy loops. This can be achieved through long-lasting design, maintenance, repair, reuse, remanufacturing, refurbishing, and recycling". The main differences between the two terms, according to [13], are:

(1) The difference in agency and responsibility. Agency and responsibility are diffused in the case of sustainability, the CE has a clear emphasis on businesses, regulators, and policy makers.
(2) Difference between commitments, goals, and interests. The sustainability prioritizes alignment between all three pillars and all stakeholders, while CE prioritizes financial advantages for companies, and less resource consumption and pollution for the environment.
(3) Difference in time frame for achieving results—CE gives relatively immediate results comparing to sustainability.

In summary, CE aims to intentionally design a circular system (in contrast to the established linear economy) with companies and governments carrying the main responsibility for establishing and sustaining the circular system. Sustainability, on the other hand, is a concept that aims at benefiting environment, economy and society, where responsibilities are shared by everyone, but not clearly defined.

Positive synergies between lean and green/sustainability have been shown in existing literature, well documented in the latest literature reviews [14–16]. In this literature, lean is mostly seen as an approach for waste reduction, which consequentially contributes to improved resource usage and better environmental performance. Even when studying impact of lean on sustainability, mostly environmental and economic dimensions are addressed from the position of waste reduction [14].

Despite the growth of research on lean and green/sustainability, consideration of how lean complement CE has been almost absent from the literature due to a mismatch between research on lean green, which has focused on internal manufacturing operations (product and process levels), and research on CE, which takes a broader, more holistic view of environmental impact (the system level) [17]. Furthermore, the same study found that pure lean and green perspective leads to viewing waste as dirty, but not a resource. CE perspective, on the other hand, allows to focus on reuse, remanufacturing, refurbishment, repair, and upgrading throughout the life cycle of products, leading to lowered emissions and less resource demand.

The conducted literature study points towards three challenges in the lean and green research.

1) Lean is seen mostly as a waste reduction method, which indirectly improves green/sustainability/CE performance [2]. There is lack of studies that look at how lean principles can help in setting and moving towards green/sustainability/CE goals.
2) There is a lack of studies that consider the combined impact of lean-green/sustainability/CE on social aspects.
3) Currently, most of the existing literature is being dominated by theoretical papers—empirical evidence is lacking [16].

In this paper, the first and third challenges are addressed. As the literature study suggests, the traditional interpretation of LP in CE is that lean is a method for the reduction of waste in the production system [6]. Even though the reduction of waste might be an outcome of LP, it is not the aim. LP, born from the constraints of the Toyota Motor Company [18], studied and presented as a full business system [19], can also be described as a people centric system for continuous learning and growth [20], from which companies can Find and face their business challenges, and frame and form solutions through developing people [21].

If CE is included in the business strategy, it is often without giving direction to day-to-day continuous improvement actions. Hoshin Kanri is precisely recognized for building the link between strategic goals and day-to-day actions [22]. Hoshin Kanri is a strategy deployment process which attempts to integrate top management goals into Continuous Improvement (Kaizen) activities [23]. It aims to [24]:

- Provide focus on corporate direction by setting annual strategic priorities
- Align strategic priorities and local plans through a process of catchball, sharing ideas back and forth towards a consensus on how to achieve the Hoshin targets.
- Integrate strategic priorities with daily management by breaking down overall challenges into more manageable problems
- Provide a structured review of the progress of the strategic priorities

Based on the presented gaps in the literature and the notion of Hoshin Kanri, we formulated the following research question: *"How can Hoshin Kanri help companies succeed in the transition towards a circular economy?"*.

3   Research Method

In contrast to traditional positivist experimental science, our research question requires an investigation that is built on socially distributed, application-oriented knowledge production. Therefore, given the practical nature of our study and being guided by our research question, we adopt action learning research, a form of action-oriented research which has collaborative learning at its core. Unlike more traditional case study research, where researchers observe the phenomenon under investigation from the outside, action learning research entails the active participation of the researcher in a reflexive questioning and learning process [25]. The action learning research process ultimately aims to create and disseminate new, actionable knowledge, contributing to a theory-building process which is situation specific, emergent and incremental [26].

In the action learning research process, data comes through engagement with others during action cycles. This means that the act of collecting data is itself an intervention. As such, the observations made during the action cycles are not simply seen as collecting data per se, but rather as generating learning for the researcher and the participants in the action. Such an approach provides a rich foundation of data with which to generate knowledge and learning. Observations and reflections were documented through notetaking during interventions, as well as through direct consultation with participants in the action learning network using telephone, email and direct conversation. Where necessary, technical and contractual documents were consulted (Fig. 1).

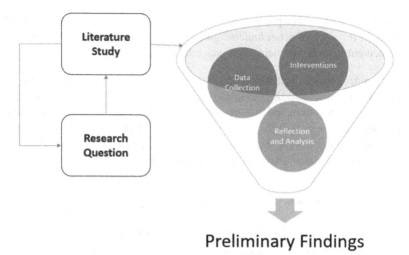

Fig. 1. Action learning research funnel

4   Company Description and Interventions

The case company is a global manufacturer of medical equipment and devices. The company has used lean production for almost 20 years. Over the last 5 years the Supply Chain & Manufacturing (SC&M) organization has shifted its use of lean production from tools- and methods-oriented approach to a more holistic learning approach focused on business development through people development. In 2020 the company conducted a thorough study of its environmental impact and set out its sustainability goals in a 2030 vision to, among other goals, reduce its carbon footprint by 50% in 2030 by implementing CE.

The hoshin system already in place was structured as follows: the company goals were updated yearly on Quality, Cost, People and Service, then a catch-ball process broke down and aligned the overall targets with local initiatives once a year. However, since the sustainability targets are 10 years ahead, the VP also decided to look further ahead on the traditional areas. To do so 5-year targets were established for all areas, including sustainability. The catch ball process will still be yearly and each plant and department in the SC&M organization has their own 1-year hoshin.

Intervention 1: The researcher discussed with the Vice President (VP) of SC&M how to achieve sustainability goals in that part of the organization. To avoid implementing a new system to follow up on CE goals, the researcher suggested adopting the hoshin system the organization had been practicing in one of their plants and include sustainability in this system. The VP then created a 5-year hoshin for the organization.

Intervention 2: The decision to include CE goals in the hoshin system triggered a discussion between the researcher, the VP and a Plant Manager (PM) on how to break down and present goals in the hoshin. The outcome was clear targets and the removal of the VPs ideas and suggestions on how to achieve these targets. It was agreed that this should be the outcome of the catch ball process.

Intervention 3: Researcher participated in the regular follow-up meetings already in place, with the intention of better understanding how this is carried out today. In addition, the management team in the main plant was interviewed.

Intervention 4: Further discussions on how to break down and create specific targets for the factory and how middle managers can contribute to these targets. Discussed the connection between system and culture after meeting with the HR-Director of another company who have successfully worked with a Hoshin process. Key take-away was that when establishing targets, they should be almost unattainable, and to have the right method, systematic Kaizen activities, to reach targets (Table 1).

Table 1. Overview of interventions and outcome

Intervention number	Type of intervention	Outcome
1st intervention	Integrate sustainability targets in the organization	Include sustainability in the SC&M organizations Hoshin
2nd intervention	Discussion on how to break down targets	Set targets and use catch ball process to challenge organization
3rd intervention	Observe follow-up meeting of current hoshin process, including interviews with managers in the plant	Refresh the hoshin process itself
4th intervention	Discussions on how to break down goals and achieve commitment to goals	Also need the right method to achieve goals

5 Preliminary Observations and Planned Interventions

The organization has faced several challenges in the preliminary stages of the 5-year hoshin process that started in mid to late 2021. First, the progress of the catch ball process has been slow as the organization has found itself in a state of constant fire-fighting due to global supply chain disruptions and a highly complex supply chain created during the years of cost reduction efforts. Second, there are issues with how the process itself has been practiced over the years that the organization has found hard to change. I.e., the conversations are driven by compliance rather than learning, possibly due to the nature of medical equipment manufacturing—there are strict regulatory measures related to clinical equipment that drives a bureaucratic compliance system within the organization. Third, the sustainability/CE terminology itself is confusing for practitioners. And finally, their complex supply chain is now under pressure also because of the covid-19 pandemic that has caused supply chains to be disrupted across the globe. Supply chain issues have left parts of the organization in a constant state of firefighting. Because of these issues, the organization is struggling to address the long-term challenges posed by its own hoshin.

In addition, the hoshin system as it is currently practiced is arguably too complex itself and needs to be simplified as current practices hinders the involvement of the front-line of the organization.

With regards to the challenges presented in the literature, findings so far suggest that the lean principles of Continuous Improvement and Respect for People can help companies face up to the sustainability challenge by engaging everyone in problem finding and problem solving, and therefore have an impact outside of the mechanical reduction of waste. Furthermore, from a practitioners' point of view, Hoshin shows promise, however there is a possibility the system can become a bureaucratic exercise and as such hinder real improvements. Furthermore, as CE issues are often complex, so-called "ultra-solutions" are likely to be sought, possibly increasing the likelihood of problem-shifting [27].

We stated our research question as *"How can Hoshin Kanri help companies succeed in the transition towards a circular economy?"* The preliminary observations are promising, but more data is needed as it is too early to indicate performative impact. Therefore, we plan to conduct further interventions together with the case company guided by our initial findings. First, we plan to test a dedicated visual management room (Obeya) for the plant-management team to follow up on the improvements they have planned for 2022 and onwards. Second, we look at how the departments engage operators and other front-line workers in improving CE. Third, we will work with the case company to simplify the language of CE, making it more suitable for practitioner context.

Acknowledgement. The authors acknowledge the support of the Norwegian research council for the research project Circulær.

References

1. Florida, R.: Lean and green: the move to environmentally conscious manufacturing. Calif. Manage. Rev. **39**, 80–105 (1996)
2. Caldera, H.T.S., Desha, C., Dawes, L.: Exploring the role of lean thinking in sustainable business practice: a systematic literature review. J. Clean. Prod. **167**, 1546–1565 (2017)
3. Garza-Reyes, J.A.: Lean and green – a systematic review of the state of the art literature. J. Clean. Prod. **102**, 18–29 (2015)
4. Winans, K., Kendall, A., Deng, H.: The history and current applications of the circular economy concept. Renew. Sustain. Energy Rev. **68**, 825–833 (2017)
5. Ciliberto, C., Szopik-Depczyńska, K., Tarczyńska-Łuniewska, M., Ruggieri, A., Ioppolo, G.: Enabling the Circular Economy transition: a sustainable lean manufacturing recipe for Industry 4.0. Bus. Strateg. Environ. **30**, 3255–3272 (2021)
6. Nadeem, S.P., Garza-Reyes, J.A., Anosike, A.I., Kumar, V.: Coalescing the lean and circular economy. In: Proceedings of the International Conference on Industrial Engineering and Operations Management 2019, pp. 1082–1093 (2019)
7. Kvadsheim, N.P., Nujen, B.B., Powell, D., Reke, E.: Realizing value opportunities for a circular economy: integrating extended value stream mapping and value uncaptured framework. In: Dolgui, A., Bernard, A., Lemoine, D., von Cieminski, G., Romero, D. (eds.) APMS 2021. IAICT, vol. 630, pp. 739–747. Springer, Cham (2021). https://doi.org/10.1007/978-3-030-85874-2_81

8. Kurdve, M., Bellgran, M.: Green lean operationalisation of the circular economy concept on production shop floor level. J. Clean. Prod. **278**, 123223 (2021)
9. Monden, Y.: Cost Reduction Systems: Target Costing and Kaizen Costing. Productivity Press, Portland (1995)
10. Akao, Y.: Hoshin Kanri: Policy Deployement for Successful TQM. Productivity Press, Cambridge (1991)
11. Furuta, K.: Welcome Problems, Find Success. Taylor & Francis, Boca Raton (2022)
12. Fujioka, K.: Toyota speeds up carbon-zero target for factories to 2035. In: Nikkei Asia (2021). https://asia.nikkei.com/Spotlight/Environment/Climate-Change/Toyota-speeds-up-carbon-zero-target-for-factories-to-2035. Accessed 31 Mar 2022
13. Geissdoerfer, M., Savaget, P., Bocken, N.M.P., Hultink, E.J.: The Circular Economy—a new sustainability paradigm? J. Clean. Prod. **143**, 757–768 (2017)
14. Bhattacharya, A., Nand, A., Castka, P.: Lean-green integration and its impact on sustainability performance: a critical review. J. Clean. Prod. **236**, 117697 (2019)
15. Farias, L.M.S., Santos, L.C., Gohr, C.F., de Oliveira, L.C., Amorim, M.H.daS.: Criteria and practices for lean and green performance assessment: systematic review and conceptual framework. J. Clean. Prod. **218**, 746–762 (2019)
16. Tasdemir, C., Gazo, R.: A systematic literature review for better understanding of lean driven sustainability. Sustainability (Switzerland) **10**, 2544 (2018)
17. Schmitt, T., Wolf, C., Lennerfors, T.T., Okwir, S.: Beyond "Leanear" production: a multi-level approach for achieving circularity in a lean manufacturing context. J. Clean. Prod. **318**, 128531 (2021)
18. Shimokawa, K., Fujimoto, T.: Birth of Lean. The Lean Enterprise Institute Inc, Cambridge (2009)
19. Womack, J.P., Jones, D.T., Roos, D.: Machine That Changed the World. Harper Perennial, New York (1990)
20. Ballé, M., Chartier, N., Coignet, P., Olivencia, S., Powell, D.J., Reke, E.: The Lean Sensei. Go, See, Challenge. The Lean Enterprise Institute Inc, Boston (2019)
21. Ballé, M., Jones, D.T., Chaize, J., Fiume, O.: The Lean Strategy: Using Lean to Create Competitive Advantage, Unleash Innovation, and Deliver Sustainable Growth. McGraw Hill Professional, New York (2017)
22. Giordani da Silveira, W., Pinheiro de Lima, E., Gouvea da Costa, S.E., Deschamps, F.: Guidelines for Hoshin Kanri implementation: development and discussion. Prod. Plann. Control **28**, 843–859 (2017)
23. Tennant, C., Roberts, P.: Hoshin Kanri: a tool for strategic policy deployment. Knowl. Process. Manag. **8**, 262–269 (2001)
24. Witcher, B., Butterworth, R.: Hoshin Kanri: how xerox manages. Long Range Plan. **32**, 323–332 (1999)
25. Coghlan, D., Coughlan, P.: Notes toward a philosophy of action learning research. Action Learn. Res. Pract. **7**, 193–203 (2010)
26. Westbrook, R.: Action research: a new paradigm for research in production and operations management. Int. J. Oper. Prod. Manag. **15**, 6–20 (1995)
27. Watzlawick, P.: Ultra-Solutions: How to Fail Most Successfully. WW Norton & Co, New York (1988)

Fostering Circular Manufacturing Through the Integration of Genetic Algorithm and Process Mining

Federica Acerbi[(✉)] , Adalberto Polenghi , Walter Quadrini , Marco Macchi ,
and Marco Taisch

Department of Management, Economics and Industrial Engineering, Politecnico Di Milano,
Via Lambruschini 4/b, 20156 Milan, Italy
{federica.acerbi,adalberto.polenghi,walter.quadrini,
marco-macchi,marco.taisch}@polimi.it

Abstract. Recently, the increasing lack of raw materials is forcing the manufacturing sector in revising the internal operating and strategic activities to embrace Circular Economy (CE) principles thus, moving towards Circular Manufacturing (CM). CE principles are pursued during product design, product realisation, as well as product end-of-life. As an enabler of end-of-life CM strategies, disassembling represents the cornerstone to facilitate other ones to take place, as remanufacturing and recycling. Indeed, nowadays, empowering companies in the disassembling process by maintaining high their environmental sustainability performances is essential. Indeed, identifying the best disassembly sequence that is also energy-effective is an open challenge to guarantee a 360° application of CM strategies. Therefore, the objective of this contribution is to develop a framework able to automatically reconstruct the disassembly sequence while minimising the energy consumption. The solution is based on process mining technique, which aims at representing the original process, and genetic algorithm, which is instead in charge of identifying the solution with minimal energy consumption. Once the framework has been developed, its feasibility has been tested first at laboratory scale and then through a simulated case. The proposed framework represents a Proof of Concept that aims at promoting the pursue of CM strategies in the product end-of-life by facilitating the identification of the disassembly sequence which is also energy-effective.

Keywords: Circular economy · Disassembly · Energy · Process mining ·
Genetic algorithm

1 Introduction

The linear production model is no longer sustainable since it is rapidly and irreversibly damaging the environment requiring drastic corrective actions [1]. Indeed, hundreds of millions of wastes are generated yearly by developed countries together with an

© IFIP International Federation for Information Processing 2022
Published by Springer Nature Switzerland AG 2022
D. Y. Kim et al. (Eds.): APMS 2022, IFIP AICT 664, pp. 407–414, 2022.
https://doi.org/10.1007/978-3-031-16411-8_47

increased energy consumption trend causing carbon dioxide and other greenhouse gasses emissions augment [2]. Moreover, the shortage of resources requires the introduction of new strategies oriented towards the adoption of Circular Economy (CE) paradigm in manufacturing companies, named as Circular Manufacturing (CM) strategies [3]. In this context, although the design phase represents the main area in which applying the CE paradigm in an efficient and effective way, it is extremely important to ensure an easy and sustainable treatment of products at their end-of life (EoL) in case they wouldn't be designed to be circular [4]. EoL-related strategies, such a recycling, remanufacturing and repair, are based on disassembly processes (DP) so to have unitary components and subassemblies available to obtain valuable parts or materials to increase economic efficiency [5].

Nevertheless, although the opportunities are many, there are still some limitations in the correct introduction and exploitation of DP, due to the uncertainty about the disassembly process itself, EoL product quality, demand and yield [4] and high skilled labour requirement to plan the entire DP [6].

In addition, to be effective, thus using few resources in terms of energy, cost and time [7], DP requires lots of data (such as component shape, size and weight, joining elements) [8] that must be available to the company in charge of disassembly.

The challenge this work aims at facing is the exploitation of advanced data analysis techniques to solve the disassembly sequence problem (DSP) in case of few data available, while keeping energy consumption minimisation as a target. The DSP repress the problem of selecting the best sequence of tasks so to minimise or maximise a certain objective function [9]. In the current work, the proposal is a framework based on process mining (PM) to automatically extract the assembly sequence to infer the disassembly one, and genetic algorithms (GA) to identify the DP whose energy consumption is the lowest amongst those DP that are feasible.

2   Background on DSP, Process Mining and Genetic Algorithm

As previously described, the DSP refers to the identification of the best disassembly sequence so to optimise a certain objective function. Hence, DSP challenges mainly refer to the identification of the feasible (set of) sequences and then the identification of the sequence whose performance optimise a certain objective. While GA are widely used to solve the DSP [10], they are usually used for both challenges. However, if the knowledge of the process is not given for granted, a workaround must be identified, and PM is identified as a well-fitted option. The overall framework is presented later in Sect. 3, after a brief excursus on PM and GA that are the ground of this work.

2.1   Process Mining

Process Mining (PM) is a process management and data analysis technique which allows to discover, monitor and improve production processes through the inspection of data coming from the information systems present in manufacturing companies [11]. Benefits like reduced complexity at low effort required from the PM usage, had been evidenced in other fields of study. Indeed, the highlighted PM potentialities are limited time needed for the initial scoping of the data, the PM fast development of an actual process model, the PM capability of mapping complex processes into simple process models and last the PM possibility to analyse and evaluate deviations from the planned process [12].

2.2 Genetic Algorithm

Genetic algorithms are meta-heuristic algorithms based on principles of biological evolution through crossover, mutation, replication, cut-paste and break-joint mechanisms. Species face a process of continuous evolution, generation after generation, intending to achieve better adaptable offspring concerning environmental conditions in which they live. The chromosomes produce offspring chromosomes in such a way that offspring are different but keeping some of the original gene fragments. Indeed, the variation between the two generations is caused by the mutation mechanism that helps to increase chromosome diversity allowing to reach new possibilities [9]. Chromosome's adaptiveness is measured by a fitness value, which is evaluated through a fitness function: an absolute value that represents the goodness of the solution proposed by the chromosome itself [13]. In DSP, GA are widely used since they are able to identify the best disassembly sequence according to specific objectives the company is pursuing.

3 Framework Development

The developed framework is based on PM and GA, which allows to determine the best energy-effective disassembly sequence with the aim of enabling EoL-related CM strategies. The framework has been developed according to three phases: i) analysis of the scientific literature to assess the selected algorithms and techniques and to mathematically define the DSP in terms of objective functions, variables and constraints; ii) framework design and development taking into account required data for each step; iii) framework testing both in a laboratory-scaled environment and through a simulated case.

The literature review was systematic through the following keywords ("Disassembly") AND ("Process Mining" OR "Data Mining" OR "Genetic Algorithm"), which, inserted in Scopus, resulted into 318 documents in the last 10 years. After title and abstract screening, and full reading, a final sample of 59 documents were selected as eligible. In addition to GA, also Artificial Bee Colony (6%) and Grey Wolf Optimizer (4%) have been used.

The optimization algorithm used for DSP usually considers as fitness function the cost (39%) and the completion time (34%). Energy-related objectives account for 24%.

The development of algorithms for DSP must consider various constraints. Worth to mention are sequential disassembly constraints (no parallel operations) and precedence constrains (some operations must be performed before other ones).

With a throughout view of the scientific state of art, it is possible to develop a framework, whose aim is to identify the energy-effective sequence and automatically identify the disassembly sequence through process mining. Indeed, this technique is used very few for DSP according to the literature. The framework is depicted in Fig. 1.

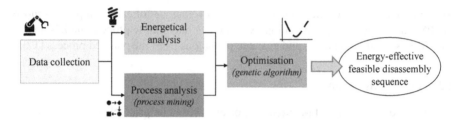

Fig. 1. Framework proposal for energy-effective DSP.

The steps of the framework are the following, going from left to right:

1. Data collection, which refers to different types of data, as operational one for energy analysis and log data for process representation.
2. Energetical analysis to identify hotspots.
3. Process analysis to identify the process sequence through process mining, to be later transformed into disassembly sequence.
4. Optimisation through genetic algorithm for the identification of the cost-effective feasible disassembly sequence.

Starting from the entire batch of data collected from the production systems, those relevant for the DSP problem must be collected. In the scope of this work, the gathered data are related to the consumed energy per machine and the data log recording values of the control variables, usually Boolean, and others like timestamp, the piece ID on which the activity is carried out and the name of the resource (machine) that performs the activity. Once available, the energy data are used to identify hotspots, which are energy demanding machines in production systems. The results are a matrix relating production system resources (machines) with their energy consumption. Furthermore, data logs are used for PM, to infer the disassembly process sequence without a direct knowledge. Indeed, the direct assembly sequence is discovered and reversed so generate a Petri Net that is then translated into a Precedence Matrix, both representing the dismantling precedence.

Finally, the GA takes as input the energy matrix and the Precedence Matrix and looks for a disassembly sequence that respects the dismantling constraints, i.e. feasible, and that also reduces the overall consumed energy, i.e. energy-effective.

4   Framework Testing

The first test sessions have been performed in the laboratory environment of the Industry4.0 Lab at Politecnico di Milano. This laboratory is a semi-automated assembly line devoted to the manufacturing of real-like smartphones, equipped with commercial PLCs and connected to a digital infrastructure compliant with the standards ISA 95 and IEC 62264. The line is composed of seven stations, realising one operation each, as reported in Fig. 2, together with the product parts. In a previous work by [14], the line has been demonstrated to be capable of some disassembling operations too. For this reason, it has been used as first testing environment for this research, although the authors are aware about key limitations currently present: the disassembly process does not include the transportations and the disassembly phases considered for this experiment are based on the simple reverse flow of the assembly phases. Specifically for this Proof of Concept (PoC), the last key limitation implies that the energy of disassembly operations is assumed through corrective coefficients.

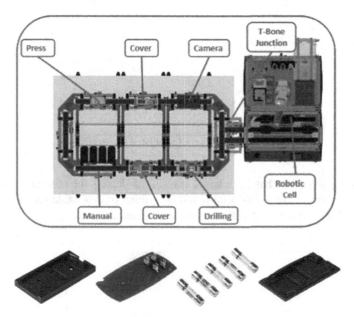

Fig. 2. Industry 4.0 Lab line (rendered).

In the PoC, after an explorative analysis, two variables of interest have been selected for acquisition (one Boolean signal describing the presence of a product in working position and the integer value of the active power consumed), then a chain of Python scripts implementing the methodology described in Sect. 3 has been developed to feed the GA with the Precedence Matrix and energy matrix. After the phases of generating the initial population, crossing-over, mutation, union of populations and selection of the best chromosome, the best and feasible disassembly sequence in terms of energy consumption have been selected, as displayed in Fig. 3.

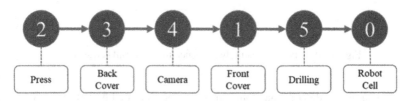

Fig. 3. Identified process sequence for the disassembly process.

Given the inherent limitations of the line (in terms of paths allowed), a second run of the procedure has been performed in a simulated environment, where more products were assumed, hence more paths were allowed (as displayed in the Petri Net of Fig. 4).

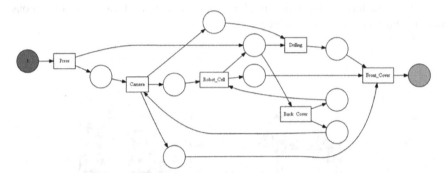

Fig. 4. Petri net of simulated scenario.

The same procedure has been hence run (Fig. 5 depicts the progresses of the GA) and the sequence of Fig. 6 has been found as optimal (unreachable for the real line of Industry4.0Lab, but coherent with the simulated scenario).

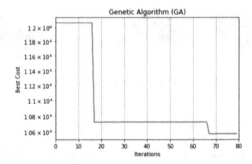

Fig. 5. GA fitness function value by iteration for the simulated scenario.

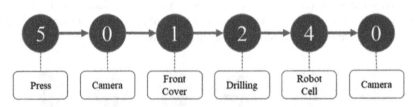

Fig. 6. Identified disassembly sequence for the simulated scenario.

At this moment, this optimal solution suffers of afore mentioned limitations. Especially, through process mining, only the assembly sequence could be discovered, while the disassembly operations should be put manually. This represents the main limitation, target of an ongoing research work, where ontological models may inform about the disassembly operations given the assembly ones.

5 Discussion and Conclusions

The present contribution aims at developing and testing a framework to support an energy-effective DSP, as one of the main strategies to pursue circularity in manufacturing companies. The design and development of the framework is based on an ensemble of several techniques and algorithms. Firstly, PM is used to extract the knowledge of the current assembly sequence and reverse it to identify a first disassembly sequence. Then, energy matrix and Precedence Matrix are inputs to the GA that allows to find the disassembling sequence that is feasible and energy-effective at the same time. To test the feasibility of the framework, two applications have been performed. Starting with a successful but simplified case at laboratory scale, the sample of data has been amplified in a simulated scenario to test the robustness. The framework shows its capability to tackle DSP with a complete data-driven approach, given that it does rely only on data gathered from the production systems.

From a theoretical point of view, the proposed framework enables to overcome the limitations identified in the extant literature about the lack of models enabling the automated creation of a precedence tool enabling the identification of the optimal disassembly sequence in a case where no prior knowledge about the dismantling process exists. From a practical point of view the model enables to empower manufacturing companies in putting in practice an optimised disassembly sequence process by receiving it in an automated way the optimal sequence of tasks to be performed to limit the energy consumptions.

Nonetheless, at the current state of advancement, the main limitations to pinpoint are: i) simple disassembly sequence based on the reverse flow of the assembly one, ii) impossibility to practically test the disassembly sequence, iii) one-type product only (more products only simulated, hence more paths), iv) hypothetical energy consumption of the disassembly phases through corrective factors and v) relatively controlled environment in which the framework has been tested. Future research will overcome these limitations, especially related to the possibility to introduce coherent disassembly operations; at the moment ongoing research is focused on the introduction of ontological models that may infer, starting from the process mining information, the disassembly operations required, and the GA could then arrange them in the most energy-effective way. Furthermore, the solution must be extended so to test it in more complex environments, both simulated for numerical experimentation and real to test industrial viability. Additionally, in future research, the authors will apply the framework in an empirical environment, where specific disassembly phases are required and may differ according to the product type.

References

1. Korhonen, J., Honkasalo, A., Seppälä, J.: Circular economy: the concept and its limitations. Ecol. Econ. **143**, 37–46 (2018). https://doi.org/10.1016/j.ecolecon.2017.06.041

2. OECD, Global Material Resources Outlook to 2060. OECD (2019). https://doi.org/10.1787/9789264307452-en
3. Acerbi, F., Taisch, M.: A literature review on circular economy adoption in the manufacturing sector. J. Cleaner Prod., 123086 (2020). https://doi.org/10.1016/j.jclepro.2020.123086
4. Slama, I., Ben-Ammar, O., Dolgui, A., Masmoudi, F.: Genetic algorithm and Monte Carlo simulation for a stochastic capacitated disassembly lot-sizing problem under random lead times. Comput. Ind. Eng. **159**, 107468 (2021). https://doi.org/10.1016/j.cie.2021.107468
5. Wang, K., Li, X., Gao, L., Li, P., Gupta, S.M.: A genetic simulated annealing algorithm for parallel partial disassembly line balancing problem. Appl. Soft Comput. **107** (2021). https://doi.org/10.1016/j.asoc.2021.107404
6. Institute of Electrical and Electronics Engineers, An Economical Approach for Disassembly Sequence Planning (2019)
7. Marconi, M., Germani, M., Mandolini, M., Favi, C.: Applying data mining technique to disassembly sequence planning: a method to assess effective disassembly time of industrial products. Int. J. Prod. Res. **57**(2), 599–623 (2019). https://doi.org/10.1080/00207543.2018.1472404
8. Zhuang, X.C., Wu, Y., Gu, J., Li, C. X.: Disassembly process management based on BOM. Liaoning Gongcheng Jishu Daxue Xuebao (Ziran Kexue Ban)/J. Liaoning Tech. Univ. (Nat. Sci. Ed.) 25(2), 268–271 (2006)
9. Tseng, H.E., Huang, Y.M., Chang, C.C., Lee, S.C.: Disassembly sequence planning using a Flatworm algorithm. J. Manuf. Syst. **57**, 416–428 (2020). https://doi.org/10.1016/j.jmsy.2020.10.014
10. Tseng, H.E., Chang, C.C., Lee, S.C., Huang, Y.M.: A Block-based genetic algorithm for disassembly sequence planning. Expert Syst. Appl. **96**, 492–505 (2018). https://doi.org/10.1016/j.eswa.2017.11.004
11. van der Aalst, W.: Process mining: overview and opportunities. ACM Trans. Manag. Inf. Syst. **3**(2) (2012). doi: https://doi.org/10.1145/2229156.2229157
12. Ortmeier, C., Henningsen, N., Langer, A., Reiswich, A., Karl, A., Herrmann, C.: Framework for the integration of process mining into life cycle assessment. Procedia CIRP **98**, 163–168 (2021). https://doi.org/10.1016/j.procir.2021.01.024
13. Ren, Y., Zhang, C., Zhao, F., Xiao, H., Tian, G.: An asynchronous parallel disassembly planning based on genetic algorithm. Eur. J. Oper. Res. **269**(2), 647–660 (2018). https://doi.org/10.1016/j.ejor.2018.01.055
14. Rocca, R., Rosa, P., Sassanelli, C., Fumagalli, L., Terzi, S.: Integrating virtual reality and digital twin in circular economy practices: a laboratory application case. Sustainability (Switzerland) **12**(6) (2020). https://doi.org/10.3390/su12062286

Sustainable Multi-period Production with Core and Adjacent Product Portfolio

Elham Jelodari, Khaled Medini$^{(\boxtimes)}$, and Xavier Delorme

Mines Saint-Etienne, Univ Clermont Auvergne, CNRS, UMR 6158 LIMOS, Institut Henri
Fayol, 42023 Saint-Etienne, France
`khaled.medini@emse.fr`

Abstract. Manufacturing and service companies need to increase service level
to ensure their survival. However, in recent years this is not the only problem with
production systems, the environmental impact became a major concern for manufacturing and service companies alike. In this article, we jointly consider time,
cost, and environmental impact for production planning. To achieve this goal,
collaborative decision-making with three decision-makers (DMs) is assumed to
adjust sustainability performance through choosing the most suitable production
type and appropriate production day. Financial managers, industrial managers, and
environmental managers are three decision-makers who collaborate to improve
responsiveness, and to reduce total production cost, and CO_2 emissions sequentially. To this end, a mixed-integer multi-objective mathematical model is suggested; $\mathcal{E}$-constraint is used to solve the model. With the proposed model, DMs
can make decisions on which products are produced on which day in a way to
have trade-off among indicators.

Keywords: Product portfolio · Collaboration · Linear programming ·
Responsiveness · CO_2 emissions · Sustainable production

1 Introduction and Related Works

Firms are increasingly extending their offering with a wide variety of products, which has
led to a lot of competition in meeting customers' demands. This led to many changes in
the firms' environment based on the changes of customers' demands. In an environment
that is constantly changing, firms must be more responsive to disruptions and manage
all external and internal threats [1, 2]. Responsiveness in supply chains is the ability
to respond to changes as quickly as possible [3]. This definition shows that there is a
close relation between agility and responsiveness [4, 5]. Actually, agility is the response
rapidly to the changes (e.g. in customers' demands) to increase the responsiveness of the
supply chain [5, 6]. Although responsiveness is one of the topics discussed in detail in the
supply chain [5, 7–11], only few studies were concerned with production management
[4, 12].

© IFIP International Federation for Information Processing 2022
Published by Springer Nature Switzerland AG 2022
D. Y. Kim et al. (Eds.): APMS 2022, IFIP AICT 664, pp. 415–422, 2022.
https://doi.org/10.1007/978-3-031-16411-8_48

A very important point in the production system is that some products may have a lower priority than other products. For example in the Covid-2019 era, the production of masks or alcohol was a priority for cosmetics companies and a specific day (period) for their production and delivery was allocated. While some other products had lower priority and their production depended on their cost-effectiveness. Generally, low priority products can be produced on different days (period window) if they are economical. In this case, the preference of the production system is to produce them on the right day and at the same time in a fast way.

Reducing cost is not the only challenges companies face. Given the nature of the production and manufacturing industry, it can greatly contribute to climate change by, e.g., emitting Greenhouse Gases (GHGs) [13]. Due to the increase in GHGs, authorities, and policymakers tightened the regulations on emissions production. Recently, the European Commission proposed the first European Climate law, aiming at achieving a climate-neutral Europe by 2050 [14]. The report asserts that one of the intermediary steps is to reduce GHG emissions by at least 55% by 2030 compared to 1990. This indeed translates to emissions targets at the country and company levels. The emergence of environmental concerns motivated researchers to focus on emissions produced in production system. Furthermore, a production system is sustainable if any interaction has an impact on the economic, social, and environment [15]. These interactions, which can be taken, done in the manufacturing system are among the popular topics of literature in the last years [16, 17]. Sustainability is a vital key for the survival of the manufacturing systems, which can cover economic, environment, and human factors at the same time [18]. Although these objectives are essential to include in the real production systems, there are not enough academic studies in this field [18].

Although in the literature of supply chain [19] examined the relationship among responsiveness, cost, risk, and agility, in production management there is not any study to include sustainability concept in terms of responsiveness. The aim of [18] was to investigate how different levels of flexibility and agility (as two important antecedents of supply chain responsiveness) lead to different levels of responsiveness. In the publication, on the one hand, environment dimension was not included and on the other hand, all demands must be satisfied.

Within the limit of the current study, we jointly consider time, cost, and environmental impact for production planning. To achieve this goal, collaborative decision-making with three decision-makers (DMs) is assumed to adjust sustainability performance through choosing the most suitable production type and appropriate production day. Financial managers, industrial managers, and environmental managers are three decision-makers who collaborate to improve responsiveness, and to reduce total production cost, and CO_2 emissions sequentially.

A mixed integer multi-objective mathematical model is proposed to model the collaborative decision making problem and $\mathcal{E}$-constraint is an approach to solve it. With the proposed model, DMs can make decisions on which products are produced on which day in a way to have trade-off among indicators.

The reminder of the article is organized as follows. Section 2 reports on the problem definition and presents the mathematical model. Section 3 presents the results of mathematical model for a small size problem to observe the value of indicators and illustrate decision making between DMs. Conclusion and future research propositions are summarized in Sect. 4.

2 Problem Description and Research Mode

Making a decision via collaboration of three DMs to determine the most efficient production plans in the appropriate period is the base of the current research. To achieve minimum costs and minimum CO_2 emissions beside maximization of responsiveness, three decision makers (financial manager, industrial manager, and environmental manager) collaborate to produce the most appropriate products. To determine optimal solutions, mathematical modelling was identified as the most appropriate approach. Mathematical models help DMs observe the effects their decisions on KPIs through multi-objective functions. A mixed integer mathematical programming model is proposed to produce two types of products in appropriate periods (the output of the model) to satisfy minimization of costs, saving CO_2 emissions, and maximization of responsiveness. The suggested model is a mixed-integer mathematical model involving binary variables (y_{it}) and integer variables (q_{it}). The two categories of products for which plans are generated are:

1. *Core products*: all the products in this category should be produced in a pre-defined period. Furthermore, if a product is set in this category, it is obligatory to be produced.
2. *Adjacent products*: products in this category are produced if they are appropriate to production (in terms of three indicators and collaboration of decision makers). These products are not compulsory and they can be produced at more than one specific period (period window). If a product is appropriate for production, it is produced in a most suitable and earliest period (to improve responsiveness).

The parameters and decision variables for the proposed model are described respectively in Tables 1 and 2.

The proposed mixed integer mathematical model is:

$$Min \sum_{i \in I} \sum_{t \in H} p\, c_{it} y_{it} \tag{1}$$

$$Min \sum_{i \in I_2} \sum_{t \in [\alpha_i, \beta_i]} y'_{it} \tag{2}$$

$$Min \sum_{i \in I} \sum_{t \in H} g\, \Theta_{it} \tag{3}$$

$st :$

$$\sum_{t \in [\alpha_i, \beta_i]} y_{it} \leq 1, \quad \forall i \in I_2 \tag{4}$$

Table 1. Parameters for the presented model

Symbols	Description
$I = I_1^h \cup I_2$	Set of total products variants (products in category 1 and products in category 2)
I_1^h	Set of products type 1 in period (day)$h \in H$
H	Time horizon
py	Production capacity
pc_{it}	Production cost of variant $i \in I$ in period $t \in H$
g	Emissions produced (g) by a production of a variant $i \in I$
D_{it}	Upper demand limit for variant $i \in I$ in period $t \in H$
d_{it}	Lower demand limit for variant $i \in I$ in period $t \in H$
α_i	Lower bound of period window for product $i \in I_2$ in second category
β_i	Upper bound of period window for product $i \in I_2$ in second category
M	Big-M

Table 2. Decision variables of the proposed model

Symbols	Description
y_{it}	1, if and only if variant $i \in I$ in period $t \in H$ is produced; 0, otherwise
q_{it}	Representing production volume of variant $i \in I$ in period $t \in H$
y'_{it}	Auxiliary variable (in the making linear of second objective function is used)
Θ_{it}	Auxiliary variable (in the making linear of third objective function is used)

$$y'_{it} \geq t \times y_{it} - \alpha_i, \quad \forall i \in I_2, \ \forall t \in [\alpha_i, \beta_i] \tag{5}$$

$$\sum_{i \in I} q_{it} \leq \sum_{i \in I} y_{it} py, \forall t \in H \tag{6}$$

$$d_{it} \leq q_{it} \leq D_{it}, \quad \forall i \in I, \ \forall t \in H \tag{7}$$

$$\Theta_{it} \leq M y_{it}, \ \forall i \in I, \ \forall t \in H \tag{8}$$

$$\Theta_{it} \leq q_{it}, \ \forall i \in I, \ \forall t \in H \tag{9}$$

$$\Theta_{it} \geq q_{it} - (1 - y_{it})M, \quad \forall i \in I, \ \forall t \in H \tag{10}$$

$$\Theta_{it} \geq 0, \ \forall i \in I, \forall t \in H \tag{11}$$

$$y'_{it} \geq 0, \ \forall i \in I_2, \ \forall t \in [\alpha_i, \beta_i] \tag{12}$$

$$q_{it} \geq 0, \ \forall i \in I, \ \forall t \in H \tag{13}$$

$$y_{it} = 0 \ for \ any \ i \in I_2 \ and \ for \ any \ t \notin [\alpha_i, \beta_i] \tag{14}$$

$$y_{it} = 0 \ for \ any \ i \in, I_1^h, \ t \neq h \tag{15}$$

First objective function minimizes total production costs (Eq. 1). Second objective function with Eqs. (5) maximizes responsiveness by minimization the difference between the lower bound (or the earlier possible production period) and the actual production period. Minimization of CO_2 emissions is indicated by third objective function (Eq. 3). Equations (4) ensures that an adjacent product can be either produced in a period within its period window or not produced. Constraints (6) and (7) check the maximum capacity of productions and demands. Constraints (8)–(10) are used to make linear the third objective function. Constraints (11)–(15) guarantee integrality and non-negativity condition for the decision variables.

3 Experimental Results

We solved the suggested mixed-integer linear programming model by $\mathcal{E}$-constraint approach due to its easy application for enterprises where there are small size instances.

In the applied small instance, the time horizon covers 5 periods (days), the period window for products in second category is generated randomly between (1, 5). The rest of data like demands, maximum capacity, and CO_2 emissions are generated randomly or adopted from [20]. GAMS 12.6 implemented the $\mathcal{E}$-constraint approach and the results are illustrated by Fig. 1 and Fig. 2. According to Fig. 1, different trade-offs between responsiveness and cost can be identified which facilitates negotiation and decision making between industrial and financial managers. In Fig. 2, the correlation between cost and CO2 emissions was depicted to observe what is the effects of increasing (decreasing) the costs on the environmental indicator. This figure is helpful for environment manager and financial manager to make decision about the environment and financial indicators by analysing the solutions on Pareto front. It is clear to save more CO_2 emissions; the enterprise has to spend more money. Generally, the proposed model is expected to be helpful for DMs to negotiate decisions on production plans based on different perspectives (financial, environmental, responsiveness).

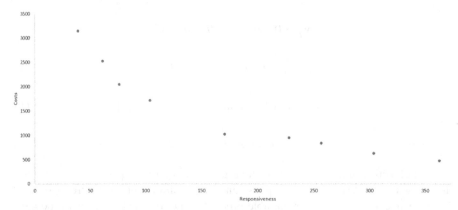

Fig. 1. Pareto front of first and second objective function (costs and responsiveness)

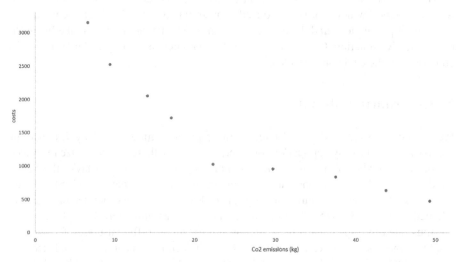

Fig. 2. Pareto front of first and third objective function (costs and CO_2 emissions)

4 Discussion and Conclusions

In this study, a mixed integer multi-objective mathematical model was suggested to produce two product categories in a time horizon. The objective is to minimize all the costs, increase responsiveness, and minimize CO_2 emissions. The problem was solved by ε-constraint approach (for small size instances) to produce the most suitable combination of products in a time horizon.

This paper contribution is threefold: first, the model considers two category of products: high priority with predefined production day (core products) and low priority products with different days of productions (adjacent products). Second, the model focuses on three indicators covering some of the broad sustainability spectrum. Actually, by collaboration among three DMs (financial, industrial, and environment managers) the most suitable level in each indicator can be identified. Third, the model takes into account collaboration among decision makers. The model is expected to be useful for managing the ramp-up phase where newly developed products (adjacent) are progressively introduced into the market. This can benefit from the work of [20].

One limitation of the current research is the fact that risk is not considered in the model while it could be a key for companies to take planning decisions. Moreover, another perspective is to solve the presented model in large size instances with heuristics and metaheuristics algorithm. To this end, the challenge of data collection should be addressed. This task is complex because required data comes from multiple sources (environmental databases, cost data, etc.). Another challenge that shall be addressed is to include stochastic parameters to have a model more close to real applications.

References

1. Battistella, C., Toni, A.D., Zan, Z.D., Pes, E.: Cultivating business model agility through focused capabilities: a multiple case study. J. Bus. Res. **73**, 65–82 (2017)
2. Yang, J.: Supply chain agility: securing performance for Chinese manufacturers. Int. J. Prod. Econ. **150**, 104–113 (2014)
3. Bernardes, E.S., Hanna, M.D.: A theoretical review of flexibility, agility and responsiveness in the operations management literature toward a conceptual definition of customer responsiveness. Int. J. Oper. Prod. Manag. **29**(2), 30–53 (2009)
4. Gunasekaran, A., Laib, K., Cheng, T.C.: Responsive supply chain: a competitive strategy in a networked economy. Omega **36**, 549–564 (2008)
5. Yusuf, M.A., Gunasekaran, A., Adeleye, E.O., Sivayoganathan, K.: Agile supply chain capabilities. Determinants of competitive objectives. Eur. J. Oper. Res. **159**(2), 379–392 (2004)
6. Chen, K., Zhao, H., Xiao, T.: Outsourcing contracts and ordering decisions of a supply chain under multi-dimensional uncertainties. Comput. Ind. Eng. **130**, 127–141 (2019)
7. Um, J., Lyons, A., Lam, H.K., Cheng, T.C., Dominguez-Peryd, C.: Product variety management and supply chain performance: a capability perspective on their relationships and competitiveness implications. Int. J. Prod. Econ. **187**, 15–26 (2017)
8. Nooraie, S.R.: Mitigating supply and demand risk of disruptions through trade off among risk, cost and supply chain capabilities. Doctoral dissertation, North Carolina Agricultural and Technical State University (2017)
9. Kim, M., Suresh, N.C., Hillmer, C.K.: An impact of manufacturing flexibility and technological dimensions of manufacturing strategy on improving supply chain responsiveness: business environment perspective. Int. J. Prod. Res. **51**(18), 5597–5611 (2013)
10. Gong, Y., Janssen, M.: From policy implementation to business process management: principles for creating flexibility and agility. Gov. Inf. Q. **29**(1), 61–71 (2012)
11. Matson, J.B., McFarlane, D.C.: Assessing the responsiveness of existing production operations. Int. J. Oper. Prod. Manag. **19**(8), 765–784 (1999)
12. Bernardes, E.S., Hanna, M.D.: A theoretical review of flexibility, agility and responsiveness in the operations management literature: toward a conceptual definition of customer responsiveness. Int. J. Oper. Prod. Manag. **29**(1), 30–53 (2009)
13. United Nations (2015). https://sustainabledevelopment.un.org/topics/climatechange
14. Jäger-Waldau, A., Kougias, I., Taylor, N., Thiel, C.: How photovoltaics can contribute to GHG emission reductions of 55% in the EU by 2030. Renew. Sustain. Energy Rev. **1**(126), 109836 (2020)

15. Sarkar, P., Rachuri, S., Suh, H.W., Lyons, K., Sriram, R.D.: A measure of product sustainability based on triple bottom line. In: ASME 2009 Int'l. Design Engineering Technical Conferences & Computers and Information in Engineering Conference IDETC/CIE, San Diego, CA (2009)
16. Labuschagne, C., Brent, A.C., Van Erck, R.P.G.: Assessing the sustainability performances of industries. J. Clean. Prod. **13**(4), 373–385 (2005)
17. Ageron, B., Gunasekaran, A., Spalanzani, A.: Sustainable supply management: an empirical study. Int. J. Prod. Econ. **140**(1), 168–182 (2012)
18. Pardo-Jaramillo, S., Muñoz-Villamizar, A., Osuna, I., Roncancio, R.: Mapping research on customer centricity and sustainable organizations. Sustainability **12**(19), 7908 (2020)
19. Shekarian, M., Nooraie, S.V.R., Parast, M.M.: An examination of the impact of flexibility and agility on mitigating supply chain disruptions. Int. J. Prod. Econ. **220**, 107438 (2020)
20. Medini, K., Wuest, T., Jelodari, E., Romero, D., Laforest, V.: A decision support system to operationalize customer-centric sustainability. Procedia CIRP **103**, 122–127 (2021)

Cognitive and Autonomous AI
in Manufacturing and Supply Chains

Dynamic Job Shop Scheduling Based on Order Remaining Completion Time Prediction

Hao Wang[1] , Tao Peng[1(✉)] , Alexandra Brintrup[2] , Thorsten Wuest[3] ,
and Renzhong Tang[1]

[1] Institute of Industrial Engineering, School of Mechanical Engineering, Zhejiang University,
Hangzhou 310027, China
tao_peng@zju.edu.cn
[2] Institute of Manufacturing, Department of Engineering, University of Cambridge,
Cambridge CB3 0FS, UK
[3] Industrial and Management Systems Engineering, West Virginia University, Morgantown,
WV 26506-6070, USA

Abstract. Emerging ubiquity of smart sensing in production environments provide opportunities to make use of fine-grained, real-time data to support decision-making. One, currently untapped opportunity is the prediction of order remaining completion time (ORCT) which can be used to improve production scheduling. Recent research has focused on the development of ORCT prediction models however, their integration into scheduling algorithms is an understudied area, especially in job shop environments where processing times can be highly variable. In this paper, an artificial neural network was developed to predict ORCT based on real-time job shop status data which is then integrated with classical heuristic rules for facilitating dynamic scheduling. A simulation study with four scenarios was developed to test the performance of our approach. The results demonstrated improved completion time, however tardiness was not reduced under all scenarios. In moving this research forward, we discuss the need for further research into combining static and dynamic characteristics and priority rule design for satisfying multiple objectives.

Keywords: Order remaining completion time prediction · Dynamic scheduling · Artificial neural network · Heuristic rules

1 Introduction

Many small- and medium-sized enterprises (SMEs) focusing on Make-To-Order (MTO) production face the challenge of providing on-time order delivery whilst operating under highly uncertain environments [1]. In a typical job shop environment, simple First-Come-First-Serve production leads to long completion times and order tardiness. Order remaining completion time (ORCT), also termed as order completion time [2] or job remaining time [3], is defined as the time that elapses between a customer's order is created and order completion in the production environment [4]. The actual order due date

© IFIP International Federation for Information Processing 2022
Published by Springer Nature Switzerland AG 2022
D. Y. Kim et al. (Eds.): APMS 2022, IFIP AICT 664, pp. 425–433, 2022.
https://doi.org/10.1007/978-3-031-16411-8_49

depends on the ORCT which impacts the efficacy of subsequent production scheduling. However, predicting the ORCT of an incoming or in-production order is quite challenging, particularly in a job shop with high product variance and production uncertainties such as fluctuating processing time and machine availability.

Due to the highly variant nature of job shops, heuristic rule-based dynamic scheduling has been implemented to create feasible schemes in near real-time. In the past decades, shortest processing time rule (SPT), earliest due date rule (EDD), least work content in the next queue rule (WINQ) and cost over time rule (COVERT) [5] have been proposed to prioritize the waiting jobs considering characteristics including processing time, lead time of jobs, and work content of machines. Once the ORCT of order at any time can be acquired, it can be considered as an important indicator for evaluating the order's priority for dynamic scheduling. Dynamic scheduling involves using these priority rules which then changes the processing order of the waiting jobs, which in turn affects their completion times. Given the interdependence of ORCT and production scheduling, there is a gap in literature exploring how these solution approaches may be combined and what would the resulting efficacy of doing so would be.

This paper explores this research gap by proposing to dispatch incoming and in-production orders based on online predicted ORCT. Firstly, production related data that will affect ORCT are analyzed and used to train an artificial neural network based prediction model (ORCTpNet). Secondly, orders are prioritized based on predicted ORCT for to minimize order completion time and tardiness.

2 Brief Review

The essence of our proposed approach relies in ORCT prediction based on real-time job shop production data. We first review existing works on ORCT prediction, mainly focusing on the use of machine learning based approaches. Next, research on heuristic rules based dynamic scheduling are introduced.

2.1 ORCT Prediction

In ORCT prediction studies have mainly concentrated on analytical methods [6, 7] by constructing mathematical models under restrictive assumptions or simulation methods [8, 9] that require long computing time to obtain sufficient samples. The asumptative nature of analytical models, and high computational times required by simulation models prohibit these from being used in real-time production scheduling.

With the increased popularity of smart sensing solutions deployed in job shop environments, production data can be continuously streamed which may be used to develop ANN models, creating a data-driven approach. In an ANN model data from machinery, WIP, materials and orders can be feature-engineered as inputs to estimate ORCT. Compared with analytical and simulation based methods, a data-driven method treats a complex manufacturing system as a black box and has the advantage of achieving higher accuracy without having to resort to restrictive assumptions. However, ANN also has the limitation of a lack of explainability and high dependency on data quality.

Researchers have highlighted many factors to be considered to predict ORCT successfully. According to Liu [10], the key features affecting ORCT include production process, buffer queue length, order content, workload and status of machines, continuous working period of machines as some of these. Huang et al. [11] developed a hybrid approach combining the Long Short-Term Memory (LSTM) network and analytical system model to predict the product completion time in a flow shop considering the product type, processing time and queue length of machines, but no dynamic events were considered. Wang and Jiang [2] proposed a deep neural network-based order completion time prediction method by using real-time job shop RFID data, which include the types and waiting list information of all WIPs, real-time processing progress of all WIPs under machining, but the breakdown of machines was not considered. In the real production environment, dynamic events such as machine failure and repair, random arrival of orders and worker shift and their impacts on the ORCT should be considered, in order to make the prediction models in accordance with the actual situations.

2.2 Dynamic Scheduling with Heuristic Rules

Dynamic scheduling does not create or update schedules. Instead, it uses heuristic rules to prioritize jobs waiting for processing. When a source becomes available, the scheduling algorithm sorts the job queue by pre-designated criteria with the first-ranked job being dispatched for processing. In real-world scenarios, construction heuristics are often the method of choice for creating feasible schedules of reasonable quality within a relatively short computation time, as fast decision-making processes are of vital importance in uncertain manufacturing environments [12]. In Blackstone's work [13], frequently used heuristic rules for scheduling were classified into four categories: processing time-oriented, due date-oriented, workload-oriented and combined rules. EDD and COVERT rules both suggest to take the due date into consideration when evaluating the priority of a waiting job, but it's challenging to provide an accurate due date of an incoming job, and an experience-dependent estimated due date, for example, the Little's law [14], make these heuristic rules fail to achieve the desired outcome.

Gyulai et al. [15] investigated a flow shop scheduling problem to adjust the job priorities based on machine learning-based prediction of manufacturing lead times. To achieve situation-awareness, dynamic scheduling should rely on the combination of static data (e.g., product attributes) and event-driven data. Therefore, online ORCT prediction should be considered simultaneously in dynamic scheduling to allow for more realistic scheduling solutions.

3 Research Methodology

In this study, a discrete MTO manufacturing job shop is investigated where each machine can process a certain task of each job. A job will be processed on each machine once and some machines may not be occupied by the job's task sequence. Each task of a job can only be processed on one dedicated machine. A simulation model has been developed to reflect the real production and act as a test bed for the proposed research framework (as shown in Fig. 1). The framework outlines four main tasks.

Task 1: production data from sensors and devices are statistically analyzed to mathematically describe the uncertainties.

Task 2: a simulation model reflecting the real situations and dynamic events is built and verified upon statistic data.

Task 3: the ORCTpNet is developed and trained based on hybrid simulation and production data.

Task 4: heuristic rules-based dynamic scheduling with online predicted ORCT is implemented in the simulation to reduce tardiness and order completion time.

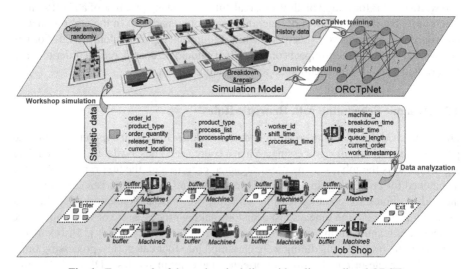

Fig. 1. Framework of dynamic scheduling with online predicted ORCT.

3.1 Problem Statement

There are five products to be processed on a same eight-machine production line and each of them has individual routes and processing times. Orders are released randomly to the job shop and the due date d_j of order j can be calculated by Eq. (1) where OR_{jt} is the predicted ORCT of order j at its release time r_j. For a given amount of orders O, C is the completion time of the last finished order as Eq. (2) and F is the sum of tardiness of all orders as Eq. (3). The objective functions of interest include the completion time C and tardiness F, depicted as Eq. (4).

$$d_j = r_j + OR_{jt}, t = r_j, j = 1, 2, \ldots, O \tag{1}$$

$$C = \max C_j, j = 1, 2, \ldots, O \tag{2}$$

$$F = \sum_{j=1}^{O} \max(C_j - d_j, 0) \tag{3}$$

$$f = \min(C, F) \tag{4}$$

3.2 ORCTpNet Training

When an order is released to the job shop or enters the waiting buffer of one machine, there are numerous production status data to be considered to predict the ORCT. Theoretically, if an order can be processed without delays at each machine, the ORCT would simply be the sum of processing times, determined by product type and quantity. In real production, the order might need to wait in the queue of an occupied or faulty machine and the processing times might fluctuate. Here, four types of production status data are selected to construct the feature set of ORCTpNet: order-related, product-related, worker-related and machine-related data as shown in Fig. 1. Product and order-related data for a given location can be acquired from ERP, whilst the remaining data are real-time and streamed from MES. By tracing back the completion time of historical orders and the work timestamps of each machine, the order remaining completion time at each machine can be calculated to train ORCTpNet as Algorithm 1.

Algorithm 1. ORCTpNet training

Input: Dataset D, train_set_size s, epochs E
   D = MinMaxScaler(D)
   train_set, test_set = split(D, s)
   construct ORCTpNet $A(\odot)$
   repeat for $A(\odot)$
        for epochs in 1,..., E do
        train $A(\odot)$ with train_set
   examine $A(\odot)$ with test_set
   until for the performance of $A(\odot)$ is satisfactory
   Save the trained $A^*(\odot)$
Output: $A^*(\odot)$

3.3 Close-Loop Production Scheduling

Numerous open-source tools have been introduced to develop and train machine learning models such as TensorFlow, Scikit-learn and PyTorch. These tools are usually implemented in Python and need to integrate with job shop environment constructed by simulation platform. Incompatibility between different programming languages induces time delays. In this paper, the connection between Java-based job shop simulation model and Python-based ORCT prediction model is realized through flask-http-client [16]. When an order enters in the waiting buffer of a machine, a request is triggered by the machine to acquire the ORCT of this order. As a response, the predicted ORCT is sent to the machine. Then, the priority of the incoming order can be calculated and the waiting orders in the queue are reordered. In this way, online ORCT prediction and close-loop dynamic scheduling can be realized with minimal time delays and instability.

4 Simulation Experiments

4.1 Parameter Setting

We investigate an office furniture manufacturing job shop. The standard processing time of each process is normally distributed with mean 12.0 min and variance 0.5. Workers change shifts 8 h one day. Order arrival follows a triangularAV distribution with the mean value of 15 min and variance of 0.5, and the quantity of product in each order follows a uniform (50, 100) distribution. The time between machine failures follows a uniform (5.0, 8.0) hour distribution and the repair time follows a triangular (0.5, 2.0, 1.0) hour distribution.

4.2 Model Training and Performance Evaluation

During the simulation, each order follows an individual route and its processing time on each machine is related to product type, quantity and the operator. When the machine breaks down, the order being processed is suspended until the machine is repaired. After model logic and trial validation, the simulation model has been run for 30 days and 36801 records were obtained to train the ORCTpNet. Each record contains the production status data when the order was entered in the waiting buffer of the machine as input features and the actual ORCT was the label. In order to meet the near-real-time requirements of online prediction, the structure of the neural network should be as simple as possible such that computational time is minimized whilst prediction accuracy maximised. A normal back-propagation network including four dense layers (100-100-50-1 units) is deployed on TensorFlow and the output of each layer is processed by batch normalization to accelerate the training and avoid over-fitting [17]. The optimizer used in this case study is AdamOptimizer with learning rate $\alpha = 0.001$ and the training batch size is 128. The training process is depicted in Fig. 2. Both training loss and testing loss decreases substantially with the training epochs.

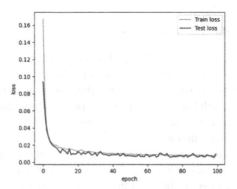

Fig. 2. Training process.

When ORCTpNet has been used at different machines, the results were satisfactory of the first four machines, whereas the prediction results were always zero for the last four machines as shown in Fig. 3. The reason was that orders were about to be completed at the last four machines so the ORCT at these locations was smaller than that of the machines forward, which led to sample values close to zero after Min-max normalization. To overcome this problem, the model was retrained by using samples from the last four machines and the resulting two networks were deployed to predict ORCT at different locations.

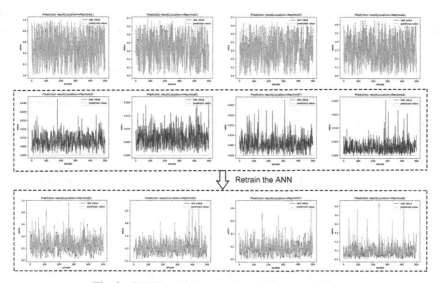

Fig. 3. ORCT prediction results at different machines.

4.3 Performance Compared with Classic Heuristic Rules

The aforementioned classic heuristic rules such as EDD and COVERT consider a fixed order due date d_j and remaining processing time R_{jm} to calculate the priority of job j in the queue of machine m at time t (ρ_{jmt}), whereas in a priority-based production environment, the expected due date is continuously fluctuating with preempt-production at each machine. We introduce the real-time ORCT OR_{jt} to calculate order due date at any time, then the EDD and COVERT rules can be adapted as Eq. (5) and (6).

$$\text{EDD}^* : \rho_{jmt} = 1/(t + OR_{jt}) \tag{5}$$

$$\text{COVERT}^* : \rho_{jmt} = \frac{1}{p_{jm}}\max[1 - \frac{\max(OR_{jt} - R_{jm}, 0)}{k_1 R_{jm}}, 0] \tag{6}$$

Four scenarios were developed to validate our approach, which differed in their order arrival interval λ in minutes, total order quantity O and product quantity Q (Scenario 1: $\lambda = $ triangularAV(2.5, 0.5), $O = 50$, $Q = $ uniform(20, 50); Scenario 2: $\lambda = $ triangularAV(7.5, 0.5), $O = 50$, $Q = $ uniform(20, 50); Scenario 3: $\lambda = $ triangularAV(2.5, 0.5),

$O = 100$, $Q =$ uniform(20, 50); Scenario 4: $\lambda =$ triangularAV(2.5, 0.5), $O = 50$, $Q =$ uniform(50, 100)). The results are shown in Table 1. Overall, SPT and WINQ rules hold a relatively low completion time but heavy tardiness. EDD and COVERT rules have good performance on tardiness reduction. The introduction of real-time ORCT to replace the fixed due date had a positive effect in completion time reduction, but the tardiness was not always reduced. The experimental results demonstrate that the consideration of real-time ORCT is somehow beneficial for the objective of completion time reduction, however, a well-designed combined heuristic rule that considers both the static and dynamic characteristics should be developed to satisfy the two objectives.

Table 1. Experimental results of heuristic rule-based scheduling.

Rule		Scenario 1	Scenario 2	Scenario 3	Scenario 4
SPT	C	31.30	34.67	61.80	95.72
	F	50.79	144.24	342.65	910.27
WINQ	C	34.80	33.57	61.84	94.32
	F	121.05	110.82	209.03	484.13
EDD	C	34.78	34.72	64.66	96.75
	F	60.35	99.85	61.52	78.82
EDD*	C	33.13	32.31	62.04	94.42
	F	57.42	64.14	237.47	421.74
COVERT	C	36.59	37.48	66.70	93.04
	F	89.39	81.62	104.43	272.08
COVERT*	C	33.98	34.69	63.93	92.90
	F	71.06	92.21	107.94	462.75

5 Conclusions and Outlook

This paper proposed an ANN-based approach to predict real-time ORCT in a dynamic job shop such that uncertainties stemming from processing times and availability of machines may realistically inform subsequent scheduling decisions. In our approach, first hybrid simulation data and production data including information of orders, products, workers and machines were feature-engineered as inputs of the ORCT prediction model. To achieve the objectives of minimal completion time and tardiness, the predicted ORCT was considered as an indicator for evaluating order priority, such that a situation-aware closed-loop production control approach could be created. Experimental results showed a positive effect in completion time reduction but tardiness was not always reduced.

Although our results demonstrate the usefulness of ORCT prediction in scheduling, feature extraction and fusion can be further conducted to analyse which variables are more influential in deterring ORCT. Simulation data can be replaced by the real data from factories to train the ANN model, and new technologies such as data cleaning and pre-processing can be employed to support practical application. For manufacturing industries, seasonal demands lead to diverse distribution of the training samples, which necessitates a robust model for prediction accuracy. Finally, a composite priority rule considering static and dynamic order characteristics can also be developed to have a good performance in all aspects.

References

1. Bender, J., Ovtcharova, J.: Prototyping machine-learning-supported lead time prediction using AutoML. Procedia Comput. Sci. **180**(5), 649–655 (2021)
2. Wang, C., Jiang, P.: Deep neural networks based order completion time prediction by using real-time job shop RFID data. J. Intell. Manuf. **30**(3), 1303–1318 (2017). https://doi.org/10.1007/s10845-017-1325-3
3. Fang, W., Guo, Y., Liao, W., et al.: Big data driven jobs remaining time prediction in discrete manufacturing system: a deep learning-based approach. Int. J. Prod. Res. **58**(9), 2751–2766 (2020)
4. Gunasekaran, A., Patel, C., Tirtiroglu, E.: Performance measures and metrics in a supply chain environment. Int. J. Oper. Prod. Manag. **21**(1), 71–87 (2001)
5. Wang, H., Peng, T., Tang, R., et al.: Smart agent-based priority dispatching rules for job shop scheduling in a furniture manufacturing workshop. In: ASME 2020 15th International Manufacturing Science and Engineering Conference, pp. 1–8. Virtual Online (2020)
6. Altendorfer, K., Jodlbauer, H.: An analytical model for service level and tardiness in a single machine MTO production system. Int. J. Prod. Res. **49**(6), 1827–1850 (2011)
7. Hu, S., Zhang, B., Zhang, X.: Order completion date estimation and due date decision under make-to-order mode. Ind. Eng. J. **15**(3), 122–129 (2012)
8. Li, M., Yang, F., Wan, H., et al.: Simulation-based experimental design and statistical modeling for lead time quotation. J. Manuf. Syst. **37**, 362–374 (2015)
9. Hsieh, L., Chang, K., Chien, C.: Efficient development of cycle time response surfaces using progressive simulation metamodeling. Int. J. Prod. Res. **52**(9–10), 3097–3109 (2014)
10. Liu, D., Guo, Y., Huang, S., et al.: A SOM-FWFCM based feature selection algorithm for order remaining completion time prediction. China Mech. Eng. **32**(9), 1073–1079 (2021)
11. Huang, J., Chang, Q., Arinez, J.: Product Completion time prediction using a hybrid approach combining deep learning and system model. J. Manuf. Syst. **57**, 311–322 (2020)
12. Braune, R., Benda, F., Doerner, K., et al.: A genetic programming learning approach to generate dispatching rules for flexible shop scheduling problems. Int. J. Prod. Econ. **243**, 108342 (2022)
13. Blackstone, J., Phillips, D., Hogg, G.: A state-of-the-art survey of dispatching rules for manufacturing job shop operations. Int. J. Prod. Res. **20**(1), 27–45 (2007)
14. Little, J.D.: OR FORUM---Little's law as viewed on its 50th anniversary. Oper. Res. **59**(3), 536–549 (2011)
15. Gyulai, D., Pfeiffer, A., Bergmann, J., et al.: Online lead time prediction supporting situation-aware production control. Procedia CIRP **78**, 190–195 (2018)
16. Flask-http-client. https://pypi.org/project/flask-http-client/
17. Loffe, S., Szegedy, C.: Batch normalization: accelerating deep network training by reducing internal covariate shift. JMLR.org (2015)

Towards Cognitive Intelligence-Enabled Manufacturing

Reuben Seyram Komla Agbozo[1], Pai Zheng[2] (ID), Tao Peng[1](✉) (ID),
and Renzhong Tang[1] (ID)

[1] Institute of Industrial Engineering, School of Mechanical Engineering, Zhejiang University,
Hangzhou 310027, China
tao_peng@zju.edu.cn
[2] Department of Industrial and Systems Engineering, The Hong Kong Polytechnic University,
Hung Hom, HKSAR, China

Abstract. Cognitive intelligence-enabled manufacturing (CoIM) uses machines
to utilize technologies that mimic human cognitive abilities to solve complex
problems in manufacturing. With the support of a cognitive intelligence-enabled
manufacturing system (CoIMS) architecture, information flow is organized and
coordinated appropriately, starting from the machine sensory system, central system to the motor system. Machine perceptive abilities monitor, sense and capture
equipment performance, aggregate data, and help gain valuable insights into the
production process. It uses the industrial internet of things, data analytics, artificial intelligence and related techniques and cognitive computing and related
technologies to address production issues in an autonomous manner. As such,
CoIMS solves complex production problems. It also transforms manufacturing
by improving product quality, productivity, and safety, reducing costs and downtimes, identifying knowledge gaps, and enhancing customer experience. Even so,
a CoIMS is not responsible for making the final decision. Instead, it supplements
information on the fly for engineers to take necessary actions.

Keywords: Cognitive intelligence · Manufacturing · Self-X cognition · Smart
decision making · Artificial intelligence

1 Introduction

Smart factories are automated production facilities that use sensors, cyber-physical systems (CPS), industrial internet of things (IIoTs), artificial intelligence (AI), robotics, and
other modern technologies to improve efficiency and reduce costs [1]. These technologies also aid in monitoring, diagnostics, and prognostics. However, cognitive intelligence
can strengthen the learning mechanism in manufacturing systems. For instance, the 5C
architecture for implementing CPS inherently supports the reasoning in making manufacturing cognitive intelligent [2]. The CPS manages the interconnected systems between
the physical assets and computational capabilities while leveraging the interconnectivity
of machines to become cognitive intelligent [3]. Besides, the CPS coupled with IIoTs

adds a layer of knowledgeability to any system through data collection and monitoring. This is established through the Data-Information-Knowledge-Wisdom (DIKW) hierarchy, which facilitates the functional relationship between data, information, knowledge, and wisdom to better understand a subject [26], a trait of human cognition. Strube (2001) defines *cognition* as "*a class of advanced control mechanisms that allow for sophisticated adaption to changing needs (e.g., learning and planning) through computations operating on mental representations*" [4]. These mental actions form the foundation for cognitive science. Cognitive science studies human thought processes, including perception, memory, language, reasoning, problem-solving, decision making, planning, and learning [5]. It has been used across many fields. For instance, Tesla electric vehicles utilize cognitive intelligence features in their vehicle maintenance program to monitor their health condition continuously, and users are signalled in case of any aberrations while proactively and independently ordering the replacement ahead of servicing schedules [6].

The human mind is a complex system otherwise described as an information processing machine that receives, stores, retrieves, transforms, and transmits information through computational processes [5, 7]. With the help of the sensory receptors, humans extract meaning from a sensation due to contact with external stimuli through perception [8]. Figure 1 illustrates the stages of information processing in humans. Humans use their senses to gather information acquired through environmental stimulation. It is then followed by perception, cognition, or recognition within the information processing region. For example, humans recognize objects by their shape, colour, size, or speech. Consequently, the human cognitive system makes decisions by identifying and comprehending these patterns. In this paper, the authors use the information processing mechanism in Fig. 1 and the general view of human cognitive architecture in Fig. 2 as the foundation and inspiration for proposing a CoIMS, where Fig. 2 details the stages of information transfer.

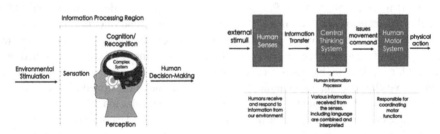

Fig. 1. Cognition, perception, and information processing

Fig. 2. A general view of human cognitive architecture

Manufacturing is evolutional, and CoIM is a phase in this advancement. This progression toward human-machine collaboration and Self-X cognitive systems is the inspiration behind CoIM and the proposed architecture of CoIMS. In addition, this paper highlights the enabling technologies of CoIMS and ongoing applications across selected industries using cognitive intelligence-enabled technologies.

2   Fundamentals of CoIMS

The CoIMS imitates ordinary brain-related skills and acts as the information processing region, including memory, attention, concentration, problem-solving, creativity, and critical thinking. A CoIMS applies these imitated skills to execute regular manufacturing tasks. The information processing capacity of humans, plus the system's mechanism, is described as cognitive architecture (see Fig. 4) [5]. Like brain-based skills, the CoIMS has different compartments with specific skills for performing categorical functions, as shown in Fig. 3.

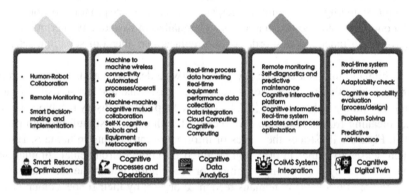

Fig. 3. CoIMS composition

Engineers have, over the years, made tremendous progress in automating the replication of human senses. These human-like sensory systems are used in smart manufacturing for system diagnostics and prognostics. For instance, machine vision [9] technologies are used in visual inspection, fault diagnostics, and product defect detection. Other machine perceptions include machine audition [10], machine olfaction [11], machine touch or tactile perception [12], and machine gustatory (the process of mimicking the perception of taste and feel experiences food at a machine level), a term coined purposely for illustration, has seen very little progress. Machine perceptions mimic human senses to gather data on the manufacturing operations and their surroundings. Data collected is forwarded for analysis and interpretation. Then, the machine motor systems coordinate certain machine motor functions as per the directives of the CoIMS to solve production issues. Based on this logic of mimicking human cognition, perception, and information processing to solve problems as described in this paper, we define *cognitive intelligence-enabled manufacturing (CoIM) as using machines to utilize technologies that mimic human cognitive abilities to solve complex problems in manufacturing.*

Generally, human cognition and learning are based on three thematic theories: "the nature of knowledge, learning and transfer, and the nature of motivation and engagement" [13]. A CoIMS is structured on the same pattern of cognition and learning. Unlike humans, machines acquire knowledge through data supply (historical and real-time). Subsequently, they learn new information from the acquired data using knowledge graphs [14] to map data points using relationships. Identical to human knowledge transfer and learning is the machine learning technique called transfer learning [17]. Transfer learning is used in transferring knowledge in different but related source domains to improve the performance of target learners on a target domain [15, 16]. As humans learn and transfer knowledge, they are motivated extrinsically or intrinsically to become better at their tasks. Likewise, machines use reinforcement learning (RL) [21]. Applications of RL are seen in robotic control, end-to-end control, recommendation systems, and natural language dialogue systems [18, 19]. However, a critical cognitive skill, Metacognition, is barely used in smart systems. Metacognitive processes refer to the ability to reflect on one's thinking processes and evaluate them for improvements [20]. Metacognitive skills such as self-monitoring and evaluation, help the system to reflect on its performance, thus enabling it to be self-motivating, engaging, and enthusiastic about finding problems. Such abilities enable machines to identify problems early and take corrective action.

3   CoIMS Characteristics and Enabling Technologies

CoIMS simulates human cognition to perform production tasks and solve problems. It learns from experience and adapts its behaviour based on system feedback. However, the CoIMS needs the support of enabling technologies, to learn from data and perform tasks efficiently without explicit programming.

3.1   Characteristics of CoIMS

A CoIMS is knowledgeable, flexible, and attentive to be adaptive. It imitates human cognitive architecture using flexible programmable systems and technology for reasoning, planning, and solving problems. A CoIMS independently performs diagnostics and prognostics. It utilizes metacognitive abilities, cognitive reasoning, learning, knowledge transfer, mapping, and graphing.

3.2   Enabling Technologies in CoIMS

CoIM is dependent on enabling technologies which are integrated and work as collaborative systems. They include cognitive computing and informatics, machine learning, deep learning, big data and analytics, robotics, CPS, IIoTs, machine vision, cloud computing, knowledge graphs, natural language processing (NLP), and reinforcement learning. These techniques and technologies are tools for mimicking human cognitive abilities and are applied to manufacturing processes. As a result, the system performs diagnostics and suggests preventive and corrective actions. For example, to take proactive measures in CoIM, the machine learning (ML) and deep learning (DL) models are trained on the data harvested within the machine sensory system. The trained models acquire knowledge to identify patterns within a defined data group and present detailed information on the right approach to solve a production issue. The CoIMS supplements relevant information to engineers for analysis and implementation, thereby enhancing an interactive change and innovation drive.

4   The Proposed System Architecture of CoIM

A CoIMS functions effectively and efficiently with a defined architecture, named CoIMS architecture in this paper (see Fig. 4). The compositions of the CoIMS architecture in Fig. 4 are depicted in Fig. 3, which are modelled using Figs. 1 and 2. Inspired by the functionalities of Figs. 1 and 2, machine sensory systems perform the role of machine perceptions in a CoIMS. The machine central systems and motor systems in a CoIMS mimic human central thinking systems and motor systems shown in Fig. 2. The machine central system is the engine of the CoIMS, where it analyzes data from the machine sensory system (to identify inefficiencies and potential production issues). The machine motor system is also responsible for coordinating real-time and historical data in the machine central system for decision making. As a result, the CoIMS interacts with cognitive machines, processors, devices, and cloud platforms to identify issues and communicate them to engineers.

The CoIMS architecture is the underlying principle behind a cognitive intelligence-enabled factory. As depicted in Fig. 5, a cognitive intelligence-enabled factory comprises enabling technologies, a Self-X cognitive manufacturing network [21], machine-to-machine cognitive-mutual collaboration, a real-time data centre, a CoIMS system, and CoIM digital twin. Robots and other manufacturing equipment in this factory adopt self-X cognitive abilities in their operations. In this factory, machines can self-learn and unlearn. Enabling technologies and techniques enhance machine-to-machine interaction while optimizing operations and making the system adaptive and flexible to understand changes in the information process flow. It identifies problems by pulling historical data if the data in the problem is incomplete by using cloud computing methodologies. Thereafter, predictive actions are forwarded to engineers for decision-making and implementation based on data analytics. Simply, the CoIMS can be described as a consultant (an expert using key enabling technologies to function), and the human is the overseer. For instance, cognitive chatbots mimic human thinking processes using NLP to engage in causal analysis and advisory interactions with engineers on ways to improve total system performance. Besides, this factory adopts a cognitive digital twin (CDT) technology, a real-time virtual cognitive system [25]. The CDT aids in analyzing real-time performance, adaptability, and cognitive capabilities. Thence, results in real-world system optimization, problem-solving, and taking proactive measures.

Solving previously unknown issues birth new information to effectively leverage manufacturing operations. For instance, if a new issue of material quality defect arises during the production process, CoIMS will refer to historical data, draw inferences, and make diagnostics or prognostics where necessary. Solving this new problem adds to the existing knowledge database. As such, the CoIMS can be described as a system equipped with the ability to gather new information in the manufacturing plant and use the acquired information to improve product quality, productivity, and safety. The same approach applies to cost and downtime reduction, identifying knowledge gaps, and enhancing customer experience.

Besides Tesla, which comprehensively applies cognitive intelligence to their systems at a product level, IBM Watson IoT perfectly illustrated how cognitive intelligence-enabled systems could dramatically enhance efficiency and maximize performance on the shop floor within the manufacturing plant.

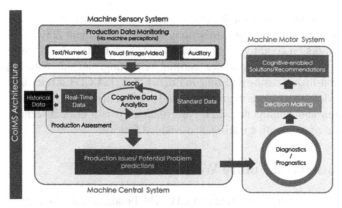

Fig. 4. A cognitive intelligence-enabled manufacturing system (CoIMS) architecture

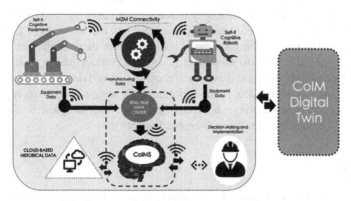

Fig. 5. A cognitive intelligence-enabled factory

For instance, in their illustrative video case study, an NLP-enabled cognitive chatbot relies on an enormous amount of manufacturing data, similar to the operation of the machine sensory systems in Fig. 3. The chatbot uses a visual inspection system to identify defective products and based on historical and production data, it recommends probable servicing actions to the maintenance team 24. After that, the engineers feed the new solution into the cognitive system for future proactive decision-making.

Furthermore, Zheng et al. (2021) highlighted the Self-X cognitive manufacturing network and focused on an industrial knowledge graph (IKG)-based multi-agent reinforcement learning approach in manufacturing networks with a higher level of automation. They used a simulated multi-robot based on their proposed IKG-based MARL-enabled approach, comprising the Self-X cognitive attributes [22]. The success of the Self-X cognitive manufacturing network lays a strong foundation for a cognitive intelligence-enabled factory in Fig. 5. Also, Zheng et al. (2022) introduced the visual reasoning-based mutual-cognitive human-robot collaborative (HRC) system. The proposed system will enable industry robots to develop visual cognitive reasoning and perception during task executions, which is relevant to activities on a manufacturing shop floor. With a holistic scene analysis, robots can logically and cognitively understand activities around them, and then predict and support human actions in that environment [23].

Lastly, works on cognitive digital twins (CDT) for manufacturing are explored for future implementations where it uses learning, reasoning, and automatic adjustment for better decision-making using real-time IoT data [25, 27]. A CDT is relevant as it requires semantic modelling, systems engineering, and product lifecycle to achieve higher levels of automation and intelligence [27]. Nevertheless, it is a critical technology for the establishment of a cognitive intelligence-enabled factory.

5   Conclusion and Future Work

This paper described the inspiration behind CoIM. Fundamentals and enabling technologies in CoIMS coupled with illustrative examples were also discussed. In addition, we echo the Self-X cognitive manufacturing network with multi-robot collaboration and envision a cognitive intelligence-enabled factory that generates a massive amount of data to enable manufacturers to gain deeper insight into the workings of CoIMS. After that, the cognitive system can gather new information in the manufacturing plant and use the acquired information to subsequently improve product quality, productivity, and safety. Others include cost and downtime reduction, identifying knowledge gaps, and enhancing customer experience. In the near future, the authors shall explore the fluidity in collaboration between varying robots (having distinct functions) with Self-X cognitive capabilities in a cognitive intelligence-enabled factory.

References

1. Li, J., Tao, F., Cheng, Y., Zhao, L.: Big data in product lifecycle management. Int. J. Adv. Manuf. Technol. **81**(1), 667–684 (2015)
2. Lee, J., Bagheri, B., Kao, H.A.: A cyber-physical systems architecture for industry 4.0-based manufacturing systems. Manuf. Lett. **3**, 18–23 (2015)
3. Baheti, R., Gill, H.: Cyber-physical systems. Impact Control Technol. **12**(1), 161–166 (2011)
4. Strube, G.: Cognitive SCIENCE: OVERVIEW. In: Smelser, N.J., Baltes, P.B. (eds.) International Encyclopedia of the Social and Behavioral Sciences, pp. 2158–2166. Elsevier, Amsterdam (2001)
5. Stillings, N.A., Chase, C.H., Weisler, S.E., Feinstein, M.H., Garfield, J.L., Rissland, E.L.: Cognitive Science: An Introduction, 2nd edn. MIT Press, Massachusetts (1995)
6. Tesla. https://twitter.com/Tesla/status/1125465424529887232. Accessed 09 Feb 2022
7. Simon, H.A.: The human mind: the symbolic level. Proc. Am. Phil. Soc. **137**(4), 638–647 (1993)
8. Levitin, D.J.: Foundations of Cognitive Psychology: Core Readings. MIT Press, London (2002)
9. Klette, R.: Concise Computer Vision. Springer, London (2014)
10. Wang, W.: Machine Audition: Principles, Algorithms, and Systems: Principles, Algorithms, and Systems. IGI Global, Hershey (2010)
11. Haddad, R., Medhanie, A., Roth, Y., Harel, D., Sobel, N.: Predicting odor pleasantness with an electronic nose. PLoS Comput. Biol. **6**(4), e100740 (2010)
12. Fleer, S., Moringen, A., Klatzky, R.L., Ritter, H.: Learning efficient haptic shape exploration with a rigid tactile sensor array. PloS One **15**(1), e0226880 (2020)

13. Greeno, J.G., Collins, A.M., Resnick, L.B.: Cognition and learning. In: Berliner, D., Calfee, R. (eds.) Handbook of Educational Psychology, pp. 15–46. MacMillan, New York (1996)
14. Hogan, A., et al.: Knowledge graphs. Synth. Lect. Data Semant .Knowl. **12**, 1–257 (2021)
15. Torrey, L., Shavlik, J.: In: Handbook of Research on Machine Learning Applications and Trends: Algorithms, Methods, and Techniques, pp. 242–264. IGI Global (2010)
16. Zhuang, F., et al.: A comprehensive survey on transfer learning. Proc. IEEE **109**(1), 43–76 (2020)
17. Pan, S.J., Yang, Q.: A survey on transfer learning. IEEE Trans. Knowl. Data Eng. **22**(10), 1345–1359 (2009)
18. Wang, H.N., et al.: Deep reinforcement learning: a survey. Front. Inf. Technol. Electron. Eng. **21**(12), 1726–1744 (2020)
19. Li, Y.: Deep reinforcement learning: an overview. arXiv preprint arXiv:1701.07274 (2017)
20. Livingston, J.A.: metacognition: an overview. U.S. Department of Education, pp. 1–9 (2003)
21. Wiering, M.A., Van Otterlo, M.: Reinforcement learning. Adapt. Learn. Optim. **12**(3), 729 (2012)
22. Zheng, P., Xia, L., Li, C., Li, X., Liu, B.: Towards self-X cognitive manufacturing network: an industrial knowledge graph-based multi-agent reinforcement learning approach. J. Manuf. Syst. **61**, 16–26 (2021)
23. Zheng, P., Li, S., Xia, L., Wang, L., Nassehi, A.: A visual reasoning-based approach for mutual-cognitive human-robot collaboration. Cirp Ann. Manuf. Technol. (2022)
24. Woolfe, T.: Cognitive Manufacturing in Action - IBM Watson IoT. https://www.youtube.com/watch?v=f3WB2e3vXWQ&t=438s&ab_channel=TobyWoolfe. Accessed 03 Mar 2022
25. Al Faruque, M.A., Muthirayan, D., Yu, S.Y., Khargonekar, P.P.: Cognitive digital twin for manufacturing systems. In: 2021 Design, Automation & Test in Europe Conference & Exhibition, pp. 440–445. IEEE (2021)
26. Mourtzis, D.: Towards the 5th industrial revolution: a literature review and a framework for process optimization based on big data analytics and semantics. J. Mach. Eng. **21**(3), 5–39 (2021)
27. Zheng, X., Lu, J., Kiritsis, D.: The emergence of cognitive digital twin: vision, challenges and opportunities. Int. J. Prod. Res., 1–23 (2021)

Distributed Manufacturing for Digital Supply Chain: A Brief Review and Future Challenges

Wangchujun Tang[1] ⓘ, Tao Peng[2] ⓘ, Renzhong Tang[2] ⓘ,
and Alexandra Brintrup[1][(✉)] ⓘ

[1] Institute of Manufacturing, Department of Engineering, University of Cambridge,
Cambridge CB3 0FS, UK
ab702@cam.ac.uk
[2] Institute of Industrial Engineering, School of Mechanical Engineering, Zhejiang University,
Hangzhou 310027, China

Abstract. The rising demand for customization and increasing convergence of the physical and digital worlds have led manufacturing companies to seek solutions to maintain competitiveness in the global business landscape. Distributed manufacturing (DM) enables small volume customized production in geographically dispersed locat and drives the supply chain (SC) to become more agile, flexible, and sustainable. This review paper aims to present future research opportunities and challenges for the facilitation of DM for digital supply chain (DSC) by emerging digital technologies and artificial intelligence (AI). After a review of DM, we identify three distinct types of DM platforms that may facilitate DSC based on transaction mechanisms. These are then explored from a technological perspective, in terms of enabling technologies and data analysis methods that support DM for DSC. We conclude by highlighting the need for empirical studies to investigate the motivations for DM platform adoption and identify a key challenge to their adoption, that is the lack of privacy-preserving AI algorithms in facilitating DM.

Keywords: Distributed manufacturing · Supply chain · Digitalization · Artificial intelligence · Machine learning · Agent-based system

1 Introduction

The rising demand for customization, has become a critical factor for companies to gain competitive advantage over their competitors [1]. Studies found that greater customization drives a 5–15% increase in revenue and a 10–30% increase in marketing-spend efficiency [2]. On the other hand, as part of globalization trends, many companies shifted their production plants to countries where labor and/or raw material costs are low, with the aim of mass producing standardized goods at a single location and achieving economies of scale [3]. The rising demand for customization poses a contrast to mass production, requiring companies to seek solutions in achieving rapid supply chain

© IFIP International Federation for Information Processing 2022
Published by Springer Nature Switzerland AG 2022
D. Y. Kim et al. (Eds.): APMS 2022, IFIP AICT 664, pp. 442–450, 2022.
https://doi.org/10.1007/978-3-031-16411-8_51

reconfigurability such that parts to produce alternative product configurations can be sourced reliably, at short notice.

In tandem, the need for more resilient supply chains has been increasing. Most recently, with Covid-19 lockdowns in place, the imperative restrictions caused production shutdowns and/or logistics disruptions. This brought another tremendous pressure to manufacturing companies worldwide. A survey shows 47% of companies cited delays at end customers are the most considerable risk [4]. In addition, more than 80% of organizations are currently experiencing difficulties in recovering from SC disruptions in the short term [4]. Many organizations have encountered challenges in adjusting their production plans to ensure timely delivery of goods when faced with supplier delays. Inappropriate decision-making due poor information exchange in the supply chain led organizations to produce unnecessary waste in production, logistics, and human resources [5].

The above two imperatives yield an urgent need to devise an effective SC strategy for overcoming these challenges. DM has been proposed to be one of the approaches for manufacturing industries to overcome these challenges [6]. DM itself involves bringing together a collaborative, rapidly reconfigurable network of producers to allow resilient mass customization. However, the concept is not widely adopted partly due to the difficulty of its implementation. Rapid reconfiguration necessitates rapid information exchange and thus digital tools to help. There is a lack of understanding of state-of-art technology applied to DM when digitalizing the production and SC. It is therefore necessary to carry out research on how to enable DM from a digital infrastructure perspective and how the current methods and tools can be integrated into DM.

The main objectives of this paper are thus to (1) investigate the state-of-the-art applications and technologies applied to DM for Digital supply chain (DSC), (2) identify digital DM implementation challenges and future research opportunities from the perspective of DSC. The rest of this paper is organized as follows: in Sect. 2, DM concept and features are described, and types of DM platforms supporting DSC are presented, in Sect. 3, current technology enablers are reviewed, followed by derived challenges and future perspectives discussed in Sect. 4, and conclusion in Sect. 5.

2 DM for Digital SC

2.1 Review Methodology

This review is conducted based on two major databases (Web of Science and Scopus) variety of internet websites such as Google Scholar, Research Gate, etc. for searching relevant publications. We focus on data collecting, exchanging, and analyzing tools and methods in DM for DSC. The key search terms "Distributed manufacturing" and "Digital supply chain" incorporated with "CPS", "IoT", "Artificial Intelligence", and "Data analytics" are selected from publications of summarized emerging digital technology enablers from production [7] and DSC [8] through April 2022. The outcome of this review is a summary of digital technology enablers in DM and their impact on production and DSC performance.

2.2 DM Concept and Features

DM is an evolving concept [9], although it has been around for more than two decades. Many studies [10–13] have attempted to define DM which was ultimately converged on 5 key characteristics: digitalization, personalization, localization, new manufacturing technologies, and multi-user participation [13]. In this study, DM is defined as *"A collaborative network of distributed manufacturing facilities that utilize new emerging advanced technologies to meet personalized and customized demand in an agile, flexible, sustainable, and demand-driven manner"* where:

"Collaborative" [14] implies the intra- and inter-organization coordination and collaboration within the network which all stakeholders are involved,

"Distributed" [13] refers to different locations of production sites which are either independent or belongs to a single enterprise. It also implies a non-hierarchical relationship between the facilities within the network and a need for flexible, rapid supply chain coordination,

"Agile, flexible, sustainable, and demand-driven" [13] emphasizes the objective of DM, which aims to tackle the current manufacturing challenges.

To adapt DM, manufacturers need to both rethink their manufacturing strategy and readjust their supply chain configuration. Manufacturing companies need to find ways to optimize procurement by extensive cooperation with a more dynamic supply network. Thus, a DSC network with reliable business relationships and shared economic interests will significantly enhance the competitiveness of enterprises.

2.3 DM Platforms

One of the key DM implementation strategies has been to outsource parts from suppliers who have available manufacturing resources at the time. Manufacturing companies decouple the primary manufacturing processes and outsource to the available suppliers when demand is increased [15] with a short-term partnership. However, it is challenging to adopt an effective DM strategy due to the long evaluation and audit processes involved in a traditional SC. As demand drives the production of customized goods, it is time sensitive and purchasing from established suppliers is not always feasible. Consequently, DM deployment may require a third-party facilitator to act as a bridge that connects organizations.

The third-party facilitator integrates information on distributed manufacturing resources and their capacity and helps allocate these resources to cater to demand. It enables cooperation, sharing, and optimization of manufacturing resources between organizations to improve their responsiveness and competitiveness in the market. Recent studies presented several platforms to coordinate manufacturing resource sharing [16–18]. The ultimate objective of the proposed platforms is aligned with the purpose of DM and share the same characteristics with DM. Therefore, this research classifies them all as DM platforms.

A DM platform consists of three main actors: supplier, client, and platform provider. The distinctions between each platform are based on the transaction mechanism and the authority exerted over distribution. Transaction mechanism refers to the mechanism with which the platform operates the process of making a deal, and authority exerted over distribution refer to the points of decision-making. One platform can have the same authority distribution with different transaction mechanisms, but not vice versa. Three types of DM platforms are identified based on transaction mechanisms as (1) **Task Assignment** [19]: The service provider dominates the transactions and facilitates quoting, matchmaking, and task assigning. Clients cannot communicate with suppliers directly. (2) **Yellow page** [20]: Supplier publishes capabilities and contact info on the server. The service provider does not involve in any transaction activities. Clients are free to communicate with suppliers. (3) **Auction-based** [14]: Client submits order to service provider, it will be either published in the system or broadcasted to the suppliers. All registered suppliers can access order information through the platform and bid. The client makes decision based on the offer(s).

DM platform benefits both ends from accessing richer manufacturing resources and leveraging idle production capacities. Different types of platforms support manufacturing companies to create values in various ways. Developing a successful DM platform involves an in-depth grasp of the business's challenges and demands. A critical factor for DM platform development involves sophisticated manufacturing and information technologies to facilitate DSC which requires better visibility of operation.

3 DM Digital Technology Enablers for SC

3.1 Agent-Based System

As a collaborative network of geographically dispersed facilities, efficient and effective collaboration between organizations is crucial to the success of DM for SC. The primary approach utilizes an agent-based system (ABS) to design cooperation mechanisms between agents to enable automated collaboration. The implementation of ABS in DM is considered from different organizational levels. Li [21] developed two-level ABS (Sub-EMAS and EA-MAS) which aim to schedule manufacturing resource sharing through both intra- and inter-organizational views.

Most ABS research in DM has focused on resource scheduling in manufacturing. There are three types of DM scheduling based on the manufacturing resource attributions [21]. (1) Manufacturing resources are owned by the same organization and located in different sites [22]. (2) Manufacturing resources belong to multiple organizations and located in different sites [23]. (3) Manufacturing resources deliver to organizations across the supply chain [24]. Due to the complex and dynamic nature of DM environment, manual decision-making processes on resource sharing is not cost-effective. Thus, one of the main objectives of ABS is to provide efficient and accurate decision-making through automation.

Several negotiation methods were proposed to solve scheduling problems in a centralized approach via a third-party agent. However, risks are exposing sensitive information to the opponents and the third-party during the negotiation process. Also, the third-party agent can be a bottleneck that will potentially impact performance. An agent-based framework was proposed to improve the efficiency of the decision-making process during multiple shipbuilding project planning using an iterative combination auction method [25]. Szaller [14] designed an auction-based DM resource sharing platform, agents place biddings to compete for production tasks in a federated architecture. Since each agent maintains production data only at local, they may use false information to bid on auctions, leading to production issues. However, local evaluation by distributed agents and lack of information exchange results in poor scheduling quality. Hsu [26] proposed an agent-based fuzzy constraint-directed negotiation (AFCN) mechanism to solve related privacy issues in heterogeneous production information sharing. Although this approach can effectively reduce the risk of information leakage from an agent, but it assumes that each agent has access to local information. Companies are less likely to allow third party agents access to their production information due to information privacy concerns. Several studies [14, 25] stated the same concerns and suggested that collaboration among agents is inefficient due to information privatization.

3.2 Data Acquisition and Transmission

Maintaining stable, efficient manufacturing resource allocation processes require sufficient data to support coordination and control between different units and facilities. The development of new Information and Communication Technologies (ICT) has empowered information flow in DM. ICT enables DM facilities integration with ERP, MES, and CRM, extracting insights from raw data and data embedded in various equipment, devices, and product objects via IoT. IoT utilizes various types of sensors to transmit and gain real-time visibility of progress, stock level, quality, energy, and logistics through wireless routers or cloud servers. For example, several IoT-based frameworks [27, 28] were proposed to monitor and analyze energy consumption for machine workshops in the DM facilities to improve energy efficiency, energy consumption and reduce cost. To achieve sustainability, Turner [29] embedded RFID tags on construction assets and materials incorporating with Building Information Model to build modular buildings in a DM scenario. IoT combines with Cyber-Physical systems (CPS) in production floor shops to enhance the data transmission and control between production units. Krishnamurthy [30] proposed an IoT-based CPS framework leveraging sensors and cameras to incorporate Virtual Reality (VR), supporting users and engineers to virtually interact with the PCB assembly process from the DM environment. Yang [31] developed a CPS-based platform to monitor automotive production sites across the globe. This platform integrated Digital Twin (DT), which creates information models to synchronize and visualize the real-time status of the part supplier, sub-assembly supplier, and OEM. The current studies on data collection and transmission mainly focus on sole organization. Capturing data from multiple parties across SC to achieve DM is still challenging.

3.3 Machine Learning

Distributed production facilities produce and collect datasets via various information collection and transmission technologies. Diverse data sources in DM include supplier, manufacturing, product, sales, customers, and financial organizations [32].

The key processes to use datasets in DM include data preprocessing [33] and data analytics. Data preprocessing methods, including data integration, reduction, and transformation, aim to eliminate inconsistency and prepare necessary data without noise for learning models. For example, text mining is applied to cleaning and extracting data from various sources such as machines, operations, materials, and manufacturing processes to prevent unnecessary bias.

Data analytics techniques can then be applied to draw managerial insights after data preparation. Previous works used the traditional mathematical methods such as mathematical programming model [34], and optimization [35] focusing on distributed shopfloors scheduling to improve efficiency and manufacturing resource utilization. Due to the high volume of real-time stream data and dynamic environments in DM, methods using deterministic models are not effective enough and researchers increasingly move to Machine Learning methods. Ramakurthi [34] presented a case study of gear industry and proposed a hybrid method using classification and mixed integer nonlinear programming (MINLP) models to select suitable suppliers with a multi-objective optimization of lead time, reliability, energy consumption, and service utilization rate. Agostino [17] applied regression models including AutoRegressive Integrated Moving Average (ARIMA) and Neural Network Auto Regressive (NNAR) to forecast production time based on historical production data and used objective functions to optimize production order allocation across multiple production facilities. Bhsekar [36] applied a similar mixed approach with a support vector machine (SVM) model to approximate feasible production regions and design an optimal DM SC network. Classification and regression are two branches of supervised learning in Machine learning (ML). ML models can effectively aid the decision-making process in identifying trends and patterns from large sets of unstructured data. Although, the current research using ML approach in DM is limited, a few studies have applied ML models to predict order lead times [37], perform preventive maintenance [38], and predict disruptions with new task arrivals [39], all of which can potentially support DM in SC. However, there is a lack of study to address information silos issues when utilizing data across organizations as well as data privacy and security concerns when integrating heterogeneous DM data.

4   Challenges and Future Perspective

The advantages of DM platforms lie in facilitating information sharing and allocation of manufacturing resources dynamically. Manufacturing companies have adopted three types of DM platforms. But attracting more participation remains a question since larger user pools make the DM platform more effective. There is a need to conduct empirical studies to develop a systematic understanding of industrial perceptions when adopting DM platforms from aspects of (1) Motivation, precisely the reason to adopt DM platforms from perspectives as the client, supplier, or platform provider. (2) Capability, determine the status of DM technology enablers' adoptions, especially for SMEs, since facilitating SC activities in DM highly demands information technology infrastructure. (3) Challenges, identifying technological and managerial barriers for DM implementation for DSC.

The study of ABS in DM has been extensively conducted, but there is still a rare number of applications that have been applied in practice. There is a lack of trust in AI in executing important task including placing order and production scheduling without human interaction [40]. It challenges the reliability of data source and the precision of analysis. The current information acquisition approaches do not specifically address production and DSC data collection method between different organizations. For example, it should clarify whether data needs to be derived from both MES and ERP systems as well as the categorizations. There is no standard of identifying the core data group and this can lead to inefficient and inaccurate analysis due to complexity of manufacturing data. Significantly, there is a need to identify the essential data categories and establish a standard which allow precise, efficient, and low-cost data acquisition process via existing information technologies.

On the other hand, data security is a vital concern when transmitting data between organizations. DM platform requires sufficient data information from various sources among stakeholders. Although there are established standards, protocols, and technologies such as Blockchain technology (BCT) [41] have been proposed to guard data security for DSC, these approaches were not utilized in a DM environment. Moreover, transparency and traceability enabled by BCT may not be sufficient for DM since companies are unwilling to transmit sensitive information including production and purchase order data, making it challenging to conduct data analytics in DM. Also, most ABS studies assumed data accessibility when acting as a third-party facilitator. Data analytics is a crucial requirement for DM platform to facilitate automated matches between suppliers and buyers. Thus, an important future research direction to advance the use of DM platforms includes developing privacy-preserving algorithms such as federated learning which allow DM stakeholders to keep their sensitive data while allowing analytics to be performed.

5 Conclusion

This research focused on DM for DSC and a review is carried out to (1) examine the existing DM implementation approaches and three major types of DM platforms are classified, (2) investigate the state-of-art DM technology enablers including data collection, exchange, and analysis technologies, and (3) provide challenges and future research opportunities which include challenges of adopting DM platform from the industrial perspective, data acquisition methods, and data privacy concerns for analysis in real life industrial practice.

References

1. Wang, X., Wang, Y., Tao, F., Liu, A.: New paradigm of data-driven smart customisation through digital twin. J. Manuf. Syst. **58**, 270–280 (2021)
2. McKinsey & Company. https://www.mckinsey.com/business-functions/marketing-and-sales/our-insights/the-future-of-personalization-and-how-to-get-ready-for-it. Accessed 2022
3. Srai, J.S., Harrington, T.S., Tiwari, M.K.: Characteristics of redistributed manufacturing systems: a comparative study of emerging industry supply networks. Int. J. Prod. Res. **54**, 6936–6955 (2016)
4. Euler Hermes. https://www.eulerhermes.com/en_global/news-insights/economic-insights/Global-Supply-Chain-Survey-In-search-of-post-Covid-19-resilience.html
5. Shareef, M.A., Dwivedi, Y.K., Kumar, V., Hughes, D.L., Raman, R.: Sustainable supply chain for disaster management: structural dynamics and disruptive risks. Ann. Oper. Res., 1–25 (2020). https://doi.org/10.1007/s10479-020-03708-3

6. Anwari, V., et al.: Development, manufacturing, and preliminary validation of a reusable half-face respirator during the COVID-19 pandemic. PLoS ONE **16**, e0247575 (2021)
7. Karnik, N., Bora, U., Bhadri, K., Kadambi, P., Dhatrak, P.: A comprehensive study on current and future trends towards the characteristics and enablers of industry 4.0. J. Ind. Inf. Integr. **27**, 100294 (2022)
8. Attaran, M.: Digital technology enablers and their implications for supply chain management. Supply Chain Forum Int J **21**, 158–172 (2020)
9. Haddad, Y., Salonitis, K., Emmanouilidis, C.: Design of redistributed manufacturing networks: a model-based decision-making framework. Int. J. Comput. Integr. Manuf. **34**, 1–20 (2021)
10. Johansson, A., Kisch, P., Mirata, M.: Distributed economies–a new engine for innovation. J. Clean. Prod. **13**, 971–979 (2005)
11. Mourtzis, D., Doukas, M., Psarommatis, F.: A multi-criteria evaluation of centralized and decentralized production networks in a highly customer-driven environment. CIRP Ann. **61**, 427–430 (2012)
12. Korn, O., Boffo, S., Schmidt, A.: The effect of gamification on emotions - the potential of facial recognition in work environments. In: Kurosu, Masaaki (ed.) HCI 2015. LNCS, vol. 9169, pp. 489–499. Springer, Cham (2015). https://doi.org/10.1007/978-3-319-20901-2_46
13. Srai, J.S., et al.: Distributed manufacturing: scope, challenges and opportunities. Int. J. Prod. Res. **54**, 6917–6935 (2016)
14. Szaller, Á., Egri, P., Kádár, B.: Trust-based resource sharing mechanism in distributed manufacturing. Int. J. Comput. Integr. Manuf. **33**, 1–21 (2020)
15. Kumar, M., Tsolakis, N., Agarwal, A., Srai, J.S.: Developing distributed manufacturing strategies from the perspective of a product-process matrix. Int. J. Prod. Econ. **219**, 1–17 (2020)
16. Hasan, M., Starly, B.: Decentralized cloud manufacturing-as-a-service (CMaaS) platform architecture with configurable digital assets. J. Manuf. Syst. **56**, 157–174 (2020)
17. Agostino, I.R.S., Frazzon, E.M., Alcala, S.G.S., Basto, J.P., Rodriguez, C.M.T.: Dynamic production order allocation for distributed additive manufacturing. Ifac Papersonline **53**, 10658–10663 (2020)
18. Lu, Y., Xu, X.: Cloud-based manufacturing equipment and big data analytics to enable on-demand manufacturing services. Robot. Comput.-Integr. Manuf. **57**, 92–102 (2019)
19. 3D hubs. https://www.hubs.com/. Accessed 11 Apr 2022
20. Casicloud. http://www.casicloud.com/. Accessed 11 Apr 2022
21. Li, K., Zhou, T., Liu, B.-H., Li, H.: A multi-agent system for sharing distributed manufacturing resources. Expert Syst. Appl. **99**, 32–43 (2018)
22. Aissani, N., Trentesaux, D., Beldjilali, B.: Multi-agent reinforcement learning for adaptive scheduling: application to multi-site company. IFAC Proc. Vol. **42**, 1102–1107 (2009)
23. Adhau, S., Mittal, M.L., Mittal, A.: A multi-agent system for distributed multi-project scheduling: an auction-based negotiation approach. Eng. Appl. Artif. Intell. **25**, 1738–1751 (2012)
24. Hamidi Moghaddam, S., Akbaripour, H., Houshmand, M.: Integrated forward and reverse logistics in cloud manufacturing: an agent-based multi-layer architecture and optimization via genetic algorithm. Prod. Eng. Res. Devel. **15**(6), 801–819 (2021). https://doi.org/10.1007/s11740-021-01069-9
25. Mao, X., Li, J., Guo, H., Wu, X.: Research on collaborative planning and symmetric scheduling for parallel shipbuilding projects in the open distributed manufacturing environment. Symmetry **12**, 161 (2020)
26. Hsu, C.-Y., Kao, B.-R., Ho, V.L., Lai, K.R.: Agent-based fuzzy constraint-directed negotiation mechanism for distributed job shop scheduling **53**, 140–154 (2016)

27. Chen, E., Cao, H., He, Q., Yan, J., Jafar, S.: An IoT based framework for energy monitoring and analysis of die casting workshop. Procedia CIRP **80**, 693–698 (2019)
28. Chen, X., Li, C., Tang, Y., Xiao, Q.: An Internet of Things based energy efficiency monitoring and management system for machining workshop. J. Clean. Prod. **199**, 957–968 (2018)
29. Turner, C., Oyekan, J., Stergioulas, L.K.: Distributed manufacturing: a new digital framework for sustainable modular construction. Sustainability **13**, 1515 (2021)
30. Krishnamurthy, R., Cecil, J., Perera, D.: ASME: An Internet-of-Things Based Framework for Collaborative Manufacturing. American Social Mechanical Engineers, New York (2018)
31. Yang, J., et al.: Integrated platform and digital twin application for global automotive part suppliers. In: Lalic, B., Majstorovic, V., Marjanovic, U., von, G., D., Romero (eds.) APMS 2020. IAICT, vol. 592, pp. 230–237. Springer, Cham (2020). https://doi.org/10.1007/978-3-030-57997-5_27
32. Soroka, A., Liu, Y., Han, L., Haleem, M.S.: Big data driven customer insights for SMEs in redistributed manufacturing. Procedia CIRP **63**, 692–697 (2017)
33. Nino, M., Saenz, F., Blanco, J.M., Illarramendi, A.: Requirements for a Big Data capturing and integration architecture in a distributed manufacturing scenario. In: 2016 IEEE 14th International Conference on Industrial Informatics, pp. 1326–1329. IEEE, New York (2016)
34. Ramakurthi, V.B., Manupati, V.K., Machado, J., Varela, L.: A hybrid multi-objective evolutionary algorithm-based semantic foundation for sustainable distributed manufacturing systems. Appl. Sci. **11**, 6314 (2021)
35. Morariu, C., Morariu, O., Răileanu, S., Borangiu, T.: Machine learning for predictive scheduling and resource allocation in large scale manufacturing systems. Comput. Ind. **120**, 103244 (2020)
36. Bhosekar, A., Ierapetritou, M.: A framework for supply chain optimization for modular manufacturing with production feasibility analysis. Comput. Chem. Eng. **145**, 107175 (2021)
37. Lingitz, L., et al.: Lead time prediction using machine learning algorithms: a case study by a semiconductor manufacturer. Procedia CIRP **72**, 1051–1056 (2018)
38. Cheng, J.C., Chen, W., Chen, K., Wang, Q.: Data-driven predictive maintenance planning framework for MEP components based on BIM and IoT using machine learning algorithms. Autom. Constr. **112**, 103087 (2020)
39. Liu, M., Yi, S., Wen, P., Song, H.: Disruption management for predictable new job arrivals in cloud manufacturing. J. Intell. Syst. **26**, 683–695 (2017)
40. Brintrup, A.: Artificial Intelligence in the Supply Chain (2020)
41. Batwa, A., Norrman, A.: Blockchain technology and trust in supply chain management: a literature review and research agenda. Oper. Supply Chain Manage. Int. J. **14**, 203–220 (2021)

Operators 4.0 and Human-Technology Integration in Smart Manufacturing and Logistics Environments

The Classification of Game Elements for Manufacturing

Makenzie Keepers, Isabelle Nesbit, and Thorsten Wuest(✉)

Industrial and Management Systems Engineering, West Virginia University, Morgantown, WV 26501, USA

{mk0004,ijn0001}@mix.wvu.edu, thwuest@mail.wvu.edu

Abstract. Gamification is the application of game elements in non-game contexts, and in manufacturing this can be applied on the shopfloor, with intralogistics, and for training. The term "game elements" is commonly used when describing an instance of gamification. In the manufacturing context, "game elements" describe the pieces of an implementation that allow the scenario to be considered *gamified*. In research, various publications have used differing terms to describe these "game elements," including mechanisms, components, technology, and various others. Since these terms are not used universally across the field, it is important to develop a framework which describes how these terms relate to one another and how they are defined in relation to gamification. This research aims to review currently used game elements from gamification for manufacturing and to classify the identified game elements more discretely for the gamification community. The resulting framework of this research will serve the gamification community in i) developing a foundation of well-established language and diction used within the field to allow for clear communication and research and ii) providing context for implementing gamification across different scenarios in the manufacturing context.

Keywords: Game elements · Gamification · Manufacturing · Production

1 Introduction

With the shift of manufacturing research to focusing more intently on human-machine interactions and human factors on the shopfloor, gamification has been a growing topic of interest for the field. Gamification is defined as "the application of game elements to non-game context" [1]. Its application has been seen in various scenarios in our daily lives, including *points programs* created by restaurants, *incentive programs* in the workplace, or *game-like effects* on language learning apps. Gamification is often implemented into scenarios that strive to improve morale and motivation, increase productivity and efficiency, and enhance learning [2]. Within the manufacturing context, gamification is still a topic of research in its infancy, particularly from a shopfloor operations perspective. To expand upon the field of gamification for manufacturing (GfM), we must consider how gamification may be effectively incorporated into particular manufacturing settings.

© IFIP International Federation for Information Processing 2022
Published by Springer Nature Switzerland AG 2022
D. Y. Kim et al. (Eds.): APMS 2022, IFIP AICT 664, pp. 453–460, 2022.
https://doi.org/10.1007/978-3-031-16411-8_52

This paper focuses on classifying the game elements often involved in GfM scenarios. The purpose of the classification framework is to provide a concrete method of identifying game elements to be used in and matched to gamified scenarios in manufacturing. Game elements are the attributes or pieces of the gamified scenario which create the game-like environment. To identify the game elements commonly mentioned in GfM research, the game elements were extracted from the results of a separate in-depth literature review recently conducted by our team [3]. A total of 35 papers, which focused on the gamification of shopfloor operations for manufacturing, production, and intra-logistics, resulted in a subset of 44 unique game elements to be considered in the development of the classification framework described in this paper.

Following this introduction, Sect. 2 describes the methodology used for gathering the game elements from literature, as well as the development of the classification framework. Section 3 provides the details and explanation of the framework. Section 4 showcases two different GfM scenarios in literature and how the framework can be used to develop a gamified scenario in manufacturing, thus validating the framework. The final section, Sect. 5, completes the paper by drawing final conclusions and providing future work recommendations.

2 Methodology

This paper stems from an in-depth literature review previously conducted by the research team [3]. In the literature review, a methodical investigation was conducted to review all papers related to our topic of interest: gamification for manufacturing. We began the literature review with searching the Scopus database with the search string: TITLE-ABS-KEY((gamif*) AND (operation* OR manufactur* OR production* OR logistic)). After systematically reviewing the search results and identifying relevant papers, a subset of 35 papers were reviewed in-depth for the literature review. This literature review is not discussed further in this paper because, as it relates to this paper, it was used for the sole purpose of identifying the 44 unique game elements related to GfM. The purpose of this paper was to analyze the 44 unique game elements to establish a classification framework.

After reviewing the list of game design elements identified through our previous literature review, different categories were identified that the game elements could be grouped into based on their characteristics. The characteristics were categorized by simple vs. complex, individual vs. group, and intrinsic vs. extrinsic. These categories were chosen for the classification framework because the first two categories are important considerations of the scenario prior to implementing gamification, while the third category is more of a choice that can depend on personal preference or history of what has seemed to work well in the past. In general, the use of these three categories provides sufficient consideration of the current state (pre-gamification) of the scenario, as well as how the gamification designer and team desire the scenario to function. Additionally, all three categories included game elements which were classified into both categories.

When grouping between simple and complex game elements, a distinction was made based on the intricacy of creating or implementing the game element. For example, *leaderboards*, *point systems*, and *badges* are most frequently used in a manner that only requires a relatively simple setup, allowing for universal use in a given scenario. For example, a *leaderboard* may display employee (or team) identifiers based on daily productivity in a manufacturing scenario where productivity is already a collected data point and reviewed metric. On the other hand, *feedback*, *storylines*, and *levels* often require more effort in the form of resources, time, and expertise for development and implementation, and in some cases may require personalization towards the user. For example, *storylines*, to be effective, require significant thought and development to ensure a clear and worthwhile result. Additionally, to provide automated feedback to users, it is likely that additional sensors and technology would need to be implemented into the scenario for data collection and accurate tracking of the employee's or team's work. In this comparison of simple vs. complex game elements, some elements were identified as being associated with both categories, where the complexity was dependent on the context in which it was used. An example of this is *badges*, as they could be made in a one-size-fits-all manner, or they could be individualized to each employee, team, or task.

Individual and group categorizations were decided based on the typical setting in which the game element is applied. Individual game elements can be applicable to a worker without the support or collaboration of anyone else. *Quests*, *progress bars*, and *achievements* are most often an individualized experience. On the other hand, group game elements include *leaderboards*, *contests*, and *competition*. These elements require more than one individual's participation to be implemented successfully and effectively.

Intrinsic motivation involves the completion of a task because of personal satisfaction, while extrinsic motivation comes from outside motivators such as prizes, money, or social status. To rank game elements between intrinsic and extrinsic motivations, it was important to take into consideration the differences between how they would be applied in a manufacturing scenario. Some elements were used as a means of enjoyment for an employee, whereas others may be used as an incentive in the workplace. For example, *strategies*, *avatars*, and *narratives* are a few game elements that primarily use intrinsic motivation. This is clear since these game elements do not lend to any external motivators. Contrarily, extrinsic motivators are elements like *leaderboards*, *levels*, and *rules*. These are known to be categorized as such because, when completed or used successfully, they lead to rewards such as increased social status, or other monetary and physical rewards. Some individual game elements could be considered either intrinsic or extrinsic motivators, depending on the context in which they were applied; *collaboration*, *interaction*, *teammates*, and *discussion boards* are a few game elements that could be considered either intrinsic or extrinsic depending on the context and objectives of the different scenarios. This was dependent on whether the collaboration was a personally rewarding experience or if it led to competitiveness, or other motivating factors.

Grouping game elements based on 'technological required' or 'technology optional' was considered, but after further assimilation, it was found that nearly every game element could belong in both categories. While technology would likely be helpful in the application of most game elements, the majority of game elements were still capable of being developed and implemented without the use of technology. For example, while *leaderboards* are most easily updated and displayed using smart systems, leaderboards can also be implemented in a manual sense where data is reviewed at the end of each time period (e.g., end of each shift) and handwritten and displayed on a white board on the shopfloor.

With these three categories identified as the basis for our assimilation, a tabulation was created that separated these categories into eight distinct groups of game elements. This tabulation created a framework layout to facilitate the classification of elements. With the classification of the game elements into the framework layout, the resulting tabulation allows for manufacturers, researchers, and designers to follow the framework to identify and select relevant, use case specific game elements when interested in implementing a gamified scenario into their operations.

Finally, based on the groupings and visualizations, a qualitative review of the findings was conducted. Using the findings and context of the use of game elements in GfM (through literature), the game elements were classified. This classification framework is the main result of this research and provides the groundwork for future implementations of gamification in manufacturing.

3   Results and Discussions

First, the classification framework (Fig. 1) was developed by determining the most logical order of the columns as when reading left to right.

The first column is simple vs. complex since this is often the first stipulation of the scenario: determining and understanding the available resources of the project for implementing gamification. This is a crucial step where the designer would consider if there were sufficient time, money, expertise, etc. to warrant a complex scenario, as well as to consider if a complex scenario is currently worth the resource investment.

The second column is individual vs. group because this then considers the current state of the workforce by scrutinizing how the shopfloor employees interact and work with one another. In some cases, group work may entice and encourage additional efforts, while in other cases, group work may lead to arguments and stress.

Lastly, intrinsic vs. extrinsic motivation is considered as a third column. This was determined to be the last question to ask because this is solely based on the designer's preferences, what they believe would be best, and how they desire the scenario to look and function.

Following the completion of the framework, which resulted in eight discrete categories, the game elements were classified into their respective group(s) (Table 1). The results show a near even split of simple and complex motivators amongst the overall 44 game elements considered, with 24/44 (54.5%) classified as simple and 28/44 (63.6%) classified as complex. (Note that the percentages exceed 100%. This is due to the repeat of game elements in both categories.) This is beneficial to the gamification designer as the near even split indicates that making one choice (simple or complex) does not immediately rule out the possible use of a wide variety and selection of elements. This also helps to quickly narrow down the list of possible game elements, reducing the decision complexity at later states of the framework.

In the next step, far more game elements were classified as individual than group. 32/44 (72.3%) were classified as individual game elements, while 15/44 (34.1%) were considered to be group game elements. It is interesting to note that nearly all of the

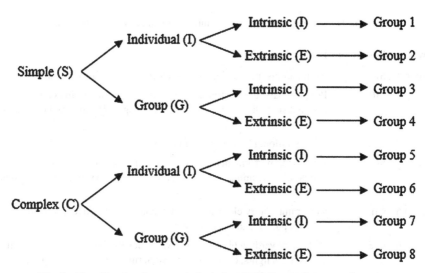

Fig. 1. Classification framework depicting the 8 groups for game elements.

elements that fell into the group category were classified as such because they include a competitive element and thus contribute to extrinsic motivation because of a possible prize or other positive outcome, such as social status.

There are far more extrinsic (33/44 = 75%) motivators amongst the game elements than intrinsic (16/44 = 36.7%). Implementing extrinsic motivators in GfM creates a simpler and more easily measurable study for developers and implementors, because people tend to respond much faster to rewards that are offered to them than they do to intrinsic motivators. Many of the game elements that were classified in both categories were dependent on the context in which they were applied and how the individuals may interpret the tasks. For example, having *teammates* could be either intrinsic or extrinsic, because an employee may simply find personal enjoyment from the social aspect of teammates, but the employee may also find outside motivation of social status when they are seen as the team leader.

Table 1. Game elements classified into their respective classification.

Group	Descriptor	Elements
Group 1	SII	Notifications, personal goals, increasing complexity, constraints
Group 2	SIE	Progress bars, goals, strategy, time constraints, increasing complexity, loss aversion, displaying performance, badges, rewards, achievements, awards
Group 3	SGI	Collaboration, interaction, teammates
Group 4	SGE	Displaying performance, collaboration, interaction, leaderboards, competition, teammates, ranking, awards, point system, scoring system, contests
Group 5	CII	Constraints, story elements, avatars, emotion, narrative, problem solving, puzzle games, scenarios
Group 6	CIE	Badges, rewards achievements, awards, levels, feedback, quests, virtual goods, boss fights, challenges, mission, rules, content unlocking, performance groups
Group 7	CGI	Discussion boards
Group 8	CGE	Awards, point system, scoring system, contests, performance graphs, discussion boards, betting, social recognition

4 Validation of the Framework

To consider the efficacy of the framework, two publications which involved detailed scenarios of GfM implementations were reviewed in parallel with the framework. Using the understanding of the scenario of the first publication [4], we worked through the framework to determine possible game elements to be used. With the second publication [5], we considered the chosen game elements used in the paper alongside the framework to show that the classification framework can be used for considering additional game elements that could be used in a similar scenario.

One publication [4] observed a lab-based environment in which two teams completed a three-step assembly process on an assembly line. The first team worked on the assembly line with gamified information, including a leaderboard, where each employee got a score for the number of products they assembled and allowed communication amongst employees, while the second team did not receive a score and were not allowed to communicate. The purpose of the game was to assemble as many test objects as possible within the allotted time frame, completely and accurately. The group that had a leaderboard to track the number of completed product produced significantly more than the group that did not. Comparing the work of this publication with the developed framework, it is clear that leaderboards were used in a simple and group environment. Based on the reactions of the gamified team, it is shown that extrinsic motivators of the leaderboard were well received due to the gamified team's discussion of their status on the leaderboard during the break. By understanding the specific situation that the researchers had (simple, group, extrinsic) our framework would have led them to using leaderboards to incorporate a gamified experience into their production processes. This evaluation result indicates that our framework is aligned with recent implementations and experimental outcomes.

In another study conducted by Korn [5], emotion recognition is used to determine whether employees in a production work setting were "happy" or "unhappy" when applying gamification methods. They were given a 10-task repetition without gamification, then the process was repeated with gamification. Participants were given real-time feedback, received performance displays, and saw their scores. Using our proposed framework, it is shown that point systems are associated with group 4 (simple, group, extrinsic). Following this, it is likely that teammates, rankings, and leaderboards would have had the same effect on the process as the two chosen game elements. Feedback is a group 6 (complex, individual, extrinsic) element, which suggests that game elements such as levels, badges, and rewards may have had similar effects on the process. This aspect of the validation process expands on the possible use of the proposed framework as a tool for implementing additional game elements that are comparable to game elements already used in a scenario.

5 Conclusions, Limitations, and Future Work

The formation and organization of this chart creates a foundation for those in industry and research to have a basis of application for GfM by providing guidance on the game elements to use. Since gamification is a growing application in manufacturing, this framework facilitates the future growth by providing concrete guidelines for implementation by considering the current state (pre-gamification) of the process.

By compiling a list of 44 game elements used across various publications, it was determined that the game elements could be separated into groupings of simple or complex, individual or group, and intrinsic or extrinsic. Using these categories, eight groups of differing game elements were created. The classification framework was validated using two different publications of GfM scenarios to exemplify two ways the framework can be utilized by stakeholders: i) in examining the pre-gamification scenario to understand potentially relevant game elements for the specific use case, and ii) in understanding the current gamified scenario to consider additional game elements which may produce similar results.

One limitation of this research is that the publications used for the validation step were part of the 35 papers from which the 44 game elements were extracted from. Thus, it is possible that a slight bias was introduced since the game elements and framework application for these publications were not entirely independent of one another. However, since the game elements were only extracted and then compiled separately into the proposed framework, the potential bias is limited. Another limitation of the research at this stage is that the evaluation is based on secondary data (publications) and the proposed framework has not yet been validated using primary research data (case studies or experiments). Additionally, the framework included in this paper does not include considerations for making decisions based on characteristics of the production system or operators involved, but only considerations which are under the control of the gamification designer. These limitations are addressed in the planned future work.

The proposed framework allows for future manufacturers to apply gamification techniques into their production processes and for GfM researchers to further explore gamification by understanding the benefits of each group of elements for manufacturing. Following the creation of this framework, the next step in the process is to validate the framework with industry partners through a case study. From this, adaptations can be made to improve the organization and implementation of the process. Additionally, one area that GfM struggles is in understanding the concrete, empirically-based benefits of gamification. This framework hypothesizes that benefits for elements within the same group are comparable, and thus the empirical testing of GfM benefits could be centered around the eight groups, as opposed to the 44 unique elements, resulting in significantly less experimentation. Another area for future research revolves around the development of a framework based on characteristics of the production system or operators involved. To support the development of this type of framework, significant research regarding the effectiveness of particular elements in different scenarios is fundamental.

Acknowledgements. This work was performed under the following financial assistance award 70NANB20H028 from U.S. Department of Commerce, National Institute of Standards and Technology.

Certain commercial software products are identified in this paper. These products were used only for demonstration purposes. This use does not imply approval or endorsement by NIST, nor does it imply these products are necessarily the best available for the purpose.

References

1. Deterding, S., et al.: From game design elements to gamefulness: defining "gamification". In: 15th International Academic Mindtrek Conference, Finland, pp. 9–15 (2011)
2. Lithoxoidou, E., et al.: Improvement of the workers' satisfaction and collaborative spirit through gamification. In: Kompatsiaris, I., et al. (eds.) INSCI 2017. LNCS, vol. 10673, pp. 184–191. Springer, Cham (2017). https://doi.org/10.1007/978-3-319-70284-1_15
3. Keepers, M., et al.: Current state of research & outlook of gamification for manufacturing. J. Manuf. Syst. (2022, accepted)
4. Ohlig, J., et al.: Human-centered performance management in manual assembly. Procedia CIRP **97**, 418–422 (2021)
5. Korn, O., Boffo, S., Schmidt, A.: The effect of gamification on emotions - the potential of facial recognition in work environments. In: Kurosu, M. (ed.) HCI 2015. LNCS, vol. 9169, pp. 489–499. Springer, Cham (2015). https://doi.org/10.1007/978-3-319-20901-2_46

Human Factors and Change Management: A Case Study in Logistics 4.0

Chiara Cimini⊙, Alexandra Lagorio(✉)⊙, Claudia Piffari⊙, Mattia Galimberti⊙, and Roberto Pinto⊙

Department of Management, Information and Production Engineering, University of Bergamo, Viale Marconi 5, Dalmine, BG, Italy
{chiara.cimini,alexandra.lagorio,claudia.piffari,
mattia.galimberti,roberto.pinto}@unibg.it

Abstract. Although the benefits and advantages are emerging more clearly, the transition of traditional manufacturing and logistics systems to Industry and Logistics 4.0 paradigms is still challenging for companies. In particular, the change management strategies suggested and employed so far lack consideration of the role of human factors to support a successful transition. Starting from the analysis of a case study conducted in a medium-sized Italian manufacturing company, this article aims to show how the critical consideration of the human factors involved in a change of operational processes in a logistics 4.0 perspective is crucial to achieve the objectives set. The article discusses the main strategies to consider from the beginning and the overall impacts on all the job profiles, tasks, and human factors involved to prevent potential resistance and inefficiencies in the implementation phases.

Keywords: Logistics 4.0 · Human factors · Change management · Case study

1 Introduction

The manufacturing paradigm of Industry 4.0 has been dominating the debate on the introduction of new technologies in manufacturing in both academic and industrial circles for several years so far. However, many studies now state that the full achievement of Industry 4.0 goals has not yet taken place [1] and that most companies are still fully addressing the transition [2]. This slowdown in exploiting the full potential of 4.0 technologies has several causes, mainly related to the fact that companies are advancing in adopting digital technologies without being ready from an organisational perspective [3]. Mainly, failures are due to employee resistance, lack of clearly defined and achievable objectives, scarce management support and commitment, and poor communication [4]. To overcome these problems, several tools and theories have been developed to support companies during the change process. In particular, among the most effective and widely adopted theories, there is change management, i.e. "a structured approach to facilitating a transition from a current state to a future state" [5]. Change management

© IFIP International Federation for Information Processing 2022
Published by Springer Nature Switzerland AG 2022
D. Y. Kim et al. (Eds.): APMS 2022, IFIP AICT 664, pp. 461–468, 2022.
https://doi.org/10.1007/978-3-031-16411-8_53

theory suggests different actions to implement in order to facilitate the transition from a traditional to an innovative state, such as defining leadership, generating awareness, defining a clear vision and strategy of change, improving communication, identifying short-term goals, identifying and managing resistance to change, monitor and consolidate change [4]. Industry 4.0, however, focuses its importance on technology and change management theory puts the organisation at the centre, the connecting element between the two, as indicated by socio-technical models, remains uncovered: the human factors (HF) [6], which are intended as "all physical, psychological, and social characteristics of the humans, which influence the action in socio-technical systems" [7]. Taking physical, cognitive and organisational HF into consideration, such as repetitive movements, memory and team work capabilities in the digital transformation of work, can avoid negative consequences for individual employees, production organisations, and society as a whole [8]. This research work's objective is to analyse the HF involved in a case study of a Logistics 4.0 change process in order to prevent possible future problems and identify possible solutions to be implemented. In particular, this paper analyses the introduction of different technological innovations (i.e., a warehouse management system, wearable devices, and fast rotation storage) applied incrementally in the logistics sector (i.e., warehouse organisation) in a medium-sized Italian manufacturing company. The paper is structured as follows. Section 2 contains an overview concerning change management challenges in Industry 4.0 and a focus on the Logistics 4.0 context. Section 3 presents the methodology of the case study analysis adopted, while Sect. 4 reports on the elements analysed in the case study. Finally, Sect. 4.3 reports a discussion with the main insights deduced from the case study, and finally, Sect. 5 summarises the conclusions of the research work.

2 Background

2.1 Change Management in the Industry 4.0 Era

Despite promising valuable competitive advantages, the transition of manufacturing companies to Industry 4.0 constitutes a complex and resource-intensive process [2]. Indeed, it is now quite commonly recognised that a successful transformation to manufacturing and logistics models adhering to the Industry 4.0 paradigm involves a variety of dimensions that relate to implementable technologies and, above all, several organisational changes in a broad sense [9]. Industry 4.0 transformation initiatives can rightly be considered change initiatives, understood as processes of transition from a less digitalised state to a more digitalised one, requiring specific change management approaches [4]. Starting from the seminal works of Lewin [10], managerial literature offers several models to design, manage and reinforce the change process. Attempts to apply these models to Industry 4.0 transformation already exist: change dimensions have been adopted in Industry 4.0 assessment [11], and some roadmaps and frameworks for successful digital transitions have been proposed according to change management strategies (e.g. [2]). Nevertheless, in the literature on the digital transformation change process, it emerges the lack of in-depth studies about how to support the business transformation with suitable organisational evolutions [12]. Indeed, Industry 4.0 contains technical and social (human-related) aspects [13]. For this reason, human-centred design is beginning to be increasingly adopted [14] to achieve the expected results in terms of productivity and efficiency, without intervening in problems related to the workforce, both in terms of the necessary skills and the actual acceptance of the process transformation in a 4.0 perspective. Thus, anthropocentric approaches are helpful to understand in advance the evolution of the human roles in the change process and promote the development of production and logistics systems in which technologies valorise human capacities, and socially sustainable interactions between machines and humans occur [15].

2.2 Logistics 4.0

Logistics has been one of the sectors most affected by 4.0 technologies due to the continuous need for process optimisation and cost reduction. Logistics 4.0 is defined as "the logistical system that enables the sustainable satisfaction of individualised customer demands without an increase in costs and supports this development in industry and trade using digital technologies" [16]. Logistics, however, like the manufacturing sector in general, suffers from the same problems described in the introductory section concerning managing the transition from traditional to 4.0 logistics. In particular, the process of technology adoption and the motivations driving this choice have not yet been extensively analysed in the literature. The role of HF or the need for new organisational structures in Logistics 4.0 has not yet been fully explored [16, 17]. Furthermore, there are some areas of logistics, such as reverse logistics or outbound logistics, where 4.0 technologies have not yet been widely exploited. Among all the gaps still present both at the academic level and in industrial application, we decided to explore in this research work the issue related to the role of HF in managing change towards a Logistics 4.0. This issue is of paramount importance also in the light of the European Union's indications to move towards a more resilient, sustainable and above all human-centered Industry and consequently Logistics 5.0 [18]. In particular, the design of human-centered logistic processes and activities helps to prevent possible problems that can be generated in the workforce, by making more evident the areas in which it is necessary to intervene with targeted action of training and empowerment of workers [8].

3   Methodology

To explore the role of the HF involved in a change process, we opted for a single case study research. Indeed, case research is useful in exploratory research to develop ideas that can be conceptualised and tested afterwards [19]. In particular, a single case study is suitable if the purpose of the research is connected to new concepts and knowledge [20]. In the specific research presented in this paper, we based the single case study on the approach provided by [21]. In particular, the industrial case presented aims to take a snapshot of the different stages of a company's change process following the decision to improve its order management and the subsequent technological introductions and modifications to its logistics processes. The choice of this company for the development of the industrial case study has been made according to the [21]'s single case study rationale selection of the "common case". The objective of the common case is to capture the circumstances and conditions of an everyday situation that could provide novelty aspects about the processes related to some theoretical interest (i.e., human factors in logistics) [21]. In order to overcome the main single case study limitation, we have adopted some strategies which, if used in the research process, contribute to enhance the validity and reliability of the case study. They have been employed to ensure congruence among literature, data collection, and analysis [11]: in particular, construct validity, internal validity, and reliability were addressed. Construct validity allows identifying correctly the operational measures for the concepts being studied. According to [21], in order to guarantee internal validity, we have developed a case study protocol. As a further element to guarantee the reliability of the research, experienced investigators, whose main values are sensibility, adaptability and ability for clarification, conducted the case study [22]. Indeed, all the authors have experience in adopting the single and multiple case study methodology.

4 Case Study

4.1 Problem Statement

The company selected for the single case study is one of Italy's largest bottling plants and packaging machines manufacturers. It designs and manufactures a wide range of machines and systems for bottling and packaging food and beverages, household cleaning products, personal care products, chemical and pharmaceutical products. The scope of the analysis encompasses all the company's logistical processes, including issuing batch orders, receiving and stowing orders within the company, handling materials, picking components, and storage of materials and work-in-progress. In the past, these processes were characterised by several problems that caused inefficiencies. Firstly, the company issued an excessively high number of orders, even for small quantities of components. This was a severe problem, especially considering the company's geographical location, which is located in a mountainous area that is difficult to reach, with high shipment costs. In addition, production components orders and spare parts orders were issued separately, causing a further increase and duplication in the number of orders to manage, which generated inefficiency due to the huge number of material acceptances and quality checks at the entrance. Incoming orders then had to be allocated to the correct areas of the company, which resulted in a high number of material and goods movements, with relevant risks of damage to the material and safety risks for operators. Indeed, the company operated with a Just-In-Time approach, ordering materials as and when customers required them. However, this approach finally resulted in delays in deliveries to customers and thus low service level, mainly concerning spare parts. All these problems could be traced back to the batch sizes used by the company to re-order materials. The logistics operators defined the batch sizes based on their own experience. Therefore, this process could easily be subject to discretionary decisions and human error. In addition, the materials and components used by the company are not standard, with dimensions ranging from a few centimetres to many metres. This increased the complexity of handling and storing materials within the company. All these problems led the company to invest in improving its logistics processes. As most of the issues were due to the small batch sizes, the company designed and implemented a management system to optimise their computation. The designed Warehouse Management System (WMS) aimed at optimising the batch size, taking into account the stock level, the trimestral budget and the bill of materials of the company's products. The main objective of these changes was to improve business efficiency by reducing the number of orders issued, shipments, and material handling. Secondly, the implementation of the WMS had the potential to improve effectiveness by reducing disservices due to delays.

4.2 Adopted Solutions

As mentioned in the previous paragraph, the design and implementation of a WMS allowed for solving the problems caused by suboptimal batch sizes. In implementing this technology, the work of the operators in charge of batches definition was fully replaced by an automatic algorithm. The implementation of the WMS had an impact on the orders-issuing process and other logistics processes. This resulted in the need to integrate and implement other technologies to enable the achievement of the company's objectives. In conjunction with the implementation of the WMS, indeed, other technologies have been introduced: some of them, such as tablets, currently support the operators' activities, while others, such as automated warehouses, are full automation technologies (Table 1). All these technologies interact with each other and especially with the WMS.

Table 1. Implemented technologies

Technology	Type	Area	Objectives
WMS	Automation	Order Mgmt	Reducing inefficiencies, measuring KPIs
Fast-rotation automated warehouses	Automation	Storage	Allowing optimal storage for high-turnover parts
Tablets	Support	Stowage/Picking	Suggesting the right material allocation to the receipt operators
PCs	Support	Picking	Suggesting the location of materials to pick for assembly
Printers	Support	Stowage/Traceability	Supporting the operators in the labelling and tracking of incoming material

4.3 Impacts on the Human Work

At first, the introduction of the WMS was designed to facilitate the operators of the purchasing and logistics management department, who, from the beginning, have responded positively to the introduction of the new technologies. Indeed, the WMS design and implementation were driven by significantly simplifying orders management. The WMS relieved operators from sizing batches of materials and issuing purchase orders, performing these operations automatically and more precisely thanks to optimisation algorithms, able to take into account simultaneously the orders of the last 18 months, the spare parts needed, the forecast of future orders, and the current available budget of the company. Along with reducing the cognitive HF required, this also introduced a formalisation into the purchasing process that had not existed before and reduced the risk of error when purchasing materials, thereby reducing the number of orders to be placed. Although the introduction of this new technology was aimed at helping the logistics office, it also affected other departments, which were not involved initially and did not initially react positively to the change. This is the case of the warehouse operators, who did not immediately understand the usefulness of the change. Before introducing the new technologies, they were in charge of checking the incoming material, sorting it, and assigning it to one of the four storage areas in the plant. Therefore, the change required an initial period of adaptation. Nevertheless, after that, the warehouse operators finally appreciated the introduction of the new technologies, as they realised that their workload had been relieved without requiring any new skills: the optimised batch sizes resulted in a minor number of checks on incoming materials, along with handlings, which has made it possible to reduce physical HF in these tasks. Another task in which the new technologies helped the warehouse operators was materials allocation. Whereas before, the operators had to decide autonomously where to place the incoming material, with the involvement of cognitive HF, such as memory, now the WMS automatically provides, by displaying it on a tablet, the destination of the material and the occupation of the location areas, suggesting the optimal route to store the materials into the assigned locations. Having a global view of the consumption and arrival of components has made it possible to transport large size pieces directly to the assembly workbenches immediately after their arrival in the warehouse, avoiding unnecessary and repetitive transportation. Moreover, this innovation enabled a further positive result, initially unexpected by the company, in simplifying the picking task for the assembly operators. Whereas they previously wasted time by looking for the necessary materials to assemble, they can now read their exact location on a PC located directly in the assembly island, which shows each operator the picking list. Finally, to exploit the introduction of the WMS, ten vertical automated warehouses for fast-rotation storage were implemented. Nevertheless, some issues for the correct allocation of materials in them emerge. If high, medium and low rotation parts are not sorted correctly, there is a risk of queues being generated during the picking operations. The WMS automatically suggests the sorting, but the warehouse operator still makes the final decision about allocation. Therefore, these new technologies introduction has also led to the generation of a new cognitive HF for these workers.

5   Discussion and Conclusion

The industrial case offered interesting insights about how process changes can affect human work and, at the same time, how proper HF analysis are crucial to drive successful change management. First, it was clear that to avoid unexpected and adverse consequences to the technology introduction, a holistic analysis of the involved job profiles, tasks, and HF needs to be performed. Indeed, since the WMS design mainly addressed the requirements of the logistics clerks, initial resistances to change occurred concerning warehouse operators, who were not fully aware of the technology impacts and expected benefits on their work. For this reason, the human-centred design of digital solutions, such as the WMS functionalities, must be performed by taking into account the requirements of usability, accessibility and user-friendliness for all the involved roles. This also suggests that involvement and communication at a broad level to employees before the change is fundamental to achieve a successful transition. Other strategies to support the change management *ex-ante* are modeling and simulation of processes that will be affected by modifications in tasks, layouts, and operational modes in relation to implementing new technology. During the transition, then, training strategies could be helpful to make employees familiar with technological solutions, and bottom-up improvement suggestions should be encouraged to align the technologies' operational settings according to user needs. In the case company, the logistics transformation journey was not planned from the beginning. However, updates in the process changes were deployed based on new requirements that emerged from the workforce after the first WMS functionalities introduction. This suggests that, along with the development of a clear change management plan, continuous feedback analysis and emerging issues diagnosis should be carried out to timely intervene with corrective actions and maximise the benefits. Generally, as literature shows, also from the case, it emerged that adopting change management strategies is highly relevant to generate the proper awareness in the workforce and managing potential resistances, with the final result of achieving consolidated process changes and improvements. This research presents a preliminary attempt to analyse change management strategies in Industry 4.0 regarding the importance of involving HF. Although only a single case study being discussed concerning the logistics area, interesting insights about the importance of deploying suitable change management strategies taking into account all the involved tasks and HF were presented. To overcome the limitations of this first research stage, further case analysis will be carried out to produce practical roadmaps for guiding HF-based change management paths in Industry and Logistics 4.0.

References

1. Eickemeyer, S.C., Busch, J., Liu, C.-T., Lippke, S.: Acting instead of reacting—ensuring employee retention during successful introduction of i4.0. Appl. Syst. Innov. **4**, 97 (2021)
2. Ghobakhloo, M., Iranmanesh, M.: Digital transformation success under Industry 4.0: a strategic guideline for manufacturing SMEs. J. Manuf. Technol. Manage. **32**, 1533–1556 (2021)
3. Machado, C.G., Winroth, M., Almström, P., Ericson Öberg, A., Kurdve, M., AlMashalah, S.: Digital organisational readiness: experiences from manufacturing companies. J. Manuf. Technol. Manage. **32**, 167–182 (2021)
4. Bellantuono, N., Nuzzi, A., Pontrandolfo, P., Scozzi, B.: Digital transformation models for the I4.0 transition: lessons from the change management literature. Sustainability **13**, 12941 (2021). https://doi.org/10.3390/su132312941
5. Balogun, J., Hope-Hailey, V.: Exploring Strategic Change, 3rd edn. Prentice-Hall, London (2008)
6. Karltun, A., Karltun, J., Berglund, M., Eklund, J.: HTO – a complementary ergonomics approach. Appl. Ergon. **59**, 182–190 (2017)

7. Stern, H., Becker, T.: Concept and evaluation of a method for the integration of human factors into human-oriented work design in cyber-physical production systems. Sustainability **11**, 4508 (2019)
8. Neumann, W.P., Winkelhaus, S., Grosse, E.H., Glock, C.H.: Industry 4.0 and the human factor – a systems framework and analysis methodology for successful development. Int. J. Prod. Econ. **233**, 107992 (2021)
9. Cimini, C., Boffelli, A., Lagorio, A., Kalchschmidt, M., Pinto, R.: How do industry 4.0 technologies influence organisational change? An empirical analysis of Italian SMEs. J. Manuf. Technol. Manage. **32**, 695–721 (2020)
10. Lewin, K.: Field Theory of Social Science: Selected Theoretical Papers. Harper & Row, New York (1951)
11. Soomro, M.A., Hizam-Hanafiah, M., Abdullah, N.L., Jusoh, M.S.: Change readiness as a proposed dimension for Industry 4.0 readiness models. Logforum **17**, 83–96 (2021)
12. Bordeleau, F.-È., Felden, C.: Digitally transforming organisations: a review of change models of Industry 4.0. In: Proceedings of the 27th European Conference on Information Systems (ECIS), p. 15 (2019)
13. Sony, M., Naik, S.: Industry 4.0 integration with socio-technical systems theory: a systematic review and proposed theoretical model. Technol. Soc. **61**, 101248 (2020)
14. Nguyen Ngoc, H., Lasa, G., Iriarte, I.: Human-centred design in industry 4.0: case study review and opportunities for future research. J. Intell. Manuf. **33**, 35–76 (2021)
15. Rauch, E., Linder, C., Dallasega, P.: Anthropocentric perspective of production before and within Industry 4.0. Comput. Ind. Eng. **139**, 105644 (2019)
16. Winkelhaus, S., Grosse, E.H.: Logistics 4.0: a systematic review towards a new logistics system. Int. J. Prod. Res. **58**, 18–43 (2020)
17. Lagorio, A., Zenezini, G., Mangano, G., Pinto, R.: A systematic literature review of innovative technologies adopted in logistics management. Int. J. Logist. Res. Appl. **0**, 1–24 (2020)
18. European Commission: Directorate General for Research and Innovation: Industry 5.0: towards a sustainable, human centric and resilient European industry. Publications Office, LU (2021)
19. Voss, C., Tsikriktsis, N., Frohlich, M.: Case research in operations management. Int. J. Opt. Prod. Manage. **22**, 195–219 (2002). https://doi.org/10.1108/01443570210414329
20. Eisenhardt, K.M.: Building theories from case study research. AMR **14**, 532–550 (1989)
21. Yin, R.K.: Case Study Research: Design and Methods. SAGE, Los Angeles (2009)
22. Morse, J.M., Barrett, M., Mayan, M., Olson, K., Spiers, J.: Verification strategies for establishing reliability and validity in qualitative research. Int. J. Qual. Methods **1**, 13–22 (2002)

Investigating the Use of Immersive Technologies for Additive Manufacturing

Gustavo Melo(✉) ⓘ, Ahmed Ercan, Moritz Kolter ⓘ,
and Johannes Henrich Schleifenbaum ⓘ

Chair for Digital Additive Production, RWTH Aachen University, 52074 Aachen, Germany
gustavo.melo@dap.rwth-aachen.de

Abstract. The demand for Additive Manufacturing (AM) is continuously increasing, so new challenges must be overcome. For instance, in the event of a pandemic, location-independent communication must be ensured so that the production and the training of workers can continue. As a result, digital learning and teaching techniques have gained traction, especially in location-independent interventions. Those techniques enable synchronous and asynchronous, location-independent transmission of information and data, however, they are mostly designed for theoretical contents. In order to ensure physical learning as well, more immersive technologies must be resorted to. Thus, this study investigates the extent to which Extended Reality (XR) technologies can be used in AM. Two workshops were held to gather expert opinions on how Virtual Reality (VR) and Augmented Reality (AR) can be utilized in AM. It turns out that the technologies can be used in a variety of ways, especially in areas such as training, visualization, information, simulation, checking, and communication. The greatest added value with minimal effort could be achieved in the location-independent training and assistance of employees.

Keywords: Additive manufacturing · Augmented reality · Virtual reality

1 Introduction

1.1 Initial Situation

The development of laser technologies has significantly increased the application potential of Additive Manufacturing (AM), especially in industry. The diverse and promising technologies that enable direct and rapid manufacturing of parts thus offer a wider range of applications for efficient production. However, production does have vulnerabilities, especially in times of a global pandemic [1]. In order to implement AM in traditional production, AM users need to be on-site. Unforeseen obstacles can cause problems, especially for training topics where participants rely on on-site instructors. To circumvent these issues, alternative methods are now being researched. Digital learning and teaching options are being taken up as a basic solution.

© IFIP International Federation for Information Processing 2022
Published by Springer Nature Switzerland AG 2022
D. Y. Kim et al. (Eds.): APMS 2022, IFIP AICT 664, pp. 469–476, 2022.
https://doi.org/10.1007/978-3-031-16411-8_54

1.2   Objective

The hypothesis to be investigated is potential for use of digital learning and teaching techniques exists in the context of training opportunities. To this end, building on the current state of AM and digital learning and teaching methods, which are currently of particular relevance, the future potential uses of immersive learning technologies will be analyzed. The work is intended to make a general contribution to the development of these technologies in order to highlight their future prospects in AM.

1.3   Research Approach

In view of the objectives, a qualitative research approach will be used in this study. To this end, a literature review of the current state of AM and digital training options, in special the immersive ones, will first be conducted. Subsequently, group discussions in the form of two workshops will be conducted in order to answer the research hypothesis. The participants of the two workshops are respectively AM researchers from academia and AM users from industry. Finally, the results will be discussed and summarized.

2   State of the Art

2.1   Additive Manufacturing

The demand for additively manufactured products has steadily increased over the years. The global 3D printing market size reached $12.6 billion in 2020 [2]. While it is predicted to increase to US$37.2 billion by 2026 [2]. Additive manufacturing, also known as 3D Printing, is a layer-wise manufacturing process in which components are manufactured by applying material layer-by-layer without the need for tools. A typical workflow consists of Design, Pre-Process, AM-Process, Post-Process and Quality Assurance. In general lines, Design step covers the construction of the part/product, Pre-Process deals with the data preparation of the file to be additively manufactured in the subsequent step. Typical Post-Processes are the removal of the part from building platform as well as surface finishing, being finalized by Quality Assurance steps covering destructive and nondestructive testing. Digital and three-dimensional models form the basis for this process. The term AM comprises several process categories. For this study, the most widespread technology for metallic materials was taken as the focus of our investigation: Laser Powder Bed Fusion. This process consists of applying layers of metallic powder which are selectively melted by a laser beam in a protected atmosphere [3].

2.2   Extended Reality

Advancing digitalization is responsible for creating new opportunities and challenges for industry. Especially in the working world of Industry 4.0, in which the interaction between human and machine plays a significant role, hence digital competencies are gaining a continuously growing importance. Thus, the interest in exploring and implementing training opportunities using Extended Reality (XR) technologies is increasing. The term XR implies immersive technologies such as Mixed Reality, Virtual Reality and Augmented Reality [4].

Augmented reality (AR) technology is based on the fundamental principle that users move around their real environment with full awareness while interacting with virtual information and objects [5]. In order to apply AR technology, the real environment must first be captured. This is usually done using a camera. The captured data is visualized on a projector. The visualization can take the form of a screen display, for example. In this case, a fixed camera is used to capture predefined markers. Depending on the position of these markers, a positional representation can be made. One option for the application of AR is the use of head-mounted displays. Here, the camera is located on the head and captures the environment from the user's viewing perspective. The device is usually worn on the head in the form of goggles, allowing flexibility of movement and position [6].

Virtual reality (VR) is based on the basic idea of presenting a computer-generated simulation of a realistic experience. The technology is used to completely block out the real world and replace it with a virtual environment [7]. Thus, the user has the sensation of being involved in the synthetically generated environment. This sensation is also called immersion. In industry, this technology is mostly used to gain a stereoscopic view of computer-generated objects. Interaction is made possible through the use of hand-held input devices. This technology creates a great advantage in that three-dimensional models and products can be spatially displayed, analyzed, and interactively handled [8].

3 Method

The present research is based on a qualitative methodology, which is particularly appropriate, compared to quantitative methods, when little information is available on a topic. The qualitative research approach is based on generating theory statements that are captured through empirical data. In qualitative research, participants report on their experiences rather than taking positions on predetermined topics. The generation of qualitative data is possible via interviews, focus groups, observations, or documents. The qualitative approach, in special the focus group discussion, is therefore the more suitable variant in the present work since the statements of the participants have a corresponding analytical reference point [9]. The participants are thus AM experts and the data collection takes place in the form of focus group discussion held in a hybrid format assisted by digital canvas and teleconference tools. The essential difference between the latter and an interview is that in a group discussion several interviewees refer to one topic of investigation at the same time [10]. In order to facilitate such a group discussion, two workshops of 2 h long each are conducted in this paper. This approach is often used for qualitative research to gather responses from a group of people on a particular topic. In this case, in order to integrate different opinions into the discussion, participants who work in different fields are specifically included. During the workshops, the participants, in total 18 individuals with 2 to 10 years of experience, were divided into six groups accordingly to their expertise to maintain clarity and cover the whole AM process chain: Design,

Pre-Process, In-Process, Post-Process, Quality Assurance, and Other. For a successful focus group discussion, the Miro platform is used. This offers participants the opportunity to work simultaneously on the same interface. This way, they can communicate their ideas and assign them to the areas through integrated functions such as creating notes, labeling or drawing. The workshops were carried out in September and November 2021 and aimed to present the XR technologies under investigation to the participants and to gather expert opinions on the extent to which these technologies can be integrated into the manufacturing steps along the AM process chain. The evaluation of the data took place via Mayring's process model, which is used for qualitative content analysis and covers the following steps: determine material, determine direction of content analysis, select form of content analysis, interpret results, define quality criteria [11]. The analysis took place in the course of this work using the analysis software MAXQDA.

4 Results

Figure 1 shows the result of the industrial workshop displaced on the Miro board covering the whole AM process chain. On the left, XR use cases in manufacturing were elucidated and on the right ideas from the AM experts were gathered and discussed. The discussion of the focus groups has been recorded, transcribed and coded using the grounded theory described by Mayring [11]. After first-order and second-order coding, six fields of usage of XR in AM have been identified namely: Information, Checking, Communication, Visualization, Simulation, Training. Each of these groups can be split up into subgroups as given in Table 1. Furthermore, the industrial workshop has been used to identify low-hanging fruits described in more detail in the next section.

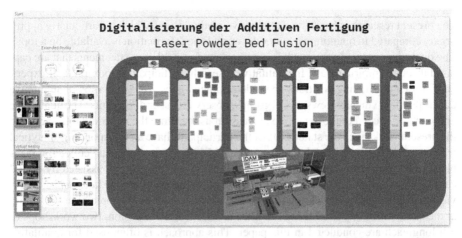

Fig. 1. Visual results from industrial workshop displaced on the digital canvas in Miro.

5 Discussion

In the industrial workshop, recommendations were voiced to filter and implement so-called low-hanging Fruits, according to Varela and Ramquist [12] and shown in Fig. 2. The term low-hanging fruit refers to items that could have a high impact with little effort. The two axes in Fig. 2. Define effort and impact. Items with low effort and a low impact are classified as 'harmless weeds'. Items with high effort and high impact are classified as 'the best of the best'. Factors that have high effort and low impact should be avoided and are classified as rotten tomatoes. Items that have a strong impact and require low effort should be prioritized.

No.	Category	Complexity	Overall Relevance
1	Information	1,82	54
2	Checking	2,12	61
3	Communication	1	22
4	Visualization	1,7	55
5	Simulation	2,6	67
6	Training	1,24	72

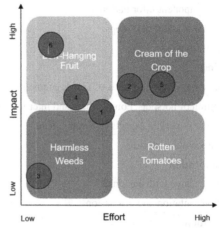

Fig. 2. Classification of the categories in the low-hanging fruit matrix (own representation after Varela and Ramquist [12]).

The strength of impact can be related to the relevance of the technologies considered, which can be scaled depending on the frequency of mention in the workshops.

The relevance is evaluated considering the following aspects:

- Number of different areas in which the points were taken up,
- Number of workshops in which the points were addressed,
- Mention of the points in the discussion,
- Picking up the points in brainstorming.

The effort, on the other hand, is reflected in the complexity and feasibility of implementation. This evaluation is performed based on the state of the art of research and the results described in the previous chapters. Complexity is ranked building on feasibility with values between 1 and 3. Table 1 shows an overview of the categories after the compilation and analysis of the data material with respective points. Figure 2 shows the classification of the categories in the low-hanging fruit matrix according to Varela and Ramquist [12]. The criteria for relevance are summed up and the criteria for complexity are averaged for each of the six key categories. It can be seen that the points of communication are classified in the 'harmless weeds' area. The reason for this could be that advanced technology is not needed for secure and stable communication.

Table 1. Categorization

Activity	Complexity	Relevance
Information		
Display powder status	2,33	9
Visualization of production status and parameters	1,75	15
Display component information	1,50	15
Display status about next steps	1,5	11
Display warnings	2	4
Checking		
Comparison of TARGET and ACTUAL geometry	2,8	14
Recognition of hotspots, complexities and internal structures	1,375	20
Verification of certain aspects of a component	1,8	15
Direct process monitoring	2,5	12
Communication		
Virtual exchange with customer	1	12
Virtual presentation and discussion	1	10
Visualization		
Virtual representation of the production process	1	11
Visualization of the component in different environments	1,6	13
Visualization of components printed in the past	2	8
Visualization and evaluation of data	2,14	15
Visualization of the component	1,75	9
Simulation		
Visualization of the component condition and the tools	2,6	14
Execution and display of simulations	2,67	14
Virtual designing	2,67	7
Dimensional accuracy check	2,875	19
Direct operation	1,75	13
Training		
Training without teacher	1,5	19
Training with instructor	1,13	22
Remote assistance, support, and maintenance	1,08	31

In addition, this category could be seen as self-evident, since communication must always be guaranteed. For the 'simulation' and 'checking' categories, the evaluation diagnosed high effort overall, but also strong impact. This suggests that participants would like to see advanced features that could add a lot of value. However, the state of the art is not advanced enough to implement them without further difficulty. If the goal is to achieve high impact with a low effort, the application areas 'visualization' and 'information' could be an efficient choice. This result is especially conditioned by the motivation to visualize information that currently can only be obtained on-site. This work hypothesized that the considered technologies can be particularly efficient in the area of training. Based on the matrix, it can be seen that the highest impact can indeed be achieved here with minimal effort. This is due, among other things, to the fact that the technology offers a new training dimension that enables the transmission of not only theory and language but also facial expressions, gestures, and physics, regardless of location and time. Thus, the hypothesis was confirmed and the subcategories of training - instructor-led, instructor-less, and remote assistance - are classified in the low-hanging fruit domain.

6 Summary and Outlook

With the present scientific work and the associated empirical investigation, a contribution regarding the use of immersive technologies along the AM process chain was made. Thus, based on the state of the art of research, it was recorded that the technologies of XR can form a basis for a practical, time-independent, and location-independent delivery of training, but it can potentially create benefits in several other areas.

For this reason, two focus group discussions were conducted in form of a hybrid workshop. The participants were experts in the field of AM. The workshop aimed to present the technologies under investigation to the participants and to gather expert opinions on the extent to which these technologies can be integrated into the manufacturing process. It was hypothesized that the technologies could achieve the greatest added value in the area of training opportunities. As a result, it was determined that the established hypothesis was confirmed. In addition to training opportunities, there is also potential in other areas such as information, visualization, checking, communication, and simulation. Using a low-hanging fruit matrix, it was shown that the implementation of technologies in the area of 'training' can achieve the greatest added value with the lowest effort. Furthermore, it was stated that in the areas of 'displaying information' and 'visualization of data' a high added value can also be achieved with little effort. The implementation of technologies in the areas of checking' and 'simulation' is more complex, although there is also a high relevance and demand here.

The workshop methodology in a hybrid format has shown to be a good approach since it was appreciated by the participants and direct follow-up projects within an XR development roadmap were initiated, especially for training. As limitation, it became apparent that the participants in the workshops were rather less engaged with the XR technologies. This was partly due to the fact that experts from the field of AM were selected for the research study. Thus, ideas were collected about the XR technologies that could potentially be implemented in the field of AM. The criteria to what extent this is feasible, to what extent the implementation is worthwhile or what challenges might arise for the development were not considered. Thus, in the next step, it must be taken into account that opinions must potentially be collected from experts who are primarily concerned with XR.

Acknowledgments. The authors would like to thank the Federal Ministry of Education and Research of Germany (BMBF) for funding the research in the project Industrialization and Digitalization of Additive Manufacturing for automobile series production (IDAM, grant number 13N15084) and the Deutsche Forschungsgemeinschaft (DFG, German Research Foundation) for funding under Germany's Excellence Strategy – EXC-2023 Internet of Production – 390621612.

References

1. Naghshineh, B., Carvahlo, H.: The implications of additive manufacturing technology adoption for supply chain resilience: a systematic search and review. Int. J. Prod. Econ. (2022). https://doi.org/10.1016/j.ijpe.2021.108387
2. Placek, M.: Share of sales revenue of additive manufacturing by industry | Statista. https://www.statista.com/statistics/1268618/share-sales-revenue-of-additive-manufacturing-by-industry/. Accessed 20 Nov 2021
3. Berger, U., Hartmann, A., Schmid, D.: 3D-Druck−Additive Fertigungsverfahren: Rapid Prototyping, Rapid Tooling, Rapid Manufacturing, 2nd edn. Haan-Gruiten: Verlag Europa-Lehrmittel−Nourney Vollmer GmbH & Co. KG (2017). https://www.europa-lehrmittel.de/downloads-leseproben/50335-2/3194.pdf. Accessed 10 Oct 2021
4. Palmas, F., Niermann, P.F.-J. (eds.): Extended Reality Training: Ein Framework für die virtuelle Lernkultur in Organisationen. Springer Gabler Wiesbaden, Germany (2021). https://doi.org/10.1007/978-3-658-34504-4
5. Azuma, R., Baillot, Y., Behringer, R., Feiner, S., Julier, S., MacIntyre, B.: Recent advances in augmented reality. IEEE Comput. Grap. Appl. **21**(6), 34–47 (2001). https://doi.org/10.1109/38.963459
6. Mehler-Bicher, A.: Augmented Reality: Theorie und Praxis, 2nd edn. Walter de Gruyter GmbH, Berlin/München/Boston (2014). https://ebookcentral.proquest.com/lib/kxp/detail.action?docID=1634280
7. Mann, S., Furness, T., Yuan, Y., Iorio, J., Wang, Z.: All Reality: Virtual, Augmented, Mixed (X), Mediated (X,Y), and Multimediated Reality, April 2018. https://arxiv.org/pdf/1804.08386
8. Bertsche, B., Bullinger, H.-J. (eds.): Entwicklung und Erprobung Innovativer Produkte−Rapid Prototyping: Grundlagen, Rahmenbedingungen und Realisierung. Springer, Berlin, Heidelberg (2007). https://doi.org/10.1007/978-3-540-69880-7, http://nbn-resolving.org/urn:nbn:de:bsz:31-epflicht-1586761
9. Brüsemeister, T. (ed.): Qualitative Forschung: Ein Überblick, 2nd edn. VS Verlag für Sozialwissenschaften, Wiesbaden (2008)
10. Hussy, W., Schreier, M., Echterhoff, G.: Forschungsmethoden in Psychologie und Sozialwissenschaften für Bachelor: Mit 54 Abbildungen und 23 Tabellen, 2nd edn. Springer, Berlin, Heidelberg (2013). https://doi.org/10.1007/978-3-642-34362-9
11. Mayring, P.: Qualitative Inhaltsanalyse: Grundlagen und Techniken. Beltz, Weinheim (2015). Print−ISBN: 9783407293930
12. Varela, G., Ramquist, K.: Low-hanging fruit matrix. https://theleansixsigmaoffice.com/2017/03/18/low-hanging-fruit-matrix/. Accessed 15 Dec 2021

Enabling Smart Production: The Role of Data Value Chain

Natalie Agerskans$^{(\boxtimes)}$ [iD], Jessica Bruch [iD], Koteshwar Chirumalla [iD], and Mohammad Ashjaei [iD]

Mälardalen University, Hamngatan 15, 631 05 Eskilstuna, SE, Sweden
natalie.agerskans@mdu.se

Abstract. To stay competitive, manufacturing companies are developing towards Smart Production which requires the use of digital technologies. However, there is a lack of guidance supporting manufacturing companies in selecting and integrating a combination of suitable digital technologies, which is required for Smart Production. To address this gap, the purpose of this paper is twofold: (i) to identify the main challenges of selecting and integrating digital technologies for Smart Production, and (ii) to propose a holistic concept to support manufacturing companies in mitigating identified challenges in order to select and integrate a combination of digital technologies for Smart Production. This is accomplished by using a qualitative-based multiple case study design. This paper identifies current challenges related to selection and integration of digital technologies. To overcome these challenges and achieve Smart production, the concept of data value chain was proposed, i.e., a holistic approach to systematically map and improve data flows within the production system.

Keywords: Digital technology · Smart manufacturing · Industry 4.0

1 Introduction

To stay competitive in the fourth industrial revolution and boost sustainability, manufacturing companies are developing towards Smart Production [1]. Smart Production is a system that generates and collects data across the entire product lifecycle and converts this data into valuable insights that are applied to optimize production processes in a smarter way [2]. Consequently, to enable Smart Production, manufacturing companies need to address aspects related to data management, i.e., the entire process from generating data at its source of origin until data is applied in to add value [3]. This requires using a combination of different cutting-edge digital technologies such as Industrial Internet of Things (IIoT), 5G, and Artificial Intelligence (AI) to fulfill the data managements tasks [4]. However, the main obstacles in accelerating Smart Production are selecting and integrating suitable digital technologies for data management in each specific production system [5]. This can be explained by the highly complex nature of advanced digital technologies [6] and the overwhelming number of continuously evolving digital technologies available on the market. Many digital technologies have several useful

© IFIP International Federation for Information Processing 2022
Published by Springer Nature Switzerland AG 2022
D. Y. Kim et al. (Eds.): APMS 2022, IFIP AICT 664, pp. 477–485, 2022.
https://doi.org/10.1007/978-3-031-16411-8_55

characteristics allowing applicability in different ways [4]. This makes it a complex task to understand what digital technologies to select and how these should be integrated in an optimal way. Further, the complex nature of a production system makes integration of new technology a challenging task. If changes are made in one part of the production system, it will affect its subsystems as well as its processes [7].

A number of studies examining Smart Production has been conducted. However, the majority of these studies focus on integrating one digital technology alone while Smart Production requires integration of several synergizing digital technologies [1, 4]. Therefore, more studies are needed to investigate how several digital technologies should be combined in an optimal way and how this problem can be approached by having a holistic perspective [1]. Further, Silva et al. [5] conducted a systematic literature review to identify recent publications on selection and integration of digital technologies. Their study confirms the findings from Müller et al. [8] which showed that Smart Production has mainly been looked at academically, but there has been limited attention on how manufacturing companies can select and integrate digital technologies. Silva et al. [5] concludes that previous studies on the topic is insufficient and more research is needed.

Considering the above motivations, there is a research gap on holistic approaches related to selection and integration of synergizing digital technologies for Smart Production. However, in order to propose such an approach and ensure all relevant aspects are considered, it is first considered necessary to identify current challenges that manufacturing companies are facing related to this topic. Therefore, the purpose of this paper is twofold: (i) to identify the main challenges of selecting and integrating digital technologies for Smart Production, and (ii) to propose a holistic concept which can be used to support manufacturing companies in mitigating the identified challenges in order to select and integrate a combination of digital technologies for Smart Production.

The outline of this paper is as follows: Sect. 2 presents a literature review, while Sect. 3 presents the research methodology. The case study findings and discussions are described in Sects. 4 and 5, respectively. Finally, Sect. 6 concludes the paper indicating some future work.

2   Literature Review on Smart Production

2.1   Digital Technologies

Although the term digital technology is frequently mentioned in previous research related to Smart Production, it is hard to find a clear definition for the term [9]. However, previous research on digital technologies and Smart Production [1, 3, 4] mainly deal with the general idea of software and hardware technologies applied for automated data management, including data collection and storage, in a digital context with the purpose of optimizing processes and increase value creating activities. There are many advanced digital technologies available on the market which can be linked to Smart Production. Focusing on the technologies that facilitate the data management, each technology is developed with a specific purpose, i.e., customized to solve a dedicated issue in the data management for Smart Production [4]. Tao et al., [3] identified the following critical phases for data management in Smart Production:

1. *Data sources and collection.* Refers to the points of origin where data is generated and the method of data collection. The technologies within this phase include sensors and data acquisition devices.
2. *Data communication.* Refers to the transmission of data from their sources to the places where they will be stored, processed, and visualized. Various technologies based on wireless and wired communication are within this category, e.g., WiFi.
3. *Data processing and storage.* Refers to the operations conducted to extract information from data and the place were collected data is stored. Typical technology examples include databases and data analytics tools.
4. *Data visualization and usage.* Refers to the techniques used to present data to end-users and the context in which data is applied to fulfill a purpose. IoT platforms are common technologies that serve this purpose.

2.2 Challenges of Selecting and Integrating Digital Technologies

Previous research has identified many digital technologies that can be connected to a Smart Production context. For instance, Klingenberg et al., [4] conducted a systematic literature review on digital technologies related to Industry 4.0 and identified more than 60 digital technologies. At the same time, since Industry 4.0 and Smart Production are new phenomenon, some digital technologies are still evolving [4]. However, companies often lack internal knowledge related to what benefits would come from integrating different digital technologies in production [6], making it challenging to select suitable digital technologies. Further, there is a lack of guidance on how to select a combination of different digital technologies that matches the existing production system elements. Instead, a common approach is to select and integrate one digital technology at the time without having a holistic perspective on the entire flow of data [4]. For instance, using smart sensors to collect large volumes of data without having a plan for how this data should be used to support production processes [10]. This can result in an extended time required until a full-fledged integration of technologies. In the worst case, selection of inappropriate digital technologies can lead to unprofitable investments [4].

Further, digital technologies will allow manufacturing companies to replace many manual work tasks with automated processes. Thus, the role and responsibilities of humans working at the shop floor will drastically change, which calls for new skills and competences, combining traditional production engineering with IT engineering [6]. Other challenges relate to the establishment of new interconnections between different actors [6, 11]. New actors will be introduced, and existing actors will play new roles. This comes with several challenges involving lack of existing IT infrastructure for data exchange, lack of IT and analytical capabilities, and new ways of collaborating using data as a resource [4, 10, 11].

3 Research Methodology

This study adopts a case study design [12] based on two reasons. First, case studies are appropriate for exploring novel subjects requiring increased theoretical insight. Second, case studies rely on empirically rich data including the context and experience of participants. This was considered essential for increasing the practical relevance of findings. A multiple case study involving companies from different industries and of different sizes was chosen to cover different contextual aspects that may contribute to the results. This was considered important to ensure results applicable for different types of companies in the manufacturing industry. The data was collected using semi-structured interviews and workshops with four manufacturing companies, two large companies and two Small Medium sized Enterprises (SMEs). An overview of the four companies and the collected data is presented in Table 1. The empirical data was analyzed using thematic analysis which is a systematic approach for capturing patterns in qualitative datasets. The data analysis included an iterative comparison of the empirical data and literature by following six concurrent activities: (i) data familiarization, (ii) generation of codes, (iii) searching for themes, (iv) reviewing themes, (v) defining and naming themes, and (vi) writing the paper [13]. In step (iv), empirical data was analyzed and sorted using the four categories identified in literature: data sources and collection, data communication, data processing and storage, and data visualization and usage. The concept of data value chain was developed based on an iterative analysis and cycles between empirical data and related literature following a case study approach. During the process, design science guidelines [14] were followed to identify priority areas of intervention and related solutions.

Table 1. Overview of studied companies and collected data

	Company A	Company B	Company C	Company D
Type of products	Heavy vehicles	Railway	Investment casted components	Electronics
Company size	Large	Large	SME	SME
Data collected:				
Interviews (No.)	6	3	2	23
Workshops (No.)	–	–	1	8

4 Challenges of Selecting and Integrating Digital Technologies

The empirical analysis showed that manufacturing companies are currently facing several challenges related to selection and integration of digital technologies for Smart Production. The identified challenges were classified in different themes which in turn were sorted into the following categories: (i) data sources and collection, (ii) data communication, (iii) data processing and storage, (iv) data visualization and usage, and (v) general challenges. These overall categories of challenges along with their reported examples are presented in Table 2. An overview of the identified themes of challenges is presented in this section, while a detailed analysis and presentation of the collected challenges are remained for the future work.

Data sources and collection included challenges related to generating data from its source of origin where three main themes of them include the following. The first theme is *manual work processes and reporting.* Operators were manually reporting data in the system which led to mistakes due to the human factors. Generating data from manual work processes was also challenging since there was no clear way how to generate this data automatically. The second theme is related to the *collection of operators data* which considers the challenges of privacy aspects when having the human operator as an object to collect from the data. The third theme is *automatic data generation and collection,* where ensuring that the collected data reflected the reality.

The second category is the **data communication** that covers themes related to transmitting the data from their sources to the places where they will be stored, processed, and visualized. The first theme considered the challenges of enabling data exchange between systems and equipment, known as *interoperability. Data accessibility* during the system failure and achieving *structured data communication,* such as attaching time labels on data, were two other themes of data communication challenges category.

The third category is **data processing and storage** which includes themes related to the operations conducted to extract information from data and the place were collected data is stored. The first theme, *pre-processing* considers the operations conducted to prepare data for analysis. This was especially considered a challenge for data which had only been used for manual analysis purposes and thus required categorization and cleaning. *Manual data analysis,* the second theme, was usually time consuming and required good data analysis skills by operators, which was in many situations not considered a good way of analyzing data. However, ensuring automatic *data analysis quality* is a complex task since the quality of the data analysis relies on the quality of the collected data. Some commonly mentioned problems were data inconsistency, data inaccuracy, and incompleteness, which all contributed to lacking quality of the data analysis. As a result, the generated data could not be used. *Data security* was the third theme within this category. The mentioned challenges were mainly regarding the data storage and giving access authorization to different roles to prevent the data being misused.

Visualization and usage of data is the fourth category which refers to themes related to the data content and techniques used to present data to end-users and the production context in which data is used. The theme *data visualization quality* considered aspects related to how data was presented to the end-user. Several companies mentioned that useful data was available to end-users, however the data was not actually used. The main reason for this was that the data was not presented in a format that was supported by the end-users in their work tasks. Another challenge was related to the *work processes,* i.e., the application area where the data should be applied to generate value. Developing current routines into work processes suitable for Smart Production was considered demanding as well as identifying digital technologies that were user-friendly for operators.

The last category is **general challenges** which covers themes that could be related to all four previous mentioned categories, yet not directly connected. The theme *usefulness and development of technologies* is considered as a challenge related to identifying how different systems can be utilized and developed in the best possible way for specific production systems. *Resources* was another theme which included challenges such as lack of skills and competence, culture, and time constrains for involvement of people

Table 2. Overview of categories and exemplary quotations

Data sources and collection

"... how to make the data that really reflects the reality, there is no errors due to forgotten reporting or not working system integration or stuff like that." (Process and IT Engineer, Company A)

"So it is difficult to find a way to, combined with the other technological aids we have, collect data and send it further so the administrative part is eliminated" (Production and Logistics Developer, Company B)

Data communication

"... it was the first time it happened that the network was down, the WiFi, and we could not produce, because it is not quality assured according to the process..." (Head of Production Planning, Company B)

"So I see this is as the biggest challenge actually, to get all of the systems connected " (Process and IT Engineer, Company A)

Data processing and storage

"...we are collecting a lot of data. And actually, we are not so great with correlating that data with some other features which we can also collect" (Process Engineer and IT Engineer, Company A)

"... we speak different languages in different domains. And how do we manage to break the language or communication barriers?" (Production Preparation Process Director, Company A)

Data visualization and usage

"Let's say that we have processed 100 products and there have been 50 quality faults (...) but I cannot tell if it these faults are on one or several products..." (Operator, Company D)

"So, I can, at any given time, see what the status is and even call operators and say "Hey, you need to stop", or whatever. But I also have a lot of other stuff to do ... " (Production Manager, Company C)

General challenges

"... I think it's easy to get lost in cool solutions and technologies that may not be value-creating..." (Production and Logistics Developer, Company B)

"Some roles, some jobs will have to change, or some jobs will disappear, but people will have to do something else or new type of jobs – so this is probably one of the main threats when you discuss with people" (Head of IT, Company A)

---

to work in Smart Production projects. The theme *defining a business case* refers to the challenges to ensure the right digital technologies are selected and invested in.

5   The Concept of Data Value Chain for Smart Production

Previous chapter presented themes of challenges related to data management within the production system. The empirical findings show that not addressing these themes of challenges can hinder manufacturing companies from achieving the desired benefits, i.e., generating value in a production context. It is therefore clear that manufacturing companies must have a holistic perspective on how to manage their entire data flow within the production system in order to convert data collected into valuable information which is applied to yield positive impacts on production.

The theoretical and empirical findings show that the concept of data value chain can be used to describe the data flow within a production system as a series of steps that are required to generate value and useful insights from the data. The data value chain can be used to describe the complete data lifecycle from a technical point of view, which includes data sources and collection, data communication, data processing and storage, and data visualization and usage. The empirical findings show that all these phases must be managed in a way that require minimum or no effort from humans. Therefore, having both efficient and effective data value chains is a key enabler for Smart Production.

Since the empirical findings show that all challenges of selecting and integrating digital technologies for Smart Production are somehow related to the data value chain, we propose the concept of data value chain as an approach to facilitate the selection and integration of digital technologies in order to move from current situation to Smart Production. The concept can be used in three steps. First, the current data flow within the production system is mapped based on the phases of the data value chain. This gives an overview of the data available, technologies, systems, and other resources used for data management, which is essential when defining compatibility requirements for new digital technology investments. Second, the mapped current situation is being analyzed by listing challenges, for example missing data, problems in current technological infrastructure, and lacking work processes. Third, by analyzing the challenges, suitable actions can be identified to mitigate the challenges. This can, for instance, involve the need for new investments or improvements regarding the integration of existing digital technology. The proposed improvements are finally mapped as a desired future data value chain, where Smart Production is the goal, to give a holistic overview before actions are taken. The data value chain concept and its pillars are shown in Fig. 1 that provides a set of knowledge to analyze the current situation that in turn will assist to select and integrate a set of digital technologies for desired Smart Production. Notice that the process is iterative which helps to update the data value chain challenges.

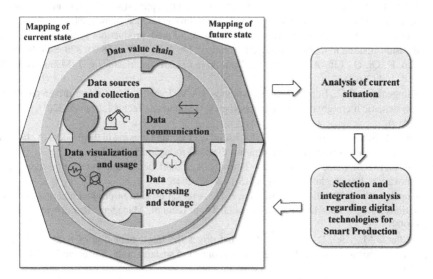

Fig. 1. The pillars of the data value chain concept and how the concept can be applied

6 Concluding Remarks

This study contributes to the ongoing discussion of selecting and integrating digital technologies to enable Smart Production [1, 5] by identifying current challenges and proposing a practical, holistic concept to overcome these challenges. More specifically, 15 themes of challenges were identified related to selection and integration of digital technologies. These themes showed that a key enabler for Smart Production is having both efficient and effective data management within the production system, where the entire flow from data generation to data usage must be considered. In this study, both large and SME manufacturing companies from different industries were selected to show that the discussed categories of challenges are applicable for different manufacturing companies. Further, the overall concept of data value chain was presented, i.e., a holistic approach which can be used to map the data flow within a production system to support engineers and managers involved in Smart Production projects when selecting and integrating a combination of digital technologies for Smart Production.

Planned future research includes a more detailed analysis of the presented themes of challenges related to Smart Production and extending the presented data value chain concept by developing a framework including application guidelines and validation of findings. Moreover, the research involves a more detailed analysis of how different digital technologies should be selected and combined to achieve Smart Production.

References

1. Choi, T.-M., Kumar, S., Yue, X., Chan, H. L.: Disruptive technologies and operations management in the industry 4.0 era and beyond. Product. Oper. Manag. **31**(1), 9–31 (2022)
2. Alavian, P., Eun, Y., Meerkov, S.M., Zhang, L.: Smart production systems: automating decision-making in manufacturing environment. Int. J. Prod. Res. **58**(3), 828–845 (2020)
3. Tao, F., Qi, Q., Liu, A., Kusiak, A.: Data-driven smart manufacturing. J. Manuf. Syst. **48**, 157–169 (2018)
4. Klingenberg, C.O., Borges, M.A.V., Antunes, J.A.V.: Industry 4.0 as a data-driven paradigm: a systematic literature review on technologies. J. Manufact. Technol. Manag. **32**(3), 570–592 (2019)
5. Silva, J., Silva, F., Silva, D., Rocha, L., Ritter, Á.: Decision making in the process of choosing and deploying industry 4.0 technologies. Gestão Produção **29**, (2022)
6. Sjödin, D.R., Parida, V., Leksell, M., Petrovic, A.: Smart factory implementation and process innovation. Res. Technol. Manag. **61**(5), 22–30 (2018)
7. Gopalakrishnan, S., Bierly, P., Kessler, E.H.: A reexamination of product and process innovations using a knowledge-based view. J. High Technol. Managem. Res. **10**(1), 147–166 (1999)
8. Müller, J.M., Kiel, D., Voigt, K.-I.: What drives the Implementation of Industry 4.0? the role of opportunities and challenges in the context of sustainability. Sustainability **10**(1), 247 (2018)
9. Berger, S., Denner, M.S., Röglinger, M.: The nature of digital technologies - Development of a multi-layer taxonomy. In: 26th European Conference on Information Systems (2018)
10. Schuh, G., Anderl, R., Dumitrescu, R., Krüger, A., ten Hompel, M.: Industrie 4.0 Maturity Index: Managing the Digital Transformation of Companies. Munich (2020)

11. Kache, F., Seuring, S.: Challenges and opportunities of digital information at the intersection of big data analytics and supply chain management. Int. J. Oper. Prod. Manag. **37**(1), 10–36 (2017)
12. Yin, R.K.: Case Study Research and Applications: Design and Methods. Sage, Los Angeles (2018)
13. Braun, V., Clarke, V.: Using thematic analysis in psychology. Qual. Res. Psychol. **3**, 77–101 (2006)
14. Takeda, H., Veerkamp, P., Yoshikawa, H.: Modeling design process. AI Mag. **11**(4), 37 (1990)

A Spontaneous Adoption of AR Technology
a manufacturing industrial context

Geir Kristian Lund[1,2] and Martina Ortova[1(✉)]

[1] Department of Industrial Economics and Technology Management in Gjøvik, Norwegian University of Science and Technology (NTNU), Postbox 191, 2802 Gjøvik, Norway
martina.ortova@ntnu.no
[2] Innlandet Hospital Trust, Postbox 104, 2381 Brumunddal, Norway

Abstract. Digital transformation is a process encompassing all organizations, requiring a proactive attitude and willingness to change. The Covid-19 pandemic highlighted the relevance of digitization through an increased awareness and implementation of digital tools for working life. The next wave of successful innovation in industry demands high-pitched adoption of technologies for production and workplace learning systems. Organizations are trying to understand which technologies to invest in, based on usability measures, cost effectiveness, and sustainability. It can be hard to predict which technology is best suited for specific tasks. This implies a growing risk regarding investments in technology. This paper describes the spontaneous use of technology for augmented reality (AR, Microsoft HoloLens 2) in a Norwegian manufacturing company during Covid-19. The case illustrates how AR technology can be used in assembling, installation and acceptance testing of machinery for selective soldering in the production of circuit boards. Data were collected through case study research and a qualitative research design, through observation and interviews with the participants. The results show that Microsoft HoloLens 2 is easy to adopt and could contribute to immediate and real value creation in industrial production companies. We believe that the spontaneous usage of AR technology in such extraordinary circumstances as a pandemic could motivate and guide other businesses facing important decisions related to technology implementation. The original value of this article is a contribution to the discussion on the Technology Acceptance Model, which is chosen as a theoretical framework for the paper.

Keywords: AR technology · Technology acceptance model · Industry 4.0

1 Introduction

Technological progress is growing exponentially, and the commercialization of modern technologies to the consumer market is steadily accelerating [15]. Thanks to global phenomena like social media, and not least unpredictable and critical events like the Covid-19 pandemic, modern technology is being distributed even faster. A wave of technological innovations affects organizations globally, and in the context of Industry

© IFIP International Federation for Information Processing 2022
Published by Springer Nature Switzerland AG 2022
D. Y. Kim et al. (Eds.): APMS 2022, IFIP AICT 664, pp. 486–493, 2022.
https://doi.org/10.1007/978-3-031-16411-8_56

4.0, companies must cope with phenomena like Internet of Things (IoT), digital twins, autonomous robots, and artificial intelligence [1]. Augmented reality (AR) has for some years been a part of this flow of new technology, and it is predicted that AR will play a key role in industrial development, especially in the areas of learning and skills training [2, 7]. To meet the demands for renewal, flexibility, and a sustainable production, industry must continuously implement new technology, which could become critical components of their competitive strategy. Making the right decisions for which technology to acquire and which models of implementation to use, and finding the potential for utilization, are resource consuming processes. Organizations must make a lot of considerations before technologies are put into operation, i.e., on technology characteristics, organization structure, management support, and human factors [3].

The purpose of the paper is to show how a complex industrial operation can be solved during extraordinary circumstances (Covid-19) through spontaneous use of new technology. This also illustrates the significance of collaboration and participation between various levels of the organization. Due to the pandemic and the encompassing restrictions a new and radical need for spontaneous usage of new technology has emerged. This paper describes a case where AR technology, already purchased by a company for research and learning purposes, gained new relevance due to the impacts of the Covid-19 pandemic. The case shows how a disruptive condition may force organizations to develop innovative decision models, skipping the usually essential steps of planning.

In the next sections we will elaborate the chosen theoretical framework, the Technology Acceptance Model (TAM), the give a brief introduction to AR technology, and discuss the applied methodology and the case of spontaneous usage of AR. Finally, we will try to contribute to the discussion about the technology acceptance model illustrated by the events of spontaneous usage of AR technology.

2 Theoretical Framework

As a theoretical framework for the present case, we are focusing on the technology acceptance model and spontaneous usage of technology. Here these two concepts will be briefly introduced. Implementing new technology in organizations can be challenging, and the success of implementation depends on how changes are planned, managed, accepted, and evaluated, and how the organization and its management consider the relation and the dynamics between technology and employees [14]. Various forms of decision-making methods in implementation of modern technology could be used, and different variables can be taken into consideration, e.g., size of investment, amount of affected employees, and the role of decision makers [13]. Decision making methods include identifying and choosing alternatives which are based on the values and preferences of decision makers [3]. Each decision maker must consider a variety of alternatives and make decisions which fit the goals of the organization.

2.1 Technology Acceptance Model (TAM)

The Technology Acceptance Model (TAM) [8] is influenced by the Theory of Reasoned Action [10], see Fig. 1. TAM is a commonly applied model to describe and measure an individual's acceptance of new information systems. The model was originally designed in 1986 and gained great interest in different scientific communities, leading to a substantial number of studies [4]. The main domain of TAM are two variables: Perceived Usefulness and a Perceived Ease of Use. Other variables was added by Venkatesh and Bala [16], including Social Pressure, Perceived Enjoyment and Fun, and Perceived Complexity.

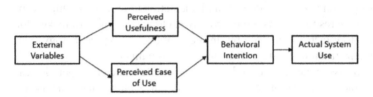

Fig. 1. Technology acceptance model (TAM) [17]

This paper focuses on the two basic variables of TAM adapted to innovative technology: the usefulness and the ease of use of AR technology (exemplified by Microsoft HoloLens2). Various studies have been performed on the use of TAM on VR- and AR adoption in learning environments and for the training on technical tasks [18–20]. Originally, TAM is studied on an individual level and not on the level of organizations. This is an important delimitation for this project since spontaneous usage of the technology primarily will be performed on the level of individuals, but within an organizational scope. This in turn implies that the use of the technology as a tool for training and learning will involve many levels of the organization, even if the practical application will take place on an individual operators' level. Assuming that the success of rapid implementation of modern technology in organizations can be caused by one employee's rapid decision to make use of technology, and that this employee for the management supports this approach, we suggest that spontaneous implementation of such technology can contribute to resolve a sudden event.

2.2 Spontaneous Usage

According to Oxford Dictionary [23] we define the adjective "spontaneous" as "not planned but done because you suddenly want to do it", or "done naturally, without being forced, practiced or organized in advance". "Usage" is defined as "the fact of something being used; how much something is used" [23]. If we merge these two terms, "spontaneous usage" can be defined as "the usage of something that was not planned to use before, but suddenly was taken into actual use." In the field of psychology, researchers are studying "spontaneous thought" [5] as an uncontrolled higher-order mental process which could arise in everyday life. The randomness of these spontaneous thoughts can contribute to the rejection of phenomena and cause them to never be realized. If we compare the terms spontaneous usage and spontaneous thought, we can assume that spontaneous usage, contrary to thought, triggers action. Thus, we choose spontaneous usage as a main term for the description of spontaneous action. In the next section, we will give a brief description of the AR technology used for specific cases.

3 The Technology

Augmented reality (AR) displays digital elements onto the real world, merging the virtual and the physical environment. Through AR the physical reality can be enriched and reinforced with digital layers and information elements, and new visual interfaces can be added to the physical surroundings. This facilitates interaction, information sharing and instruction in an interconnected and distributed manner [7].

In this paper we discuss the spontaneous usage of Microsoft's AR headset HoloLens 2 in an industrial context. Microsoft HoloLens 2 differs from AR in other contexts, like AR-apps on mobile phones, or head-up-displays in cars, in that the HoloLens 2 are a stand-alone, head-worn stereoscopic display equipped with processing power, sensors, camera, battery, etc. [22]. The headset has pre-installed software (Microsoft Teams, Assist, Guides), facilitating collaboration, instruction and guiding. There are some cons; the glasses are still restricted for professional tasks due to technical limitations, they offer a relatively small field-of-view (FOV), limited GPU and battery, and a mobile processor less powerful than AR-technology combined a pc.

4 Methodology

The described event coincided with the company's participation in a research project, including two other companies and partners from the public sector. This project is focused on the innovation, testing, and demonstration of systems for training, guiding, and learning using digital technology like AR and VR. Methodically, the study builds on a qualitative design approach, specifically based on case study design [9, 21] and collaborative action research approach [6, 12]. Case study research builds theory not as objective truth, but as interpretation of practical cases in their respective contexts. "The case study is a research strategy which focuses on understanding the dynamics present within single settings (...)" [9]. Data is collected through observation studies, field work and interviews. This approach encourages the active engagement of the actual users of the technology and close collaboration between these users and the researchers. This collaborative method proved useful when the company during the pandemic received a new machinery with high importance to keep production running, and the supplier's technicians could not travel from Germany to Norway due to Covid-19 restrictions. The acute situation hastened the company to find a solution, and encouraged the researchers to turn around quickly and participate in the session.

During the writing process, the researchers have been working with the implementation of AR technology in the company, actively observing and participating in the case. Interviews with participants were performed during and after the event.

4.1 Observation and Interviews

Date: April 20, 2021; Duration: 3 h; Participants: 3 technicians, manager of learning; Observers: CEO, PhD candidate, facility manager; Role of researcher: Observer, participant in some of the conceptual and technical preparations; Number of interviews: Three, the learning manager, two technicians.

TAM was used to analyze and sort results, not least to document the extent to which the employees found the technology useful. See Fig. 1 for an illustration on how the project followed the five steps in the TAM-model.

5 The Company and the Case

The case company was established in 1973, its core production is in industrial electronics, i.e., circuit boards, smart chargers, and communication components for the petroleum industry. The 22 000 sq. m. production facilities are co-located with the administrative functions in Eastern Norway. The company is one of several Norwegian Centers of Expertise (NSE), and has a total of approximately 250 employees, and reached 598 MNOK in sales in 2020. The case company is a part of the innovation project FAbL (Faster Assembly by Learning), described under"Acknowledgements". In the following chapter the spontaneous usage of AR technology will be described.

5.1 Case: Real-Time Augmented Instruction for the Assembly Machinery

The case shows a spontaneous usage of AR technology for the installation and acceptance testing of production machinery. In 2020, one of the participating companies in the R&D project FAbL purchased a fully automated machine for selective soldering for the production of circuit boards. Assembling the parts of the production machinery is an extensive series of tasks, requiring high competence in mechanics and electronics. These tasks include assembling of mechanical and electronic parts and circuits, installment of computerized systems, and final accept testing of all functions. All this is performed by trained technicians, guided by the German manufacturers' experts on the field, usually spending some days in Norway during the installation and testing. However, due to Covid-19, the manufacturer's technicians were prevented from travelling, and the case company's staff were unable to install the machine without the assistance from the German experts. New routines had to be established in a hurry, as the soldering machine was essential for maintaining the production capacity.

By a coincidence, the case company had acquired a pair of AR glasses (Microsoft HoloLens 2) due to their participation in the FAbL project, exploring digital technologies for faster assembly by learning. The company's manager of learning had a brief knowledge of AR technology after some testing, and he saw an opportunity to simultaneously solve the assembly situation and get more data on the use of AR for spontaneous instruction. He gave a couple of the factory employees a crash course in the use of HoloLens 2 and the Assist/Teams software. Through this, they could have instructions and mixed reality annotations in an "immersive digital meeting" during the installation of the soldering machine.

The technicians mastered HoloLens 2 after 2 h of on-site tutorial by the manager of learning. The German expert was then invited to a Teams meeting through the AR-glasses, and was given a quick tutorial on how to use the tools and functions for instruction and annotation in the meeting app (the software Assist works through Teams). Then they started the augmented collaboration and assembly process. During the session, the CEO of the company participated both through the Teams-meeting in the HoloLens 2, and physically through visits to the premises. This provided a unique opportunity to "live audit" the installation of the machinery.

Experiences from the manager of learning:
Quote 1: "During the installation, I did not wear the glasses myself, but the technicians told me that they experienced an immersive proximity to the instructor seated in Germany. Eventually, we became more confident that the technology worked as planned. Overall, we experienced that HoloLens 2 was a key factor in assembling and getting the machinery up and running."

Quote 2: "Several other machine suppliers now are considering shipping HoloLens 2 with their machines, to instruct and communicate via AR during assembly, installation, and accept testing. During Covid-19, we experienced that the cost of a AR headset equaled the cost of shipping two technicians from Germany to Norway. The investment is then estimated to have been saved in at the first installation."

6 Findings and Discussion

The case is evaluated using TAM (Fig. 1), level of spontaneous usage, and rapid implementation. The objective was the study of two main variables: Perceived Ease of Use and Perceived Usefulness. Due to the company's participation in project FAbL, they were familiar with the AR technology and HoloLens 2 before the spontaneous event. The manager of learning is a technology enthusiast and worked in advance on utilizing the AR glasses for simple tasks, like making a guide for the use of the copier. Based on this, and collaboration with the IT department, he observed that the usage of AR technology could be done without great technical thresholds. A challenge was the coupling between the AR technology and the organization's IT system, and between the AR-software Teams, Assist and Guides and the user's MS business account. Solving these challenges, the glasses were recognized as a specific computer on the company's network. Regarding the parameter Perceived Ease of Use, we can conclude that a strong individual interest in technology, familiarity with the organization and easy access to managers and a variety of companies' human and technical resources played an essential role in the case event.

We experienced that the Perceived Usefulness was affected by the Covid-19 situation, and that the spontaneous usage of technology in the case event was partly due to the strict rules for travel and entry between exposed countries. Additionally, the avoidance of expenditures due to already possessed AR equipment may have amplified the perceived usefulness. The perceived usefulness on an individual level seems to be lower than on an organizational level. Previous studies on TAM are generally focused on individual experiences and perceived usefulness [19]. Our results may indicate that TAM should be more studied on an organizational level, not least related to the implementation of modern technology in an Industry 4.0 context.

7 Conclusion

Technology implementation is usually a time-consuming process. A quick summary of the results reveals that the following variables played a significant role in this case: The

Covid-19 context, one enthusiastic employee's interest in AR-technology, the management's belief that this was profitable and substantially important for innovation, and the employees' and the organization's ability to convert these variables into action. The study encompasses only one event of spontaneous usages of AR technology, and in just one single company. Considering these limitations, the reported findings may open for new discussions on faster adoption and adaptation of innovative technology in organizational practice. The case offers some evidence that the spontaneous utilization by one single individual may support faster adoption of modern technology at an organization level. Although spontaneous usage proves to be particularly suitable under certain conditions, more experience is necessary to figure out if this provides an interesting path for further research. We suggest the following guidance: What is the role of the individual (the technology enthusiastic employee) in the implementation of modern technology? Which role does spontaneous usage play in the TAM model? How can the TAM model be used on an organizational level?

Acknowledgments. Project FAbL (Faster Assembly by Learning) is a four-year Innovation and Research Project for the Industrial Sector. Funded by The Research Council of Norway (NFR) - no. 309427. Partners: Hapro Electronics, IDT Solutions, Forestia, NTNU, Sykehuset Innlandet HF.

References

1. Ashrafian, A., et al.: Sketching the landscape for lean digital transformation. In: Ameri, F., Stecke, K.E., von Cieminski, G., Kiritsis, D. (eds.) APMS 2019. IAICT, vol. 566, pp. 29–36. Springer, Cham (2019). https://doi.org/10.1007/978-3-030-30000-5_4
2. Bailenson, J.: Experience on Demand: What Virtual Reality is, how it Works, and What it Can do. WW Norton & Company (2018)
3. Benders, J.: Robots: a boon for working man? Inf. Manag. **28**(6), 343–350 (1995)
4. Chang, S., Chou, C., Yang, J.: The literature review of Technology Acceptance Model: a study of the bibliometric distributions. Pacific Asia conference on information systems, PACIS 2010 Taipei, Taiwan (2010)
5. Christoff, K., Gordon, A., Smith, R.: The role of spontaneous thought in human cognition. In: Vartanian, O., Mandel, D.R., (eds.), Neuroscience of Decision Making. Psychology Press, pp. 259 – 284 (2011)
6. Coghlan, D., Brydon-Miller, M.: The SAGE Encyclopedia of Action Research. Sage (2014)
7. Dalton, J.: Reality Check: How Immersive Technologies Can Transform Your Business. Kogan Page (2021)
8. Davis, F.D.: Perceived usefulness, perceived ease of use, and user acceptance of information technology. MIS Q. **13**, 319–339 (1989)
9. Eisenhardt, K.M.: Building theories from case study research. Acad. Manag. Rev. **14**(4), 532–550 (1989)
10. Fishbein, M., Ajzen, I.: Belief, Attitude, Intention, and Behavior: An Introduction to Theory and Research. Addison-Wesley, Reading, MA (1975)
11. Gartner Hype Cycle Research Methodology, https://www.gartner.com/en/research/methodologies/gartner-hype-cycle, Gartner (n.d.) (2022)
12. Greenwood, D.J., Levin, M.: Introduction to Action Research: Social Research for Social Change. SAGE Publications. (2007)

13. Kimmerle, J., Cress, U., Held, C.: The interplay between individual and collective knowledge: technologies for organizational learning and knowledge building. Knowl. Manag. Res. Pract. **8**(1), 33–44 (2010). https://doi.org/10.1057/kmrp.2009.36
14. Orlikowski, W.J.: The Duality of technology: rethinking the concept of technology in organizations. Organ. Sci. **3**(3), 398–427 (1992). http://www.jstor.org/stable/2635280
15. Roser, M., Ritchie, H.: Technological progress. Our World in Data; 2013 (2013). https://ourworldindata.org/technological-progress. Accessed 21 Dec 2021
16. Venkatesh, V., Bala, H.: Technology acceptance model 3 and a research agenda on interventions. Decis. Sci. **39**(2), 2008, 273–315 (2016)
17. Venkatesh, V., Davis, F.D.: A model of the antecedents of perceived ease of use: development and test. Decis. Sci. **27**, 451–481 (1996). https://doi.org/10.1111/j.1540-5915.1996.tb00860.x
18. Jang, J.Y.K., Shin, W.S., Han, I.: Augmented reality and virtual reality for learning: an examination using an extended technology acceptance model. IEEE Access **9**, 6798–6809 (2021). https://doi.org/10.1109/ACCESS.2020.3048708
19. Sagnier, C., Escande, E.L., Lourdeaux, D., Thouvenin, I., Valléry, G.: User acceptance of virtual reality: an extended technology acceptance model. Int. J. Hum. Comput. Inter. **36**(11), 993–1007, (2020). https://doi.org/10.1080/10447318.2019.1708612
20. Fussell, S.G., Truong, D.: Accepting virtual reality for dynamic learning: an extension of the technology acceptance model. Interact. Learn. Environ. (2021). https://doi.org/10.1080/10494820.2021.2009880
21. Yin, R.K.: The case study as a serious research strategy. Knowledge **3**(1), 97–114 (1981)
22. Microsoft HoloLens (n.d.) (2016). https://www.microsoft.com/microsoft-hololens/en-us/hardware
23. Simpson, J.A, Weiner, E.S.C.: Oxford University Press.: The Oxford English Dictionary. Oxford: Clarendon Press (1989)

Supporting Resilient Operator 5.0:
An Augmented Softbot Approach

Lara P. Zambiasi[1]([⊠]) [iD], Ricardo J. Rabelo[2] [iD], Saulo P. Zambiasi[3], and Rafael Lizot[1]

[1] IFSC – Federal Institute of Santa Catarina, Chapecó, Brazil
zambiasi.lara@gmail.com
[2] UFSC - Federal University of Santa Catarina, Florianopolis, Brazil
ricardo.rabelo@ufsc.br
[3] UNISUL - University of Southern Santa Catarina, Florianopolis, Brazil

Abstract. Industry 4.0 and 5.0 have been posing new challenges to industries. From a focus on supporting resilience at a corporate level, there is a need to do it at a more operational level, enabling people to act with resilience as well. The *resilient operator 5.0* is a new concept emerged from this need. It has the aim of providing more intuitive, symbiotic, human-centered, and cognitive working computing environments to enhance human adaptation capabilities, productivity, and mental health. In this direction, this paper presents an approach that combines softbots and augmented reality, called '*augmented softbot*'. Looking at a specific company, a software prototype has been implemented to evaluate how this approach can be useful and feasible for preventive maintenance. Three scenarios have been devised for that, and they are summarized in the paper. The achieved results are discussed, showing the high potential of the approach.

Keywords: Industry 5.0 · Industry 4.0 · Softbots · Virtual assistants · Augmented reality · Resilient operator 5.0 · Operator 4.0 · Maintenance

1 Introduction

A key goal in the Industry 4.0 model refers to building smart resilient manufacturing systems [1]. In this context, resilience relates to "*the ability of manufacturing activities to withstand or quickly recover from operational disruptions that pose as threats to the continuity of manufacturing operations at the desired level*" [2].

Industry 5.0 also includes being resilient, but it extends it to the companies' workforce, via a socially and cognitively sustainable environment [1], putting people in the (control) loop. This means transforming people into protagonists of several activities, making them to act more collaboratively, enabled by more symbiotic human-machine interactions, and strongly supported by advanced technologies [1, 4].

At shop floor level, literature has presented different approaches to support this higher symbiosis. This work focuses on the use of softbots, a kind of virtual assistant software that helps humans in the execution of tasks, and whose potentials in manufacturing have

© IFIP International Federation for Information Processing 2022
Published by Springer Nature Switzerland AG 2022
D. Y. Kim et al. (Eds.): APMS 2022, IFIP AICT 664, pp. 494–502, 2022.
https://doi.org/10.1007/978-3-031-16411-8_57

been demonstrated in some works [e.g., 3]. More recently, augmented reality has arisen as another powerful technology to increase that symbiosis in manufacturing [4]. The union of these two technologies – to what we call as *'augmented softbot'* – can provide an environment where operators can be guided or interact with cyber-physical systems via voice and real-life-like images in the execution of tasks. This can decrease operation errors and time as well as increase productivity, continuous learning and improvement, and human satisfaction [1, 3, 4]. Despite this potential, no works have been found out in the literature or in commercial products with this combination in the industrial context.

This paper has the goal of showing some industrial shop floor scenarios where soft-bots and augmented reality are combined to create a working cognitive environment for the so-called "Resilient Operator 5.0" [1], extending the concept of *'augmented operator'* [5]. In terms of domain problem, this work has focused on preventive maintenance, one of the most relevant issues being dealt by industries in their chasing for higher operational efficiency, zero error, and lower production costs [6]. The importance of maintenance operators to be assisted by such technologies relies on an increasingly complexity in their daily activities, which includes: continuous training as new products and versions are developed; manual maintenance in several and very different equipment; planning activities and lots of information to be constantly checked about each equipment; the different levels of expertise and operators experience, leading to longer maintenance times and more errors; among others [6, 7].

This work has adopted the *Action-Research* methodology, which aimed at interactively and incrementally developing a Proof-of-Concept (PoC) software prototype to demonstrate the envisaged concept for a particular company; in this case, on how softbots and augmented reality can be a suitable approach for supporting the resilient operator 5.0 in the maintenance of industrial equipment.

This company is a medium-sized enterprise placed in the State of Santa Catarina, Brazil, specialized in producing customized industrial automated assembling solutions for the food sector, attending customers from Brazil and other countries. A machine called *"hamburger cartoning automated system"* has been chosen for the PoC. This machine is responsible for receiving ready pieces of raw hamburgers and packing them into ready-to-deliver paper boxes. This PoC is one of the company's initiatives towards developing *smart machines* to the market.

This article is organized as follows: Sect. 1 highlights the problem paper's goal. Section 2 summarizes the main theoretical fundamentals related to the proposed approach as well as related works. Section 3 describes the experimental setup, implementation cases, and results. Section 4 presents the preliminary findings of this research and its next short-term steps.

2   Basic Foundation and Related Works

The term Resilient Operator 5.0 is defined as *"a versatile and resourceful worker who uses creativity, skill and innovation enhanced by information and technology as a way to break paradigms in search of generating economic innovations that ensure the sustainability and well-being of operation tasks in the face of possible unexpected or difficult conditions that may encounter"* [1].

Augmented Reality (AR) can be defined as a human-machine interaction technology to supplement a real-world environment with computer-generated inputs with the aim of enhancing users' perception of reality and enriching the provided information content. It overlays computer-generated information on the real-world environment, and can be described as a set of three key features: combination of real and virtual objects in a real environment; real-time interaction with the system, able to react to user's inputs; geometrical alignment of virtual objects to real ones in the real world [8].

A softbot can be defined as *"a virtual system deployed in a given computing environment that automates and helps humans in the execution of tasks by combining capabilities of conversation-like interaction, system intelligence, autonomy, proactivity, and process automation"* [3]. It is the one that interfaces humans and a target system. A softbot can represent, act on behalf of, or respond to one or several users, computing systems, digital twins, and industrial equipment [9].

In terms of related works, a systematic literature review (SLR) has been carried out over the most important scientific databases looking for papers written in English that have addressed the equivalent problem and technologies in the last ten years.

More than 100 papers have been found out, but all of them covered only partial aspects of the envisaged approach. For example, papers combining softbots with maintenance; maintenance with AR; AR as a powerful technology for the operator 4.0 and 5.0; etc. Yet, most of the papers are conceptual, without computing implementations. Actually, and from the best of our knowledge, only one work [6] has suggested that combination, but "only" proposing a comprehensive conceptual architecture for that.

From a broader perspective on AR, Egger et al. [10] evaluated that its interfaces should allow two-way communication in order to be more effective. Wang et al. [11] seems to be the first one who proposed an AR-based system to support hands-free actions. Majewski et al. [12] have introduced speech recognition in AR-based systems. Palmarini et al. [7] found out, in their literature review on AR applications for manufacturing maintenance, that 2D and 3D visualizations combined with text or audio is the most common approach. It could be also observed from the SLR that the implemented AR mechanisms are basically reactive, responding to users as they request information. The approach with *augmented softbots* includes automatic and proactive actions to warn and guide users before and during their maintenance operation.

Some works can be mentioned here to briefly illustrate how AR or softbots have been viewed as useful technologies to help operators at industrial shop floors.

Fite-Georgel [13] and Mourtzis et al. [4] have discussed the potential of AR and other technologies to better support workers in their production environments. Hořejší et al. [14] evaluated that the available smart glasses present some hardware limitations, but advocate that they will be a strong candidate tool in future smart factories, combined with the use of voice commands. In this line, König et al. [15] implemented a prototype system using *Microsoft HoloLens* with AR and data glove, in which an inexperienced operator has been guided in an assembly process. Almeida et al. [16] proposed an approach where operators are provided with voice-enacted real-time reports and logs about the actions they should do and did as a means to increase operational efficiency and to decrease error rates.

The research of Rabelo et al. [2, 4] showed the use of softbots to help in creating more symbiotic human-machine interfaces close to industrial cyber-physical systems (CPS) and CPS's digital twin as well as a means to support CPS's autonomy and inter-CPS interactions.

3 Implementation Scenarios and Results

The first part of the work was related to identifying the needs and requirements in terms of how to do maintenance using the potentials of the proposed approach. After meetings with the company, a *cartoning system* module called *"Cam"* has been selected given its complexity and large number of parts (44), which require professionals with large experience to make maintenance on it.

The main professional responsible for doing the maintenance in this equipment helped to refine requirements and needs. This made possible the identification of the modeling needs, the dynamics of the softbot-AR model, and the ergonomics of the user interface and dialogs. Scenarios were devised based on this, being further implemented.

3.1 Implementation Resources and PoC Setup

The prototype has been developed as a 3D AR model. The cartoning system's parts had already been designed by the company in a CAD system (*Solid Works*). After being converted into a proper AR format, colors and textures were added to the parts using the *Blender* software. The whole environment was implemented within the *Unity* framework/tool. *Vuforia* software was used to get the modeled parts and to load them in the Unity environment. Once there, all the parts' animations and choreographies, the design of buttons and heads-up displaying, functionalities programming (via scripts coded in C#), etc., can be implemented.

This prototype was devised as an App to run on a smartphone, although the development environment supports other devices, such as tablets and smart glasses.

In what the softbot implementation is concerned, the *ARISA Nest* web platform [3] has been used. It allows the derivation of particular instances of service-oriented bots for given domains and their deployment in the cloud. The interaction between the derived softbot with the App is done through a web service developed in the *GO* programming language using the *REST* standard.

In general, when the softbot needs something (previously designed) from the App, a message is sent out to it, and vice-versa. This message can be sent due to a direct user's request, or be automatically and internally sent between the softbot and the App depending on the softbot's behavior associated with the desired action (see next section). Some description on how messages are modeled and processed can be found in [3] as well as how the softbot interacts with the equipment. Figure 1 shows the general architecture implemented in this PoC.

The operator uses the App for visualizations and interactions, and the softbot for voice and text interactions. The App's *engine* module centralizes all the general actions and reasoning. At the right side of Fig. 1 the main AR's GUI is showed (in Portuguese). The operator can ask for some information [*"informações"*] (e.g., see Fig. 4). The option

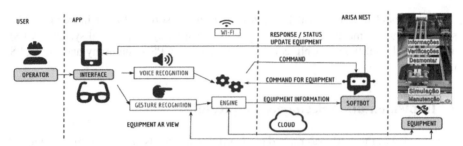

Fig. 1. General systems architecture

verification ["*verificações*"] allows checking the most important maintenance operations to be done. The option *disassembly* ["*desmontar*"] graphically shows how the *Cam* should be correctly disassembled for maintenance purposes. The option *simulation* ["*simulação*"] shows how the *Cam* can be assembled. Finally, the option *maintenance* ["*manutenção*"] shows a step-by-step process how to do the maintenance itself.

3.2 Implementation Scenarios

There are many possible scenarios related to how maintenance operators can be assisted by AR with or without softbots, as discussed in e.g. [1, 3–5, 7].

Considering the main goals of this PoC for the target company, three scenarios have been devised and implemented having the Resilient Operator 5.0 [1] in mind[1].

These scenarios also tried to exploit some of the *Arisa Nest*'s potentials, where softbots can be configured to have three behaviors: (i) *reactive*, allowing the softbot to act in response to direct user's requests via chatting or voice (e.g., to ask about some specific information from a given equipment); (ii) *planned*, allowing the softbot to act in response to (predefined) scheduled tasks, bringing their results to users after their execution (e.g., to generate consolidated equipment performance reports after every working shift); and (iii) *pro-active*, allowing the softbot to perform predefined tasks autonomously on behalf of users or of the equipment(s) it represents, bringing their results to users - if needed (e.g., to continuously check sensors' information, to anticipate problems and to promptly take measures to solve them, to send warnings and alarms, etc.).

Proactive Behavior Scenario. This scenario refers to when maintenance operators leave the maintenance office and go to the shop floor for their daily routine after knowing which machines should be checked and maintained. During their walk the machine's softbot warns them that the respective machine has an issue after receiving some information from sensors. This warning is sent out in an AR way (Fig. 2) when the softbot detects that a maintenance operator is close by the machine (this automatic 'detection' has been so far implemented only in a simulated way), or via sending a SMS message to the operator's smartphone.

---

[1] A partial demo can be visualized (menus are written in Portuguese) at https://youtu.be/V6S mVK4-R9Y.

Fig. 2. Proactive case, warning about the machine's situation

Reactive Behavior Scenario. This scenario refers to when the operator is doing the maintenance, starts an interaction with the softbot, and has some doubts about what or how to do, whether experienced or beginner operators. A very simple 'expert system' inside the softbot is implemented, guiding the operator during the operation. All interactions happen via the AR environment, running on the operator's smartphone (Fig. 3 left side), and they can be made both via voice and text.

In the case the operator wants more information about some specific aspect, an auxiliary interface pops up; in this case, the operator needs information about the *'casquilho'* part and the explanation is showed (Fig. 3 right side).

Fig. 3. Reactive case, assisting the operator during a maintenance

Planned Behavior Scenario. This scenario refers to when the operator is about to end his shift and wants to check the current status of the maintenance activities against what was planned. Reports are made available via the App and are automatically generated by the softbot, as planned. As Arisa Nest does not support *per se* graphical interfaces, the reports are stored and accessed at the derived softbot's web area (Fig. 4).

3.3 Implementation Evaluation

Being a PoC tested in a controlled environment, more formal quantitative performance indicators could not be applied and measured (for example, to measure the decrease of number of errors, the decrease in the maintenance time, etc.).

The designed functionalities worked as planned. The main limitation of this PoC was that the operator had to hold the mobile phone with the hands to do the maintenance.

From a more qualitative and general preliminary evaluation, some operators stated that this creates a more symbiotic operation environment. It can provide more confidence when they do the maintenance as they would be guided, warned, or aided by a correct and up to date maintenance information as machines are many and different. This may decrease their mental stress and perhaps decrease training time and costs.

In the case of the particular manufacturer industry which the PoC was developed for, this could decrease enormously the need for the company's employees to travel to customers for maintenance support as the customers' operators would be supported by the software. This means saving global maintenance and waiting times as well as costs from both sides when customers have problems in some equipment.

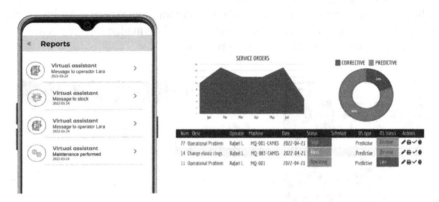

Fig. 4. Planned case, generating reports automatically

4   Conclusions

This article has presented a PoC implementation about how augmented softbots can be used as a viable approach to support the *Resilient Operator 5.0* concept at shop floor.

Three scenarios have been devised to evaluate the approach. The preliminary results confirmed its potential, in which the integration of a softbot with AR could help overcoming some of the challenges operators used to face in maintenance activities on industrial equipment. This includes the possibility to do some maintenance via voice and AR without using their hands (although this was not implemented), and without being very expert on given industrial machines. For example, the conversation with the softbot provided step-by-step instructions to the operator while showing the exact location of the actions for doing preventive maintenance.

Solutions based on the proposed approach can be helpful to train operators, both experienced and beginners, decreasing training time and hence costs. Besides this, they decrease the enormous effort and mental stress of maintenance operators to keep very up to date about every different equipment as new products, versions, automation devices, etc., are often introduced in the industry and so in the way maintenance is done.

Modeling the diverse parts of a single equipment in a CAD system and dealing with the design itself and implementation of the AR application takes time and requires specialized people for doing that. For example, the implementation of this prototype (with all the parts being previously designed in a CAD system) took about 150 h of work. Once deployed, and even having a good level of intuitiveness, solutions like that require training of operators in "using diverse tools" in their daily maintenance activities, which may be an additional point of stress.

The main next steps of this research are twofold. Firstly, there is a need to make more tests with AR-related technologies and products in wider scenarios. Secondly, to add machine learning techniques in the softbot so that it can adapt its answers and actions according to operators' experience as well as it can generate performance operation reports for identifying training needs.

Acknowledgments. This work has been partially supported by *CAPES Brazilian Agency for Higher Education*, project PrInt "Automation 4.0".

References

1. Romero, D., Stahre, J.: Towards the resilient operator 5.0: the future of work in smart resilient manufacturing systems. Procedia CIRP **104**, 1089–1094 (2021). https://doi.org/10.1016/j.procir.2021.11.183

2. Kusiak, A.: Open manufacturing: a design-for-resilience approach. Int. J. Prod. Res. **58**, 4647–4658 (2020). https://doi.org/10.1080/00207543.2020.1770894

3. Rabelo, R.J., Romero, D., Zambiasi, S.P.: Softbots supporting the operator 4.0 at smart factory environments. In: Moon, I., Lee, G.M., Park, J., Kiritsis, D., von Cieminski, G. (eds.) APMS 2018. IAICT, vol. 536, pp. 456–464. Springer, Cham (2018). https://doi.org/10.1007/978-3-319-99707-0_57

4. Mourtzis, D., Angelopoulos, J., Panopoulos, N.: Operator 5.0: a survey on enabling technologies and a framework for digital manufacturing based on extended reality. J. Mach. Eng. **22**, 43–69 (2022). https://doi.org/10.36897/jme/147160

5. Romero, D., Stahre, J., Wuest, T., et al.: Towards an operator 4.0 typology: a human-centric perspective on the fourth industrial revolution technologies. In: CIE 2016: 46th International Conference on Computers and Industrial Engineering. Tianjin, China, pp. 1–11 (2016)

6. Wellsandt, S., Klein, K., Hribernik, K., et al.: Hybrid-augmented intelligence in predictive maintenance with digital intelligent assistants. Ann. Rev. Control (2022). https://doi.org/10.1016/j.arcontrol.2022.04.001

7. Palmarini, R., Erkoyuncu, J.A., Roy, R., Torabmostaedi, H.: A systematic review of augmented reality applications in maintenance. Robot Comput. Integr. Manuf. **49**, 215–228 (2018). https://doi.org/10.1016/j.rcim.2017.06.002

8. Dini, G., Mura, M.D.: Application of augmented reality techniques in through-life engineering services. In: Procedia CIRP, pp 14–23 (2015)

9. Rabelo, R.J., Romero, D., Zambiasi, S.P., Magalhães, L.C.: When softbots meet digital twins: towards supporting the cognitive operator 4.0. In: Dolgui, A., Bernard, A., Lemoine, D., von Cieminski, G., Romero, D. (eds.) APMS 2021. IAICT, vol. 634, pp. 37–47. Springer, Cham (2021). https://doi.org/10.1007/978-3-030-85914-5_5

10. Egger, J., Masood, T.: Augmented reality in support of intelligent manufacturing – a systematic literature review. Comput. Ind. Eng. **140**, 106195 (2020). https://doi.org/10.1016/j.cie.2019.106195

11. Wang, X., Ong, S.K., Nee, A.Y.C.: Multi-modal augmented-reality assembly guidance based on bare-hand interface. Adv. Eng. Inform. **3**, 406–421 (2016). https://doi.org/10.1016/j.aei.2016.05.004

12. Majewski, M., Kacalak, W.: Human-machine speech-based interfaces with augmented reality and interactive systems for controlling mobile cranes. In: Ronzhin, A., Rigoll, G., Meshcheryakov, R. (eds.) ICR 2016. LNCS (LNAI), vol. 9812, pp. 89–98. Springer, Cham (2016). https://doi.org/10.1007/978-3-319-43955-6_12

13. Fite-Georgel, P.: Is there a reality in industrial augmented reality? In: 2011 10th IEEE International Symposium Mix Augment Reality, ISMAR 2011, pp. 201–210 (2011).https://doi.org/10.1109/ISMAR.2011.6092387

14. Hořejší, P., Novikov, K., Šimon, M.: A smart factory in a smart city: virtual and augmented reality in a smart assembly line. IEEE Access **8**, 94330–94340 (2020). https://doi.org/10.1109/ACCESS.2020.2994650

15. Konig, M., Stadlmaier, M., Rusch, T., et al.: MA2RA - manual assembly augmented reality assistant. In: IEEE International Conference on Industrial Engineering and Engineering Management, pp. 501–505 (2019)

16. Almeida, B., Bolas, J.M., Santos, R.J., et al.: Application of assisted reality at maintenance activities: e-redes' pilot project results, 1260–1264 (2022). https://doi.org/10.1049/icp.2021.2090

Evaluation of AI-Based Digital Assistants in Smart Manufacturing

Alexandros Bousdekis[1](✉), Gregoris Mentzas[1], Dimitris Apostolou[1,2], and Stefan Wellsandt[3]

[1] Information Management Unit (IMU), Institute of Communication and Computer Systems (ICCS), National Technical University of Athens (NTUA), Athens, Greece
{albous,gmentzas}@mail.ntua.gr
[2] Department of Informatics, University of Piraeus, Piraeus, Greece
dapost@unipi.gr
[3] BIBA - Bremer Institut für Produktion und Logistik GmbH at the University of Bremen, Bremen, Germany
wel@biba.uni-bremen.de

Abstract. Industry 5.0 complements the Industry 4.0 paradigm by highlighting research and innovation as drivers for a transition to a sustainable, human-centric and resilient industry. In this context, new types of interactions between operators and machines are facilitated, that can be realized through artificial intelligence (AI) based and voice-enabled Digital Intelligent Assistants (DIA). Apart from the existing technological challenges, this direction requires new methodologies for the evaluation of such technological solutions that will be able to treat AI in manufacturing as a socio-technical system. In this paper, we propose a framework for the evaluation of voice-enabled AI solutions in Industry 5.0, which consists of four dimensions: the trustworthiness of the AI system; the usability of the DIA; the cognitive workload of individual users; and the overall business benefits for the corporation.

Keywords: Industry 5.0 · Evaluation methodology · Trustworthy AI · Voice-enabled assistant

1 Introduction

Industry 4.0 has revolutionized the manufacturing sector by integrating several technologies, such as Artificial Intelligence (AI), the Internet of Things (IoT), cloud computing, and Cyber Physical Systems (CPS). On the other hand, Industry 5.0 complements the existing Industry 4.0 paradigm by highlighting research and innovation as drivers for a transition to a sustainable, human-centric and resilient industry [1]. In this context, new types of interactions between operators and machines are facilitated, thus fostering the hybrid-augmented intelligence paradigm [2]. This paradigm can be realized through voice-enabled Digital Intelligent Assistants (DIA), which is more than a voice-based human-computer interface; its intelligence rests with the integration of diverse AI functionalities that have the capability to interact with the user via voice [2, 3].

© IFIP International Federation for Information Processing 2022
Published by Springer Nature Switzerland AG 2022
D. Y. Kim et al. (Eds.): APMS 2022, IFIP AICT 664, pp. 503–510, 2022.
https://doi.org/10.1007/978-3-031-16411-8_58

Although industrial applications of DIAs have emerged only recently, they are expected to play a significant role in the collaboration between humans and AI systems [4–6]. Apart from the existing technological challenges, this direction requires new methodologies for the evaluation of such technological solutions that will be able to treat AI in manufacturing as a socio-technical system.

In this paper, we propose a framework for the evaluation of voice-enabled AI solutions in Industry 5.0, which consists of four dimensions: the trustworthiness of the AI system; the usability of the DIA; the cognitive workload of individual users; and the overall business benefits for the corporation.

The rest of the paper is organized as follows. Section 2 describes the four dimensions of the proposed evaluation framework and reviews the state-of-the-art in each dimension. Section 3 presents the proposed evaluation framework. Section 4 presents three use cases in which we will apply the proposed framework, while Sect. 5 concludes the paper and outlines our plans for future work.

2 Dimensions of Evaluation for Voice-Enabled AI Solutions in Industry 5.0

In this Section, we describe the four dimensions of the proposed evaluation framework, i.e. AI trustworthiness, system usability, cognitive workload, business benefits. For each dimension, we review the governing principles, and we review the state-of-the-art of related approaches tools in the literature.

2.1 AI Trustworthiness

To maximize the benefits of AI, while at the same time mitigating its risks, the concept of Trustworthy AI (TAI) promotes the idea that individuals, organizations, and societies will only ever be able to achieve the full potential of AI if trust can be established in its development, deployment, and use [7]. The TAI concept has been studied in several works (e.g. [8–10]. The increasing literature implies that although human-centricity is an indispensable feature of AI, it has not suited to be used by data scientists in the development of AI-based services or products [9, 11].

Therefore, AI should be: Lawful, complying with all applicable laws and regulations; Ethical, ensuring adherence to ethical principles and values; Robust, both from a technical and social perspective [7]. These requirements serve the need for trust [8, 10]. Despite their value for a realization of TAI, the outlined principles and the corresponding frameworks and guidelines face two major limitations [9]. First, several TAI principles may conflict with each other. Second, they are so general that do not provide sufficient guidance on how they can be transferred into practice. To this end, the High-Level Expert Group on Artificial Intelligence (AI-HLEG) has created the Assessment List for Trustworthy Artificial Intelligence (ALTAI) tool that helps organizations to self-assess the trustworthiness of their AI systems [7].

2.2 System Usability

Usability and user experience has become an important performance measure in the evaluation of interactive systems, since improving the end-user satisfaction leads to a greater adoption of the products [12]. A large number of usability evaluation tools are available, such as: The Usability Metric for User Experience (UMUX) [13], The Computer System Usability Questionnaire (CSUQ) [14], Software Usability Measurement Inventory (SUMI) [15], AttrakDiff [16], System Usability Scale (SUS) [17].

The SUS is the most widely used questionnaire for the assessment of perceived GUI usability that has significantly attracted the researchers and practitioners' interest [12, 18]. However, the application of SUS in voice assistants is limited [18]. Voice-interfaces face some distinct challenges, such as: the ability to understand non-conversational cues (i.e., pauses in the middle of a conversation) [18, 19], difficulty with back and forth navigation [20], absence of a visual feedback that increases the cognitive workload [21], users' pre-conceived expectations as to how a conversation should proceed [19], the effect of the quality of the synthetic voice to the perception of the users [22].

In the past, there had been an explosion of usability evaluation approaches, metrics and scales focusing on conversational interfaces, chatbots and intelligent assistants. Examples include: Subjective Assessment of Speech System Interfaces (SASSI) [23], Speech User Interface Service Quality (SUISQ) [24], SUXES [25]. However, recent literature on the usability of AI-based voice-assistants is lagging [12, 18]. To this end, an extension of SUS targeted explicitly to chatbots and voice-enabled interfaces has been developed, called Voice Usability Scale (VUS) [19].

2.3 Cognitive Workload

When attempting to solve a problem, humans call upon their limited cognitive resources. The degree of their utilization is described as cognitive load [26]. While the number of parameters to be considered and to be processed by modern-day knowledge workers increases, their cognitive resources do not [27]. The evaluation of cognitive workload is a key point in the research and development of human–machine interfaces, in search of higher levels of comfort, satisfaction, efficiency, and safety in the workplace [28]. The workload level experienced by an operator can affect task performance, since too high a load can increase stress and failure rates and decrease the work satisfaction and performance of employees [29].

The existing evaluation tools fall into three categories [30]: (a) performance-based measures, (b) subjective measures, and (c) physiological measures. The performance-based measures are grounded on the assumption that any increase in task difficulty will lead to a decrease in performance. Subjective procedures assume that an increased power expense is linked to the perceived effort. Physiological indexes assume that the mental workload can be measured by means of the level of physiological activation.

As human–machine systems have become more complex and automated, evaluations based on the operator's performance have become prohibitively difficult. To this end, subjective measures are becoming an increasingly important tool [28]. The reasons for their frequent use include their practical advantages (ease of implementation, non-intrusiveness) and current data which support their capability to provide sensitive measures of operator load. The most well-established and widely used subjective method is the NASA-TLX, which allows a detailed analysis of the workload source (Task Load Index) (e.g., [28, 29, 31, 32], which was proposed by [33].

2.4 Business Benefits

The business benefits are defined in the form of business Key Performance Indicators (KPIs). KPIs are the quantifiable operational and strategic measurements that reflect the success factors of the manufacturing processes that adopt a technological solution. In this sense, they are used to quantify the efficiency and effectiveness of manufacturing processes [34]. Acknowledging the contributions and support of the KPIs, the decision-makers can evidence the existing gap between the before and after situation in terms of performance. According to the manufacturing process under examination and the business requirements, different KPIs can be defined and measured.

3 The Proposed Evaluation Framework

In this Section, we present our proposed evaluation framework for voice-enabled trustworthy AI solutions in Industry 5.0. As shown in Fig. 1, it is structured across the four dimensions of Sect. 3: AI trustworthiness, system usability, cognitive workload, business benefits. Below, we present the methods that address these dimensions.

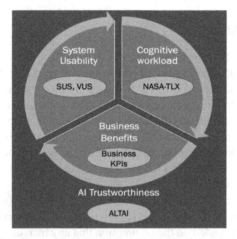

Fig. 1. The proposed evaluation framework for AI-based digital assistants in manufacturing.

AI Trustworthiness: In the proposed framework, AI trustworthiness is addressed by the ALTAI questionnaire which adopts the Ethics Guidelines for Trustworthy Artificial Intelligence proposed by the AI HLEG in order to self-assess its compliance to the seven requirements of Trustworthy Artificial Intelligence (TAI) [7]: Human agency and oversight; Technical robustness and safety; Privacy and data governance; Transparency; Diversity, non-discrimination and fairness; Societal and environmental well-being; Accountability. Interdisciplinary expertise is required to answer since the very first questions.

System Usability: Voice-enabled AI solutions are implemented with a Digital Intelligent Assistant (DIA) as an interface, while they are usually accompanied by a GUI for visualization. The GUI can be evaluated through the well-established SUS which has proved to have high reliability, validity, while it is sensitive to a wide variety of independent variables. Drawing parallels to SUS, the VUS scale is also a 10-item one, a 7-point Likert scale having declarative statements of opinion to which the participants will respond with their rate of agreement, allowing meaningful comparisons to be made between the two [18]. The problem of developing a usability measure for voice-assistants is that there are no commonly accepted usability dimensions.

Cognitive Workload: This dimension is addressed by the NASA-TLX, a well-established and widely used subjective method, which includes six dimensions: Mental Demand; Physical Demand; Temporal Demand; Overall Performance; Effort; Frustration Level. The adoption of emerging AI technologies poses new challenges to both employers and employees of manufacturing companies who need to adapt to new processes requiring an efficient management of workload [35, 36]. Virtual assistants provide opportunities to reduce the workload by assisting in the execution of repetitive tasks that require the fast retrieval and processing of data [27, 37]. It was only recently that there is some preliminary evidence that virtual assistants are able to reduce the cognitive load when performing tasks [27]; however, evaluation in real manufacturing environments is still at its early stages [38].

Business Benefits: The business benefits are defined in the form of business KPIs by the use cases in which the voice-enabled AI solution under evaluation is deployed. Various categories of KPIs can be examined according to the scope of the technological solution, the manufacturing processes under consideration, and the business goals, such as: organizational, financial, business, operational, technology, health & safety, environmental sustainability.

4   Use Cases

In this Section, we briefly describe three use cases in which we will apply the proposed framework.

On-the-Job Training in Textile Production: This scenario addresses the shortage of qualified labor force in processes from raw materials to fabric delivery and, to clothing sale to consumers. A key goal is to maintain the worker's autonomy instead of promoting the unquestioned execution of instructions. A voice-enabled AI solution will identify the worker's current skill level and will adapt the advising behavior according to the learning experience, accompanied by explainability functionalities. In this way, the training support will contribute to the defects reduction that are caused by human errors.

End-of-Line Quality Control in White Goods Production: This scenario addresses the support of operators at the end-of-line quality control through a Digital Intelligent Assistant (DIA) in order to adopt a predictive quality strategy that will link the quality control of the finished product with the design stage and the shop floor. By integrating all available information sources (e.g. sensor data, historical operational data, and expert knowledge), it will be able to predict low-quality products and to plan mitigating actions in order to proactively identify their root causes in order to, among others, reduce organization, warranty but also reputation costs.

Line Re-configuration in Hygiene Products Manufacturing: This scenario addresses the setup and change-over of production lines that require trained workers capable of (re)configure machines, align production speeds, and adjust machine settings within a given amount of time. To address these problems, the company aims to standardize the reconfiguration process by capturing the best practices and by sharing them through a digital intelligent assistant which will guide the workers towards optimum configuration of the production line. This will reduce the change-over time, time pressure caused by downtime, and lessen the cognitive workload of workers in solving unpredictable complex tasks.

5 Conclusion and Future Work

Although industrial applications of DIAs have emerged only recently, they are expected to play a significant role in the collaboration between human and AI. This direction requires new methodologies for the evaluation of such AI solutions.

In this paper, we proposed a framework for the evaluation of AI-based Digital Assistants in smart manufacturing, which consists of four dimensions: AI trustworthiness, system usability, cognitive workload, business benefits.

We are currently in the process of applying the evaluation framework in the three aforementioned real-life scenarios. An early application of the ALTAI framework with a first demonstration version of the DIA has already demonstrated the benefits, and also some limitations, of the approach. In the near future we will apply all four dimensions and examine their suitability and usefulness for digital intelligent assistants in manufacturing use cases.

Acknowledgements. This work is partly funded by the European Union's Horizon 2020 project COALA "COgnitive Assisted agile manufacturing for a LAbor force supported by trustworthy Artificial Intelligence" (Grant agreement No 957296). The work presented here reflects only the authors' view and the European Commission is not responsible for any use that may be made of the information it contains.

References

1. Maddikunta, P.K.R., et al.: Industry 5.0: a survey on enabling technologies and potential applications. J. Ind. Inf. Integr. **26**, 100257 (2021)

2. Wellsandt, S., et al.: Hybrid-augmented intelligence in predictive maintenance with digital intelligent assistants. In: Annual Reviews in Control (In Press, Corrected Proof) (2022)
3. Dhiman, H., Wächter, C., Fellmann, M., Röcker, C.: Intelligent assistants. Bus. Inf. Syst. Eng. 1–21 (2022)
4. Rabelo, R.J., Romero, D., Zambiasi, S.P.: Softbots supporting the operator 4.0 at smart factory environments. In: Moon, I., Lee, G., Park, J., Kiritsis, D., Von Cieminski, G. (eds.) Advances in Production Management Systems. Smart Manufacturing for Industry 4.0. APMS 2018. IFIP Advances in Information and Communication Technology, vol. 536, pp. 456–464. Springer, Cham (2018). https://doi.org/10.1007/978-3-319-99707-0_57
5. Bousdekis, A., et al.: Human-AI collaboration in quality control with augmented manufacturing analytics. In: Dolgui, A., Bernard, A., Lemoine, D., von Cieminski, G., Romero, D. (eds.) Advances in Production Management Systems. Artificial Intelligence for Sustainable and Resilient Production Systems. APMS 2021. IFIP Advances in Information and Communication Technology, vol. 633, pp.303–310. Springer, Cham (2021). https://doi.org/10.1007/978-3-030-85910-7_32
6. Wellsandt, S., Hribernik, K., Thoben, K.D.: Anatomy of a digital assistant. In: Dolgui, A., Bernard, A., Lemoine, D., von Cieminski, G., Romero, D. (eds.) Advances in Production Management Systems. Artificial Intelligence for Sustainable and Resilient Production Systems. APMS 2021. IFIP Advances in Information and Communication Technology, vol. 633, pp. 321–330. Springer, Cham (2021). https://doi.org/10.1007/978-3-030-85910-7_34
7. High-Level Independent Group on Artificial Intelligence (AI HLEG). Ethics Guidelines for Trustworthy AI. https://ec.europa.eu/digital
8. Floridi, L.: Establishing the rules for building trustworthy AI. Nat. Mach. Intell. 1(6), 261–262 (2019)
9. Baneres, D., Guerrero-Roldán, A.E., Rodríguez-González, M.E., Karadeniz, A.: A predictive analytics infrastructure to support a trustworthy early warning system. Appl. Sci. 11(13), 5781 (2021)
10. Thiebes, S., Lins, S., Sunyaev, A.: Trustworthy artificial intelligence. Electron. Mark. 31(2), 447–464 (2020). https://doi.org/10.1007/s12525-020-00441-4
11. Georgieva, I., Lazo, C., Timan, T., Van Veenstra, A.F.: From AI ethics principles to data science practice: a reflection and a gap analysis based on recent frameworks and practical experience. AI Ethics 1–15 (2022)
12. Kocaballi, A.B., Laranjo, L., Coiera, E.: Understanding and measuring user experience in conversational interfaces. Interact. Comput. 31(2), 192–207 (2019)
13. Finstad, K.: The usability metric for user experience. Interact. Comput. 22(5), 323–327 (2010)
14. Lewis, J.R.: IBM computer usability satisfaction questionnaires: psychometric evaluation and instructions for use. Int. J. Hum. Comput. Interact. 7(1), 57–78 (1995)
15. Kirakowski, J.: Software usability measurement inventory SUMI. SUMI (2011). http://sumi.uxp.ie/en/index.php
16. Hassenzahl, M., Burmester, M., Koller, F.: AttrakDiff: a questionnaire to measure perceived hedonic and pragmatic quality. Mensch Comput. 57, 187–196 (2003)
17. Brooke, J.: SUS-A quick and dirty usability scale. Usability Eval. Ind. 189(194), 4–7 (1996)
18. Zwakman, D.S., Pal, D., Arpnikanondt, C.: Usability evaluation of artificial intelligence-based voice assistants: the case of Amazon Alexa. SN Comput. Sci. 2(1), 1–16 (2021). https://doi.org/10.1007/s42979-020-00424-4
19. Murad, C., Munteanu, C., Cowan, B.R., Clark, L.: Revolution or evolution? Speech interaction and HCI design guidelines. IEEE Pervasive Comput. 18(2), 33–45 (2019)
20. Holmes, S., Moorhead, A., Bond, R., Zheng, H., Coates, V., McTear, M.: Usability testing of a healthcare chatbot: can we use conventional methods to assess conversational user interfaces? In: Proceedings of the 31st European Conference on Cognitive Ergonomics, pp. 207–214 (2019)

21. Cowan, B.R., et al.: What can i help you with? Infrequent users' experiences of intelligent personal assistants. In: Proceedings of the 19th International Conference on Human-Computer Interaction with Mobile Devices and Services, pp. 1–12 (2017)

22. Babel, M., McGuire, G., King, J.: Towards a more nuanced view of vocal attractiveness. PLoS ONE 9(2), e88616 (2014)

23. Hone, K.S., Graham, R.: Towards a tool for the subjective assessment of speech system interfaces (SASSI). Nat. Lang. Eng. 6(3–4), 287–303 (2000)

24. Polkosky, M.D.: Machines as mediators: the challenge of technology for interpersonal communication theory and research, pp. 48–71. Routledge (2008)

25. Turunen, M., Hakulinen, J., Melto, A., Heimonen, T., Laivo, T., Hella, J.: SUXES-user experience evaluation method for spoken and multimodal interaction. In: Tenth Annual Conference of the International Speech Communication Association (2009)

26. Sweller, J.: Cognitive load during problem solving: effects on learning. Cognit. Sci. 12(2), 257–285 (1988)

27. Brachten, F., Brünker, F., Frick, N.R., Ross, B., Stieglitz, S.: On the ability of virtual agents to decrease cognitive load: an experimental study. Inf. Syst. e-Bus. Manag. 18(2), 187–207 (2020)

28. Rubio, S., Díaz, E., Martín, J., Puente, J.M.: Evaluation of subjective mental workload: a comparison of SWAT, NASA-TLX, and workload profile methods. Appl. Psychol. 53(1), 61–86 (2004)

29. Cao, A., Chintamani, K.K., Pandya, A.K., Ellis, R.D.: NASA TLX: software for assessing subjective mental workload. Behav. Res. Methods 41(1), 113–117 (2009). https://doi.org/10.3758/BRM.41.1.113

30. Meshkati, N., Hancock, P.A., Rahimi, M., Dawes, S.M.: Techniques in mental workload assessment (1995)

31. Hart, S.G.: NASA-task load index (NASA-TLX); 20 years later. In: Proceedings of the Human Factors and Ergonomics Society Annual Meeting, vol. 50, no. 9, pp. 904–908. Sage publications, Sage CA: Los Angeles, CA (2006)

32. Castro, S.C., Quinan, P.S., Hosseinpour, H., Padilla, L.: Examining effort in 1d uncertainty communication using individual differences in working memory and NASA-TLX. IEEE Trans. Vis. Comput. Graph. 28(1), 411–421 (2021)

33. Hart, S.G., Staveland, L.E.: Development of NASA-TLX (Task Load Index): results of empirical and theoretical research. In: Advances in psychology, vol. 52, pp. 139–183. North-Holland (1988)

34. Zhu, L., Johnsson, C., Varisco, M., Schiraldi, M.M.: Key performance indicators for manufacturing operations management–gap analysis between process industrial needs and ISO 22400 standard. Procedia Manuf. 25, 82–88 (2018)

35. Galy, E., Cariou, M., Mélan, C.: What is the relationship between mental workload factors and cognitive load types? Int. J. Psychophysiol. 83(3), 269–275 (2012)

36. Matt, C., Hess, T., Benlian, A.: Digital transformation strategies. Bus. Inf. Syst. Eng. 57(5), 339–343 (2015)

37. Dellermann, D., Ebel, P., Söllner, M., Leimeister, J.M.: Hybrid intelligence. Bus. Inf. Syst. Eng. 61(5), 637–643 (2019)

38. Mirbabaie, M., Stieglitz, S., Brünker, F., Hofeditz, L., Ross, B., Frick, N.R.: Understanding collaboration with virtual assistants–the role of social identity and the extended self. Bus. Inf. Syst. Eng. 63(1), 21–37 (2021)

Supporting Data Analytics in Manufacturing with a Digital Assistant

Stefan Wellsandt[1](✉), Mina Foosherian[1], Katerina Lepenioti[2], Mattheos Fikardos[2], Gregoris Mentzas[2], and Klaus-Dieter Thoben[3]

[1] BIBA – Bremer Institut für Produktion und Logistik GmbH, Hochschulring 20, 28359 Bremen, Germany
{wel,fos}@biba.uni-bremen.de

[2] Information Management Unit (IMU), Institute of Communication and Computer Systems (ICCS), National Technical University of Athens (NTUA), Athens, Greece
{albous,gmentzas}@mail.ntua.gr

[3] Faculty of Production Engineering, University of Bremen, Badgasteinerstr. 1, 28359 Bremen, Germany
tho@biba.uni-bremen.de

Abstract. The shortage of skilled workers is a barrier to applying data analytics. Augmented analytics is an approach to lower it by using machine learning to automate related activities and natural language applications to assist less-skilled employees. Public information about augmented analytics case studies in manufacturing is hardly available. Therefore, this article presents a related case study from the white goods industry. It focuses on a quality test lab in a production line where workers use a digital assistant prototype to interact with descriptive and predictive data analytics. This article derives a framework from this case study to organize how an assistant could augment analytics. The framework has five areas: training data modification, model training, starting an analysis, retrieval of results, and decision support. The latter is relevant to the other four areas and includes, for instance, suggesting options to customize analytics. Four scenarios of different complexity concretize the framework's areas. Finally, this article outlines four questions for future research.

Keywords: Augmented analytics · Digital intelligent assistant · Voice assistant · Natural language understanding · Assistance technology

1 Introduction

When producers adopt and practice data analytics, they need skilled employees familiar with its approaches, activities, and tools. Often, this includes machine-learning (ML) expertise. The employees also need a deep understanding of the data's context, including the target audience that will use the results at work. A critical barrier that slows down the adoption of data analytics in production is the shortage of skilled employees [1].

© IFIP International Federation for Information Processing 2022
Published by Springer Nature Switzerland AG 2022
D. Y. Kim et al. (Eds.): APMS 2022, IFIP AICT 664, pp. 511–518, 2022.
https://doi.org/10.1007/978-3-031-16411-8_59

Drivers for this situation are that the education of data analysts takes a long time, and more companies want to employ these experts, which increases the demand.

Technology providers aim to reduce data analytics' skill floor and the education time by automating activities and supporting employees who work with related tools [2–4]. **Augmented analytics** a) uses technologies such as ML to automate data analysis activities and b) assists employees with data preparation, processing, and understanding results [5]. The latter includes the application of artificial intelligence (AI) and natural language processing (NLP) in chatbots and voice assistants. Such tools augment human cognitive capabilities, so less-skilled employees can use data analytics tools.

Public information about augmented analytics in manufacturing is sparse—especially case studies with sufficient depth. Consequently, advancing research in this field is challenging because researchers cannot build on previous work.

This article provides a *case study* and a related *framework* for augmented analytics in manufacturing. It includes the architecture for a voice-enabled digital intelligent assistant (DIA) and dialogs outlining how users interact with data analytics through it. The remainder of this article has four sections. Section 2 summarizes aspects of augmented analytics to scope this paper, while Sect. 3 presents the case study and example conversations. Section 4 introduces a framework to augment different analytics activities. Finally, Sect. 5 concludes the paper and outlines research directions.

2 Related Work

Augmented analytics is a term brought up by Gartner to summarize the use of AI in analytics [1]. It is a broad concept proposing ML and conversational user interfaces (CUI) to get insight from data. CUIs allow users to interact with software through natural language and are an essential characteristic of a DIA [6].

2.1 Automated machine learning in manufacturing analytics

Automated machine learning (AutoML) is a sub-topic of augmented analytics. It focuses on the progressive automation of manual ML tasks [7] and aims at minimizing human intervention to save time and make analytics accessible to non-experts.

The application of AutoML in manufacturing concerns, for instance, the prediction of lead times and process quality. Bender, Trat, and Ovtcharova [8, 9] applied AutoML to predict lead times in two small and medium-sized enterprises. They found that it created superior prediction models in one case. The authors reported mixed results for the other case because the error rates were too high for some production steps. Besides, the applied AutoML approach could not support highly labor-intensive tasks, such as data understanding, transformation, filtering, pre-processing, and feature engineering. Denkena et al. [10] used AutoML to optimize shape error prediction in milling processes. They could significantly decrease prediction errors with AutoML, which is a substantial advantage in their targeted application area. However, the authors reported that applying AutoML requires much expertise in ML compared to manually making all decisions. The two example applications above do not provide clear answers on how automation lowers the skill floor of analytics tasks.

2.2 Digital assistants in manufacturing analytics

The application of DIAs and similar systems in manufacturing is a comparably new research area with few articles on the topic and even less related to analytics. The following two articles cover assistants in combination with analytics.

Abner et al. [11] describe a software robot that provides descriptions, diagnostic information, predictions, and prescriptions. It interacts with users via chatting and providing URLs to dashboards with multi-dimensional information, such as time series. Listl, Fischer, and Weyrich [12] applied a chatbot as an alternative user interface for a plant simulation tool. Their prototype lets users adjust simulation parameters, model topology, and schedules via chatting.

Besides academic case studies, some commercial assistants support analytics in manufacturing. Software, such as Oracle Digital Assistant [13], SAP Conversational AI [14], and SPIX [15], ground their features on connectors to existing business software, including analytics services. We did not identify specific case studies about assistants and analytics among commercial tool providers, but feature descriptions contain cues. For instance, SAP has augmented analytics and conversational AI (digital assistant) services. The former offers a conversational user interface to query descriptive analytics results [16]. A demo video from 2020 [17] presents the following query text: *"show order value by product by customer segment for product [...] for previous year"*. Such natural language queries are helpful if analytics results are complex and navigating through a dashboard overloads the user.

The case studies above demonstrate that users can query results and parameterize analyses through natural language. However, they remain rather unspecific about how they augment the analytics process. They do not provide deeper insight into the type of support they provide to the users. Without this information, it is hard to understand how and in which areas augmentation can reduce the skill floor of analytics.

This paper contributes preliminary findings from a DIA case study in manufacturing and proposes an augmentation framework to address the issue above.

3 Case study

This article bases on a case study in the white goods industry where an assistant supports employees during quality tests in a laboratory at the end of the production line. Lab operators perform various manual tests to identify deviations from the expected product behavior or characteristics (e.g., correctly printed and placed labels). Lab supervisors assess deviations and use analysis results to decide how to manage them.

3.1 Context and process

Product and process quality concerns most manufacturing firms because negative consequences only show in production or worse when the customer returns with a complaint [18]. Producers must prevent adverse effects of quality flaws before they become evident in the product's use [18, 19] or even before they cause inefficiencies in the production process.

One approach to minimizing production quality issues is applying predictive quality analytics. It extracts valuable insights from various data sources by determining patterns, revealing correlations between products and defects, and predicting future outcomes (e.g., product defects and fault localization) [18–21]. Data sources include measurements performed by technical systems and information that employees create, for instance, through reports.

3.2   Assistant architecture

Access to predictive quality analytics typically requires expertise, as outlined in the introduction. Therefore, we developed a DIA to support, amongst other tasks, this analytics process. It uses open-source technology to transcribe the human voice, understand the resulting natural language texts, decide how to respond, and return responses in synthetic speech. Our augmented manufacturing analytics (AMA) assistant combines the digital assistant framework Mycroft and the chatbot framework Rasa. A custom Mycroft skill manages the exchange of messages between these two frameworks. Users interact with the assistant through a tablet with a custom App providing different conversation modes and rich-media contents (e.g., buttons, images, and videos). The Rasa chatbot contains a custom dialog model and actions to transform user utterances into formalized queries for the quality analytics component. Besides, it builds natural language responses out of the computer-readable analysis results.

3.3   User story and augmentation examples

Test laboratory supervisors inspect defects and search for root causes. They need quality analytics to better understand which product types and how many items had a specific defect. Besides, they need predictions for the quality to become aware of emerging issues that require inspection or sophisticated root cause analysis.

The assistant can recognize and manage several intents related to augmented analytics. Most involve a specific product with a unique identifier, such as a serial number or stock-keeping unit (SKU) code. The user scans the item's matrix or barcode with the tablet to add this identifier in a conversation. Scanning proved to be the most viable option because typing is slow, and speech transcription is error-prone. However, the assistant supports the latter two to help in specific situations (e.g., scanning issues and hands-free interaction).

Once the assistant knows which product the user is interested in, the user can request follow-up information. For example, the assistant could provide statistics and performance indicators as a text response or link to an online dashboard. Each time, the assistant triggers an analysis process according to the user's request. Besides, the assistant can make predictions on request. In some situations, the assistant takes the initiative after a trigger event. Measurements or automated software processes can create these events. For example, when a new product arrives in the test lab, the assistant communicates which defect groups the user can expect based on a prediction. Figure 1 summarizes augmented analytics conversations with our voice assistant. Some responses contain encoded identifiers that future versions will decode.

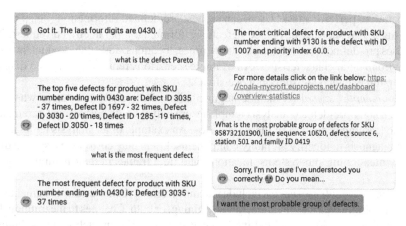

Fig. 1. Product registration, requesting descriptive analytics for an item, and predictions

4 Analytics support framework

The case study above outlines how a DIA could augment employees that interact with data analytics. We summarize our preliminary findings and the planned features in the framework illustrated in Fig. 2.

A. Modify training data	B. Train a model	C. Start analysis process	D. Retrieve results
Change data labeling	Select a training template	Select analysis template	Get a fixed or parameterized set of analysis results created earlier.
Add or remove samples	Customize parameter values	Customize parameter values	
	Select an algorithm		

E. Decision support
Inform about available templates, parameter values, and algorithms
Reminder about valid input values
Suggestion for one or more options
Make aware of potential consequences choosing an option

Fig. 2. Augmented analytics framework for digital intelligent assistants in manufacturing

The framework above has five areas with one or more augmentable activities. Areas A, B, and C represent typical steps in data analytics. Area D concerns retrieving analysis results and, therefore, is not a typical analytics task but necessary to access information. Areas A to D represent the logical sequence of a data analytics process using machine learning. Finally, area E focuses on decision support for the augmentable activities in all other areas – representing augmentation in the narrow sense. Its activities help users understand decision options, valid input values, and potential consequences of choosing options. The areas A-D refer to augmentation in the broader sense. Here, users may interact with analytics via natural language, granting intuitive access to information.

In the framework, the smallest possible augmented analytics scenario is the retrieval of existing results. Many users in manufacturing may only retrieve existing analytics information to perform a task. Users can request pre-defined information (i.e., a named view), such as a shortlist of ranked defects, or formulate a parametrized request. The latter uses pre-defined parameters like dates, times, locations, and other product, process, and environmental characteristics. An example scenario is requesting a Pareto diagram (e.g., top three defects) to support a decision.

More complex scenarios include augmentation of the analysis process where the user can trigger pre-defined analysis templates or analyses with customized parameters. Machine learning is not part of these scenarios. An example of an analysis template is a system diagnosis to identify all faulty components. Users may customize a system diagnosis by mentioning sub-systems, locations, and time frames in their natural language request.

Even more complex scenarios include machine learning. In these cases, augmentation can cover training data modification, model training, or both. Changes to the training data are relevant for hybrid-augmented intelligence systems [22]. In such systems, humans and AI support each other's learning and improvement. For example, users could inspect new quality issue reports through a DIA and instruct it to add specific ones as training data. The next model training would include these changes.

The *most complex augmentation scenarios* include decision support for one or more activities in areas A to D. The assistant could **inform** users about available options (e.g., parameters, templates, and algorithms) at the beginning of a task. Second, it could **remind** users about valid input values after providing invalid ones. Valid means that values are allowed because they relate to existing information such as components, defect groups, and locations. This support could be a response to faulty transcriptions or when users accidentally provide invalid input. Third, the DIA could **suggest** adding or removing a sample, selecting a template, or using a specific parameter value. The specific suggestion is the result of a deterministic or probabilistic model. An example is a user who requests a prediction for quality incidents by a given date, such as tomorrow, next week, or the month's end. If the prediction accuracy for the next week is below a threshold, the assistant could suggest using the timeframe just above the minimum allowed accuracy. Fourth, the assistant could **make the user aware** of the potential consequences of choosing a template, algorithm, or parameter value. For example, if the user removes training data samples via the assistant, the model training will likely produce an overfitting model. A second example is an assistant that tests training data changes for bias and warns the user if it finds them.

5   Conclusion

The case study and the framework above provide concrete examples of how a DIA could help employees perform descriptive and predictive analytics. We did not realize all scenarios in the framework with an assistant yet. Our current prototype focuses on areas C, D, and E, and we expect it will provide additional results for more profound theoretical and applied research. Future research could cover the following questions:

- *How deep should the assistance be to be most efficient?* Sophisticated assistance requires more development effort, which is costly. Besides, it leads to more complex software that is more difficult to maintain and error-prone because the assistant can be confused easier.

- *How could the assistant explain its predictions to users?* The capability to explain predictions (and other results based on machine learning) is an essential aspect of trustworthy AI. Explanations can be quite technical and thus difficult to understand by non-experts.
- *How can developers transfer dialog models for augmented analytics from one case to another?* There are many training data formats, machine learning algorithms, and parameters. Transferable dialog models could significantly reduce the effort to build DIAs for augmented analytics.
- *How does the augmentation affect the skill floor of using data analytics in manufacturing?* Literature suggests that augmented analytics helps less-skilled employees perform analytics, but it seldomly backs this claim with evidence. Since augmented analytics solutions tend to become more available, researchers could use them for systematic evaluations.

Our future work will focus on the assistant's evaluation in factory environments and the extension of its features to cover more areas in the framework above.

Acknowledgments. This work is funded by the European Union's Horizon 2020 research and innovation program via the project COALA, "COgnitive Assisted agile manufacturing for a LAbor force supported by trustworthy Artificial Intelligence" (Grant agreement No 957296).

References

1. Prat, N.: Augmented Analytics. Bus. Inf. Syst. Eng. **61**(3), 375–380 (2019). https://doi.org/10.1007/s12599-019-00589-0
2. SAP: Augmented and predictive analytics features (2022). https://www.sap.com/germany/products/cloud-analytics/features/augmented-analytics.html. Accessed 27 Jun 2022
3. Avidon, E., Kronz, A.: Gartner: augmented analytics, ecosystem for BI now key (2022). https://www.techtarget.com/searchbusinessanalytics/news/252515720/Gartner-Augmented-analytics-ecosystem-for-BI-now-key. Accessed 27 Jun 2022
4. Tableau Software: Augmented analytics explained: definition, use cases, benefits, features, and more (2022). https://www.tableau.com/learn/articles/augmented-analytics. Accessed 27 Jun 2022
5. Gartner: Gartner Glossary: Augmented Analytics (2022). https://www.gartner.com/en/information-technology/glossary/augmented-analytics. Accessed 12 Apr 2022
6. Wellsandt, S., Hribernik, K., Thoben, K-D.: Anatomy of a digital assistant. In: Dolgui, A., Bernard, A., Lemoine, D., et al. (eds) Advances in Production Management Systems. Artificial Intelligence for Sustainable and Resilient Production Systems, vol. 633, pp. 321–330. Springer International Publishing, Cham (2021). https://doi.org/10.1007/978-3-030-85910-7_34
7. Hutter, F.: What is AutoML? (2022). https://www.automl.org/automl/. Accessed 13 Apr 2022
8. Bender, J., Trat, M., Ovtcharova, J.: Benchmarking automl-supported lead time prediction. Procedia Comput. Sci. **200**, 482–494 (2022). https://doi.org/10.1016/j.procs.2022.01.246
9. Bender, J., Ovtcharova, J.: Prototyping machine-learning-supported lead time prediction using AutoML. Procedia Comput. Sci. **180**, 649–655 (2021). https://doi.org/10.1016/j.procs.2021.01.287

10. Denkena, B., Dittrich, M-A., Lindauer, M., et al.: Using AutoML to optimize shape error prediction in milling processes. SSRN J. (2020). https://doi.org/10.2139/ssrn.3724234
11. Abner, B., Rabelo, RJ., Zambiasi, SP., et al.: Production management as-a-service: a softbot approach. In: Lalic, B., Majstorovic, V., Marjanovic, U., et al. (eds) Advances in Production Management Systems. Towards Smart and Digital Manufacturing, vol. 592, pp. 19–30. Springer International Publishing, Cham (2020). https://doi.org/10.1007/978-3-030-579 97-5_3
12. Listl, FG., Fischer, J., Weyrich, M.: Towards a Simulation-based conversational assistant for the operation and engineering of production plants. In: 2021 26th IEEE International Conference on Emerging Technologies and Factory Automation (ETFA), pp. 1–4. IEEE (2021)
13. Oracle: Oracle digital assistant for ERP and SCM (2022). https://www.oracle.com/chatbots/digital-assistant-for-erp-scm/. Accessed 24 Feb 2022
14. SAP: SAP Conversational AI (2022). https://www.sap.com/germany/products/conversational-ai.html
15. Spix Industry: Spix: Industry-ready chatbot technology (2022). https://www.spix-industry.com/en/products-chatbot-for-industrial-software-development-spix/. Accessed 24 Feb 2022
16. SAP: Augmented Analytics (Smart Features) (2022). https://www.sap.com/products/cloud-analytics/features.html. Accessed 14 Apr 2022
17. SAP Analytics: Augmented analytics in SAP analytics cloud (2020)
18. Nalbach, O., Linn, C., Derouet, M., et al.: Predictive quality: towards a new understanding of quality assurance using machine learning tools. In: Abramowicz W, Paschke A (eds) Business Information Systems, vol. 320, pp. 30–42. Springer International Publishing, Cham (2018). https://doi.org/10.1007/978-3-319-93931-5_3
19. Berger, D., Zaiß, M., Lanza, G., et al.: Predictive quality control of hybrid metal-CFRP components using information fusion. Prod. Eng. Res. Dev. **12**, 161–172 (2018). https://doi.org/10.1007/s11740-018-0816-1
20. Bai, Y., Sun, Z., Deng, J., et al.: Manufacturing quality prediction using intelligent learning approaches: a comparative study. Sustainability **10**, 85 (2018). https://doi.org/10.3390/su10010085
21. Gittler, T., Relea, E., Corti, D., et al.: Towards predictive quality management in assembly systems with low quality low quantity data – a methodological approach. Procedia CIRP **79**, 125–130 (2019). https://doi.org/10.1016/j.procir.2019.02.026
22. Wellsandt, S., Klein, K., Hribernik, K., et al.: Hybrid-augmented intelligence in predictive maintenance with digital intelligent assistants. Ann. Rev. Control (2022). https://doi.org/10.1016/j.arcontrol.2022.04.001

Cyber-Physical Systems for Smart Assembly and Logistics in Automotive Industry

Characterizing Digital Dashboards
for Smart Production Logistics

Erik Flores-García[1]([✉])(iD), Yongkuk Jeong[1](iD), Magnus Wiktorsson[1](iD),
Dong Hoon Kwak[2](iD), Jong Hun Woo[2](iD), Thomas Schmitt[3,4](iD),
and Lars Hanson[3,5](iD)

[1] KTH Royal Institute of Technology, Södertälje 151 36, Sweden
{efs01,yongkuk,magwik}@kth.se
[2] Seoul National University, Seoul 08826, Republic of South Korea
{s2arta2s,j.woo}@snu.ac.kr
[3] Scania CV AB, Södertälje 151 38, Sweden
{thomas.schmitt,lars.hanson}@scania.com
[4] Uppsala University, Uppsala 752 36, Sweden
[5] University of Skövde, Skövde 541 28, Sweden

Abstract. Developing digital dashboards (DD) that support staff in
monitoring, identifying anomalies, and facilitating corrective actions are
decisive for achieving the benefits of Smart Production Logistics (SPL).
However, existing literature about SPL has not sufficiently investigated
the characteristics of DD allowing staff to enhance operational performance. This conceptual study identifies the characteristics of DD in SPL
for enhancing operational performance of material handling. The study
presents preliminary findings from an ongoing laboratory development,
and identifies six characteristics of DD. These include monitoring, analysis, prediction, identification, recommendation, and control. The study
discusses the implications of these characteristics when applied to energy
consumption, makespan, on-time delivery, and status for material handling. The study proposes the prototype of a DD in a laboratory environment involving Autonomous Mobile Robots.

Keywords: Digital dashboards · Smart production logistics ·
Autonomous mobile robots

1 Introduction

Smart Production Logistics (SPL) is critical for enhancing the operational performance and increasing the competitiveness of manufacturing companies [3].
SPL refers to applying the Industrial Internet of Things (IIoT) and digital technologies (e.g., cyber physical systems, artificial intelligence, or digital twins) for
achieving the active perception, response, and autonomous decisions regarding
the movement of information and materials in a factory [1]. SPL presents several benefits to manufacturing companies including the timely and automatic

© IFIP International Federation for Information Processing 2022
Published by Springer Nature Switzerland AG 2022
D. Y. Kim et al. (Eds.): APMS 2022, IFIP AICT 664, pp. 521–528, 2022.
https://doi.org/10.1007/978-3-031-16411-8_60

identification of exceptions, self-organizing configuration and self-adaptive collaboration of resources [2].

Presenting information to staff with the purpose of monitoring, identifying anomalies, and facilitating corrective actions is decisive for achieving the benefits of SPL [4]. This need originates from the increasing level of automation facilitated by the implementation of digital technologies, and improving the work and conditions of humans at manufacturing companies [5]. Therefore, interacting with and presenting information to staff for enhancing operational performance is complementary to existing research efforts in SPL. For example, recent studies describe the importance of integrating monitoring systems that collect data in real-time, and predictive analytics that examine the performance of production logistics [6]. Additionally, the literature identifies the need for interfaces where humans can directly take decisions about strategies, control, or activities in production logistics [7].

The purpose of this conceptual study is to identify the characteristics of DD in SPL for enhancing operational performance of material handling. The study presents preliminary findings from an ongoing laboratory development. To achieve this purpose, the study applies the concept of DD according to [20], and discusses six characteristics for enhancing operational performance in material handling. These include monitoring, analysis, prediction, identification, recommendation, and control. Then, the study describes the implications of the six characteristics of DD for addressing energy consumption, makespan, on-time delivery, and status of resources in material handling. Finally, we propose a prototype of DD in a laboratory environment involving Autonomous Mobile Robots (AMRs) in material handling. The remainder of this study includes the following structure. Section 2 presents related works involving SPL and DD. Section 3 discusses the implications of DD in SPL. Section 4 proposes a prototype of a DD for enhancing operational performance in a laboratory environment. Section 5 concludes this study.

2   Related Works

2.1   Operational Performance in Smart Production Logistics

The implementation of digital technologies in SPL has critical implications for monitoring and interacting with resources enhancing the operational performance of material handling. SPL includes the use of IIoT with the purpose of connecting all industrial resources (e.g., machines and control systems) with information systems for understanding the flow of materials in factories [2]. This facilitates the real-time acquisition of data necessary for increasing material visibility [9], and the development of services for monitoring, controlling, optimizing, and making autonomous decisions that identify anomalies and facilitate corrective actions [16]. Taken together, these advances are critical for realizing dynamic and customer-oriented activities supporting the goals of logistics (e.g., right time, delivery, quality, and cost) [10].

In this study we give precedence to four salient concerns for enhancing operational performance in SPL according to recent research efforts [2]. These include energy consumption, on time delivery, makespan, and status of resources. For example, [11] monitor the status of Automated Guided Vehicles (AGVs) for planning and scheduling problems with the use of Cyber Physical Systems (CPS). [12] monitor the energy consumption and on-time delivery of AGVs when applying a proactive material handling method for a CPS enabled shop floor. [2] focus on waiting time, makespan, and energy consumption during a self-adaptive collaborative control mode for material handling in SPL. [14] monitor energy consumption, on time delivery, and deviations in process cycle times when developing a decision support system capable for shop-floor decision-making activities. [14] target energy consumption, delivery, and makespan when developing a real-time production and logistics self-adaption scheduling.

IIoT is a critical aspect for monitoring and interacting with resources in SPL including AGVs or autonomous mobile robots (AMRs). IIoT facilitates sensing data, processing information, and realizing services [16]. Recent research efforts suggest applying an IIoT architecture including a sensing, networking, and applications layer for monitoring and interacting with resources in material handling [1]. The sensing layer comprehends all physical resources responsible for material handling (e.g., parts, AMRs, or pallets) and IIoT devices generating data about the location or status of equipment. The networking layer involves the real-time capture of data, its processing into information, and transfer to databases or applications. Finally, the applications layer contains service that establish links with the enterprise tier that implements domain-specific applications and provides end-user interfaces. Applying a similar IIoT architecture, [13] suggest measuring resource consumption in production processes, using open source tools for data collection (Node-Red), storing (InfluxDB) data and visualization (Grafana) information. The study addresses issues such as hardware and software compatability, and allows for a customizable and scalable architecture.

2.2 Digital Dashboards Supporting Operational Performance

DD include visual applications that summarize information aligning the goals and processes of organizations, and help users take and improve decisions [20]. DD involve multiple coordinated visualizations and interactive features for rapid understanding. Its benefits include increased communication, transparency and agility, and understanding of process context, performance, and remedial actions [18].

DD for enhancing operational performance target frontline workers, and address the identification of problems and their corrective actions [22]. Accordingly, recent research efforts on DD underscore the importance of proactively supporting and improving decisions of staff at an operational level. For example, [3] proposes a digital twin framework including a DD for the real-time monitoring of machines and interconnected system for with the purpose of improving overall equipment effectiveness and order scheduling. [19] present a CPS including a dashboard displaying the real-time status of a production system providing staff with tools for supervision and intervention in case of failure.

This study applies the six characteristics of DD for enhancing operational performance identified by [20] including monitoring, analysis, prediction, identification, recommendation, and control. This choice is informed by the recency of these findings, and the need for efficiently providing information to productive areas and feeding DD with adequate data sources. Monitoring refers to the intuitive display of information and associated activities for staff responsible for operational performance [20], which is essential for triggering alerts in reduced performance [22]. Identification comprehends activities determining the root cause of problems in operational performance [21]. Analysis involves the examination of relevant information to demonstrate the consistency and effectiveness of resources or processes [20]. Recommendations focus on transmitting information about strategic objectives and enable staff and resources to measure, monitor, and manage key activities and processes [18]. Communication concerns the transmission of information about strategic objectives, and enable staff and resources to measure, monitor, and manage key activities and processes. For example, [3] suggest the use of digital technologies including IIoT or digital twins for achieving real-time prediction of expected behavior, recommendations of actions, and communication with resources for enhancing operational performance. Control consists of the interaction between systems for regulating and promoting activities for dealing with non-conforming problems.

3   Implications of Digital Dashboards in Smart Production Logistics

The purpose of this conceptual study is to identify the characteristics of DD in SPL for enhancing operational performance of material handling. This section discusses the implications of the six characteristics of DD (e.g., monitoring, analysis, prediction, identification, recommendation, and control) on energy consumption, makespan, on-time-delivery, and status of resources.

The literature underscores the importance of reducing energy consumption in material handling leading to improved sustainability [11]. For example, [13] suggests an IIoT architecture including a dashboard solution, visualizing the environmental footprint of production to help users understand resource patterns and improve eco-efficiency of processes. DD can contribute to this goal in a number of ways. For example by monitoring the energy consumption of one or a fleet of AMRs during a period (e.g., electricity in kilowatts per hour). Analyzing historical trends, informing, or alerting staff about failure to achieve goals of energy consumption. Predicting and presenting recommendations for meeting energy consumption goals in the following period according to historical data (e.g., energy management and control policies, vehicle charging, or execution of material handling operations). Presenting information to staff about strategic goals of energy consumption, and controlling resources in material handling with the purpose of achieving these goals.

Traditional measurements of operational performance in production logistics remain decisive for securing manufacturing competitiveness [3,14,15]. To this extent, the use of DD in SPL has important implications for makespan, on-time delivery, and resource utilization. For example, DD provide benefits to makespan by monitoring the current and historical patterns involving the maximum time to complete tasks in material handling. Further, DD may facilitate identifying tasks, stations, or AMRs contributing to an extended makespan. Additionally, these can present information to staff including predictions of makespan considering current resources and material handling tasks, or provide recommendations such as the need for additional resources for meeting goals in makespan. Finally, DD may facilitate the control of resources in material handling such as a change of speed in AMRs or preference for routes.

DD present distinct benefits for on-time delivery of material handling in SPL. In relation to monitoring, DD help determine the status of delivery tasks including their on-time or late delivery. Also, they can provide time series analysis of on-time delivery percentage for a period and its comparison with established goals. Furthermore, DD can present critical information to staff including the identification of the root cause of problems for late delivery (e.g., changes to production schedule, production problems, failed equipment, or poor quality).

The use of DD contributes to improving the use of resources in material handling including AMRs. This can reveal their real-time movement and status including idle, loading and unloading, moving with and without products, charging or failure times. Furthermore, DD are decisive for aggregating historically this information and identifying failed performance (e.g., excessive movement without products). Finally, DD are crucial for communicating expected goals on the use of resources or executing missions for an AMR with the purpose of controlling behavior (e.g., assigning a resource to an area).

4   Proposed Digital Dashboard for Enhancing Operational Performance

This section proposes a prototype of a DD for enhancing operational performance in a laboratory environment involving AMRs. The features of the DD that make it applicable to the case of AMRs include the need from staff for understanding dynamic resources and monitoring and controlling remotely operations of this equipment [23]. Figure 1 presents the proposed prototype of a DD for enhancing operational performance involving AMRs.

The case involves the picking and delivering of parts in the machining area of an automotive manufacturer. Material handling includes the delivery of supplies from a warehouse to machining stations and transfer of work-in-progress parts and finished products. Management will implement AMRs and IIoT devices with the purpose of increasing visibility in material handling and enhancing operational performance. Accordingly, there is a need for monitoring the energy consumption, makespan, on-time delivery, and status of the AMRs. The prototype application utilizes a three-layered IIoT architecture according to the International Electrotechnical Comission (2016) [1,13]. These include perception, networking, and application layers for achieving real-time collection of data, and active perception and response of resources.

The perception layer includes physical resources and IIoT devices in material handling. Physical resources comprehend products, pallets, buffers, or storage units. IIoT devices involve sensors and actuators capable of transmitting data and receiving information to execute actions. This involves the use of pallets for transporting products, and radio frequency identification devices for identifying the position of resources, and an AMR for executing material handling tasks in the prototype application. Input data includes three aspects. First, a schedule including a description of tasks for material handling. Second, the layout delimiting the activity of the AMR. Third, data collected from the AMR with application programming interfaces including position, energy consumption, and speed.

The networking layer establishes the communication between the physical world and digital applications including those necessary for achieving the characteristics of a DD. This layer captures data, and processes data into information, and transfers information to achieve material handling tasks, and coordinated visualizations and interactive features for rapid understanding. The prototype application applies Node-RED as a middleware for connecting hardware devices, application programming interfaces, and online services. Additionally, the database management system MariaDB stores information generated during material handling including the energy consumption, orders in material handling, AMR missions, and results from makespan, on-time delivery, and AMR status.

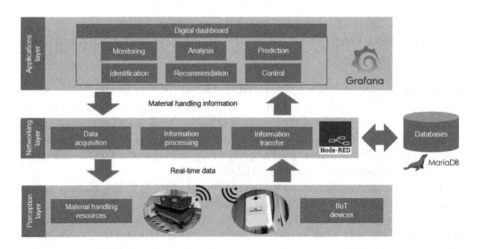

Fig. 1. Proposed prototype of a DD for enhancing operational performance involving AMRs.

The applications layer provides personalized services according to the needs of staff. Therefore, this layer contains the applications realizing a DD for enhancing operational performance in material handling. The prototype application applies the multi-platform open source analytics and interactive visualization application Grafana in this layer. The DD utilizes data sources facilitated by the networking layer for visualizing operational performance.

5 Conclusions

This conceptual study identified the characteristics of digital dashboards in SPL for enhancing operational performance of material handling. The study discussed the implications of the six characteristics of DD (e.g., monitoring, analysis, prediction, identification, recommendation, and control) on energy consumption, makespan, on-time-delivery, and status of resources in material handling. The study proposed prototype of a DD for enhancing operational performance in a laboratory environment including AMRs. Future research will focus on two aspects. First, presenting empirical results about the implications of DD in operational performance of material handling. Second, proposing a data model for transferring information across layers in an IIoT architecture for securing DD.

Acknowledgement(s). The authors would like to acknowledge the support of Swedish Innovation Agency (VINNOVA), and its funding program Produktion2030. This study is part of the Explainable and Learning Production & Logistics by Artificial Intelligence (EXPLAIN) project.

References

1. Zhang, Y., Guo, Z., Lv, J., Liu, Y.: A framework for smart production-logistics systems based on cps and industrial IoT. IEEE Trans. Ind. Inf. **14**(9), 4019–4032 (2018)
2. Guo, Z., Zhang, Y., Zhao, X., Song, X.: CPS-based self-adaptive collaborative control for smart production-logistics systems. IEEE Trans. Cybern. **51**(1), 188–198 (2021)
3. Wang, K.J., Lee, Y.H., Angelica, S.: Digital twin design for real-time monitoring - a case study of die cutting machine. Int. J. Prod. Res. **59**(21), 6471–6485 (2021)
4. Klummp, M., Hesenius, M., Meyer, O., Ruiner, C., Gruhn, V.: Production logistics and human-computer interaction-state-of-the-art, challenges and requirements for the future. Int. J. Adv. Manuf. Technol. **105**(9), 3691–3709 (2019)
5. Wang, L.: A futuristic perspective on human-centric assembly. J. Manuf. Syst. **62**, 199–201 (2022)
6. Sgarbossa, F., Grosse, E.H., Neumann, W.P., Battini, D., Glock, C.H.: Human factors in production and logistics systems of the future. Ann. Rev. Control **49**(1), 295–305 (2020)
7. Cimini, C., Lagorio, A., Romero, D., Cavalieri, S., Stahre, J.: Smart logistics and the logistics operator 4.0. IFAC-PapersOnLine **53**(2), 10615–10620 (2020)

8. Zhou, B., He, Z.: A material handling scheduling method for mixed-model automotive assembly lines based on an improved static kitting strategy. Comput. Ind. Eng. **140**, 106268 (2020)

9. Winkelhaus, S., Grosse, E. H.: Logistics 4.0: a systematic review towards a new logistics system. Int. J. Prod. Res. **58**(1), 18–43 (2020)

10. Kache, F., Seuring, S.: Challenges and opportunities of digital information at the intersection of big data analytics and supply chain management. Int. J. Oper. Prod. Manag. **37**(1), 10–36 (2017)

11. Lian, Y., Yang, Q., Xie, W., Zhang, L.: Cyber-physical system-based heuristic planning and scheduling method for multiple automatic guided vehicles in logistics systems. IEEE Trans. Ind. Inf. **17**(11), 7882–7893 (2021)

12. Wang, W., Zhang, Y., Zhong, R.Y.: A proactive material handling method for CPS enabled shop-floor. Robot. Comput. Integr. Manuf. **61**, 101849 (2020)

13. Schmitt, T., Sakaray, P., Hanson, L., Urenda Moris, M., Amouzgar, K.: Frequent and automatic monitoring of resource data via the internet of things. In: Swedish Production Symposium 2022, pp. 75–85. IOS Press (2022)

14. Yao, F., Alkan, B., Harrison, R.: Improving just-in-time delivery performance of IoT-enabled flexible manufacturing systems with AGV based material transportation. Sensors **20**(21), 6333 (2020)

15. Yang, W., Li, W., Cao, Y., Luo, Y., He, L.: Real-time production and logistics self-adaption scheduling based on information entropy theory. Sensors **20**(16), 4507 (2020)

16. Guo, Z.X., Ngai, E.W.T., Yang, C., Liang, X.: An RFID-based intelligent decision support system architecture for production monitoring and scheduling in a distributed manufacturing environment. Int. J. Prod. Econ. **159**, 16–28 (2015)

17. Pan, Y.H., Qu, T., Wu, N.Q., Khalgui, M., Huang, G.Q.: Digital twin based real-time production logistics synchronization system in a multi-level computing architecture. J. Manuf. Syst. **58**, 246–260 (2021)

18. Gröger, C., Stach, C., Mitschang, B., Westkämper, E.: A mobile dashboard for analytics-based information provisioning on the shop floor. Int. J. Comput. Integr. Manuf. **29**(12), 1335–1354 (2009)

19. Franchesci, P., Mutti, S., Ottogalli, K., Rosquete, D., Borro, D., Pedrocchi, N.: A framework for cyber-physical production system management and digital twin feedback monitoring for fast failure recovery. Int. J. Comput. Integr. Manuf. 1–14 (2021). https://doi.org/10.1080/0951192X.2021.1992666

20. Vilarinho, S., Lopes, I., Sousa, S.: Developing dashboards for SMEs to improve performance of productive equipment and processes. J. Ind. Inf. Integr. **12**, 13–22 (2018)

21. Yigitbasioglu, O.M., Velcu, O.: A review of dashboards in performance management: implications for design and research. Int. J. Account. Inf. Syst. **13**(1), 41–59 (2012)

22. Eckerson, W.: Performance Dashboards: Measuring, Monitoring, and Managing your Business, 2nd edn. Wiley, New York (2011)

23. Oyekanlu, E.A., et al.: A review of recent advances in automated guided vehicle technologies: integration challenges and research areas for 5G-based smart manufacturing applications. IEEE Access **8**, 202312–202353

Human Digital Twin System for Operator Safety and Work Management

Goo-Young Kim[1] , Donghun Kim[1] , Sang Do Noh[1(✉)] , Hong Ku Han[2],
Nam Geun Kim[3], Yong-Shin Kang[4], Seung Hyun Choi[4], Dong Hyun Go[5],
Jungmin Song[5], Dae Yub Lee[5], and Hyung Sun Kim[5]

[1] Sungkyunkwan University, Suwon 16419, Republic of Korea
sdnoh@skku.edu
[2] Shinsung E&G, Seongnam 13543, Republic of Korea
[3] Shinsung CS, Seongnam 13543, Republic of Korea
[4] Advanced Institute of Convergence Technology, Suwon 16229, Republic of Korea
[5] DEXTA Inc, Suwon 16677, Republic of Korea

Abstract. The value-driven Industry 5.0 has brought a shift in the approach towards worker well-being. However, the understanding of the effects on workers due to technological advancements of Industry 4.0, based on a human-centric approach, is limited. The reason for this limitation is that the tools are scarce, which is quantitatively evaluating and analyzing various factors in the workplace. To solve this problem, we propose a human digital twin system supporting decision-making regarding safety management and work management of workers. The human digital twin system consists of a digital twin module, an analysis module, and a visualization module. The proposed system connects a physical human and a virtual digital human model; analyzes the location, posture, and motion-time of workers; and delivers information about safety and work management. This information enables workers and managers to improve the work environment by making them resilient to workplace factors.

Keywords: Industry 5.0 · Operator 4.0 · Human digital twin system

1 Introduction

Industry 5.0, announced by the European Commission, has modified the approach of industries towards worker well-being [1]. Technological advancements of Industry 4.0 based on a human-centric approach affect workers who are essential resources in manufacturing systems [2]. For allowing workers to respond flexibly to various factors existing in a workplace, a method was proposed, which is making the manufacturing system more agile and flexible [3]. Additionally, it was argued that future research to create a worker-centered work environment is necessary through reliable and quantifiable technology [4]. In other words, the problem is the lack of skills to quantitatively evaluate and analyze factors in the work environment for workers. To solve this problem, we propose

© IFIP International Federation for Information Processing 2022
Published by Springer Nature Switzerland AG 2022
D. Y. Kim et al. (Eds.): APMS 2022, IFIP AICT 664, pp. 529–536, 2022.
https://doi.org/10.1007/978-3-031-16411-8_61

a human digital twin system that supports decision-making regarding safety management and work management of workers. The human digital twin mirrors the physical environment into a virtual world and enables the monitoring of workers of the physical environment. Furthermore, the digital twin aids decision-making for workers and managers by synchronizing and analyzing field data. This study utilizes motion capture devices and mobile devices to implement the digital human model (DHM) of the human digital twin and connects physical and virtual workers. Through visualization, the workers and managers confirm quantitatively evaluated and measured analysis results. The analysis results, such as safety level and process smoothness, support improvement in the work environment for workers by making workers and managers resilient to workplace factors.

2 Research Background

2.1 Operator 4.0

Under the technology-driven Industry 4.0, a human-centric approach has attracted global attention because of the value-driven Industry 5.0 announced by the European Commission [1]. Operator 4.0 was presented as a smart and skilled operator of the future that involves leveraging the collaboration between cooperative robots and accurate machinery and the human being's ingenious unique potential [5]. In the Operator 4.0 typology, the healthy and smart operator has the ability to detect problems and suggest solutions in machines and systems that build predictive models for proactive actions [6]. In addition, Healthy Operator 4.0 architecture was suggested, which is composed of smart connection, integration and communication, modeling, and cognition layer [7]. Through this architecture [7], the gathered data sources are analyzed in real-time with advanced modeling technologies to derive insightful inferences. Similarly, a framework of human cyber-physical system was presented for symbiosis between Operator 4.0 and artificial intelligence to facilitate feedback and decision-making from the shop-floor [8]. Moreover, with the upcoming Industry 5.0 phase, the focus of research is shifting towards Operator 5.0. An argument is being made that a new collaborative framework for Operator 5.0 should be designed using advanced digital technologies such as mixed reality, deep learning, and digital twins [9].

2.2 Digital Twin

Digital twin is a data-driven digital replica model of a product, machine, and manufacturing process that reflects the property and state of the object and explains how a physical and virtual model behave. According to [10], the digital twin not only supports real-time monitoring and tracking of diverse situations in the physical environment by reflecting it in the cyber environment, but also the interaction between the physical and cyber environments through repetitive communication and convergence. Based on these characteristics of the digital twin, digital twin-based services assist shop-floor workers and factory managers to share information about the production sites and create a safe environment for workers by predicting collisions through real-time location information

[11]. Through the digital twin application, workers' motions were synchronized between the physical and cyber environments and analyzed by using motion capture technology [12]. Meanwhile, a framework was proposed to support monitoring and decision-making by implementing human digital twin [13]. In addition, a digital twin concept and prototype were proposed to represent human operators in the cyber environment for acquiring and analyzing data by using a simulation-based framework [14]. Similarly, a human-centric digital twin architecture was suggested to improve operator capabilities by using derived context information as a solution [15].

3   Human Digital Twin System

Human digital twin system (HDTS) for operator safety and work management consists of digital twin, analysis, and visualization modules, as shown in Fig. 1. The digital twin module composes DHM, an important element of the human digital twin, by connecting the worker in the real environment with the worker object in the virtual environment. The analysis module analyzes real-world worker-related data acquired through a virtual environment for worker safety and work management. The visualization module delivers the analysis results to the workers and managers who make decisions by checking and reflecting on the data from results.

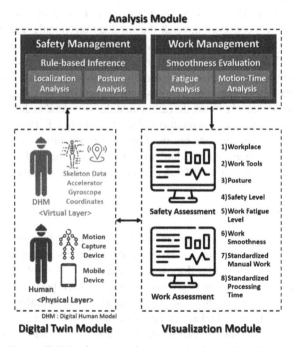

Fig. 1. Human digital twin system for operator safety and work management

3.1 Digital Twin Module

To connect the physical world and virtual world, it is necessary to create an object in the virtual world for an object in the physical world and synchronize data between the two objects. The proposed architecture introduces mobile devices and motion capture equipment to synchronize between the real world and virtual world. Real-time location coordinates of workers are acquired through mobile devices and access points installed in the real environment. Musculoskeletal data is acquired through the accelerometer and gyroscope sensor values of the mobile device and the data of the motion capture equipment worn by the operator. The data acquired through mobile sensors and motion capture equipment connects real-world workers and virtual-world objects. The position of the worker object in the virtual environment is matched according to the position of the worker in the real environment, and the movement of the worker object in the virtual environment is also synchronized according to the movement of the worker in the real environment. Finally, the DHM in the virtual environment is implemented through the acquired sensor data of the worker.

3.2 Analysis Module

The acquired data is not only used to implement the DHM, but also for data analysis, such as identification of the worker's workplace, posture and work fatigue analysis, and safety assessment. The location coordinate data of the worker is used to identify specific locations of the worker through the localization module; that is, through the localization module, it is possible to identify the work-center where the operator and tools are located. The accelerometer and gyroscope of the mobile device are used to analyze the movement and posture of the operator through the posture detection module. The worker's location and surrounding tools, motion, and posture data analyzed through the localization module and posture detection module embedded in the expert system are used to evaluate worker safety through rule-based reasoning. Furthermore, the motion capture equipment's skeleton data are used to analyze the fatigue of workers and the execution time of the operator's standard work using a fatigue analysis module, which is a rapid upper limb assessment (RULA), and the motion-time analysis module.

3.3 Visualization Module

The accident safety level of workers and work performance fatigue obtained through the analysis of the acquired data is used by safety managers and process managers to monitor shop-floor workers. Shop-floor workers detect the safety of accident and adjust their posture according to the safety level determined by their posture in relation to their location and the work they conduct. The safety manager performs safety management for all workers located on-site and takes precautions against possible accidents. The process manager understands the fatigue and work smoothness of the shop-floor workers and ensures the process productivity and safety from musculoskeletal injuries. Furthermore, standardized worksheets required for production planning can be prepared and used by standardizing worker processing time through working time analysis.

4 Case Study

4.1 Experiment

We implemented the proposed HDTS for the human-based assembly process of fan filter-producing units. A worker performs a task using the upper body to take assembly tools and materials from a workbench connected to a conveyor belt. To create DHM, workers on the shop-floor wear motion capture devices and carry mobile devices to acquire joint data such as accelerometer and gyroscope data from their skeletons and coordinate data from their shop-floor map. For the shop-floor map, we analyzed the production line and factory layout and developed a virtual factory using Unity. Figure 2 shows workers wearing motion capture devices in a physical factory and avatars representing shop-floor workers in a virtual factory. The avatar of the virtual environment is connected with the worker of the physical environment through the data acquired from the physical environment. The avatar's data, representing the worker's data, is transferred to the analysis module of the HDTS.

Fig. 2. Implementation of digital human model. (a) Actual worker. (b) Virtual avatar

The coordinates of a shop-floor map and sensor values such as accelerometers and gyroscopes are used for safety management. The indoor localization model yields a workplace and equipment that the worker can locate by using shop-floor map coordinates. The posture detection model returns the actions of the worker, such as standing, walking, walking down, walking up, sitting, and lying down by using the accelerometer and gyroscope of the mobile device. The rule-based reasoning model of safety management generates the safety level of the worker by utilizing the outcome of the indoor localization and posture detection model. The skeleton data from the motion capture device is used for work management. The fatigue analysis model utilizes data from the accelerometer, gyroscope, and magnetometers, which are acquired from sensors attached to the joints of the human body. The fatigue level of DHM is calculated through RULA, and the change in fatigue level flow during the process is checked to calculate the work smoothness of the process. These sensor data are also used in the motion-time analysis model. The motion-time analysis model identifies standard tasks that compose the assembly process and calculate the working time of each standard task. By analyzing the pattern of the acquired data, each standard operation is classified, and the working time is calculated by evaluating the start and end times of each standard operation of the DHM. The visualization module aggregates and shows the results of the analysis module, helping the manager monitor the current safety level of all workers by expressing the safety level of workers in real time, as shown in Fig. 3.

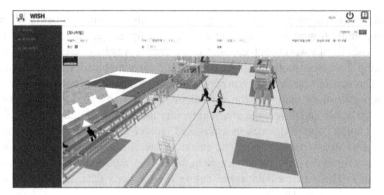

Fig. 3. Dashboard for worker's safety level visualization

4.2 Empirical Results

The result of applying the HDTS helps managers' decision-making by visualizing the analysis module. Figure 4 depicts (a) worker's posture in physical environment, (b) avatar's posture in virtual environment depending on worker's posture in physical environment, and (c) the workplace, surrounding equipment, posture and accuracy, and safety level. According to the current situation, the worker's safety level is "MIDDLE." The safety level is considered appropriate because there are ladders around the worker in the physical environment and the worker is in a sitting position. Likewise, safety managers are able to monitor the safety levels of all workers even if they are not on the shop-floor sites.

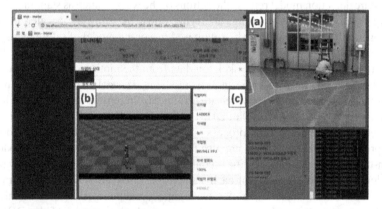

Fig. 4. Analysis results of rule-based inference in safety management

Work management shows work smoothness, standard tasks, and standard processing times. Figure 5 demonstrates the work smoothness of workers in the assembly process. Each worker performs the same assembly process but with different work smoothness because they have dissimilar detailed tasks. Conversely, each worker has a different level of work smoothness even when assigned to the same assembly process due to the variety of standard tasks performed by the workers, and the safety from injury is also different because the workers experience different fatigue levels while performing the same process.

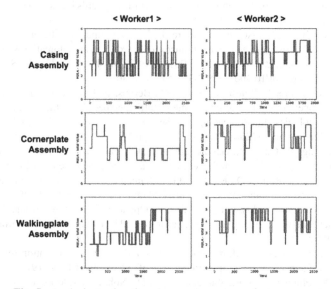

Fig. 5. Analysis results of work smoothness in work management

5   Conclusions

This study presented and implemented an HDTS to support decision-making about safety management and work management of operators. The proposed system, composed of digital twin, analysis, and visualization modules, implemented a DHM of an actual worker, calculated safety and fatigue levels, and expressed analysis results. Future research could focus on verifying results by enhancing the accuracy of machine learning models used in safety and work management. Furthermore, the digital twin module not only has a chance to apply DHM with a collaborative robot in a factory, but also to utilize augmented and virtual reality devices for workers in the physical environment to accept feedback.

Acknowledgement. This research was financially supported by the MOTIE and KIAT through the Inter-national Cooperative R&D program [P0009839] and supported by project for Smart Manufacturing Innovation R&D funded Korea Ministry of SMEs and Startups in 2022 [RS-2022–00140261].

References

1. Breque, M., De Nul, L., Petridis, A.: Industry 5.0: towards a sustainable, human-centric and resilient European industry. Luxembourg, LU: European Commission, Directorate-General for Research and Innovation (2021)
2. Pinzone, M., et al.: A framework for operative and social sustainability functionalities in human-centric cyber-physical production systems. Comput. Ind. Eng. **139**, 105132 (2020)
3. Romero, D., Stahre, J.: Towards the resilient operator 5.0: the future of work in smart resilient manufacturing systems. Procedia CIRP **104**, 1089–1094 (2021)
4. Lu, Y., et al.: Outlook on human-centric manufacturing towards industry 5.0. J. Manuf. Syst. **62**, 612–627 (2022)
5. Romero, D., Bernus, P., Noran, O., Stahre, J., Fast-Berglund, Å.: The operator 4.0: human cyber-physical systems & adaptive automation towards human-automation symbiosis work systems. In: Nääs, I., et al. (eds.) APMS 2016. IAICT, vol. 488, pp. 677–686. Springer, Cham (2016). https://doi.org/10.1007/978-3-319-51133-7_80
6. Romero, D., Stahre, J., Wuest, T., Noran, O., Bernus, P., Fast-Berglund, Å., Gorecky, D.: Towards an operator 4.0 typology: a human-centric perspective on the fourth industrial revolution technologies. In: Proceedings of the International Conference on Computers and Industrial Engineering (CIE46), Tianjin, China. pp.29–31 (2016)
7. Sun, S., Zheng, X., Gong, B., Garcia Paredes, J., Ordieres-Meré, J.: Healthy operator 4.0: a human cyber–physical system architecture for smart workplaces. Sensors **20**(7), 2011 (2020)
8. Bousdekis, A., Apostolou, D., Mentzas, G.: A human cyber physical system framework for operator 4.0–artificial intelligence symbiosis. Manuf. Lett. **25**, 10–15 (2020)
9. Mourtzis, D., Angelopoulos, J., Panopoulos, N.: Operator 5.0: a survey on enabling technologies and a frame-work for digital manufacturing based on extended reality. J. Mach. Eng. **22**, 43–69 (2022)
10. Park, K.T., et al.: Design and implementation of a digital twin application for a connected micro smart factory. Int. J. Comput. Integr. Manuf. **32**(6), 596–614 (2019)
11. Kim, G.-Y., Flores-García, E., Wiktorsson, M., Do Noh, S.: Exploring economic, environmental, and social sustainability impact of digital twin-based services for smart production logistics. In: Dolgui, A., Bernard, A., Lemoine, D., von Cieminski, G., Romero, D. (eds.) APMS 2021. IAICT, vol. 634, pp. 20–27. Springer, Cham (2021). https://doi.org/10.1007/978-3-030-85914-5_3
12. Nam, Y.W., Lee, S.H., Lee, D.G., Im, S.J., Noh, S.D.: Digital twin-based application for design of human-machine collaborative assembly production lines. J. Korean Instit. Industr. Eng. **46**(1), 42–54 (2020)
13. Greco, A., Caterino, M., Fera, M., Gerbino, S.: Digital twin for monitoring ergonomics during manufacturing production. Appl. Sci. **10**(21), 7758 (2020)
14. Sharotry, A., et al.: A digital twin framework for real-time analysis and feedback of repetitive work in the manual material handling industry. In: 2020 Winter Simulation Conference (WSC), pp. 2637–2648. IEEE (2020)
15. Löcklin, A., Jung, T., Jazdi, N., Ruppert, T., Weyrich, M.: architecture of a human-digital twin as common interface for operator 4.0 applications. Procedia CIRP **104**, 458–463 (2021)

Asset Description of Digital Twin for Resilient Production Control in Rechargeable Battery Production

Kyu Tae Park[1]([⊠]), Yang Ho Park[1], Yun-Hyok Choi[1], Moon-Won Park[1], and Sang Do Noh[2]

[1] Micube Solution, Inc., Seoul, Republic of Korea
parkkyutae0201@gmail.com
[2] Sungkyunkwan University, Suwon-si, Republic of Korea

Abstract. In rechargeable battery production—a component of mass customization—high quality, low cost, efficient delivery, and flexibility must be ensured. Efficient production operation can be achieved by solving the performance degradation problem, which is a limitation of mass customization. This degradation can be prevented through resilience, which can be achieved by satisfying four core functional requirements, which are as follows: (1) selecting robust actions; (2) measuring performance indicators; (3) notifying impermissible fluctuations; and (4) extracting the adjusted reactions. A digital twin (DT) is an advanced virtual asset that represents configuration, reflects functional units, and synchronizes information objects. This article describes DT application to satisfy the four core functional requirements and reflect the operational characteristics of three heterogeneous stations in rechargeable battery production. Analyses of the measures taken to achieve the resilience and operational characteristics of stations in rechargeable battery production are provided to present an appropriate design of the description. The asset description is designed with P4R classes based on this analysis. The designed asset description is applied to stations in rechargeable battery production, and the proposed method is verified with the implemented DT application. The proposed asset description presents an efficient method of satisfying the core activities and technical functionalities corresponding to the DT. The proposed method is an early case of DT usage in rechargeable battery production and can be considered as a reference for smart manufacturing technologies in the manufacturing domain in the future.

Keywords: Cyber physical production system · Digital twin · Mass customization · Production control · Rechargeable battery production · Resilience

1 Introduction

Rechargeable battery production is a component of mass environment and involves the fabrication of highly diversified products; hence, high quality, low cost, efficient

© IFIP International Federation for Information Processing 2022
Published by Springer Nature Switzerland AG 2022
D. Y. Kim et al. (Eds.): APMS 2022, IFIP AICT 664, pp. 537–547, 2022.
https://doi.org/10.1007/978-3-031-16411-8_62

delivery, and flexibility must be ensured [1–5]. However, mass customization often results in performance degradation caused by the complexity of the production processes, dynamic situations, and increased preparation time [6–8]. Therefore, the production process and systematic efficiency must be enhanced to minimize the negative effects of unpredictable changes and dynamic disturbances by achieving resilience [9–11]. This concept is more effective at dynamically handling the events because robust solutions cannot be considered beforehand for all potential fluctuations [9, 12].

Four core functional requirements must be satisfied for a simulation aspect to achieve resilient production control in rechargeable battery production: (1) selection of robust actions; (2) measurement of performance indicators; (3) notification of impermissible fluctuations; and (4) extraction of the adjusted reactions [9]. These technical functionalities ensure the overall production efficiency improvement and dynamic performance degradation prevention in production operation [9, 12].

A digital twin (DT) is a core element of the cyber physical production system, which is necessary to meet the aforementioned requirements. A DT is an advanced virtual asset that represents a configuration of the physical asset, reflects functional units corresponding to the operational characteristics, and synchronizes the information objects derived from the entire value stream [13–16]. The DT must provide the following three types of execution procedures to satisfy the requirements: virtual commissioning, which is used to select a robust action; prognostic simulation, which is implemented to provide notifications about impermissible fluctuations; and reactive simulation, which is provided to extract the adjusted reactions [17]. The measurement performance indicators are realized by three types of DT-based execution [17, 18]. Similar to other smart manufacturing technologies, the most important aspect of DT is the use of information. Specifically, DT requires a large variety and volume of information elements to provide suitable technical functionalities [3, 15, 19]. The asset description is an abstract information structure that provides specific inputs to the DT. However, the existing asset descriptions of virtual factory technology are required for improved DT implementation [19–25]. In addition, an asset description for rechargeable battery production has not been proposed.

This report proposes an asset description for DT application in rechargeable battery production. This description implements the asset administration shell (AAS) concept with high-level object orientation and "type and instance" concepts. The measures taken to achieve resilience and operational characteristics of stations in rechargeable battery production were analyzed for efficient design of the description. Accordingly, the asset description was designed with the product, process, plan, plant, and resource (P4R) classes based. The designed asset description was applied to stations in rechargeable battery production, and the proposed method was verified with the implemented DT application.

2 Research Background

From a work center perspective, a DT is an advanced virtual factory, which represents a configuration of a physical work center, reflects functional units corresponding to operational characteristics, and synchronizes information objects derived from the entire value stream [13, 26–28]. The DT application creates, synchronizes, and executes a DT and has core elements such as an asset description, operation module, configuration data library (CDL), and DT engine. Table 1 presents the detailed descriptions of these elements [17, 19].

Table 1. Detailed descriptions of core elements of DT application [17, 19].

Element	Description
Asset description	An information schema that abstracts the inputs to create and synchronize a DT and is instantiated through aggregation from heterogeneous information sources
Operation module	A module that implements the creation, synchronization, and execution procedures. These three procedures are defined as follows: • The creation procedure represents the configuration and reflects the functional units of a physical work center. This step is classified in resource-centric, process-centric, and hybrid creations • The synchronization procedure synchronizes the input information objects to prepare for the execution of the DT. This step is classified in snapshot and footprint synchronizations • The execution procedure operates the created and synchronized DT and provides technical functionalities. This step includes virtual commissioning, prognostic simulation, reactive simulation, and representation
CDL	A library that manages the composition of elements, which are divided into base model, logic, and metadata; it is used in the creation procedures to represent configuration and reflect functional units

The asset description is a core element for the use of information to create and synchronize the DT. The main components of asset description include core manufacturing simulation data (CMSD); commercial-off-the-shelf simulation package interoperability (CSPI); neutral simulation schema (NESIS); product, process, plan, and resource (P3R); and virtual representation for a digital twin application (VREDI). Table 2 summarizes the scope, coverage, and characteristics of the asset descriptions [19–25]. All descriptions are classified according to the object-oriented classes to represent the physical assets. However, only VREDI supports vertical integration, which is the most important characteristic of a DT. Further, only VREDI considers the repeated derivation of performance indicators in terms of service composition. Moreover, other descriptions have insufficient interoperability for high-level object orientation and "type and instance" concepts, which are required by AAS principles [19].

Table 2. Asset descriptions for virtual factory technology [19–25].

Name	Item	Contents
CMSD [20–22]	Scope	Simulation of operations in the job shop environment
	Coverage	Part information, layout, resource information, production operation, production planning, support
	Vertical integration	No specific support
	Horizontal integration	No specific support
CSPI [23]	Scope	Supports interoperability between simulation packages
	Coverage	Entity transfer, shared resource, shared event, shared data structure
	Vertical integration	No specific support
	Horizontal integration	Support for exchange between simulation models
NESIS [25]	Scope	Exchange of simulation models between simulation and other manufacturing applications
	Coverage	Product, process, resource, Sim_List, configuration
	Vertical integration	No specific support
	Horizontal integration	Support for information exchange between simulation models and manufacturing applications
P3R [24]	Scope	Simulation of material flow analysis
	Coverage	Product, process, plant, resource
	Vertical integration	No specific support
	Horizontal integration	No specific support
VREDI [19]	Scope	Implementation of DT with supporting vertical and horizontal integrations
	Coverage	Product, process, plan, plant, resource
	Vertical integration	Support for information exchange with a physical work center
	Horizontal integration	Support for information exchange between advanced engineering applications

3   Asset Description of Digital Twin in Rechargeable Battery Production

3.1   Concept Definition of Digital Twin in Rechargeable Battery Production

The asset description provides appropriate technical functionalities to enable resilient production control in rechargeable battery production [24, 25]. The proposed DT must satisfy the four core requirements, which were explained earlier.

The DT provides virtual commissioning for alternatives to extract the performance indicators to select robust actions. In addition, the impermissible fluctuation can be predicted by prognostic simulation, and notifications can be provided about the potential negative effects on the performance indicators. Furthermore, the adjusted reactions are extracted based on the reactive simulation, and subsequently, performance indicator degradation is prevented and decreased. The performance indicators are quantitatively measured based on the three types of simulation-related execution.

The technical functionalities require the synchronization of the production plan and schedule alternatives for virtual commissioning. In addition, the dynamic information, which indicates the status of the physical work center, must be synchronized with the DT. The dynamic information, which includes the dynamic fluctuations, ensures that the DT can predict the potential negative effects of the performance indicators. Furthermore, the dynamic information and the reactive plan and schedule alternatives must be synchronized with the DT. The reactive plan and schedule alternatives can be evaluated appropriately based on the dynamic information.

The rechargeable battery production includes three main stations: (1) mixing and electrode production, (2) winding and assembly, and (3) formation. From the analysis results of the manufacturing domain, it can be inferred that these three stations have heterogeneous operational characteristics, which must be transmitted to the DT as functional units. The mixing and electrode production is a hybrid flexible flow shop that involves a batch process, which further enables production with inconsistent process operation. This station produces the cathode and anode electrodes separately and moves the batches to the next station. The mixing process causes the ripple effect owing to the inconsistency of outputs and complexity that result from the sequence-dependent setup time [29]. Furthermore, a massive number of works in process (WIPs) is required to meet the due date of the next station.

The winding and assembly station is a parallel flow shop with the bottleneck processes that are required for the entire rechargeable battery production process. Therefore, this station should efficiently maximize the utilization rate to improve all the performance indicators. The previous station must deliver the required electrodes before the production processes in the next station start. The tardiness values in this station can be used to study the considerable negative effects on the entire production operation. The production plan and schedule for this station should be revised if the order is changed by the customer. Furthermore, the production plan and schedule of the previous station must be adjusted.

The formation station is a reentrant job shop that includes the reentrancy, which is a tray visits identical resource instances [30]. This situation further increases the complexity of managing and controlling this station [30, 31]. Therefore, the performance indicators cannot be measured dynamically and are calculated conceptually using the master information. Additionally, the station faces logistics congestion, which may negatively affect the overall performance indicators.

3.2 Design of Asset Description of DT in Rechargeable Battery Production

The proposed asset description was adapted from the VREDI based on the defined concept for the DT [18, 22]. This VREDI applies the AAS concept with high-level object-orientation and the "type and instance" concept. This asset description supports vertical and horizontal integrations, which are the key characteristics of DTs.

The proposed asset description contains the object-oriented P4R classes, as described in Fig. 1. The *Product* class contains the information elements of various forms of materials, from slurries to cells. These constitute the batch units and different operational characteristics for each operation. Therefore, the information elements related to the manufacturing domain are considered in the design of this class.

In the *Process* class, the information elements of the process and material handling operations are indicated. The information elements corresponding to rework, defect, and sequence-dependent setup time are included in this class.

The *Resource* class describes the information elements of resource types, such as machine, buffer, material handling conveyor (MHC), and material handling vehicle (MHV).

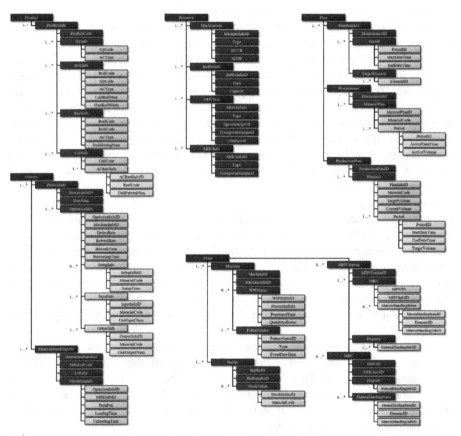

Fig. 1. Asset description for a DT in rechargeable battery production (adapted from Park et al. [18, 22]).

The *Plan* class describes the information elements that correspond to the maintenance, procurement, and production plans. The business policy is described by the elements in this class, which includes the instance information.

The *Plant* class contains the information elements with the status and dynamic information of the resource instances, including machine, buffer, MHC, and MHV. The WIP and failure status are described in this class, and these information elements are synchronized with the DT dynamically.

4 Industrial Case Study

The proposed asset description for the DT in rechargeable battery production was implemented and applied to three stations. The defined concept of the DT and asset description to satisfy the requirements were applied for verification.

The information objects based on the proposed method were implemented using the JavaScript object notation (JSON) message format. The JSON messages were provided using the service platform, which was implemented using the OSGi framework. This platform enables loosely coupled integration through a web service. The implemented information objects were provided according to the required technical functionalities.

The DT application was implemented based on the S-Prodis engine. This DT engine is a discrete event simulation engine, which is an efficient tool used to predict production-related performance indicators. Figures 2 and 3 present the created and synchronized DTs of the implemented DT application. The creation and synchronization procedures were selected for resource-centric creation and snapshot synchronization. Resource-centric creation improves the decision-making process because the elements are more intuitive than those corresponding to other creation types. The proposed asset description enables snapshot synchronization. The information objects, which were based on the P4R classes with dynamic information, were synchronized with the DT application.

The virtual commissioning, prognostic simulation, and reactive simulation were provided in the execution procedures. These execution types are required to achieve resilience, as described in Sect. 3.1. Furthermore, the operational characteristics of the three stations in the rechargeable battery production are represented in the proposed method. The proposed asset description indicates the sequence-dependent setup time, WIPs, due date, and reentrancy for appropriate simulation-based technical functionalities. Consequently, the proposed method satisfies the four core requirements.

Fig. 2. Created and synchronized DTs in mixing and electrode production station.

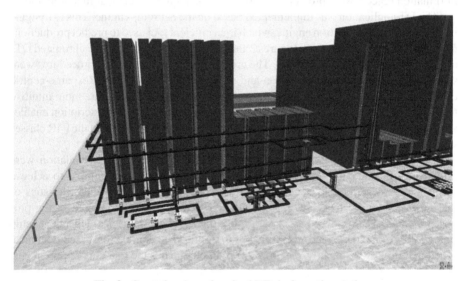

Fig. 3. Created and synchronized DTs in formation station.

5 Conclusion

The four core requirements defined in Sect. 1 must be satisfied for resilient production control. The DT must perform three primary execution procedures to satisfy the requirements: virtual commissioning, prognostic simulation, and reactive simulation. The measuring performance indicators are realized by the three DT-based executions.

The proposed asset description enables the DT to support the core requirements. This description implements the AAS concept with the high-level object orientation and "type and instance" concepts. These concepts improve the interoperability and efficiency of information management. This description was adapted from VREDI [22], which was previously proposed by the authors. Furthermore, the operational characteristics of three heterogeneous stations in rechargeable battery production were considered in the design of this description. The specific requirements corresponding to the manufacturing domain were generalized and projected onto the description.

The proposed asset description presents an efficient means of satisfying the core requirements and technical functionalities corresponding to the DT. Suitable technical functionalities and input information objects are necessary to satisfy each requirement. The proposed method is an early case of DT usage in rechargeable battery production, and the results of this study can be used as reference information in the smart manufacturing technology domain in the future. In addition, the adaption of asset descriptions for specific manufacturing domains can contribute to DT application in various manufacturing domains. The architectural design of the DT application in rechargeable battery production is required for robust and efficient application to the manufacturing domain in future research.

Funding Acknowledgement. This study was partly supported by the Smart Manufacturing Innovation Technology Development Programs under Grant [2022-0-01024, Development of International Standard-based Digital Twin Management Technology for Large-scale Optimal CPPS Operation] and Grant [2022-0-00131, Development of an AI-based Production Planning Technology for Reconfigurable Manufacturing Systems] funded by Ministry of Science and ICT.

References

1. Kwade, A., Haselrieder, W., Leithoff, R., Modlinger, A., Dietrich, F., Droeder, K.: Current status and challenges for automotive battery production technologies. Nat. Energy **3**(4), 290–300 (2018). https://doi.org/10.1038/s41560-018-0130-3

2. Thiede, S., Turetskyy, A., Kwade, A., Kara, S., Herrmann, C.: Data mining in battery production chains towards multi-criterial quality prediction. CIRP Ann. **68**(1), 463–466 (2019). https://doi.org/10.1016/j.cirp.2019.04.066

3. Wiktorsson, M., Do Noh, S., Bellgran, M., Hanson, L.: Smart factories: South Korean and Swedish examples on manufacturing settings. Procedia Manuf. **25**, 471–478 (2018). https://doi.org/10.1016/j.promfg.2018.06.128

4. Coito, T., et al.: A middleware platform for intelligent automation: an industrial prototype implementation. Comput. Ind. **123**, 103329 (2020). https://doi.org/10.1016/j.compind.2020.103329

5. El Kadiri, S., et al.: Current trends on ICT technologies for enterprise information systems. Comput. Ind. **79**, 14–33 (2016). https://doi.org/10.1016/j.compind.2015.06.008

6. Kumar, A.: From mass customization to mass personalization: a strategic transformation. Int. J. Flex. Manuf. Syst. **19**(4), 533–547 (2007). https://doi.org/10.1007/s10696-008-9048-6

7. Du, X., Jiao, J., Mitchell, M.T.: Understanding customer satisfaction in product customization. Int. J. Adv. Manuf. Technol. **31**(3), 396–406 (2006). https://doi.org/10.1007/s00170-005-0177-8

8. Son, J.Y., et al.: IoT-based open manufacturing service platform for mass personalization. J. Korean Inst. Commun. Sci. **33**(1), 42–47 (2015)
9. Ivanov, D.: Structural Dynamics and Resilience in Supply Chain Risk Management, vol. 265. Springer International Publishing, Berlin, Germany (2018). https://doi.org/10.1007/978-3-319-69305-7
10. Kwade, A., Haselrieder, W., Leithoff, R., Modlinger, A., Dietrich, F., Droeder, K.: Designing a resilient production system with reconfigurable machines and movable buffers. Int. J. Prod. Res. 1–16 (2021). https://doi.org/10.1080/00207543.2021.1953715
11. Bagozi, A., Bianchini, D., De Antonellis, V.: Designing context-based services for resilient cyber physical production systems. In: Huang, Z., Beek, W., Wang, H., Zhou, R., Zhang, Y. (eds.) WISE 2020. LNCS, vol. 12342, pp. 474–488. Springer, Cham (2020). https://doi.org/10.1007/978-3-030-62005-9_34
12. Fertier, A., et al.: Managing events to improve situation awareness and resilience in a supply chain. Comput. Ind. **132**, 103488 (2021). https://doi.org/10.1016/j.compind.2021.103488
13. Grieves, M.: Digital twin: manufacturing excellence through virtual factory replication. White Pap. **1**, 1–7 (2014)
14. Gabor, T., Belzner, L., Kiermeier, M., Beck, M.T., Neitz, A.: A simulation-based architecture for smart cyber-physical systems. In: 2016 IEEE International Conference on Autonomic Computing (ICAC). IEEE (2016). https://doi.org/10.1109/ICAC.2016.29
15. Cimino, C., Negri, E., Fumagalli, L.: Review of digital twin applications in manufacturing. Comput. Ind. **113**, 103130 (2019). https://doi.org/10.1016/j.compind.2019.103130
16. Semeraro, C., et al.: Digital twin paradigm: a systematic literature review. Comput. Ind. **130**, 103469 (2021). https://doi.org/10.1016/j.compind.2021.103469
17. Park, K.T., Lee, D., Noh, S.D.: Operation procedures of a work-center-level digital twin for sustainable and smart manufacturing. Int. J. Precis. Eng. Manuf. Green Technol. **7**(3), 791–814 (2020). https://doi.org/10.1007/s40684-020-00227-1
18. Park, K.T.: Autonomous digital twin for resilient decision and production control. Sungkyunkwan University, Ph. D. dissertation (2021). UCI: I804:11040-000000165664
19. Park, K.T., Yang, J., Noh, S.D.: VREDI: virtual representation for a digital twin application in a work-center-level asset administration shell. J. Intell. Manuf. **32**(2), 501–544 (2020). https://doi.org/10.1007/s10845-020-01586-x
20. Lee, Y.T.T., Riddick, F.H., Johansson, B.J.I.: Core manufacturing simulation data–a manufacturing simulation integration standard: overview and case studies. Int. J. Comput. Integr. Manuf. **24**(8), 689–709 (2011). https://doi.org/10.1080/0951192X.2011.574154
21. Leong, S., Lee, Y.T., Riddick, F.: A core manufacturing simulation data information model for manufacturing applications. In: Simulation Interoperability Workshop, Simulation Interoperability and Standards Organization (2006)
22. Riddick, F.H., Lee, Y.T.: Core manufacturing simulation data (CMSD): a standard representation for manufacturing simulation-related information. In: Fall Simulation Interoperability Workshop (Fall SIW). SISO (2010)
23. Taylor, S.J.E., et al.: Commercial-off-the-shelf simulation package interoperability: Issues and futures. In: Proceedings of the 2009 Winter Simulation Conference (WSC). IEEE (2009). https://doi.org/10.1109/WSC.2009.5429326
24. Lee, J.Y., et al.: Concurrent material flow analysis by P3R-driven modeling and simulation in PLM. Comput. Ind. **63**(5), 513–527 (2012). https://doi.org/10.1016/j.compind.2012.02.004
25. Lee, J.Y., et al.: NESIS: a neutral schema for a web-based simulation model exchange service across heterogeneous simulation software. Int. J. Comput. Integr. Manuf. **24**(10), 948–969 (2011). https://doi.org/10.1080/0951192X.2011.608726
26. Cheng, Y., Zhang, Y., Ji, P., Xu, W., Zhou, Z., Tao, F.: Cyber-physical integration for moving digital factories forward towards smart manufacturing: a survey. Int. J. Adv. Manuf. Technol. **97**(1–4), 1209–1221 (2018). https://doi.org/10.1007/s00170-018-2001-2

27. Liu, Q., et al.: Digital twin-driven rapid individualised designing of automated flow-shop manufacturing system. Int. J. Prod. Res. **57**(12), 3903–3919 (2019). https://doi.org/10.1080/00207543.2018.1471243
28. Uhlemann, T.H.-J., et al.: The digital twin: demonstrating the potential of real time data acquisition in production systems. Procedia Manuf. **9**, 113–120 (2017). https://doi.org/10.1016/j.promfg.2017.04.043
29. Abreu, L.R., Cunha, J.O., Prata, B.A., Framinan, J.M.: A genetic algorithm for scheduling open shops with sequence-dependent setup times. Comput. Oper. Res. **113**, 104793 (2020). https://doi.org/10.1016/j.cor.2019.104793
30. Kumar, P.R.: Re-entrant lines. Queueing Syst. **13**(1–3), 87–110 (1993). https://doi.org/10.1007/BF01158930
31. Hu, R., Wu, X., Qian, B., Mao, J., Jin, H.: Differential evolution algorithm combined with uncertainty handling techniques for stochastic reentrant job shop scheduling problem. Complexity 9924163 (2022). https://doi.org/10.1155/2022/9924163

Cyber-Physical System Platform and Applications for Smart Manufacturing in Global Automotive Industry

Jinho Yang[1] ⓘ, Jonghwan Choi[1] ⓘ, Joohee Lym[1] ⓘ, Sang Do Noh[1(✉)] ⓘ,
Yong-Shin Kang[2], Sang Hyun Lee[3], Hyung Sun Kim[4], Je-Hoon Lee[5],
and Hyun-Jung Kim[5]

[1] Sungkyunkwan University, Suwon 16419, Republic of Korea
sdnoh@skku.edu
[2] Advanced Institutes of Convergence Technology, Suwon 16229, Republic of Korea
[3] Yura, Seongnam 13494, Republic of Korea
[4] Dexta Inc., Suwon 16677, Republic of Korea
[5] Korea Advanced Institute of Science and Technology, Daejeon 34141, Republic of Korea

Abstract. The modern manufacturing industry ought to solve various problems amid increasingly fierce competition. Particularly, the supply chain network of the manufacturing industry is expanding globally. Therefore, there is an increasing necessity for smart manufacturing. Smart manufacturing is an integrated manufacturing system that applies information and communication technologies to manufacturing, rendering the entire manufacturing process smart, for obtaining real-time responses to internal and external variations in factories, supply networks, and customer requirements. Although there are several technologies that promote smart manufacturing, the cyber-physical system (CPS), introduced into the manufacturing environment is the primary technology. Global manufacturing enterprises have limitations in that it is difficult to collect information generated at distributed manufacturing sites with independent applications, and it is impossible to make quick decisions. To build smart manufacturing at such global manufacturing scales, a platform that integrates information and provides various applications in a distributed environment using the CPS ought to be built. This paper proposes an integrated platform for smart manufacturing implementation. The primary components and functions of the platform are defined. Finally, the effectiveness of the proposed platform is verified through a case study.

Keywords: Cyber-Physical System (CPS) · Platform · Smart manufacturing

1 Introduction

The modern manufacturing industry is required to solve various problems, such as dynamic global market demand, short product life cycles, greater product variety, and lower production costs [1, 2]. These requirements increase the complexity of manufacturing systems and promote the introduction of various information and communication

© IFIP International Federation for Information Processing 2022
Published by Springer Nature Switzerland AG 2022
D. Y. Kim et al. (Eds.): APMS 2022, IFIP AICT 664, pp. 548–555, 2022.
https://doi.org/10.1007/978-3-031-16411-8_63

technologies (ICTs) into the existing manufacturing system. Starting with industry 4.0, which was proposed by Germany, various advanced manufacturing countries, such as the United States, Korea, and Sweden, are trying to attain a competitive edge in manufacturing [3–5]. Various technologies, such as smart manufacturing [3], the cyber-physical system (CPS), internet of things, and big data, are commonly considered essential [3, 5] and believed to promote the fourth industrial revolution in the manufacturing field. When these technologies are applied to manufacturing, the entire manufacturing process can become smart and respond to the internal and external variations in systems such as factories, supply networks, and customer requirements in real time [4, 6]. The CPS is a core technology of the industry 4.0 architecture. It is a concept for managing systems connected to physical resources in the cyber world through communication networks [5, 7]. The cyber-physical production system (CPPS), which corresponds to the CPS in the manufacturing environment, constitutes autonomous and cooperative elements and subsystems, based on information obtained from the overall production site and logistics system, intelligence, connectedness, and responsiveness toward internal and external variations as its primary features [8].

Global manufacturing companies dispersed in several countries ought to overcome obstacles such as differences in cultures, languages, regulations, policies, and manufacturing units [9]. Particularly, the automotive parts industry is a representative assembly industry in which a small number of automakers procure tens of thousands of parts from a large number of automotive part makers to produce automobiles. It constitutes highly complex and extensive value chains [10, 11]. Therefore, the collection of information in a distributed field with an independent application is difficult. Moreover, localized platforms exhibit limitations toward acceptance and distribution in the industry [12]. To facilitate cooperation among different enterprises and responsiveness to global competition, a standardized open platform, in lieu of existing independent platforms, is needed.

This paper proposes an integrated platform for the efficient implementation of smart manufacturing for global manufacturing companies. Various ICTs used in the CPS platform are discussed, and the applications provided through this platform are introduced. Finally, industrial case studies are performed by applying this platform to the assembly and production line of a Korean automotive part manufacturing company.

2 Research Background

The CPS is an innovative technology that enables data access, processing, analysis, and utilization between physical assets and computational entities through an interconnected system [8, 13, 14]. The CPPS can configure the production environment more flexibly, in addition to providing more differentiated management and control processes than conventional manufacturing systems do [8, 15]. To effectively implement the CPPS, the most important consideration is the integration of analytics technology and a simulation-based approach for big data collected in large quantities at the manufacturing site [8]. Particularly, the most core technology among the various elements constituting the CPPS is the digital twin (DT), defined as a virtual model that enables the analysis, evaluation, optimization, and prediction of the current situation by synchronizing and simulating real-time information and functions collected at the production site [16]. The core technical functionality of the DT is simulation. Additionally, it is essential for deriving the performance indicators of various production control techniques [17]. To provide various services by integrating information in a distributed environment using the CPS and DT technologies discussed, a platform that provides a large-scale service system ought to be constructed [12]. In a smart manufacturing environment, this platform is a middleware technology that delivers information collected from devices to services and applications. The platform builds various services and applications by converging technologies such as CPS, big data, and cloud computing. Through this platform, people, things, and systems can be connected [5]. In particular, the CPS platform, with ICT technologies, provides intelligent capabilities to predict various situation at production sites, and encapsulate and virtualize distributed manufacturing resources into cloud manufacturing services to support tasks such as product design, simulation, testing, and management [18–20]. Accordingly, we propose an integrated platform using the DT and various ICTs to construct an efficient CPS environment.

3   CPS Platform and Applications

3.1   CPS Platform

The proposed technology in this study is a CPS platform for building a smart assembly system for automotive part makers through converging with legacy systems, such as the manufacturing execution system, or enterprise performance management using various ICT and applications for production site application. The purpose of this platform is to support various services such as production quality prediction and production management for the development of a smart manufacturing system. Figure 1 depicts the architecture of the proposed platform.

The proposed CPS was classified into the automotive part assembly line (corresponding to the physical world) and the platform (corresponding to the virtual world). The definitions of the components composing the CPS are as follows.

- Automotive part assembly line: It is an assembly line that produces various automobile parts and is a manufacturing site comprising resources such as workers and assembly parts. Information with respect to workers, equipment, and products on the assembly line are transmitted to the CPS platform and legacy system through media.
- Core technologies of the platform: It is the core basis of basic functions and application services for engineering in the platform. The functions comprise the DT, which can perform various functions by configuring a virtual model using real-time data collected from the manufacturing site, and can perform advanced analytics to analyze and utilize the collected data. Finally, it comprises big data management for manufacturing, which processes and refines the data collected at the manufacturing site.
- Basic functions: These are provided by the platforms utilizing core functions. The basic functions available on the platform were real-time monitoring, simulation, visualization, prediction, and analysis.

- Application services: These are services that can be utilized according to the characteristics and circumstances of the manufacturing site using the basic functions described previously.

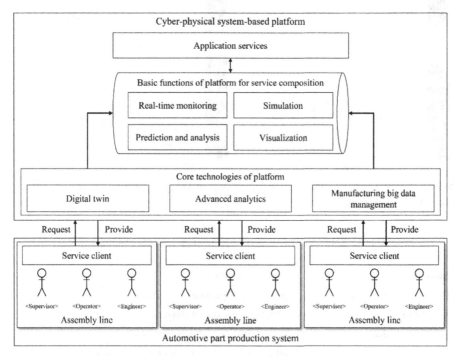

Fig. 1. Conceptual architecture of the proposed platform.

Figure 2 shows the driving screens of the basic functions of a platform implemented in a cloud computing environment. The CPS platform dashboard allows service clients to check and respond to the status of the system based on real-time data from various manufacturing sites. Using this data, real-time monitoring can generate a DT model at the manufacturing site and monitor the situation of a particular production line or factory. The simulation on this platform provides more accurate results than existing simulation models by utilizing the generated DT model. Additionally, the platform facilitates the visualization of various production-related data such as simulation, prediction, and diagnosis results. This function includes charts, reports, and visualization of 3D models. Table 1 summarizes the relationship between the core technologies used in basic functions. The basic functions of the platform are built by combining one or more core functions. The application services can be built using these basic functions. Although various application services can be configured on the platform, based on the requirements of a global manufacturer, this paper introduces smart production management and smart quality prediction systems.

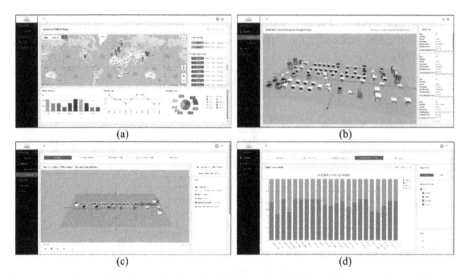

Fig. 2. Snapshots of the CPS platform (a) dashboard [21] (b) real-time monitoring [21], (c) simulation, and (d) visualization.

Table 1. Relationship between basic functions and core technologies.

Basic function	Core technologies
Real-time monitoring	Digital twin; big data management
Simulation	Digital twin; big data management; advanced analytics
Prediction and analysis	Big data management; advanced analytics
Visualization	Digital twin; big data management; advanced analytics

The platform shown in Fig. 2 applied a standardized information model for data collection from the distributed manufacturing sites to ensure versatility. The information model was defined based on international industry standards [21]. We have omitted the detailed descriptions in this paper for conciseness.

3.2 Applications of the CPS Platform

Various service applications can be implemented using the functions of the proposed platform. To build a smart assembly line, this platform primarily comprises two service applications. The first application is a smart quality prediction system that can predict the quality of products in advance by analyzing the quality impact analysis between the processes. The core function of this system is advanced analytics; the algorithms are implemented by preprocessing and training data using various machine learning models. The second application is a smart production management system, which utilizes an optimization algorithm to provide an optimal task allocation function considering the skill of workers at the production site and the amount of work required for each production line. The periodic verification of the working status of workers on the production line facilitates the relocation and optimization of the work process for problems caused by workers for various reasons. Figure 3 is a screen for these service applications provided by the platform.

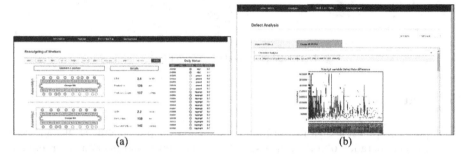

(a)   (b)

Fig. 3. (a) Smart production management and (b) smart quality prediction systems.

4 Industrial Case Study

To validate the proposed CPS platform and applications, they were applied to an actual industrial site of a global automotive parts manufacturer in Korea. The target factories located in Vietnam, China, and Korea were virtualized using the platform. Research is currently underway toward applying the developed technologies to the smart factory test bed located in Sweden. This study was conducted as a part of the international joint research of Korea and Sweden. Figure 4 shows the DT models of the target factories for which the proposed technology was applied. The proposed platform and services application results for the three target production lines were as follows.

- The average performance calculation accuracy of the DT model virtualized on the platform agreed with more than 90% of the observations in the real production line.
- With optimized assembly process control, the productivity of the assembly line was improved by more than 3%.
- The average quality prediction accuracy was more than 90% on average, for the identification of defects and responding in advance, contributing toward productivity improvement.

The details of the application results are not completely disclosed, owing to the confidentiality conditions of the manufacturer applying the technologies.

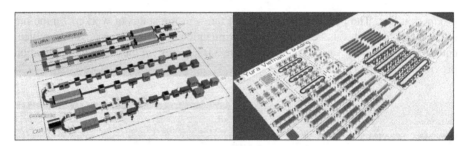

Fig. 4. Digital twin models of target factories.

5 Conclusion

This paper proposed a CPS platform and application for the systematic management and efficient operation of a Korean-based global automotive part manufacturer. For the smartization of the manufacturing system, we discussed advanced technologies, such as the DT and advanced analytics. The contributions of this study are as follows. First, the architecture of the CPS platform was presented, and the primary components were defined. Based on this, the practically implemented technologies were introduced. In addition, service applications that can be utilized in the CPS environment were explored. By applying the proposed technology to the actual manufacturing site, improvements over the existing manufacturing system were derived. However, the proposed platform exhibited the following limitation: there is a large gap in the technology that can be applied depending on the required level of virtualization and automation of the production line. Therefore, in the future, it is necessary to identify a method that can reflect the various levels of the production site and to develop a platform technology tailored for the site.

Acknowledgement. This research was financially supported by the MOTIE and KIAT through the International Cooperative R&D program [P0009839] and supported under the Smart Manufacturing Innovation R&D program funded by the Korea Ministry of SMEs and Startups in 2022 [RS-2022–00140261].

References

1. Koren, Y., Gu, X., Guo, W.: Reconfigurable manufacturing systems: principles, design, and future trends. Front. Mech. Eng. **13**(2), 121–136 (2017). https://doi.org/10.1007/s11465-018-0483-0
2. Bortolini, M., Francesco, G.G., Cristina, M.: Reconfigurable manufacturing systems: literature review and research trend. J. Manuf. Syst. **49**, 93–106 (2018). https://doi.org/10.1016/j.jmsy.2018.09.005
3. Kang, H.S., et al.: Smart manufacturing: past research, present findings, and future directions. Int. J. Precis. Eng. Manuf.-Green Technol. **3**(1), 111–128 (2016). https://doi.org/10.1007/s40684-016-0015-5

4. Wiktorsson, M., Noh, S.D., Bellgran, M., Hanson, L.: Smart factories: South Korean and Swedish examples on manufacturing settings. Procedia Manuf. **25**, 471–478 (2018). https://doi.org/10.1016/j.promfg.2018.06.128

5. Kagermann, H., Wahlster, W., Helbig. J.: Securing the future of German manufacturing industry: Recommendations for implementing the strategic initiative INDUSTRIE 4.0. Final report of the Industrie 4.0 (2013)

6. Kusiak, A.: Smart manufacturing. Int. J. Prod. Res. **56**(2), 508–517 (2018). https://doi.org/10.1080/00207543.2017.1351644

7. Schroeder, G.N., Steinmetz, C., Pereira, C.E., Espindola, D.B.: Digital twin data modeling with automationml and a communication methodology for data exchange. IFAC-PapersOnLine **49**(30), 12–17 (2016). https://doi.org/10.1016/j.ifacol.2016.11.115

8. Monostori, L., et al.: Cyber-physical systems in manufacturing. Cirp Ann. **65**(2), 621–641 (2016). https://doi.org/10.1016/j.cirp.2016.06.005

9. Ivanov, D., Sethi, S., Dolgui, A., Sokolov, B.: A survey on control theory applications to operational systems, supply chain management, and Industry 4.0. Annu. Rev. Control **46**, 134–147 (2018). https://doi.org/10.1016/j.arcontrol.2018.10.014

10. Yang, J., et al.: Integrated platform and digital twin application for global automotive part suppliers. In: Lalic, B., Majstorovic, V., Marjanovic, U., von Cieminski, G., Romero, D. (eds.) APMS 2020. IAICT, vol. 592, pp. 230–237. Springer, Cham (2020). https://doi.org/10.1007/978-3-030-57997-5_27

11. Jung, J.S.: Logistics Innovation in the Automotive Industry. Research Report, Korea Institute for Industrial Economics & Trade, Sejong (2001)

12. Yun, S., Jun-Hong P., Won-Tae, K.: Data-centric middleware based digital twin platform for dependable cyber-physical systems. In: 2017 Ninth International Conference on Ubiquitous and Future Networks (ICUFN), p. 17063600. IEEE, Milan (2017). https://doi.org/10.1109/ICUFN.2017.7993933

13. Lee, J., Behrad, B., Hung-An, K.: A cyber-physical systems architecture for industry 4.0-based manufacturing systems. Manuf. Lett. **3**, 18–23 (2015). https://doi.org/10.1016/j.mfglet.2014.12.001

14. Rajkumar, R., Lee, I., Sha, L., Stankovic, J.: Cyber-physical systems: the next computing revolution. In: Design Automation Conference, pp. 731–736. IEEE (2010). https://doi.org/10.1145/1837274.1837461

15. Ribeiro, L., Björkman, M.: Transitioning from standard automation solutions to cyber-physical production systems: an assessment of critical conceptual and technical challenges. IEEE Syst. J. **12**(4), 3816–3827 (2017)

16. Tao, F., Zhang, M., Nee, A.Y.C.: Digital twin driven Smart Manufacturing. Technology & Engineering. Academic Press, London (2019

17. Rosen, R., von Wichert, G., Lo, G., Bettenhausen, K.D.: About the importance of autonomy and digital twins for the future of manufacturing. Ifac-PapersOnline **48**(3), 567–572 (2015). https://doi.org/10.1016/j.ifacol.2015.06.141

18. Lin, Y.C., et al.: Development of advanced manufacturing cloud of things (AMCoT)—a smart manufacturing platform. IEEE Rob. Autom. Lett. **2**(3), 1809–1816 (2017)

19. Xu, X.: From cloud computing to cloud manufacturing. Rob. Comput.-Integr. Manuf. **28**(1), 75–86 (2012)

20. Hung, M.H., Li, Y.Y., Lin, Y.C., Wei, C.F., Yang, H.C., Cheng, F.T.: Development of a novel cloud-based multi-tenant model creation service for automatic virtual metrology. Rob. Comput.-Integr. Manuf. **44**, 174–189 (2017)

21. Choi, J., et al.: Design and implementation of digital twin-based application for global manufacturing enterprises. In: Dolgui, A., Bernard, A., Lemoine, D., von Cieminski, G., Romero, D. (eds.) APMS 2021. IAICT, vol. 634, pp. 12–19. Springer, Cham (2021). https://doi.org/10.1007/978-3-030-85914-5_2

Digital Twin-Based Services and Data Visualization of Material Handling Equipment in Smart Production Logistics Environment

Yongkuk Jeong[1]([✉])(iD), Erik Flores-García[1](iD), Dong Hoon Kwak[2],
Jong Hun Woo[2], Magnus Wiktorsson[1](iD), Sichao Liu[3](iD), Xi Vincent Wang[3](iD),
and Lihui Wang[3](iD)

[1] KTH Royal Institute of Technology, Södertälje 151 36, Sweden
{yongkuk,efs01,magwik}@kth.se
[2] Seoul National University, Seoul 08826, Republic of Korea
{s2arta2s,j.woo}@snu.ac.kr
[3] KTH Royal Institute of Technology, Stockholm 114 28, Sweden
{sicliu,wangxi,lihuiw}@kth.se

Abstract. Smart production logistics has introduced in manufacturing industries with emerging technologies such as digital twin, industrial internet of things, and cyber-physical system. This technological innovation initiates the new way of working, working environment, and decision-making process. Especially the decision-making process has changed from experience and intuition to knowledge and data driven. In this paper, digital twin-based services, and data visualization of material handling equipment in smart production logistics environment are presented. There are several applications of digital twin in manufacturing industries already, however feedback from the virtual environment to physical environment and interactions between them which are the essential features of digital twin are very weak in many applications. Therefore, we have developed digital twin-based services in the laboratory scale including feedback and interaction. In addition, data visualization application of material handling equipment in automotive industry is presented to provide insights to the users. Both applications have developed based on the same framework including database and middleware, so it has possibilities to develop further in the future.

Keywords: Digital twin · Digital service · Data visualization · Smart production logistics

1 Introduction

New technological solutions such as Cyber-Physical Systems (CPS), Industry 4.0, and Internet of Things (IoT) are creating opportunities in various industries

© IFIP International Federation for Information Processing 2022
Published by Springer Nature Switzerland AG 2022
D. Y. Kim et al. (Eds.): APMS 2022, IFIP AICT 664, pp. 556–564, 2022.
https://doi.org/10.1007/978-3-031-16411-8_64

including the production logistics [1]. These solutions enabled researchers to develop new paradigm of production logistics called, "Smart Production Logistics (SPL)", which addresses to fully autonomous systems to increase the performance of the production system [2]. The SPL can be achieved with the ability of logistic objects to process information, to render and to execute decisions on their own [3]. Various technologies are contributing to this goal including CPS, IoT, interfaces, decentralized applications, automatic identification, virtual environments like Digital twins, and the branches of data science like machine learning, data mining, and big data analytics [4]. The demand of digitization and digitalization in production logistics to maximize the performance and the efficiency of the system adopting the technologies has increased the most [5].

The virtual environments are used in production logistics to simulate various scenarios that couldn't be conducted in reality due to limitations like cost and time. Digital twins, simulations, augmented reality, and virtual reality could be classified as the virtual environments [6]. Digital twin (DT) is defined as "a virtual representation of a physical system that is updated through the exchange of information between the physical and virtual system" [7]. Thus, DT should include physical system, virtual environment, and connection between the physical system and virtual environment generating data and information flow. The characteristics of the DT enables the system to ensure the improvement of data driven approach to the monitoring, management, and knowledge [8]. Due to its capability of high-fidelity reflection of physical system, the DT has been highly contributed in smart manufacturing system design phase where it demands to minimize the gap between the design domain and operation domain [9].

Therefore, this study aims to provide a prototype service of DT technology in SPL improving the efficiency of decision making process. The study is conducted in production logistics design process involving multiple material handling equipment, so called, Autonomous Mobile Robot (AMR). To assist the decision making process in the service, data visualization derived from production logistics environment is also addressed in this study.

The rest of the paper is organized as follows. A background of the recent studies of DT application and production logistics data visualization are provided in Sect. 2. The applications of DT and data visualization in production logistics environment are presented in Sect. 3. The overall objective of this study and future challenges are described in Sect. 4.

2 Related Works

2.1 Digital Twin Applications in Manufacturing

With rapid growth of interest toward the smart manufacturing system, there has been significant efforts on DT implementation for integrating information technologies and operation technologies in various industries [10]. DT application not only includes connection between the cyber and physical world, but also emphasizes the synchronization between the two by offering monitoring and optimization services and capability to control from the cyber world to enhance decision making process [11].

These aspects of DT has made significant improvements in different manufacturing services from entire business processes to operational procedures [12]. For instance, [13] proposed DT based production process design framework in automobile assembly line to minimize design errors that can lead to significant delays in the design process. The reflection of physical system in virtual environment enabled designers to test different designs of luminaire in different application scenarios with DT framework [14]. [15] conducted DT-driven methodology for designing automated flow-shop manufacturing system in pre-production phase considering static configuration and dynamic execution at the same time. There are also implementations of DT monitoring and optimizing the operation procedures [11]. [16] proposed a system architecture for the virtualization of manufacturing machines as a middleware to monitor and control the physical machines. [17] proposed a DT-based process knowledge model including real-time equipment status and accumulation of process knowledge for reuse in future planning. [18] presented a case study evaluating energy efficiency reduction using simulations of the DT. In this study, buffering-based solution was introduced for improving the energy efficiency in surface mount technology PCB assembly line. To provide safe and productive interaction between human and mobile robot, [19] proposed augmented reality solution and supporting system architecture for smart warehouse.

DT can be utilized more than a static environment in cases where the situation frequently changes dynamically, such as in a production logistics environment. However, although many DT application cases have already been studied, it is very difficult to find a case that fully applies the interaction between the physical and virtual environments.

2.2 Production Logistics Data Visualization

Data analytics is necessary for the implementation of SPL by enabling to analyze the acquired data in more advanced level [20]. Thus, big data technology from data collection to data analysis and visualization should follow to create value improving the performance level of the SPL [21]. Especially, the complexity and variety of data has reached to the peak that emphasized the importance of data visualization empowering managers to derive valuable managerial insights for process innovation and efficiency [22]. Therefore, data visualization has been introduced in various industries studying data analytics in recent years.

[23] introduced Google Web Toolkit and HTML5 as dynamic user interfaces developed to display real-time values. [24] proposed a framework of sensitivity analysis and visualization tool for multidimensional nuclear simulation data for multipurpose probabilistic risk assessment and uncertainty quantification framework so called, Reactor Analysis and Virtual Control Environment (RAVEN). [25] introduced LiveGantt for planning production schedule that helps users explore highly-concurrent large schedules from various perspectives. The study

is conducted to multiple engineering researchers and showed significant improvement in scheduling due to its exploration capability in multiple-perspectives. [26] introduced an interactive visual analytics system for monitoring and controlling manufacturing industries for operators to enhance performance level.

As big data analysis technology developed and many interactive visualization toolkits were released, various studies on big data visualization were performed. However, many studies have not yet been found in the field of production logistics.

3   Digital Twin-Based Services and Data Visualization

This section presents digital services based on DT to material handling equipment and data visualization in SPL system. The DT-based services are developed and tested in a laboratory level environment that represents a simplified version of internal production logistics environment with AMR. The physical and virtual environments are connected through the middleware to interchange data between the two environments.

The data visualization application is developed with the data from an automotive manufacturing industry. The data is related to production logistics and we developed interactive heat map, frequency analysis map, and time-based trajectory map using open-source libraries.

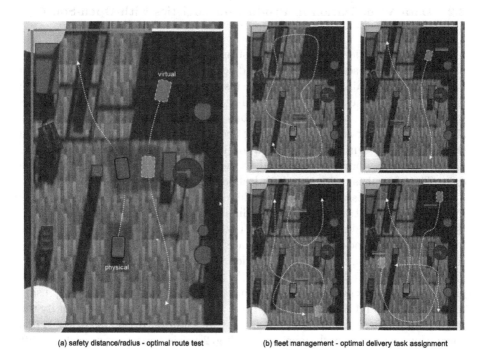

(a) safety distance/radius - optimal route test   (b) fleet management - optimal delivery task assignment

Fig. 1. DT-based AMR monitoring and controlling application

3.1   Digital Twin-Based Monitoring and Controlling Application

The service involves interactions between AMRs between physical and virtual environment. Figure 1 (a) is visualizing the safety radius around AMRs from both physical and virtual environment in DT. When the two AMRs interfere their safety distance and radius each other, the path will be adjusted to avoid collision between them. This informs that the AMR in the physical environment is capable of sensing and interacting with the virtual AMR in the virtual environment and re-calculate its direction.

This application can be used for the fleet management service in the design phase of the production logistics system. This service could be adopted as an optimization tool in decision making process of finding an optimal number of fleets in the production logistics system. Figure 1 (b) provides results of scenarios with different number of fleets assigned to execute the same schedule. There are 6 tasks in the schedule, and each AMR in each scenario has assigned the tasks to complete the schedule. The routes are the optimized route regarding the interference between all AMRs. Thus, the real process is promised to follow the simulation result unless there's unexpected disturbance such as malfunction of the AMR, variability of process time of each task, human disturbance, etc. Then, the result is could be considered in decision making process of how many fleet to be purchased regarding the strategic goal of the system.

3.2   Data Visualization in Production Logistics with Open-Source Library

The DT-based service is focused in assisting decision making process in terms of providing different scenarios in time and cost effectively. The data visualization has conducted in this paper to get more insight from the historical location data of the forklift in the automotive manufacturing company. The forklifts deliver products from one station to another but they don't have structured schedule since the logistics tasks are supporting activities in the production system. In this paper open-source data visualization library is used to develop interactive dashboard. This library is connected to the database which is storing real-time data. Therefore it is easy to update dashboard with the real-time data.

In this case we can acquire different kinds of data from forklifts; name of forklift, location (longitude, latitude, coordinate, and predefined zone), and timestamp. Figure 2 (a) shows a heat map of the frequency of forklifts' location in the factory using the location data (longitude, latitude) in the map. The red color represents high frequency of the location, whereas the green color represents low frequency of the location. Figure 2 (b) shows the time-serial zone frequency graph that presents number of forklifts in each zone throughout timestamp using predefined zone and timestamp data. From this graph, managers can identify the real-time forklift distribution in the factory, in addition to the historical traffic congestion records in each zone. Lastly, Fig. 2 (c) is trajectory of each forklift through time using name of forklift, location data (longitude and latitude), and

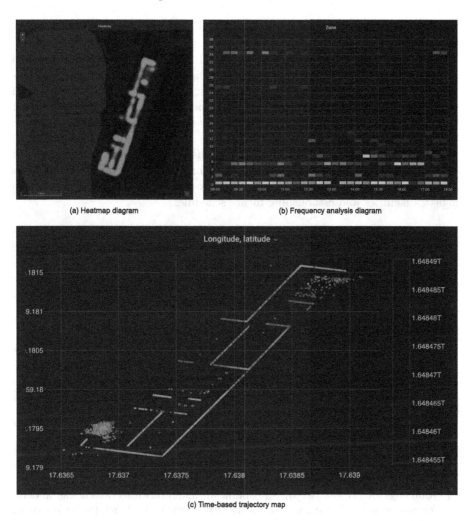

(a) Heatmap diagram

(b) Frequency analysis diagram

(c) Time-based trajectory map

Fig. 2. Data visualization in production logistics with open-source library

timestamp. The color of trajectory is differed through time. Recent trajectory is marked with red dots, while old records are marked with blue dots.

Data visualization can be utilized by various stakeholders related to internal logistics operations. First, logistics operators such as forklift drivers can make decisions based on quantitative results rather than their own experiences or intuition, which can be used to improve inefficient driving habits. Also, from the perspective of a logistics manager who establishes logistics plans, data visualization can be used to compare whether planning and operation strategies have been applied accurately. From a more macroscopic point of view, factory managers can be usefully used for short-term, mid-to-long-term performance analysis.

4   Conclusions

Digital twins are already being developed in many places, but most are focused on product development, and it is difficult to find many cases that derive examples of interaction between virtual and physical environments even for digital twins targeting production systems. In this study, several cases that can support decision-making through interaction between virtual and physical environments in a production logistics environment are presented. In addition, we developed an interactive dashboard that can provide insight to users based on location data of production logistics facilities stored for digital twin development. This can be used as useful input when analyzing the operating patterns of production logistics facilities and establishing future schedules.

Acknowledgement. The authors would like to acknowledge the support of Swedish Innovation Agency (VINNOVA). This study is part of the Cyber Physical Assembly and Logistics Systems in Global Supply Chains (C-PALs) project. This project is funded under SMART EUREKA CLUSTER on Advanced Manufacturing program.

References

1. Douaioui, K., Fri, M., Mabroukki, C., Semma, E.: The interaction between industry 4.0 and smart logistics: concepts and perspectives. In: 2018 International Colloquium On Logistics And Supply Chain Management, LOGISTIQUA 2018, vol. 21266798, pp. 128–132 (2018)
2. Klumpp, M., Hesenius, M., Meyer, O., Ruiner, C., Gruhn, V.: Production logistics and human-computer interaction-state-of-the-art, challenges and requirements for the future. Int. J. Adv. Manuf. Technol. **105**, 3691–3709 (2019)
3. Windt, K., Böse, F., Philipp, T.: Autonomy in production logistics: identification, characterisation and application. Robot. Comput. Integr. Manuf. **24**, 572–578 (2008)
4. Kaiblinger, A., Woschank, M.: State of the art and future directions of digital twins for production logistics: a systematic literature review. Appl. Sci. (Switzerland) **12** (2022)
5. Woschank, M., Rauch, E., Zsifkovits, H.: A review of further directions for artificial intelligence, machine learning, and deep learning in smart logistics. Sustainability (Switzerland) **12** (2020)
6. Woschank, M., Kaiblinger, A., Miklautsch, P.: Digitalization in industrial logistics: contemporary evidence and future directions. In: Proceedings of the International Conference On Industrial Engineering And Operations Management, pp. 1322–1333 (2021)
7. VanDerHorn, E., Mahadevan, S.: Digital twin: generalization, characterization and implementation. Decis. Support Syst. **145** (2021)
8. Jones, D., Snider, C., Nassehi, A., Yon, J., Hicks, B.: Characterising the digital twin: a systematic literature review. CIRP J. Manuf. Sci. Technol. **29**, 36–52 (2020). https://doi.org/10.1016/j.cirpj.2020.02.002

9. Liu, M., Fang, S., Dong, H., Xu, C.: Review of digital twin about concepts, technologies, and industrial applications. J. Manuf. Syst. **58**, 346–361 (2021). https://doi.org/10.1016/j.jmsy.2020.06.017

10. Lu, Y., Liu, C., Wang, K., Huang, H., Xu, X.: Digital twin-driven smart manufacturing: connotation, reference model, applications and research issues. Robot. Comput. Integr. Manuf. **61**, 101837 (2020). https://doi.org/10.1016/j.rcim.2019.101837

11. Cimino, C., Negri, E., Fumagalli, L.: Review of digital twin applications in manufacturing. Comput. Ind. **113**, 103130 (2019). https://doi.org/10.1016/j.compind.2019.103130

12. Qi, Q., Tao, F., Zuo, Y., Zhao, D.: Digital twin service towards smart manufacturing. Procedia CIRP **72**, 237–242 (2018). https://doi.org/10.1016/j.procir.2018.03.103

13. Caputo, F., Greco, A., Fera, M., Macchiaroli, R.: Digital twins to enhance the integration of ergonomics in the workplace design. Int. J. Ind. Ergon. **71**, 20–31 (2019). https://doi.org/10.1016/j.ergon.2019.02.001

14. Martin, G., et al.: Luminaire digital design flow with multi-domain digital twins of LEDs. Energies **12** (2019)

15. Liu, Q., Zhang, H., Leng, J., Chen, X.: Digital twin-driven rapid individualised designing of automated flow-shop manufacturing system. Int. J. Prod. Res. **57**, 3903–3919 (2019). https://doi.org/10.1080/00207543.2018.1471243

16. Angrish, A., Starly, B., Lee, Y., Cohen, P.: A flexible data schema and system architecture for the virtualization of manufacturing machines (VMM). J. Manuf. Syst. **45**, 236–247 (2017). https://doi.org/10.1016/j.jmsy.2017.10.003

17. Liu, J., Zhou, H., Tian, G., Liu, X., Jing, X.: Digital twin-based process reuse and evaluation approach for smart process planning. Int. J. Adv. Manuf. Technol. **100**, 1619–1634 (2019)

18. Karanjkar, N., Joglekar, A., Mohanty, S., Prabhu, V., Raghunath, D., Sundaresan, R.: Digital twin for energy optimization in an SMT-PCB assembly line. In: Proceedings–2018 IEEE International Conference On Internet Of Things And Intelligence System, IOTAIS 2018, pp. 85–89 (2019)

19. Papcun, P., et al.: Augmented reality for humans-robots interaction in dynamic slotting "chaotic storage" smart warehouses. In: IFIP International Conference on Advances In Production Management Systems, pp. 633–641 (2019)

20. Witkowski, K.: Internet of things, big data, industry 4.0–innovative solutions in logistics and supply chains management. Procedia Eng. **182**, 763–769 (2017). https://doi.org/10.1016/j.proeng.2017.03.197

21. Zafarzadeh, M., Wiktorsson, M., Baalsrud Hauge, J.: A systematic review on technologies for data-driven production logistics: their role from a holistic and value creation perspective. Logistics **5**, 24 (2021)

22. Zhou, F., et al.: A survey of visualization for smart manufacturing. J. Vis. **22**, 419–435 (2019). https://doi.org/10.1007/s12650-018-0530-2

23. Vrba, Pavel, Kadera, Petr, Jirkovský, Václav., Obitko, Marek, Mařík, Vladimír: New trends of visualization in smart production control systems. In: Mařík, Vladimír, Vrba, Pavel, Leitão, Paulo (eds.) HoloMAS 2011. LNCS (LNAI), vol. 6867, pp. 72–83. Springer, Heidelberg (2011). https://doi.org/10.1007/978-3-642-23181-0_7

24. Maljovec, D., et al.: Rethinking sensitivity analysis of nuclear simulations with topology. In: IEEE Pacific Visualization Symposium, 2016-May, pp. 64–71 (2016)
25. Jo, J., Huh, J., Park, J., Kim, B., Seo, J.: LiveGantt: interactively visualizing a large manufacturing schedule. IEEE Trans. Vis. Comput. Graph. **20**, 2329–2338 (2014)
26. Wu, W., Zheng, Y., Chen, K., Wang, X., Cao, N.: A visual analytics approach for equipment condition monitoring in smart factories of process industry. In: IEEE Pacific Visualization Symposium

Trends, Challenges and Applications of Digital Lean Paradigm

Industry 4.0 Technologies as Drivers for Eliminating Waste in Lean Production: A French-Norwegian Study

Anne Zouggar Amrani[1(✉)] and Daryl Powell[2,3]

[1] University of Bordeaux, Ims-Lab, UMR CNRS, 5218 Talence, France
anne.zouggar@ims-bordeaux.fr
[2] Norwegian University of Science and Technology, Trondheim, Norway
daryl.powell@sintef.no
[3] SINTEF Manufacturing, Raufoss, Norway

Abstract. The aim of this paper is to provide insights about the operational performance improvements that may arise from the combination of Industry 4.0 technologies with the tools of Lean Production. Indeed, companies and their decision makers are looking for actionable knowledge around the usefulness of Industry 4.0 technologies and their inclusion in existing operational excellence programs. Lean is a tried and tested means of promoting better thinking in organizations, contributing to an increase in customer satisfaction and business performance. The emergent technologies of industry 4.0 are also influencing performance improvement in both the development and delivery of products and services. Yet actionable knowledge of the combination of Lean Production and Industry 4.0 is relatively immature and requires deeper analysis. This paper presents insights into the possible integration of Lean Production and Industry 4.0 technologies by analyzing multiple case studies in France and Norway. We suggest an approach that depicts the way in which such integration can reduce and ultimately eliminate waste.

Keywords: Lean Production · Industry 4.0 · New technologies · Operational performance

1 Introduction

For many decades, Lean Production (LP) has proven itself to be a powerful way of thinking, an adapted managerial approach and set of tools to reduce inefficiency and improve the operational performance. However, lean thinking spans beyond the simple tools of operational and productivity improvement. It is a global learning approach that empowers teams and individuals, enabling them to solve problems by engaging in their own learning process – discovering and exploring problems and discussing interesting, novel solutions. Many companies around the world have experimented with LP and have been satisfied by the positive results.

D. Y. Kim et al. (Eds.): APMS 2022, IFIP AICT 664, pp. 567–574, 2022.
https://doi.org/10.1007/978-3-031-16411-8_65

The emerging technologies of Industry 4.0 (I4.0) are nowadays grasping the interest of many decision makers in various companies of different sizes, in different sectors, and on different hierarchical levels in the company. Indeed, the new technologies may be useful for large companies and SMEs alike, from automotive industry to food and pharmaceutical, from engineer-to-order (ETO) [1] context to make-to-stock (MTS), and from research and development services to production and maintenance departments. However as stated in [2] the competencies and the know-how about the use, choice, and deployment of these new technologies is still problematic. The decision makers are often tackling the problem of the relevancy of the tools to their contexts [3], the contribution of their choice to ecological standards [4], and the difficulty to match the technologies contribution with LP initiatives. Grasping the relevancy of using both LP and I4.0 is therefore an interesting step which leads to greater combined optimization potential, accelerated operational improvement, and increased learning within and across teams [5].

In the following section, we present a literature review to position our contribution in the research community. The problem statement is provided in Sect. 3 summarizes the current challenges for decision makers and outlines the remaining gap. Thus consolidating the research topic and offering insights may increase our understanding of the association of both LP and I4.0 technologies.

2   Literature Review

Many research publications mention the benefits of combining LP and I4.0 [6–14]. For example, Perreira et al. [6] analyzes over 54 articles and finds that 55% present I4.0 as enhancing LP efficiency. Among the technologies presented are cyber-physical systems (CPS), additive manufacturing (3D printing), and cloud computing. Bittencourt [7] highlights the essential fact that the enhanced process capability of LP is further improved through the integration of I4.0.

Only 45% of the documents reviewed highlighted the support of LP for I4.0. Buer et al. [8] points out that a high Lean implementation level enables successful digitalization. As such, the literature often reveals a lean first, then digitalize approach (e.g., Powell et al. [9]). However, it is also interesting to analyze situations when I4.0 is adopted and perceive how LP can also be considered thereafter. Ciano et al. [10] remind that when I4.0 is implemented first, managers can take benefit of value stream mapping (VSM) to reinforce vertical integration and succeed in technology deployment. Rosin [11] establishes a wide analysis to find the linkage between LP and I4.0 without an in-depth analysis into how they influence performance improvement.

Regarding the useful combination of both paradigms stated in the literature, we would like to go deeper in this analysis to understand not only if one is influencing the other and in which chronology but also to perceive in which ways both paradigms can be linked to influence operational performance.

3   Problem Statement

As authors resident to France and Norway, we notice that companies in these countries have demonstrated an increase in performance and productivity when using LP and

I4.0 in isolation and indeed in association. The combination of the two approaches obviously exists, and the intention of using both paradigms for operational improvement is obviously perceived, however the way this combination has been done remains unclear. Is it just managerial choice? Is it a coincidental feeling of experience? Is it a benchmark done with competitors? Is it a technological opportunity? For the moment there is no clear model or roadmap helping managers to perceive similarities and common points of LP and I4.0 integration to allow a replicable deployment and help as a decision-support tool towards a common deployment.

In the following figure (Fig. 1) we have chosen to analyze the situation regarding the common deployment of LP and I4.0 in France and Norway. Four case studies will be described (two from each country, from aerospace and automotive sectors) to perceive the strengths and/or weaknesses during the deployment of both paradigms. Indeed, an analysis of real situations reveals actionable knowledge as to how a successful combination of LP and I4.0 is possible. We also identify gaps to pursue with further research. This combined study is useful for understanding how to propose a better parallel transformation using LP and I4.0 in different companies.

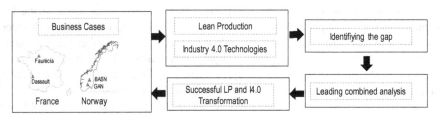

Fig. 1. Positioning of the paper – Problem statement

3.1   Lean and Industry 4.0 – French Cases

Dassault Aviation in France (Mérignac – Bordeaux) is a French producer of the Falcon business jet. It has based its lean approach upon its *Amelioration de la réactivité en Production* (ARP) program, which means "Improvement of the reactivity in Production". In parallel the company is leading technological transformation through adoption of Digital twin, the use of Fabrication laboratories (fablabs) for production, and 3D printed components for spare parts, reducing the waiting times in production lines and speeding up the maintenance repair times. Sensors and internet of things (IOT) have also proved useful, deployed to pursue and monitor the state of the machines (Temperature, vibration, etc.), with many parameters monitored in real time remotely to enable the predictive maintenance program. Evidence of both LP and I4.0 are prominent in this large Aeronautic Group [15] and the relevance of LP tools adoption in aerospace has already been demonstrated in [16].

In the automotive industry, we chose the example of Faurecia (Caligny), a French producer of several automotive systems. They have been labelled in France, in 2017, by AIF Alliance Francaise de l'industrie, as being an example of the factory of the Future. Indeed, this company, beside the typical tools-oriented LP approach (e.g., Just-in-Time, which is well implemented), has built up a strategic approach to LP called Faurecia Excellence System (FES). Faurecia has undertaken a big plan of new technologies integration in association with LP. The evidence coming from their development is well represented by the "digital Kanban". Kanban is an essential Lean tool [17]. A recent transformation project at Faurecia (in 2018) has been led to associate the principle of Just-in-Time in Logistics with new technologies. Near Field Communication (NFC) has been chosen as a solution to pick up the Kanban cards in production shop floors. When previously production points in different workshops were waiting the arrival of physical Kanban cards (with a risk of lost cards). Now the sourcing of the different components from the different shops is ensured by NFC terminals positioned in specific places to get by digital information (tags) the required quantities to trigger the delivery of the different points in the production shop.

3.2 Lean and Industry 4.0 – Norway Cases

GKN Aerospace Norway (GAN) is a Norwegian producer of complex jet engine components for military and civilian aero-engine programs. With the goal of reducing activities that add cost without adding any value (often referred to as waste in the lean terminology) and to improve operational efficiency, GAN introduced LP in its shopfloor operations in 2012. In 2018, GAN extended the focus of LP to other business areas, under the umbrella of business process improvement (BPI). This is because much of the waste and inefficiencies in the company were found outside of the manufacturing shopfloor. In these back office areas, the digitalization of otherwise manual/analogue business processes has contributed significantly to increased effectiveness. GAN was in fact awarded the prestigious title of Norway's smartest company in 2016 – having reduced its quality costs by 70% using digitalization and automation to provide real-time surveillance and self-optimizing, adaptive control of processes to drive systematic operational improvement.

In the automotive sector, we describe the case of Benteler Aluminum Systems Norway (BASN), a Norwegian producer of aluminum bumper beams and crash protection systems. The company has its own operational excellence program, Benteler Operating System – Lean Enterprise (BOSLE), and has more recently adopted several I4.0 technologies including IOT and big data applications to promote reliability and efficiency and to enhance the quality and sustainability of its products and processes. For example, Benteler's Production and Process Database (PPDB) and Smart Production Data Platform (SPDP) allows the company to continuously evaluate its wide range of process and product data easily and quickly. As a result, the company can understand technical issues in real time and recognize otherwise unknown correlations – supporting the BOSLE culture of continuous improvement and learning. This means better maintenance, higher output, and even greater quality.

Regarding the insights from these four cases, we can suggest for both practitioners and the research community a global framework which will help to perceive the common points between the improvement approaches presented through integrating LP and I4.0 technologies.

4 How to Combine Lean and Industry 4.0: The Elimination of Wastes as a Common Ridge

Using one of both paradigms (LP or I4.0) in industry is sufficient for improving operational performance. However, combining the two appears to hold greater promise, as the two paradigms positively influence the global performance of companies and increase the possibilities for the teams to continuously learn and improve their products and processes. Enabling managers to lead both with increased visibility, understanding how to transform the company and knowing the steps to establish coherent deployment would be highly appreciated in practice. Indeed, often the companies reveal to be "lost" when exposed to such mammoth transformations. We suggest in this section a combined approach.

As shown in the Fig. 2, even LP and I4.0 technologies are commonly targeting increase operational performance (costs, lead-times, quality, conformity, flexibility, robustness, service increase, energy consumption) and also increase the teams involvement and the skills development by building supporting learning systems [18]. Lean helps to develop managerial skills through key visual management techniques, helping individuals and teams to learn how to solve problems.

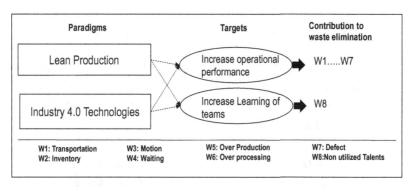

Fig. 2. Combined analysis: Waste as a common ridge between LP and I4.0

Emerging I4.0 technologies also help to empower the operator – contributing to the development of skills through real-time connectivity and monitoring, which also increases the learning abilities and enhances the company capabilities [19]. If a company is wondering whether to use LP or I4.0, we suggest that the common contribution is that towards the elimination of waste.

The 8 wastes are used as a discovery mechanism to find problems, through recognizing symptoms and exploring their underlying syndromes when doing Gemba walks [20]. If such problems and wastes go unaddressed, company's turnover may drop and the demotivation of the teams may rise. Active employee participation in the identification and reduction of such waste promises to improve the global process and helps to increase the outputs and the performance of the production system. The elimination of the 7 wastes in LP can be perceived as contributing to operational performance. The addition of the 8th waste (unutilized talent), as identified by Jeffrey Liker [21] is interesting to consider in LP and I4.0 integration, as it promotes a human-centric approach to its achievement. Indeed, many interesting technical and managerial skills are already existing in the company. As such, integration of LP and I4.0 may contribute to enhancing the learning system that empowers teams and helps to maintain high level of capability.

When highlighting that the elimination of waste is enhanced by combining LP and I4.0 technologies, we can proceed with the next analysis, showing paradigm by paradigm, tool by tool, the contribution to the elimination of the 8 wastes. For example, Table 1 presents how LP tools and I4.0 technologies are more likely to contribute to waste elimination. The assignment of the wastes was derived according to practical insights from the industrial cases described in the previous section. The choice of the relevant LP tool or I4.0 technology would become possible regarding this common ridge analysis.

Regarding the used operational performance (Service rate, conformity level, reliability rate, on-time-delivery, time-to-market, etc.) the manager can jointly follow up the impact of technologies of industry 4.0 used and the impact of lean practices implemented. The learning of teams can be measured by another set of managerial indicators (number of improvements/lean projects implemented, absence rate, level of involvement of the teams, etc.). The more the teams are consulted and included in the implementation, the more the team becomes autonomous and able to enlarge lean deployment.

Table 1. Lean and Industry 4.0 contributions to waste elimination

Paradigm	Analysed LP tools/I4.0 tech	Contribution to waste elimination
Lean production	Kanban	W2, W3, W4, W5, W8
	Poka Yoke	W1,W4, W5, W7
	Andon	W2, W7
	Visual management	W2, W3,W4, W5, W7
	SMED	W2, W3,W4, W5, W6
	5S	W3,W4, W5, W6, W7
	Plant layout	W1,W4, W5, W6
	Value stream mapping	W1–8
	Heijunka	W2,W4, W5, W6
Industry 4.0	Internet of things (IOT)	W2, W3,W4, W5, W6, W7
	RFID	W1, W2, W3,W4,W7
	Digital twin	W1, W3,W4, W6, W7
	Augmented reality/Virtual reality	W1,W2, W3,W4, W7
	Articial intelligence/Machine learning	W3,W4, W7
	Cloud computing/Edge computing	W3, W4, W6
	Robotics/Cobots	W1, W2, W3,W4, W7, W8

5 Conclusion and Perspectives

LP and I4.0 are two paradigms of upmost importance in the current economic context, where resource consumption must be reduced, ecological considerations are high, and customer requirements are extremely diversified. This preliminary analysis of LP and I4.0 integration for waste elimination is an initial attempt to figure out the linkages existing between the two paradigms for leading common transformations. From a technical point of view: waste such as over processing, waiting times, inventory, transportation, motion, overproduction, defects and non-utilized talents are the main elements to be aware of. From a managerial perspective, leading in tandem lean and I4.0 transformation requires careful consideration of pain-points (problems) to allow people to agree on the underlying problems, followed by convincing the team to lead transformation showing respect to them in order to get them on board. Initial "quick wins" demonstrating the effect of Lean and I4.0 implementation makes it easier to extend the approach to remaining departments. The next step would be to develop a global framework to provide a roadmap for companies and get feedback regarding the adoption of a structured approach – compared to the otherwise common, traditional approach to transformation (which is likely full of intuition, experience, and some benchmarking, but certainly not structured, modular, designed and detailed). At the moment we conclude that there is no "cookie-cutter" approach to standard sequencing a lean and I4.0 implementation. However, this will be investigated in a further study. Yet we strongly support the view presented in [9], which adopts a lean first … the digitalize approach. Further findings will be revealed in future work from the collaboration between France and Norway.

Acknowledgements. The authors would like to acknowledge support from the Research Council of Norway for funding the research project Lean Digital.

References

1. Powell, D.J., Strandhagen, J.O., Tommelein, I., Ballard, G., Rossi, M.: A new set of principles for pursuing the lean ideal in engineer-to-order manufacturers. Procedia CIRP **17**, 571–576 (2014)
2. Zouggar Amrani, A., Vallespir, B.: Lean production and industry 4.0 technologies: link and interactions. In: Dolgui, A., Bernard, A., Lemoine, D., von Cieminski, G., Romero, D. (eds.) APMS 2021. IAICT, vol. 630, pp. 697–703. Springer, Cham (2021). https://doi.org/10.1007/978-3-030-85874-2_76
3. Possik, J., Zouggar-Amrani, A., Vallespir, B.: Lean techniques impact evaluation methodology based on a co-simulation framework for a manufacturing system. Int. J. Comput. Integr. Manuf. IJCIM **35**, 91–111 (2021)
4. Powell, D.J., Lundeby, S., Chabada, L., Dreyer, H.: Lean six sigma and environmental sustainability: the case of a norwegian dairy producer. Int. J. Lean Six Sigma (2017)
5. Powell, D., Romero, D., Gaiardelli, P., Cimini, C., Cavalieri, S.: Towards digital lean cyber-physical production systems: Industry 4.0 technologies as enablers of leaner production. In: Moon, I., Lee, G.M., Park, J., Kiritsis, D., von Cieminski, G. (eds.) APMS 2018. IAICT, vol. 536, pp. 353–362. Springer, Cham (2018). https://doi.org/10.1007/978-3-319-99707-0_44
6. Pereira, A., Dinis-Carvalho, J., Alves, A., Arezes, P.: How Industry 4.0 can enhance lean practices. FME Trans. **47**, 810–822 (2019)

7. Bittencourt, V.L., Alves, A.C., Leão, C.P.: Industry 4.0 triggered by lean thinking: insights from a systematic literature review. Int. J. Prod. Res. **59**, 1496–1510 (2021)
8. Buer, S.V., Semini, M., Strandhagen, J.O., Sgarbossa, F.: The complementary effect of lean manufacturing and digitalisation on operational performance. Int. J. Prod. Res. **59**(7), 1976–1992 (2021)
9. Powell, D., Morgan, R., Howe, G.: Lean first ... then digitalize: a standard approach for Industry 4.0 implementation in SMEs. In: Dolgui, A., Bernard, A., Lemoine, D., von Cieminski, G., Romero, D. (eds.) APMS 2021. IAICT, vol. 631, pp. 31–39. Springer, Cham (2021). https://doi.org/10.1007/978-3-030-85902-2_4
10. Ciano, M., Dallasega, P., Orzes, G., Rossi, T.: One-to-one relationships between Industry 4.0 technologies and Lean Production techniques: a multiple case study. Int. J. Prod. Res. **59**(5), 1386–1410 (2020)
11. Rosin, F., Forget, P., Lamouri, S., Pellerin, R.: Impacts of Industry 4.0 technologies on Lean principles. Int. J. Prod. Res. **58**, 1644–1662 (2020)
12. Akkari, A.C.S., Valamede, L.S.: Lean 4.0: a new holistic approach for the integration of lean manufacturing tools and digital technologies. Int. J. Math. Eng. Manag. Sci. **5**, 851–868 (2020). https://doi.org/10.33889/IJMEMS.2020.5.5.066
13. Salvadorinho, J., Teixeira, L.: Stories told by publications about the relationship between Industry 4.0 and lean: systematic literature review and future research agenda. Publications (Basel) **9**(3), 29 (2021)
14. Santos, B.P., Enrique, D.V., Maciel, V.B.P., Lima, T.M., Charrua-Santos, F., Walczak, R.: The synergic relationship between Industry 4.0 and lean management: best practices from the literature. Manag. Prod. Eng. Rev. **12**(1) (2021)
15. Zouggar-Amrani, A.: Dassault Aviation using 4.0 Technologies - France. European I4EU project (2021). https://www.i4eu-pro.eu/wp-content/uploads/sites/2/2021/07/Dassault.pdf
16. Zouggar-Amrani, A., Ducq, Y.: Lean practices implementation in aerospace based on sector characteristics: methodology and case study. Int. J. Prod. Plan. Control **31**, 1313–1335 (2020)
17. Powell, D.J.: Kanban for lean production in high mix, low volume environments. IFAC-PapersOnLine **51**, 140–143 (2018)
18. Powell, D.J., Reke, E.: No lean without learning: rethinking lean production as a learning system. In: Advances in Production Management Systems: Production Management for the Factories of the Future. Springer, Heidelberg (2019)
19. Powell, D.J., Coughlan, P.: Rethinking lean supplier development as a learning system. Int. J. Oper. Prod. Manag. **40**, 921–943 (2020)
20. Balle, M., Chartier, N., Coignet, P., Olivencia, S., Powell, D., Reke, E.: The Lean Sensei. Go. See. Challenge. Lean Enterprise Institute, Inc (2019)
21. Liker, J.: The Toyota Way – 14 Management Principles. McGraw-Hill, London (2004)

Cyber-Physical Visual Management Systems in the Digital Lean Manufacturing World

David Romero[1]([⊠]) [iD], Matteo Zanchi[2] [iD], Daryl J. Powell[3] [iD], and Paolo Gaiardelli[2] [iD]

[1] Tecnológico de Monterrey, Monterrey, Mexico
david.romero.diaz@gmail.com
[2] University of Bergamo, Bergamo, Italy
{matteo.zanchi,paolo.gaiardelli}@unibg.it
[3] Norwegian University of Science and Technology, Trondheim, Norway
daryl.j.powell@ntnu.no

Abstract. The importance of Visual Management (or "Mieruka" as it is called in Japanese) has been largely demonstrated over the last few years, especially when it comes to the creation and management of data-rich environments for effective and efficient data-driven decision-making, such as digital lean smart factories. Although the different functions of visual systems are already known by the scientific community, further analysis of the capabilities and benefits provided by these tools, especially when enhanced with modern digital technologies, has yet to be provided. Therefore, this paper aims to frame a list of capabilities of the current physical visual systems, and their cyber/digital equivalents, according to a reference framework called the "7Is", which was extracted from a review of the current literature available. This may serve as a valid common reference for future research on this topic.

Keywords: Digital manufacturing · Smart manufacturing · Lean manufacturing · Digital lean manufacturing · Visual management · Mieruka · Digitalization

1 Introduction

Digital technologies have given rise to a new era of lean manufacturing, which extends the *lean philosophy* to the cyber world, known as "Digital Lean Manufacturing (DLM)". This new DLM world is characterised by "new data acquisition, data integration, data processing and data visualization capabilities to create different descriptive, predictive and prescriptive analytics applications to detect, fix, predict and prevent unstable process parameters and/or avoid quality issues inside defined tolerance ranges that may lead to any type of waste within the cyber- and physical- worlds" [1].

In this paper, from a *Visual Management perspective*, particular attention is given to the new *data visualization capabilities* offered by novel *digital technologies,* which play a significant role in spreading the right information; in the right visualization type, medium, and frequency; to the right person(s); at the right time for decision-making

D. Y. Kim et al. (Eds.): APMS 2022, IFIP AICT 664, pp. 575–585, 2022.
https://doi.org/10.1007/978-3-031-16411-8_66

and/or action-taking. Furthermore, this paper aims to create awareness of the potential *information overload phenomena* [2] in smart factories that are data-rich environments with the "danger" of exceeding the information processing capacity of their workers, which may lead to counteract the benefits of data availability for data-driven decision-making. Hence, proper *information visualization* is key to minimising the workers' cognitive load (and avoiding *Cognitive Muri/Overburden*) in data-rich environments for effective and efficient data-driven decision-making and action-taking.

The ultimate goal of this paper is to deepen the knowledge regarding the implications of adopting new *digital technologies* to support traditional *visual management practices and systems' functions*. Based on a literature review, the functions that characterize present *Visual Management Systems* are first identified and then used by a team of lean and digital lean experts to create a map of the opportunities and limitations arising from their digitization: *Digital Visual Management Systems*.

2 Visual Management

Visual Management (VM) (or *Mieruka* as it is called in Japanese) is "the lean practice of connecting and aligning organisational information with the process environment and stakeholders, employing stimuli that directly address one or more human senses to call for action" [3]. VM is encouraged in lean management because workers respond to and process *visual information* much better than with any other of their senses [4]. In fact, 90% of information transmitted to the brain is "visual", and workers tend to remember only 20% of what they hear, yet 80% of what they saw [4]. Moreover, VM is also promoted, particularly for shopfloor/factory management, because it helps to understand the state of production, whether it is running correctly or not, as well as the configuration of different working areas and stations, and how to reach them and what to pay attention to—e.g. for troubleshooting [5].

VM has been mainly developed, over the years, through practitioner efforts rather than theoretical insights; therefore, there is actually a lack of a solid, shared theoretical background about its development and practice [6]. In particular, it is unclear which *Mieruka functions* [3] lead to which specific benefits, and which are the challenges associated with their application [6]. This "uncertainty" becomes even more relevant today because of the *digitization* and/or *digital-enhancement efforts* of many of the *Mieruka functions* as lean researchers and practitioners rethink traditional VM systems and tools for the new DLM world (or Industry 4.0) [7]. Furthermore, the *digitization of information* and *digital transformation of processes* can lead to new forms of waste and overload [1, 8]. Therefore, it becomes of significant importance to understand whether and to what extent *digitization* changes the different functions of *Mieruka*, improving or worsening their relative effects.

3 Methodology

This research work was developed in two steps. First, a literature review on *Mieruka*, contextualized within the Lean Manufacturing paradigm, was carried out to understand the distinctive characteristics and functionalities of VM practices, systems, and tools.

Web of Science, Scopus, and Google Scholar databases were consulted to collect useful papers related to the topic under analysis. The analysis was conducted independently by the authors of this paper with a theoretical and practical experience in (digital) lean manufacturing to identify the distinctive characteristics and functionalities of *Mieruka*.

An initial research attempt, carried out by inputting combinations of different keywords belonging respectively to the semantic fields of *Lean Manufacturing* (i.e. *Mieruka*) and *Visual Management* (with respective synonyms) allowed, by setting up appropriate filters related to the scientific areas of competence (mostly related to the engineering field) and the required type of document (journal or conference papers or book chapters), to obtain an initial selection of 99 papers which, following the reading phase of the abstracts, was then narrowed down to a total of 75 analysed documents.

Some subsequent meetings have allowed resolving any differences of opinion, thus arriving at the construction of a shared map of VM characteristics and functions. Afterwards, and as the second step, a brainstorming session with factory managers and lean experts took place to understand how current *digitization* and *digital transformation efforts* are "affecting" traditional VM practices, systems, and tools on the shop floor, resulting in a final table (see Table 2) reporting the main benefits and the drawbacks regarding each of the *digitized* and/or *digitally-enhanced* features and functionalities identified in the literature review on *Visual Management Systems (VMSs)*.

4 Literature Review

The key importance of VM in working environments has been evidenced by the fact that this practice has always been a cornerstone of the Lean Manufacturing philosophy, and it is probably the most famous and adopted lean practice and tool in the world for its effectiveness. Indeed, *visual communication* is crucial to achieving better operational performance [9] and continuous improvement [10], as it facilitates instant monitoring of production activities while supporting staff involvement, by making information accessible to everyone for decision-making and action-tacking.

Scientific and managerial research suggests that *Mieruka practices* serve different operations management functions, but there are no studies in the literature that can provide a complete and comprehensive overview. The literature review conducted identified seven different functions absolved by *Visual Management,* which were called the "7Is", each of these may actually bring benefits to one or more principles underlying the Lean Manufacturing paradigm as stated in the "4P Model": Philosophy, Process, People & Partners, and Problem Solving [11]. A brief description of each of the seven "I" is reported in Table 1 with their main relationship with the 4Ps of Lean.

Table 1. Correlation between Mieruka's functions (7Is) and Liker's [11] 4P dimensions

Mieruka's Functions (7Is)	Involved P of Liker's model
Identify	Process (waste)
Inform	People about Process
Instruct/Illustrate	People on how to develop a Problem Solving
Involve	People (in the Process of optimization)
Instil/Inspire	Philosophy of lean
	Problem Solving approach
Improve	Process (transparency and performance)
Indicate	(How to) Plan a Process optimization

4.1 The 7Is in Traditional Mieruka Systems

Identify—*Visual systems* have the function of helping people identify an object (be it a product, a piece of equipment, or a document) in the shortest possible time, resulting in increased production efficiency. For instance, during *5S programs,* the adoption of "red tags" to identify unnecessary or unneeded items in workplaces can speed up the sorting process. Again, the use of tapes, symbols, and coloured shapes, facilitates the identification of spaces in which to store documents, materials, and equipment according to the principle of *"a place for everything and everything in its place",* while the use of floor and wall signs allows the identification of special areas or areas where access is limited to personnel and authorized vehicles. In the case of *Kanban,* instead, the tag is used to identify the contents of a specific container clearly and unambiguously, as well as the areas where the material is to be used, to avoid any risks of error during the delivery phase. Finally, *visual system tools* also serve to rapidly identify problems that may arise in the manufacturing field, for instance, the *Value Stream Map (VSM)* is an effective map for providing a precise and immediate image of the production process, allowing operators and managers to grasp faster and more clearly the problems inherent in the operational processes, to quickly draw up effective interventions [3].

Inform—Getting all the most important information directly to a single location, such as a machine status update or the latest production news, is a distinctive feature of visual systems [12], particularly those referred to as *Visualization Boards.* The creation of an information point of reference for people within the company simplifies the flow of information, as it makes it possible to become aware of the organisational context simply and at a single glance. Through *Andons,* for example, light signals and messages on visualization boards allow personnel to be informed almost instantaneously about various critical issues that have arisen, from a machine downtime, unsatisfactory production yields, and quality problems, to missing items in the production line or the warehouse. On the other hand, the QCDSM dashboards placed close to a workstation or production line can allow the area or department manager to promptly check whether the daily safety, quality, efficiency, and productivity objectives have been reached, to establish the most appropriate corrective actions. The use of these dashboards has proven to be fundamental in providing continuous feedback regarding the state of a production system, as this practice provides an observer with a snapshot of the performance trend and relative deviations from company targets, again at a glance. *Visual tools,* though, not only simplify 'top-down' and 'bottom-up' communication between management and departments but also facilitate the sharing of information between departments and functions operating at the same hierarchical level. For example, through a standard graphical language, the VSM eases the exchange of opinions and ideas among optimization team members.

Instruct/Illustrate—*Visual signals* are often designated to ensure manufacturing consistency through operator training. Operators can be instructed using visuals and simple diagrams on standards and procedures related to work cycles and quality control, equipment maintenance, safety management, and material picking and unloading. This category typically includes *One Point Lessons (OPLs),* simple written instructions aided by visual details (such as images, diagrams, and photos) designed to formalize an element of guidance and training on which steps, tools, and documents need to be used to efficiently carry out an operation, whether it be executive, control, or improvement. Making this kind of information available at the "point-of-use" for operators is key to reducing the amount of non-value-added activities [13]. Also, the *Kanban board* is a practical tool for instructing the operator, indicating with its three-coloured (i.e. red, yellow, and green) layout the logic of priorities that (s)he must adopt in production.

Involve—The adoption of *visual tools* such as *Visualization Boards* fosters a sense of shared ownership and connection to a team through a clear and public representation of team performance. For example, presenting operational results from individual teams on the corporate dashboard, rather than reporting the best team or operator on the boards in common areas of the factory, fosters positive internal competition and stimulates operators to challenge themselves for recognition from the company and their colleagues [12]. This climate of "positive" competition, which publicly rewards worthy teams without putting other crews in the shadow, improves *morale* among personnel through the encouragement of openness and willingness to share ideas and information by streamlining the flow of information and delivering it at the "point of use". For example, the QCDSM boards that allow operators to intervene directly in the feedback process through reporting their productivity, safety, quality, and cost issues, stimulate the workforce to proactively participate in the decision-making processes, fostering commitment, and self-esteem. If implemented correctly, *VM* can provide a solid foundation for continuous improvement, which requires a systematic, incremental, and iterative approach throughout the company that involves employees at all levels.

Instil/Inspire—*Visual tools* create a positive tension within the workgroup that drives people to pursue discipline [14], especially in terms of *"building a habit of maintaining correct procedures"*. In this regard, both the adoption of OPL systems and operating instructions for the execution of production, control, maintenance, or material management processes help to define an operational and behavioural discipline to be followed, which compliance favours the reduction of uncertainty, reduces process variability, and improves the monitoring and control of activities. Another key aspect characteristic of any *Visual Management project* resides in its ability to increase information transparency. In this case, the implementation of *visual planning tools* such as *Kanban boards* and *A3 sheets,* characterized by a focus on the visibility of information inherent in production planning, quality management, and problem-solving processes, contributes to the creation of a clear information network that, in turn, sensitizes staff to seek greater awareness and control of organisational and decision-making processes. This leads to the empowerment of workers operating inside an organisation, as *visual tools* create the conditions for capturing more quickly and more effectively the inherent tacit knowledge, thus, speeding up the training process of workers as well as the development of a creative approach and orientation towards continuous improvement and problem-solving.

Improve—The adoption of *visual procedures* often allows to cut down non-quality and time-wasting connected to production and control activities, thus, generating a significant increase in the speed of execution [5]. The use of *Kanban,* for instance, helps to reduce production stops due to lack of material or delivery errors, if adequately supported by suppliers able to work according to the same kind of logic. *Visual Management* also encourages management by facts, namely the management of people and processes based on data and statistics rather than guesswork and intuition, which helps managers and team leaders guide and improve the quality of tasks and projects through the use of a rigorous methodology. *VSM,* for example, proves to be particularly adherent to this benefit, as it shows new opportunities for improvement at a glance through the creation of the future state value stream map.

Indicate (how to plan)—Thanks to their high versatility, *visual tools* facilitate planning processes of production activities and more. While the *Heijunka board* helps to visually scan the pace of production in accordance with customer needs, the *Kanban board* supports the planning of improvement projects by displaying the contents of the work (by theme, assignment, deadline) and the optimization of the interventions, by separating actions in relation to the capabilities and availability of individuals in a specific period of time [14]. In line with the scientific method of problem-solving, the *PDCA cycle* supports the team for optimisation in defining objectives, constructing a plan of action, and its execution and control. The adoption of *visual tools,* finally, enables the corrective actions necessary for the realignment between objectives and performances achieved. In this sense, the *X-Matrix* is a powerful method for effective strategy deployment and communication of long-term goals.

4.2   The 7Is in Digital or Digitally-Enhanced Mieruka Systems

Identify—This *Mieruka function* has been digitally-enhanced in the DLM world with the use of *Auto-ID (Automatic Identification) technologies* such as RFID (Radio-Frequency Identification) and NFC (Near Field Communication) that offer numerous benefits over traditional paper-based tagging and labelling solutions in the Industrial Internet of Things (IIoT). For example, offering proactively or passively not only the description of a *smart object* but also information about its location, availability, condition, usage, etc. [15]. Moreover, *Computer Vision Systems* are becoming big allies for automatic product quality inspection [16]. When it comes to the identification of spaces, *LED tapes, e-labels, and projection mapping technologies* can offer digitally-enhanced solutions to provide clear indications for fast picking and storage tasks to workers based on pick-to-light & put-to-light solutions aimed at reducing or eliminating the human error in these finding & storage operations in warehouses and supermarkets in the production line [17] (i.e. a kind of *Digital Poka-Yoke*). In the case of *e-Kanban, smart bins* enhance visual feedback (with e-labels), eliminate manual counting (with the help of sensors), and enable automatic e-notifications for restocking tasks, assisting workers in efficiently managing their inventory levels [18]. Finally, *IIoT-enabled Value Stream Maps (VMSs)* can offer, thanks to smart sensors, accurate and always actual (a.k.a. real-time) information about machine and human workstations performance to avoid material still standings due to lack of instructions [19].

Inform—*Visualization* [20] and *Digitalization* [21] are of the utmost relevance when improving information sharing and visualization methods in the DLM world. The creation of *IIoT-based Visualization Boards* offers great benefits like the automatic gathering of shopfloor data and its updated display in digital dashboards for supporting data-driven decision-making processes [22]. Moreover, the *digital-interactive interfaces* of modern digital dashboards offer the opportunity to display information (i.e. data visualization) according to their user requirements providing the right amount of information, in the right format depending on the complexity of the decision to be made, so information overload and misinterpretation be avoided [22]. Furthermore, through *Digital Andon devices* (i.e. tablets, smartphones, smartwatches, and head-mounted displays), information can be proactively delivered and visualized by the right workers using targeted e-notification systems to quickly react to any production abnormalities [23]. Lastly, the use of *QCDSM Digital and IIoT-based Dashboards* allows instant (i.e. display of "real-time" information) and proactive (i.e. alerting based on predictive analytics) feedback regarding the present and possible future state of a production system [22, 23].

Instruct/Illustrate—*Visual signals* are designated to ensure production consistency through operator training. In the DLM world, such signals have become also "digital" by means of *Augmented Reality (AR) devices,* such as smart glasses and projectors, that overlaid in real-time information to the worker. Hence, AR can be considered a key enabling technology for improving the transfer of information from the digital to the physical world in a non-intrusive way for the operator, becoming an enabler of *Digital Assistance Systems* for reducing human errors (i.e. a *Digital Poka-Yoke*) and at the same time reducing the dependence on printed work instructions, computer screens, and operator memory for augmented operator performance [24].

Involve—*Digital and IIoT-based Leaderboards,* as "gamified" visual performance boards [25], can provide real-time performance information and foster positive internal competition and stimulate operators to challenge themselves for recognition from the company and their colleagues at the same time that the workforce is driven to the desired QCDSM production objectives. Furthermore, also the DLM world, the use of *Visualization Boards* with *Digital-Interactive Interfaces* (i.e. with dimmed visual elements, drop-down menus, slicers, etc.) promotes workforce engagement with the visual information displayed on the boards by offering workers the possibility of customizing their dashboards, faceting the data in these through data filters and slicers, and cross-highlighting and annotating the data available for a more personal analysis of the data items that are relevant for him/her [26] – e.g. for performance monitoring and continuous improvement action.

Instil/Inspire—In the DLM world, *Digital Poka-Yokes* can provide digitally-enhanced visual aids and light/voice-guided steering mechanisms to prevent deviations from Standard Work or Operating Procedures (SWOs/SOPs) so defects can avoid, and the speed of work be increased in a reliable way [27]. Furthermore, *Digitally-enhanced Visual Planning Tools* such as *Kanban boards* and *A3 sheets* offer new planning and control as well as problem-solving features based on integrated simulation technologies for testing and scheduling of countermeasures before their life implementation, and later progress tracking based on IIoT technologies [28].

Improve—The adoption of *AR-enhanced Visual Procedures* in the DLM world often allows for higher productivity rates and error-proof processes with the help of *Digital Poka-Yokes*. *Digital Assistance Systems* can act as guiding and fail-safe mechanisms, as well as teaching-learning mechanisms, facilitating making the correct action far easier than the mistake and detecting any mistake for immediate correction [24, 27]. Furthermore, the use of *e-Kanban* helps to identify the exact amount of what and when is needed [18]. Lastly, *Visual Management* promotes a data-driven approach for decision-making using descriptive, predictive, and prescriptive data analytics to detect, fix, predict and prevent unstable process parameters and avoid quality issues (e.g. VSM 4.0 [19], Quality 4.0 [29]).

Indicate (how to plan)—In the DLM world, *IIoT-based Heijunka boards* are able to automatically scan the pace of production, thanks to smart sensors, and support a "truly holistic" production (re-)scheduling in real-time and just-in-sequence logic for avoiding waste risk creation due to the lack of a systemic scheduling approach [1, 30]. Furthermore, a *Digitally-enhanced PDCA cycle* can automate and/or augment its data acquisition, data integration, data processing, and data visualization activities with the use of IIoT, data analytics, and real-time visualization technologies for avoiding continuous improvement decisions/actions based on obsolete data [31].

5   Discussion

A growing interest in benefits and criticalities concerning the application of *Digital Technologies* in the field of *Visual Management* has risen in recent years [32], but whether and to what extent the adoption of these technologies is effectively useful or not is still unclear. Based on the interpretation of the "7Is" functions, a discussion with some lean and digital lean manufacturing experts has enabled the building of Table 2, where the pros and the cons of emerging *digital technologies* supporting *Mieruka* are summarized.

Table 2. Benefits and criticalities of the influence of digital technologies on Mieruka

	Pros	Cons
Identify	• Computer vision systems can be used to identify product quality deviations and communicate these to the operators • Pick-to-light and put-to-light devices serve as digital poke-yokes	• Over-reliance on technology may cause operators to feel redundant, causing boring work
Inform	• Augmented Reality (AR) and Intelligent Personal Assistants (e.g. chatbots) can enhance the transmission of relevant information to human operators • Smart devices (e.g. phones/tablets) can serve as digital andons	• AR headsets still cause motion sickness in many users; projection mapping solutions and digital widescreens may be a safe middle-ground
Instruct/ Illustrate	• AR can be used to instruct operators on standard work procedures, both in training and in the operation phase. AR can also be used to illustrate important knowledge points (quality critical data)	• AR headsets still cause motion sickness in many users, consequently, traditional means of communicating knowledge points may remain the preferred choice of workers
Involve	• Mobile computing and wearables can be used to proactively involve operators in problem-solving (e.g. quality control circles)	• General Data Protection Regulation (GDPR) and observation of operators' habits may cause issues with their involvement (the connectivity paradox)
Instil/ Inspire	• Karakuri IIoT (low-cost IIoT) can be used to inspire operators to discover new means of triggering and communicating visual information • Digitalization of the A3 process on smart devices	• IIoT-push could lead to the creation of digital waste rather than contributing to solving genuine problems • A3 reports writing with a pen and paper requires more mental energy and engages more areas of the brain than when pressing keys on a computer keyboard or smart device
Improve	• The visual communication of real-time data using big data analytics and cloud/ edge computing can serve as a driver for improvement activity (e.g. descriptive, predictive, and prescriptive analytics)	• Operators may become dependent on the data to identify "improvement" rather than using their own eyes and hands to find facts at the Gemba
Indicate	• Electronic transmission of visual production instructions and signals/ cues (e.g. e-Kanban)	• e-Kanban may be falsely optimized, disengaging human creativity to further improve the process

6 Conclusions and Further Research

A general overview of various *Visual Management* (or *Mieruka*) lean practices were presented in this paper, which looks at its seven main functions (here referred to as the "7Is") that have been supported by classic *physical* visual practices, systems, and tools out from the traditional Lean Manufacturing world, and now are aimed to be supported as well by new *cyber/digitally-enabled ones* emerging from the novel *Digital Lean Manufacturing world* [1]. Furthermore, a first effort to understand the pros and cons of this *digitalization phenomenon of Visual Management* was conducted. Nevertheless, this should be considered as further research work as lean researchers and practitioners continue to rethink traditional VM practices, systems, and tools in light of new their potential digital capabilities, which are yet to be studied in detail to clearly determine their specific benefits and implementation challenges so these contribute to digitally-enhanced value-creation and not digital waste (e.g. information overload).

References

1. Romero, D., Gaiardelli, P., Powell, D., Wuest, T., Thürer, M.: Digital lean cyber-physical production systems: the emergence of digital lean manufacturing and the significance of digital waste. IFIP, AICT **535**, 11–20 (2018)
2. Edmunds, A., Morris, A.: The problem of information overload in business organisations: a review of the literature. Inf. Manag. **20**, 17–28 (2000)
3. Tezel, B.A., Koskela, L.J., Tzortzopoulos, P.: The functions of visual management. international research symposium, pp. 201–219 (2009). http://usir.salford.ac.uk/10883/
4. Sivak, M.: The information that drivers use: is it indeed 90% visual? Perception **25**(9), 1081–1089 (1996)
5. Galsworth, G.D.: Visual workplace/visual thinking. Visual-Lean Enterprise Press, Portland (2005)
6. Koskela, L., Tezel, A., Tzortzopoulos, P.: Why visual management? 26th annual conference of the international group for lean construction, pp. 250–260. Chennai, India (2018)
7. Fenza, G., Loia, V., Nota, G.: Patterns for visual management in industry 4.0. Sensors 21(19), 6440 (2021)
8. Romero, D., Gaiardelli, P., Powell, D., Thürer, M., Wuest, T.: Cyber-physical waste reduction and elimination strategies in the digital lean manufacturing world. IFIP, AICT **566**, 37–45 (2019)
9. Bititci, U., et al.: Impact of visual performance management systems on the performance management practices of organisations. Int. J. Prod. Res. **54**(6), 1571–1593 (2015)
10. Olszewski, L., Bhattacharya, A., Harrington, T.S.: Exploring visual management and continuous improvement in a manufacturing context: a structured bibliometric analysis. 23rd Cambridge INT'l. Manufacturing Symposium (2019). https://doi.org/10.17863/CAM.45890
11. Liker, J.K.: The Toyota Way, 14 Management Principles from the World's Greatest Manufacturer. McGraw-Hill, New York (2004)
12. Eaidgah, Y., et al.: Visual management, performance management and continuous improvement: a lean manufacturing approach. Lean Six Sig. **7**(2), 187–210 (2016)
13. Badger, A.S., et al.: A methodology to enhance equipment performance using the oee measure. Eur. J. Ind. Eng. **2**(3), 356–376 (2008)
14. Tezel, A., et al.: Visual management in production management: a literature synthesis. J. Manuf. Technol. Manag. **27**(6), 766–799 (2016)

15. Rahmadya, B., et al.: Ultra-high frequency band radio frequency identification tag enabling color-change for inventory management systems: a color-change tag. IEEE J. Radio Freq. Identif. **4**, 101–106 (2020)
16. Vergara-Villegas, O.O., Cruz-Sánchez, V.G., de Jesús Ochoa-Domínguez, H., de Jesús Nandayapa-Alfaro, M., Flores-Abad, Á.: Automatic product quality inspection using computer vision systems. In: García-Alcaraz, J., Maldonado-Macías, A., Cortes-Robles, G. (eds.) Lean Manufacturing in the Developing World, pp. 135–156. Springer, Cham (2014). https://doi.org/10.1007/978-3-319-04951-9_7
17. Hofmann, E., Rüsch, M.: Industry 4.0 and the current status as well as future prospects on logistics. Comput. Ind. **89**, 23–34 (2017)
18. El Abbadi, L., El Manti, S., Houti, M., Elrhanimi, S.: Kanban system for industry 4.0. Eng. Technol. **7**(4.16), 60–65 (2018)
19. Hartmann, L., Meudt, T., et al.: Value stream method 4.0: holistic method to analyse and design value streams in the digital age. Procedia CIRP **78**, 249–254 (2018)
20. Lindlöf, L., Södererg, B.: Pros and Cons of lean visual planning: experiences from four product development organisations. Technol. Intell. Plann. **7**(3), 269–279 (2011)
21. Fast-Berglund, Å., Harlin, U., Åkerman, M.: Digitalisation of meetings—from white-board to smart-boards. Procedia CIRP **41**, 1125–1130 (2016)
22. Steenkamp, L.P., Hagedorn-Hansen, D., Oosthuizen, G.A.: Visual management system to manage manufacturing resources. Procedia Manuf. **8**, 455–462 (2017)
23. Mohamad, E., et al.: Framework of andon support system in lean cyber-physical system production environment. In: Manufacturing Systems Division Conference, pp. 404–405 (2019)
24. Rodriguez, L., Quint, F., Gorecky, D., Romero, D., Siller, R.: Developing a mixed reality assistance system based on projection mapping technology for manual operations at assembly workstations. Procedia Comput. Sci. **75**, 327–333 (2015)
25. Keepers, M., Romero, D., Hauge, J.B., Wuest, T.: Gamification of operational tasks in manufacturing. IFIP, AICT **591**, 107–114 (2020)
26. Sarikaya, A., Correll, M., et al.: What do wetalk about when we talk about dashboards? IEEE Trans. Vis. Comput. Graph. **25**(1), 682–692 (2019)
27. Sposito-Valamede, L., Santos-Akkari, A.C.: Lean 4.0: a new holistic approach for the integration of lean manufacturing tools and digital technologies. Int. J. Math. Eng. Manag. Sci. **5**(5), 851–868 (2020)
28. Nakazawa, S., Tanaka, T.: Development and application of kanban tool visualizing the work in progress. In: 5th IIAI International Conference on Advanced Applied Informatics (IIAIAAI), pp. 908–913 (2016)
29. Romero, D., Gaiardelli, P., Powell, D., Wuest, T., Thürer, M.: Total quality management and quality circles in the digital lean manufacturing world. IFIP, AICT **566**, 3–11 (2019)
30. Kjellsen, H.S., et al.: Heijunka 4.0—key enabling technologies for production levelling in the process industry. IFIP, AICT 630, 704–711 (2021)
31. Peças, P., Encarnação, J., et al.: PDCA 4.0: A new conceptual approach for continuous improvement in the industry 4.0 paradigm. Appl. Sci. 11(16), 7671 (2021)
32. Tezel, A., Aziz, Z.: From conventional to it-based visual management: a conceptual discussion. Inf. Technol. Constr. **22**, 220–246 (2017)

Lean Product Development for a Circular Economy: An Operations Management Perspective

Kristina Kjersem[1](✉), Bella Nujen[2], Eivind Rekke[3], Natalia Iyakmenko[3], and Daryl Powell[4]

[1] Møreforsking AS, Ålesund, Norway
Kristina.kjersem@moreforsking.no
[2] Faculty of Economics and Management, Department of International Business, NTNU, Ålesund, Norway
[3] SINTEF Manufacturing, Raufoss, Norway
[4] Faculty of Economics and Management, Department of Industrial Economics and Technology Management, NTNU, Ålesund, Norway

Abstract. For years, manufacturing companies have been working with developing and implementing lean thinking to continuously improve the management of their operations. Since lean thinking provides tools and approaches to solve problems enterprise-wide, there is an ambition among lean companies to use the lessons learned while applying lean, to develop and implement a more circular economy approach to their operations. However, extant research combining lean and circular economy concern mostly the business model level and there is a lack of research on how to bring circular economy thinking to the operations. Even though both lean thinking and circular economy emphasize the importance of designing products that can be manufactured in an efficient way, using as few resources as possible, and without waste, the extant literature combining these concepts refers mainly to the processes concerning the product's end of life. This paper deploys the 'by design' aspect of circularity through the lens of lean product development, a key element within the lean thinking concept.

Keywords: Circular economy · Lean product development

1 Introduction

The pressure on becoming sustainable challenges industry to shift existing business models and disrupt the way their operations are managed and performed. Even though business models and operations management (OM) models are deeply interrelated, they embody two different concepts. The first refers to how an organization realizes its revenues by capturing and delivering value to its customers. By contrast, OM refers to how an organization creates that value. OM includes the location where value adding activities are done, the information system supporting these operations, the network of contributing suppliers, as well as the management system that coordinates the overall value chain [1]. As such, OM entails a wider process of developing products that add value to the customer and society [2].

However, becoming sustainable implies to adapt or to change both the business and the operating models to deliver products that fit within the requirements imposed through the UN's sustainable goals. Among the tools developed for achieving these goals is the Circular Economy (CE) concept that aims at eliminating any types of waste from the design phase of a product throughout the manufacturing process, as well as its beginning of life to the end-life [3, 4]. Indeed, the concept of CE differs from the linear approach (i.e., produce-consume-dispose) by replacing the idea of 'throughput' with the idea of 'roundput' where resources are used but not used up [5] by the means of cyclical thinking [6].

In general, CE is considered a superior concept for achieving sustainability goals, but methods to implement CE in manufacturing operations are still scarce. Researchers have recommended combining lean thinking with CE to facilitate a better implementation of the latter [7–9]. Yet, despite these efforts, there is a lack of published work that provide viable results of the combination of these concepts towards sustainable OM [7]. In most extant research, CE has been introduced predominantly as a pathway for product life-cycle design and business model development while the CE concept in the context of OM has received a lesser amount of attention [10].

Furthermore, most research on lean and CE focuses on the waste reduction part of lean and on proposing models that combine lean (or green-lean) solutions with CE elements [7, 8]. Consequently, the focus is predominantly put on the direction of how to handle companies' current products but miss to introduce circularity at the product development phase from the OM perspective. This is rather interesting since CE is about products that are regenerative by design. Achieving that implies a radical change in the way products are designed and the way materials are selected and combined for each product. The challenges inherent in the required efforts might be solved by applying tools belonging to the Lean Product Development concept (LPD). To our knowledge, there is limited research where LPD is proposed as an approach to embrace when designing circular products. LPD was developed by Toyota as an integrated part of their OM system. They created each product by considering people, the whole manufacturing process as well as the technology needed for producing each new product. Such an approach allowed Toyota to focus on choosing the most appropriate materials, modularization elements, and other characteristics of a product while considering the constraints of the manufacturing line at theirs, as well as at suppliers' facilities [2].

With respect to a more holistic understanding of the topic, we derive this paper from theoretical and conceptual works to delineate potential opportunities of LPD within the context of CE. Thus, the following research question is posed: How can CE implementation benefit from LPD principles to realize more sustainable OM strategies?

2 Theoretical Background

2.1 Circular Economy

Among the most cited definitions of CE is the one provided by the Ellen MacArthur foundation who states that CE is "*an industrial system that is restorative or regenerative by intention and design*" [11]. The same organization identifies five pillars of the CE concept: 1) design out waste, 2) build resilience through diversity, 3) shift to renewable energy sources, 4) think in systems, and 5) think in cascade. Succinctly put, CE enables effective flows of materials, information, human resources, energy so that the natural and social capital can be rebuilt. The idea is to optimise systems rather than components, thus context is everything and, in order to provide productive and robust flows through continuous rebuilding of the capital stock, "design for fit" is an essential element [12].

While the concept of CE presents a great potential for achieving sustainable operations, the challenges for its adaptation and operationalization within most management styles of today, seem to remain unclear. An increasing number of new techniques, methods and models are being developed and most of these induce a complete change of the existing OM system. This requires investments in machines and materials as well as in upskilling the existent labor force. For most small and medium sized companies, it is rather challenging to accomplish such transitions due to higher capital and skills requirements [8]. In many aspects, the challenges are similar to those being aired with regards to lean thinking implementation.

Hence, while CE is rich in concepts and approaches, examination of pragmatic steps toward implementation often falls short [3]. Thus, to achieve a favourable integration of CE with OM, companies must identify specific meanings relevant to the manufacturing domain [10]. For that, there is a need to apply a form of system thinking across the whole life cycle of the product. A systematic approach can predict and avoid creating environmental problems by addressing and eliminating the root causes of these problems from the design phase [13]. To incentivize that, there is also a need for tangible design and engineering targets that can function as environmental key performance indicators [14].

2.2 Lean Product Development

Within OM, lean thinking is acknowledged as one the most successful paradigms for managing operations and in many cases implies a high beneficial impact on sustainability [15]. According to [16], understanding lean thinking requires a close look at every step in the value creation process, beginning with the process of developing and engineering the product and then continuing along the entire manufacturing chain until the customer is reached. Another perspective on lean thinking is provided by [17] who emphasizes the view of lean as a socio-technical system based on systematic routines that underlines scientific reasoning at all organizational levels.

Lean thinking as a concept was first introduced in the 1980's to describe a manufacturing system that transformed the traditional logic of mass production following a longitudinal study of the automotive industry [18]. A lean approach is capable of manufacturing a broad range of products in relatively low volumes at competitive costs

[18]. LPD seeks to enhance value and reduce cost from a product perspective [19]. As such, LPD practices can be described as 13 principles that together can help organizations design better products by " *appropriately integrating people, processes, tools, and technology to add value to the customer and society*" [2].

According to [2], the thirteen principles of LPD are: 1) Establish customer-defined value to separate value-added activity from waste. 2) Front-load the product development process while there is maximum design space to explore alternative solutions thoroughly. 3) Create a leveled product development flow. 4) Utilize rigorous standardization to reduce variation and create flexibility and predictable outcomes. 5) Develop a chief engineer system to integrate development from start to finish. 6) Organize to balance functional expertise and cross-functional integration. 7) Develop towering technical competence in all engineers. 8) Fully integrate suppliers into the product development. 9) Build in learning and continuous improvement. 10) Build a culture to support excellence and relentless improvement. 11) Adapt technology to fit your people and processes. 12) Align your organization through simple, visual communication. 13) Use powerful tools for standardization and organizational learning. These principles are grouped under three categories: process (principles 1 to 4), people (principles 5 to 10), and technology (principles 11 to 13) [2].

Adding to these principles, Toyota developed tools and guiding rules that can be applied when implementing each of these principles (for a detailed description, see [2]). To exemplify, among of the tools developed to support decision making in the design and engineering process while considering a holistic view of the entire value chain is the one called Obeya. This tool facilitates the process of making decisions through direct communication and information sharing, team integration, and maintaining partnerships [20]. The term defines systematic meetings with specialists from each department within the company. Each of these specialists brings specific knowledge to the process of developing a new product. Succinctly put, LPD is a holistic approach to manufacturing products through an integrative process where quality is built in, while waste is eliminated starting at the design and engineering phase [2].

Still, the implementation of lean thinking is perceived by many as a concept that does not concern for the environment since its focus is on improving the business processes. Meanwhile, several other authors do agree that lean thinking alongside improving business performance, also contributes to improving the environment [7, 9, 21]. The latter studies have indeed concluded that holistic frameworks are essential in deepening our understanding of how to jointly use lean while being environmentally and socially responsible [21]. This is also in line with E. Deming's ideas of modifying or replacing industrial processes to consume fewer resources and eliminate any form of waste [14].

3   Method

This paper is based on a literature study in two main domains: CE and LPD. Literature studies represent an essential element of any research as they: 1) enable mapping, summarizing, and evaluating the knowledge base relevant for a studied topic, and 2) provides guidance for future studies to address knowledge gaps [22]. To better understand the phenomenon under investigation, a literature review was carried out using the search terms: 'lean product development and circular economy' in several different styles within the following scientific databases: Science Direct, Google Scholar, and Web of Science. From an initial collection of 139 articles, non-peer-reviewed papers, theses, foreign texts, and duplications were removed. As such, 48 articles proceeded to be reviewed in full. Among these, several articles consider LPD as a tool towards sustainability at the business model level e.g., [14, 23] while CE is mentioned as an element within the sustainability approach. Other articles bring LPD as a supporting tool for knowledge exchange or learning within and among organizations aiming to become circular e.g., [24, 25]. However, none of the reviewed articles provide research about the applicability of LPD's principles and tools as an OM supporting model in the process of implementing CE.

4 Discussion

For most companies, implementing a CE involves radical changes of the business and the operating models. This is partly due to CE being applied as a disruptive and innovative economic model that relates to government policy, businesses, and consumers. At its core, CE is restorative and regenerative by design, structure, and objective. Through CE, products, components, and materials are designed to continuously add, recreate, and sustain value at all times. As such, CE challenges the existing business models and forces a rethinking of the many various aspects of OM and product utilization across the entire value chain [3]. To achieve circularity, products must be designed with the disassembly process in mind leading in this way to more predictable material recovery rates while generating more value and less waste [26]. Most of the articles combining lean and CE assume the elimination of waste as one of the main connecting principles. However, real circularity can be achieved only by designing the product in a way that eliminates any form of waste along the whole value chain.

Reviewing the existing research that combines lean thinking and CE implemented at the OM level proved to show a lack of published work on this particular topic, also in line with the conclusions of [7]. At the same time a contrasting difference between lean and CE is, according to [8], that lean focuses on the immediate and effective usage of the resource within a specific process, while CE takes a more holistic approach from systems perspective, as to enhance the value of the resource even after the ended life cycle of the product. Yet, this analysis lacks to consider the systematic approach provided by LPD where people, processes, and technology are integrated towards a holistic view of the entire value chain.

Nevertheless, there is a large gap on the literature combining LPD and CE. The literature on CE accentuate that companies should focus on the design phase, if not, companies can risk missing out the cost-and environmental benefits that can be reaped from disassembly, reuse, refurbish, or remanufacture each element of the product to be disposed. Without such effort, there will always be a poor rate of circularity within the whole OM process. It is here LPD can provide valuable insights and methods. LPD argues that many of the attributes of a product are established during the design phase and the decisions taken at the early design stage therefore determine the scale of the environmental impacts. Sutherland et al. [13] capture the essence of this idea:

'a poor design, from an environmental standpoint, cannot really be remedied during manufacturing'. Thus, in order to succeed with CE in OM, companies need to include circular targets in the design and development of each new product.

LPD aspires to provide a system and structure to enable people to bring their best selves and contribute to making great products that are design efficient from both a financial and environmental perspective. One of the LPD principles refers to adapting technology to fit company's people and processes (principle 11). Applying this principle could reduce the amount of investment needed for implementing CE as without focusing on the people dimension, no transformation of product development will be able with regards to the business model aimed at. LPD emphasizes the collaborative aspects of developing a product and by using tools like Obeya rooms it gives the possibility of including issues connected to the end-of-life of the product within the design and engineering phase. Extending the number of participations in the product development process with specialists that address this part of the value chain will create better opportunities at the OM level and uncover uncaptured value within the existing business model. Since product development is a team sport, it takes effective collaboration to meet the targets, which are supported through having compatibility before completion and using Obeya rooms effectively.

Table 1 provides a tentative framework that depicts the applicability of the LPD within the five CE principles. The first five LPD principles resonate well with the first principle of circularity, which is design out waste. This can be done through building CE competence at both design and production levels while considering customers' requirements. Building resilience through diversity, the second CE principle, can be accomplished through developing people and by involving suppliers to be part of developing circular products (cf. Principles 6–9). Such approach is also necessary when applying a systematic thinking throughout the whole OM process so that the company can effectively adapt its processes and technology to support a circular model. The third and fifth CE—shift to renewable energy sources and think in cascade - can be added as desirable elements of the entire OM process that needs to be redesigned and improved continuously. Yet, this type of association needs to be tested in lean companies who are willing to apply LPD tools when implementing CE.

Implementing CE at the operational level in a company, is, like for lean, dependent on the level of understanding at the leadership level, the context of the implementation, and the level of training among the employees. There is no "one-solution fits all" type of approach and each company should first ensure at least a basic level of training of its people through continuous improvement possibilities. This literature-based study has found that while LPD in itself might appear agnostic to circular thinking, it is a system that could be effectively used to support adaptation of CE by using the tools developed for a successful LPD implementation. A circular product can be achieved through a close collaboration among all stakeholders including both the ones at the beginning of life as well as the ones dealing with the product after its lifecycle was completed.

Table 1. LPD and CE principles

	LPD Principles	CE Principles
1	Establish customer-defined value to separate value-added activity from waste	
2	Front-load the product development process while there is maximum design space to explore alternative solutions thoroughly.	
3	Create a leveled product development flow	
4	Utilize rigorous standardization to reduce variation and create flexibility and predictable outcomes	1) design out waste,
5	Develop a chief engineer system to integrate development from start to finish	
6	Organize to balance functional expertise and cross-functional integration	
7	Develop towering technical competence in all engineers.	2) build resilience through diversity
8	Fully integrate suppliers into the product development.	
9	Build in learning and continuous improvement.	3) shift to renewable energy sources
10	Build a culture to support excellence and relentless improvement.	
11	Adapt technology to fit your people and processes.	4) think in systems
12	Align your organization through simple, visual communication.	5) think in cascade.
13	Use powerful tools for standardization and organizational learning.	

5 Concluding Remarks

An important aspect of CE is to understand what customers consider valuable in regards to the final product and to include sustainable aspects as well as circularity aspects [14] from the design phase throughout the whole OM process.

Collaboration across departments and stakeholders create an understanding of the environmental implications of decisions at the design stage with clear roles and responsibilities for execution. Promoting a culture of sustainable development that integrate product development with circularity can become a key objective in lean companies. Part of a successful implementation of CE lays in training engineers in the principles, strategies, tools, and methods of CE so that these become a part of their professional development not just a constraint. LPD tools may be the missing holistic approach that most lean companies can use in becoming circular.

Acknowledgements. The authors acknowledge the support of the Research Council of Norway for the research project CIRCULÆR.

References

1. Joglekar, N., Parker, G., Srai, J.S.: Winning the race for survival: How advanced manufacturing technologies are driving business-model innovation, p.19 (2020)
2. Morgan, J., Liker, J.: The Toyota product development system. USA (2006)
3. Esposito, M., Tse, T., Soufani, K.: Introducing a circular economy: new thinking with new managerial and policy implications. Calif. Manage. Rev. **60**(3), 5–19 (2018)

4. Webster, K.: The Circular Economy: A Wealth of Flows, ed. E. MacArthur and W. Stahel.: Ellen MacArthur Foundation Publishing (2017)
5. Webster, K.: What might we say about a circular economy? some temptations to avoid if possible. World Futures: J. Gen Evol **69** (2013)
6. Homrich, A.S., et al.: The circular economy umbrella: trends and gaps on integrating pathways. J. Clean. Prod. **175**, 525–543 (2018)
7. Lim, M.K., et al.: Circular economy to ensure production operational sustainability: a green-lean approach. Sustain. Prod. Consumption **30**, 130–144 (2022)
8. Nadeem, S., et al.: Coalescing the lean and circular economy keywords (2019)
9. Nadeem, S., Garza-Reyes, J., Leung, S., Cherrafi, A., Anosike, A.I., Lim, M.K.: Lean manufacturing and environmental performance – exploring the impact and relationship. In: Lödding, H., Riedel, R., Thoben, K., von Cieminski, G., Kiritsis, D. (eds.) APMS 2017. IAICT, vol. 514, pp. 331–340. Springer, Cham (2017). https://doi.org/10.1007/978-3-319-66926-7_38
10. Korhonen, J., et al.: Circular economy as an essentially contested concept. J. Clean. Prod. **175**, 544–552 (2018)
11. MacArthur, F.: Towards a Circular Economy: Business Rationale for an Accelerated Transition, p. 20. Ellen MacArthur Foundation, UK (2015)
12. MacArthur, F.: Towards the Circular Economy - Opportunities for the Consumer Sector, p. 112. Ellen MacArthur Foundation, UK (2013)
13. Sutherland, J., et al.: Industrial sustainability: reviewing the past and envisioning the future. J. Manuf. Sci. Eng. **142**, 1–33 (2020)
14. Cooper, D.R., Appell, K.: Exploring how lean product and process development can promote industrial sustainability. In: ASME 2021 International Design Engineering Technical Conferences and Computers and Information in Engineering Conference (2021)
15. Kurdve, M., Bellgran, M.: Green lean operationalisation of the circular economy concept on production shop floor level. J. Clean. Prod. **278**, 123–223 (2021)
16. Womack, J., Jones, D., Roos, D.: The Machine That Changed The World. Rawson Associates, New York (1990)
17. Rother, M.: Toyota Kata: Managing People for Improvement, Adaptiveness and Superior Results. McGraw-Hill, New York (2009)
18. Krafcik, J.F.: Triumph of the Lean Production System. Sloan Manag. Rev. **30**, 41–52 (1988)
19. Reke, E., Powell, D.: Rethinking value – a means to end the whispering game. Procedia CIRP **104**, 1041–1045 (2021)
20. Schaeffer, J.A., Bellgran, M.: Spatial design and communication for improved production performance. In: The International 3rd Swedish Production Symposium. Göteborg, Sweden: Swedish Production Academy (2009)
21. Martínez León, H.C., Calvo-Amodio, J.: Towards lean for sustainability: understanding the interrelationships between lean and sustainability from a systems thinking perspective. J. Clean. Prod. **142**, 4384–4402 (2017)
22. Baker, M.: Writing a literature review. Mark. Rev. **1**, 219–247 (2000)
23. Schmitt, T., et al.: Beyond "Leanear" production: a multi-level approach for achieving circularity in a lean manufacturing context. J. Clean. Prod. **318**, 128531 (2021)
24. Agyabeng-Mensah, Y., et al.: Organisational identity and circular economy: are inter and intra organisational learning, lean management and zero waste practices worth pursuing? Sustain. Prod. Cons. **28**, 648–662 (2021)

25. Kvadsheim, N., Nujen, B., Powell, D., Reke, E.: Realizing value opportunities for a circular economy: integrating extended value stream mapping and value uncaptured framework. In: Dolgui, A., Bernard, A., Lemoine, D., von Cieminski, G., Romero, D. (eds.) APMS 2021. IAICT, vol. 630, pp. 739–747. Springer, Cham (2021). https://doi.org/10.1007/978-3-030-85874-2_81

26. Pawlik, E., et al.: Exploring the application of lean best practices in remanufacturing: empirical insights into the benefits and barriers. Sustainability **14**(1), 149 (2022)

Intelligent Poka-Yokes: Error-Proofing and Continuous Improvement in the Digital Lean Manufacturing World

David Romero[1]([⊠]) [iD], Paolo Gaiardelli[2] [iD], Daryl J. Powell[3] [iD], and Matteo Zanchi[2] [iD]

[1] Tecnológico de Monterrey, Monterrey, Mexico
david.romero.diaz@gmail.com
[2] University of Bergamo, Bergamo, Italy
{paolo.gaiardelli,matteo.zanchi}@unibg.it
[3] Norwegian University of Science and Technology, Trondheim, Norway
daryl.j.powell@ntnu.no

Abstract. Poka-Yoke devices have always been regarded by lean manufacturing companies as essential quality control and assurance tools to support efficient and effective manufacturing processes and procedures. Thanks to their ease of use and low cost, these devices help maintain high-quality standards and also encourage organisations to undertake Kaizen continuous improvement activities. With the advent of new digital and analytical technologies, these devices have undergone significant transformations. Based on a study of the scientific literature and the results of brainstorming sessions conducted with factory managers and lean experts, this paper analyzes how and to what extent digitalization changes the definitions, functions, approaches, and perspectives of traditional Poka-Yokes. Furthermore, it examines how the change in data collection, sharing, analysis, processing, and feedback (interpretation) approaches brought by the digitalization and smartification of Poka-Yoke devices affects the operational performance of modern Digital Lean Cyber-Physical Production Systems.

Keywords: Digital manufacturing · Smart manufacturing · Lean manufacturing · Digital lean manufacturing · Poka-Yoke · Error-proofing · Error prevention

1 Introduction

Digital Lean Manufacturing (DLM) leverages the potential of *cyber-physical quality management systems* (i.e. tools, techniques, and practices), particularly *quality control systems*, to increase the stability and performance of production processes towards (near-)zero-defect manufacturing [1]. One of those practices is the use of traditional and digitally-enhanced *Poka-Yokes* as one of the means to detect and predict errors and defects in *Digital Lean Cyber-Physical Production Systems (CPPSs)* [2]. These modern production systems can be composed of advanced automation, collaborative, and/or manual subsystems, where humans are involved in activities such as monitoring

© IFIP International Federation for Information Processing 2022
Published by Springer Nature Switzerland AG 2022
D. Y. Kim et al. (Eds.): APMS 2022, IFIP AICT 664, pp. 595–603, 2022.
https://doi.org/10.1007/978-3-031-16411-8_68

and/or operating production equipment and individually and/or collaboratively performing manual operations to ensure the right functioning of these three types of subsystems. In such activities, human inadvertent mistakes can influence the *operational reliability* of production equipment and manual operations, and therefore their quality output. Hence, *Poka-Yokes* play a fundamental role in achieving (near-) zero defects or errors in such complex production systems. This paper explores the digitally-enhanced evolution of *Poka-Yokes* from a twofold perspective, first from an *error-proofing perspective* as these progress towards "error prevention" rather than "error correction" devices, and second from a *Kaizen perspective* as these gain additional "intelligence" to digitally understand human and machine errors and provide insights on how to mistake-proof production processes and procedures by (re-)design.

2 Methodology

This research work was developed based on a scientific literature review focused on *Poka-Yoke devices*. The main outcomes of the literature analysis were then grouped according to five distinctive dimensions, namely: definitions, functions, approaches, perspectives, and examples. Several brainstorming sessions were then conducted with factory managers and lean experts on the evolution of these error-proofing devices in light of their new potential digital and analytical capabilities in the emerging Digital Lean Manufacturing world [2]. After introducing the main characteristics of *traditional Poka-yoke devices* concerning definitions, functions, approaches, perspectives, and examples, factory managers and lean experts were asked to give their points of view on their "digitization" impact. Common views were then incorporated and transcribed. On the other hand, in case of different or apparently conflicting interpretations, a subsequent meeting with the parties concerned was held to find a common point of view, avoiding any bias.

3 Poka-Yokes: Definitions, Functions, Approaches and Perspectives

3.1 Definitions

Traditional *Poka-Yokes* (*Poka*—inadvertent error, and *Yoke*—avoidance) are defined as devices that perform 100% inspection of automated and manual operations for the prevention, detection, elimination, and correction of process and procedure errors and defects at their source to avoid affecting product quality and operators' health and safety [3, 4]. Being made of physical, functional, or symbolic barriers [5], *Poka-Yokes* contribute to facilitating the making of the correct action far easier than the mistake and mitigate the effects of the mistake if the error cannot be eliminated. Moreover, as *technology* has evolved, *Poka-Yokes* have also too from simple and economic jigs, pins, locks, fixtures, sensors, visual signals, warning devices, and go/no-go gauges [6, 7] to advanced quality controls used to predict and prevent errors rather than detect and correct such, and to collect error data for real-time and post-analysis to provide immediate feedback for corrective measures and later insights for the continuous improvement of a process or procedure (re-)design. Hence, *Poka-Yokes'* evolution has progressed towards an "error prevention" tool and a "continuous improvement" mechanism.

An *Intelligent Poka-Yoke* is a device that works with smart sensors, real-time data, and instant feedback mechanisms to predict if a human or machine error will occur based on task-tracking and intent prediction methods or in-process controls to prevent a mistake in a process or procedure. *Intelligent Poka-Yokes* are characterized by their new "assisting" nature towards zero defects and errors rather than their traditional error detection approach as well as by their new role as a *Kaizen mechanism* collecting and providing error data for processes or procedures continuous improvement.

An *Intelligent Poka-Yoke device* is different from other *smart IoT devices* from the viewpoint that its *primary function* is oriented to reducing human and machine errors and improving processes and procedures in a production line. Furthermore, *Intelligent Poka-Yokes* should be particularly developed following an integrated "process-centric" and "human-centric" design approach, and incorporating different digital and analytical technologies that must provide real-time feedback to the operators for error-proofing processes and procedures towards (near-)zero-defect manufacturing.

3.2 Functions and Approaches

Traditional *Poka-Yoke devices* have three main features, being (i) inspection methods, (ii) function setters, and (iii) function regulators [8, 9]. As *inspection methods*, these offer three types of inspection [8]: (a) *judgment inspection*, which aims to sort out defective products so they do not reach the customer; this type of inspection does not prevent defects nor does it provide instant feedback so the next defects in the process can be avoided right away, (b) *informative inspection*, which purpose is to provide "after the fact" feedback to improve a process or procedure and prevent future product defects (e.g. control charts), and (c) *source inspection*, which focuses on determining "before the fact" the process conditions that will create an error-free production. As *function setters*, these provide four "setting methods" to support inspection [8, 9]: (a) *physical methods* that determine whether an error exists in a process or procedure based on contact mechanisms such as switches, limits, proximity sensors, position sensors, displacement sensors, and pass sensors or a defect in a product by testing its size, shape, colour or any other similar physical attribute, (b) *grouping and counting methods* (also known as fixed value methods) that use counting or measuring approaches to ensure no errors have occurred when a specific number of movements are not made (e.g. fulfilling a picking or delivery order, which must be correct and complete), (c) *sequencing methods* (also referred as motion-step methods) that verify that a standard sequence (i.e. standard operating procedure) has occurred, and (d) *information enhancement methods* that ensure required information for a process or procedure is available at the correct time and place. And as *function regulators*, these deliver two "regulatory mechanisms" for processes and procedures [8]: (a) *controls*, which stop a process or procedure once an error has been detected—using jigs, pins, and locks—restricting its continuation till the problem has been eliminated, and (b) *warnings*, which purpose is to only alert the operator—using bells, buzzers, or warning lights—without stopping the process or procedure that an error has occurred or is about to occur so the corrective action can be made when considered appropriate.

Furthermore, traditional *Poka-Yoke devices* work using two main strategies [10, 11]: (a) a *prevention-based strategy* (or proactive strategy) aiming to avoid the occurrence of an error or defect, or (b) a *detection-based strategy* (or reactive strategy) focusing on detecting that the error or defect has happened, and two main approaches [12]: (a) a *passive-approach* by suggesting the need of corrective action, or (b) an *active-approach* by forcing correcting action.

On the other hand, *Intelligent Poka-Yokes* still have their three main features, but these have been focused, renewed, and digitally enhanced, and one more new feature, a fourth one, has been added as *Kaizen tools*. As *inspection methods*, these now mainly focus on (a) *informative inspection* with an extended purpose to support data-driven processes and procedures continuous improvement by recording in real-time, using smart sensors and computer vision systems, all errors and defects (i.e. big data) for their post-analysis and use for discovering improvement possibilities [13], and on (b) *source inspection* by using task-tracking and intent prediction methods in human constrained procedural tasks (e.g. maintenance and assembly tasks) to track these and provide in real-time guidance and prompt feedback if necessary to a technician or an operator, using AR-based or light-based guide systems, on the correct course of action according to the standard operating procedure so errors can be prevented from occurring in the first place or allow the human to fix the error as soon as it occurs [14], or in-process controls by using smart sensors and actuators to monitor and if necessary to adjust a process (parameter) to prevent an error in a machine and as a result a product out of specifications [15]. As *function setters*, these use new and advanced versions of the original four "setting methods" to support inspection: (a) *virtual methods*, in the past physical methods, such as non-contact mechanisms like electromagnetic induction, laser imaging, optical method, electrical method, ultrasonic method, etc. that measure the work-piece without producing any deformation in it—due to contact with it [15], (b) *grouping and counting methods* such as computer vision grouping [16, 17] combined with projection mapping technology to overlay light on the identified parts or products to be easily grouped, smart bins equipped with weight sensors for real-time recognition of their filling levels and the automatic triggering of their withdrawal e-Kanban cards for inventory replenishment (control) and with smart labels based on e-paper tech for offering updated product information as well as real-time order status and delivery date [18], and pick-to-light and put-to-light systems driving operators in their picking and placement activities in the assembly line and warehouse so they can easily and quickly pick the right part or product and the placed it in the right place [19], (c) *sequencing methods* such as pick-to-sequence and put-to-sequence, including picking and placing verifications, based on AR-based or light-based guide systems and smart sensors (e.g. break beams to detect whether the operator has reached into the correct bin) so operators can diligently assemble and distribute parts in the right order [20], and (d) *information enhancement methods* such as e-Kanban systems [18], digital Andons [20], and other digital "push" information systems based on mobile computing and smart wearable technologies that allow notifying and delivering the right information to the right person at the right time for problem-solving or troubleshooting. And as *function regulators*, these deliver improved "regulatory mechanisms" with more sophisticated (a) *controls* that early-detect, diagnose a problem, and in some cases correct it before it actually occurs to avoid procedures or processes stoppage based on intent prediction methods [14] and in-process controls [15] to prevent error, and (b) *(early-)warnings* that based on "predictive" approaches and digital Andons (i.e. tablets, smartphones, smartwatches, smart-glasses, etc.) can provide at any time and at any place "early" alerts and other "proactive" e-notifications to the right person to call it for countermeasure actions [20].

In summary, *Intelligent Poka-Yoke devices* work using a *prevention-based strategy* and an *active approach* to error-proofing.

3.3 Perspectives

From an *error-proofing (tool) perspective*, "Intelligent Poka-Yokes" aim to become preventive, proactive, and active devices creating the right conditions before executing a process or procedure step and assisting humans and machines during the execution of a sequence of steps to avoid errors and defects. A clear manifestation of this evolution is the emergence of new digital operator assistance systems providing AR-based visual aids to the workers so they can make the right judgements and if needed steer their actions or intended actions to drive the next "right" step [21, 22], and new or renewed smart manufacturing technologies for in-process controls based on closed-loop and real-time feedback systems compensating for a process instability to avoid a rejected work-piece (e.g. in-process gauging systems) [23].

From a *Kaizen (mechanism) perspective*, "Intelligent Poka-Yokes" will collect error data for real-time and post-analysis to provide first immediate feedback to operators and machines to solve problems right away (i.e. short-term countermeasures), and second address their root cause by providing later insights coming out from real-data based simulations (e.g. digital twinning) for the continuous improvement of processes and procedures by redesign (i.e. long-term countermeasures) to prevent errors or defects happen again. Furthermore, *Intelligent Poka-Yokes* will enhance the *Kaizen continuous improvement cycle* by (i) documenting reality with the help of automatic data collection systems (e.g. smart sensors and computer vision systems), which can provide more reliable (big) data in comparison to manual systems, (ii) identifying waste with the support of advanced analytical and prediction tools capable of anticipating problems, (iii) eliminating non-value-added steps with the assistance of real-time optimization techniques, (iv) developing and (v) implementing short and long-term countermeasures with the help of advanced modelling and simulation techniques, (vi) verifying change with the support of task-tracking systems, (vii) measuring (improvement) results with the assistance of IoT-based performance measurement systems, and (viii) making (new) standard operating procedures digitally available to aid workers with AR-based guide systems in their jobs. One further emergent enhancer is foreseen in the near future, (viii) short-run machine learning algorithms for AI-based support of small-batch and one-of-a-kind production systems management, where large repetitive datasets are difficult to realize.

4 Discussion and Examples of Intelligent Poka-Yokes

Generally speaking, the development of an *Intelligent Poka-Yoke device* consists of four steps: (i) selecting the sensing technology (e.g. smart sensor(s) and/or computer vision system) to "detect" an error or defect, (ii) analysing the error or defect with data analytics tools, (iii) determining the error or defect root cause with the help of real-data based simulations (e.g. a digital twin), and (iv) (re-)designing and implementing tools to avoid the error or defect recurrence with the support of advanced modelling and simulation tools.

The most promising technologies supporting the development of *Intelligent Poka-Yokes* are smart sensors (or IoT-based sensors), computer vision systems (and AI-based cameras), augmented reality, (big) data analytics, and machine learning. Examples of their usage to add "intelligence" to *Poka-Yoke devices* are: Auto-ID technologies such as barcoding and RFID systems for parts and products always right identification, intelligent in-process controls at machine tools auto-correcting process deviations automatically, torque drivers and callipers to perform manual operations to exact specifications, computer vision systems and AI-based cameras for parts and products detail inspection, AR-based guide systems for always correct assembly sequences, machine learning-based measurement systems analysis for efficient low volume, high mix production management, etc.

Consistent with Table 1 where the main features of a *traditional Poka-Yoke* vs. an *Intelligent Poka-Yoke* are shown, the following statements can be made:

- If compared to traditional Poka-Yokes, *Intelligent Poka-Yokes* perform better in terms of both reliability, quality, and response time, therefore, to operational performance. Indeed, thanks to their ability to collect, analyze, and interpret a large amount of data and their mutual relationships in real-time, these devices facilitate the recognition of problems that are hidden or have not yet emerged in products and processes but will arise in the near future.
- On the other hand, *Intelligent Poka-Yokes* may lead to incorrect interpretations, considering risky situations that are not, with a consequent increase in quality management costs, or rather unrisky critical situations, if the data interpretation system has not been properly set up, or the amount of data is so large that it overloads the decision-maker, leading him/her to error.
- Since *Poka-Yoke devices* can also be used for supporting setup activities, the improvement in quality and response times allowed by their digitalization means less time for production changes, with a consequent improvement in the flexibility of the manufacturing system. Moreover, adopting digital tools such as *Intelligent Poka-Yokes* increases the flexibility of the decision-making system as "intelligent" systems can reprocess the decision-making logic in relation to the experience gained over time.
- Despite the continuous hardware and software cost-cutting, *Intelligent Poka-Yokes* can result very costly in economic terms, or at least too expensive when compared to traditional ones which, in line with lean principles, must be easy to use and cheap.

Table 1. Traditional Poka-Yoke vs Intelligent Poka-Yoke

Function	Traditional Poka-Yoke	Intelligent Poka-Yoke
Collection	• Manual Data Collection • Limited Data Collection • Historical Data Collection	• Automatic Data Collection (with Smart Sensors) • Big Data Collection • Real-Time Data Collection
Sharing	• Delayed Data Sharing	• Instant Data Sharing (IoT-enabled)

Analysis	• Basic Data Analytics Tools
	  – Statistical Process Control
	  – Root-Cause Analysis
	  – Correlation Analysis
		• Big Data Analytics Tools
		  – Machine Learning
		  – Data Mining
		  – Predictive Analysis

Optimization	• Post-Optimization	• Real-Time Optimization
Feedback	• Real-Time Feedback	• Real-Time Feedback (IoT-enabled) • Enriched Feedback (AR-enabled)

Although *Intelligent Poka-Yokes* can offer great benefits to perfect error-proofing, these smart devices can also come with some drawbacks, which are referred to here as the "Poka-Yoke Paradox". On the one hand, *Intelligent Poka-Yokes* promise to enhance "error prevention" in *Digital Lean Cyber-Physical Production Systems*, while on the other hand may uncover an inherent risk in which operators may become "too dependent" on such smart devices to detect potential errors and defects, rather than rely on their human senses to care about quality and think deeply about potential *Kaizen* opportunities. Thus, the *Poka-Yoke Paradox* can be formulated in such a way that the reliance on *Intelligent Poka-Yokes* may incur a detrimental effect on the "Thinking People System" of lean manufacturing, something that *traditional Poke-Yokes* and *Jidoka systems* were actually designed to improve.

5   Conclusions and Further Research

Recent developments in digital and analytical technologies have opened up a variety of data-driven possibilities for error-proofing processes and procedures towards (near-) zero-defect manufacturing. Implementing *Intelligent Poka-Yokes* can be the starting point for evolving from an "error detection" to an "error prevention" paradigm and to enhance the *Kaizen* continuous improvement cycle for years to come. However, the need to safely access and manage reliable (big) data in real-time on the shop floor, calls for the necessity to adopt also new data management technologies like 5G, blockchain, and metadata analysis.

Though this paper presents several useful reflections around the digitalization and smartification of *Poka-Yoke devices*, it is suggested that further research could benefit from practical insights from applied research, for example, case studies and/or action research projects. Furthermore, it is particularly suggested the development of research works addressing the definition of criteria to decide between the use of traditional Poka-Yokes vs. Intelligent Poka-Yokes on the shop floor, the identification of manufacturing environments and processes/procedures that are most suitable for the deployment of Intelligent Poka-Yokes, and the explanation of more concrete examples for the use of Intelligent Poka-Yokes in Kaizen mechanisms.

Acknowledgements. The authors would like to acknowledge the support of the Research Council of Norway for the research project: *Lean Digital.*

References

1. Romero, D., Gaiardelli, P., Powell, D., Wuest, T., Thürer, M.: Total quality management and quality circles in the digital lean manufacturing world. In: Ameri, F., Stecke, K.E., von Cieminski, G., Kiritsis, D. (eds.) Advances in Production Management Systems. Production Management for the Factory of the Future. IFIP Advances in Information and Communication Technology, vol. 566, pp. 3–11. Springer, Cham (2019). https://doi.org/10.1007/978-3-030-30000-5_1
2. Romero, D., Gaiardelli, P., Powell, D., Wuest, T., Thürer, M.: Digital lean cyber-physical production systems: the emergence of digital lean manufacturing and the significance of digital waste. In: Moon, I., Lee, G.M., Park, J., Kiritsis, D., von Cieminski, G. (eds.) Advances in Production Management Systems. Production Management for Data-Driven, Intelligent, Collaborative, and Sustainable Manufacturing. IFIP Advances in Information and Communication Technology, vol. 535, pp. 11–20. Springer, Cham (2018). https://doi.org/10.1007/978-3-319-99704-9_2
3. Robinson, H.: Using Poka-Yoke techniques for early defect detection. In: 6th International Conference on Software Testing Analysis and Review, pp. 1–12 (1997)
4. Fisher, M.: Process improvement by Poka-Yoke. Work-Study **48**(7), 264–266 (1999)
5. Saurin, T.A., Ribeiro, J.L.D., Vidor, G.: A framework for assessing Poka-Yoke devices. J. Manuf. Syst. **31**(3), 358–366 (2012)
6. Grout, J.R., Downs, B.T.: Mistake-proofing and measurement control charts. Qual. Manag. J. **5**(2), 67–75 (1998)
7. Kattman, B., Corbin, T.P., Moore, L.E., Walsh, L.: Visual workplace practices positively impact business processes. Benchmarking: Int. J. **19**(3), 412–414 (2012)
8. Shingo, S.: Zero Quality Control: Source Inspection and the Poka-Yoke System. Productivity Press, Cambridge (1986)
9. Chase, R.B., Stewart, D.M.: Mistake-Proofing: Designing Errors Out. Productivity Press, Portland, Oregon (1995)
10. Bayers, P.C.: Using Poka-Yoke (Mistake-Proofing Devices) to ensure quality. In: Proceedings of IEEE Applied Power Electronics Conference and Exposition, vol. 1, pp. 201–204 (1994)
11. Chao, L.P., Ishii, K.: Design process error-proofing: strategies for reducing quality loss in product development. In: ASME International Mechanical Engineering Congress and Exposition, vol. 118, pp. 255–264 (2005)
12. Gamberini, R., Gebennini, E., Rimini, B., Spadaccini, E., Zilocchi, D.: Low-cost automation and Poka-Yoke devices: tools for optimising production processes. Int. J. Prod. Qual. Manag. **4**(5–6), 590–612 (2009)
13. Buer, S.-V., Fragapane, G.I., Strandhagen, J.O.: The data-driven process improvement cycle: using digitalization for continuous improvement. IFAC-PapersOnLine **51**(11), 1035–1040 (2018)

14. Bovo, R., Binetti, N., Brumby, D.P., Julier, S.: Detecting Errors in Pick and Place Procedures: Detecting Errors in Multi-Stage and Sequence Constrained Manual Retrieve-Assembly Procedures. 25th International Conference on Intelligent User Interfaces, ACM, New York, NY, USA, pp. 1–10 (2020)
15. Junaid, A., Siddiqi, M.U.R., Mohammad, R., Abbasi, M.U.: In-Process Measurement in Manufacturing Processes. In: Khan, W.A., Rahman, K., Hussain, G. (eds.) Functional Reverse Engineering of Machine Tools, pp. 105–134. CRC Press, Boca Raton (2019)
16. Buhmann, J.M., Malik, J., Perona, P.: Image recognition: visual grouping, recognition, and learning. Proc. Natl. Acad. Sci. U.S.A. 96(25), 14203–14204 (1999)
17. Belu, N., Ionescu, L.M., Misztal, A., Mazăre, A.: Poka-Yoke system based on image analysis and object recognition. IOP Conf. Ser.: Mater. Sci. Eng. 95, 012138 (2015)
18. Peron, M., Alfnes, E., Sgarbossa, F.: Kanban system in industry 4.0 era: a systematic literature review. In: Wang, Y., Martinsen, K., Yu, T., Wang, K. (eds.) Advanced Manufacturing and Automation XI. Lecture Notes in Electrical Engineering, vol. 880, pp. 12–19. Springer, Singapore (2022). https://doi.org/10.1007/978-981-19-0572-8_2
19. Battini, D., Calzavara, M., Persona, A., Sgarbossa, F.: A comparative analysis of different paperless picking systems. Ind. Manag. Data Syst. 115(3), 483–503 (2015)
20. Mohamad, E., et al.: Framework of Andon support system in lean cyber-physical system production environment. In: Manufacturing Systems Division Conference, pp. 404–405 (2019)
21. Moencks, M., Roth, E., Bohné, T.: Cyber-physical operator assistance systems in industry: cross-hierarchical perspectives on augmenting human abilities. In: IEEE International Conference on Industrial Engineering and Engineering Management, pp. 419–423 (2020)
22. Mark, B.G., Rauch, E., Matt, D.T.: Worker assistance systems in manufacturing: a review of the state of the art and future directions. J. Manuf. Syst. 59, 228–250 (2021)
23. Shi, J.: In-Process quality improvement: concepts, methodologies, and applications. IISE transactions (2022)

A Benchmarking Study on Existing VSM Software

Matteo Zanchi$^{(\boxtimes)}$ ⓘ, Roberto Sala ⓘ, and Paolo Gaiardelli ⓘ

Department of Management, Information and Production Engineering, University of Bergamo,
Viale Marconi 5, Dalmine, BG, Italy
{matteo.zanchi,roberto.sala,paolo.gaiardelli}@unibg.it

Abstract. Every Lean optimization path typically starts with the mapping of a process, to identify criticalities and wastes embedded in manufacturing processes. Value Stream Mapping (VSM) represents the main and most suitable Lean technique to this purpose, thanks to its simplicity and immediacy residing in its visual effectiveness. Originally designed as a "draw by hand" mapping technique, VSM is moving on digital platforms; different software has in fact been developed over the last few years, each with its own functionalities and characteristics, reason why a software may not be always valid, but useful only within certain contexts. According to a classification of software based on mapping, analytical and collaborative functionalities, crucial aspects for a successful VSM application, the paper aims to depict, through a benchmark analysis, the current situation regarding VSM software and, therefore, serve as a reference model to orient manufacturing companies towards best suited VSM applications.

Keywords: Lean management · Value stream mapping · Industry 4.0 · Benchmark · Software

1 Introduction

The many benefits that the implementation of Lean Management (LM) tools and principles provides to companies, leading them to gain of a relevant competitive advantage [1], has led in the last four decades to an increasing interest of scientific community towards this topic [2]. Embarking on such a path is not, though, a simple matter but rather requires undertaking different steps through adopting appropriate methods and tools. Among others, the Value Stream Mapping (VSM) technique manages to provide a precise, immediate, and easy-to-understand representation of the whole production process, combining process inputs, outputs, activities, actors and information flows (mapping) [3]. Moreover, according to the customer's needs [4], VSM is helpful to pinpoint the non-value-added sources (e.g., main criticalities and wastes) nestled into the process [5], thus identifying the best management approach towards optimization, by orienteering the necessary improvement interventions into a structured roadmap (analysis). Finally, it

© IFIP International Federation for Information Processing 2022
Published by Springer Nature Switzerland AG 2022
D. Y. Kim et al. (Eds.): APMS 2022, IFIP AICT 664, pp. 604–612, 2022.
https://doi.org/10.1007/978-3-031-16411-8_69

helps the development of teamwork based on a common language and a systematic process that lays the foundations for a strategic and shared improvement plan (collaboration) [6].

Originally born as a "draw by hand" tool [6], VSM has yet proven to be ineffective in production contexts characterized by process uncertainty [7] due to frequent changes of products, short product life cycle or high fluctuations of customer orders [8]. However, with the advent of digital technologies, much new mapping software has been developed, which has indeed contributed to exceeding the constraints typical of traditional VSM. Thanks to a permanent and continuous visualization of the value stream, achieved by means of real-time monitoring systems which allow for a high level of sensitivity in relation to possible production fluctuations, operation managers can obtain a constantly updated view of the processes under observation [9]. In addition, supported by the simulation functionalities provided by software, they can test several improvement proposals and identify the best approach among a set of potential future scenarios. The achieved benefits lie not only in more frequent, fast, and accurate control of data coming from the field, but also in a greater integration and transparency of information, as well as in the possibility of studying and comparing several improvement alternatives simultaneously, by analyzing the interactions of different material and information flows in a simpler and more effective way, in order to identify time and economic savings at an early stage [10].

Despite the manifest benefits of the new VSM software applications, it is not yet clear what functionalities are compulsory for creating VSM suitable for dynamic and uncertain contexts, and to what extent the software available on the market cover these functionalities. On these premises, aim of the paper is to outline an overview regarding the current VSM software available on the market and their distinctive functionalities, to understand to what extent they match the main VSM characteristics, namely mapping, analysis and collaboration.

Following this brief introduction, the paper is then structured as follows: Sect. 2 describes the research methodology; Sect. 3 provides an overview of the current software and functionalities available on the market, whose benchmark results are then reported in Sect. 4. Section 5 includes a discussion over the main outcomes of the analysis, whose most relevant considerations are then reported in the conclusive section of the paper, along with hints regarding possible future research.

2 Methodology

From a methodological standpoint, the research was built upon three main phases, each one composed of one or more subphases (Fig. 1). Three researchers participated in the whole research process.

The first phase, carried out through two parallel streams, aimed at identifying the main functionalities required and offered for VSM projects. The literature review focused on case studies reporting VSM applications aimed at understanding the relevant information necessary to conduct a VSM analysis. On the other hand, exploratory research of VSM software was carried out to identify the main commercial solutions available on the market and the functionalities (i.e., "any aspect of software application or any computing

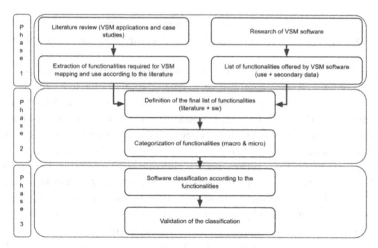

Fig. 1. Research methodology and related steps

device can do for the user") [11] offered. From this research, 18 software was found and analyzed in detail. When both free and paid versions of the software were available, the 'full version' - i.e., the one with the greatest number of available functionalities - was considered. Functionalities were identified both by using the software and analyzing secondary data (e.g., tutorials, marketing material).

The second phase involved the preparation of the final list of functionalities. Such a list was created by merging the results of the literature review and exploration of the commercial software. Eventually, a list of 64 functionalities was defined. Starting from this list, functionalities were clustered into micro- and macro-categories, where the former represent a specification of the latter: for example, the macro-category "Mapping" includes the micro-categories "Data", "Formatting", "Icons", "User experience". In turn, each micro-category entails one or more functionalities. For instance, the micro-category "Formatting" contains the functionalities "Customization of color of the stencil", "Highlight value added processes" and "Taking and integrating pictures".

Finally, each software was classified according to their distinctive functionalities. After testing the software and collecting data from secondary sources, each researcher ran the classification independently. Then, the classification was validated by comparing and, when necessary, discussing the analysis of each researcher. Such approach was carried out until reaching an agreement on the software classification.

3   Overview of VSM Software Functionalities

As stated in the previous section, the literature review and exploratory research phase enabled the identification of 64 different functionalities characterizing VSM applications. These functionalities can be clustered into 10 micro-categories and, in turn, be grouped into 3 main macro-categories according to the dimensions of VSM found in literature. Table 1 reports the list of micro-categories and relevant macro-categories. The latter are briefly described in the following.

Table 1. List of software functionalities, grouped in micro and macro-categories

Macro-category	Micro-category	Description
Mapping	Data	Calculate data boxes variables
	Formatting	Format personalization of mapping stencils
	Icons	Standard or customized icons and stencils
	User Experience (UX)	Software supportive tools for the drawing phase
Process Analysis and Optimization	Basic	Calculate basic KPIs and production indexes typical of a VSM representation (LT, OEE, Takt Time, EPEI etc.)
	Optimization	Compute line balancing and Kanban optimization, compare multiple what-if scenarios
	Personalization	Generate customized reports
	Simulation	Capability to simulate a production process, through discrete-event models
	Visualization	Display mode of reports generated at the end of the simulation
Collaboration	Asynchronous	Possibility for several people to access, edit and collaborate on the same map, not simultaneously
	Synchronous	Possibility for several people to access, edit and collaborate on the same map simultaneously

- **Mapping.** It covers all the functionalities concerning the drawing phase, including the customization of templates, icons, symbols, and areas for data and information management. Formatting options and other supporting functionalities to enrich the User Experience in the mapping phase, with particular mention to the auto-draw capabilities, are also taken into account;
- **Process analysis and optimization.** It refers to functionalities concerning the software's ability to process data and find solutions to static or dynamic problems [12], i.e., when the amount of input data changes continuously, in terms of fluctuations in demand and resources, product and variant mixes, and non-sequential production processes [13]. In other words, it specifies the set of functionalities concerning graphs, calculations and simulations, in the form of discrete events or of scenario analysis, to support the simultaneous comparison of multiple what-if scenarios. The category also

considers the possibility to represent analysis results through 'ad hoc' performance indicators, designed by the user;

- **Collaboration.** It concerns the ability of a VSM software to engage multiple users to cooperate, working simultaneously on a specific document. It also includes those functionalities pertaining to the ability of the software to facilitate feedback through the use of real time chats, or a system for tracking changes.

18 software applications, identified in the first phase of the research and reported in Table 2, were then assessed according to the mentioned criteria.

Table 2. List of analysed software

Software (alphabetical order)		
BlueSpring LeanView	Ifakt	Simcad Simulation
BreezeTree	iGrafx	SimVSM
ConceptDraw	LeanLab Visual Factory VSM	SmartDraw
Creately	Lucidchart	Systems2win
EdrawMax	Profit Surge VSM	TecnomatixPlantSimulation
eVSM Mix	ProModel	Visual Paradigm

4   Results

The final assessment of VSM functionalities owned by each application is reported in the benchmark analysis depicted in Fig. 2. The enumeration of software applications in the list is purely coincidental and is not in any way related to the sequence of Table 2..

The bubble chart shows the functionalities owned by the 18 software considered within the benchmark analysis. In accordance with the three characteristic dimensions of VSM systems, the x-axis refers to the amount of functionalities concerning "Process analysis and optimization" possessed by each software, while the y-axis as the "Mapping" functionalities. The diameter of each bubble represents, on the other hand, the number of "Collaboration" functionalities available for each software program. To avoid tracking of applications that do not possess any "Collaboration" tool, the minimum value for this variable has been set equal to one. In all cases, the higher the number of functionalities available, the higher the score achieved in each category.

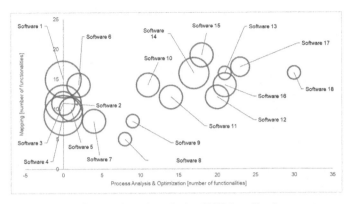

Fig. 2. Benchmark analysis of VSM applications

5 Discussion

The diagram of Fig. 2 shows that the different VSM software considered in the benchmark analysis widely ranges among the dimensions in terms of owned functionalities. In particular, three main different clusters can be identified, as highlighted in Fig. 3:

- **"Drawing" (blue):** the first cluster is made up of software used exclusively to draw processes. Located along the y-axis software belonging to this cluster, it may be of particular interest to users who only necessitate a map representation tool. Indeed, this kind of software possesses several "Mapping" functionalities to the detriment of "Process analysis and optimization" ones which, for the majority of cases, are completely absent, excluding for software 6 and 7 which respectively includes a couple of functionalities concerning process analysis;
- **"Static Analysis" (red):** the second cluster, that is located in the central area of the diagram involves software applications that possess a fair amount of both mapping and process analysis and optimization functionalities. In particular, "Process analysis and optimization" functionalities featured by software belonging to this category mainly refer to numerical analyses of the key indicators associated with a process, mostly in stationary conditions;
- **"Dynamic Analysis" (yellow):** the last cluster groups software tools that, through simulation, enable the study of alternative scenarios characterized by different flows of material and information, also in non-stationary and highly variable conditions. These applications, which are also characterized by a high number of both "Mapping" and "Process analysis and optimization" functionalities, are particularly useful for the analysis of the process current state, as well as for evaluating alternative improvement strategies.

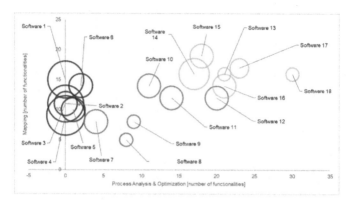

Fig. 3. Clustering of VSM software according to main software utility

Finally, an overall view on different software categories identified, a synthetic bubble diagram, which thickens all the different applications belonging to the same category into a single point, has been elaborated in Fig. 4. The chart shows that, on average, "Drawing" applications have more "Collaboration" functionalities (4,2 on average) compared to the remaining tools available on the market (which count respectively 1,3 and 1,5 available functionalities on average for the "Static Analysis" and "Dynamic Analysis" applications). This distinguishing difference is probably due to the fact that, most likely, software built on a simulation architecture gives the opportunity to evaluate alternative process configurations autonomously, without any need for external support, as opposed to "Drawing" software tools which are, instead, enhanced by the possible inclusion of such functionalities.

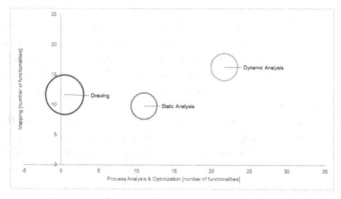

Fig. 4. Cluster mid-points for each VSM software category

6   Conclusion

The benchmark analysis described throughout this paper provides a general overview on the current state of VSM software available on the market, identifying the distinctive software functionalities as well as its main differences with other proposed solutions. The benchmark analysis, therefore, can work as a reference point for both manufacturing and software development companies. On one hand, it may support manufacturing companies in a VSM software selection process, directing them on the alternative solution that best suits their needs in terms of number and type of functionalities. On the other hand, the benchmark analysis may act as a comparison tool to provide software companies some hints regarding new possible functionalities to be implemented, or orient the policy of development towards the specialization on a specific field of usability (i.e. drawing or static/dynamic analysis). Finally, the utility of the analysis undertaken also resides in the fact that the different utilities of VSM identified in literature (namely mapping, analysis and collaboration) are indeed reflected on the software utilities available on the market, confirming the usefulness of such applications in properly drafting a VSM coherently with the theoretical principles.

Further research may be oriented towards the inclusion of software that covers additional semantic areas within the traditional context of a VSM, such as the environmental, sustainability, economic/financial and societal dimensions, as well as taking into account cost, usability, or customer satisfaction in the software assessment. One final aspect of interest could relate the readiness of VSM mapping applications to be integrated with Process Mining methodologies [14] to manage the complexity and variability of modern production systems, through event log-based business process analysis. This new line of research would be instrumental for the creation of what can be called as Dynamic Value Stream Map (DVSM) [15].

References

1. Belekoukias, I., Garza-Reyes, J.A., Kumar, V.: The impact of lean methods and tools on the operational performance of manufacturing organisa-tions. Int. J. Prod. Res. **52**(18), 5346–5366 (2014)
2. Netland, T.H., Powell, D.J.: A lean world. In: Netland, T.H., Powell, D.J. (eds.) The Routledge Companion to Lean Management, pp. 465–473. Taylor and Francis, New York (2017)
3. Romero, L., Arce, A.: Applying value stream mapping in manufacturing: a systematic literature review. IFAC-PapersOnLine **50**(1), 1075–1086 (2017)
4. Maskell, B.H.: Lean accounting. McGraw-Hill Education (2015)
5. Wakamatsu, Y.: Il valore della produzione nel Toyota Production System. FrancoAngeli Edizioni (2016)
6. Rother, M., Shook, J.: Learning to see: value stream mapping to add value and eliminate muda. Lean Enterprise Institute (2003)
7. Luz, G.P., Tortorella, G.L., Narayanamurthy, G., Gaiardelli, P., Sawhney, R.: A systematic literature review on the stochastic analysis of value streams. Prod. Plann. Control **32**(2), 121–131 (2021)
8. Tamás, P.: Application of value stream mapping at flexible manufacturing systems. Key Eng. Mater. **5**, 168–173 (2016)

9. Sanders, A., Elangeswaran, C., Wulfsberg, J.: Industry 4.0 implies lean manufacturing: research activities in industry 4.0 function as enablers for lean manufacturing. J. Industr. Eng. Manag. **9**(3), 811–833 (2016)
10. Luz, G.P., Tortorella, G.L., Bouzon, M., Garza-Reyes, J., Gaiardelli, P.: Proposition of a method for stochastic analysis of value streams. Prod. Plann. Control **33**(8), 1–17 (2020)
11. Salleh, M.A., Bahari, M., Zakaria, N.H.: An overview of software functionality service: a systematic literature review. Procedia Comput. Sci. **124**, 337–344 (2017)
12. Lugert, A., Völker, K., Winkler, H.: Dynamization of value stream management by technical and managerial approach. Procedia CIRP **72**, 701–706 (2018)
13. Paul, S.K., Sarker, R., Essam, D.: Managing real-time demand fluctuation under a supplier–retailer coordinated system. Int. J. Prod. Econ. **158**, 231–243 (2014)
14. Knoll, D., Reinhart, G., Prüglmeier, M.: Enabling value stream mapping for internal logistics using multidimensional process mining. Expert Syst. Appl. **124**, 130–142 (2019)
15. Tran, T.A., Ruppert, T., Abonyi, J.: Indoor positioning systems can revolutionise digital lean. Appl. Sci. **11**(11), 5291 (2021)

Author Index

Printed in the United States
by Baker & Taylor Publisher Services